Empire's Twilight
Northeast Asia Under the Mongols

Harvard-Yenching Institute
Monograph Series 68

Empire's Twilight

Northeast Asia Under the Mongols

David M. Robinson

Published by the Harvard University Asia Center
for the Harvard-Yenching Institute
Distributed by Harvard University Press
Cambridge (Massachusetts) and London 2009

Printed in the United States of America

The Harvard-Yenching Institute, founded in 1928 and headquartered at Harvard University, is a foundation dedicated to the advancement of higher education in the humanities and social sciences in East and Southeast Asia. The Institute supports advanced research at Harvard by faculty members of certain Asian universities and doctoral studies at Harvard and other universities by junior faculty at the same universities. It also supports East Asian studies at Harvard through contributions to the Harvard-Yenching Library and publication of the *Harvard Journal of Asiatic Studies* and books on premodern East Asian history and literature.

Library of Congress Cataloging-in-Publication Data

Robinson, David M., 1965–

Empire's twilight : northeast Asia under the Mongols / David M. Robinson.

p. cm. -- (Harvard-Yenching Institute monograph series ; 68)

Includes bibliographical references and index.

ISBN 978-0-674-03608-6 (cl : alk. paper)

1. Mongols--East Asia--History--14th century. 2. East Asia--History--14th century. I. Title.

DS23.R63 2009

950'.24--dc22

2009022545

Index by the author

Printed on acid-free paper

Last number below indicates year of this printing

18 17 16 15 14 13 12 11 10 09

In memoriam
Joan M. Robinson
(1937–2005)

Acknowledgments

This book would have been impossible without the generous help of colleagues and friends in the United States and East Asia. Yi Hŭi-sŭng of the Andong Folk Museum kindly provided me with materials relating to the local religious shrines in Andong devoted to King Kongmin and his queen. Professor Kim Ho-dong proved a gracious host during my brief stay at Seoul University, providing stimulating conversation and introductions to his energetic graduate students. One of these, Mr. Sŏl Paek-wan, was particularly helpful in tracking down difficult-to-find articles. Professor Min Hyŏn-gu of Koryŏ University patiently answered my questions about the reign of Kongmin, and Chang Tong-ik of Pukkyŏng University provided valuable bibliographic suggestions for the late Koryŏ period. Professor Hong Sŏng-gu, now also of Pukkyŏng University, arranged access to the rare book collection at Koryŏ University. I especially thank Professors Cho Yong-hŏn of Hong'ik University and Cha Hye-wŏn of Yŏnse University for introducing me to scholars in Korea. Over the years, Professor A Feng of the Chinese Academy of Social Sciences (CASS) has been invaluable in navigating the library collections of Beijing. I also thank Professor Chen Gaohua for his kind support of my work for the past decade and Professor Liu Xiao (also of CASS) for his valuable assistance in Yuan sources. Professor Morihira Masahiko provided an expert synopsis of Mongolian and Koryŏ sources in Seoul for me, a nearly total stranger. Yagi Takeshi, Nakasuna Akinori, and Yang Longzhang saved me from a number of translation blunders. Martin Heijdra has patiently fielded my bibliographic queries over the years. Finally, I owe a great debt to Professor Fuma Susumu for his limitless generosity during my time at Kyoto University (1992–93, 1999–2000, 2003–4) in providing guidance with sources, reading drafts, and giving me the opportunity to present early versions of this work.

Research takes time and travel, which requires financial support. I am deeply grateful to the Research Council of Colgate University for making possible Korean-language study and two trips to Seoul. Generous fellowships from the American Council of Learned Societies and the National Endowment for the Humanities provided essential support for research stints at Kyoto University and CASS. The tenure of the former forced me to fundamentally recast my project, and the tenure of the latter permitted me to complete the bulk of my research. This book would have been impossible without their support.

I have presented portions of this work at several conferences and seminars, including the Fritz Mote Memorial Conference (Princeton University), the Ming Taizu and His Age Conference (Chinese University of Hong Kong), the International Order in East Asia and Exchange, Third International Symposium (Kyoto University), and the Chinese Humanities Seminar (Harvard University). I owe a debt of gratitude to those who offered criticisms, suggestions, and encouragement. Professors Thomas Allsen, Elizabeth Endicott-West, William Atwell, and John Duncan offered insightful comments on early versions of this book and saved me from many embarrassing mistakes. Two anonymous readers for the press provided me with a wealth of invaluable suggestions and corrected many problems of romanization in Korean and Mongolian. I am also indebted to students of my Mongol Empire and Late Imperial China courses at Colgate University, who good-naturedly suffered various iterations of the manuscript.

D.M.R.

Contents

Koryŏ Kings During the Mongol Period

Adapted from Pak Yong-un, *Koryŏ sidaesa*, pp. 794–96.

Kojong 高宗 (1213–59)
Wŏnjong 元宗 (1259–74)
Ch'ungnyŏl 忠烈王 (1274–98.1)
Ch'ungsŏn 忠宣王 (1298.1–8)
Ch'ungnyŏl 忠烈王 (1298.8–1308.7)
Ch'ungsŏn 忠宣王 (1308–13)
Ch'ungsuk 忠肅王 (1313–30)
Ch'unghye 忠惠王 (1330–32)
Ch'ungsuk 忠肅王 (1332–39)
Ch'unghye 忠惠王 (1339–44)
Ch'ungmok 忠穆王 (1344–48)
Ch'ungjŏng 忠定王 (1349–51)
Kongmin 恭愍王 (1351–74)
U 禑王 (1374–88)
Chang 昌王 (1388–89)
Kongyang 恭讓王 (1389–92)

Mongolian Rulers

Adapted from *Cambridge History of China*, 6: xxviii.

Mongolian Name	Chinese Temple Name
Chinggis khan (Temüjin) (1206–27)	Taizu 太祖
Ögödei (1229–41)	Taizong 太宗
Güyük (1246–48)	Dingzong 定宗
Möngke (1251–59)	Xianzong 憲宗
Qubilai (1260–94)	Shizu 世祖
Temür (1295–1307)	Chengzong 成宗
Haishan (1308–11)	Wuzong 武宗
Ayurbarwada (1312–20)	Renzong 仁宗
Shidebala (1321–23)	Yingzong 英宗
Yisün-Temür (1324–28)	Taiding di 泰定帝
Aragibag (1328)	Tianshun 天順
Tuq-Temür (1328–29)	Wenzong 文宗
Qoshila (1329)	Mingzong 明宗
Tuq-Temür (1329–32)	Wenzong 文宗
Irinchibal (1332)	Ningzong 寧宗
Toghan-Temür (1333–70)	Huizong 惠宗 (Shundi 順帝)
Ayushiridara (1371–78)	Zhaozong 昭宗
Toghus-Temür (1379–88)	

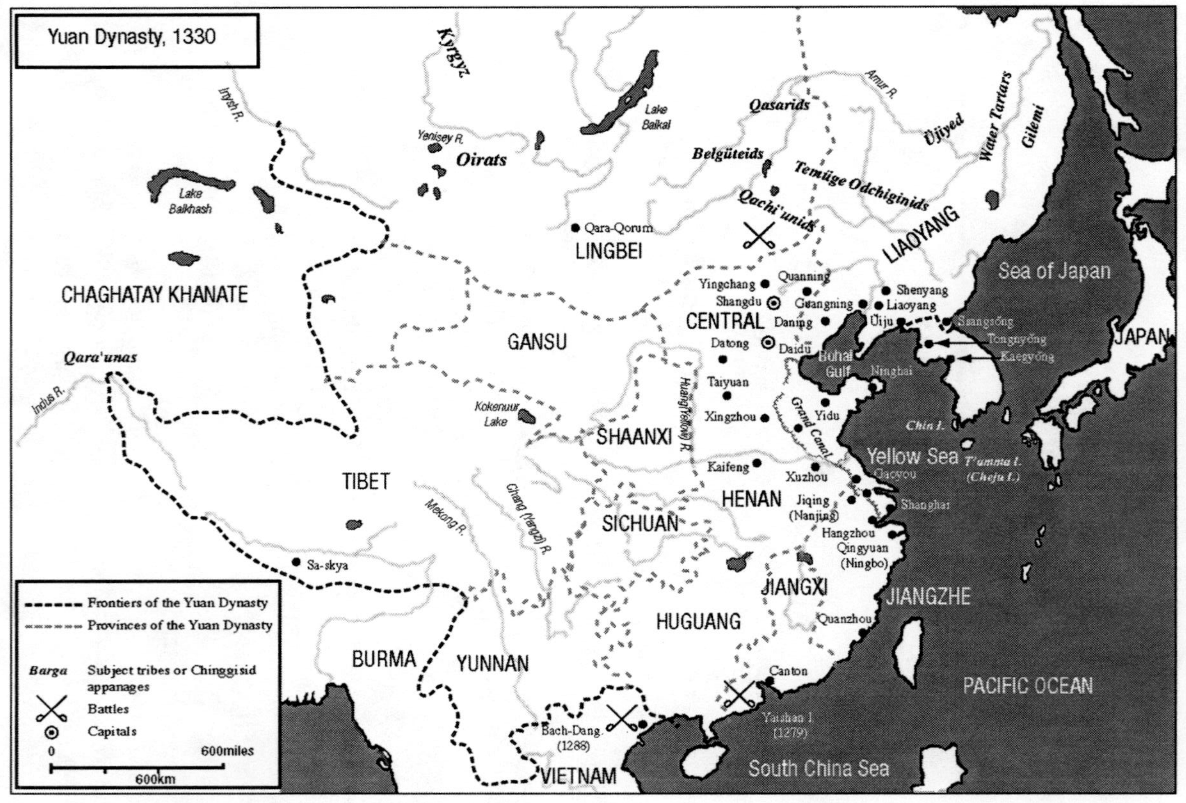

Map 1 Yuan dynasty, 1330 (adapted from Christopher Atwood, *Encyclopedia of Mongolian and the Mongol Empire* [New York: Facts on File, 2004]).

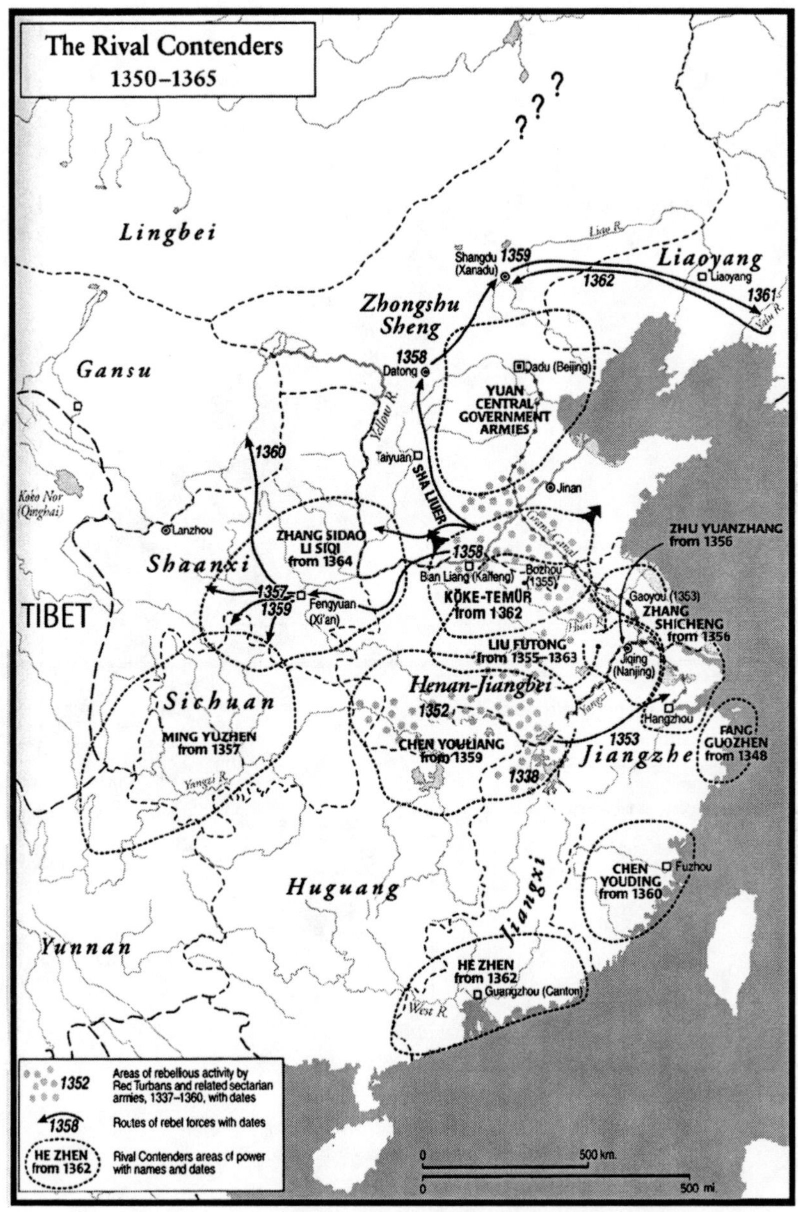

Map 2 The rival contenders, 1350–65 (adapted from Frederick Mote, *Imperial China* [Cambridge: Harvard University Press, 1999]).

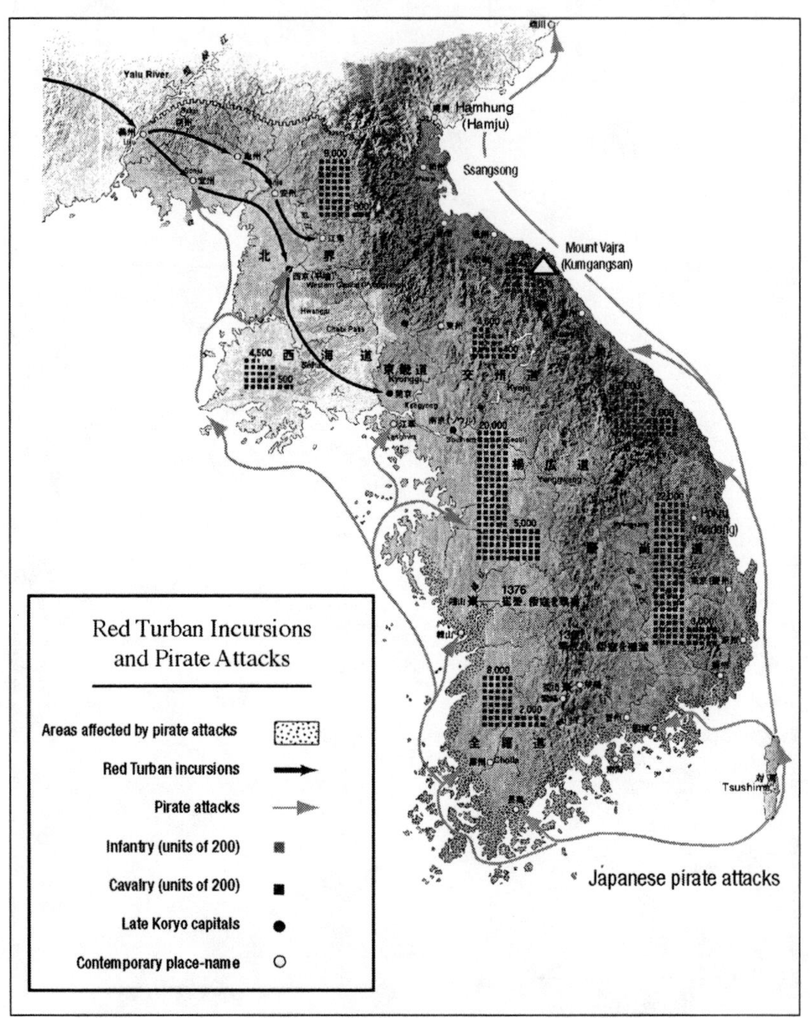

Map 3 Red Turban and pirate attacks (adapted from *Kankoku rekishi chizu* [Tokyo: Heibonsha, 2006].

Empire's Twilight
Northeast Asia Under the Mongols

Introduction

Six centuries after the collapse of the Mongol empire, it continues to confound historians. The Mongols integrated a wide variety of regions and peoples, each with its own local traditions, beliefs, and forms of organization. Few scholars possess the daunting linguistic and historical training necessary for comprehensive study of the Mongol empire. At a minimum, scholars need a firm command of classical Persian and Chinese, the major documentary languages of the empire, and preferably some Arabic, Turkish, and Mongolian. One might easily expand the list to a dozen classical and modern languages. In addition is the small matter of reading and contextualizing all those documents. Finally, and perhaps most challenging, is the task of synthesis, looking beyond the fragmented parts to perceive the greater whole.

Understandably, scholars often focus on one slice of the empire, most commonly units that correspond fairly well to contemporary nation-states. These studies often trace the unfolding of native political, cultural, economic, social, or intellectual traditions, with various degrees of attention to the impact of Mongol rule. A second major concern has been the interaction between the metropole—various Mongol courts throughout Eurasia—and local elites. Especially valuable has been the investigation of how local elites, both the well established and *arrivistes*, sought to advance their own interests within the matrix of the Mongolian empire. This dynamic of accommodation constitutes an essential element of empire. As Charles Maier has observed, "Empire is a form of political organization in which the social elements of those who rule in the dominant state . . . create a network of allied states in regions abroad who accept subordination in international affairs in return for security of their position in their administrative unit."[1] Several studies have drawn attention to ways that local elites from Armenia, Kart, and Rus to Tibet, North China, and Koryŏ forged ties with the Mongols to consolidate their position at home.

Single-slice studies are invaluable and provide the nuanced analysis possible only through mastery of the intricacies of difficult documentary traditions and careful consideration of prior cultural and political developments in a given area. Unfortunately, this kind of training and perspective can easily result in a balkanization of research and a fractured sense of the Mongolian empire.

Less examined but equally vital are the frameworks of empire within which both elites and commoners from disparate allied (or subjugated) lands interacted. The Mongols relocated sizable populations throughout Eurasia, often taking technical specialists from one part of the empire and resettling them in areas where the Mongols found their presence most convenient. Elite intermarriage between ruling houses, the practice of sending young princes as hostages to the Mongol court, service in the personal guard of the Mongol khans, great state banquets, and regular gift-exchanges were among the ways the Mongol empire fostered political allegiance and integration among a variety of regions and peoples. Single-slice studies only poorly capture this critical synchronic dimension of the Mongol age.

Another imbalance plagues the study of the Mongol empire—diachronic perspective. The dramatic early decades of world conquest and the glories of the mature empire during the mid- to late thirteenth century have been studied in great detail. The Mongols' decline and fall have in contrast languished in relative neglect. All the world knows Chinggis Khan; few recognize Toghan-Temür (1320–70) or Abu Sa'id (d. 1335), the last khans of khans to control East and West Asia, respectively. The fading decades of Mongol empire lack the larger-than-life figures and the clear plotline of war, conquest, and glory. With expansion came greater complexity; with decline, chaos. The parade of short-lived rulers, endless court intrigues, and countless regional uprisings across the page seems more an avalanche of unfamiliar names, dates, and places than a coherent narrative. Nonetheless, the age of Mongol domination did not end in the thirteenth century, and generalizations about the empire are impossible until we better understand the fourteenth century.

This work is an effort to address some of these problems. Inevitably it is a compromise. Although informed by considerations of the Mongol empire as a whole, it focuses on a discrete geographical area—Northeast Asia. I use "Northeast Asia" to refer to the kingdom of Koryŏ (918–1392) on the Korean peninsula, southern Liaodong (southern Manchuria), Shandong, and the territory northeast of the primary Mongol capital in eastern Eurasia, Daidu (present-day Beijing). Thus, I am looking at more than a single kingdom but far, far less than the entire empire. Similarly, although it considers the emergence of Mongol structures of empire in Northeast Asia throughout the thirteenth century, this study analyzes warfare during the tumultuous mid-fourteenth century and its impact on Mongol rule. Finally, I argue that a more nuanced appreciation of dynamics in Northeast Asia during a time of crisis can shed light on similar developments elsewhere in Eurasia and, more generally, on the nature of the Mongol empire.

The Red Turban Wars

The largest rebellion of the fourteenth-century world occurred in its most affluent and powerful empire, the Great Mongol Nation (*Yeke Mongghol ulus*), or the Great Yuan *ulus* (*Dai Yuwan ulus*), as it was known in East Asia.[2] The Great Yuan *ulus* controlled territory corresponding to today's People's Republic of China, Mongolia, and southern Siberia and exercised profound influence over Tibet and Korea. At the core of the rebellion, or more accurately many related rebellions, were the Red Turbans. Loosely organized and inspired by a heady brew of apocalyptic millenarianism rooted in Buddhism, the Red Turbans produced dozens of important military and religious leaders. During the mid-fourteenth century, these leaders clashed with Yuan imperial regulars, locally organized Chinese militias, and largely autonomous Chinese and Mongolian warlords. They also established regional regimes that shaped the lives of millions of people during the 1350s and 1360s.

The destructive Red Turban wars are most commonly approached from the perspective of Chinese history. The battles were fought largely on Chinese soil, nearly all the leaders and followers were Chinese, and they contributed to the fall of an alien regime (the Mongol Yuan) and the rise of the last Chinese dynasty, the Ming (1368–1644). Thus, in recent decades and in past centuries, most scholars have tended to approach the reconfigurations of the late Yuan as a prelude to the Ming dynasty's rise.[3] Distant from the epicenter of early Ming rule in Jiangnan (the arc of affluent cities and their hinterlands radiating out from present-day Shanghai), developments in Northeast Asia, in contrast, are frequently shunted to the margins.[4] Few have considered the significance of these rebellions in the wider context of the Mongol Empire or East Asia.

The fighting in the Northeast Asian theater of the late Yuan wars was a major international event. It is difficult to imagine that an episode of similar magnitude in European history—hundreds of thousands of imperial regulars, royal troops, local militias, and rebel soldiers fighting for more than five years across approximately 250,000 square miles (about the size of France or the state of Texas) in a strategic region with consequences that would be felt for decades—might be passed over in near silence. Yet, not a single English-language study has examined this important facet of the Mongolian empire's collapse. Consideration of the Red Turban wars in Northeast Asia deepens our understanding of several major developments of the mid-fourteenth century: the renewed importance of military men, intensified diplomatic activities among an unusually wide variety of actors, and precarious state control of local society and resources.

The Red Turban campaigns were both a cause and a symptom of the growing prominence of military men. The rise of military warlords in the Yuan during the mid-fourteenth century has been well studied in the context of Chinese history. Scholars of Korean history, too, have noted the emergence of powerful generals, one of whom ended the Koryŏ kingdom and established the Chosŏn (1392–1910). Closely linked, these developments should be seen as a regional trend that also included the rise of such Mongolian figures as Naghachu and Gaojianu in Liaodong. The Red Turban wars illumine both points of commonality and significant variation in the role and impact of military men across the region.

Similarly, the intensification of diplomatic activity within Northeast Asia occasioned by the Red Turban wars sheds light on patterns that normally do not emerge with such clarity in dynastic chronicles. Simultaneously, these shifting military and political exigencies altered relations both between the ruling houses of the Great Yuan *ulus* and Koryŏ and between the thrones and their nominal, but increasingly autonomous, servants. Powerful Mongol leaders in Liaodong struggled to adjust to a world in which Daidu's writ seemed increasingly distant and allies closer to home grew more vital. These Mongol military commanders alternately cajoled, threatened, and courted the Koryŏ throne (and more local figures along the northwestern and northeastern borders of Koryŏ). The Koryŏ court's triumph in the Red Turban wars threw into relief its strategic importance to competing interests within the Mongol court and showed how closely intertwined political elites in Northeast Asia had grown. During the 1350s, 1360s, and 1370s, Great Yuan *ulus* ministers, the Koryŏ court, local Mongol commanders in Liaodong, and Chinese warlords far to the south all invoked the Red Turban campaigns to advance their interests. The particular ways that they employed the Red Turban wars illumine the increasingly precarious balance of alliance and autonomy, of past ties and future opportunities.

Finally, the Red Turban wars provide insight into more local political and socioeconomic developments throughout Northeast Asia. The Red Turban campaigns held a different strategic importance for Koryŏ's King Kongmin (1330–74) than they did for the Great Yuan *ulus*'s khan of khans, Toghan-Temür; their impact on domestic political dynamics mirrored that divergence. The Red Turban wars throw into relief the precarious position of the Koryŏ king vis-à-vis the aristocracy in his own capital, Kaegyŏng, his uncertain control of material and labor resources in the countryside, and questions about the loyalty of the military to the throne. Red Turban forces twice invaded Koryŏ in large numbers, occupying both Sŏgyŏng 西京 (hereafter referred to as the Western Capital, present-day P'yŏngyang) and Kaegyŏng 開京 (the dynasty's main capital and site of the central government, modern Kaesŏng), driving the court south to Pokju 福州 (present-day Andong) severing government control over much of northern Koryŏ, throwing royal finances into chaos, providing fertile ground for deadly intrigue at the Koryŏ court, and greatly increasing the prominence of military leaders in regional and dynastic politics.

Although Red Turban forces sacked Toghan-Temür's secondary capital of Shangdu, his primary capital, Daidu, held firm. Developments to the south in the economically critical regions of present-day Jiangsu, Zhejiang, and Fujian commanded more of his attention and resources than did the Red Turban campaigns in the northeast. Nonetheless, the Red Turban wars in Shandong and Liaodong reveal the limitations of local Yuan governance, the steady militarization of society, and how overland and maritime transportation networks that once united the empire could be turned to its subversion. They facilitated the flow of war refugees beyond government control and the movement of rebel forces to vulnerable areas in the Great Yuan *ulus*.

Themes of This Study

Four related themes run through my attempt to place the Red Turban wars in the wider context of Northeast Asia and the Mongol empire: the need for a regional perspective versus that of dynasty or country; the process and consequences of integration under the Mongols; the tendency for individual and family interests to trump those of dynasty, country, or linguistic affiliation; and finally, the need to see Koryŏ as part of the wider Mongol empire.

Several scholars, perhaps most notably Thomas Allsen and Sugiyama Masaaki 杉山正明, have undertaken global studies of the Mongol empire.[5] Lacking their linguistic and historical gifts, I have taken up a more modest project—exploration of the northeastern corner of the empire during the chaotic mid-fourteenth century. This study eschews an exclusive focus on any one country. The Great Yuan *ulus* encompassed much more than just China proper. In fact, the term "Yuan dynasty," with its misleading connotations of a Chinese-style dynasty, is perhaps best avoided.[6] It directly administered the vast expanses of Mongolia, Liaodong, and the transitional zone between the steppe and the sown only intermittently controlled by Chinese dynasties. The Yuan also expanded southward into areas never before subjugated by the Chinese. Finally, the Yuan exercised greater influence in Koryŏ and Tibet than almost any Chinese regime. Given the enormous scale of the Great Yuan *ulus*, developments in one of its regions frequently had significant repercussions elsewhere in the empire. Exclusive focus on a single component of the story—whether China, Korea, or the steppe—misses the big picture. Such a perspective also risks miscasting even the disaggregated elements.

Northeast Asia formed an important part of the Mongol empire. Developments there are fundamental to understanding the nature of both the Mongol empire and the new post-empire world emerging in the 1350s and 1360s. In Northeast Asia, Jurchen, Mongol, Chinese, Korean, and Japanese interests intersected (and would continue to intersect until the last days of imperial East Asia). The collapse of the Great Yuan *ulus* reshaped Northeast Asia perhaps more dramatically than any other region of East Asia. To understand this transition, or series of transitions, one cannot examine single dynasties in isolation. Neighboring polities nearly always influence one another, and the Mongol period witnessed much intensified interaction.

My decision to focus on the region of Northeast Asia rather than China, Korea, or Liaodong is linked to a second theme of the book—the unprecedented integration under the Mongols. During the thirteenth and fourteenth centuries, Mongol rule extended from the Pacific coast to eastern Europe, from the forests of Siberia to subtropical southern China. The largest contiguous land empire in history, it ushered in a new scale of global integration. Under the Mongols, everything from people, textiles, and foodstuffs to religion, art, and precious jewels, from scientific technologies, military hardware, and administrative ideals to microbes, spices, and sartorial fashions flowed more broadly and more rapidly than ever before.[7] Entire peoples were uprooted, and ethnic identities remade.[8]

In the context of East Asian history, many have noted that the Mongols unified "Greater China" for the first time in centuries, bringing the north and south together under one rule and greatly facilitating economic integration and cultural developments in areas as varied as theater, painting, thought, and geography. The incorporation of southern Chinese territories into the Mongols' global empire "exploded the cramped, localist perspective of the Southern Song, a perspective imposed as much by geopolitical confines as by politics and ideology."[9] At the same time, as numerous studies have elucidated, such groups as Tibetans, Turks, Muslims, Jurchens, and Khitans played a large role in the Great Yuan *ulus*.[10] In Northeast Asia, the Mongols forcibly relocated tens of thousands of Koryŏ subjects to southern Liaodong. Later, other inhabitants of Koryŏ followed voluntarily in search of economic and political opportunities. New administrative structures of the empire cut across old dynastic borders: the Mongols established bureaucratic offices in the Koryŏ capital of Kaegyŏng; they created military zones in northern Koryŏ that reported to Daidu rather than Kaegyŏng; and they set up overlapping jurisdictions in Liaodong under Mongol nobles, former Koryŏ military men, and a variety of Chinese, Jurchen, and Koryŏ bureaucrats. Overland and maritime transportation networks bound the region more tightly than in previous centuries, facilitating the flow of personnel, material, and culture from Kaegyŏng to Liaodong, Daidu, and beyond.[11]

If we think in terms of region rather than nation or dynasty and if we bear in mind the new levels of economic, political, military, and social integration, it is easy to understand why personal and family interests often trumped those of dynasty, country, or linguistic affiliation. This, my third theme, was particularly true in time of rapid change. If the rise of the Mongols transformed world history and culture, the empire's collapse in the mid-fourteenth century had similarly profound consequences. The sprawling, loosely knit polity's fall not only brought decades of suffering, death, and unrest but also created new political dynamics, opportunities, and vacuums. The patterns of integration forged by the Mongols profoundly shaped behavior during the empire's twilight. Half a century ago, Henry Serruys, a clear-eyed scholar of daunting industry and exacting standards, observed apropos Sino-Mongol relations, "A national feeling in the modern sense that one belonged to a definite nation, or was a member of a specific race sharply distinct from any other one, hardly existed in China in the fourteenth century. Loyalty was loyalty to a reigning house, a dynasty, a leader, a general, an army commander."[12] In fact, I would argue that political, military, and economic ties transcended those to individual dynasties or countries. The integrative structures of the Mongol empire provided those who lived through the chaotic decades of the fourteenth century a wider perspective that facilitated cooperation and alliance across dynastic or linguistic affiliations.[13] The empire's collapse reflected its quiddity.

Finally, this book argues for the need to see the Koryŏ kingdom as part of the Great Yuan *ulus*. The ruling Wang dynasty was part of the Eurasian elite created under the Mongol empire. The Wangs were *küregen*, Chinggisid in-laws, and full participants in a set of institutions that incorporated elite Tibetans, Uyghurs, Persians, Georgians, Armenians, and others into the Great Mongol Nation. Much Korean scholarship casts Koryŏ's position vis-à-vis the Mongols as unique or anomalous. Scholars have debated how Koryŏ under the Mongols should be characterized: defeated in battle but still administratively distinct; conquered and subjugated; or autonomous but subject to Mongol interference. Others argue that since Koryŏ culture and identity survived, the country must have been independent. The focus on independence or identity in the face of empire is understandable given the context of aggressive, invasive Japanese colonization of Korea during the first half of the twentieth century and the succeeding cold war. However, framing the question in such terms obscures more than it illuminates. The Mongols generally showed little interest in converting their subject lands to Mongolian culture or custom.[14]

Koryŏ was far from unique. Its position was analogous in many ways to several small and midsize polities throughout Eurasia, such as the Sa skya regime of Tibet, the Uyghurs of Turfan, the regional "lords" (*naxarars*) of Armenia, the princes of Rus, the Qutlugh Khanid dynasty of Kirman, or the Karts of Herat, whose regimes the Mongols either incorporated or created.[15] The destruction of the Song, the Jurchen Jin (1115–1234), and the Khwārazmanshāh were the exceptions, vitally important, but still not the rule. The Mongols incorporated polities and ethnic groups, both steppe and sedentary, whenever feasible. As the following chapters demonstrate, Koryŏ during the thirteenth and fourteenth centuries must be considered in the global context of the Mongol empire.[16] Although the depth and accuracy of their understanding varied widely, observers from Western Europe and West Asia understood that Koryŏ had fallen under Mongol dominion and that Koryŏ envoys regularly traveled to Mongol capitals.[17] Their knowledge of Koryŏ derived, of course, from the Mongolian matrix that facilitated the flow of information throughout most of Eurasia.

Two Men and a Woman

This study is also the story of two men and a woman. The men were the rulers of the Great Yuan *ulus* and the Koryŏ dynasty—Toghan-Temür and King Kongmin, respectively. The woman was Toghan-Temür's Korean-born wife, Empress Ki. Less renowned than his illustrious forefathers Chinggis Khan (1167–1227) and Qubilai Khan (1215–

94), Toghan-Temür nonetheless held the throne longer than any other Yuan ruler and more than four times as long as any other Mongol emperor of the fourteenth century—from 1333 to 1370. King Kongmin, too, enjoyed an unusually long reign for fourteenth-century Korean rulers (1352–74).

Both men have mixed reputations. Many have noted Toghan-Temür's efforts to revitalize the Great Yuan *ulus* in the early years of his reign. Perhaps more ink has been spilt about his shortcomings: contemporary observers criticized Toghan-Temür for his lack of interest in matters of state; some decried his debilitating enthusiasm for Tantric Buddhism, sex, and elaborate ceremonies; still others struggled to square his obvious intellectual abilities with his failure to conform to Confucian ideals of a moral sage. Later historians further excoriated him as a cynical manipulator who cast aside powerful ministers once they were no longer of use or had grown dangerously powerful. In some ways, he was an odd figure. In contrast to most Mongolian nobles, he disliked alcohol. Instead he found solace in painting, calligraphy, and boating. Ultimately, however, he is known as the last Mongolian emperor to rule China, the man who lost the jewel of Qubilai's empire.

Most accounts hold that King Kongmin also began auspiciously. Editors of the mid-fifteenth century *Official History of the Koryŏ Dynasty* praised the king for his intelligence, compassion, and early successes in wresting greater autonomy from the Mongols. Writing in the wake of five decades of Japanese colonial rule and in the midst of the cold war period, Korean historians of the twentieth century also warmed to these elements of Kongmin's legacy. Like Toghan-Temür, he was a gifted painter, a man of refined sensibilities who disliked the hunt but appreciated the ferocity of his prey. Scholars often see the death of his beloved Mongolian queen in 1365 as a turning point. Overwhelmed by grief, the king is said to have lost interest in government, yielded the reins of power to an unprincipled Buddhist monk, and turned to handsome young men to fill the gaping hole created by his wife's death. Prominent scholars such as the late Kim Sang-gi 金庠基 hold that these actions hastened the Koryŏ dynasty's fall.[18] Thus, for some he is a romantic, even tragic, figure, who began well but was destroyed by loss and grief.

The two men struggled to maintain power in a time of accelerating change: bloody purges at court, growing militarization of local society, and a series of devastating floods, epidemics, and famines throughout the empire. The campaigns against the Red Turbans shaped the worlds of Toghan-Temür and King Kongmin. They affected economic resources, social policy, personnel decisions, and military strategy. The course of the campaigns figured in the fortunes of leading ministers and generals at the courts of both men and in the relations of the two rulers to their respective servitors. Finally, the rebellions had a palpable impact on relations between emperor and king, between the Great Yuan *ulus* and the Koryŏ dynasty.

And what of the woman? Beautiful, ambitious, and a brilliant politician, Empress Ki was the most influential woman in mid-fourteenth-century Eurasia. Having won Toghan-Temür's affection and secured her status as empress, she built a powerful patronage network that stretched from the Yuan court to the provinces, from the Mongolian capitals of Daidu and Shangdu to the corridors of power in Kaegyŏng. Empress Ki's ambitions for her son, the heir apparent, would imperil both her husband and King Kongmin. Although Chinese and Korean accounts portray her as conniving, unprincipled, and dangerous, Ki reflected the more general status of women in the Mongol empire, which allowed significant political power to women, even non-Mongolians. At the same time, her particular passions and ambitions shaped domestic and international relations throughout Northeast Asia in specific ways.

To tell this story, I have brought together several bodies of scholarship that usually stand separate, principally studies of the late Koryŏ period, the late Yuan period, and the Mongol empire in general. I have drawn on court chronicles, private histories, policy proposals, letters, essays, temple inscriptions, and poems written in classical Chinese from the Great Yuan *ulus*, the Koryŏ dynasty, and to a lesser extent the later Ming and Chosŏn dynasties. In order to make sense of Northeast Asia under the Mongols, I have made liberal use of the excellent work of scholars working in English, Chinese, Japanese, and Korean who have examined everything from art patronage, religious practices, and political reform to military institutions, maritime trade, and cultural transmission. My debt to them is great and gratefully acknowledged.

Organization of This Book

Better capturing the interlocking connections of this period, a regional perspective gives due consideration to discrete political borders but also makes clear the larger developments of the day. The organization of this book reflects this approach. It begins with a bird's-eye view of the Mongol consortium during the mid-fourteenth century to better contextualize events in East Asia. From there, it reviews the challenges that the Yuan faced during its last decades. Having established the problems, approaches, and resources available to the Yuan court, I then focus on developments in the Northeast, that is, present-day Shandong province, Hebei province northeast of Beijing, southern Liaodong, and Koryŏ. Another way to think about the region under examination would be to say the lands bordering Bohai Bay and the northern Yellow Sea and their hinterlands.

Chapter 1 examines the integration of Northeast Asia under the Mongols. It begins with a consideration of governance, most especially that of Liaodong and Koryŏ, under the Mongols. These structures incorporated several key groups, including powerful Mongolian nobles, ethnic groups placed under the control of Korean allies, and finally administrative and military units in northern Korea and Kaegyŏng that reported directly to the Great Yuan *ulus*. The chapter concludes with a survey of other forms of integration such as culture, religion, economics, and the military.

Chapter 2 argues that the collapse of Mongol rule in North China, most especially the Capital Region during the fourteenth century, was not a foregone conclusion in 1350. It then traces the spread of banditry, famine, and disease, the rise of the Red Turban commander Mao Gui, his seizure of Shandong, his attack on Daidu, and the Yuan government's successful military campaign against the Red Turbans in the Capital Region and Shandong. It closes with a brief review of Master Guan and other Red Turban leaders whose troops sacked Shangdu and threatened Liaodong and beyond.

Chapter 3 considers the place of Koryŏ in the Mongol empire. After reviewing the marriage ties that linked the ruling houses of the Great Yuan *ulus* and the Koryŏ dynasty, it looks at the fate of several of King Kongmin's predecessors during the fourteenth century. It ends with

Kongmin's response to the spreading rebellions in China and his efforts to bolster the power of the throne at home.

Chapters 4 and 5 narrate the Red Turban wars in Northeast Asia. Chapter 4 chronicles the first years of Red Turban wars in Liaodong and Koryŏ from 1357 to 1360; Chapter 5 treats the Red Turban wars in Koryŏ to their conclusion early in 1362. It considers Koryŏ's military response and war's impact on domestic politics. In particular it shows that widespread fighting increased the power and standing of military commanders and argues that King Kongmin tacitly approved the elimination of the generals who had just won back his capital.

Chapters 6, 7, and 8 consider the impact of the Red Turban wars on Northeast Asia. Chapter 6 looks briefly at Liaodong and Koryŏ in the wake of the Red Turban wars. Chapter 7 analyzes the ways in which the Red Turban wars became imbricated into diplomatic relations between the Koryŏ and Yuan courts through a study of Tash-Temür, a Koryŏ royal clansman the Mongols attempted to put on the Koryŏ throne. Chapter 8 widens to examine the shifting international landscape of East Asia during the 1360s, with special attention to the place of Koryŏ. It argues that the Red Turban wars figured in international perceptions of the Koryŏ dynasty and that King Kongmin attempted to exploit his military success in those wars during his negotiations with such varied players as the Mongol generals Naghachu and Köke-Temür, and the Chinese warlord Zhang Shicheng. The study concludes with a brief consideration of shifting memories of the Red Turban wars and a look forward to the emerging order of the late fourteenth century.

I

Northeast Asia and the Mongol Empire

The Mongol Empire in the Fourteenth Century

By the mid-fourteenth century, the glory days of the Mongol empire were decades in the past.[1] From its earliest days on the steppe, the Mongols' regime had been characterized by flexibility, pronounced regional autonomy, and an ever-shifting balance of interests within the Mongol aristocracy.[2] However, even after the famed "dissolution" of the Mongolian realm during the 1260s and emergence of several major, largely autonomous *ulus*es (the Golden Horde in Rus and the Qipchaq steppe, the Il-khanate in western Asia, the houses of Ögödei and Chaghatay in Central Asia, and the Great Yuan in East Asia),[3] certain bureaucratic practices such as taxation, population censuses, investiture rituals, and revenue-sharing provided the empire a loose structural coherence.[4] The Mongols' deservedly famous communication system facilitated the movement of personnel, goods, and information across Eurasia. Many of these structures and practices would outlive the Mongols' reign, surviving in various successor regimes from China to Persia.

By the 1330s, Mongol control over much of Eurasia was under immense strain. In the Il-khanate, increasingly violent competition for political legitimacy and control of modern-day Iran, Iraq, and Afghanistan began with the death of Abu Sa'id, whose lack of an heir ended the direct line of the house of Hülegü. Early in the fourteenth century, intra-Mongol rivalry brought an end to the house of Ögödei in Turkestan. Despite the impressive success of Qaidu (1236–1301), who had dramatically improved Ögödeid fortunes during the second half of the thirteenth century, by 1307 the house had been largely subordinated to the Chaghatayid line. During the mid-fourteenth century, the power of the Chaghatayid house became restricted to eastern Turkestan and even there faced increasing challenges.[5] In contrast, although its authority was periodically challenged during the fourteenth century, the Golden Horde retained its rule over Rus well into the fifteenth century. Beginning in the 1330s, the Great Yuan *ulus* confronted a series of natural disasters, civil wars, and local revolts. As the following chapters show, however, the Mongol regime in East Asia demonstrated vigorous and occasionally brilliant leadership until a surprisingly late date.

The Last Decades of the Yuan

The Mongol conquest of first the Jurchen Jin dynasty (1115–1234) and then the Chinese Southern Song (1127–1279) over the course of the thirteenth century is well known and requires little comment here; scholars have examined its political, economic, and military facets in great detail.[6] Under Chinggis Khan's grandson, Qubilai (r. 1260–93), all Song territory fell under Mongol control. The Great Yuan *ulus* came to include neighboring lands that had not previously been subject to Chinese rule. In addition to Manchuria, Mongolia, and Tibet, such areas as Yunnan and the oasis-cities west of Shanxi were now more thoroughly tied to the major population and economic centers of China than ever before. Although such Great Khans as Möngke (r. 1251–59) and Qubilai strove to bring greater control over local revenues into the hands of the central government,[7] Mongol rule was relatively indirect. After incorporation into the Mongol polity through formal submission and investiture, local rulers were often left in place. As long as they guaranteed the flow of tribute, taxes, and personnel to the Mongol court, local powerholders enjoyed considerable autonomy. Few efforts were made to impose religious preferences, social practices, or cultural orientations on local populations.

Similarly, members of the Mongol nobility maintained a relatively high degree of autonomy from central authorities. The idea that the entire empire, and all the large and small *ulus*es that constituted the whole, was the joint patrimony of the Mongols proved highly resistant to challenge. As Michal Biran has noted, the conflicts of Qubilai and later Great Khans with fellow Mongolian aristocrats are often cast in terms of ideology. Ariq Böke (d. 1266), Qaidu (1235–1301), and Nayan may have felt some measure of distaste for Qubilai's so-called Chinese ways. More fundamental to the armed struggles among Mongolian nobles was, however, the tension over control of lands, revenue, and personnel.[8] Qubilai vanquished most of his Mongol enemies on the battlefield (Qaidu was the primary exception), but the basic conflict remained unchanged. Long after Qubilai's death, flexibility and strong local autonomy remained hallmarks of the Mongol empire.

Steppe patterns of deliberative government and shared authority shaped Mongol governance in China.[9] Yuan emperors never became reliant on Chinese methods of governance. Nor did they ever exclusively patronize Chinese governmental officials, religious figures, or cultural pursuits. The Mongols adopted financial, administrative, military, and artistic technologies from Chinese, Persian, Uyghur, Khitan, Jurchen, and European traditions to suit their own needs and inclinations. Such borrowings inevitably also prompted reinterpretations of both foreign and Mongolian traditions.

The Great Yuan *ulus* united the economic resources and administrative infrastructure of China with the Mongols' strategic vision and global concerns.[10] Although the initial conquest of China involved considerable brutality, destruction of the agricultural base, social dislocation, and widespread land flight, in time Chinese society and the economy thrived. This was especially true in the territories of the former Southern Song, which suffered far less extensive damage from warfare and political turmoil than North China. As was true in the Il-khanate in West Asia, publishing, painting, and many fields of scholarship flourished under the Great Yuan *ulus*. Although debate continues about the impact of incorporation into the Mongol empire on the Chinese economy,[11] there are strong indications that it thrived. In fact, the burgeoning economy made possible the growth of commercial publishing, the spread of Confucian academies, and the development of theater, to name just a few areas that flowered under the Great Yuan *ulus*.[12] The current re-evaluation of the Mongols' impact on China has close parallels in reassessments of developments in Rus and West Asia under the Golden Horde and the Il-khanate.[13]

The Last Great Khan in China

The study of the history of the Great Yuan *ulus* is curiously unbalanced. The Mongol court maintained a primary capital at Daidu until 1368. Powerful Mongol commanders held sway over much of the southwestern, northwestern, and northeastern regions of the Great Yuan *ulus* for decades longer. Most scholars, however, have focused their attention either on the dramatic rise of Chinggis Khan and the early years of the Mongol empire or on Qubilai's long and glorious reign. With some notable exceptions, understanding of the latter half of the Yuan remains rudimentary. A review of recent Japanese scholarship describes the field of post-Qubilai political history as "rather lonely."[14] This is even truer of English-language scholarship. The Great Yuan *ulus*, however, continued to evolve over the course of the fourteenth century. Developments in politics, economics, the military, culture, and society did not end with Qubilai's death. Closer examination of these events is essential for balanced evaluations and generalizations of the Mongol period in East Asia.

The last Mongol emperor to rule China, Toghan-Temür (known posthumously in most Chinese sources as Shundi 順帝), ascended the throne in 1333. He was a compromise candidate who came to the throne as a frightened boy. As a result of court intrigue, his father, Qoshila (1300–1329), had been exiled to distant Yunnan in the southwest and then escaped to the safety of the Chaghatay court before being recalled to the Great Yuan *ulus*. Qoshila held the throne for several months, before dying suddenly in 1329 (quite likely poisoned by a political rival). At this point, Toghan-Temür might simply have been eliminated. As his father's experiences illustrate, the Mongols, however, often exiled their elites rather than execute them immediately. Shunted to the side, Toghan-Temür was sent first to an isolated island off the southwest coast of Koryŏ and then to Jingjiang 靜江 (present-day Guilin) deep in the Chinese south, where he began his study of the Chinese classics and calligraphy. In 1333 he was summoned to Daidu and placed on the throne. During the early years of his reign, powerful senior Mongol nobles dominated the boy emperor. Plots to remove him from power began almost as soon as he ascended the throne. Not until 1340, when Toghan-Temür reached his early twenties, did he begin to rule as well as reign.[15]

Although far from an outstanding political or military leader, Toghan-Temür surely does not deserve the abuse heaped on him over the centuries. It was his misfortune that the Great Yuan *ulus* crumbled during his reign. To consign him to the category of degenerate last rulers whose personal faults trigger a dynastic collapse fits nicely into well-established Confucian historiographical traditions.[16] For those who wish to understand the last Mongol emperor to control China, court dynamics, and conditions in Northeast Asia, however, such a perspective is quaint at best.

Critics of all stripes found much that was objectionable about Toghan-Temür. To give just one example, Confucian officials seized on the emperor's keen interest in Tibetan Buddhism as evidence of his depravity and poor political judgment. Contemporary officials complained to the throne that he spent far too much time in the pursuit of tantric rituals with Tibetan monks and a circle of boon companions.[17] Compiled by the succeeding Ming dynasty largely on the basis of extant Chinese materials, the *Official History of the Yuan Dynasty* dismissed these pursuits as mere debauchery. Even when the *Official History of the Yuan Dynasty* includes documents revealing that the emperor and Tibetan monks understood these ritual practices in a more profound spiritual sense, editorial comments stress the vain and foolish aspects. One Tibetan master pointed out the fleeting nature of this world to the Yuan ruler. "Although Your Highness holds the esteemed position of supreme monarch and is blessed with the wealth of all the world, these may be held for no more than this lifetime. How long does life last? [Your Highness] should accept this Hevajra Samadhi (Chin. *Da xile chanding* 大喜樂禪定)." Editors of the *Official History of the Yuan Dynasty* characterized this and other tantric rites as "all arts of the bedroom" and Toghan-Temür's practices as "exclusively licentious amusements in this pleasure."[18]

Compiled at the order of Ming founder, Zhu Yuanzhang 朱元璋 (1328–98), the *Official History of the Yuan Dynasty* was simultaneously a historical chronicle of the past and a political message intended for contemporary audiences. The Mongol court posed a military menace to the fledgling Ming dynasty; it also constituted a threat to Zhu's political legitimacy. Zhu Yuanzhang's rush to complete the *Official History of the Yuan Dynasty* was motivated by the political need to underscore that the Yuan had lost the Mandate of Heaven. The *Official History* was intended to serve as evidence of its demise.[19] Discrediting Toghan-Temür fit neatly into a Chinese historiographical tradition that emphasized the moral failings of last emperors as an explanation for dynastic collapse and loss of legitimacy.[20]

Tibetan Buddhism's sophisticated visual meditation techniques and rich iconographic art did not exhaust its attractions for Toghan-Temür. Following a decades-long tradition strongly associated with Qubilai, Toghan-Temür also sought protection of the state and his rule in Tibetan Buddhism. Located north of Beijing, the famed Juyong Gate (Juyong guan 居庸關) bears silent testimony to late Yuan efforts to bolster the position of both the Great Khan and the dynasty.[21] Constructed at great expense in the mid-1340s, the Juyong Gate featured "a stupa (reliquary) gate in the Tibetan style (the uppermost stupa structure is now lost), and may have been one of four planned gates intended to guard the four directions surrounding the Yuan capital at Beijing."[22] Guardians of the four directions and other images drawn from a strongly Tibetan tradition were carved into the arched, stone passageway through which travelers and armies would have passed on their way from the north to Beijing.[23]

Perhaps the most striking feature of the Juyong Gate is the set of inscriptions in six languages—Chinese, Uyghur, Xixia (Tangut), Tibetan, Sanskrit, and the Mongols' universal phonetic system, 'Phags pa. In slightly different ways, they articulate the divine and universal character of the Mongol rulers. The Mongol inscription reads in part as follows: "That blessed bodhisattva, the Emperor Secen [Qubilai] possessed vast wisdom, about whom the prophecy was made that there would be someone named 'The Wise One from the vicinity of Mount Wutai [Mañjuśrī], who would become a great emperor.'"[24] The passage identifies Qubilai Khan as the reincarnation of Mañjuśrī, the bodhisattva of wisdom who in some traditions was considered a protector of China. Thus, Qubilai was no mere Mongol ruler who controlled Chinese territory through virtue of superior military force but the reincarnation of a Buddhist deity who was to protect and shield China. He was a universal ruler.[25]

For Toghan-Temür, whose paternity was impugned, whose personal power was uncertain, and whose dynasty was deteriorating, Juyong Pass with its complex cosmological and political message was an attempt to assert a direct tie to a glorious forefather, to reassert claims to the tradition of universal rulership first articulated by the thirteenth-century Tibetan polymath, the cleric 'Phags pa, on behalf of Qubilai, and to bolster the supernatural defenses of his capital in a time of growing crisis. Toghan-Temür was clearly interested in Qubilai; in the twelfth lunar month of 1354, he ordered the production of a tapestry portrait of his forefather.[26] Toghan-Temür also continued tantric Buddhist rites in the capital first introduced under Qubilai. As he explained to the empire's most powerful minister in 1354, "In the past, We held a *gdugs dkar* Dharma ritual (Chin. *duosigeerhaoshi* 朵思哥兒好事),[27] welcomed the White Umbrella, and circumambulated the walls of the Imperial City. In reality this was done on behalf of [all] the sentient beings in the realm." He ordered a leading Tibetan Buddhist cleric to select 108 monks to continue the rites.[28]

The Juyong Pass formed one element in a larger project designed to revitalize the Great Yuan *ulus*. Also during the 1340s, the Yuan throne sponsored a series of important political and cultural measures: the court restored the state civil service examination in 1342; it ordered the completion of the official histories of the Jin, Liao, and Song dynasties; it compiled and published an updated version of legal statutes; and it announced tax reductions and tax amnesties for many groups in society.[29] All these measures were designed to bolster the emperor's authority and prestige. The new regime also tried to alleviate deeply felt grievances among the Mongolian nobility by restoring many key figures to their former titles and positions.[30] The results of the reforms were mixed, but the Yuan remained committed to meeting the changing challenges of the day. One strategic region essential for the survival of the Great Yuan *ulus* was Liaodong and, more broadly, Northeast Asia.

Liaodong Under the Mongols

A rough and ready designation, Liaodong (literally, "east of the Liao [River]") referred during the Yuan period to a broad swath of territory corresponding to the three provinces of Liaoning, Jilin, and Heilongjiang in the People's Republic of China as well as most of the eastern half of Siberia and Sakhalin Island. It included deep forests, several major river systems including the Amur River in the northeast and Liao River in southwest, extensive swamplands (largely along the Amur), as well as great tracts of fertile lands, rolling hills, and a few mountain chains. In the north, fishing and hunting tended to predominate. To the south, sedentary agriculture was more common. The mountainous Liaodong peninsula extends two hundred miles into the Bohai Gulf.[31]

With the fall of the Han dynasty early in the third century, Liaodong moved beyond the control of Chinese central governments. For the next thousand years, a succession of Chinese, Korean, Khitan, Jurchen, and other rulers held sway in the region. Both the Khitan Liao dynasty (947–1125) and the Jurchen Jin dynasty established a capital in Liaoyang, on the southern bank of the Taizi River 太子河, a tributary of the Liao. As political and military control of Liaodong shifted over the centuries, the complexity of its ethnic, linguistic, cultural, and social composition increased. Newly ascendant conquerors did not eradicate local populations.[32] They were too valuable as sources of labor, revenue, and potential military support.[33] New political regimes frequently incorporated existing populations by co-opting tribal leaders and their followers or by replacing chieftains but retaining the basic tribal organization beneath them.

As a Liao, and especially Jin, capital, Liaoyang was situated at the juncture of the steppe, the sown, and the forested mountains. This geographical position facilitated economic and cultural exchanges with formerly Chinese territory along the border as well as with the Koryŏ and the Song dynasties (960–1279).[34] Khitan and Jurchen tribesmen were also affected. During the early years of the Liao dynasty, the Khitan leader Abaoji (872–926) relocated considerable numbers of Jurchen households to the region south of Liaoyang. His goal was to prevent Jurchen tribes from developing into a united threat against his growing dominion.[35]

Succeeding the Liao and Jin dynasties, the Mongols ushered in a new age. Encompassed by the roughly triangular arrangement of Daidu, Liaoyang, and Kaegyŏng, southern Liaodong experienced levels of political, economic, social, and ethnic integration not seen for nearly one thousand years. Political borders that had formerly demarcated discrete dynastic concerns (the Koryŏ, the Jin) lost much of their significance. In their place, the Mongols established new administrative, ethnic, economic, social, and military orders. They drew on but did not slavishly reduplicate previous models and structures.

Liaodong in Northeast Asia Under the Mongols

Similar patterns of greater integration were at work in Liaodong. Even before the Mongol conquests, developments in China had touched Liaodong. As a relatively porous frontier region, under the Liao and Jin Liaodong afforded educated men and women access to painting styles, Confucian thought, literature, and administrative structures from China. As Chikusa Masaaki 竺沙雅章 has observed, in such fields as Buddhist studies and painting these Chinese influences were not those of the contemporaneous Song dynasty but those of the preceding Tang (618–907).[36] With Mongol unification and the expansion of administrative, educational, religious, and cultural institutions centered in Daidu, new influences from the continent, the steppe, and the peninsula shaped Liaodong.

As Thomas Allsen, Nicola Di Cosmo, and others have argued in different contexts, the unprecedented economic, technological, cultural, and artistic exchanges of the thirteenth and fourteenth centuries were not accidental. The Mongols consciously shaped these exchanges even as they purposely invested resources into the transportation and commercial infrastructure that made them possible. Mongol tastes did much to determine the flow of specific materials (for instance, textiles woven with gold thread), styles, and personnel. Things did not simply happen.[37] The following account of regional integration does not deny unintended consequences; it does, however, give great weight to Mongol desires and objectives.

Beginning early in the thirteenth century, Mongol military expansion brought important changes to Liaodong. Shortly after unifying the

Mongolian steppe early in the thirteenth century, Chinggis Khan began to probe Jin borders. Because of its strategic importance as "the root of the [Jin] dynasty," Liaodong was one of the Mongols' early targets. Major Mongol raids, including the capture of the Jin's Eastern Capital at Liaoyang in 1212 and 1215, seriously undermined Jin control in the region. Khitan aristocrats chafing under Jin control saw the Mongols as a way to secure greater autonomy from the Jurchens. In some cases, undermanned, isolated, but still ambitious Jurchen military officers in Liaodong turned their backs on the Jin dynasty. The most famous of these military commanders even established a short-lived dynasty. As Jin control faltered, local Chinese magnates also joined the Mongols. The Mongols formed temporary alliances of convenience with many local groups, but by 1233 they had terminated many such relations and established military dominance in Liaodong.[38]

The Mongols' punctuated conquest of Liaodong finds ready parallels elsewhere in Eurasia. Having destroyed existing governmental structures and displaced political elites, the Mongols did not immediately establish firm control. The resulting vacuum brought welcome opportunities to some, crushing defeat to others, and a sense of uncertainty to nearly all. In some cases, the lack of clear centers of power and authority led to widespread violence and social collapse. George Lane describes conditions in the wake the collapse of the Khwārazmanshāh in Persia as "a state of anarchy with its city states at the mercy of warring armies, marauding bandits, and rival warlords."[39] In North China, the Mongols smashed Jin political and military control during the first decades of the thirteenth century. One observer wrote at the time: "Countless too were those who assembled the people, who joined together to protect their families and homes, who banded together as robbers; who amassed grain, silk, gold and tools, boys and girls, as their private property; who trampled over land boundaries and seized dwellings, or fastened upon whole districts and prefectures as their own property."[40]

A new elite emerged, composed of ambitious local Chinese families from a variety of backgrounds, locally prominent Khitans who surrendered to the Mongols with large contingents of military followers, Jurchens who joined their fortunes to the Mongols, and Chinggis Khan's own followers. Not until the mid-thirteenth century did the Mongol court attempt to rein in this new North China elite. Nearly two decades elapsed between the end of effective Jin governance in Liaodong and the establishment of firm Mongol control in the region. As later chapters show, the Chinggisid collapse in the mid-fourteenth century ushered in a similar time of opportunity, instability, and conflict.[41]

Over the course of the thirteenth century, the Mongols developed a fluid system of governance in Liaodong designed to extract economic and military resources while maintaining local stability. As was the case in other parts of their empire, the Mongols developed a composite system of governance in Liaodong. At its core, especially during the thirteenth century, were the territories and populations granted to Mongol nobles and leading military men. Greatest among them were the three brothers of Chingghis Khan and their descendents. During much of the thirteenth century, these imperial princes and their extensive appanages not only formed the most important element of Mongol control in Liaodong but also were among the most influential actors in the entire empire. Communities of relocated Koreans, placed under the control of the Mongols' key Korean allies, constituted the second facet of rule in Liaodong. Most prominent among them were the Hong family and the royal Wang family. Finally, the Mongols established the Liaoyang Branch Secretariat to oversee much of local administration, especially in the southern half of Liaodong. Although these three elements of Mongol rule are treated separately in the following account, as will become clear, they overlapped in terms of territory, populations, and personnel.

The Three Princely Houses of the Eastern Regions

Liaodong was home to an unusual concentration of Mongol princes. The most important of them were often referred to in the aggregate as the Three Princely Houses of the Eastern Regions (*Dongfang sanwangjia* 東方三王家). The Three Princely Houses of the Eastern Regions refer to the three full brothers of Chinggis Khan, Joči Qasar, Qači'un, and Temüge Odchigin. Following Mongol custom, the youngest brother, Temüge Odchigin, protected the homelands while the others campaigned abroad. During the seven years Chinggis Khan led campaigns in Central and West Asia early in the thirteenth century, Temüge Odchigin acted as de facto regent for much of the Mongolian plain, Liaodong, and northern Koryŏ. Although Temüge Odchigin appears to have suffered Chinggis Khan's occasional displeasure for overstepping his authority, when Chinggis divided the broad Mongol empire among his followers, Temüge Odchigin and his brothers received some of the choicest pasturelands. These were located in eastern Mongolia, along the Khingan Mountains (Xing'anling 興安嶺).[42] Chinggis Khan also granted them control of far more households than anyone else. Because of his particularly privileged status, Temüge Odchigin and his successors exercised unusually firm (but never absolute) control over the members of his house, his brothers' houses, and the five lineage units (五投下) that Muqali, Chinggis's vicegerent in North China, had overseen as a Polity Prince (*guowang* 國王). Taken as a whole, these Eastern Princes represented the most powerful military bloc in the Mongol empire.[43]

As Ebisawa Tetsuo and Sugiyama Masaaki have stressed, Qubilai's rise to power and triumph over his younger brother and rival Ariq Böke owed much to the support of the Three Princely Houses of the Eastern Regions.[44] Especially critical was the decision of Tāčar, the head of the Temüge Odchigin house at the time, to join Qubilai.[45] He wielded great influence over the other two houses and the various subordinate clans. During the first half of his reign, Qubilai showered rewards and honors on Tāčar.[46] However, the expanse of their lands, the size of their populations, the strength of their warriors, and their long standing as the empire's elite would in time create tensions between the Eastern Princes and the Mongol court.

These princes and their establishments enjoyed considerable autonomy, maintaining their own military forces and administrative staffs.[47] Throughout much of the thirteenth century, they influenced local governance by appointing their own men to key posts. In some cases, the prime ministers of the princes' *ulus*es were drawn from Uyghur and Jurchen officials resident in appanages located in agricultural lands.[48] Like other *ulus* leaders, the Eastern Princes regularly dispatched representatives to the central courts to protect their interests and secure their share of the Mongols' expanding patrimony.[49] During his reign, Qubilai attempted to strengthen the position of the court vis-à-vis Mongolian princes throughout the empire through such administrative institutions as branch central secretariats. Like princely establishments elsewhere, the Eastern Princes guarded their prerogatives vigorously.[50] In 1287, tensions between the princes and the court erupted into open warfare (more on this below).[51] In the wake of the fighting, the central government periodically (which suggests not entirely successfully) upgraded the Liaodong Branch Secretariat's authority in the hope of undercutting the princes' powers.

Although most of their lands were located in Eastern Mongolia, populations subject to the Eastern Princes also figured in the administration of Liaodong and even Koryŏ. In 1275, an official from Liaoyang complained to the throne: "The territory of Liaodong is vast. Princely encampments and the people of various appanages live scattered throughout [these lands]. They use their position to encroach on others. . . . Five men close to the imperial prince of Liaoyang seized goods from local residents and in addition beat them. Local officials did not dare pursue the matter."[52] In 1280, another official serving in Liaoyang faced similar challenges. At the time, he wrote, "The falconers of the princes of the east are violent and unrestrained. The people suffer grievously."[53]

As late as the mid-fourteenth century, "servants of noble households and lictors of government offices" in Liaoyang forced rural farmers to sell their goods at "half their value." When Dorjibal, himself a seventh-generation descendent of Muqali, took his post as a senior official in the Liaoyang Branch Secretariat, he warned that "if guilty, not even senior ministers of meritorious service will be spared." The phrase "senior ministers of meritorious service" indicates not members of the civil bureaucracy but families that had shown great loyalty and courage in the service of Chinggis Khan and his descendents. According to Dorjibal's biography, "the princely residences and the various officials heard the news and were terrified."[54]

The influence of these Liaodong princes extended into northern China and Koryŏ. Great Khans granted the princes revenue-producing territories in Shandong and Hebei, where they also recruited administrative talent to manage their wealth. Like other Mongol princes, the Three Princely Houses of the Eastern Regions derived a portion of their income from taxes assessed on households in the territory of the former Southern Song. In both cases, Yuan government officials collected the taxes and then remitted them to the princes.[55] In contrast, Korean chronicles suggest that in the 1270s, if not earlier, several areas near the Chabi Pass, which marked the northern extent of the Koryŏ throne's jurisdiction, had placed themselves under Tāčar's control and that Tāčar's administrative officials maintained census records for the population.[56] In 1261, Qubilai granted another Mongolian prince, Basdar (Ch. Basidaer 巴思答兒), permission to establish a border market on the western bank of the Yalu River. Half a year later, the market was at least temporarily abolished for unspecified reasons. Qubilai allowed Tāčar to establish an iron foundry in 1262, but rejected his request to establish a border market.[57] Fear of the expansion of the princes' economic and military influence into Koryŏ may have figured in Qubilai's decision. Although the power and stature of Three Eastern Princely Households may have suffered permanent injury as a result of the 1280s revolts,[58] they would survive the Yuan's withdrawal to the steppe in 1368 and became important military allies of the new Ming dynasty.

Governance of Relocated Korean Communities

Expansion of the Mongol empire changed the composition of Liaodong's population and shaped its administrative contours. The Mongols established firm control over Liaodong early in the 1230s and relocated large numbers of people from northwestern Koryŏ to southeastern Liaodong. Between 20,000 and 30,000 Koreans under the control of the Mongols' principal Korean ally, Hong Pok-wŏn 洪福源, were settled in the region between Liaoyang and Shenyang. Grain production and tax revenues were among the Mongols' reasons for encouraging Korean emigration to Liaodong.[59] During the 1230s, the Mongols appointed Hong Senior Official of Koryŏ Military and Commoner Populations (*Gaoli jun min zhangguan* 高麗軍民長官).[60] Shortly thereafter, the Mongols charged Hong with conquering those Koreans he could not convince to surrender. The position became hereditary; until the early fourteenth century, Hong's son and then grandson held the post.[61]

Later in the thirteenth century, the Mongol court divided leadership of the Korean communities in Liaodong between the Hong family and a member of the Koryŏ royal clan. In 1263, a royal clansman was appointed Pacification Commissioner of the Koryŏ Military and Commoner Populations Supervisorate-in-Chief (*an fu Gaoli junmin zongguanfu* 安撫高麗軍民總管府). His sons succeeded him in the position and likewise led military forces in the campaigns against Japan and against the Mongol noble Nayan (see below).[62] In 1292, the Yuan court appointed one of the then-deceased royal clansman's sons to head the recently established Chief Myriarchy of Koryŏ, Jurchen, and Northern Chinese Troops (*Zongguan Gaoli Ruzhen Han jun duwanhufu* 總管高麗女眞漢軍都萬户府). He oversaw approximately 10,000 Koreans in Shenyang.[63]

During the late thirteenth and early fourteenth centuries, Hong men also figured prominently in the highest levels of the general Liaoyang administration (see below). As the Mongol court attempted to consolidate its control of Liaodong in the wake of armed challenges by Nayan and Qadan (descendents of Belgütei [Chin. Bieligutai 别里古台], a younger brother of Chinggis khan), three members of the Hong family headed the Liaoyang Branch Secretariat (all had fought with Qubilai and his generals on the battlefields of the northeast). The Hong family was a proven ally of the Mongol throne entrusted with much of the governance of Liaodong, not just Korean communities.[64]

In addition to securing governmental positions in Liaodong and the Yuan's colonial administration in Koryŏ, members of the Hong family served in the Great Khan's imperial bodyguard (the *keshig*) and fought in some of the Mongols' most critical campaigns of the thirteenth century. Whereas Hong Pok-wŏn's activities were restricted to Koryŏ and Liaodong, his brother, son, and grandson played important roles in campaigns against Japan, the Southern Song, and Mongolian aristocrats who challenged the Great Khan. They also served in administrative positions from Koryŏ and Liaodong to the Jiangnan region. Hong Pok-wŏn's fifth son, Hong Kun-sang 洪君祥, held a position as Grand Academician in the Jixian Academy (Jixianyuan 集賢院, a kind of brain trust for Mongol emperors) and served in Bureau of Military Affairs (Mizhisi 密直司) for sixteen years.[65] In exchange for their efforts, the Hong family gained privileged access to the elite of the Great Yuan *ulus*.

They also circulated among educated literati in Daidu. The following undated poem by Jie Xisi 揭傒斯 (1274–1344) illustrates many important features of northeast Asia under the Mongol empire.[66]

The Hong family rose in Liaohai,	洪氏起遼海
Its reputation has spread to all points of the compass.	流章耀八紘
Their filial piety and brotherly love are based in generations of study,	孝友根世學

Their loyalty and devotion are from Heaven. 忠貞自天成
At the court, they serve in the emperor's honor guard, 入爲帝羽儀
In the provinces, they are entrusted with weighty matters of state. 出秉國鈞衡
Their great thriving residence, 洋洋高門居
Is full of great ministers. 濟濟羅公卿
Well-known Cheng and Lan,[67] 籍甚澄與瀾
Esteemed for their excellence. 玉質金爲聲
Their discernment penetrates to the smallest matters, 折理貫秋毫
Their literary excellence exceeds a spring day. 擒藻艷春晴
In the morning, they report for duty at the court, 朝趨承明内
In the evening, they welcome worthy friends and scholars. 暮進賢友生
Over gowns of silk, they wear a modest top of coarse cotton, 衣錦絡尚絅
Their pleasant looks cover keen abilities. 穆然含粹精
Phoenixes, they did not pursue recognition, 靈鳳非求知
They amazed the world when they came forward. 出爲世所驚
Precious uncarved jade they hide among the immortals' mountains, 奇璞隱崐岫
Polished, they serve among the court's elites. 采充清廟英
Yao and Tang assembled the ranks of the talented, 堯湯攬群才
The way of the sage ruler grew brighter every day. 聖道日光明
How could only the men of the Yin be handsome and capable, 豈惟殷膚敏
Helping with offerings at the capital. 裸將在周京
Although Heaven is as high as the clouds, 蒼天雖云高
It still cares for people from afar. 乃心此黎氓
Both the ruler and the minister have their difficulties, 君臣兩不易
Both wish for peace in the realm. 相期底隆平
The ruler's virtue is precious for its inclusiveness, 君德貴並包
The way of the minister guards against overweening pride. 臣道戒驕盈
Establishing the worthy must be without favor, 立賢必無方
Selecting successive men of talent leads to a common goal. 拔茅思彙征
First in the empire, [the Hong brothers must] be circumspect to the end. 最哉敬厥終
These two worthies are truly pillars of the empire.[68] 兩賢信國桭

Jie Xisi lavished great praise on the Hong brothers and their lineage as men of the empire. Several times Jie referred to their twin identities. The family had its roots in Liaodong but established an empire-wide reputation. Similarly, they served both as members of the emperor's *keshig* in the capitals and as high officials in the provinces. Men of formidable talents hailing from the margins, the Hongs realized their potential only through service to the Mongols.

Rather than focusing on the conqueror and the vanquished, Jie Xisi cast the Hongs' relationship with the Mongol emperor in terms of minister and ruler. He notes their mutual dependence and common hopes. For a ruler to succeed, he must be inclusive, drawing talent from wherever it is found. The minister, in turn, is warned against undue pride. Jie concluded the celebratory piece with praise for the Hong's success and an admonition for continued loyalty to the dynasty.

Perhaps even more striking is the encompassing rhetoric of empire. Nowhere did the author mention that the Hong family was Korean. Nor did he make explicit reference to the conquest of either Liaodong or Koryŏ. He invoked the venerable example of the men of the defeated Shang dynasty (1766–1122 BCE) who aided the conquering Zhou dynasty (1122–249 BCE) in carrying out sacrifices. Instead of a foreign people conquering a neighboring country, Jie portrayed the transfer of power and loyalties in terms of dynastic succession, one that could be successful only with the Mandate of Heaven. Rather than Koreans who betrayed their sovereign king, the Hong family followed in the footsteps of historical worthies who perceived Heaven's will and offered their special skills to serve a greater good.

In complementary fashion, Heaven (which can be seen as analogous to the emperor), exalted and almighty, cares equally for all within the realm. Jie's choice of the word *meng*, which often referred specifically to people relocated from afar, was particularly apt for both the Hong family, which had moved to Liaodong, and the larger Korean community, which had settled in the region. The overall effect is to efface dynastic borders and to highlight the notion of a center and its borders, all contained within the Mongol empire.

On the orders of the Sim Prince 瀋王 (Ch. Shen wang) (Wang Chang), these same Hong brothers traveled to the contemporary cultural heartland of China, the Jiangnan region, to purchase books. There, they met local officials and literati. In a short poem commemorating the visit, a noted Chinese literatus Gong Su 龔璛 (1266–1331) acknowledged Koryŏ's place in the cultural empire.

Located on the map, the princedom of Shen is in the southeastern region.[69]	輿圖瀋國東南境
Your family's place of residence for generations, Liao City, is close to the ruler.[70]	家世遼城尺五天
There is no harm in a man of purpose serving as a retainer, exalted.	志士何妨曳裾貴
The esteemed prince wishes to provide a cart for purchasing books.	賢王欲與購書傳
Your cultivated bearing surpasses that of Jiangnan.	文風物色先江左
The court spreads glory to these distant lands.	使指光華下日邊
I, too, commonly held the land of the Ming and Bo Seas in little regard.	我亦平生小溟渤
[Now] I want to follow Jizi to visit Chaoxian.[71]	要隨洪範過朝鮮

Gong registered surprise at Hong's unexpectedly impressive bearing. He paid the ultimate compliment—it surpassed that of the inhabitants of Jiangnan, China's most culturally sophisticated region. Although Hong was Korean and acting on the orders of a Koryŏ prince, Gong still associated Hong's mission with the throne in Daidu. This is expressed both in the title (with reference to imperial permission to use government highway stations) and the line noting the spread of glory from the capital to "distant lands," here a self-deprecating description of Jiangnan. In the last lines, Gong wrote that his experience with Hong has changed his previous low opinion of the area surrounding the Bohai Sea. He now wishes to be like the author of the classical work *The Great Plan* (*Hong fan* 洪範), Jizi 箕子, a scion of the Shang royal house who fled the Central Plains and was traditionally thought to have established the state of Chosŏn in 1122 BCE. One assumes that Gong meant to say that he now found Koryŏ worthy of attention, rather than that he planned to bring advanced culture to a marginal backwater as Jizi (Kija) had. Gong's attitude may mirror the shifting perception of Koryŏ among many Chinese educated men. Through closer integration into the Mongol empire, Koryŏ forged ties to the ruling imperial house and gained access to the culturally rich Jiangnan region. These ties were often mediated through the Liaoyang area.

Another Korean, the Sim Prince, figured importantly in the political terrain of Liaodong. In 1307 or 1308, the reigning king of Koryŏ, Ch'ungnyŏl 忠烈王 (r. 1274–1308), was invested as Simyang wang

瀋陽王, or Simyang Prince. Simyang (Ch. Shenyang) referred to the Shenyang region, just northeast of Liaoyang, where by the 1330s, an estimated 30,000–35,000 Koryŏ subjects had settled.[72] The title soon passed to the next Koryŏ king, Ch'ungsŏn 忠宣王 (r. 1308–13), a grandson of Qubilai.[73] Ch'ungsŏn was among many in the empire who received promotions and titles for their assistance in putting a new emperor on the throne, Haishan (posthumous Chinese title Wuzong 武宗, r. 1308–11).[74] The title Prince Simyang was upgraded to Prince Sim, a status that put Ch'ungsŏn in the highest rank of imperial Mongol princes. Following common practice, the title came with a portfolio of revenue lands, properties, warehouses, and residences that supplemented earlier gifts from the throne. The Sim Prince received income from lands in Jiangnan, properties and warehouses in Yizhou 懿州 (western Liaodong), and revenue lands and a residence in Daidu and its environs. The title also included control over several Korean communities located midway between Kaegyŏng and Daidu. They were to provide for the king's needs when he and his entourage moved between the two capitals.[75]

The Hong family perceived the Sim Prince as a potential threat to its power in Liaodong, because he enjoyed direct access to the reigning emperor.[76] It quickly made its concerns manifest to the Yuan throne. The family pointed out that King Ch'ungsŏn now held two official seals of investiture as *wang* (king or prince), a highly irregular practice. In an effort to mollify the Hong family, which represented an important bastion of Yuan rule in Liaodong, without offending Ch'ungsŏn, the emperor offered a compromise. Ch'ungsŏn would maintain control over most of his financial resources but essentially forfeit any real power in the Liaodong region. Although involved in political intrigues in Daidu and Kaegyŏng, later successors to the title of Sim Prince (especially Ch'ungsŏn's nephew, Ko) had little or no influence in Liaodong.[77]

Evident here is the Mongols' proclivity for assigning responsibility in terms of populations rather than strictly defined territorial units.[78] Authority over Korean communities was granted as a reward for allegiance to the Mongols. There were sufficient numbers of Koryŏ subjects in the Liaodong region to allow the Mongols to divide them among the Hong family, the Wang family, and the Koryŏ king. Such an arrangement imposed minimal additional administrative or economic burdens on the Mongol court itself. It also fostered competition rather than cooperation among the Koreans. As was common elsewhere in the Mongol empire, communities in Liaodong were largely self-governing.[79]

Liaoyang Branch Secretariat

The third element of Mongol governance in Liaodong was the Liaoyang Branch Secretariat, which oversaw seven circuits (*lu* 路).[80] The beginnings of civilian administration appeared during the 1230s and 1240s in the form of offices devoted to taxation and registration. During the middle decades of the thirteenth century, a branch secretariat with officials appointed by the central government was established and abolished several times. Only late in the century did the Liaoyang Branch Secretariat become a more entrenched feature of the Liaodong political landscape.[81] Even then, its administrative offices were shuffled among at least three different cities in western Liaodong. During most of the fourteenth century, the Liaoyang Branch Secretariat was located in Yizhou 懿州. A strategic military and transportation hub, Yizhou was home to important grain warehouses. By the late Yuan, it exported grain and salt to other regions of the empire. It was also the site of horse markets that drew buyers from as far away as Koryŏ.[82]

It would be misleading to portray the Liaoyang Branch Secretariat as a purely civilian administration staffed by career bureaucrats. As noted above, as members of the Northeast Asian elite, the Hong family dominated the Liaoyang Branch Secretariat during the late thirteenth and early fourteenth centuries. After fighting in the campaigns against the Mongolian princes Nayan and Qadan (Ch. Hadan, K. Tapdan 哈丹), who resisted efforts by the court to curtail their autonomy, in 1287 Hong Tagu 洪茶丘 headed the Branch Secretariat. When Qadan resumed his revolt and attacked the Koryŏ capital of Kaegyŏng, "all the 2000 *li* [from there] to Liaoyang were in a tumult." The Yuan Central Secretariat "specially appointed Tagu to pacify the region east of the Liao River" and granted him wide latitude to accomplish this task.[83] Tagu's younger brother and son would later hold this post during the last decade of the thirteenth century and the first decade of the fourteenth. Perhaps the prominence of Koreans in its administration and population accounts for Rashīd al-Dīn's description of the Liaoyang Secretariat as "the province of Jürcha [Manchuria] and Solangqa [Korea]."[84]

Mongolian nobles also served in senior positions in the general Liaoyang administration. For instance, Dorji 朶兒只, a fifth-generation descendent of Muqali and a Polity Prince,[85] held territory in Liaoyang and served periodically as a senior member of the Liaoyang Secretariat. According to his biography in the *Official History of the Yuan Dynasty*, in 1329 Dorji was invested as a Polity Prince and ordered to take up his lands in Liaoyang.[86] A decade later in 1338, the court transferred his status of Polity Prince to another member of the Muqali house but appointed Dorji Minister of the Left of the Liaoyang Branch Secretariat.[87] For most of the 1340s, he served in several provincial administrations and in the central government, sometimes coming in for criticism as "following the Han people in his heart." In 1349, Dorji left his post as prime minister, resumed his status as Polity Prince, and returned to his lands in Liaoyang.[88] A commemorative poem by Nasen 迺賢 (1309–68), a well-regarded poet of Qarluq descent, also notes that in 1349 Dorji was made a prince, went to his lands in Liaodong, and received the congratulations of the minister of the left, presumably of the Liaoyang Branch Secretariat.[89] In mid-1352, the court ordered Dorji and a certain Temür to defend Longqingzhou 龍慶州, about forty-five miles northwest of Daidu.[90] Responding to calls for members of the Mongolian nobility to rally round the throne during a time of spreading warfare, in 1354 he led troops to Huainan under the overall command of Toqto'a. The next year, he died fighting in the same theater.[91]

The extant of Dorji's lands and subordinate populations in Liaoyang is unclear.[92] The *Official History of the Yuan Dynasty* provides no clues as to what, if any, troops Dorji might have assembled from Liaoyang in 1354 to fight in the south or if he brought his own men to defend Longqingzhou in 1352. A 1331 entry notes that the court ordered the Liaoyang Branch Secretariat to issue 15,000 piculs of relief grain "to the six appanages 部 of Mongolian military and civilian households [of] Prince Dorji, Naqur 納忽兒, and others."[93] Four months later, the court issued 15,000 *ding* 錠 of cash to aid 30,312 households of "starving Mongolians [of] the nine appanages of Prince Dorji and others."[94] These entries suggest that Dorji was responsible for some subordinate Mongolian populations, presumably in the broad Liaoyang region. Conditions in the region seem to have been difficult. That same spring, the Liaoyang Branch Secretariat had provided famine relief grain to other Mongolians,[95] and the court issued two months of grain for 3,500 households under the jurisdiction of the Liaoyang Eastern Circuit Mongolian myriarch.[96] The widespread famine at this time was probably linked to politics. As Chen Gaohua has noted, large numbers of nomadic pastoralists fled the steppe in the wake of the devastation wrought by such succession crises as the 1328 War of the Two Capitals.[97]

Relief grain and other gifts from the imperial throne were most typically distributed to Mongolians in Liaoyang through Mongolian princes. In this way, the princes maintained a stake in the larger imperial patronage system that ultimately linked the Great Khan with the most humble members of the Great Yuan *ulus*. At least that was the theory; during the fourteenth century, poverty among Mongolians on the steppe steadily deepened, further complicating the Great Yuan *ulus*'s effort to redistribute the empire's wealth, a linchpin of Mongol order.

Balancing Interests

Balancing interests among various members of the imperial family, the Mongol aristocracy, and local elites posed a perennial challenge for the enormous Mongol empire. The Yuan throne periodically faced grave challenges to its authority and power from Mongol princes invested by Chinggis Khan. Wishing to preserve the autonomy traditional in steppe society, these princes resented the Yuan throne's efforts to consolidate power in the hands of the central government. Long chafing under Qubilai's reforms, Qaidu revived the Ögödeid house and asserted the autonomy of Central Asia by force of arms. A serious military and political threat, Qaidu occupied much of the Yuan's attention from the 1260s to the 1280s.[98]

Facing such difficulties to the west, Qubilai could ill afford trouble on his eastern flank. Liaodong, with its concentration of Mongol imperial princes and other Mongol aristocrats, represented special challenges. Too much freedom, it was feared, would allow Mongol elites either to impose unsustainable burdens on the local Chinese, Jurchen, and Korean populations or to form alliances with their leaders. Overly close control from the center, however, risked alienating Mongol princes and aristocrats, whose loyalty and support were critical to the regime. After receiving reports of misgovernance in 1274, Qubilai dispatched one of his most respected senior statesmen, the Uyghur Lian

Xixian 廉希憲 (1231–80), to Shangdu to serve as Director of Political Affairs in the Regional Secretarial Council of the Northern Capital (*Beijing xingsheng pingzhang zhengshi* 北京行省平章政事).[99] In his parting instructions to Lian Xixian, the emperor wrote: "There are no less than several hundred thousand households in Liaoxi 遼霫 [Liaodong]. It is where imperial princes and imperial in-laws have their lands of investiture. All of them are very familiar with your abilities. Thus, I have sent you to oversee things. Heed my meaning." To this point, local officials appointed by central government had proved to be no match for Mongol princes, who considered them with a measure of disdain when they bothered to consider them at all. As a senior advisor who enjoyed Qubilai's confidence, Lian brought considerably greater prestige and influence to his duties than most. Lian, however, was only a temporary expedient; basic tensions between the princes and the throne remained unaltered.

By the mid-1280s, Qubilai began to receive reports that the most dominant of the Eastern Princes, Nayan (Ch. Naiyan, K. Nae'an 乃顏), a direct descendent of Belgütei, was planning a revolt. In the second lunar month of 1287, Qubilai sent the eminent general Bayan to Nayan's camp to investigate. His fears confirmed by Bayan's report, Qubilai immediately stripped Nayan of his right to rule his lands. Two months later, Nayan was in open revolt.

With decades of political experience, Qubilai responded with speed, subtlety, and ultimately overwhelming force. He immediately ordered officials of the Pacification Bureau of the Northern Capital and Other Such Regions (*Beijing deng chu xuanweisi* 北京等處宣慰司) to restrict the movement of Nayan's followers in or out of the city. They were forbidden to ride horses or carry bows and arrows. He also sent Bayan to Qara Qorum (Ch. Helin) in order to keep the steppe princes in line and to prevent Nayan from joining forces with Qaidu. At the same time, he undermined Nayan's support among the Princes of the Left Hand, persuading Prince Naya'a 納牙 (another descendent of Belgütei) to come to Daidu as a gesture of allegiance to the court. Finally, having assembled a military force composed of Mongol cavalry and Chinese infantry, Qubilai, now a 77-year-old man suffering from gout, rheumatism, and obesity, set forth from Shangdu in a large battle carriage mounted on elephants.

Fierce battles ranged across a broad swath of eastern Mongolia and northern Manchuria. Driven from his main camp, Nayan attempted flight but was quickly captured. In recognition of his special status as a member of the imperial family, Nayan's blood was not allowed to touch the ground. Wrapped in a carpet, he was crushed to death under the hoofs of Mongolian horses.[100] Qubilai commemorated the victory by minting ingots impressed with the characters "Liaodong" from silver captured during the campaign.[101]

One of Nayan's principal lieutenants, the Mongol Qadan, remained at large for several more years. Ranging through much of Liaodong, north to modern-day Heilongjiang province, and east into Jurchen and later Koryŏ territory, Qadan and Yuan forces fought a number of inconclusive battles. Although not nearly as well known as Qaidu or Nayan, Qadan posed such a serious threat that Qubilai announced that he would personally lead an expedition against him.[102] King Ch'ungnyŏl volunteered troops for the campaign. Qadan's destructive raids into the northern half of Koryŏ prompted Ch'ungnyŏl to evacuate much of his capital, relocate his court to Kanghwa Island, and request immediate military assistance from Qubilai.[103] The Mongols sent more than 30,000 troops. Until his death in 1291, Qadan illustrated the limits of Yuan control in the northeast corner of the empire.

Qubilai's efforts to restore order in the region reflect the complex nature of Northeast Asia under the Mongols. As 1288 drew to a close, he re-established the Secretariat for State Affairs of Such Regions as Liaoyang (*Liaoyang deng chu shangshusheng* 遼陽等處尚書省) to consolidate control over Liaodong. He also appointed such loyal generals as the Korean Hong Kun-sang (the fifth son of Hong Pok-wŏn) to senior posts within Liaodong's administration. In a move likely intended to win support from the Koryŏ court, in 1290 Qubilai formally abolished Tongnyŏngbu (Ch. Dongningfu 東寧府), the military administrative center located in northwestern Koryŏ, which to this point had been directly subordinate to the Yuan throne.[104] Qubilai also granted greater control over the Mongolian colonial administration in Koryŏ to the Korean throne.[105] In exchange for greater authority, the king of Koryŏ was expected to provide troops for fighting in Liaodong, Jianzhou, and even for a campaign against Qaidu.[106] Qubilai also insisted that Koryŏ provide 100,000 piculs of grain to offset agricultural shortfalls in

Liaodong caused by fighting against Nayan.[107] Finally, Qubilai was careful to permit Nayan's relatives to retain his lands and privileges.[108] The Yuan court needed the allegiance of the Mongol aristocracy as a whole even when Daidu was forced to strike against individual members.[109] Qubilai strove to balance the interests of the Koryŏ throne, local Mongol nobles, leaders of the Korean community in Liaodong, and his own court to restore order in the northeast.

During the fourteenth century, no open military conflict marred relations between the Mongol court and imperial princes in Liaodong. The Branch Secretariat of Liaodong exercised more local control than in previous decades. However, the central government still felt the need to periodically dispatch special emissaries to assist Liaodong officials in tours of inspections. One important goal was to prevent Mongolian princes from extracting so much from local populations that they were driven to abandon their lands or turn to revolt.[110] The court also wished to ensure the flow of tribute and taxes from Liaodong to the capital. At the same time, however, the court remained cognizant of the need to "reward the princes in order to keep them at ease."[111] In other words, the Mongol court continued to work at a balance among its own interests, Chinese populations, center-oriented local administration, and Mongol princes in the region.

During the fourteenth century, princes in Liaodong continued to figure prominently in the wider political developments of the empire. In mid-August 1328, the Great Khan Yisün-Temür (Taiding di 泰定帝) died. The designated heir, Yisün-Temür's son Aragibag, was enthroned at the summer palace in Shangdu. At the main capital in Daidu, however, bold action was taken to restore the throne to the sons of Haishan, either Qoshila (Toghan-Temür's father, who was in exile in Central Asia at the time) or Tuq-Temür (who was cooling his heels in southern China). The clash between the two groups "was the bloodiest and most destructive succession in all Yuan history."[112] It is often called the War of the Two Capitals.

Learning that Daidu had fallen into hostile hands, the loyalists committed nearly all their military resources to a multipronged attack on the southern capital. The plan was to overwhelm the critical military passes protecting Daidu and then attack the capital from all sides. Under the inspired field command of the young Qipchaq Turk, El-Temür, however, restorationist troops repeatedly defeated individual loyalist columns, including men from Liaodong, before they could assemble as scheduled around Daidu.[113] The fighting would have continued but for a surprise attack on the now nearly undefended Shangdu by the head of the Eastern Mongolian Chief Military Command and several eastern Mongolian princes.[114]

Important here is that Mongolian princes and high-ranking Mongolian officials based in Liaodong and eastern Mongolia fought on both sides of the War of the Two Capitals.[115] The Eastern Princes and others were not more conservative or traditional than other Mongolian aristocrats. The War of the Two Capitals was less about ideology and more a struggle to advance individual and family interests through political alliances and military strength. The fighting devastated large swaths of territory in such areas as Yongping prefecture between the capital and Liaodong. The *Official History of the Yuan Dynasty* notes, "In the wake of the military battles of Tianli 天曆 [1328–29], no residents were left in the countryside."[116]

El-Temür conducted an extensive purge in the wake of the succession crisis, executing enemies and confiscating the properties of more than a hundred Mongolian aristocrats. In order to increase its control over the Eastern Princes, the court implemented several measures. In 1329, it established the Military Commission (*Dudufu* 都督府), headed by El-Temür himself.[117] Convinced that the administrative personnel in the appanages of Mongolian princes who had opposed him were more loyal to their princes than to the court, El-Temür then purged most of them.[118] "Because military commanders in the Mongol, Koryŏ, and Zhaozhou Myriarchs of the Liaoyang Branch Secretariat (*Liaoyangsheng Menggu Gaoli Zhaozhou san wanhu* 遼陽省蒙古高麗肇州三萬户) supported the rebellion, raised troops, and attacked the Capital Region," early in 1329 the court "seized their seals of command and imperial orders" (*fuyin zhichi* 符印制敕).[119] The details of this second measure are unclear. Neither a Mongol nor a Koryŏ myriarch in the Liaoyang Secretariat appears in the *Official History of the Yuan Dynasty*. The closest match seems to be the Chief Myriarchy of Koryŏ, Jurchen, and Northern Chinese Troops.[120] Also unclear is whether all commanders were cashiered, if all were replaced, and if so, by whom. Korean chronicles such as *Official History of the Koryŏ Dynasty* and the *Abridged History of the Koryŏ Dynasty* (*Koryŏsa chŏryo*) shed no light on this edict. The order does show that into the mid-fourteenth century, Liaodong interests continued to figure prominently in court politics and that alliances cut across such labels as "Mongol" and "Koryŏ."

In addition to Mongol princes, Uyghur ministers, and the Hong family, Koryŏ subjects also staffed the administration of Liaoyang, albeit often in more humble posts. Until the resumption of the civil service examination early in the fourteenth century, men from Koryŏ like others in the empire gained position through proximity to the Great Khan. Han Yong's 韓永 (1285–1336) path to Liaodong led through the imperial *keshig*. Han's father had been among the young men selected from Koryŏ's leading families to be hostages at Qubilai's court. Han grew up in Daidu, where he studied and remained after his father returned to Koryŏ.

In 1303, the eighteen-year-old Han began service in the *keshig* of the heir apparent, Ayurbarwada, the future emperor.[121] For nearly twenty years, he held a series of posts at the Mongol court, many within the sensitive Armaments Court. In 1320, he took up his duties as prefect of Jinzhou 錦州, Daning circuit, in southwestern Liaodong. Two years later, the court transferred him to the northeastern corner of Daning, to a place called Gaozhou 高州. One Chinese funerary account notes that Han "was thoroughly acquainted with the customs of the two subprefectures," without offering any explanation for how he acquired that knowledge or what those customs might be. A Koryŏ account sheds no light on what, if any, previous connection might have tied Han to the region but does provide a rare description of local society. Gaozhou, the author writes:

> was formerly Khitan land. It had repeatedly experienced warfare. The people's property had been devastated. It is a place where frontier barbarians and miscellaneous breeds gathered. There was no agriculture or sericulture. They commonly lived off brigandage. His Excellency knew what it was like. . . . He strove to transform them through virtue and to move them through sincerity. The villainous who did not change their ways, he forcefully reined in through the law.[122]

Han apparently enjoyed a successful tenure in Jinzhou and Gaozhou but fell short in his next assignment in Liaodong, Yizhou, one of the region's most important cities and the future site of Liaoyang's administrative seat. His lackluster performance, however, did not prevent him from enjoying a long career in local government in northwestern China.[123] Han set an important precedent; in the following decades several more men from Koryŏ would serve in administrative positions in Liaodong, often in exactly the same places Han had.

These later servants of the Mongol empire, however, took a different road to Liaodong. One of the greatest honors a Koryŏ scholar could achieve was passing the Yuan civil service examinations, a feat managed by only a handful of men. They received posts within China, in the Yuan's colonial administration within Koryŏ, and in Liaodong. Having passed the Yuan civil service examination in 1321, Ch'oe Hae 崔瀣 (1287–1340) was appointed assistant prefect (*panguan* 判官) of Gaizhou 蓋州 in the Liaoyang circuit. Ch'oe appears to have considered Gaizhou a backwater and his post beneath him. After only five months, he returned to Koryŏ, pleading illness.[124] Three years later in 1324, An Ch'uk 安軸 (1287–1348) passed the Yuan examination and took up the same post as assistant prefect of Gaizhou. It is not clear how long An held this position, but he remained involved in the politics of both Daidu and Koryŏ from his new post in Liaodong. An wrote to King Ch'ungsuk, under detention at the time in Daidu, who felt isolated and vulnerable. An complained to the Yuan throne that Ch'ungsuk lacked a proper residence in Daidu. Grateful for An's words of support and profession of loyalty, the king granted An a promotion in the Koryŏ administration.[125] Thus, during An's service in Liaodong in the Yuan administration, he participated in Koryŏ politics in Daidu and received a concurrent post in the Koryŏ bureaucracy.

In 1345, An Chuk's younger brother, An Po 安輔, passed the Yuan civil service examination.[126] An Po was appointed to serve concurrently as a Recorder and Concurrent Dispatch Forwarder and Archival Administrator (*zhaomo jian chengfa jiageku* 照磨兼承發架閣庫).[127] An apparently felt overqualified for this low-level (8b), largely clerical position. "Having received an order, not to serve in this post would be disrespectful. Further, a record keeper does no more than handle documents; there are no other duties. I should go." An's abilities reportedly impressed his superiors who treated him with courtesy. After an indeterminate period in Liaoyang, claiming filial responsibilities, An abandoned his post and returned to Koryŏ to care for his parents.[128]

Also during Ch'ungsuk's reign, Cho Yŏm 趙廉 (1290–1343) passed the Yuan examinations. He was appointed to the far more important position of Director-General of Liaoyang and Such Places (*Liaoyang deng lu zongguan zhifu* 遼陽等路總管知府).[129] Having passed the Yuan civil service examination in 1342, Yi In-bok 李仁復 (1308–74) was appointed assistant prefect of Jinzhou 錦州, Daning circuit 大寧路, the same position that Han Yong had held two decades earlier.[130] He may never have left Daidu to take up his duties in Jinzhou and seems to have tried to advance his career through contributions to the throne. Politically well connected, Yi would become an important figure at Kongmin's court, serving as the king's special envoy to the Yuan.

Yi Kok 李穀 (1298–1351), a distinguished Koryŏ scholar-official who also passed the Yuan civil service examination, highlights the universality of the Yuan court. For Yi, the Mongol empire provided opportunities for advancement regardless of place of origin. In an undated mid-fourteenth-century poem dedicated to two investigation commissioners (*lian fang* 廉訪) of Koryŏ origin, he wrote:

In [matters of] civilization, there is no north and south.[131] 聲教無南北
In regard to fortune there is ease and difficulty. 遭逢有易難
To the Sagely Court come the ten thousand countries. 聖朝來萬國
Men of excellence appear from Korea.[132] 佳士出三韓

Yi Kok's rhetoric of universality (also seen in Jie Xisi's description of the Hong family), however, was belied by Mongol personnel policy in Liaodong. Of the dozen Koryŏ scholars known to have passed the Yuan civil service examination during the fourteenth century, at least five served in the Liaodong administration. For the most part, they did not welcome these assignments, which they considered unworthy of their talents. The Mongol court, however, apparently considered Koryŏ men particularly appropriate for Liaodong. As noted above, during the late thirteenth and early fourteenth centuries, men from the Hong family figured prominently in the highest levels of the Liaoyang Branch Secretariat. This was in addition to the Mongol court's use of Korean allies to oversee relocated Korean populations in Liaodong for more than a century beginning in the 1230s. At least through the 1350s, descendents of the Hong family and others of Korean descent held posts in the Directorate-General of Koryŏ Military and Civilian Households on the Shenyang and Other Such Circuits (*Shenyang deng lu Gaoli jun min zongguanfu* 瀋陽等路高麗軍民總管府) and the Myriarchy of Koryŏ, Jurchen, and North Chinese Military Households.[133]

Just as Mongols, Koreans, Chinese, and Uyghurs figured in the administration of Liaoyang during the thirteenth and fourteenth centuries, military institutions and campaigns also united diverse peoples in the imperial enterprise.

Military Institutions in Liaodong

Military institutions exercised a wide-ranging influence over Liaodong. Absorption of local personnel resources formed a critical part of the Mongol control. In 1215, the Mongols liquidated a Chinese magnate based in southwestern Liaodong who had "privately supported 12,000 'dare-to-die troops' who were called the Black Army." They were immediately integrated into the ranks of the Mongol forces.[134] During his campaigns early in the thirteenth century, the great Mongol general Muqali absorbed Khitan, Jurchen, Chinese, and Parhae men into his armies.[135] Defeated Jin garrison troops formed the core of new local defense forces in many areas throughout Liaodong.[136]

"Newly subjugated armies" were used extensively as farmers on agricultural colonies established to provide a portion of the army's food. The term referred primarily to Chinese troops from the recently defeated Song army.[137] In addition to the Koryŏ farmers settled in Liaodong mentioned above, military personnel from many parts of China were also relocated to Liaodong. Zhang Cheng 張成 is one of the better-documented cases illustrating how Mongol military and economic imperatives facilitated integration.

A native of Qizhou, Huguang province (southern central China), in 1275 Zhang surrendered to Mongol armies and received a post as supervisor of the newly surrendered troops of Qizhou (*Xinfujun zongguansi* 新附軍總管司). Four years later, he traveled north to the Mongol capital at Daidu to serve in the Imperial Guard (*Shiwei* 侍衛) as a chiliarch. He retained command over 86 men from his days in Qizhou. In

1281, he and his men saw action in the western islands of the Japanese archipelago.

The remainder of his career centered in the northeast. During the mid-1280s, he and his company were sent to the northeastern corner of the Mongol empire deep in Jurchen territory ("to the northeastern extreme of the Amur River"), where they established an agricultural colony as part of Qubilai's efforts to consolidate Yuan control.[138] By mid-1286, his company was traveling south again to fight against Nayan in Manchuria. He then held a rapid succession of assignments related to growing and transporting grain, first in the Agricultural Colony Myriarchy of the Right Wing (*Youyi tuntian wanhufu* 右翼屯田萬户府), then Yangcun taoyuhe 楊村桃御河, and in the Linqing Grain Transport Myriarchy (*Linqing yunliang wanhufu* 臨清運糧萬户府) located south of the capital along the Grand Canal. He served his last years (1293–94) in the southern tier of Liaodong in several agricultural colonies. His descendents settled there (in Jinzhou 金州). By the time they erected a stele in his memory in 1348, Zhang's great-grandsons had adopted names distinctive to the Mongol period, such as Gouer 狗兒, Heisi waitou 黑廝歪頭, Basukaiwang 八速開往, and Zhaijianu 寨家奴.[139] Although few details survive, at some point the Yuan court established a myriarch of subjugated troops in Liaoyang Branch Secretariat. During the mid-fourteenth century, the title was still in use.[140]

In other cases, Chinese families from Liaodong ended up elsewhere in the empire. For instance, during the Mongol conquest of Liaodong early in the thirteenth century, the Xing family 邢氏 "encouraged the people of their locality to surrender." The head of the family was appointed a provisional chiliarch in Yizhou 義州, in southwestern Liaodong, charged with control of the local population. During the early fourteenth century, first his son (who also served in the imperial *keshig*) and then his grandsons would serve at Ayurbarwada's court, responsible for the Great Khan's food and drink. "Daily they enjoyed great imperial favor and within a few years, they held posts among the ranks of ministers." The emperor granted them residences in Daidu, where they settled. Attributing the family's success to their grandfather, they bought land south of the capital, made a funeral plot, erected stone markers, and solicited a funeral inscription from a leading Chinese official and man of letters to be inscribed in stone. Early during the fourteenth century, the son served as Director-General of Daning circuit (*Daninglu zongguan* 大寧路總管), which subsumed Yizhou where his father had served during the thirteenth century; this suggests that perhaps family interests continued there. All three grandsons used Mongol names, Salji'ud 山而, Qaiju 海住, and Maimai 買買. The youngest served in the imperial *keshig*.[141]

It is worth noting in passing that the Yuan court, like the later Ming dynasty, exiled criminals from China proper to the northeast, particularly the Nurgan area, which produced Haiqing gyrfalcons in southern Siberia. In contrast, Jurchens and Koreans were exiled to Huguang in central China, presumably because they originated in Northeast Asia.

Koryŏ in Northeast Asia Under the Mongols

If early in the thirteenth century the Yalu River had marked the northwestern edge of Koryŏ territory, events soon complicated claims of authority and rule by the Wang royal family.[142] First, a succession of ambitious families in the Northern Border Regions of Koryŏ joined the Mongols. The most influential of these, the Hong, relocated its base of power west of the Yalu River into the Liaodong region. As noted above, the Mongol throne granted them extensive powers over the Korean communities between the Liao and Yalu Rivers.

The Mongols maximized their influence by capitalizing on tensions between local military officers and the Koryŏ court.[143] They established competing political and administrative authorities within Koryŏ itself. In 1258, several military officers in northeast Koryŏ surrendered to the Mongols.[144] The Mongol throne established the Ssangsŏngbu Directorate-General (*Ssangsŏngbu ch'ongkwanbu* 雙城總管府) to control northeast Koryŏ as well as access to Jurchen communities to the north. The Mongol throne appointed one of the surrendered Koryŏ officers, surnamed Cho 趙, and his descendents as myriarchs in charge of the Ssangsŏngbu administration. The Korean communities under the jurisdiction of the Ssangŏng administration would remain beyond effective control of the Koryŏ court until 1356.

Exploiting a revolt in 1269–70 in the Northwest Territory by the Koryŏ military officer Ch'oe T'an 崔坦 against the Koryŏ throne, the Mongols set up the Directorate-General of Tongnyŏngbu (*Tong-*

nyŏngbu ch'ongkwanbu 東寧總管府) as an administrative and military center to oversee territory as far south as the Chabi Pass. Tongyŏngbu was directly subordinate to the imperial Yuan throne until it was abolished in 1290, when the need for Koryŏ military assistance in the wake of Nayan's and Qadan's revolts in Liaodong made Koryŏ requests for the return of the Northwest Territory more compelling to the Yuan court.[145] Efforts by Möngke and Qubilai to secure greater control of the empire's resources for the center may explain why Ssangsŏngbu and Tongnyŏngbu were more directly controlled by the court rather than being granted the autonomy enjoyed by the Hong family in Liaodong.[146]

Other lesser regional figures also joined the Mongols, bringing with them local populations. Outside the control of the Koryŏ court, these territories attracted Korean families who wished to avoid taxes and government service obligations, those who wanted to escape their social status as "base people," and criminals who hoped to avoid punishment. Although exact figures are scarce, the loss of territory and people may have posed long-term problems of finance and social control for the already beleaguered Koryŏ throne. Both the crown's efforts to woo local populations back and its efforts to persuade Yuan authorities to return Koryŏ subjects met with limited success.[147]

The Branch Secretariat for the Eastern Campaigns (*Zhengdong xingzhongshusheng* 征東行中書省) grew out of the Mongols' efforts to invade Japan late in the thirteenth and early fourteenth centuries. The branch secretariat oversaw the mobilization of personnel and matériel for the military campaigns.[148] Simultaneously, it served as a Mongol tool of political control within Koryŏ. However, as noted above, in order to gain fuller Koryŏ support against Nayan's revolt, beginning late in the 1280s Qubilai granted greater power to the Koryŏ throne. The secretariat continued to serve as a key administrative instrument for supervising and controlling Koryŏ. At the same time, however, the Koryŏ king, as head of the secretariat, used this administration as a way to bolster his position within Koryŏ and in the broader Mongol empire. The secretariat was staffed primarily by Koreans; most owed their posts to the king's patronage. Thus, the power and prestige associated with the secretariat maintained Mongol control over Koryŏ; it also strengthened the position of the Koryŏ king within his kingdom. The fortunes of Mongol and Koryŏ rulers in Northeast Asia were inseparably linked.[149]

Thus, during the Mongol period, the ideal of a single Koryŏ king commanding supreme political control or even legitimacy over the entirety of his dominion, always intensely contested, was compromised even further. Although the early decades of the Mongol period brought much violence and destruction, local leaders and communities throughout Northeast Asia enjoyed more choices about allegiance.[150] Dynastic borders meant less. As Peter Yun has shown, Koryŏ kings made frequent use of Mongolians, Chinese, and Central Asian émigrés with literary, diplomatic, and military skills as a way to bolster their domestic position and to strengthen ties to other parts of the Mongolian empire.[151]

Others Strands of Integration Under the Mongols

Economically, the Mongols created what the Japanese scholar Sugiyama Masaaki has termed the "Eurasian Trade Sphere." Deeply committed to expanding global trade as a way to increase their wealth, the Mongols developed an extensive transportation infrastructure, issued paper currency based on an empire-wide silver standard, and forged close links with international commercial groups (often Turkestani and Uyghur merchant consortiums).[152] One facet of this pan-Eurasian development was intensified trade between the Yuan and Koryŏ, linking Northeast Asia together more closely than in the past. In contrast to the state-to-state trade that had dominated Korea's economic exchanges with previous Chinese dynasties, more varied forms of trade characterized the Mongol period. The so-called tribute trade continued under the Mongols. The Koryŏ court fulfilled Mongol demands for porcelains, nuts, furs, fans, papers, silver, and gold. Like all other parts of the empire, Koryŏ was expected to provide the Mongols a variety of personnel, including palace women (more on this below), eunuchs, Buddhist monks, and others. The Mongol court reciprocated with gifts to the Koryŏ royal family.

In contrast to earlier Chinese practice, however, the gifts bestowed by the Yuan throne were generally only a fraction of the value of the Koryŏ tribute. Further, as Peter Yun has observed, the number of tribute missions to the Mongols increased nearly eightfold over those to the Liao and Jin.[153] The Mongols imposed heavy burdens on subjugated polities, but part of this steep increase arose out of an extensive "gift-exchange" with the imperial family and various Yuan princes. An integral part of Mongolian political culture, these gift-exchanges constituted a defining characteristic of the Northeast Asian economy during the thirteenth and fourteenth centuries.[154] Another dimension to economic links between Koryŏ and the Yuan was the maintenance of several substantial royal Korean residences in Daidu.[155] This included securing provisions, services, and, when ready funds grew short, loans from merchants based in the Yuan.[156]

One consequence of these varied economic ties was Koryŏ's partial incorporation into the "Yuan paper currency bloc." Yuan paper currency flowed into Koryŏ in the form of imperial gifts and payments for a wide variety of goods and services. During the mid-fourteenth century, this meant that the Yuan's inflationary policies directly influenced large segments of Koryŏ, especially the royal economy based in Kaegyŏng.[157] Members of the royal Koryŏ family, government officials, and newly ascendant elites with close ties to Daidu were those most likely to receive gifts of paper currency from the Yuan throne. They also incurred expenses in the Yuan that might be covered in the Mongols' paper currency.[158] Exposure to the Mongol imperial family's active involvement in trade during their stay in Daidu may have influenced some Koryŏ kings' notions of commerce, especially the idea of tapping rich merchants to conduct overseas trade on the state's behalf.[159] Although levels of commercialization in Liaodong lagged behind those in economic centers like the Jiangnan region, archeological and documentary evidence suggests that the southern regions of Liaodong were relatively well integrated into the larger Yuan economy.[160] It is not coincidental that the basic plotline of perhaps the most important Koryŏ primer for the study of colloquial Chinese at the time follows a Koryŏ merchant who travels to Daidu for business accompanied by a merchant from Liaodong who demonstrates an easy familiarity with both the Yuan and the Koryŏ markets.[161]

Many kinds of people flowed in great numbers throughout Northeast Asia under the Mongols.[162] Over the course of the thirteenth century, hundreds of thousands of people left northern Koryŏ. Most had been seized as captives by Mongol forces during their destructive invasions of the mid-thirteenth century. Others chose to surrender to the invaders. Some were relocated to southern Mongolia and China proper, but the vast majority settled in the Liaodong region, where they worked as farmers.[163] Koryŏ eunuchs, translators, and literary figures sought their fortunes in the major metropolitan areas of Yuan China, usually Daidu or Shangdu.[164] Common farmers and their families from Koryŏ's Northern Border Regions took advantage of looser government control to flee tax and labor service obligations to form sizable Korean communities in and near Liaoyang and Shenyang.[165] As many as a quarter-million Koreans may have lived scattered throughout China as a whole.[166]

Liaodong itself was home to significant numbers of other groups such as Mongols, Jurchens, and Khitans and to lesser numbers of Uyghurs, Qipchaqs, and Parhae.[167] Some populations predated the Mongol empire, but, as noted above, many were relocated as a result of Mongol military and administrative policies. Real differences in lifeways, economic structures, and social organization distinguished Jurchen tribesmen located near Liaoyang from those farther to the north and northeast. Over time, however, incorporation into the Mongol empire probably reduced these differences.

Mongol domination introduced an extensive communication and transportation infrastructure to Eurasia. The Mongols routinely demanded that conquered territories demonstrate their subordinate status in tangible ways: local rulers were to visit the khan's court (wherever it might be at the time); the rulers' sons were to be held hostage and serve in the khan's bodyguard; rulers were to submit tax and population records. Finally, they were to construct and maintain an extensive network of relay stations. These measures were intended to bind the newly integrated lands and rulers to the Mongol empire.

Designed to facilitate the flow of trade, intelligence, official orders, and military forces, relay stations dotted the main overland routes of Eurasia, including Northeast Asia. The Mongols established approximately 200 overland relay stations in Liaodong. Dozens more spanned the length of Koryŏ. Stations were most densely concentrated along the main highways running between such political, military, and economic centers as Daidu, Shangdu, Liaoyang, the Western Capital, and Kaegyŏng. In addition, other subroutes stretched deep into Jurchen lands and beyond. Horses were the preferred animal of transport, but dogs and reindeer were maintained in stations to the north with their heavy snow and long winters.[168]

Despite their origins in the steppe, Mongols also exploited and expanded maritime routes throughout Eurasia. Linking East and West Asia, these maritime trade routes formed an essential part of their trade empire.[169] Although slightly more perilous than overland highways, the maritime routes in Northeast Asia were important for the rapid shipment of bulk items like grain and soldiers. Beginning no later than the mid-1270s, the Yuan court periodically moved grain between Liaoyang and Koryŏ as an emergency relief measure against drought and famine. Sea routes also connected Koryŏ to Shandong province and the port of Zhigu, an entry point for access to Daidu. For instance, in 1295, a Koryŏ official shipped 14,000 bolts of linen to coastal Shandong, from whence they were transported overland to Yidu 益都. The Eastern Princes maintained a strong presence in Yidu and dispatched their representatives there to protect their interests, which included a portion of Yidu's tax revenues granted by the Yuan throne as part of the princes' share of the jointly held patrimony that constituted the Mongol empire. The fabric was exchanged there for Yuan paper currency to be used by the Koryŏ heir apparent in Daidu.[170] Koryŏ goods transported to Shandong were also transshipped along the Grand Canal to the capital.[171] In the mid-fourteenth century, a close friend of Kongmin died when his ship went down on the return trip from Daidu to Koryŏ.[172]

As one might expect, given the Mongols' dominant political and military status within the empire and their extensive transportation infrastructure, Mongol customs penetrated throughout much of Northeast Asia. Mongolian hairstyles, hats, garments, and boots found a receptive audience among many segments of Koryŏ's court elite. The Mongolian diet, with its roots in pastoral nomadism and emphasis on animal husbandry, is often said to have exercised a broad and lasting influence on Korean eating habits.[173] Mongol names appeared among Chinese and Korean populations. Whether out of a desire to advance their careers or out of fashion, some Chinese adopted Mongol names.[174] Other Chinese, Khitans, Jurchens, and Koreans received Mongolian names from the Yuan court in recognition of their contributions to the empire in a wide variety of fields, including the military, administration, craftsmanship, cuisine, medicine, and culture.[175]

Cultural interaction was not an exclusively top-down spread of Mongolian ways to subject populations. Mongolian rulers stocked their kitchens and banquet halls with such standard steppe fare as mutton, *kumis*, and butter. However, as the empire expanded, the Mongols' foodways diversified. Especially at the tables of elites, spices and cooking techniques from Persian, Turkish, and Chinese culinary traditions grew common.[176] The empire facilitated the spread of regional fashions. Early in the thirteenth century, at least one son and several wives (both Jurchen and Mongol) of the prominent Mongol general Muqali wore turbans and other clothes from West Asia. The famous *jisün* robes often worn at grand banquets in the Mongol capitals, which fascinated observers like Marco Polo, probably originated in West Asia.[177] During the thirteenth and early fourteenth centuries, Koryŏ clothing styles became fashionable in many elite circles in Daidu.[178]

Koryŏ women were inseparable from the popularity of things Korean. The first waves of Koryŏ women into the Mongol empire arrived as captives seized during the bloody fighting of the mid-thirteenth century. These women were variously used as slaves, married to recently surrendered Southern Song soldiers, or distributed as war booty to Mongol warriors. Late in the thirteenth century, Qubilai and other Mongol aristocrats began to demand women from elite Koryŏ families as wives and consorts. Despite initial efforts to avoid these demands, the Korean government eventually responded by establishing government bureaus to organize and control the flow of Koryŏ women to the Mongol empire.

What had begun as the seizure of women as war booty evolved into a complex system of formal tribute between the ruling houses of Koryŏ and the Mongol empire. Yuan envoys regularly traveled to Koryŏ to secure women on behalf of the emperor, who often redistributed them as gifts to leading ministers. Yuan envoys and Yuan officials stationed in Koryŏ also requested Koryŏ brides for themselves.[179]

The number of Koryŏ women in Daidu increased steadily over the late thirteenth and first half of the fourteenth centuries. Nearly 1,500 Koryŏ tribute women are noted in official Yuan and Koryŏ court annals. The actual number of women was certainly much higher since elite Koryŏ women nearly always traveled with their own maids and servants. Lesser-known women were not deemed sufficiently significant to merit mention in official records.[180] Many Koreans married their womenfolk to members of the Yuan elite as a way to secure official posts and advance family interests.

Mongolian, Muslim, and Uyghur elites appreciated Koryŏ beauties, and the acquisition of Korean concubines became something of a fad.[181] As one fourteenth-century Chinese observer familiar with the court in Daidu observed:

> Among prominent officials and influential people in the capital city, acquisition of a Koryŏ woman has become *de rigueur* for one to be considered a leading light. The Koryŏ women are amiable and yielding; they excel in serving [their lords] to such a degree that they often win [his] favor [away from other women]. Since the Zhizheng reign period, most of the palace stewards and attendants in the imperial palace are Koryŏ women. For this reason, everywhere clothes, shoes, hats, and utensils all follow the Korean style.[182]
>
> 京師達官貴人必得高麗女然後爲名家。高麗婉媚善事人至則多奪寵。自至正以來宮中給事使令大半爲高麗女。以故四方衣服鞋帽器物皆依高麗樣子。

Probably because of the prestige associated with imperial patronage, Koryŏ clothing fashions made inroads even into China proper's most affluent and culturally sophisticated area, the Jiangnan region.[183] Not surprisingly, these Koryŏ beauties were valued as "eyes and ears," valuable sources of intimate intelligence gathered through their privileged access to the Yuan's most powerful families.[184]

The influence of Korean women at the late Yuan court had consequences beyond clothing fashions and sexual politics. In an environment in which personal connections were critical, some degree of Korean-language competence probably offered an advantage. In *Poem of the Capital* 輦下曲, Zhang Yu 張昱 wrote: "Soldiers of the guard have learned the speech of Koryŏ" 衛兵學得高麗語.[185] Simple conversational skills would have facilitated communication with Korean-born eunuchs, palace women, and the consorts and servants of elite Mongol families. Even a smattering of Korean probably lent a certain élan to men in the capital guard.

Daidu's Korean tint during the mid-fourteenth century struck the poet Nasen,[186] who contrasted Chinese villagers' grinding poverty with

Koryŏ women's privileged luxury in the capital. In 1355, Nasen was traveling north from his hometown, the port city Qingyuan 慶元 (present-day Ningbo), to Daidu. The poem was inspired by conditions in the first county entered after reaching the northern bank of the Yellow River, Xinxiang 新鄉.[187] After describing the cold and hunger, crushing government taxes and labor service, and the constant harassment of dunners that he witnessed in Xinxiang, Nasen offered a vision of imperial pampering in Daidu.

Uncombed hair and barefoot,
  The Old Woman of Xinxiang. 蓬頭赤腳新鄉媼
Her black gown patched in a hundred places,
  She is an elder of the village. 青裙百結村中老
During the day, she cooks rice,
  To feed her husband in the field. 日間炊黍餉夫耕
At night, she spins cotton into thread,
  Until the dawn breaks. 夜紡綿花到天曉
She weaves the cotton into fabric,
  To pay military taxes. 綿花織布供軍錢
She requests someone to hull her grain,
  To pay land taxes. 倩人輾穀輸公田
Officials from the county office,
  Demand that she pay. 縣裏公人要供給
[Unable to comply], they tear away her clothes,
  She suffers the blows of bastinadoes and whip. 布衫剝去遭笞鞭
It has been three months,
  Since her sons have left. 兩兒不歸又三月
She can only worry about their cold and hunger,
  Their clothes in tatters. 秪愁凍餓衣裳裂
Her eldest son transports wood,
  For the construction of government offices. 大兒運木起官府
Her younger son carries dirt,
  To repair a broken dike. 小兒擔土塡河決
A thatched roof house in falling snow,
  Dim light from her lamp. 茆櫩雨雪鐙半昏
Powerful families collect their debts,
  They bang at the gate incessantly. 豪家索債頻敲門
No cash in her purse,
  No grain in the pantry. 囊中無錢甕無粟

Now she has only,
  Her grandson holding himself up along the bed. 眼前只有扶牀孫
The next day she takes her grandson,
  Into the city to sell. 明朝領孫入城賣
She asks a pathetic price,
  Onlookers look on in surprise. 可憐索價旁人怪
The painful parting of blood family,
  It goes without saying. 骨肉生離豈足論
She wants only to pay off,
  Her immediate debts. 且圖償却門前債
In three days,
  It will be New Year. 數來三日當大秊
At her mother-in-law's grave,
  She has no paper money. 阿婆墳上無紙錢
She sprinkles cold water,
  Into the weeds in front of the grave. 凉漿澆溼墓前草
She lowers her head and sobs,
  Her cries reach Heaven. 低頭痛哭聲連天
I rue not being born
  a woman of Koryŏ. 恨身不作三韓女
[Suitors] fill carts with gold and pearls,
  As they compete to acquire her. 車載金珠爭奪取
In a silver ewing, she warms wine,
  She drinks from a jade cup. 銀鐺燒酒玉杯飲
To music in a great hall,
  She sings and dances at night. 絲竹高堂夜歌舞
Gold bangles cover her arms,
  Pearl hairpins fill her hair. 黃金絡臂珠滿頭
Kingfisher clouds patterns on silk fabric,
  Mandarin ducks embroidered in silk. 翠雲繡出鴛鴦裯
Drunkenly she calls her eunuch servant
  to part the silk curtains [of her sleeping platform] 醉呼閹奴解羅幔
And to add incense to the warmer
  at the foot of the bed.[188] 床前爇火添香篝

Like Nasen's other poems that contrast desperate rural conditions in central China with the luxury of the court, this work draws attention to the yawning divide between the suffering of commoners in the countryside and the fantastic wealth of elites in the capital. If the old woman of Xinxiang really did express her envy of Koryŏ women in Daidu as Nasen wrote, it would suggest that in the popular imagination, Koreans formed a critical feature of elite life in the empire.

High culture also spread through the matrix of the Mongolian empire. Koryŏ scholars traveled to Daidu and elsewhere within China, where they studied with the leading lights of various strains of Neo-Confucian thought and purchased canonical works, which they brought back to Koryŏ.[189] On at least one occasion (in 1314), the Mongol ruler Ayurbarwada donated 17,000 fascicles or chapters (Ch. *juan* 卷, K. *kwŏn*) from the former Southern Song imperial archives to the Koryŏ court.[190] In Daidu and in the Jiangnan region, Koreans studied government-approved commentaries by Zhu Xi on the classics as they prepared for the Yuan civil service examinations.[191] Neo-Confucian thought and scholarship gained influence in Koryŏ through a second and more direct route. Some Chinese administrators dispatched by the Yuan government to serve in the Koryŏ Branch Secretariat shared their intellectual and literary tastes (including developments in Neo-Confucianism) with Koryŏ scholars through scholarly and cultural exchanges.[192]

The empire also facilitated cultural exchanges among such subjugated peoples as the Jurchens, Chinese, Uyghurs, and Koreans. Before the Mongol invasions, some Jurchen scholars had developed a deep engagement with Chinese intellectual, artistic, and literary traditions. Mongol control provided easy interaction with Chinese populations, and the Yuan period saw the emergence of dozens of Jurchen scholars, playwrights, poets, painters, and calligraphers who developed reputations as renowned cultural figures. Evidence from fourteenth-century household encyclopedias demonstrates that Jurchen traditions left their mark on things like Chinese culinary tastes. Intermarriage between Jurchens and Chinese grew even more common than it had been during the preceding Jin period.[193]

The Mongol matrix stimulated the growth of religious patronage networks that stretched across much of East Asia. Tibetan Buddhism, so lavishly patronized by Yuan emperors, spread both east and west.[194] Early Il-khans supported Tibetan Buddhism in Persia, and the Koryŏ court, especially Mongol women there, apparently subsidized the casting of several bells and bronze figures rendered in the Tibetan style.[195]

From the time of Qubilai, the spiritual resources of Koryŏ, like those of Rus, China, and elsewhere, came under Mongol dominion.[196] Qubilai and his descendents summoned outstanding Koryŏ Buddhist monks to Daidu and Shangdu, where they were expected to put their spiritual prowess at the service of the imperial family.[197] Several were lodged in Daidu temples. On designated days (usually the emperor's birthday, the first day of the lunar year, etc.) the Koryŏ king and his officials were expected to offer prayers at temples in Koryŏ for the prosperity and longevity of the reigning Yuan emperor. Preliminary studies of a badly damaged remnant of a Yuan-period order written in Tibetan and housed in the Songgwangsa Temple 松廣寺, a center of Sŏn (Zen) Buddhism, suggest that Koryŏ Buddhism institutions may have fallen under the loose supervision of the imperial preceptor (*dishi* 帝師), who oversaw Buddhist temples and personnel throughout the empire.[198] Some scholars have suggested that Yuan rulers attempted to impose a measure of uniformity on the production of Buddhist sutras as a way to promote political unity within the empire.[199]

Lines of religious patronage extended beyond the Yuan throne. In exchange for blessings and religious services, various members of the imperial Yuan family granted tax exemptions and other protections to Koryŏ temples.[200] Korean women serving in the Yuan palace or married to political elites contributed generously to Buddhist institutions in Daidu. Korean eunuchs at the Yuan court, sometimes acting on behalf of palace women and sometimes on their own, supported Buddhist temples in the capital and its environs.[201] Korean women and eunuchs in Daidu also funded Buddhist temples in Koryŏ through gifts of Yuan paper currency and gold.[202]

Mongol domination profoundly influenced Koryŏ military structures. After finally subjugating Koryŏ late in the thirteenth century, the Mongol court instituted a series of changes designed to ensure both Mongol control and domestic Korean stability. To a large degree, Koryŏ fell under the Mongolian military umbrella. Koryŏ's vaunted northern defenses were sharply pared back and its standing armies were abolished. In their place, the Koryŏ court mobilized men from among the general population on an ad hoc basis when a military crisis occurred. Perhaps more important, Yuan forces north of the Yalu River and the Yuan-controlled Ssangsŏngbu became the bulwarks of Koryŏ's northern defenses. The Palace Guard (*Suk'wigun* 宿衛軍) became known more for its numerous sinecures than for its fighting prowess. Consequently, by the mid-fourteenth century, Koryŏ kings were poorly prepared to face either the challenges of increasing international turmoil or rivals at home. As a way to ensure the safety of his person, his family, and the palace, several kings of the fourteenth century developed sizable personal guards, modeled explicitly after the Mongolian *keshig*. The official designation of some prestigious units in the royal guard was in the Mongolian tongue.[203]

The Yuan *tümen* or myriarchy (萬户府: Ch. *wanhufu*; K. *manhobu*) system was also introduced into Koryŏ.[204] Although troop strength seldom reached the prescribed ten thousand men, these myriarchies were generally stationed in the environs of the capital and along the southern coastal regions. Manned with Koryŏ soldiers and staffed by Koryŏ officers, the myriarchies represented a degree of autonomy from the Mongols. Through the mid-fourteenth century, however, the Mongols maintained effective control over officer appointments and thus some measure of control over the military forces as a whole.[205] Koryŏ kings could never take for granted the political loyalties of their officer corps. The Mongol court also reserved the right to mobilize Koryŏ military personnel for its own purposes and for campaigns of its own choosing.[206]

Thus, by the mid-fourteenth century, a far-ranging set of political, economic, cultural, and military connections tied Northeast Asia together more tightly than ever before in history. Peoples, goods, money, fashions, and ideas flowed across political borders with ease. The fates of Koryŏ, southern Liaodong, and northeastern China proper became inseparably intertwined. This is not to say that previous traditions disappeared; new imports were subject to local interpretation and were often changed in the process. Likewise, during the Mongol century, former political borders became far more permeable, but old rivalries and underlying tensions could re-emerge during times of crisis.

Integration under the Mongols proved contentious within Koryŏ. As Kim Hyŏng-su and others have observed, throughout the fourteenth century, debates raged about how closely Koryŏ should align its political, economic, social, and military structures with those of the Mongol empire. Some advocated adopting Yuan legal codes, military organization, and Neo-Confucianism. To gain Qubilai's acceptance and forestall even more onerous demands for materials and manpower, King Ch'ungnyŏl (r. 1298–1308) donned Mongol garb, cut his hair in the Mongol fashion, and acquiesced to Mongol demands to rename Koryŏ administrative bureaus to reflect their subordinate status within the empire.

During the fourteenth century, this trend accelerated under his son King Ch'ungsŏn (Wang Chang), Qubilai's grandson. As heir apparent, Wang Chang had spent much of his youth in Daidu, where through his connections to Mongol and Chinese elites, he gained firsthand knowledge of how the Great Yuan *ulus* was ruled.[207] As king, Ch'ungsŏn and his advisors favored adoption of Yuan legal codes, which would have meant far-ranging changes to Koryŏ socioeconomic foundations. Especially heated were debates over Yuan efforts to reduce the size of Koryŏ's slave population, a critical pillar of the kingdom's entire socioeconomic structure. King Ch'ungsŏn saw himself as both the king of Koryŏ and a prince of the empire. These reforms would simultaneously improve relations with the Yuan, undermine the economic foundations of many potential rivals within Koryŏ, and increase revenue flow to the throne.

These reforms sparked vociferous opposition. Many elites feared that the proposed changes would lead to social and economic chaos. In appeals to the king, some officials argued that such close integration would mean the end of Koryŏ's sovereignty. They reminded the king that Qubilai had ordered that Koryŏ's "dynastic customs" be respected. Fourteenth-century efforts to align Koryŏ's social and legal institutions with those of the Yuan violated Qubilai's will, they insisted. Those who wished to conserve traditional Koryŏ practices related to marriage, social status, and the balance of power between the throne and the country's aristocratic families walked a dangerous line. Insisting too loudly on Korean custom could be perceived as a rejection of Mongol authority. That being said, in the face of periodic efforts by the Yuan bureaucracy, the Koryŏ throne, and portions of the Koryŏ bureaucracy, advocates of "dynastic customs" staved off fundamental social, legal, and economic reform of Koryŏ.[208]

Kim Hyŏng-su argues persuasively that responses to Mongol rule illustrate the inadequacy of many past characterizations of the late Koryŏ period. These characterizations are often cast in such dichotomous terms as the rise of new literati versus aristocratic houses, the king versus aristocratic lineages, and Yuan supporters versus the new literati. Kim suggests that more attention to personal responses to the questions of the day may provide greater explanatory power. Although approaching the question of the "Yuan faction" in Koryŏ differently, Paek In-ho also stresses the importance of individual choice.[209] Chapter 8 returns to the question of how to understand Koryŏ during the age of the Mongols.

Incorporation of Koryŏ and Liaodong into the Great Yuan *ulus* did not mean complete unification, much less homogenization, of all facets of political, social, economic, military, and intellectual life. Yuan legal codes systematically distinguished Koryŏ from subjects in southern China. Despite extensive Yuan influence, Koryŏ remained administratively distinct from the Great Yuan *ulus*. During the thirteenth and fourteenth centuries, many viewed Liaodong as separate and distinct from the Central Plains. Such imperially commissioned compilations as the early fourteenth century *Da Yuan hunyi fangyu shenglan* 大元混一方輿勝覽 (Compendium of the unified territories of the Great Yuan) reflect this perception of Liaodong. In maps from this collection, Liaodong is conspicuously north of the Great Wall, which marks the northern limit of the Central Plain provinces.[210] The Red Turban wars would throw into clear relief the unprecedented degree of integration in Northeast Asia under the Mongols and at the same time place those relations under enormous stress.

2
A Precarious Restoration

Reform Efforts

In hindsight, it might seem obvious that the devastating epidemics, droughts, floods, and the attendant social instability of the mid-fourteenth century were bound to overwhelm the economic and political infrastructure of the Mongols' vast, loosely knit empire in East Asia. Historians of the past several centuries have noted that the Mongols' inability to devise a more stable system of succession only hastened the end of their rule in China. Nevertheless, the impending collapse of the Great Yuan *ulus* was anything but clear to contemporaneous observers.

During the mid-fourteenth century, the Mongol court implemented a series of ambitious projects designed to overcome the economic and political challenges of the day. The central aim was to consolidate control of North China, especially the Capital Region. From this strong base, the Mongol court hoped to continue its relatively loose rule over the rest of the Yuan *ulus*. Its thinking was neither foolish nor groundless. Such a strategy had brought great wealth and prosperity to the Yuan elite for nearly a century. There was every reason to believe that a revitalized dynasty based in Daidu would survive for many generations.

The man who stood at the center of these wide-ranging efforts was Toqto'a (1314–55).[1] Tall, strong, an accomplished rider and powerful bowman, Toqto'a had served a decade in an heir apparent's *keshig* and had engineered the purge of his uncle (and adoptive father) Bayan

(d. 1340), whose exuberant dominance during the 1330s had alienated much of the upper echelon of the Yuan elite, including the young Great Khan, Toghan-Temür. For eliminating Bayan and for his widely acknowledged talents in administration and politics, Toqto'a enjoyed the young emperor's confidence and widespread support among both Mongols and Chinese officials.[2] Over the next several years, Toqto'a spearheaded a wide-ranging series of reforms designed to reinvigorate Yuan infrastructure, finances, political morale, law, personnel, and cultural policies. Some scholars have termed the period the Toqto'a Restoration;[3] others, recognizing the emperor's role in the reforms, call it the Zhizheng Restoration after the name of the reign period.[4]

Beginning in the mid-1340s, under Toqto'a's leadership, the Mongol court began a series of massive hydraulic projects designed to improve the economic and transportation foundations of North China. In 1344, the Yellow River changed its course. The resultant flooding had disastrous social and economic consequences.[5] The poet Nasen used the striking image of "fish and turtles for a thousand *li*" scattered by the rushing waters flooding through the ruptured dikes of the Yellow River to capture the devastation. He also drew attention to the heavily armed brigands who entered walled cities in Shandong to plunder in broad daylight in the wake of the disaster.[6]

Toqto'a gained the court's support to redirect the river's flow eastward to its previous path. Many at the court vociferously objected to the plan: it would be expensive; it might not work; if it was such a good idea, why had it not been done in recent centuries? Mobilizing more than 150,000 men from thirteen administrative routes and 20,000 soldiers from eight divisions, the project reopened the Yellow River to boat traffic in ten months. Two months later the entire project was completed. The court heaped rewards and titles upon Toqto'a. Memorial steles describing the construction and its merits were composed and erected.[7]

The Yellow River construction project is frequently cited as evidence of poor planning and the court's growing isolation from the realities of China.[8] Wags at the time mocked the Yellow River project in doggerel for "throwing the realm into chaos."[9] During the project, enterprising rebels planted a one-eyed stone statue in the dirt along the banks of the Yellow River for workers to unearth. Such an image figured in a prophecy of imminent apocalypse circulating in much of southern China at the time. Assembling nearly 200,000 poorly paid men under loose supervision at a time of spreading crisis no doubt entailed risks but might be described as a form of working welfare. Suddenly cutting them loose with no wages when the work was done was without question shortsighted. Yet, this should not obscure the fact that the Yuan court was acting decisively to solve major problems confronting the empire.[10]

A similarly bold effort to reshape the physical environment of North China involved the introduction of wet-rice cultivation to the capital region. Beginning in the early 1350s, again under the supervision of Toqto'a, the Mongol court tried to reduce its dependence on grain from the south by growing more rice in areas closer to Daidu. Results were mixed. In 1352 efforts to grow rice in Shandong ended in failure as the harvest was insufficient to justify the costs. Farmers abandoned their fields rather than incur further losses.[11]

The court's efforts to reshape the local agricultural economy continued. Later in the 1350s, after the court provided local officials with 100,000 *ding* of cash to organize agricultural colonies manned by farmers and soldiers, southwest Shandong reported strong harvests.[12] At approximately the same time, government officials established agricultural colonies in the counties south of the capital (Xiongzhou 雄州, Bazhou 霸州) to supply Daidu with grain. This was a direct response to the interruption of tribute grain from the south caused by the growing power of Zhang Shicheng 張士誠 (1321–67).[13] Contemporaries considered these counties critical to the capital's survival. In a discussion of military developments in the mid-1350s, one writer described the troops garrisoned in places like Bazhou as the "right arm of the imperial forces," which could not be relocated.[14] As the Yuan court lost control of critical economic zones in the affluent Jiangnan region and important international ports of trade like Quanzhou 泉州, it attempted to consolidate its foundations in the Capital Region.

North China

The Mongols changed the dimensions and perspectives of China in ways that continue to the present day. One of the clearest examples of this was the establishment of the main capital of the Yuan, Daidu 大都

(Chinese for "the Great Capital") or Khan-baliq (Turkish for "City of the Khan"), in what we know today as Beijing. Although Beijing is now synonymous with China, it was not a traditional center for Chinese imperial capitals; the most important of those had been located in Northwest China or on the Yellow River plains in central China. In fact, the Beijing area had been outside Chinese control since early in the tenth century. Even then the region had been part of a precariously held northern frontier.

Scholars sometimes characterize the Mongols' decision to construct a self-consciously Chinese-style capital as an important concession to their Chinese subjects and a landmark in the Mongols' growing acceptance of "Chinese ways."[15] Beijing may be well within Chinese territory now, but during the thirteenth century, Daidu was in a frontier zone. In establishing Daidu, the Mongols were successors more to Jurchen than Chinese tradition. The Jurchen Jin dynasty had established one of its five capitals in this region for largely the same reason as the Mongols—to serve as a strategic bridge between the steppe and the agricultural regions of China.[16]

By the early fourteenth century, Daidu had largely eclipsed Shangdu to become the primary political center of the Great Yuan *ulus*. Its diverse population expanded rapidly during the late thirteenth century and by the early fourteenth century may have numbered as many as one million.[17] The Yuan court relocated communities of Chinese, Koreans, Persians, and even Russians to function as, among other trades, artisans, cooks, astronomers, textile workers, and silversmiths in their capital and its suburbs.[18] As Marsha Weidner has noted, a variety of Chinese and non-Chinese artistic traditions converged at the Mongol court, creating an environment for innovation and interaction.[19] These new residents of Daidu provided the Mongols with all the trappings that the world's richest court might desire. Spread by such accounts as Marco Polo's *Travels*, tales of the Yuan capital's legendary wealth and opulence inflamed West European imaginations for generations. Late in the fifteenth century, Christopher Columbus traveled to the Americas with a well-worn copy of the *Travels*.

Like many other empires, the Great Mongol *ulus* was transformed as a result of the imperial enterprise. Personnel and cultural practices from subjugated lands did much to shape the look and feel of the Mongols' capital in Daidu. For instance, the influence of Tibetan Buddhism at the Yuan court was striking enough that even European observers took notice. Marco Polo's *Travels* mentioned the monks' ability to perform such miracles as controlling the weather and levitating objects.[20] In fact, Tibetan Buddhism and Tibetan clergy constituted critical elements of both court life in Daidu and the Great Yuan *ulus* polity more broadly. As one scholar has recently remarked, "Tibetan Buddhist art became the most important form of official and public art of the Yuan dynasty, flourishing not only in Tibet but also in China and Mongolia."[21] Tibetan traditions even influenced how the Mongol rulers and their loved ones looked and remembered the ancestors; they commissioned painted and tapestry portraits of themselves that grew out of Tibetan media and styles.[22] Imperial patronage ensured that a steady stream of Tibetan monks trekked back and forth between Tibet and Daidu. In one six-month period in 1306, more than 850 monks, holding official travel documents issued in the 'Phags pa script, traveled along the imperially maintained postal relay routes. They transported thousands of pounds of gifts from the imperial family to Tibetan monasteries.[23] As a successor to Qubilai, Toghan-Temür was heir to the ideology, imagery, architecture, and ritual that developed out of the interface between Tibetan Buddhism and the Mongolian empire. In fact, many of the patterns of patronage and faith established by Qubilai during the latter half of the thirteenth century in regard to Tibetan Buddhism would continue to shape the court practices of both the Chinese Ming (1368–1644) and Manchu Qing (1636–1911) dynasties.[24]

Drawing on tantric Buddhist sutras, the polymath Tibetan monk 'Phags pa articulated a vision of Qubilai as a universal ruler, a *cakravartin*, or "wheel-turning sage king" (*zhuanlun shengwang* 轉輪聖王).[25] Just as bodhisattvas pledged themselves to saving all sentient beings before allowing themselves to escape the cycle of suffering, temporal rulers were to ensure the prosperity and happiness of their subjects. From there it was a short step to see the *cakravartin* as an earthly manifestation of a bodhisattva.[26]

In Daidu, this vision of Qubilai as a *cakravartin* took a number of visible forms. In 1267, Qubilai agreed to 'Phags pa's request to erect a large golden wheel above the main gate to the capital, Chongzhengmen 崇正門. The wheel symbolized Qubilai's identity as a wheel-turning sage king who unified the world. Slightly later, the court instituted the practice of suspending above Qubilai's throne a white umbrella made of plain silk with the Sanskrit letter *om*, or wisdom, written in gold. The umbrella was to suppress malevolent spirits and to protect the dynasty. In the Tibetan tantric tradition, the white umbrella was an emblem of the White Umbrella Buddha Mother, who protected Qubilai. White was an auspicious color in the Mongolian tradition. Both the gold wheel above Chongzhengmen Gate and the white umbrella figured in a procession held each year on the fifteenth day of the second lunar month. Members of the imperial honor guard, Tibetan priests, and Qubilai all participated. The richly dressed participants began at Qubilai's throne in the main hall of the palace, the Hall of Great Illumination (Damingdian 大明殿), passed through Chongzhengmen, and then circumambulated most of the Forbidden City before returning to the throne.[27] This religico-political tradition of Yuan emperor as *cakravartin* continued to the end of the dynasty. As noted in Chapter 1, Toghan-Temür maintained such practices as veneration of the white umbrella, the ritual circumambulation of the imperial city, and generous patronage of Tibetan Buddhist monks.

Tibetan influences were also manifest in the many imperially sponsored Buddhist temples in Daidu and the nearby Western Hills. Between 1270 and 1328, a dozen Tibetan-style temples were constructed by imperial order. Funded by the throne and imperial family members, these temples were lavishly appointed with jade altars, gold-covered Buddhist statues, and ornately wrought ceilings. By 1331, these temples lodged 3,150 monks and an unspecified number of service personnel.[28] Each temple commonly housed memorial portraits of former emperors and their empresses used in ritual offerings. These portraits were produced with Tibetan pigments and materials. The ceremonies also followed Tibetan customs. Today, the White Pagoda Temple (or more formally the Miaoyingsi 妙應寺) in Beijing is the only surviving example of these imperially sponsored temples; the Tibetan influences on it are unmistakable.[29]

Daidu and the Capital Region During the Fourteenth Century

The Mongols' administrative control in China, especially at the local level, was generally less centralized and less efficient than was typical of other, late imperial Chinese regimes.[30] Daidu and the Capital Region, however, were subject to relatively close supervision and control by the central government.[31] The area was home to the empire's elite: Mongols, Qipchaqs, Uyghurs, Jurchens, Persians, Chinese, and Koreans. It was garrisoned by the imperial guard, itself a critical political and military institution of empire.

By no later than the 1340s, however, imperial control faced growing challenges even here. Throughout the 1340s and early 1350s, brigand bands, often mounted, attained sufficient scale in the Capital Region to merit note in court chronicles.[32] During the spring of 1346, a band of several dozen mounted riders managed to raid 300 merchant ships plying the Grand Canal and escape with impunity.[33] The Grand Canal was a critical lifeline linking Daidu to the grain- and tax-producing provinces of the southeastern coast. Even the most sacrosanct objects in the capital were vulnerable. The same month that bandits made off with Grand Canal grain, "thieves" pilfered an undisclosed number of spirit tablets from the Imperial Ancestral Temple (*Tai miao* 太廟), the main dynastic temple.[34] From the mid-1350s on, reports of banditry in the Capital Region appear less frequently in court chronicles. The relative silence probably reflects the eclipsing of routine banditry by more pressing military conflicts elsewhere in the empire rather than improved security in Daidu's environs.

A second and related challenge for the court was securing an adequate food supply for Daidu's residents.[35] The imperial government maintained between twenty and twenty-five imperial rice shops in the capital in part as a relief measure.[36] During grain shortages caused by locusts, droughts, or disease, these rice shops were to sell rice below market prices. During the winter of 1338, each of these twenty-odd shops was ordered to sell approximately fifty piculs of rice each day "to assist the poor." Sales were to end with the autumn harvest.[37] When refugees flooded into Daidu, as happened during the spring of 1345, the government distributed "travel rice" and ordered them back to their native places.[38] One Korean observer at the time wrote that "more than half" of them died despite government relief efforts.[39] He further noted that as a result of the desperate conditions, a slave market appeared in Daidu, which officials chose to ignore.[40]

During the mid-fourteenth century, constant worry over maintaining an adequate food supply for Daidu drove the Yuan court to search for new ways to secure grain. As noted above, the court attempted to introduce wet-rice agriculture cultivation in the Capital Region. Although the powerful Mongol minister Toqto'a, the project's principal backer, fell from power in 1354, this ambitious and expensive initiative continued.

These various efforts did not prevent food shortages. In 1348, "the people of the capital starved,"[41] and in 1354, "a great famine [afflicted] the capital."[42] Local officials in rice-producing regions such as Jiangyou 江右 (present-day Jiangxi province) were encouraged to purchase rice locally and then somehow transport the grain to Daidu. One official won praise from the throne when in 1354 he managed to acquire one million piculs of grain this way.[43] Less than two decades earlier, as much as three times that amount had routinely been shipped to the capital by sea.[44] By 1360, the court was grateful for 100,000 piculs.[45]

The link between food and security was not lost on officials of the day. This relation had formed a core element of the Chinese statecraft tradition for centuries. Not only did the government declare tax amnesties for farmers in areas hit by fighting and natural disaster,[46] but it also tried to make imperial military forces more self-sufficient.[47] This would at one stroke lessen farmers' tax burdens and help ensure that soldiers would have enough to eat. If all went according to plan, both of these critical groups would be less likely to turn against the government. Late in 1355, the court established Grand Offices of Soldier-Farmers in four counties of the Capital Region. Stationed in regions with the newly introduced wet-rice agriculture, men assigned to these branch offices were to fight when necessary and farm when possible.[48] In the spring of 1357, as Daidu faced a growing threat from rebel forces based to the south in Shandong province, officials urged the court simultaneously to bolster the capital's defenses and to put soldiers to work in the fields whenever they recaptured territory.[49] There is no evidence that this strategy worked well for the Yuan during these tumultuous years. In some cases, it was counterproductive. Early in 1359, the Office of Soldier-Peasants of the Chief Military Commission (*Daidu dubing nongsi* 大都督兵農司) incurred intense local resentment when it illegally seized lands.[50]

The grain pinch led the Yuan to negotiate with such powerful maritime warlord-merchants as Fang Guozhen 方國珍 (1320–74) and Zhang Shicheng. In exchange for the delivery of grain from southern

China, the court granted them amnesties and bestowed positions within the imperial bureaucracy. Such policies led to vociferous objections by some officials. One official of Xixia descent, Mailigusi 邁里古思, argued, "Fang Guozhen began as a pirate. Although he has now surrendered to the dynasty and serves as a high official, he has begun to prey upon the people once more. How can we permit this to stand?!" Violating court orders, he began a military campaign against Fang. On the pretext of seeking his counsel, Baizhuge 拜住哥, an official with close ties to Fang Guozhen, summoned Mailigusi to the residence of one of his subordinates. Once there, Mailigusi was beaten to death with steel hammers. His decapitated head was then thrown into the privy. Mailigusi's enraged supporters then butchered most of Baizhuge's household, recovering their lord's head only after three days of searching.[51] These coastal pirates never delivered the promised amounts of grain, but the court felt that it had little choice other than to hope for the best. The court also experimented with the controversial policy of selling government posts in exchange for grain contributions.[52]

By late in the 1350s, conditions in North China and Daidu were grim. When epidemic disease compounded famine, some were driven to violate the ultimate taboo—fathers and sons reportedly consumed each other's flesh in cannibalism.[53] Beginning in 1358, people fleeing the fighting in much of eastern North China sought refuge in the capital. Severe famine and an outbreak of an unidentified epidemic took tens of thousands to their graves.[54] Despite all the Yuan government's efforts, in 1361 again "a great famine afflicted the capital."[55] Some of Daidu's residents resorted to pseudo-Daoist prescriptions to stave off starvation, with tragically predictable results.[56] Relief efforts were often privately organized and funded. For instance, in Xiongzhou, about fifty miles south of Daidu, a local man won praise for organizing efforts to bury the corpses of famine victims and distributing fish to the starving.[57]

These desperate conditions affected many areas in China and moved some men of the brush to give voice to the sufferings of the day. In 1355, Nasen began a month-long journey on horseback from his home in Qingyuan (present-day Ningbo, along the southeastern coast of China) to Daidu in pursuit of fame and a government position. During most of the late imperial period, cultivating potential patrons was a critical part of any young man's career. Since the Mongols generally avoided the examination system as a bureaucratic recruiting tool, the search for patrons and influential backers who would provide financial support or recommend talented scholars for government service became especially important. Many ambitious Jiangnan literati sought their fortune in the main Yuan capital, where they socialized with cultural and political leaders in a way they bemoaned as demeaning. The process required time, money, and determination. As they made the rounds of places like Daidu and Jinling (Nanjing), many young men collected portfolios of recommendations by literary and political figures in the form of "prefaces."[58] With any luck these "endorsements" might impress a potential patron. Some succeeded in their quests; most, like Nasen, returned home frustrated after years of wasted effort.[59]

In "Song of the Old Man of Yingzhou" ("Yingzhou laoweng ge" 潁州老翁歌), Nasen poignantly related the fate of an impoverished old man, who in better times had been a wealthy landowner with rich fields and a prosperous household of several hundred people. It is no accident that the region that Nasen describes, Yingzhou, was an area of intense Red Turban activity. It would become synonymous with rebellion during the mid-fourteenth century.

In recent years, the area south of the Huai River
  has suffered repeated droughts. 河南秊來數亢旱
The burned ground extends for one thousand *li*,
  yellow dust blows in the air. 赤地千里黃塵飛
Wheat withers and die,
  the rice does not grow to maturation, 麥禾槁死粟不熟
The hoe is hung upon the wall [idle],
  the plow rusts [with disuse]. 長鑱掛壁犁生衣
The magistrate eats and sleeps
  to his content. 黃堂太守足宴寢
He drives the commoners with whips,
  he seizes their wealth. 鞭扑百姓窮膏脂
Music blaring,
  at night, he grows mellow with drink. 聒天絲竹夜酣飲
Filled with himself,
  he ignores the people's cries of starvation. 陽陽不問民啼饑
The price of a peck of grain
  reaches ten thousand cash. 市中斗粟價十千

The starving
eat bracken for breakfast. 饑人煮蕨供晨炊
The bark has been completely stripped from the trees,
the roots of the weeds are all dead. 木皮剝盡草根死
My wife and children face one another,
their brows raised with trepidation. 妻子相對愁雙眉
Emaciated and exhausted,
their mouths spout fire [like hungry ghosts
parched for drink]. 鵠形累累口生燄
They cut up the corpses of those who starved to death,
none of the dead remained whole. 臠割餓莩無完肌
Villainous people exploit the situation,
to act as great rebels. 姦民乘隙作大盜
On the waists, they wear bows;
mounted on horses, they thunder about. 腰弓跨馬紛驅馳
They call out to the deep woods,
gathering the evil and vicious. 嘯呼深林聚兇惡
Wielding swords and halberds,
they wave battle pennants. 狎弄劍槊搖旌旗
During the third lunar month last year,
they seized the prefect's administrative complex. 去年三月入州治
They sat in the magistrate's chair,
like fierce bears. 距坐堂上如熊羆
Senior officials went out to welcome [them],
clerks then bowed down in salutations. 長官邀迎吏再拜
They presented [the rebels] gifts of cattle and wine,
they arrayed [these gifts] on the dais [where the
rebel leaders sat]. 饋進牛酒羅階墀
The wealthy families of the city
were thoroughly looted, 城中豪家盡剽掠
While signs of habitation
in the countryside grew scarce. 況在村落人煙稀
[Pillaging rebels] shredded bags and ripped apart baskets,
seizing gold and silks. 裂囊剖筐取金帛
They killed and boiled the chickens and dogs,
they used whips and bastinadoes [upon the country
folk]. 煮殺雞狗施鞭笞
This year, cruel disaster,
has reached to Chen and Yingzhou. 今年災虐及陳潁

The poison of disease has arisen in all quarters,
  the people have fled their homes. 疫毒四起民流離
Village after village, home after home,
  the dead are stacked one upon another. 連村比屋相枕藉
Even if they had medicine,
  it would be difficult to save them. 縱有藥石難扶治
A family of ten,
  in less than three days. 一家十口不三日
They are wrapped in straw mats
  and buried on a deserted hill. 藁束席卷埋荒陂
In matters of life and death,
  who gives a second thought to blood and kin? 死生誰復顧骨肉
Survival hangs
  by the slightest thread. 性命喘息縣毫氂
My eldest grandson, ten years old,
  Sold for five thousand cash. 大孫十歲賣五千
My youngest grandson, three years old,
  Thrown in the clear waters of the river. 小孫三歲投清漪
By now, in the waters
  beneath Peaceful Rule Bridge, 至今平政橋下水
White bones are piled high
  like a mountain precipice 髑髏白骨如山崖.
Envoys in embroidered clothes,
  [arrive] to restore proper moral order. 繡衣使者肅風紀
They dismount from their palanquins,
  to investigate the people's suffering. 下車訪察民瘡痍
Their memorials explaining conditions
  reach the emperor. 緣章陳辭達九陛
His musical instruments stowed, his viands reduced,
  the emperor worries over the dangers of the day. 徹樂減膳心憂危
At sundry meetings in the court halls,
  he confers with senior officials on relieving
  the disasters, 朝堂雜議會元老
And to march against the rebels.
  they labor over their deliberations. 恤荒討賊勞深機
In Shandong, the emperor's envoy
  established a special office. 山東建節開大府
He should execute the rebels,
  to make manifest the court's authority. 便宜斬石／著揚天威

The imperial guard marches forward in all directions,
the rebels flee in disorder. 親軍四出賊奔潰
The rebel leaders beheaded,
the realm restored to peace. 渠魁梟首乾坤夷
The court gives posts to those who contribute grain,
following established practice. 拜官納粟循舊典
Righteous men are moved to action,
all are pleased. 義士踴躍皆懽怡
The private coffers of Huainan,
their grain has long spoiled. 淮南私廩久紅腐
Transporting the grain [from other areas],
could they begrudge a thousand in gold? 轉輸豈惜千金資
The court dispatches officials out on inspection,
to help console [the suffering]. 遣官巡行勤撫尉
Grain and cash are supplied,
to aid the people's suffering. 賑粟給幣蘇民疲
Old and weak,
I was saved to see today. 獲存衰朽見今日
My sick and thin body is still thus,
Supported with difficulty. 病骨尚爾難撐持
If it were not for the emperor,
caring for his children, 鄉非聖人念赤子
My corpse would certainly have been,
thrown in a roadside ditch. 塡委溝壑應無疑
The old man lifts his face to the sky,
his tears fall like rain. 老翁仰天泪如雨
I am also moved,
sighing with worry. 我亦感激愁歔欷
When will the realm
be peaceful and prosperous? 安得四海康且阜
When will the weather
return to normal? 五風十雨斯應期
Head officials who are honest and fair,
magistrates who are good. 長官廉平縣令好
The common people sing and clap,
the song of peaceful times. 生民擊壤歌清時
I want to tell the poet,
who records the people's conditions: 願言觀風采詩者
Do not pass over my poem of
the Old Man of Yingzhou's suffering.[60] 慎勿廢我潁州老翁哀苦辭

Nasen dutifully criticized the "villainous people [who] exploit the situation to act as great rebels," yet he reserved his most withering remarks for local officials who ignored the people's misery and toadied to outlaw bands occupying administrative offices. One wonders whether potential patrons in Daidu appreciated the stark contrast that Nasen drew between the misery and suffering of Yingzhou and the world of privilege and power in which they themselves moved.

Despite the toll of famine, epidemics, and death during the last years of Yuan rule, the city's prosperity did not vanish completely. In the autumn of 1368, when officials of the newly founded Ming dynasty took possession of Daidu, many complained about the capital's extravagance and conspicuous consumption. Although cast as a social and moral problem, the wealth was real and attributed directly to Mongol rule.[61] The affluence of Daidu's elite could not, however, forestall concerns about the growing threat of the Red Turbans.

The Red Turbans

Yuan imperial authorities and contemporaneous Chinese observers lumped a wide variety of rebels under the rubric Red Turbans. Red Turban ideology drew on a rich variety of traditions, perhaps the most important being a millenarian faith, derived from White Lotus doctrines, in the imminent collapse of the existing temporal order and its replacement by a world in which believers' suffering and oppression would be washed away. The end would be violent. One near-contemporary wrote of the savior's arrival.

What kind of god is this Maitreya, who has sown so many seeds
of misfortune?
The flying squirrels shake the earth, and stir up huge dust storms.
Smoldering smoke blankets the land, and people's livelihood has
been made unbearable.
Blood stains all the rivers, while the ghosts and spirits wail bitterly.
Only once in a hundred years will people encounter such disasters.
As of when have the punishing weapons of Heaven, which stretch
for thousands of miles, announced their arrival?
Even in a barren field [wicked world] there may be hidden precious
jade [good people].
But alas! They all perish into a heap of ashes![62]

In place of the corrupted order would come an age of social justice, material plenty, and infinite joy. For hardworking farmers who daily struggled to pay their taxes, meet labor obligations to the government, tend their crops, and care for their families, this millenarian vision held great appeal. For those living during the tumultuous mid-fourteenth century, battered by merciless drought, famine, epidemic, and spreading violence, the message was often irresistible. A contemporary observer critical of the Red Turbans acknowledged the power of their "sweet words to mislead the people."[63]

Yet White Lotus teachings encompassed far more than apocalyptic visions and desperate farmers. White Lotus believers included political and cultural elites, including Chinese literati, Mongol nobles, and even an early fourteenth-century Koryŏ heir apparent, Wang Chang. Far from being members of covert, underground cells, some White Lotus faithful gathered in temples that formed an important feature of the social and religious landscape of the Yuan period. They venerated several figures, including the Amidha and Maitreya Buddhas. The Mongols offered protection and patronage for White Lotus communities. Beginning early in the fourteenth century, however, the Yuan government's policies occasionally shifted, outlawing some groups of White Lotus believers, razing a few (but far from all) temples associated with this tradition, and laicizing a portion of the faithful. The court periodically reissued its ban on Maitreya Buddhism. Such prohibitions did little to dampen people's faith. In fact, the Mongol court continued its patronage of White Lotus teachings.

What unsettled Mongol authorities were groups that operated beyond their control and who saw in the teachings of Maitreya a call for subversive activities. In 1325 and again in 1337 on a larger scale, Yuan military forces suppressed religious groups in southern Henan province, claiming that they had found a Maitreya pennant, seals, and forged edicts. White Lotus leaders such as Pudu 普度, who enjoyed elite patronage, struggled vainly to eliminate "heterodox" practices that sullied correct religious teachings and made all White Lotus faithful susceptible to doubt and persecution.[64]

There was no centrally organized Red Turban church. Most believers belonged to small local cells, with diffuse leadership and fluid memberships. During the 1340s, however, a few gained far broader powers.

Part of this growth resulted from spreading master-disciple relations and closer ties between individual religious communities over a much wider geographical expanse. Exactly how this happened on the ground is not clear. Government officials and later historians tended to view myriad disparate and only distantly related groups as parts of a massive, if loosely, organized movement.

The most prominent of the early Red Turban leaders was Han Lin'er 韓林兒 (d. 1367).[65] A religious leader devoted to a folk variety of Buddhism, Han's grandfather hailed from the county of Luancheng 欒城, a day's ride south of modern Beijing. Because of his missionary work, Han's family was exiled to a county northeast of Daidu, near the border of Liaodong.[66] Although Han Lin'er may have possessed some religious charisma, his name would never have become synonymous with late Yuan rebellion without the support of people like Liu Futong 劉福通 and others. These men provided the organizational skills, ambition, daring, and military resources that transformed the millenarian vision of a future paradise into paramilitary organizations that openly challenged local elites and the imperial government. As the violence spread, some who fought in Han Lin'er's name offered justification for their actions. Han, they claimed, was the ninth-generation descendent of Emperor Huizong, the Northern Song sovereign who in 1126 had overseen the loss of the northern third of the Song dynasty's territory to Jurchen invaders from Manchuria. Song restorationism added a patina of respectability to Han's actions in at least some quarters.[67]

The millenarianists acquired their name because of their frequent use of the color red. They donned red turbans and red clothes. When marching into battle, they wielded red pennants. Contemporary observers noted with dread that when the millenarian forces massed for combat, "all the fields were completely red" and that "red pennants covered the field."[68] According to the eminent Yuan specialist Chen Gaohua, the Red Turbans were not alone in their affinity for red. In fact, he argues all rebel forces wore red. Thus, he cautions against the scholarly convention of labeling groups associated with the millenarian movement the "Red Turbans." More accurate would be to designate them by the various dynastic names that individual rebel leaders selected. For instance, the forces associated with Liu Futong and Xu Shouhui 徐壽輝 might be better termed the Song 宋 Red Turbans and Tianwan 天完

Red Turbans, after the dynastic titles they adopted for their respective regimes.[69]

Local militias, in contrast, often used dark blue-green or yellow to identify themselves. In order to deceive the enemy into letting down their guard, rebel forces occasionally decked themselves out in these colors. To approach the still formidable walls of beleaguered Haozhou, in 1355 Zhu Yuanzhang (the future founder of the Ming dynasty) ordered local militia forces that had recently surrendered to him to "braid their hair in ringlets, button their gowns on the left, and wear dark blue-green clothes to pose as Yuan forces."[70] Hair ringlets and gowns buttoned on the left were Mongolian fashions. In this case, the stratagem worked. The city opened its massive gates to what its defenders believed to be reinforcements transporting desperately needed grain. The rebels quickly overwhelmed the defenders.

Despite the storied military prowess of the Mongol armies, such victories were increasingly common. The Yuan's response to the growing rebellion was shaped in part by the spread of Confucian political and moral rhetoric. According to the *Official History of the Yuan Dynasty*, the revolts infuriated Toghan-Temür, who initially favored a determined campaign of extirpation and who vowed "not to stop until all [the rebels] were dead." A senior minister of Jurchen descent and Confucian orientation reportedly dissuaded his lord from such a course of action, arguing "Pacification of the rebels consists of winning the people's hearts in order to win back Heaven's favor. [Too] much killing is not the Way."[71] The emperor relented and offered pardons as a way to defuse the situation. The rebel forces continued to grow, and within a few years Toghan-Temür would turn again to his armies.

The Yuan Military

During the thirteenth century, the Mongol military established a fearsome reputation for discipline, speed, technological sophistication, and ferocity. After subduing their enemies, the Mongols faced the even greater challenge of maintaining control in their spreading dominion. During the Yuan, the Mongols organized a palace guard (*suwei* 宿衛) in the capitals of Daidu and Shangdu and a system of garrisons in the provinces. These were the military resources with which Toghan-Temür attempted to restore imperial order in the Great Yuan *ulus*.

Befitting a regime that drew heavily from both steppe tradition and Chinese institutional models, the Yuan Palace Guard comprised two major elements. The first, the *keshig*, evolved directly from steppe practices whereby ambitious tribal leaders assembled bands of followers or companions who owed personal loyalty to the leader rather than to a clan or tribe. These men served not only as the their leader's personal bodyguard but also as household staff and government advisors. Chinggis owed much of his initial success to his band, and by 1206 he had expanded their ranks to include approximately 10,000 men. Although the *keshig*'s scope of duties and power diminished somewhat as Qubilai introduced more Chinese institutions into his government, the *keshig* continued to play several key roles in the Yuan *ulus*.[72] The *keshig* symbolized the imperial Mongol family's power, facilitated relations with other aristocratic steppe families, and figured in the maintenance of Mongolian identity.[73] Finally, as Chapter 3 describes in more detail, by incorporating elites from conquered polities and regions, the *keshig* fostered a sense of shared interests and perspectives; members of the *keshig* were the Eurasian elite.

As a military institution, the *keshig* represented the khan's personal forces. It answered not to the Bureau of Military Affairs but to the emperor. Largely drawn from the empire's elite families, the *keshig* was dominated by Mongols and Central Asians: Jurchen, Korean, and Chinese members were a distant second. These men enjoyed privileged political, economic, and social status within the Yuan *ulus*. According to most scholars, as early as the waning decades of the thirteenth century, a strong sense of superiority and entitlement eroded much of the *keshig*'s martial prowess and self-discipline.[74] *Keshig* units did not play a decisive role in the late Yuan wars against the Red Turbans and other Chinese rebel forces.

The second major component of the Palace Guards was the Imperial Guard Corps (Weijun 衛軍). Also intended as a way to bolster the strength of the central government, especially the emperor, the Imperial Guard Corps were drawn from a less prestigious stratum of the Yuan empire. Beginning as early as 1260, Qubilai established the first Imperial Guard Corps unit by skimming 6,500 superior troops from various Chinese contingents. The number of Imperial Guard Corps garrisons expanded steadily; by late in the dynasty, thirty-four had been established. Of these thirty-four garrisons, twelve were composed primarily of Central Asian troops and five of Mongolian personnel. Chinese soldiers staffed the remainder. The Imperial Guard Corps defended the two capitals (and parts of North China), protected the Yuan imperial family, served on military farms, and provided much of the labor needed for construction and repairs within Daidu.[75] Like the provincial garrison troops discussed below, Imperial Guard Corps soldiers were responsible for supplying their own weapons, horses, and feed. This burden was especially heavy for members of the Great Khan's guard during his trips to and from the northern capital of Shangdu.

During the fourteenth century, Imperial Guard Corps units increasingly shaped dynastic fortunes. Ambitious high-ranking ministers gained control over specific units and used them to make and break emperors. During the early years of Toghan-Temür's reign, the powerful minister Bayan concurrently served as the chief military commissioner of seven Imperial Guard Corps garrisons. During the mid-fourteenth century, another leading minister, Toqto'a, oversaw four units. These military units represented an essential dimension of ministers' bases of power. At the same time, through the first half of the 1350s, Imperial Guard Corps garrisons figured prominently in efforts to protect the dynasty against spreading Chinese rebellions. Imperial Guard Corps units saw action in fighting against Liu Futong and Zhang Shicheng.[76] As we shall see below, during the 1350s, regional and local forces, often times with no particular affiliation with the Yuan throne, began to supplant Palace Guard units as well as provincial garrisons.

The enormous variation in the geography, economic significance, political importance, physical proximity to the capital, and ethnic composition of the Yuan imperium posed great challenges for the Mongols. Given the relatively limited number of Mongol and Central Asian troops available, the Yuan court developed a provincial garrison system that stressed flexibility and clear priorities. Mongol and Central Asian units, thought to be the most reliable politically and militarily, were concentrated in and around the dual capitals, the Mongolian steppe, Manchuria, and North China.[77] These were the areas of the greatest strategic importance to the dynasty, and military resources were allocated accordingly. Geography too was a consideration. The topography and climate of these regions were believed better suited to steppe warriors and steppe warfare.

South of the Huai River, the Mongol military was less omnipresent. Provincial garrisons were commonly manned with Chinese soldiers, both from North China and surrendered Southern Song troops. Key urban areas and critical transportation hubs, such as those in Jiangnan and along the Yangzi River, were heavily garrisoned, often with contingents of Mongol troops. Outlying regions with less strategic value were more lightly defended. Again, the Yuan court felt that the warmer climate, prevalence of rivers and lakes, and frequently mountainous terrain favored the use of Chinese troops over Mongols and Central Asians.

Mongol units differed from Chinese units in their relation to the central government. The Mongol garrisons, especially those stationed in North China, the Mongolian steppe, and Manchuria were directly subordinate to the Bureau of Military Affairs in the capital. In contrast, the Chinese garrisons south of the Huai River reported to individual provincial governments. The Yuan court hoped that this decentralized command structure would suffice to maintain military control in the south and prevent a dangerous concentration of power in any single commander. As a way to improve political reliability, the highest posts in the provincial government generally went to Mongols and Central Asians, and the top military spots were appointed directly by the Bureau of Military Affairs.[78]

By early in the fourteenth century, economic, institutional, and political developments placed growing strains on the Yuan garrison system. Troops drew modest monthly stipends in rice and salt, received several acres of tax-free land from the government, and at least in theory, enjoyed exemptions from labor service obligations. However, they had to supply their own arms, horses, and equipment. They also bore the expense of relocation to distant garrisons. Desertion became endemic. Institutions designed to replace troops first deteriorated and then in 1345 were abolished.[79] As political intrigue surrounding succession often came to monopolize the attentions of the Yuan court in Daidu and Shangdu, the garrison system was left to atrophy. Underpaid, undermanned, and demoralized provincial garrison units proved inadequate to stem the growing tide of revolt and unrest that began in the 1330s and gained momentum in successive decades.[80]

Society's Militarization

During the mid-fourteenth century, this spreading violence led to the rapid militarization of much of China proper, which in turn increased the number of people willing and able to use arms to pursue their goals. Fortresses and stockades sprang up in many parts of the empire. These ranged from hastily constructed wooden affairs built on slight hills to elaborate complexes that boasted stone walls, beacons, and watchtowers. The largest of these defensive forts could accommodate several tens of thousands of people, including not just fighting men, but women, children, and the elderly. Whenever possible, precious livestock was brought within the walls during rebel attacks. In many cases entire communities sought shelter within these defensive complexes. When raiding parties attacked, local men took up arms in defense of their families and property.

The spreading violence and chaos of the mid-fourteenth century wrought many changes on Chinese society. The fortresses noted above were often organized by those who had the most to lose during these uncertain times—local elites. Although local government officials occasionally took the lead in organizing fortresses, more commonly the task fell to locally prominent landholders. Local elites dipped deeply into their store of social and financial capital to defend their interests in other ways. Throughout China, local magnates paid with cash and food for the fighting services of a growing variety of men.[81] These included professional mercenaries, salt workers, fishermen, farmers, and others.[82] These locally organized military forces were commonly called "righteous armies," indicating that they fought on behalf of the righteous cause, that is, in defense of the dynasty.[83]

Sacrifice on behalf of the dynasty, however, was seldom the most burning motivation for anyone. To be sure, local Yuan officials (both Mongol and Chinese) sometimes disbursed imperial funds to assemble and arm men to keep rebels at bay. In fact, the court in Daidu actively encouraged this trend, promulgating orders for the establishment of

Righteous Army Bureaus throughout the realm. The court's hope was that these new military forces would be used to supplement the hopelessly overburdened imperial regulars.

The reality, however, was that most of these righteous armies (or, less grandly but more accurately, local militias), were local affairs that contributed little to imperial campaigns of suppression.[84] County magistrates and men of local stature were concerned more with security in their backyard than with the preservation of such an amorphous thing as the "dynasty." Funerary inscriptions composed for men who led these local defense efforts consistently stress their concern with "protecting their hometowns."[85] Although few openly acknowledged it, most would have immediately appreciated the truth of one writer's observation about the escalating violence and lack of order: "Government troops and the hordes of rebels went back and forth among each other, pillaging, murdering, and wreaking havoc. The people could not go on. . . . Later, villagers took advantage of the rebels' strength and butchered one another."[86] Survival outweighed grand principles.

There were, of course, exceptions, men who displayed unwavering devotion to the dynasty. The experiences of Bayan 伯顏 (1295–1358) reveal much about the complexity of identity and cultural identification during the Yuan. His forefathers were of Turkic background (Qarluq), who had fought in Mongol armies against the Southern Song in the mid-thirteenth century. After the final conquest of China, they were registered in a Mongol military household, given livestock, and settled in Puyang 濮陽 county (located in present-day Henan province).[87] By early in the fourteenth century, he and his brothers had adopted many Chinese customs. All of them wore Chinese clothes and footwear. Alone among the brothers, however, Bayan developed an interest in Confucianism. Deeply learned in Chinese history and thought, he eventually became a teacher. As the number of his followers grew, he built a complex with more than a hundred bays and a temple dedicated to Confucius.

When in 1353 rebel groups raided near Puyang, Bayan and his family sought refuge in the mountains. Again in 1357, Bayan, now in his mid-sixties, fled mounting violence in Puyang. This time, he was accompanied not only by his family but by hundreds of his followers and their families. Once they arrived in Zhangde 彰德 (in present-day northern

Henan province), Bayan and his group built fortifications. One biography describes their motivation in the following terms: "Above, they could defend the dynasty against rebels. Below, they could fortify themselves and defend their families. They achieved both loyalty and righteousness. The plan was unsurpassed."[88] News of Bayan's stand spread widely, and "nearly ten thousand" sought refuge within his walls.

Bayan, however, proved less inspired as a military leader than a teacher. He apparently encountered difficulties maintaining order within the community; more important, in the fifth lunar month of 1358, Red Turban forces under Sha Liuer 沙劉二 attacked and quickly overran the fortifications. Sha and his men would soon advance into Liaodong and Koryŏ.

Bayan's interaction with the rebel leader gives a sense of the negotiations that played out through China during these years. The rebel leader warned his men before the assault: "Master Bayan is an eminent Confucian of Hebei. Be careful not to harm him!" On the second day the defenses fell; Bayan's wife and children were captured. Sha personally untied their bonds and tried to persuade Bayan to join him. Sha said, "Master is familiar with the past and conversant with the present. I now control more than half of the realm. If you would submit and join me, you could join me in the riches and high position." Bayan offered a counterproposal, "You were originally a good person. However, you have misled the people with heterodox teachings. If you repent and change your ways, I will inform the court and have you made a prince or official. Don't continue to take orders from a false leader [i.e., the Red Turban pretender]."

Bayan's righteous tone amused Sha. Laughing, Sha answered, "The pedantic scholar doesn't grasp the situation. It is a case of 'Not knowing the will of Heaven.'" Unsheathing his sword, one of Sha's subordinates stood up and challenged Bayan. "Do you see this? Say 'Disobedient' [i.e., not obeying the emperor's orders] one more time, and I'll kill you with a single stroke." Bayan cried out, "Disobedient! Disobedient! I would rather suffer the sword than suffer the corruption of [joining] you."[89] Bayan, his wife (a Kereyid Mongol), his children, and other clan members—a total of more than thirty people—were then slaughtered. The Yuan court eventually recognized Bayan's exemplary loyalty to the court, granting him posthumous offices and titles.

Whereas Bayan was Turkic by descent, Mongol by political affiliation, and Confucian by intellectual inclination, the most effective military man to remain loyal to the Yuan dynasty's very last days was Köke-Temür, a Chinese by birth who identified with both elite Chinese culture and the Mongol aristocracy of his uncle, the powerful general Chagha'an-Temür (himself a highly Mongolized Naiman), and felt at home in both the Chinese and the Mongol traditions. The Yuan emperor met Köke-Temür and accepted him as Mongol, granting him a Mongolian name. He campaigned extensively with his father and succeeded to his uncle's troops when Chagha'an-Temür was assassinated in 1362 (more on this below).[90] Köke-Temür became one of the Yuan throne's most important generals. Toghan-Temür would seek his aid repeatedly during the desperate years of the 1360s.

Yet, even these men on whom the Yuan court lavished commendations and high government posts were often driven to husband their military and financial resources against rival Mongol warlords, who ostensibly fought for the same Yuan cause. Again and again, Chagha'an-Temür and his nephew (and adopted son) consolidated their position in anticipation of attack by fellow loyalists rather than press ahead with the campaign against the rebel forces.[91] Some early Ming observers criticized the father and son for their unwillingness to sacrifice everything in the interests of the dynasty. However, pursuing court orders that would have resulted in certain destruction would not have benefited the dynasty—no matter how glorious posterity may have found their martyrdom. The lack of trust among leading Yuan field commanders found its counterpart in the atmosphere of suspicion and calculation that dominated the court in Daidu. In 1354, the link between court intrigue and military campaigns emerged with painful clarity in events at Gaoyou, a strategic city located on the Grand Canal.

In what would prove to be the last full-scale effort to mobilize the empire's financial and military resources to destroy the growing rebel threat in Southeast China, the powerful prime minister Toqto'a gathered an enormous host that included Mongolian, West Asian, Tibetan, Koryŏ, and Chinese troops, including at least five thousand local salt workers from the coastal city of Xuzhou. The campaign began well, and Toqto'a appeared to be on the brink of a decisive military victory over Zhang Shicheng and other rebel leaders. In December 1354, however, the Yuan court stripped Toqto'a of his military command, eliminating a potential threat to the crown but also emasculating the Yuan's most effective fighting force.[92] The debacle at Gaoyou was a turning point in the history of the Yuan *ulus*.[93] Writing centuries later, the noted historian Tan Qian 談遷 (1594–1658) remarked in his 1653 *Guo que* 國榷, "The establishment of the [Ming] dynasty and the creation of a base in the southeast were largely gifts of the Yuan court."[94]

The Yuan decision gave rebel leaders desperately needed time to regroup. One of them, Zhu Yuanzhang, would eventually topple the Yuan and establish the Ming. Many of the now-disbanded Yuan troops joined rebel groups or turned to brigandage.[95] Toqto'a's dismissal dealt a mortal blow not only to Yuan military strength but also to dynastic finances. Toqto'a's monetary reforms languished without his forceful presence, and rampant inflation resulted.[96] The fallout from the debacle also tarnished the Yuan's image abroad. Koryŏ troops returned home with tales of events in China: the enormous social dislocations caused by the fighting, the precarious state of Yuan control, and the deleterious influence of court jealousy on the execution of military campaigns. As Chapter 3 shows, the Koryŏ court exploited the Yuan's faltering control. Finally, the 1354 debacle eroded Mongol rule in North China. Prior to this point, the Yuan generally maintained firm control over North China, home to the capital and a relatively secure base from which to organize and outfit expeditions against rebellions south of the Huai and Yellow rivers.

This is not to say that unrest was unknown in North China before 1354. Scattered references to Shandong "bandits/rebels" appear several times during the 1340s; on at least one occasion Asud (present-day Ossetian) units, Caucasian mountaineers absorbed into the Mongol empire in the thirteenth century and eventually deployed to East Asia, were dispatched to crush them.[97] To improve governance throughout the empire, in 1345 the Yuan court had sent officials from the capital to investigate local conditions. The Chinese official sent to Shandong reported back that bandit groups were growing increasingly bold. In the past they had attempted to conceal their identities by painting their faces for fear of discovery. Later, the bolder groups "went so far as to beat drums and raise pennants. They did not fear apprehension by the government." He found that "[officials] of prefectures and counties flee when they hear news [of the bandits], and the local constabulary personnel abscond when they see [the bandits'] shadows."[98]

Despite his disturbing discoveries, these outlaw groups paled in comparison with the size of rebel armies during the 1350s and 1360s. The largest band the official mentions numbered less than two dozen men. He recommended that the throne immediately fill the many empty posts in local government, replace elderly and enfeebled officials, provide effective relief to farmers suffering from drought and onerous tax and service obligations to the state, and finally conduct further investigations into the large number of people languishing in local jails whose cases had been left pending for years at a time.[99]

After 1354, northern China, including the capitals of Daidu and Shangdu, came under increasingly direct threat.[100] As rebel forces crossed the Yellow River, many felt vulnerable. One official passionately exclaimed, "The rebels have now forded north across the Yellow River, but imperial troops do not repulse them. If the strategic defenses of the Yellow River can no longer be defended, what more can the people north of the river depend on? Once the hearts of the people north of the river begin to sway, what will become of the dynasty?"[101]

Mao Gui and Central Shandong

The aggressive military strikes by the Red Turban leader Mao Gui 毛貴 illustrate the increasingly beleaguered position of the Yuan court, even in its most closely controlled lands. Mao began as subordinate of a better-established Red Turban leader in the Jianghuai region. He quickly demonstrated his military skills, apparently playing a critical role in the capture of the important city of Huai'an in 1356.[102] By the second lunar month of 1357, fleeing from Yuan forces, Mao and his men had embarked at Haizhou 海州 (present-day Donghai 東海, Jiangsu province) and landed on the Shandong peninsula at Jiaozhou 膠州.[103] In so doing, Mao was exploiting a well-established coastal route developed by the Yuan government to transport grain and many other products from the affluent southeast to Daidu; he may have been traveling in government ships seized in Haizhou.[104]

The maritime connection is worth noting; Red Turban forces would later travel by sea from Shandong to the southwestern coast of Koryŏ.

In 1351, rebel forces had boarded ships at Dengzhou, Shandong, crossed Bohai Bay, and seized Jinzhou, located on the southern tip of the Liaodong peninsula. When Yuan forces rallied, the rebels crossed the bay again and returned to Shandong.[105] Maritime routes facilitated rather than impeded intraregional travel. In fact, as fighting disrupted many overland routes, maritime routes became even more important. In 1364, one Chinese official wrote that with the unrest, "The roads of the Central Plains are closed. In the coming and going of envoys, the seas are used as roads."[106]

In 1358, Mao's forces seized control of most of Shandong province. Mao first established a base in Yidu 益都, a large and important city located in central Shandong, putting to flight a Mongol prince who abandoned his lands as the price for his life.[107] By the second lunar month of 1358, Mao took stoutly defended Ji'nan 濟南, a Yuan stronghold straddling important communication and commercial routes.[108]

Extant records do not make clear local perceptions of Mao Gui, which probably varied widely. The *Official History of the Yuan Dynasty*'s account of the stubborn resistance of one veteran campaigner famous in his youth for his skill with double swords suggests the ambiguity of contemporary conditions. When Mao Gui seized control of Yidu, Wang Ying 王英 was 95 years old but apparently still full of spirit. He informed his son:

> For generations we have received dynastic favor. We have fully enjoyed prestigious posts and generous emoluments. I am old now, but even though I cannot serve in the military to repay [my debt of gratitude to] the emperor, could I still be willing to eat the [salary] grains of a [regime of] a different surname in order to save my life?
>
> 我世受國恩，美官厚祿，備嘗享之。今老矣，縱不能事戎馬以報天子，尚忍食異姓之粟以求生乎![109]

Refusing even water or gruel, Wang died within days. Mao dispatched an underling to provide Wang with a coffin and burial shroud in recognition of his exceptional loyalty.

This snippet suggests that uncompromising loyalty to the Yuan was rare enough to merit special praise. Like much of the rest of China, Shandong witnessed the rapid proliferation of local militias. In fact early in 1357, in an attempt to gain some control over the growing ranks of armed men, the Yuan court issued orders that each subprefecture and county in Shandong was to appoint an additional official to oversee these local militias.[110] Some of these forces resisted Mao Gui and other Red Turban forces.[111] More, however, either defected to Mao or fled with their families to less turbulent regions.[112]

One can also infer that Mao was attempting to win a measure of local support through public praise of moral exemplars. The Yuan court also strove to generate loyalty through public recognition of those who died in defense of the dynasty, no matter how humble their background.[113] It was an uphill battle. The most visible representatives of the Yuan state—ill-disciplined and poorly fed Yuan soldiers—frightened commoners. Tales spread of destruction and looting in the wake of these troops.[114]

The Yuan court was fully aware of the wanton brutality exhibited by its forces. It actually conferred honors and titles on a local deity for protecting residents against rampaging Yuan troops. Despite desperate efforts by the government to secure food and supplies for imperial troops, in the spring of 1359 commanding generals "pillaged the people for food" and sacked the localities south of the capital. In April, Zhuozhou 涿州, a prosperous county south of Daidu, also fell victim. According to a temple account for the local deity, "those among the people who oiled [with their own fat] the [troops'] cooking caldrons numbered hundreds and thousands each day."[115] The phrasing here and elsewhere in the account is ambiguous, suggesting either torture or, more likely, cannibalism. In any case, residents gave thanks that their suffering ended after only fifteen days, when the soldiers left the county seat. "Without divine aid that caused them to leave, there would have been no survivors."

A year later in the midst of famine, again imperial troops garrisoned in the surrounding area descended on Zhuozhou at dawn, pillaging and torching most of the town. Although the soldiers left the same day at dusk, they had seized "men and women without count" to haul equipment and supplies. Residents again offered prayers to the local deity, who interceded to ensure the safe return of five hundred of the captives, who otherwise would have died at the soldiers' hands. In recognition of the god's proven efficacy (in protecting imperial subjects from imperial generals and troops), the Yuan court approved a new more illustrious title for the deity and invested it with the rank of duke.[116] In other words, the court acknowledged that sometimes nothing but the gods could save the people of China from Yuan military forces.

One way the Yuan court attempted to assuage local uncertainty was through general pardons in areas where rebel forces had been suppressed. Rebel leaders were publicly punished as a deterrent, but the majority of followers were exonerated, often on the pretext that they had been forced to join the rebels. It was hoped that in this way, local populations would return to the imperial fold rather than join rebel regimes out of fear of government prosecution.[117]

Although only scarce details about Mao's political organization survive, he apparently attempted to establish at least a skeleton government in the region. He recruited Yuan officials, opened agricultural colonies, improved transportation, collected land taxes, and set up a branch secretariat for Yidu.[118] Due consideration was given to strengthening city walls, whose poor state had often facilitated the Red Turban victories.[119] Mao Gui himself took the title Administrator 平章 of Yidu Branch Secretariat, suggesting that he considered himself a subject of the newly declared Song dynasty established by the rebel leaders Han Lintong and Liu Futong.[120] During this time, the regime also cast official seals of office that faithfully followed Yuan government practice but were issued in the name of the Song dynasty and used its calendar.[121]

Mao soon began a military drive northward toward Daidu. Advancing by both overland and river routes, Mao's troops were closing rapidly on the capital by the third lunar month of 1358. The Yuan court panicked. One senior Chinese minister, Li Shizhan 李士瞻 (1313–67), painted a picture of administrative collapse: "The residents of all regions have panicked and scattered in all directions. [They] lack any firm resolve. All the prefectures and counties throughout the Capital Region have been left empty."[122] Officials left their cities undefended, and the cities' inhabitants fled.[123] While the court attempted to bolster capital defenses, some high officials recommended either flight to the steppe or relocation of the capital to the northwest.[124] At least one Chinese official noted that the loss of Shandong would likely result in the loss of Daidu.[125] Writing slightly after the fact, another observer opined, "The strength of the rebels was rampant, no different from the rebels at the end of the Tang dynasty."[126]

In the end, Mao's hesitance obviated the need for dramatic decisions by the Yuan court. As Mao vacillated, the Yuan strengthened Daidu's military forces and began its counterattack. High-ranking ministers like Taiping 太平 (He Weiyi 賀惟一), a Chinese official whose family had served the Yuan dynasty since its inception, argued forcefully for bolstering the capital's defenses rather than flight.[127] Yuan victories in initial engagements south of the capital made the argument more palatable, as did Mao's subsequent decision to withdraw to his base in Shandong.[128]

This marked the end of the Eastern Red Turbans as a serious threat to the Yuan. Internal tensions within the Red Turban leadership quickly undermined its military strength. In the fourth lunar month of 1359, Zhao Junyong 趙均用 arrived at the headquarters of his putative subordinate, Mao Gui. For reasons that are not entirely clear, Zhao killed Mao. Less than three months later, several of Mao's leading lieutenants avenged his death by murdering Zhao. By 1360, a large force of crack troops under the command of the renowned Mongol generals Chagha'an-Temür and Köke-Temür began their advance into Shandong. By 1361 they had reclaimed control of the region for the Yuan dynasty.[129]

Late in 1361, Chagha'an-Temür announced the victory over the rebels with offerings at the Temple of Confucius in Qufu. A Qing period scholar suggests quite plausibly that Chagha'an-Temür and the Mongol court did not take local support for granted. "Because Tian Feng [a prominent military officer who turned against the Yuan] had long controlled Shandong, military and civilian households supported him," the scholar argued, and Chagha'an-Temür "dispatched a communiqué explicating the principles of obedience and rebellion."[130]

Prospects for the Future

Contemporaries were able to convince themselves that the Yuan had turned the corner and that better days lay ahead. By this time, reports of military successes elsewhere in China began to reach the court. This news, combined with the successful defense of the capital, led to optimism—"the hearts of those in the capital and those in provinces are at peace; there are now prospects for a restoration."[131] A similar message of hope and restoration found expression in art of the day. For instance, the painting *Auspicious Harvest*, dated 1350, is a rebus containing a wealth of symbols related to good harvest, which was in turn predicated on good rulership and a healthy dynasty. Based on an analysis of the content, style, and inscriptions of Zhao Yong 趙雍's 1352 painting *Noble Steeds* (*Junma tu* 駿馬圖), Jerome Silbergeld has argued that the work suggested a message of "the continuing vitality and legitimacy of the Yüan imperial tradition."[132]

More prosaically, the re-establishment of Yuan control in Shandong is an important reminder that even during the last years of the dynasty, the Mongol court and its military forces could be effective. Some Chinese officials denounced the Yuan court for leniency toward lackadaisical and incompetent military commanders,[133] and Yuan generals were bitterly criticized for not pursuing the campaign against Mao Gui in Shandong more aggressively.[134] Yet in the end, they successfully exploited internal problems within the ranks of the Red Turbans to force Mao out of the Capital Region and to crush the Red Turbans in Shandong. Recovery of Shandong allowed partial resumption of the transmission of salt monopoly income to the capital, since critical nodes of the network ran through western Shandong. This salt income "was especially important, because it did not feed off the people [but instead] was a profit secured naturally from Heaven and Earth." Its loss led to the deterioration of government offices and to local administration. Köke-Temür had now "succeeded to his father's ambitions for restoration, pacifying Shandong, and re-establishing the Tax Transport and Salt Monopoly Commission."[135]

Yuan military success in North China grabbed the attention of powerful men in the south. As Chen Gaohua has noted, in 1359, when Chagha'an-Temür drove the Song regime out of its capital in Kaifeng, Zhu Yuanzhang did not offer to assist the Song court (his putative sovereign). Instead he sent an envoy with an offer of friendship to Chagha'an-Temür. Chagha'an-Temür's initial victories against Red Turban forces in Shandong had another effect, as many rebel leaders, again including Zhu Yuanzhang, expressed an interest in an alliance with him. The Yuan court seized the opportunity, sending an envoy bearing garments, imperial wine, and prestigious jewel-encrusted cap tops, to negotiate Zhu Yuanzhang's surrender. Thus, even the most cynical operators had not written off the Great Yuan *ulus* less than a decade before its final collapse. Chagha'an-Temür's untimely murder and the resultant uncertainty, however, scuttled the deal.[136]

This is not to say that contemporaries viewed events with unwavering confidence. Just about this time, the literatus Song Lian 宋濂 (1310–81) abandoned the Yuan and offered his allegiance and counsel to the rebel leader (and future emperor) Zhu Yuanzhang. His writings abound with graphic images of rotting, exposed corpses, savage plunder, and desperate refugees.[137] Even those who remained faithful to the Yuan displayed a certain desperation in the way they grasped at military victories as evidence of a dynastic revival. In a letter to a powerful Mongolian commander of the important southern port of Quanzhou, Li Shizhan rhapsodized:

Now the Central Plains have been pacified; [those] south of the [Huai] river have surrendered in all sincerity. Not a day goes by without presentations of prisoners and memorials of victory [at the court]. The dynasty is refounded. The land has returned to peace after chaos. The foundations of the Great Peace unfold before our eyes.

今中原底平，江南款附。獻俘奏凱，無日無之。乾坤再造，日月重明，太平之基，進在目下。[138]

Li was trying to convince the official to resume the flow of vital salt monopoly revenue to the central government. With a generous emperor on the throne, an heir apparent at the height of his powers, wise ministers to shape policy, and the dynasty on the cusp of a major revival, the official would be shortsighted to abandon his loyalty to the throne, Li implied. Li was not an idle observer. In 1359, the court sent him to Fujian to exchange salt for grain to be transported to Daidu, a mission that drew him into correspondence with Chen Youding 陳友定 (1330?–68), a Chinese military leader, basically loyal to the Yuan regime, who resisted the overtures of Zhu Yuanzhang.[139]

Li's praise of Köke-Temür's victories reveal the same mix of bright optimism and brutal realism. His celebratory memorial written on the occasion of the general's victory in Shandong opens with imperial rhetoric that stressed the dynasty's divine favor. "I have heard," he wrote, "that the term of rulers is determined by Heaven 帝王之歷數在天; those who vainly interfere destroy themselves. The dynasty's territory extends to the ends of the earth; those areas wrongfully seized must naturally be returned [to imperial control]."[140]

Passing from the brilliant conquests of Chinggis and Qubilai, Li's tone grew far darker in his discussion of Köke-Temür's recent campaigns in Shandong. After the defeat of the generals who betrayed his father in Shandong, Köke-Temür

> first ground their children into mincemeat. Then he carved up their fathers, wives, and daughters. Tian Feng and Wang Shicheng, their hearts were cut out and offered as sacrifices [to the soul of Köke-Temür's father]. He minced the meat [of their corpses] and distributed [it to his generals] to eat. He sent their decapitated heads to be displayed in the streets. He exposed their bones on high earthen mounds. As to their [subordinates] Feng, Chen, Yang, Li, and their like, the dismembered body parts of some were displayed on pikes in the public markets. Others were transported in prisoner carts to the capital. All Qi [northeast Shandong] was in this way reduced to order. Zou and Lu [southwest Shandong] were in this way pacified. Only in this way were the blades hardened and the swords sharpened. The roots of the usurpers were destroyed. Additionally, all imperfections were removed. He eliminated the spread of confusion, the violent and the social transgressors, and those unruly ones who violate the borders. All these should be promulgated as cautionary examples; they should all be forewarned.[141]
>
> 初膾剉其童孩、次脤斮其婦女。田豐、王士誠、刳心以侑祭，醢肉以分餐。傳首藁街，暴骨高垤。其馮，陳，楊，李等或竿磔于市，或轞送於京。全齊由是而削平，鄒魯由是鏟定。方將淬礪鍘鍔，勦僭僞之根；且復搜索舋瑕，除狂惑之蔓。強梁瀆紀之輩，跋扈犯關之徒，毋[努][142]怒蛙膺，敢擎螳臂。悉宜播誡[143]，咸使知懲.

Such harsh measures may have seemed increasingly necessary to some as Red Turban armies continued their despoliations throughout North China, southern Liaodong, and eventually Koryŏ. Public terror, however, was not the only response.

During the early 1360s, the Yuan court continued its efforts to revitalize local governance in North China. However, it had to overcome the hesitation of officials who dreaded local posts where fighting had devastated agriculture, destroyed such symbols of government authority as yamen offices, and left them unable to maintain local defenses on anything but a perilously ad hoc basis.[144] As private writings from the time indicate, many chose to withdraw from service and become recluses. Convincing officials to return to the broken countryside was essential to restoring Yuan control. The Red Turban attacks would raise similar questions in Koryŏ.

Shangdu and the Road to Koryŏ

Early in January 1359, Master Guan 關先生, Cracked-Head Pan 破頭潘 (also known as Pan Cheng 潘誠), and Sha Liuer 沙劉二 (also known as Master Sha Liu 沙劉先生) led Red Turban forces into Koryŏ.[145] Modern scholars sometimes call this group the Red Turbans' Middle Route Army 中路軍. It originated in southwestern Shandong province and by August 1357 had taken such major cities as Daming 大名 and Weihui 衛輝 in what is now southern Hebei province.

The Yuan court quickly dispatched the Mongol general Tash-Bātur 答失八都魯 (d. 1367) to crush the insurgents. After suffering initial losses, he refused to engage the Red Turbans. Suspecting that his actions grew out of a desire to preserve his military forces for his own purposes, the Yuan court dispatched an envoy to investigate. Red Turban forces apparently bamboozled the court envoy. They planted a forged correspondence that suggested that Tash-Bātur was attempting to negotiate a settlement with the rebels rather than extirpate them. When the Mongol general died soon thereafter, the estimable Bolod-Temür took command of the Yuan forces charged with crushing the Middle Route Red Turbans.

For the next year, Red Turban forces proved highly mobile, fighting throughout much of North China. During the early winter of 1357, they crossed the Taihang Mountains into Shanxi province. By spring 1358, they had seized Jiangzhou 絳州 and the strategic city of Datong 大同 and briefly occupied a number of other cities. Deeply concerned about a military threat so close to Daidu, the Yuan court transferred one of its leading generals, Chagha'an-Temür, to deal with the Red Turbans. He and his generals attempted to prevent the rebels' movement eastward by seizing critical passes in the Taihang Mountains. By the sixth lunar month of 1358, however, the Middle Route forces under Sha Liuer had slipped the blockade and moved into northwest Hebei province, while by the ninth lunar month Master Guan had struck against Baoding in southern Hebei.[146]

Chen Gaohua has suggested that Sha and Guan were attempting to join Mao Gui in preparation for an attack on Daidu. When the Eastern Route Turbans encountered military difficulties, Guan and Sha instead tried to return to their bases in southwestern Shandong. Stymied by Chagha'an-Temür, they moved northward again. From Datong, they marched north and then west. Early in January 1359, Master Guan, Cracked-Head Pan, and their men arrived in Shangdu.

By the mid-fourteenth century, Daidu had eclipsed Shangdu (Superior Capital) as the Mongols' chief political center in East Eurasia. Shangdu, however, remained important for the Yuan *ulus*. From the fourth to ninth lunar months, the emperor, the imperial family, and the majority of the court resided in Shangdu. From there they set out on hunting trips and other excursions that lasted anywhere from a few days to a few weeks. The majority of the *ulus*'s government continued to follow the seasonal migrations of the Great Khan as did his sizable military forces. When the court resided in Shangdu, it hosted enormous banquets for elites that offered opportunities to forge alliances, reaffirm loyalty, redistribute material wealth, and hammer out political and military strategies. Although modest when compared with Daidu, Shangdu boasted a palace complex and a set of year-round administrators. Thus, Shangdu was an important symbol of Mongolian imperial prestige, an administrative center, and military depot with stores of arms and grain.[147] Like Daidu, Shangdu had recently experienced famine. Early in 1355, 20,000 piculs of grain were sold at reduced prices and the production of alcohol was forbidden by imperial order in response to famine in the Mongol's northern capital.[148] The famine apparently continued throughout the spring.

The Red Turban armies spent only a week in Shangdu—time enough to burn the imperial palace and inflict considerable damage on the rest of the capital. Shangdu never recovered. With the benefit of hindsight, we know that 1359 marked the end of more than a century of annual sojourns in Shangdu.[149] However, no one at the time viewed it with such finality. In the fifth lunar month of 1360, the emperor sought to revive this vital feature of Mongolian political culture. He ordered large-scale repairs of the imperial palace. His efforts met with immediate opposition in some quarters. The Chinese court official Chen Zuren

陳祖仁 (1314–68) expressed sympathy for the emperor's "heartfelt desire" to restore the Shangdu palaces. He acknowledged that such restorations were a natural complement to restoring the dynasty and to reviving the glory of the emperor's ancestors.

Chen, however, argued that the court simply could not support such an expense. "At present," he observed, "the realm is in turmoil, the scars [of warfare] have not healed, the storehouses are empty, and our finances are nearly depleted." What difference, he asked, was there between forcing struggling men to serve in the construction gangs and "grabbing them by the throat and seizing their food?"[150] Chen concluded the emperor should put the dynasty's strained resources to more pressing tasks. For Chen, a Chinese minister, this certainly meant directing the court's attention away from the steppe to the Central Plain. Although the emperor reportedly praised and accepted his proposal, no details are available about how much reconstruction was accomplished. Nor is it clear how representative Chen's views were.

During the following years, Shangdu continued to figure in political struggles among the Mongolian aristocracy. In 1360, Alqui-Temür (a descendent of Ögödei and current holder of the title Yangdi Prince 陽翟王) exploited chaos within the realm to challenge the emperor. Moving eastward from his base in what is today the Xinjiang Autonomous Region, he sought allies among disaffected Mongolian nobles and charged the emperor with having betrayed the legacy of their ancestors. Although Chinese sources indicate that Toghan-Temür remained unfazed by Alqui-Temür's accusations, he did move to counter the "several hundreds of thousands" of rebel troops, which "harassed the northern border and pressured Shangdu." The Yuan heir apparent attempted to use the situation to his advantage by appointing a political rival to defend Shangdu, believing that the northern capital would soon fall to the rebels, who would naturally dispose of the city's chief defender.[151]

Initial efforts to contain the revolt seemed to confirm the heir apparent's judgment. Yuan forces fell to rebels and the commanding general escaped alone to the relative safety of Shangdu. In 1361, Toghan-Temür again mobilized "100,000" imperial troops to attack Alqui-Temür. This time, however, the Mongol court was able to recruit one of Alqui-Temür's brothers as well as one of his leading commanders, who delivered Alqui-Temür to the throne.[152] With his capture, the Yuan throne regained some control over the northern border, and Shangdu won a reprieve.

Late in 1360, a group of Red Turban rebels again attacked Shangdu, defeating relief forces under the Yuan commander Möngke-Temür 忙哥帖目兒.[153] The attack suggests that Shangdu was still important enough to bother with; the defeat indicates the continuing power of the Red Turbans.

To return to early 1359, Master Guan and Cracked-Head Pan left Shangdu, passed through Liaoyang, and then entered the kingdom of Koryŏ.[154] The Red Turban armies under Guan and Pan would have an even more profound impact on Koryŏ than they had on their native land of China.

3
Koryŏ in the Great Yuan Ulus

During the 1350s, the Koryŏ court followed developments in the Great Yuan *ulus* with keen interest. It was well positioned to track the growing severity of social unrest there. As Chapter 1 noted, during the mid-fourteenth century, tens of thousands of people from Koryŏ resided in the main capital of Daidu and as many as a quarter million Koreans may have lived scattered throughout the Yuan as a whole. They included successive generations of the Koryŏ heir apparent, his sometime rival the Sim Prince, scholars, monks, merchants, and thousands of women, who served at court and mingled with the Mongolian elite. Accurate, timely information was invaluable to all these groups.

On occasion officials in the Mongolian bureaucracy found Korean intelligence networks disturbingly efficient. In 1333, Darma 答里麻, a Gaochang 高昌 Uyghur, had just taken up his post as second privy councilor of the Liaoyang Branch Secretariat. Among the first to meet with him was a royal Koryŏ envoy en route to Daidu from Kaegyŏng. The envoy presented four bolts of fabric and an official diplomatic communication to officials in the secretariat. Darma was doubtful about the envoy's motives and methods.

Darma observed, "When you left Koryŏ, I was still in the capital and was not yet an official in the Liaoyang Branch Secretariat. How could [the king] have a letter for me?"[1] Although it is entirely possible that the Koryŏ envoy engaged in some form of duplicity (perhaps adding Darma's name to what should have been a sealed letter), it is at least equally plausible that the Koryŏ king had learned of Darma's appointment long before he arrived in Liaoyang to take up his new duties. In any case, Darma declined to accept either the correspondence or the gifts.

The Ties That Bind: Marriage and the Great Khan's Guard

Among those who paid minute attention to events in the Mongol empire was Wang Ki 王祺, or, as he is better known to history, King Kongmin 恭愍王 (r. 1351–74).[2] Twenty-two-years old in 1351, the year he formally took the Koryŏ throne, he did not look like a Korean in many ways, or at least not one that the dynastic founder would have recognized immediately. He and most of his court plaited their hair in Mongol fashion[3] and wore Mongolian felt caps. Many donned tight-fitting riding tunics with pleated robes and sleeves that narrowed at the wrist and left the bow-arm free for action.[4] Formidable equestrian skills were esteemed and on frequent display; polo matches were common in his capital.[5] Like the Mongols, the Koryŏ court valued the matches as entertainment, military training, and a way to strengthen elite cohesion. The king frequently viewed archery contests, including events that featured shooting at small targets while mounted on horses galloping at breakneck speeds. Kongmin enjoyed watching members of his bodyguard wrestle, again both as entertainment and as a test of prowess.[6] Even the king's "throne" was the platform that could seat several people (the so-called barbarian bed 胡床) commonly used by rulers throughout the Mongolian empire.[7]

Like nearly all the Koryŏ kings during the Mongol period, the young monarch used both Mongol and Korean names, depending on the context.[8] In his interactions with the empire (and on occasion with the founder of the Ming dynasty), Kongmin was known as Bayan-Temür, a solid if common Mongol name. In 1349, as a member of the Koryŏ royal family, he married a young Mongol woman, Budashiri. Her title was the Huiyi Luguo Imperial Princess 徽懿魯國大長公主. Her father was Bolod-Temür, the Wei Prince 魏王.[9] The princess's family was part of the imperial clan, but more distant from the throne in terms of blood and political influence than the families of earlier Mongol princesses married into the Koryŏ royal family during the thirteenth century.

A well-established strategy for forging strategic alliances on the steppe, marriage ties linked the Yuan imperial family to many leading Mongol lineages.[10] Koryŏ's status as a "son-in-law" country began late in the 1260s and signaled a critical shift in Yuan-Koryŏ relations.[11] In 1269, the Koryŏ heir apparent (better known later as King Ch'ungnyŏl) requested the hand of a Mongol princess; this act changed the Yuan court's attitude about Koryŏ's loyalty. Up to this point, court ministers in Daidu had debated several options for dealing with the Wang royal family in Koryŏ. One was extermination. The Koreans had after all resisted the Mongols for decades and had murdered more than a dozen high-ranking Mongol officials during a revolt in 1240.[12] The Yuan court viewed Ch'ungnyŏl's gesture as evidence of Koryŏ's new commitment to loyalty.

The Mongols' decision to interpret Ch'ungnyŏl's behavior positively owed much to the larger geopolitical conditions of the empire. Qubilai was still engaged in his mighty conflict with the Chinese Song dynasty. His Chinese ministers, such as Ma Heng 馬亨 (1207–77), counseled that improved relations with Koryŏ would prevent a damaging alliance between the Song and the Koreans. Ma Xiji 馬希驥, another official, also argued that Koryŏ's men and material could be profitably turned to the planned conquest of Japan. Both men held that the Yuan court should seize on Ch'ungnyŏl's apparent change of heart to bind the Koryŏ throne to the Yuan. Renewed war with Koryŏ would prove a dangerous and expensive distraction from the Mongols' strategic aims.[13] Qubilai probably also saw the Koryŏ royal family as a useful check against the powerful Eastern Princes of the Liaodong region. If convinced of the congruence of its interests with those of the Yuan court, the Koryŏ throne would be more inclined to resist the princes' overtures and threats.[14] Finally, in the succession struggle with his brother Ariq-Böke, the submission of Koryŏ bolstered Qubilai's credentials as Great Khan and removed it as a potential source of manpower and material to his rival.[15]

What did Ch'ungnyŏl hope to gain? The marriage alliance promised benefits to Koryŏ's ruling family, the Wangs. When Ch'ungnyŏl's distant forefather, Wang Kŏn 王建 (r. 918–43), established the Koryŏ dynasty early in the tenth century, he had attempted to strengthen the power of the monarch vis-à-vis the aristocracy, in part by forging ties with local elites (*hyangni*). However, by the 1260s, the monarch's power had been under siege for centuries. During much of the first half of the thirteenth century, military officers controlled the government, reducing the Wang family to little more than figureheads. Political infighting and the ghastly toll of decades of fighting against the Mongols eventually helped end the military dictatorship.[16] The king's position, however, remained tenuous. Increasingly powerful and self-aware, aristocratic families who owned extensive tracts of rural land but held bureaucratic posts in the capital challenged both the throne and its principal institutional ally, the *hyangni* "on whom the dynasty relied to maintain order and collect taxes, corvée, and local tribute."[17]

As the most powerful regime in Eurasia, the Mongols presented an invaluable opportunity for the Wang family and its supporters. In 1269, King Wŏnjong 元宗 (r. 1259–74) lost his throne in a coup d'état led by the military general, Im Yŏn 林衍. The king's desperate son, Ch'ungnyŏl, hit on the idea of reviving family fortunes through a marriage alliance with the Mongol imperial family. As noted above, the request matched Mongol strategic interests. In 1270, as a Mongol envoy at the Koryŏ court led Im Yŏn to believe that such a marriage was imminent, the Yuan dispatched troops to ensure Wŏnjong's return to power. The first Mongol princess did not actually arrive in Koryŏ until 1274, after the Wangs had restored a modicum of order at home and assisted in preparations for the invasion of Japan. They had demonstrated that they were worthy of a Mongol princess and Yuan commitment.

Even with Yuan support, the Wang house faced considerable challenges from aristocratic families who held important posts in the central government and enjoyed the status of ascriptive titles. Further complicating tensions between the throne and this central aristocracy, as John Duncan has termed it, was the emergence of families and individuals with ties to the Mongolian ruling elite. This helps explain why King Ch'ungnyŏl would make the arduous three-week trip between Kaegyŏng and Daidu more than a dozen times during his reign.[18] Early in Ch'ungnyŏl's reign, Koryŏ's elite military units, the Sambyŏl-ch'o 三別抄, rejected his authority (partly in response to his new alliance with the Mongols), established a pretender on their provisional island capital off the southern coast of Koryŏ, and continued the struggle against the Mongols. The Sambyŏl-ch'o were put down only when royal Koryŏ troops and Mongol forces launched a joint campaign against them.[19] The Wang family needed the Yuan ruling house, and the Yuan khan needed the Wangs.[20] Marriage cemented the bond. The young Kongmin was heir to nearly a century of such close relations.

As noted above, Kongmin's Mongol bride was not from the most influential branch of the imperial family. This general trend became increasingly pronounced over the course of the fourteenth century. One senior Korean scholar, Min Hyŏn-gu, has argued that the match reflected the Great Yuan *ulus*'s enfeeblement. With the Yuan's obvious decline, he reasons, a marriage to a princess closely related to the throne was no long imperative to the interests of the Koryŏ throne.

More recent research draws a different conclusion. At least in the case of Kongmin, the choice of marriage partner was shaped by past ties between the Koryŏ and Yuan ruling houses. Kongmin's new Mongolian bride was the granddaughter of Amuga (Chin. Amuge 阿木哥, d. 1324). Amuga was the elder brother of emperors Haisan and Ayurbarwada.[21] In 1324, one of Amuga's daughters married King Ch'ungsuk 忠肅王 (r. 1313–30), Kongmin's father.[22] Marriage ties to the close relatives of the imperial Yuan throne may well have become less critical for Koryŏ interests. In one sense, however, the Koryŏ ruling house had become so tightly intertwined with the house of Qubilai that it formed marriage ties without regard to the imperial throne itself.[23]

Mongolian women at the Koryŏ court made their presence felt and seen in many ways. Women in steppe societies often played a more visibly powerful role in politics than was common in many sedentary cultures. Such women as Chinggis khan's mother and his principal wife and, more recently, Qubilai's mother and his principal wife were powerful figures in the empire. Mongolian princesses who married into the Koryŏ royal house wielded great influence at the Koryŏ court and with their male and female attendants immediately formed alternative nodes of political power in Kaegyŏng.[24]

Their tastes in cuisine, clothing, music, and religion also shaped court culture. Like many women at the Koryŏ court, Kongmin's queen favored Mongolian fashion. Among these was the striking *boqta* (Ch. *gugu*), an elaborate Mongolian woman's hat. Worn by married Mongolian women, *boqta* for elite women could be as tall as one foot in height and were commonly adorned with precious stones or peacock feathers.[25] When in 1311, the Yuan empress dowager bestowed a *boqta* on one of Ch'ungsŏn's 忠宣王 (r. 1308–13) consorts, all understood it as evidence of the king's favored status at the Mongol court; a banquet with all Koryŏ officials in attendance was held to mark the occasion.[26] We do not know whether the queen made use of the *ger* or felt tents that King Ch'ungnyŏl had built for his Mongolian queen in 1296 on the platform of the Such'ang Palace 壽昌宮 in Kaegyŏng.[27]

King Kongmin and his queen were deeply attached. When she died in childbirth in 1365, the loss cut the king deeply. At a time when the country was experiencing severe privations, he lavished vast sums to construct a new hall in her memory and had Mongolian music played when her death was commemorated. Some scholars have argued that her death plunged the king into a long period of depression, withdrawal from affairs of state, and an interest in comely young men.[28]

Their marriage had been arranged during the king's decade-long sojourn in Daidu. Through its marriage alliances to the imperial Yuan family, the Koryŏ royal house vaulted into the ranks of Eurasia's true elites. Although many, particularly Korean scholars, emphasize the compromising consequences of the tie, Koryŏ kings' position as *küregen*, or "son-in-law kings," nearly immediately raised their status at home and abroad. Observers as far away as the Il-khanate knew of Qubilai's Korean son-in-law.[29] These advantages explain at least in part why elite Tibetans, Uyghurs, Öngüt, Kereyid, Qipchaq Turks, and others proved eager to marry into the imperial Mongolian family.[30] Morihira Masahiko has argued that the status as son-in-law king put the Koryŏ ruling house on a par with Mongolian and Central Asian princes with comparable privileges and responsibilities. The valued status of Chinggisid "son-in-law" outlasted the empire. As Beatrice Forbes Manz has observed, Tamerlane (d. 1405) would later use his status as *küregen* to legitimate his rule in the post-Mongolian world.[31]

Put in other words, the Koryŏ ruling house was integrated into the larger political structures of the Mongol empire. Administrative posts associated with princely establishments elsewhere in the Mongol empire had their counterparts in Koryŏ. Just as the Great Khan bestowed appanages on Mongol princes and other favorites, so Koryŏ kings received similar lands. Koryŏ was regarded as the king's appanage, and smaller communities in southern Liaodong were organized as a way to support the king's progresses from Kaegyŏng to Daidu and Shangdu.[32] The Koryŏ royal family served an analogous function to Qubilai's sons and grandsons, who were invested in strategic border regions to defend the interests of the Yuan throne.[33]

Another critical feature of the Mongols' system of political and military control that deeply influenced the Koryŏ ruling house was the practice of holding hostage the sons of influential leaders throughout the empire. At one level, this practice was designed to ensure the loyalty and cooperation of men who might otherwise ignore or challenge the Yuan ruling house. Yet, the system performed a far more important function. Incorporating these elite hostages into the Great Khan's bodyguard, the *keshig*, bound these future leaders of the Mongol empire to the imperial family and its interests.[34] Enjoying privileged access to the Great Khan's charisma, hostages who served in the *keshig* were marked as the empire's elite.[35] They also gained access to an exclusive world of power and connections, a world rooted in the Yuan ruling house. Through participation in this system, young elites throughout Eurasia were encouraged to view themselves as the select few who would rule over their own lands and peoples but also be part of the ruling stratum of the wider Mongol empire. Elites from as far away as Tibet and Central Asia traveled to Daidu.[36]

Beginning late in the thirteenth century, young males from the Koryŏ royal family traveled to Daidu as hostages and served successive generations of Great Khans.[37] Through their years in the Yuan capitals, young Koryŏ elites gained access to what must have been an intoxicatingly rich cultural world. Daidu and Shangdu were far from spartan military outposts—they boasted towering walls, lavish palaces, exquisitely appointed living quarters, entertainment quarters, and a full panoply of services—from chefs, courtesans, doctors, and silver artisans to leather workers, carpenters, professional scholars, artists, and religious specialists.[38]

The capitals were also the sites of the week-long state-sponsored "Colors Banquets," which featured sumptuous foods, fine serving vessels, munificent gifts to guests, and abundant quantities of alcohol.[39] As Sugiyama, Allsen, and others have noted, establishing personal bonds, developing political consensus, and forging potential alliances among the empire's elite were the principal aims of these lavish feasts.[40] The political dimensions of the banquets may have eluded some contemporary Chinese. As Frederick Mote has observed, "Although the Chinese recognized some crude analogies to their own formalized etiquette in aspects of Mongol behavior, they could not accept Mongol ritual and ceremonial as more than curiosities from the steppe way of life. The great Mongol ceremonial banquets were displays of barbaric splendor in their eyes."[41] However, to judge from the lovingly detailed descriptions of opulent clothing and the attention to the participants' exalted political and social status contained in numerous "palace poems," the underlying significance of Mongolian banquet culture did not completely escape fourteenth-century Chinese literati.[42] King Ch'ungnyŏl was fully alive to his privileged status as he took his place in 1300 among other princes of the Great Yuan *ulus* at a Colors Banquet in Shangdu.[43]

His successors also circulated among the empire's well-connected elite. In the 1330s, the dethroned King Ch'unghye (忠惠王, r. 1330–32, 1339–44) passed his days of detention in Daidu drinking with young Mongol supporters of his former patron. His love affair with a Uyghur girl in the capital proved so bewitching that on occasion he failed to report for duty at the Great Khan's *keshig*.[44] He also pursued such favored Mongolian pastimes as hunting, drinking, and dancing with the most powerful ministers of the day. Ch'unghye and El-Temür, a Qipchaq Turk who was among the most dominant figures at the Mongol court, hunted together with falcons at Hichetü (Ch. Liulin 柳林), southwest of Daidu where the Mongol court spent the late winter and early spring.[45]

Koryŏ Court Politics and Daidu

One member of the Koryŏ royal family developed into an important patron of Buddhism and Confucian scholarship during his sojourn in the capital. In fact, Kongmin's grandfather, Wang Chang 王璋 (1275–1325, who reigned as King Ch'ungsŏn), was loath to leave the sparkling world of Daidu to take up his duties as king in Kaegyŏng. In 1984 workers discovered three different Buddhist sutras stored within the body of a statue of the Tathagata Buddha in Beijing's Zhihua Temple 智化寺. Produced by exquisitely crafted woodblocks on expensive paper, the sutras bear Wang Chang's official seals as both the King of Koryŏ and the Sim Prince.[46] The discovery reflects the cosmopolitan nature of Buddhism in Daidu during the early fourteenth century and Wang Chang's role as a religious patron.[47]

Wang Chang's refusal to leave Daidu, however, arose most fundamentally from his conviction that the Yuan capital was the ultimate source of political power in Asia.[48] Even after his enthronement, Wang Chang remained in Daidu, transmitting his orders to trusted ministers who supervised daily governance in Koryŏ. Both the Yuan throne and many Koryŏ officials pressured Wang Chang to return to Kaegyŏng. Instead, he yielded the throne to his son, who ruled as King Ch'ungsuk (r. 1313–30, 1332–39).

From Daidu, Wang Chang continued to wield great power in Koryŏ, controlling the critically important personnel administration and the royal fisc. He also attempted to limit his son's authority and rule as Koryŏ king by investing his nephew Ko with the title Shen Prince (Sim Prince). This Sim Prince became a potential candidate for the Koryŏ throne, complicating political power in Korea and engendering considerable political intrigue throughout Northeast Asia. For his machinations, intransigence, but most especially for his political ties to the recently deceased emperor Ayurbarwada (r. 1312–20, Chinese temple name Renzong 仁宗) and perhaps more important Ayurbawada's mother, the Empress Dowager Targi (Ch. Daji 答己, d. 1322), the newly enthroned Shidebala (Chinese temple name Yingzong 英宗, r. 1321–23) exiled Wang Chang to distant Turfan.[49] He also dethroned Kongmin's father, King Ch'ungsuk, and kept him in Daidu under house arrest for several years. Wang Chang was right about the ultimate source of power in the fourteenth century.

In 1341, the twelve-year-old Kongmin began his service in the Yuan *keshig*, where he would experience the capital's rich cultural offerings and its hard-edged politics. He did not make the journey alone. Several score of trusted civil officials, lower-level military officers, close attendants, eunuchs, and other servants accompanied the young prince. Korean scholars tutored him in classical learning and the histories of Korean and Chinese dynasties. He may have absorbed the "Confucian atmosphere" from Chinese Confucian scholars who taught at the Hall of the Upright Root (Duanbentang 端本堂), an academy founded for the heir apparent, Ayushiridara (d. 1378; born of a Korean mother, Empress Dowager Ki).[50]

Whatever scholarly interests Kongmin may have pursued, he was still a teenage boy at the time. He developed a deep affection for one member of his entourage who was strong enough to lift him with one arm.[51] He almost certainly hunted with Mongols of royal blood, met Central Asians from elsewhere in the Mongolian empire, and mixed with the large Korean expatriate community in Daidu.

The international circle of acquaintances made at the Mongol court would survive Kongmin's return to Koryŏ. The Uyghur scholar Xie Xun 偰遜 (*js.* 1345), who served as the Yuan heir apparent's tutor at the Upright Root Academy, was among Kongmin's companions in the capital. During the Red Turban rebellions of the 1350s and 1360s, Xie would seek refuge at the Koryŏ court, where Kongmin received him warmly.[52] Korean scholar Min Hyŏn-gu has argued that Kongmin owed his crown to Toqto'a, the powerful Yuan prime minister who had supervised the Hall of the Upright Root while Kongmin had been in the capital.

In Daidu, Kongmin gained his education in Eurasian politics and developed ties with the men who would later attain high office at his court.[53] During these years he became acquainted with a wide variety of other Koreans who enjoyed independent ties to the Great Khan and his court. These included Koryŏ scholars, translators, eunuchs, palace women, and imperial in-laws. The young Kongmin witnessed up close the complexity of Koryŏ politics under Mongol domination.

Consider the case of Kongmin's older brother, King Ch'unghye.[54] In 1341, the year that Kongmin arrived at Daidu, King Ch'unghye was in the second year of his second reign. The Yuan court had removed him from the throne in 1332 and replaced him with his father, Ch'ungsuk, who in turn the Mongols had deposed in 1330 after his initial reign of seventeen years. To what did Ch'unghye owe the dubious honor of being twice deposed? The question provided rich food for his young brother, Kongmin, and his circle of advisors.

Like Kongmin, Ch'unghye's political odyssey began at the Yuan court, as required by his status as the Koryŏ heir apparent. Dissatisfied with the Koryŏ king, in 1330 the Mongols persuaded Ch'ungsuk to yield the throne and replaced him with the young Ch'unghye. At one point,

Ch'unghye appeared before his father in Mongolian clothing to offer a Mongolian-style salutation. Ch'ungsuk exploded, "Both your parents are Korean. Why, when you see me, do you observe Mongolian etiquette? Further, your gown and headgear are too lavish. How do you [have the face to] see people? Hurry up and change your clothes." The father's stern upbraiding reportedly shook his son, who left the former king's presence in tears.[55]

The competition for the Koryŏ crown throws into relief the intricacies and international complexion of politics under the Mongols. To regain his position as king, Ch'ungsuk assiduously lobbied Mongols, Koreans, and Chinese with ties to the Yuan throne, forged an alliance with the Sim Prince, and promised important posts in the Branch Secretariat for the Eastern Campaigns to Koryŏ officials who supported his cause. Due partly to the fall of his Turkic patron, El-Temür, and the rise of Bayan (who was trying to eliminate all El-Temür's allies), Ch'unghye eventually was forced to return the scepter to his father.

When his father died in 1339, Ch'unghye immediately began a campaign to regain the Koryŏ throne. His envoy requested the Yuan emperor to allow him to succeed his father as king. The most powerful man at the Mongol court, Bayan, brushed away the plea. Undeterred, Ch'unghye next dispatched two generals to Daidu to spread gifts of cash among important Yuan officials. This strategy was not unique to Ch'unghye. The costs of securing positions of leadership within the Mongol empire, including the Yuan *ulus* throne, inflated rapidly throughout the fourteenth century.[56] Ch'unghye's actions were completely in keeping with the proven practices of the day. He also convinced ranking Koryŏ ministers to petition the Yuan throne on his behalf. Within a year of his father's death, Ch'unghye had regained the crown, despite ugly accusations of illicit sexual relations with his father's Mongolian bride, Bayan-Qutuq (known also as Princess Qinghua/Kyŏnghwa 慶華公主 in Chinese and Koryŏ sources).[57] Again, Ch'unghye owed his reversal of fortunes in part to changes at the Yuan court. After meticulous preparation, Toqto'a had engineered the removal of his uncle Bayan, who had alienated much of the court.[58] Toqto'a was apparently less opposed to Ch'unghye.

If Toqto'a and other senior Mongol ministers had hoped for a pliable vessel in the new king, they were mistaken. Ch'unghye implemented a series of measures designed to strengthen the power of the Koryŏ throne. One of his first steps was to bolster significantly the size and strength of his personal entourage. Some of these men, described disparagingly in Korean court annals as "young ruffians" (K. *akso* 惡少), had formerly served as guards in the Directorate-General of Hunting and Falconry (K. *ŏngbang horjŏk* 鷹坊忽赤). As Kim Tang-t'aek has observed, other contemporary criticisms of Ch'unghye—his excessive interest in such apparently frivolous activities as hunting, polo, and wrestling—should be understood in terms of the king's effort to recruit and train a body of personally loyal retainers sufficient to offer a modicum of physical security.[59] Ch'unghye's methods were inspired by the example of the Great Khan's own personal bodyguard, the *keshig*.

Ch'unghye strove to expand royal control in other directions. For instance, he attempted to improve both the royal fisc and general socioeconomic stability within Korea. He abolished the royal salary lands (*sa'kŭpjŏn* 賜給田), attempted to bring temple lands (*sawŏnjŏn* 寺院田) and meritorious subject lands (*kongsinjŏn* 功臣田) under more effective royal control, invested money from the Royal Privy Purse in commercial trade in China, and attempted to establish a levy on officials' salaries (*chikse* 職稅). Although the details of its functions are unclear, Ch'unghye established the Directorate-General for the Evaluation of Statutes to Benefit the People. One Korean scholar characterizes it as primarily an instrument to keep powerful ministers in check and to raise funds for the throne through confiscation of elites' properties.[60] Perhaps out of a desire to clarify lines of jurisdiction and responsibility, he also petitioned (unsuccessfully) the Yuan court to repatriate Chinese, Jurchen, and Koreans from the complex and overlapping administrative zones of southern Liaodong.

Kim Tang-t'aek explains Ch'unghye's actions as anti-Mongolian. During the past century, anachronistic notions of nationalism have often colored historical research produced in areas that were once under Mongol domination.[61] In its most extreme form, such a perspective renders all Koreans tied to the Yuan as traitorous, conniving, small-minded people who pursued selfish personal ends at the expense of a vaguely defined Korean people or nation. Even such evenhanded scholars as Kim occasionally fall victim to this tendency. In the case of Ch'unghye, Kim observes that the king was an exceptionally bright man and thus acutely aware of the Yuan's oppression.[62] Ch'unghye's own father had been detained in Daidu for four years and then exiled to distant Turfan. These factors, according to Kim, account for Ch'unghye's "anti-Mongolian" stance. Kim interprets Ch'unghye's development of a personal bodyguard, taxes on his officials, greater control over economic resources, and the construction of lavish new royal palaces as evidence of the king's desire to reduce his reliance on the Mongol court. Conflict with the Yuan was thus, he concludes, "inescapable."

Ch'unghye's actions were, however, guided more by the desire to strengthen the throne against threats at home and abroad than protonationalism.[63] In his efforts to forge a more secure position within Koryŏ, King Ch'unghye, like all ambitious political players in Eurasia at the time, had to come to terms with the Mongols. Certainly his domestic rivals (aristocratic members of the civil bureaucracy, *arrivistes* who owed their rise to marriage ties to the Mongol elites, and others) did. In attempting to regain the throne, Ch'unghye made repeated overtures to the Mongol emperor and high-ranking Mongol ministers. Ch'unghye also attempted to exploit various Koreans who enjoyed special influence at the Mongol court. The most dominant political and military presence in Eurasia, the Mongols constituted a critical resource to be manipulated in the pursuit of family rather than "national" ends.

In the end, domestic rivals at the Koryŏ court persuaded the Mongols that Ch'unghye should be replaced. Ch'unghye's various reforms challenged the economic and political interests of many elites within Koryŏ. Among the most vocal of the king's critics was the Ki family. That the Ki family owed its special prominence to marriage ties with the Mongol imperial family did not predetermine its opposition to King Ch'unghye. It does, however, explain why its efforts to remove the king proved so efficacious. One member of the Ki family, Ki Ch'ŏl 奇轍, complained to the Yuan throne that the king was "lascivious and unrighteous." A final indication that the central tension of the day was the distribution of power within Koryŏ rather than nationalism is the relative apathy with which the Korean bureaucracy greeted news of Ch'unghye's final fall. Few tears were shed when Yuan officials dragged him off.[64] Later Korean historians portrayed him as a vainglorious, morally suspect, and ineffective ruler who preferred the company of ill-mannered wastrels to men of proper breeding and lineage.

King Ch'unghye's saga unfolded during young Kongmin's formative teenage years in Daidu. The political jockeying, the international lobbying, the secretive efforts to forge alliances for and against the king, tensions between the throne and the aristocratic elite, and Ch'unghye's ultimate death in exile drove home the importance of cultivating a broad network of support throughout Northeast Asia. Among the most critical of these potential backers (or dangerous enemies) was the Ki family noted above. Its most influential member was Empress Ki, favorite of the emperor and mother of the heir apparent. The empress would play a critical role both in Kongmin's accession to the throne and in later Yuan efforts to depose him.

In summary, like his brother, father, and grandfather before him, the young Kongmin spent much of his youth under the careful eyes of the Mongol court in Daidu. Privileged as a member of the *keshig*, it was hoped the Koryŏ youth would develop loyalty to the Mongol Great Khans and come to see himself as an elite member of the cosmopolitan pan-Eurasian Mongolian empire. Koryŏ was a "son-in-law" of the great Mongol empire, a subordinate but privileged member of the Mongols' sprawling imperium.[65]

Wavering Fortunes and Royal Autonomy

Given such extensive and deep ties with the Mongol empire, at first blush it might seem surprising that from the earliest days of his reign, King Kongmin sought to assert greater autonomy for the Koryŏ throne. Less than a month after his return to Koryŏ in 1351 to take the throne upon the death of his nephew, King Kongmin lavished praise on a senior official's remonstrance. The official argued, "Plaited hair and barbarian raiment are not [in accord with] the ways of former kings. I would that Your Majesty not emulate [these barbarian ways]." Pleased and impressed, the young monarch "promptly undid his plaits."[66]

The new ruler's willingness to distance himself from his Mongol overlords even in this small way owed much to the growing perception that the once-great Great Yuan *ulus* was in decline. The dizzying speed with which emperors fell from the throne in Daidu during the early fourteenth century, the paralyzing factional battles that hobbled effective governance in the Great Yuan *ulus*, and the hydra-headed revolts raging through the central and southeastern provinces suggested that the Mongols' best days were already in the past.

The Koreans quietly registered more subtle but no less fundamental signs of Yuan decline. By the fourteenth century, the marking of time had constituted a critical element of political legitimacy in East Asia for more than two millennia. Astronomy's significance for the Mongols was if anything greater than for Chinese dynasties. Mongol courts considered astronomy a variety of divination, a way to predict meteorological phenomena, and a method to influence such vital enterprises as military campaigns. Contemporary western observers like Roger Bacon believed the Mongol's success derived from their talented astronomers.[67] Having assembled a pool of men and astronomical techniques of unprecedented variety from across Asia, the Yuan court at its height had established new levels of precision for the prediction of lunar and solar eclipses.[68] The Great Yuan *ulus* demanded that all subjugated states use its calendar in official documents and diplomatic communiqués.

However, in the fourth month of 1352, less than half a year into young Kongmin's reign, the Koryŏ court noted in official records that the Yuan's official predictions for an eclipse proved false.[69] Just months later, the court again noted a similar lapse.[70] It was not merely a technical or scientific mistake. The broader political and charismatic significance of such an error would not have been lost on contemporaries. The Great Yuan *ulus* was slipping, and Koryŏ was watching.

However tempted King Kongmin and his advisors may have been to assert greater autonomy, the Mongol empire was still a daily reality, a presence rendered more pressing by the lack of any absolute borders between domestic and international affairs. Marriage, government service, and place of residence bound many leading Koryŏ families to the ruling Mongol elite in China. These families wielded tremendous power and influence in Koryŏ and ranked among the young king's most formidable rivals (and potential allies). A 1352 controversy surrounding efforts to recruit Koryŏ troops for the Yuan armies illustrates the importance of links to the Yuan throne for domestic Korean affairs.

In the third lunar month of 1352, several Korean residents of Daidu, including Ch'oe Yu 崔濡, proposed to the emperor, Toghan-Temür, that he recruit a staggering 100,000 troops from Koryŏ to assist Yuan troops in restoring order within China. Ch'oe was far from a disinterested party. His father had served in the Koryŏ government as an administrator in the Bureau of Military Affairs, and Ch'oe himself held a string of military posts in Koryŏ beginning in the 1340s. For his role in suppressing an abortive coup d'état,[71] Ch'oe was named a merit official of the first degree. Shortly thereafter, he was appointed a censor at the Yuan court. Despite repeated charges of rape,[72] he accompanied the heir apparent (Kongmin's nephew), later invested as King Ch'ungjŏng 忠定 (r. 1349–51), to Daidu. After taking the throne in 1349, Ch'ungjŏng rewarded Ch'oe's service, investing him with the title Lord of Ch'wisŏng 鷲城君.

Despite these new titles and status, or perhaps because of them, Ch'oe and his brothers grew increasingly dissatisfied under the young new king. After a series of clashes with the throne, in 1350 Ch'oe and his brother left Koryŏ to seek refuge at the Mongol court in Daidu. Ch'oe did not, however, sever ties with his native land. In fact, while at the Yuan court, he apparently cultivated relations with the reigning king's uncle, the future King Kongmin. Their relationship is unclear, but Ch'oe accompanied Kongmin on the return trip to Korea to take the throne in 1351. At the last minute, however, Ch'oe thought better of his decision to return home. When the royal entourage reached Liaoyang, midway between the Yuan and Koryŏ capitals, Ch'oe returned to Daidu. Again we know little of his motivation, but according to the *History of the Koryŏ Dynasty*, upon his arrival in the Yuan capital, Ch'oe began to "conspire" against the Koryŏ throne.[73]

Toghan-Temür's decision to use Koryŏ troops met with vociferous opposition from a second group of Koreans resident in Daidu, those apparently more closely tied to the Koryŏ throne. They argued that Koryŏ was "small, suffers from Japanese piracy, and furthermore is too distant" to supply troops.[74] Persuaded by their protests, the emperor canceled the order for Koryŏ soldiers and recalled Ch'oe to Daidu. This would prove only a temporary setback. During the next fifteen years, military conditions in China would provide Ch'oe with ample opportunity to increase his influence at both the Yuan and the Koryŏ courts.

Initial Koryŏ Involvement with the Red Turbans

Late in June 1354, an embattled senior Koryŏ official, Ch'ae Ha-jung 蔡河中, Lord of P'yŏnggang 平康府院君, returned to Kaegyŏng with important news from Daidu. The Great Yuan *ulus*'s powerful prime minister Toqto'a wanted the Koryŏ king to dispatch elite troops to fight in the imperial host that Toqto'a was assembling against the Red Turbans in Huainan.[75] Ch'ae had proposed the use of Koryŏ military personnel to Toqto'a, recommending the names of generals known for their bravery and battle sense.[76] Many of these men had served previously in the emperor's *keshig* and fought against Japanese marauders along Koryŏ's coasts.[77]

As shown in Chapter 2, by the early 1350s, revolts wracked much of the Great Yuan *ulus*, compromising local control and reducing the flow of grain and taxes to the central government. Toqto'a's expedition was a critical part of the Mongol court's efforts to restore military and administrative strength in China. The throne ordered wealthy Muslims and Jews (Ch. *zhuhu* 朮忽) throughout the realm to report to the capital for duty. Skilled archers from as far away as the northwestern province of Ningxia were also summoned.[78] A week later, diplomatic envoys from the Yuan arrived at Kaegyŏng. They announced that the Koryŏ contingent was to assemble in Daidu by the tenth day of the eighth lunar month (August 28, 1354)—that is, in less than two months.[79]

One scholar has argued that "politicians consumed with desire for political power" had engineered this military assistance to the Yuan to advance their selfish personal ends and that Kongmin was forced to acquiesce to their pressure.[80] Be that as it may, the military ties between the ruling houses of the Great Yuan *ulus* and Koryŏ were nearly a century old by this time. Kongmin's forefathers had repeatedly contributed troops, commanders, and grain to Mongol campaigns. Later, in 1362, Kongmin himself would propose joint action in Liaodong against Red Turban forces. This particular instance of military cooperative was the rule rather than the exception.

In the context of the Great Yuan *ulus*, it was axiomatic that a major rebellion in southern China was a matter of concern to all members of the empire's elite, including the king of Koryŏ. The Mongol court took pains to ensure that, as a member of the extended imperial family,

Kongmin was informed of important developments regarding the Great Yuan *ulus*. When Ayushiridara was invested as heir apparent, the Yuan court issued a pardon for "all under heaven." It dispatched an envoy to Kaegyŏng with an imperial proclamation announcing this critical decision, which had implications for all members of the Great Yuan *ulus*'s ruling elite. In accord with protocol, Kongmin welcomed the envoy at the Guests' Hall and issued a pardon for criminals within his kingdom.[81] Soon after Kongmin had assumed the throne in 1351, he had greeted a Yuan envoy at the offices of the Branch Secretariat in Kaegyŏng who brought news of Yuan victory against a "Henan rebel leader" and general empire-wide pardon to celebrate the triumph.[82] Rebellion in China directly touched Kongmin's family. At one point, the father of Kongmin's queen was seized in the field by Red Turbans in southern China.[83] The Yuan would continue to send periodic updates on important victories and campaigns.

Preparations began immediately. An official from the Yuan Ministry of Works soon arrived with 60,000 *ding* in paper currency to be distributed among the Koryŏ troops as rewards.[84] King Kongmin granted titles to many of his leading generals as encouragement for the coming battles. Titles and honorary positions figured prominently in court efforts to rally military resources throughout the country to the dynasty's defense.[85] He also ordered his court officials and the religious clerics of the capital to make horses available to his soldiers at reasonable prices. Perhaps in reaction to extortionate prices, Koryŏ soldiers preparing for the campaign in China had been forcing residents to sell horses at reduced prices. In some cases, they had seized them outright.[86]

On July 23, 1354, King Kongmin personally reviewed the 2,000-man crack unit before it left for China under the command of Yu T'ak 柳濯 (1311–71), Yŏm Che-sin 廉悌臣 (1304–82), and three dozen other elite commanders.[87] Whether through previous service in the Koryŏ heir apparent's household in Daidu or through marriage ties, most of these Koryŏ military officers were linked to the Yuan court.[88] Ch'oe Yu, the man who had failed to incorporate Korean troops into Yuan forces in 1352, was now appointed by Toghan-Temür to oversee the army's progress to Daidu.[89]

The men did not go willingly. Just before crossing the Yalu River, the cold, fearful, and frustrated force nearly ran amok. The men plotted to send a small elite group of riders back to Kaegyŏng to cut down the officials responsible (primarily Ch'ae) for sending them to die in distant China. Only after one of the commanding generals warned that there could be no escape from royal justice did they abandon their plans for assassination.[90]

During these years, Chinese unrest would repeatedly complicate intra-Korean political competition. For his role in brokering the joint Korean-Mongol expedition, early in August 1354 the Koryŏ court appointed Ch'oe finance commissioner (*samsa usa* 三司右使) and then invested him with the aristocratic title Lord of Yongsŏng 龍成府院君.[91] The court also granted titles to members of the Ki family.[92]

By the end of the year, General In An 印安 had returned from the Great Yuan *ulus* with information about the debacle at Gaoyou 高郵. Although the Koryŏ court was undoubtedly well aware of the political intrigue surrounding Toqto'a, In concentrated on how the disaster at Gaoyou related to Korean interests. According to In, the 2,000-man elite unit from Koryŏ and more than 20,000 other Koreans resident in Daidu served as the vanguard of Toqto'a's massive host. Rather than focus on the court's fears of Toqto'a's growing power, In stressed Mongol jealousy of Koryŏ military prowess. Rebel forces ensconced within the walls of Gaoyou were on the brink of collapse. "Senior Tatar military men" (*dadan zhiyuan laozhang* 韃靼知院老長), In reported, "resented that our men would monopolize the military credit [for the triumph]" and thus intentionally stalled the attack for a day.[93] This allowed the Red Turbans sufficient breathing room to firm up the city's defenses.[94] More important for the fate of the Yuan, the court removed Toqto'a from command.[95] As noted in Chapter 2, this greatly weakened the Yuan. Rebel forces gained critical time to regroup, while the dynasty's most effective military force collapsed. From this time on, the Yuan court would find itself increasingly beleaguered throughout East Asia.

The Koryŏ court continued to track developments in China closely. Late in January 1355, the Yuan court notified Kongmin that the Red Turban leaders Han Shantong 韓山童 and Han Yao'er 韓咬兒 had been executed and that Toqto'a had been pardoned.[96] Han Yao'er was among a half dozen or so men who had been spreading word in the Huainan and Henan regions that the Red Turban leader, Han Shantong, was a direct descendent of the Song dynastic house and should assume the throne of China.[97]

Although Toqto'a had been stripped of his posts and his forces had begun to disintegrate, the Koryŏ contingent continued to fight in China. Sometime during the fifth lunar month of 1355, the Southern Campaign Myriarchs Kwŏn Kyŏm 權謙 (d. 1356), Wŏn Ho 元顥, and In Tang 印璫 returned from China with reports that "the southern rebels grow stronger by the day." More positively, they informed the king that Koryŏ troops had taken the city of Luhe 六合 and that they had just been transferred to defend the Huai'an Circuit.[98] As the Yuan campaign against the Red Turbans in southeast China devolved, members of the Koryŏ contingent began to return home with firsthand accounts of the spreading chaos.[99]

Intensifying disorder within the Great Yuan *ulus* affected the Koryŏ ruling house in others ways. Perhaps in an effort to shore up support within the Koryŏ ruling stratum, in 1354 the Yuan throne invested a new Sim Prince. The title had been vacant since the death of Wang Ko in 1334.[100] The Yuan court now invested Wang Ko's grandson, Toqto'a-Buqa 脫脫不花, as the new Sim Prince.[101] Like previous holders of the title, Toqto'a-Buqa was a member of the Koryŏ royal house. Born and raised in the Mongol capital, however, he seems to have identified strongly with the Yuan. In 1350, he had begun service in the Yuan heir apparent's *keshig* (*Donggong qiexueguan* 東宮怯薛官), where he developed a close relationship with the heir apparent, Ayushiridara, the son of Toghan-Temür by his Korean wife, Empress Ki.[102] Whatever the Yuan throne's initial motivation for investing him as the Sim Prince, Toqto'a-Buqa did not participate in the military campaigns of the 1350s or 1360s. He did, however, figure in the increasingly tumultuous relations between the Koryŏ and Yuan courts (see Chapter 7).

Kingly Ambitions

Early in January 1356, the Yuan court recognized King Kongmin's contributions to the war against the Red Turbans, bestowing on him an impressive string of titles.[103] Granting such titles was a well-established way to maintain unity within the empire and to encourage loyalty to the emperor. The Yuan's declining fortunes, however, struck the king and others at the Koryŏ court as an opportunity to reassert royal authority. In mid-June 1356, the fifth year of his reign, the king moved boldly on a number of fronts in what scholars have almost universally characterized as "anti-Yuan" or nationalistic policies intended to gain greater autonomy for Koryŏ.[104] In fact these measures constituted one facet of the Koryŏ throne's periodic efforts to consolidate its domestic control.[105]

The first strike was directed against the powerful Ki family and others who enjoyed special status in Koryŏ through their links to the Yuan throne and Mongol aristocracy. On the eighteenth day of the fifth lunar month of 1356, the king held a banquet to which he invited many high-ranking officials. Taken unaware, Ki Ch'ŏl, three other Ki males, and another prominent Korean with ties to the Yuan, Kwŏn Kyŏm (noted above as the Southern Campaign general who fought against Chinese rebels), were executed on the spot. Another to meet his end was Ch'ae Ha-jung, the senior Koryŏ official who in 1354 had suggested dispatching Korean military personnel to the Yuan to suppress Chinese rebels. During the next two days, Kongmin authorized the executions of nineteen men. He exiled many more, charging them with threatening the dynasty.[106]

By any standard, the purge was audacious. Many of those killed held titles granted by either the Yuan or Koryŏ throne. No Ch'aek's 盧頙 daughter was a consort to the Yuan emperor, Kwŏn was father-in-law to the Yuan heir apparent, and Ki Ch'ŏl was Empress Ki's elder brother.[107]

Empress Ki

Born and raised in a Koryŏ family with a long history of government service, Empress Ki (her Mongolian name was Öljei-Qutuq 完者忽都) was the most powerful woman in Eurasia at the time.[108] Early in the 1330s, she began her remarkable career within the imperial Yuan household. She started as a lowly serving girl responsible for the emperor's tea. She quickly gained the favor of the newly enthroned Toghan-Temür. Only fifteen years old, under the thumb of his senior ministers, and regarded with disdain by his wife, the domineering Empress Danashiri 答納失里 (?–1335, the daughter of El-Temür), the beleaguered emperor was immediately drawn to the beautiful and sympathetic Ki.

Unlike most Mongol emperors, Toghan-Temür was not a heavy drinker. He found solace instead in painting, poetry, and astronomy. Blessed with beauty, Ki was also a woman of artistic and educational accomplishment. Worried that this young Korean servant might gain dangerous influence over the Mongol Son of Heaven, the empress abused Ki. On one occasion, Danashiri is said to have tortured Ki with a white-hot iron brander.[109] In time, she might have removed the girl altogether. Fortunately for Ki, political change at the court intervened. In 1335, the powerful minister Bayan removed the empress's father, El-Temür, from power and purged most of his relatives. Danashiri was put under house arrest and later executed.[110]

Immediately following Danashiri's death, Ki secured investiture as an official escort. Although this rank represented an enormous leap for Ki, it fell short of the emperor's hopes. Instead, following past precedent and bowing to the political counsel of Bayan, in 1337 Toghan-Temür selected a young Mongol girl from the prestigious Qonggirad tribe as his primary empress. Her name was Bayan-Qutuq 伯顏忽都 (1324–65). Contemporary observers and official court annals describe her as a retiring woman free of jealousy. She did not openly begrudge Ki's favored status with the emperor.[111] There was a sense within the empire, however, that Ki's position was still unfinished business. When Bayan fell from power in 1340, new opportunities arose.

Among the quickest to seize the moment was the Koryŏ throne. One month after Bayan fell, the Koryŏ throne appointed Ki's older brother, Ki Ch'ŏl, to head the diplomatic mission to offer birthday felicitations to Toghan-Temür. The Koryŏ throne wished to exploit the emperor's fond feelings for Ki and anticipated that, with Bayan's death, Ki might rise to even higher status.[112] The Koreans were right. One month later, Ki was invested as second empress. The decision was not popular in all quarters. In 1348, a Chinese censor complained that Ki wielded too much power at the Mongol court. In classic fashion, he justified his criticism through reference to abnormalities in the cosmic order. "The Yellow River has burst its dikes and earthquakes have occurred; bandits increase without end. All these are signs that *yin* dominates and *yang* is weak." If the emperor reduced Empress Ki's status to that of a consort, that is, if he diminished the *yin*, "the disasters would end," promised the official. Toghan-Temür ignored his plea and those of others.[113]

Befitting someone who enjoyed the emperor's favor and the rank of second empress, Ki oversaw a considerable establishment in Daidu. In 1340, a new administration, the Empress's Bureau (*Zizhengyuan* 資政院), was established to supervise the empress's financial resources. Revenues flowed in from various appanages throughout the empire, especially the rich agricultural lands of affluent Jiqing circuit 集慶路. In 1359, at Empress Ki's request, the emperor increased her holdings.[114] He placed the lands of the Chaghan-na'ur Pacification Office (*Chahannaoer xuanweisi* 察罕腦兒宣慰司) in present-day Inner Mongolia under the control of her administration.[115] Throughout most of the fourteenth century, various empresses had drawn revenue from these lands.[116] The additional revenue may have been intended to offset the loss of properties in Jiqing (present-day Nanjing), which in 1356 had become an administrative center of the rebel Song regime under the control of Zhu Yuanzhang.[117] It seems likely that Empress Ki, like her predecessors, also derived income from investment in international maritime trade.[118]

To survive the constant and often brutal competition of the Mongol court, Ki cultivated supporters within the palace, the most prominent of whom were Korean-born eunuchs who held posts within the Empress's Bureau.[119] Among those closest to her was Pak Buqa 朴不花 (?–1364), who hailed from her hometown in Koryŏ. A longtime intimate, Pak would receive prestigious court honors and serve in the Empress's Bureau.[120] She also increased the number of Korean palace women. According to one well-informed observer of the time, "Empress Ki maintained many Koryŏ beauties in her palace. When great ministers grew powerful, [she] would send them one of these women."[121] As a poet intimately familiar with affairs of the Mongol court put it:

During the previous dynasty, of Korean women admitted to the palace,	昨朝進得高麗女
More than half all claimed to be relatives of the Ki family.	太半咸稱奇氏親
Most trying was the difficulty of assigning female officials [throughout the palaces],	最苦女官難派散
The Overseer sent them to serve as attendants to the two empresses.[122]	總教送作二宮嬪

Her strategy succeeded. One of these Korean palace women would eventually gain the favor of her son, Ayushiridara.[123]

Empress Ki's hopes and energies revolved around Ayushiridara, born in 1339. She ensured that her son received an education that would prepare him for rulership. He studied the Uyghur script used to write Mongolian. Later he would take up classical Chinese and works from the Sinic canon. One well-known anecdote regarding his education involved the Dynastic Teacher, the leading Buddhist cleric in the Great Yuan *ulus* (a Tibetan monk). The Dynasty Teacher protested to Empress Ki, "Up until now, the Heir Apparent has studied the Buddhist *dharma* and has gradually reached some measure of enlightenment. Now, however, he receives instruction in the teachings of Confucius. I fear that this may harm the Heir Apparent's true nature." Empress Ki responded that although Buddhism was a fine moral foundation, Confucian teachings were essential for the heir apparent's ultimate calling, "ruling all under heaven."[124] As part of this education, in 1349, Confucian scholars prepared a primer that drew upon political history, Confucian texts, and biographies. Patterned after Zhen Dexiu's 眞德秀 well-known 1229 *An Explication of the Great Learning* (*Da xue yan yi* 大學衍義), the primer was put in the heir apparent's study hall for his instruction.[125] Thus, the heir apparent was literate in both written Chinese and Mongolian and had a grounding in Confucianism, Tibetan Buddhism, and Chinese statecraft.

Ki's first major victory for her son came in 1353, when Ayushiridara was invested as the heir apparent.[126] On at least two occasions late during the 1350s and early during the 1360s, Empress Ki attempted to force her husband into retirement and to turn the reins of power over to Ayushiridara. Toqto'a's fall may have owed something to his opposition to Empress Ki's hopes for the heir apparent.[127]

Simply put, Ki was a pivotal figure at the Yuan court, whose influence extended to military and political decisions of the day. When one of her supporters, a military officer, was captured by the powerful Chinese warlord Fang Guozhen, she intervened, arranging a special imperial amnesty for Fang in exchange for the release of the officer.[128] When the emperor's primary consort, the retiring Bayan-Qutuq, died in 1366, the emperor would finally declare Lady Ki his legal consort; he bestowed on her the family name of Solongqa 肅良合, Mongolian for

"Korean."[129] When in 1368 the Yuan court fled Daidu before the fast-approaching Ming armies, Empress Ki accompanied her husband and son into the steppe. To this day, when, where, and how she died remain a mystery.

Like many other female members of the Yuan imperial family, Empress Ki was an important religious patron, funding temples, rites, prayers, and art.[130] What distinguished Empress Ki was that her munificence extended to Koryŏ. In 1343, 1344, and 1345, she made sizable contributions to refurbish the Chang'an Temple 長安寺 on the holy Korean Buddhist mountain of Mount Vajra (Kŭmgangsan 金剛山).[131] The monks were to pray for the prosperity of the emperor and Empress Ki's son, the heir apparent. In 1346, she dispatched (duly authorized by the emperor's order) members of her household staff to Koryŏ with copper coins to have a bell cast at a temple on the same mountain.[132] King Ch'ungsuk's Mongol queen Irinjinbal (Chinese Yilinzhenban 亦燐眞班) felt that some gesture in kind was required.[133] Addressing court officials, the queen said, "Mount Vajra is located within our territory. Now the sagely Son of Heaven has in this way dispatched a trusted official in order to invigorate the Buddhist faith and spread it without end. However, we have done absolutely nothing to repay Him."[134] The queen approved her courtiers' suggestion to recast the temple bell of Yŏnboksa Temple 演福寺. Inscribed on four square panels on the bell's upper register in Chinese characters are the following set of parallel constructions: "The Wheel of Dharma ever turns; long life to the Emperor; Buddha increases in brilliance daily; long live the King" 法輪常轉，皇帝萬歲，佛日增輝，國王千秋. The phrases highlight parallels and links between the Yuan emperor and the Koryŏ king as well as between the two temporal sovereigns and the eternal and limitless realm of Buddha. Passages from the Buddhist magical formula *Usnisa-vijaya dharani* 佛頂尊勝陀羅尼 written in Lan-tsha script and the True Word Dharani 眞言陀羅尼 written in a neat Tibetan script also adorn the bell.[135] As Yuyama Akira 湯山明 has noted, these same Buddhist texts were inscribed on the famous Juyong Pass north of Daidu at just about this same time. Other inscriptions on such Buddhist religious objects as incense burners from this period offer similar wishes for the long life of the Yuan emperor and the Koryŏ king.[136] At least in elite circles, dynastic borders did not impede the flow of religious merit.[137]

Empress Ki's religious patronage was also a boon to the local economy. In 1346, Mount Kŭmgang's neighboring counties suffered from famine. Competition to work on the casting project was keen, and the food given as wages often meant the difference between life and death.[138]

Empress Ki's largesse extended to the Mongol capital of Daidu, where she was a prominent sponsor of Buddhist rites and welfare measures. In 1358, famine and disease struck the bloated population of Daidu. In an effort to escape the growing military chaos of the time, refugees from much of eastern North China streamed into the capital. In the name of Empress Ki, Pak Buqa coordinated a philanthropic effort to care for the sick and bury the dead. He first sought and received permission from the throne to purchase lands for burial sites. The emperor, the two empresses, the heir apparent, and the heir apparent's consorts contributed gold, silver, cash, and goods. The Yuan central bureaucracy also "made donations beyond calculation."

The project's scale suggests the severity of the crisis. Deep trenches stretched from Daidu all the way to Lugou Bridge (Lugou qiao 盧溝橋) several miles to the west. Men and women were buried separately.[139] Cash was distributed to those who carried the corpses to the burial grounds. Once the trenches were filled and covered with earth, the court commissioned the Wan'an shouqing Temple 萬安壽慶寺 (the present-day White Pagoda Temple) to hold a Panca(varskika)parisad 無遮大會. This ceremony stressed the essential equality of all, lay and clergy, without regard to relative social status or wealth. A central feature of the festival was the distribution of alms to participants. According to an account in the *Official History of the Yuan Dynasty*, from 1358 to spring 1364, 200,000 were buried. Costs surpassed 27,090 *ding* of cash and 560 piculs of rice. Later, for three days and nights the Great Compassion Temple 大悲寺 would hold a "festival of water and land" (*shuiluhui* 水陸會), a memorial mass for the souls of the deceased.[140]

Ki's rising star meant honor and titles for her family.[141] As the talented Ming imperial prince, Zhu Youdun 朱有燉 (1379–1439), wrote:

Woman Ki's family resides east of the Yalu.	奇氏家居鴨綠東
Only in her mature years did she gain the status of empress.	盛年纔得位中宮
Yesterday the Hanlin scholars newly drafted an edict.	翰林昨日新裁詔

Three generations [of her relatives] were graced with imperial favor; exalted titles and emoluments [were theirs].[142] 三代蒙恩爵祿崇

The parents of Empress Ki enjoyed extraordinary prestige within Koryŏ.[143] Not only did they receive aristocratic titles from the Yuan throne (in the case of her father posthumous titles), from the 1340s on Koryŏ kings demonstrated their respect for Empress Ki's mother, Madame Yi, through official visits to her residence in the capital. King Kongmin, for example, marked the beginning of the new lunar year of the second year of his reign by calling on Madame Yi at her residence.[144] As an elite member of greater Mongolian empire, Madame Yi enjoyed banquets hosted by both envoys of the Yuan and the Koryŏ king and queen. For instance, in September 1353, King Kongmin petitioned Toghan-Temür to hold a "betrothal feast" (Mongolian *bu'uljar*, Chinese *boerzhayan* 孛兒扎宴) on behalf of Madame Yi.[145] The emperor dispatched two envoys to Koryŏ, where they first held a *bu'uljar* at Yi's home and then days later at the royal palace, with Kongmin and his queen in attendance.[146]

I have heard that among the practices of the August dynasty is something called a *bu'uljar*. The joy of assembling relatives joined by marriage and the celebration of progeny, in antiquity it was already so; how could it be otherwise now? If I were granted [permission] by Your Highness to hold on behalf of Wife of the Grand Master, Madame Yi 大夫人李氏, the lavishness of a grand ceremony; to demonstrate the harmony and joy of the extraordinary benevolence [shown us by the throne], our entire [royal] clan would feel the principle of harmony and friendship among kin by blood and marriage [and we] would swear an oath of generations everlasting and never forget [these ties]. The entire country would offer praise with complete sincerity and offer wishes for longevity and long life.

竊聞，皇朝之法，有所謂孛兒扎者，合姻亞之懽，爲子孫之慶，古既如是，今胡不然，若蒙陛下爲大夫人李氏，舉盛禮之優優，示殊恩之衎衎，則九族感睦親之義，誓永世而不忘，一邦殫歸美之誠，祝後天而難老.[147]

Officials at the time inveighed against what they painted as the unconscionable extravagance of the banquets. Some Korean scholars today may bristle at the apparent self-abasement demonstrated in Kongmin's petition to the Mongol throne, offering the Mongol envoy alcohol on his knees, or the fawning attitude taken toward Empress Ki's mother. The Koryŏ king in fact knew exactly what he was doing—playing Mongolian banquet politics, politics that were all about personal relationships, loyalty, and conspicuous consumption. Empress Ki's son, Ayushiridara, had just been formally invested as heir apparent, and Yuan envoys had arrived in Kaegyŏng to announce the event.[148]

By hosting the *bu'uljar*, Kongmin asserted the Koryŏ royal family's place within the larger Mongolian empire.[149] The banquet was emphatically Mongolian: it featured Mongolian music, song, dance, meat-eating competitions, and the distribution of gifts.[150] The right to attend such events as the Colors Banquets and the *bu'uljar* marked one's privileged status within the *ulus*. To host such an occasion for the empress's mother, the heir apparent's grandmother, was an even more emphatic statement of status and family ties. To express his gratitude for this honor and to remind Toghan-Temür of Koryŏ's ties to the Great Yuan *ulus*, Kongmin dispatched an envoy to Daidu with a formal declaration of thanks shortly after the banquet.[151]

Empress Ki's brothers aggressively exploited her influence at the Yuan capital to pursue family interests. Early in 1345, the Mongol court promoted Ki Bayan-Buqa 奇伯顏不花 to Minister of the Left of the Liaoyang Branch Secretariat (*Liaoyang xingsheng zuocheng* 遼陽行省左丞) and Manager of Governmental Affairs (*pingzhang zhengshi* 平章政事).[152] Slightly more than a year later, he gained further honors, being named Grand Minister of Education (*dasitu* 大司徒).[153] In 1353, Ki Ch'ŏl would also serve as a manager in the Liaoyang Branch Secretariat.[154]

Carried to excess, such efforts to improve family fortunes were counterproductive, incurring the resentment of the Koryŏ throne and, one suspects, aristocratic families with better pedigrees. As a canny politician, the empress was aware of such dangers and attempted to forestall disaster for her clansmen. In 1344, she issued an edict to the new king, Ch'ungmok 忠穆王 (r. 1344–48), in which she ordered: "None of my clansmen are to abuse their position to seize people's lands. If there are violations, [you] must punish them. [You] also should punish those judicial officials who know of such abuses but ignore them."[155] Her efforts proved futile.

In 1351, one of Empress Ki's younger brothers, Ki Sam-man 奇三萬, was charged with misusing his influence to seize lands and with other unspecified crimes. The Koryŏ court executed him. Paek Mun-bo 白文寶 (d. 1374), an eminent scholar-official then serving in the recently established Directorate for Ordering Politics, a government bureau created to check the power of *arrivistes*, especially those who associated with the Yuan court, played a critical role in Ki Sam-man's prosecution. Perhaps as a way to deflect any demand for vengeance against the throne itself, the Koryŏ court punished and imprisoned Paek. In 1352, one of Kongmin's senior ministers (likely with the king's tacit approval) attempted to assassinate several members of the Ki family and others with ties to the Yuan throne who appeared to threaten the young king's position. The plot failed, but the conspirators did seize and kill one of Empress Ki's brothers.[156]

On the other hand, whenever possible, King Kongmin tried to use the Ki family in his relations with the Yuan. Each year, he sent gifts to Empress Ki on her birthday.[157] He appointed the empress dowager's elder brother, Ki Ch'ŏl, to head the Branch Secretariat for the Eastern Campaigns. This effort to capitalize on the Ki family's influence at the Yuan court was a consistent policy through much of the first half of the fourteenth century.[158] Late in 1347, King Ch'ungmok had dispatched Ki Ch'ŏl to offer New Year's felicitations to the emperor on behalf of the Koryŏ court. The king had honored Ki with a farewell banquet.[159] As noted above, Kongmin used formal banquets in honor of Empress Ki's mother to renew his own family ties to ruling Mongolian aristocracy.[160]

Through strategic marriages to other established elite families in Korea, the Ki family tried to bolster its status and prestige. Ki Ch'ŏl married one of his daughters to the son of Wang Hu 王煦, one of the young king's most influential supporters. Ki Ch'ŏl's nephew was married to a granddaughter of Yi Che-hyŏn 李齊賢 (1287–1367), a prominent aristocratic scholar official and key Kongmin backer.[161]

Thus, during the entirety of Kongmin's sojourn in Daidu, Empress Ki and her family were among the most important personages in the Great Yuan *ulus*. As noted above, they held important posts in Daidu, Liaoyang, and Kaegyŏng. While at the Yuan court, Kongmin attended the empress dowager's son, Ayushiridara, the Yuan heir apparent, thus forging a personal bond to the Ki family.[162] Empress Ki had initially rejected the future King Kongmin as a candidate for the throne. However, when in 1351 the empress dowager offered her critical support for

Kongmin's enthronement, she hoped that her young protégé would remember his obligation. Having put him on the throne, the empress dowager clearly expected Kongmin to reciprocate by cementing the Ki family's position at his court. Instead, he executed her elder brother, seized a portion of his slaves to fill out the ranks of the Koryŏ military, and distributed his assets to his eunuchs and high-ranking ministers.[163]

Simultaneous with the purge of the Ki family, Korean military forces clashed with Yuan troops. The Koryŏ general In Tang, just returned from fighting Chinese rebel forces, seized eight imperial relay stations along the western bank of the Yalu river.[164] Koryŏ forces also took control of Ssangsŏngbu Directorate-General, an administrative territory directly subordinate to the imperial Yuan throne and strategically located in northeastern Koryŏ with access to Jurchen communities.

Tensions among the leading military families of Ssangsŏng made possible King Kongmin's dramatic assertion of royal authority. As Min Hyŏn-gu has shown, by the mid-1350s, conflict over the succession to the post of myriarch of Ssangsŏng had riven the Cho family. Although the man who secured the post, Cho So-saeng 趙小生 (?–1362), remained tied to the Yuan throne, the Koryŏ court emerged as a possible ally for potential rivals. For King Kongmin, the fissiparous nature of power in the northeast opened a path to greater control from the center.[165]

Similarly, succession struggles within the Yi family to the post of myriarch of Hamju 咸州 meant new opportunities for the Koryŏ court. Related through marriage to a branch of the Cho family frustrated in its attempt to win Yuan backing for the post of myriarch of Ssangsŏng, Yi Cha-ch'un 李子春, myriarch of Hamju, also began to reconsider the balance of power in Northeast Asia. In 1355, Yi met with Kongmin in Kaegyŏng to discuss the nettlesome question of population registration in Ssangsŏng. Like many of his predecessors, Kongmin wanted more control over his subjects who fled Koryŏ territory. Late in 1355, the Yuan throne relented and ordered officials from Koryŏ, the Ssangsŏngbu Directorate-General, and the Branch Secretariat for the Eastern Campaigns to hold talks. During the spring of 1356, Yi would meet again with the king. The encounters convinced each man that their interests might converge. The king hinted at future clashes with the Ki family (Ki Cho'l had been appointed manager of Liaoyang Branch Secretariat in 1355) and urged Yi to "obey my commands."[166] Clearly, the

Koryŏ king did not take the obedience of his military officers for granted, especially in Ssangsŏng.

During the sixth lunar month of 1356, Koryŏ military forces seized Ssangsŏng with little effort, in part because officers garrisoned there were divided. Some transferred their loyalties to the Koryŏ throne, and others such as the commander Cho So-saeng fled northward into Jurchen lands. Cho and his followers remained a nagging problem for the court for much of the next decade. Cho Ton 趙暾 (1308–80) contributed to the Koryŏ recovery of the Ssangsŏng area, for which he received a series of appointments. His sons continued to hold high offices throughout the rest of the Koryŏ and into the Chosŏn dynasties.[167] Yi Cha-ch'un also remained allied with the Koryŏ throne. His son Yi Sŏng-gye 李成桂 (1335–1408; future founder of the successor Chosŏn dynasty) would gain his first fame fighting for the Koryŏ throne against the Red Turbans later in the decade. By offering itself as an ally in family succession struggles and claims for local domination, the Koryŏ throne gained the initial support of key military families in the northeast. Given his limited political, economic, and military resources, King Kongmin was forced to achieve his ends—greater autonomy for the throne (both domestically and internationally)—through constant negotiation, manipulation, and strategy.

Kongmin attempted to bolster control in other ways at this time. To reassert more effective control over the Korean military, he demanded that all military officers turn in their credentials 牌. Typical of the Mongol empire in which lines of command and loyalty transcended national or dynastic borders, many officers had received their credentials from the Yuan court rather than the Koryŏ court.[168] Kongmin presumably planned to confirm the posts of only those military men he felt had demonstrated proper loyalty to the Koryŏ throne. Deeply concerned about threats to royal authority both at home and abroad, during the summer of 1356 Kongmin announced plans to reinvigorate the Koryŏ central army. He focused on reviving the economic foundations of hereditary military households, increasing manpower levels, and improving command structures.[169]

Finally, late in July 1356, the Korean throne abolished the use of the Yuan's Zhizheng reign period to mark time. This was tantamount to a declaration of independence from the Great Yuan *ulus*.[170]

The Yuan court reacted angrily to Kongmin's actions. Learning of the purge of her relatives, Empress Ki went wild with rage. She attempted to remove Kongmin from the Koryŏ throne and to replace him with the newly invested Sim Prince, Toqto'a-Buqa, also a member of the Koryŏ royal family.[171] After imprisoning a Koryŏ envoy, a Yuan spokesman in Liaoyang announced that "800,000" troops were on their way to chastise Koryŏ. The Koryŏ military commander of the northwest, In Tang, was not cowed. He instead urged the throne to expand the Koryŏ army.[172] Over the next six months, diplomatic communiqués flew back and forth between the Koryŏ and Yuan courts.[173] In the end, the practical limitations of Kongmin's brash efforts to assert royal authority became apparent. King Kongmin did the politically expedient thing, appeasing the Yuan throne and removing a potential political rival. He ordered the execution of In and ended Koryŏ's openly aggressive military and political posture vis-à-vis the Yuan.[174] In exchange, the Yuan court pardoned "the crimes of executing the Ki family and attacking the border."[175] Although each viewed the other with some suspicion,[176] larger developments in Northeast Asia reminded both courts that the fates of the Yuan and Koryŏ were still inextricably intertwined.

4
The Red Turban Wars

Waiting

As the 1350s drew to a close, the first wave of Red Turban armies reached Liaodong and northern Koryŏ. Red Turban forces overran the defenses of most major urban and administrative centers in Liaodong and occupied Koryŏ's Western Capital in present-day P'yŏngyang. The fighting marked the most widespread and damaging warfare in Northeast Asia in more than a century. The simultaneous conduct of major military campaigns in both Liaodong and Koryŏ indicates either a high level of strategic coordination or, as seems more likely, considerable operational autonomy for Red Turban commanders. In either case, neither Koryŏ nor Yuan commanders ever faced the full force of a unified Red Turban army.

As was true of other parts of the Great Yuan *ulus*, the Red Turban wars would bring major political and military changes to Liaodong and Koryŏ. Although observers in Northeast Asia certainly knew of the destruction and chaos in China, no one could have predicted exactly what rebellion would bring. They did, however, try to prepare for the coming storm.

The firsthand knowledge gained by Koryŏ forces during fighting with the Red Turbans in China, the 1356 Koryŏ strikes along the Yalu River, and the threat of Yuan retribution made clear to King Kongmin and his advisors the need to bolster military defenses on the northern border. Late in August 1357, more than sixteen months before Red Turban forces crossed the Yalu River, the Koryŏ court appointed Kim Tŭk-pae 金得培 (1312–62) northwestern regional commander, responsible for defenses against the Red Turbans and Japanese pirates.[1] Although born into a family with a tradition of government service and a successful graduate of the civil service examination, Kim spent most of his career in military posts.[2] He enjoyed close relations with the king, having served in Kongmin's entourage during his decade-long sojourn in Daidu. Upon taking the throne, Kongmin appointed Kim a senior official within the Bureau of Military Affairs.[3] Late in December 1357, the court increased Kim's portfolio by appointing him Chief Inspector of the Northwest,[4] magistrate of the Western Capital, and superior myriarch. Kongmin selected a former minister of revenue, Kim Wŏnbong 金元鳳 (?–1359), who had served in the 1356 campaign to recover Ssangsŏng, as vice-myriarch and the new commander of northwestern defenses against the Red Turbans and Japanese pirates.[5]

Korean court annals reveal little of the intelligence regarding Red Turban activities in northern China available to King Kongmin and his advisors during the following months, but they must have followed developments closely. The first confirmation comes in an entry of the *Official History of the Koryŏ Dynasty* from early in May 1358. The king upbraided officials from Chŏngju 靜州 on the northwestern border and Ch'olla 全羅 in southwestern Koryŏ who had traveled to the capital in order to see the king: "At present, the dynasty faces many difficulties: to the west, we worry about the Red Turbans; to the east, we suffer at the hands of the Japanese dogs. How dare you leave your jurisdictions without permission?" They were immediately taken into custody.[6] Security concerns to both the northwest and southeast sparked discussion of strengthening the capital's walls at this time.[7]

As the Koryŏ dynasty braced itself against military incursion by the Red Turbans, it also faced the ongoing despoliations of Japanese pirates, who were ravaging the country's coasts. Like the Great Yuan *ulus*, the Koryŏ throne had to divide its attention and resources among several concurrent military and political threats. Korean ships had once dominated the seas of East Asia. As recently as the late thirteenth century, the Koryŏ navy had been a potent military force. Much of the fighting between Koryŏ loyalists and the elite Sambyŏl-ch'o units that revolted against the throne took place off the southern coast of Korea. Koryŏ ships and naval personnel formed the backbone of the Mongol's first abortive attack on Japan in 1274. In 1281, they also participated in the second disastrous campaign. The damage was never repaired. Protected by the Mongols' military umbrella, the Koryŏ throne channeled its limited resources elsewhere.

However, as the military efficacy of the Great Yuan *ulus* deteriorated during the fourteenth century, Koryŏ found itself vulnerable to the increasingly brazen attacks of Japanese pirates. By the 1350s, the size of pirate fleets grew to hundreds of ships. In coastal raiding in the south, they often targeted deliveries of tax grain to the capital. They also seized slaves.[8] An estimated 115 pirate raids occurred during King Kongmin's reign alone.[9] In response, the Koryŏ government slowly rebuilt its military, constructing more ships, granting greater power to military generals, and trying to raise and train an army. Within the first few months of King Kongmin's accession, he announced rewards to induce both elites and humble commoners to bolster the ranks of his military and proposed measures to offset the grain shortages that hobbled his armies.[10] Despite these measures, the Koryŏ court watched developments in the Great Yuan *ulus* with mounting alarm.

As spring turned to summer, drought tightened its grip over much of Northeast Asia. As Chapter 2 showed, the late 1350s and early 1360s witnessed repeated crop failures and famines in Daidu and its environs. During the fourth lunar month of 1358, the Koryŏ court attempted to alleviate the drought through a series of ritual responses. The court "cut back on food, removed the musical instruments from court, and prohibited [the imbibing or production of] wine."[11] In mid-May, Kongmin expressed his grave concern over the four-month-old drought, noting, "I have been unable to eat or sleep night or day." In order to restore cosmic equilibrium, the king declared a general pardon for all offenses of the second degree or less.[12] Two days later, the king prayed for rain at Poknyŏng Temple 福寧寺.[13] Although the king's supplications brought rain days later,[14] the drought and subsequent economic dislocation continued.[15]

As the Koryŏ court struggled with drought and famine, it braced against the growing threat of rebels in the Capital Region, Shandong, and Liaodong. Throughout the summer months, the court made a series of personnel changes in the northwest.[16] Among these measures, King Kongmin established a myriarchy at Yisŏng 泥城 along the Yalu River east of Ŭiju. This unit oversaw four military contingents commanded by superior vice-chiliarchs.[17] These would be among the first Koryŏ units to engage any invading force to cross the Yalu River. Developments in Liaodong lent growing urgency to Koryŏ military preparations along the northern border.

The Red Turbans in Southern Liaodong

Beginning late in 1358 and continuing into the first months of 1359, Red Turban forces sacked the most important cities in the northeastern corner of the Great Yuan *ulus*. Control of the region was critical to the Mongol court. It was the gateway to Koryŏ and to the Jurchen lands, and home to important members of the Mongol aristocracy. Although the area's population declined during the early fourteenth century,[18] Liaodong was the site of extensive agricultural colonies.

As the rich agricultural and highly developed commercial regions of such southeast coastal regions as Jiangnan slipped beyond Mongol control during the 1340s and 1350s, the northern half of the Great Yuan *ulus* became even more vital. The court established agricultural colonies throughout Shandong and the Capital Region. In 1354, the court set up the Liaoyang Grain Transport Office (*Liaoyang caoyun yongtian shisi* 遼陽漕運庸田使司), presumably to facilitate the flow of tax grain from Liaoyang to Daidu and elsewhere. If neither the density nor the productivity of Liaodong's agricultural colonies ever matched those of such regions as Shandong, the Capital Region, or even Shanxi, the region's farming was not negligible. For instance, in 1352, the Liaoyang Circuit was ordered to sell 500,000 piculs of grain and legumes at reduced prices to ameliorate the effects of rising prices.[19]

If the Yuan court lost command of Liaodong, Mongol prestige, tax revenues, and intelligence from this strategically critical area would suffer. Such a loss would also open the door to ambitious Mongol, Jurchen, and Chinese military men to expand their own bases of power and authority. The Yuan court had already seen the dire consequences of such a scramble in much of southeastern China, where rebel leaders had established rival political regimes.

Even before the Red Turban forces arrived in Liaodong, the Yuan faced challenges in the region.[20] During the 1340s, periodic Jurchen unrest had prompted the Yuan throne to dispatch both senior administrators and military generals to pacify the region. Beginning in 1343, Üjiyed "Wildmen" (Ch. Wuzhe yeren 吾者野人) and Water Tatars 水達達 tribesmen "revolted."[21] Few details survive, but Yuan court chronicles note Jurchen resentment against supplying gyrfalcons for the Mongol throne.[22] Initial efforts to suppress the Jurchens failed, and in 1347 the court dispatched a new Mongol commander to a higher-level post in the Liaoyang Branch Secretariat, where he tried to restore control.[23] By 1348, at least two Jurchen groups had rejected Yuan authority, their leaders claiming to be descendents of the Jin imperial family.[24]

The Üjiyed were most active in the northern half of the Liaoyang Circuit, in what would be present-day Sakhalin Island and along the northern reaches of the Amur River.[25] Further, early in 1350s, the Yuan retained sufficient appeal in these distant lands that several score Üjiyed decided to ally themselves with the Yuan. Their leaders came with offerings of furs. In exchange, the Yuan granted them silver badges of authority and put them in charge of the Üjiyed.[26] In 1355, the Mongols attempted to consolidate control through the establishment of a myriarchy in Haerfen 哈兒分 (near the convergence of the Amur and Anyuy Rivers in what is now Russia) to oversee the Üjiyed Wildmen and other Jurchens in region. Thus, the Great Yuan *ulus* continued to exert considerable if uneven control in Jurchen lands past the midpoint of the fourteenth century.

Red Turban attacks on the primary agricultural regions and major cities of Liaodong posed a more direct danger to the Great Yuan *ulus*. The rebels' seizure of Daning Circuit 大寧路 meant hard choices for local elites. Established in 1215, Daning was the first administrative circuit that the Mongols established in Liaodong. It spanned territory that includes present-day southeastern Inner Mongolia and northeastern Hebei and southwestern Liaoning provinces. By the mid-fourteenth century, Daning was among the most affluent circuits in Liaodong and enjoyed the most extensive economic ties to Chinese provinces. As news of the Red Turban force's advance spread, some elites left the region altogether. For instance, Xie Xun (K. Sŏl Son), a member of a politically well connected Uyghur family that served the Yuan, fled

Daning in 1358, where he had been observing ritual mourning for his father, and sought refuge in Koryŏ.[27] With his superb education and valuable connections to Yuan elites in Daidu, Xie received a warm welcome at Kongmin's court in Kaegyŏng. In fact, Xie and the king had served together in the Yuan *keshig* in Daidu. Based on their skills in literacy and administration, generations of Uyghurs had served the Mongol empire since the early thirteenth century. Both Toghan-Temür and his father chose Uyghurs as their personal tutors.[28] Kongmin held Xie in great respect, granting him the title of earl in mid-September 1360.[29] At least one of Xie's sons would later serve at Kongmin's court, which valued his education and Central Asian pedigree.[30]

Other members of the Xie family joined Chinese warlords to the south. Xie Xun's younger brother, Xie Si 偰斯, had served as the prefect of prosperous Jiading county located on the southeastern coast of China. When it fell to rebels in 1366, Xie Si joined Zhu Yuanzhang. Zhu exploited the Xie family connections in East Asia and the familiarity with international conditions that Xie Si had gained at this critical port. Late in 1368, Zhu dispatched Xie Si as a diplomatic envoy to the Koryŏ court to announce the establishment of the Ming dynasty.[31] Again in 1369–70, Xie traveled to the Koryŏ court where he presented Kongmin with the Ming calendar and patents of investiture.[32]

The Red Turbans' arrival in Liaodong forced the less swift to choose among hiding, surrender, or resistance. Several women from elite families took refuge in Buddhist temples and nunneries. For instance, Esen-Qutuq 也先忽都, a Qipchaq Turk and wife of the Daning Circuit *darughachi*, Temür-Buqa 鐵木兒不花, and his Chinese consort, Jade Lotus, fled to a nunnery, where the rebels discovered them. The Turkic woman refused to join other captives in mending the rebels' clothes, even when threatened at knifepoint. She railed against them, exclaiming, "I am the wife of the *darughachi*; you are nothing more than curs [rebels]. I will not wield a needle in order to serve you rebels."[33] The enraged captors murdered her. After the Chinese consort attempted to hang herself three times, the Red Turbans simply killed her themselves.

Esen-Qutuq and Jade Lotus were not the only members of the family to meet their ends during the rebel occupation. Prior to this, the *darughachi*'s fourteen-year-old son, Öljei-Temür 完者帖木兒, had ventured outside the city's walls with his father, only to be discovered by rebels. The son pleaded with the Red Turbans to take him and release his father. The bargain struck, the handsome youth joined the rebels, and the father was released. The son eventually escaped and returned to Daning, where he found and buried the corpses of his mother and the Chinese consort Jade Lotus.[34] Although Chinese records cast the *darughachi*'s son's behavior in terms of filial piety, this example suggests that the Red Turbans were recruiting members of the empire's political elite.

Liaoyang, one of the most important administrative, cultural, and economic cities between Daidu and Kaegyŏng, also fell to the Red Turbans in 1359. Zhao Zhu 趙洙, supervisor of Confucian schools in the Liaoyang Circuit, and his wife, nee Xu 許, the niece of famed scholar and official Xu Youren 許有壬 (1267–1364), took refuge in the Zishan Temple 資善寺 during the attack.[35] When discovered, Zhao upbraided the rebels. They killed him.

The Red Turbans then attempted to win the support of Zhao's wife with promises of a portion of the booty that they had seized. She responded with scorn: "I am of an established family of learning and office. I have had the misfortune to encounter calamity, but I know that I am to preserve my honor and die. Of anything else, I remain ignorant." Although she did not flinch when threatened at knifepoint, upon learning of her husband's murder she collapsed to the floor in tears. Xu cursed the rebels. Her mother had died at rebel hands in Wuchang 武昌, as had her daughter, brothers, and sisters. "Now my husband has also died at your hands. If I could take my revenge upon you, I would mince your flesh into a thousand pieces." The rebels then killed her.[36]

During the first lunar month of 1359, groups of Red Turbans also occupied Guangning 廣寧 (modern-day Beizhen 北鎮), Jinzhou 金州 (Jin county 金縣), and Fuzhou 復州 (Fu County 復縣). At some time prior to 1358, the court appointed Guo Jia 郭嘉 to serve concurrently as supervisor and encampment official (Mong. *a'uruq*, Ch. *aolu* 奥魯)[37] of Guangning Circuit in charge of encouraging agriculture and military defenses. After receiving his *jinshi* degree in 1326, Guo had served in a variety of posts, including those in local and central government that required both civil and military skills. Most recently, in response to intensifying pirate raids along the coast, the Yuan court had dispatched him to assess the value of establishing a coastal defense myriarchy in Zhejiang.[38]

On taking up his duties in Liaodong, Guo confronted several challenges, including the heavy burden upon the local population occasioned by the costs of repeated military campaigns. Illegal exactions by unprincipled clerks only exacerbated the problem. Guo implemented measures designed to base each household's tax burden on the number of family members; presumably this reduced local clerks' opportunities for illegal surcharges. Guo Jia also involved himself in the most important state ritual of the region, the offerings at Beizhen Temple 北鎮廟 to the deity of Yiwulü Mountain 醫巫閭山. In his capacity as the leading civil official of the region, Guo provided the calligraphy for a 1357 stele account commemorating what would prove to be the last of the Yuan dynasty's dozen offerings, which had begun in 1298.[39]

As noted above, in 1357 the Yuan court ordered local officials throughout the realm to bring local militias under their control. Guo organized a militia of several thousand men and drilled them in marching and obeying commands. He also attempted to instill some measure of discipline into them through a strict system of rewards and punishments. According to his biography in the *Official History of the Yuan Dynasty*, through these efforts, "Among the eastern prefectures, in terms of [securing] a wealth of taxes and grain and [maintaining] the quality of troops and arms, Guo Jia was praised as the best."[40]

When in 1358 rebel forces sacked the northern Yuan capital of Shangdu,[41] Guo "personally led the militia out in defense"; when shortly later Liaoyang fell, he again led patrols in the areas surrounding Guangning. One day, miles outside the city walls, Guo encountered a hundred-man contingent with green uniforms (*qing hao* 青號), who claimed to be imperial troops. Red Turban forces often attempted to deceive opposing forces by disguising themselves in the uniforms of imperial regulars. Guo's suspicions were confirmed when the men removed their green clothing to reveal their true colors—red. Initial skirmishes went well for Guo, who split his forces to attack the rebels with a pincer formation. Wielding bow and arrow while mounted on a horse, Guo reportedly injured at least one rebel in the fighting.

Rebel forces, however, were not deterred. With the fall of critical Yuan cities in Northeast Asia like Shangdu and Liaoyang, Guangning now stood isolated. The Yuan government followed a consistent policy of greater decentralization and autonomy for local government than had the preceding Song dynasty. The incessant crises of the late Yuan had further exacerbated this trend. Local officials were increasingly left to their own resources in meeting the challenges of the day. This was particularly true in southern Liaodong, with its greater distances between county seats and sparser population. Guo held the fate of the city in his hands.

Frustrated with fellow officials' inability to formulate any plans for the defense of the city, Guo announced, "My strategy is settled." He then distributed all the garments and property in his household to "righteous men," that is, to volunteers willing to defend Guangning. In an effort to inspire his men to greater valor, Guo made clear his own intentions: "From the time of my ancestors, we have rendered meritorious service to the throne. [To offer] the ultimate loyalty [through my death] today is only to be expected from a man of my position. Furthermore, as an official defending this region, I must live or die here. Nothing else is worth worrying about!"[42]

The rebel forces soon arrived, surrounding the city. One of the attackers bellowed, "Liaoyang is already ours. Why don't you come out and surrender?" Guo reportedly let fly with an arrow, which struck his tempter's left cheekbone, knocking him out of the saddle to the ground. The man died in the fall. When the Red Turbans retreated slightly, Guo opened the western gate of the city to pursue them. The ranks of the rebel forces only increased, eventually overwhelming the city's defenses. Guo died in the fighting. As might be expected from a dynasty in desperate straits, the Yuan court lavished posthumous posts and titles on the fallen Guo as an exemplar of loyalty and courage.[43]

In mid-January 1359 the Yuan court dispatched troops under Soju 瑣住 from the Bureau of Military Affairs to retake Liaoyang.[44] His presence did little to stem the tide in the Liaodong region. Less than a month later, the court received news that the Liaoyang Branch Secretariat had fallen to rebel forces. The circuit commander of Yizhou 懿州 in western Liaodong died in the fighting there; the court was again quick to grant him a posthumous promotion and title of nobility.[45] At nearly the same time, forces under Cracked-Head Pan and Master Guan raced toward Quanning 全寧 (in present-day Inner Mongolia), burned the residential complex of Prince Lu 魯王, and encamped in Liaoyang.[46] Late in April, Jinzhou 金州 and Fuzhou 復州 in southern

Liaodong also fell. The Yuan court did not forsake Liaodong. Fojianu 佛家奴, a Bureau of Military Affairs manager, was ordered to "mobilize troops to suppress" the rebel forces.[47]

The Red Turbans may have established a governmental administration in Liaoyang. No textual evidence survives of such an administration, but Red Turban commanders established branch secretariats, issued seals to county officials, and printed paper money in other areas that they conquered. Mao Gui implemented many of these measures from his base in Yidu, Shandong. During the late 1350s, Zhu Yuanzhang pursued similar policies in areas he controlled. Finally, as Qiu Shusen has noted, Korean records refer to several of the Red Turban leaders active in Northeast Asia by their title, administrators (K. *p'yŏngjang*, Ch. *pingzhang*).[48]

Thus by mid-1359, Red Turban forces controlled most of Shandong and the region east of Daidu to the Koryŏ border.[49] Some rebel forces were active in both areas. For instance, in August 1359, one of Mao Gui's lieutenants, Xu Jizu 續繼祖, traveled from Liaoyang to Yidu to avenge Mao by killing Zhao Junyong, Mao's murderer.[50] Given the thriving maritime trade in the region, Xu and his men likely crossed Bohai Bay by sail from Liaoyang to Yidu.

Despite the repeated military losses, the Yuan central government never wavered in its commitment to regain control of Liaodong. It appointed a number of prominent Mongols and well-connected Chinese officials to re-establish imperial authority in these strategic lands.[51] The Yuan court actively participated in negotiations between rebel leaders and the dynasty's local representatives such as government administrators and field commanders. Although most extant accounts of late Yuan rebellions pay far greater attention to events in China proper, Liaodong's critical geopolitical position ensured that the Yuan (and the Koryŏ) court would remain vitally engaged in the region.

Late in July 1359, the Yuan court named one of its most experienced and capable men to a senior post in the Liaoyang Branch Secretariat, granting him extensive discretionary powers.[52] In a distinguished administrative career that spanned more than two decades, a Mongol whose name was transliterated in Chinese as Shuosijian 搠思監 (?–1364) had held critical posts in both the central and local governments throughout the realm.[53] Shuosijian also possessed battle experience, having fought rebel forces in Huainan during the fall of 1354. Stories circulated that Shuosijian had remained unfazed after being struck in the face by an arrow during the fighting there. He served for a time in Daidu, where he oversaw agricultural colonies. While there, Shuosijian made a deep impression on the emperor, in part for his prominent facial scar from the arrow wound. By 1358, he was one of the highest-ranking officials at court.

Unfortunately, he had also become one of the most embattled. He developed a notorious reputation for corruption and avarice. More specifically, during the winter of 1358, an imperial censor had implicated Shuosijian in a high-level counterfeiting scheme and a murder. The emperor temporarily relieved Shuosijian of his duties and forced him to return his seals of office. He escaped further punishment, however. The outbreak of fighting in Liaoyang proved a godsend to Shuosijian and to the emperor, who wished to rehabilitate a Mongol of proven ability. Shuosijian thus was named head of the Liaoyang Branch Secretariat.

This able administrator and brave warrior, however, never went to Liaoyang. He remained in Daidu until the next year, when he was given a high post in the central government. A general amnesty at the time removed whatever obstacles may have stood between Shuosijian and his former glory.[54] Instead, in mid-August 1359, the court placed a contingent of *tammachi* troops 探馬赤軍 under the joint command of the imperial prince Nanggiyadai 囊加歹, a manager of the Bureau of Military Affairs, Heilü 黑驢, and two managers in the Liaoyang Branch Secretariat, Fojianu 佛家奴 and Esen-Buqa 也先不花 (both descendents of the famous early thirteenth-century commander Mukhali, who had played a prominent role in the initial Mongolian conquest of Liaodong). They were to retake Liaoyang.[55]

As was the case in most empires, military action proved a ready path to promotion, reward, and redemption. On occasion, well-placed fathers tried to engineer promising military assignments for their sons. As noted above, early in 1359, rebel forces had advanced nearly 360 miles due east from Shangdu to Liaoyang. That winter, the emperor appointed Esen-Qutuq 也先忽都 to serve as administrator of the Bureau of Military Affairs. Esen-Qutuq was the son of the eminent Chinese official Hei Weiyi 賀惟一, also known as Taiping 太平.[56] Taiping had firsthand experience of conditions in Liaoyang, having in 1356 or 1357 headed the Liaoyang Branch Secretariat. At that time, he had bought local grain for shipment to Daidu.[57] Through his father's connections, Esen-Qutuq had held a series of senior posts in the central government and was now given the concurrent titles of Director of Military Affairs and Director of the Heir Apparent's Bureau. The son was charged with the suppression of rebels in Liaoyang. The account in the *Official History of the Yuan Dynasty* maintains that Taiping worried that his son was too young for such responsibility and repeatedly but futilely tried to persuade the throne to appoint someone else. Arriving in Liaoyang Circuit, he dispatched his generals to retake the administrative seat of Liaoyang, located in Yizhou. Rather than engage in battle, the rebel forces crossed the Liao River and fled eastward. As a result of calumny at court, Taiping was relieved of his duty, presumably for failing to eradicate the rebels. Instead, he took up duties as the regent of Shangdu, which by this point had been sacked and lost much of its political significance.[58]

In his privately compiled account of the late Yuan, Quan Heng gives a strikingly different account. Quan reports that Taiping requested that his son be appointed to lead the expedition to regain control of Liaoyang. He based his request on an assessment of Master Guan's past behavior. Guan and his men had raided throughout much of North China, from Shaanxi province in the west to Liaodong in the east, without ever establishing any lasting bases. Anticipating that Guan's force would soon withdraw from Liaoyang on its own, Taiping believed that the throne would attribute the rebels' departure to his son's military prowess and grant him commensurate awards. According to Quan, however, the troops under Master Guan and Cracked-Head Pan showed no intention of retreat and instead prepared to do battle. Esen-Qutuq hesitated to engage the enemy, and his forces scattered without ever having crossed swords. Humiliated, he returned to Daidu in the dead of night.[59]

No matter which version deserves greater credence, by the late 1350s, Yuan control in southern Liaodong was precarious. Early in February 1360, "Daning Circuit fell," which might indicate that the entire circuit fell to Red Turban attacks for the first time or more likely that Red Turbans forces regained control over most of the region.[60] In any case, Red Turban attacks severely handicapped (and sometimes completely destroyed) local Yuan government without establishing an effective replacement. The result was a highly fluid situation in which no one could count on lasting stability or even passable roads and communications.

Flight was a common solution; exactly how common would later become a matter of great contention. Former Mongol Yuan administrators would later claim that more than 40,000 households fled to Koryŏ because of the fighting in 1359 and 1361. More than two decades later, the Ming central government would dispatch officials to Koryŏ with demands for the return of these households.[61] Koryŏ authorities protested that such a figure was ludicrous. "In 1359 and 1361," they wrote, "rebel armies entered the area of Liaodong and Shenyang. Their seizure of prisoners and pillaging completely emptied the region. [Residents] dispersed and scattered in all directions. There may have been a few who came [to Koryŏ] to settle. How could there have been as many as 40,000?"[62] Although the Koryŏ response begs the question of where all those people went, it does suggest the massive destruction and social dislocation caused by the Red Turban wars.

Although the Ming and Koryŏ governments did not see eye to eye on this question, the records of both sides note that people bearing mixed Sinic-Mongol names were among those who fled to Koryŏ. The *Official History of the Koryŏ Dynasty* lists a Yi Dörbudei 李朵里不歹 (K. Yi T'ari-pudae, Ch. Li Duoli-budai), and the entry in the *Ming Veritable Records* mentions a Nai Dörbudei 奈朵里不歹 (K. Nae T'ari-pudae, Ch. Nai Duoli-budai). It seems likely that they refer to the same man, with the Sinic surname Yi, which was miscopied as Nai in Chinese records.[63] If this is the case, some of those who sought refuge in Koryŏ were of Koryŏ descent.

In any case, the Yuan court now appointed one of the dynasty's most experienced and capable field commanders, the Mongol Yesü 也速, to retake this strategic area of eastern Liaodong. Like many other elites in the Great Yuan *ulus*, Yesü began his career in the *keshig* and soon established an enviable reputation as a tough, effective officer. Beginning in 1354, he was in the field nearly continuously, fighting various enemies of the Great Yuan *ulus*. He had served under Toqto'a, offering valuable battle strategy during fighting to recapture the strategically located city of Xuzhou (he urged the use of massive catapults that hurled stones against the city walls) and later leading charges against the city gates. He had also seen extensive fighting in Shandong and the area south of Daidu.

After engaging rebel forces in a battle that lasted throughout the night, Yesü dispatched another officer to circle around the enemy. Attacked from both the front and the rear, the rebel forces suffered a major defeat. Not only did Yesü retake Daning; he also captured nearly three dozen rebel leaders, whom he publicly executed in the city, presumably to deter residents from cooperating with rebel groups in the future. Recalling him for a court audience, the emperor lavished rewards, promotions, and honors on Yesü.

Yesü had little time to enjoy the glow of imperial praise. Yongping 永平, approximately 130 miles due south of Daning, soon fell, and Yesü was dispatched to reassert government control in the region. Yongping was one of the last areas in Liaodong to fall to rebel forces, and it had massive stockpiles of grain and fodder. Thus, when rebels infiltrated the city, took control, strengthened the city walls, and created defensive moats by taking advantage of the river, it was a serious blow to Yuan control of the entire region.

Yesü immediately laid siege to the well-provisioned and stoutly defended city. He established armed camps around the city walls, severing its supply of firewood and grain.[64] In engagements with rebel forces outside the city walls, Yesü captured "more than two hundred rebel leaders." He also "pacified several dozen mountain fortresses" 山寨.[65] This last detail shows the sort of fortified sanctuaries established by local communities that had sprung up through so much of China proper had counterparts in Liaodong. Yesü also retook two smaller nearby cities, capturing one of the rebel leaders, Lei Temür-Buqa 雷帖木兒不花, who had led the initial capture of Yongping. Lei is a Chinese surname, and Temür-Buqa is Mongolian. Many Chinese and Koreans used mixed Sinic-Mongolian names during the Mongol period. Adopting a Mongolian name clearly did not necessarily reflect political or cultural identification with the Great Yuan *ulus*.

The rebels countered Yesü's military successes with delaying tactics. When Yesü sent the captured leader to the capital for execution, the remaining rebel forces in Yongping turned to diplomacy rather than combat. One account in the *Official History of the Yuan Dynasty* claims that they panicked and requested permission to surrender to Cherig

Temür 徹力帖木兒, an assistant grand councilor, who requested further instructions from the court. The court granted the rebels permission to surrender to Cherig Temür, and Yesü was ordered to withdraw his troops.[66] Another account maintains that Lei Temür-Buqa's capture only stiffened the rebels' resolve and a special court envoy, Örlög-Buqa 月魯不花 (1308–66), was dispatched to negotiate their surrender. Örlög-Buqa's biography maintains that he entered the captive city to remonstrate with the rebels. This version, perhaps a bit fancifully, maintains that "the rebels all were moved to tears; prostrating themselves all around [Örlög-Buqa], they begged him to accept their capitulation."[67]

In the end, the rebels engineered a surrender on their own terms. Suspicious that their sudden docility was a ploy to lower the guard of the Yuan army, Yesü maintained a high degree of vigilance among his troops. Rather than turn themselves over to imperial authorities, the rebels eventually abandoned Yongping and attempted to flee. Yesü's forces pursued the rebels eastward to Ruizhou, where in battle they killed thousands of the enemy. The remaining rebel forces moved further eastward to Jinzhou 金州 and Fuzhou 復州. Instead of pursuing the rebels further, however, Yesü reported to Daidu.[68]

Ordered to the capital, Yesü was appointed to head the Liaoyang Branch Secretariat and the Branch Bureau of Military Affairs. In addition to continuing his previous military responsibilities, Yesü was to "pacify the soldier-farmers of the east." From Yongping, where the administrative offices of the Branch Secretariat had been relocated with the fall of Liaoyang, Yesü enjoyed some latitude to pursue his expanding range of duties. At this time, rebel forces were apparently active through much of the southern coastal area of Liaodong along the Bohai Bay. They were reportedly traveling by ship along the bay on their way to Yongping. When they learned that the formidable Mongol general Yesü had taken over the city, however, they abandoned their plans. They instead turned their attention to Daning, approximately 130 miles due north of Yongping. The local military commander there, however, managed to drive the rebels off after killing one of their leaders.

The remaining rebel forces headed west, and Yesü, anticipating that they might attack Shangdu, dispatched his subordinate Qurimtai 忽林台 at the head of a small elite force in pursuit. Yesü's hunch proved right, and the rebels suffered a serious defeat at Shangdu. In fact, if the *Official History of the Yuan Dynasty* is to be believed, Qurimtai's victory at Shangdu scattered the rebel forces and restored imperial control to Yongping and Daning.

Building on recent military successes, Yesü attempted to consolidate social order in his jurisdiction. He dispatched officials to win over local populations with morality and to compile population registers. Clearly, Yesü believed that the rebels enjoyed at least a modicum of support in the region. Thus, he strove to win the hearts and minds of the people. At the same time, he organized them in mutual responsibility units for the purposes of security and agriculture.[69]

One Family's Fortunes

Extant Yuan and Koryŏ records skip lightly over individuals' fortunes during this time of turmoil. The case of the Gao family, however, gives some sense of the rich cultural mix of Liaodong during the mid-fourteenth century. The story begins in a fairly typical fashion for the female martyr genre: Woman Liu, a native of Gushi county 固始 (in Guangzhou subprefecture 光州), Henan, was married to a Gao Xifeng 高希鳳, a native of Yingtian 應天, who was stationed in Liaodong.[70] During the fall of 1358, Red Turban forces captured her husband at Old Duck Fort (Laoyazhai 老鴉寨).[71] After Gao's short and futile resistance, the rebels cut off his right hand. Gao quickly died from the wound. The rebels then took captive his wife Liu, who kept up a hail of vituperative abuse for several miles before being struck down by her captives.

Gao Xifeng's younger brother, Gao Yaoshinu (Slave of Bhaisajya—Buddha of Healing 高藥師奴), also died during the fighting. To avoid the chaos in Liaodong, his young bride, Woman Yi 李氏, set out for Koryŏ with their son, Manjusri 文殊, and an orphaned nephew, Sengbao 僧保. Along the way, she realized that she could not complete the arduous trip with two boys in tow. She abandoned her son, since he was slightly older and marginally better able to fend for himself. With the return of relative stability after the establishment of the Ming dynasty, Woman Yi was able to recover her son. They then returned home to watch over her husband's grave.

Another of Gao Xifeng's younger brothers, Gao Bayan-Buqa 高伯顏卜花, was killed by the Mongol general Naghachu. Gao's wife,

Woman Guo/Kwak 郭氏, also from Koryŏ, hanged herself.[72] Finally, Gao Xifeng's nephew, Gao Tashi-Ding 高塔失丁, was apparently done in by the machinations of his father's enemies, whereupon his wife and aunt both committed suicide.[73]

The experience of the Gao family reveals much about the period in Liaodong. One clearly sees the influence of Mongol rule on the subject population. Although the Gaos maintained a Chinese surname, most of the male family members adopted Mongolian personal names. Chinese and Koryŏ elites regularly used Mongolian names in both formal and informal contexts; commoners also adopted the practice. The prevalence of the naming custom is reflected in the Ming founder's lavish praise for the exemplary behavior of the Gao family women. The Ming founder periodically called for the purification of Chinese names and customs "polluted" by the alien Mongols. Yet nowhere in his comments did he disparage the Gao men's names.

Second, the composition of the family suggests the great variety of people who lived in Liaodong. The Gao males hailed from affluent Yingtian prefecture in the middle coastal region of China. The Gao men married women from the central province of Henan and from Koryŏ. With their husbands' deaths, the wives and their children fled the borderland of Liaodong. One woman returned to her husband's native place, while another sought refuge in her native land of Koryŏ. The decision to seek refuge in Koryŏ suggests that Woman Yi and Woman Kwak may have maintained connections to family in their native lands. Since the accounts do not specify the women's hometowns in Koryŏ, it is difficult to determine the breadth of these regional family networks.

To turn from the fortunes of one family to macrolevel generalizations about Liaodong during the Red Turban wars, the absence of some groups is striking. For instance, the Three Princely Houses of the Eastern Regions discussed in Chapter 1 seem to have played no role in the Red Turban wars. Given their prominence in Liaodong to this point, their close ties to the Yuan throne, and their survival into the early Ming period, one might have expected them to form a bulwark of Mongolian defenses in the region. Mongolian nobles in the northwestern province of Shaanxi played just such a role in the Red Turban wars.[74] Also noteworthy is the lack of powerful local Chinese warlords or militias organized by regional elites common elsewhere within the

Yuan *ulus* during these years. As the next chapter shows, by the end of the Red Turban wars, the Mongol general Naghachu had emerged as an influential military commander in Liaodong. By the mid-1360s, at least one Chinese military man had also developed a major base in southern Liaodong. Mountain fortresses are mentioned in passing, but they do not seem comparable in prevalence or prominence to those in either Chinese or Koryŏ areas to the south. The extant documentary record suggests that the most important military commanders to fight the Red Turbans in Liaodong were Mongol officers dispatched by the Yuan court. The defenses of Koryŏ would prove to be organized along similar lines, that is, Korean generals appointed by the Koryŏ throne.

The Red Turban Invasion of Koryŏ

Soon after seizing Liaoyang, the Red Turbans turned their attention to Koryŏ. In the eighth lunar month of 1359, the reality of the Red Turbans arrived at the Koryŏ court in the form of a communiqué from the Chinese rebels.

> Aggrieved that the people have long fallen under the Mongols, we have taken up the righteous cause and raised troops in order to recover the Central Plains. To the east, we have moved beyond the Shandong region; to the west we have gone beyond Chang'an; to the south, we have passed beyond Fujian and Guangdong; to the north, we have reached the Capital Region. All have joined us in good faith, like the starving who receive meat and grain or the ill who happen upon medicine. We have now ordered our generals to strictly prohibit their soldiers from disturbing the people. We will succor those people who join us; we will chastise those who resist in battle.[75]
>
> 慨念生民久陷於胡，倡義舉兵恢復中原。東踰齊魯，西出函秦，南過閩廣，北抵幽燕悉皆款。如饑者之得膏粱，病者之遇藥石。今令諸將戒嚴士卒毋得優民。民之歸化者撫之。執迷旅据者罪之。

Here, in what appears to the sole surviving example of the rebels' formal proclamations, the Red Turbans stress their military puissance, their support among the people, and the discipline of their troops. They also adopt the long-standing Chinese imperial rhetoric of succor for those who accept legitimate authority and punishment for those who stubbornly cling to their misguided ways. They open by noting their dissatisfaction with Mongol rule in China and by announcing their plans to "restore the Central Plains." This anti-Mongolian rhetoric is striking; warlords like Zhu Yuanzhang would not play this card for nearly another decade.[76] Perhaps they believed that the people of Koryŏ were less wedded to the Great Yuan *ulus* than the landed elites of China appeared to be.

By mentioning victories in Shandong, Chang'an, the Capital Region, Fujian, and Guangdong, the authors make clear that they are referring to the Red Turbans polity in its entirety. No single leader ranged over such a wide swath of territory. In this communication with the Koryŏ court, however, they draw no distinctions between the people of China or Korea. This inclusive rhetoric was a logical extension of Confucian political philosophy. It may also have reflected contemporary lack of concern with dynastic or ethnic borders under the Great Yuan *ulus*. Finally, it may have been a matter of expedience. Why highlight differences when trying to forge ties with a foreign court against a common enemy? In any case, the Red Turbans closed with a threat of punishment for resistance.

For the next nine months, the Red Turbans remained an imminent threat rather than a present danger. That the Red Turbans did not immediately move into Koryŏ territory had perhaps less to do with Koryŏ's daunting defenses than with developments west of the Yalu River. The rebels' proximity and the imperial troops' inability to halt their progress deeply worried many in the Yuan capital. Some officials at court advocated relocating the capital to the north.

As Chapter 2 has shown, despite the tangible fear that gripped Daidu, the Red Turbans did not advance on the capital, prolonging Yuan control of China for several more years. The court mobilized elite troops from Henan. After several unsuccessful encounters with these newly transferred troops, the Red Turbans under Mao Gui withdrew to Shandong, where he was murdered in 1359.[77]

Late in 1359, Koryŏ's respite ended. In December 1359, a reported 2,300 households from the Liaodong region streamed across the Yalu River, seeking Koryŏ protection. The Koryŏ court ordered that they be settled in the country's northwestern counties and be provided with grain. Like the cases of Women Yi and Kwak noted above, these households hailed originally from Koryŏ but had settled in the Liaodong region, presumably to take advantage of less onerous tax and corvée labor demands. Despite the repeated efforts of the Koryŏ throne and the orders of the Yuan court, few Koryŏ subjects had returned during the previous decades.[78] Dire conditions in Liaodong drove them now to willingly forfeit the political and economic advantages of Liaodong for what would prove to be the chimerical safety of Koryŏ.[79]

More alarming still, the Red Turbans launched the first of many raids across the Yalu River. On December 19, more than 3,000 Red Turbans pillaged Koryŏ territory before withdrawing west of the Yalu. Lack of timely intelligence slowed the court's response. The local military officer in command attempted to cover up the raid, either feeling that the raid did not represent a serious security threat or fearing a rebuke from the court for his failure to defend the border.[80]

Why would the leaders of the Red Turban movement, who were Chinese and had no previous ties to either Liaodong or Koryŏ, decide to commit men and resources to incursions into Koryŏ? They had no base of support there, shared no common language, and enjoyed no detailed knowledge of military, economic, political, or geographic conditions. Although renegade Khitans and Jurchens had raided along the Koryŏ border, and full-scale Chinese, Mongolian, and Jurchen armies had taken Korean territory in past centuries, no large-scale Chinese rebel group had ever done so.

Chinese and Korean scholars have offered a variety of explanations. Some have stressed questions of strategic vision. In order to consolidate their control of Liaodong, the Red Turbans needed to prevent an attack from Koryŏ.[81] Another explanation is that the invasion of Koryŏ formed an element of the greater campaign against the Yuan. Koryŏ, as an important ally of the Yuan and with "exactly the same political attitudes" toward the Red Turbans, became an important target for the Red Turbans. King Kongmin's decisions to contribute troops to the Yuan's 1354 counteroffense against Chinese rebels is offered as evidence of the congruence of Yuan and Koryŏ political outlooks. At one point, Toghan-Temür was said to have contemplated escape from Daidu to Cheju Island.[82] One scholar has argued that the Red Turbans deemed control of Koryŏ (as well as Liaodong and Shangdu) essential if they were to isolate and break Daidu.[83]

Others, more persuasively, have focused less on strategic vision than opportunism. With its weaker military and absence of Mongolian forces, Koryŏ was an attractive alternative to areas within the Great Yuan *ulus*. With no greater physical barrier than the Yalu River, Koryŏ seemed an easy target for plunder.[84] Finally, at least one scholar has suggested that the attacks on Koryŏ can be traced back to the Red Turbans' hurt feelings. Korean communities in Liaodong had spurned the Red Turbans' overture for a common stand against the Yuan. The Red Turbans invaded Koryŏ to take revenge on Koreans.[85]

The most likely explanation for the first major attack on Koryŏ is military exigency. During the fall of 1358, the superior forces of Chagha'an-Temür had driven Master Guan out of North China into southern Liaodong. Southern Liaodong was not only geographically distant from the areas Master Guan and Liu Sha knew best, its highly mixed ethnic population also differed from those areas in North China. Red Turban forces had considerable success against major administrative centers in Liaodong, but they showed no inclination to hold them permanently. This owed something to Master Guan's lack of political organization, weak local support, and Yuan military pressure. Not yet militarized and without direct Mongol military protection, Koryŏ offered a way to avoid Mongol forces and a place for raiding. Many places in North China still suffered from famine at this time, and the question of food was never far from the minds of military commanders.

Once informed of the raid, the Koryŏ court again shuffled personnel, appointing Kyŏng Ch'ŏn-hŭng 慶千興 (n.d.) as supreme commander of the northwest and ordering An U 安祐 (d. 1362) to serve as second in command.[86] Both Kyŏng and An were members of Kongmin's inner circle. Kyŏng was related by marriage to the king. Like many of the day's leading military officers, An U was closely linked to the Mongols. He went by a Mongol name in Daidu, where he spent his youth. He apparently first arrived in Koryŏ in 1348 as an imperial incense envoy in the employ of the Yuan court. Under King Kongmin, he enjoyed a series of rapid military promotions. In 1358, he had taken up duties as the myriarch of Anju, located on the northwestern border of Koryŏ.[87] He would eventually occupy the highest military position in Koryŏ, Supreme General of the Soaring Eagles Army (*Ŭng'yanggun sang-janggun* 鷹揚軍上將軍).[88]

Unwilling to engage surprisingly effective Mongol forces, on December 28, 1359, Red Turban troops crossed the frozen Yalu River under the command of Mao Jujing 毛居敬. Although Koryŏ estimates of 40,000 men may strain credulity, the Red Turbans quickly overwhelmed border defenses and seized Ŭiju 義州, strategically located along the main route between Daidu and Kaegyŏng. During the fighting, Chu Yŏng-se 朱永世, a high-ranking Koryŏ officer, and a thousand residents of Ŭiju met their deaths.[89] Red Turban forces continued their advance, raiding and pillaging as they went. Part of the relative ease with which the rebels penetrated Koryŏ territory was due to inadequate fortifications. Some border counties lacked the protection of stone walls around the county seat. According to the compilers of the mid-sixteenth-century work on administrative geography, *Sinjŭng Tongguk yŏji sŭngnam* 新增東國輿地勝覽, the Red Turbans entered Koryŏ at Ch'angsŏng 昌城, which lacked city walls. "Instead," the editors noted, "the people of the county depended on the mountainous terrain to avoid disaster."[90] The next day, the invading riders brushed aside defenses at Chŏngju 靜州 and Inju 麟州, southeast of Ŭiju.[91] By December 31, they had pushed as far southeast as the coastal county of Ch'ŏlju 鐵州.[92]

Here they met their first setback at the hands of General An U and Commander Yi Pang-sil 李芳實 (d. 1362), who temporarily repulsed the invaders.[93] Yi had served the preceding Koryŏ king during his stay in Daidu and more recently had held a series of high-ranking military posts at the Koryŏ court, including the royal guard (*hogun* 護軍). Yi had proved his military prowess and political reliability to King Kongmin in a 1354 surgical strike against a governor (*darughachi*) along the northern border who had revolted against the throne.[94]

After withdrawing to their positions at Chŏngju and Inju, the Red Turbans plundered the surrounding counties. On January 5, 1360, they again attacked Ch'ŏlju.[95] The marauders clashed with several dozen cavalry troops under An U at Ch'ŏnggang 清江. According to the *Official History of the Koryŏ Dynasty*, General An played a pivotal role in the fighting, raising confidence and morale in his troops through his sangfroid. When rumors circulated of an imminent attack by the feared rebel leader Mao Gui, fear gripped the Koryŏ troops.[96] An calmly attended his morning grooming much as on any other day. Inspired by his example, An's troops regrouped sufficiently to secure a key bridge at Ch'ŏnggang and prevented the Red Turbans from crossing.[97]

Although only scarce details of the size and composition of either force survive, the Koryŏ forces were not so fortunate in subsequent battles, and An's men withdrew to Chŏngju 定州.[98]

Although General An inspired the court's confidence,[99] fellow commander Kyŏng Ch'ŏn-hŭng incurred the king's wrath. Learning that Kyŏng had failed to press the attack against the rebels, the king wanted to execute him summarily for his apparent cowardice and military ineptitude. One of Kongmin's senior and trusted civil officials, Hong Ŏn-bak 洪彥博 (1309–63), counseled against such rash action. "Kyŏng is upright and honest," Hong noted, "but he is not familiar with military strategy. It is those who employed him who have erred." The king accepted the implicit criticism with grace and spared Kyŏng's life.[100] It proved to be a prescient decision. Kyŏng would eventually help end the Red Turban threat.

The rebel forces were driven in part by hunger. As noted above, late in the 1350s, famine held in its grip Daidu, Shangdu, much of Liaodong, and northern Koryŏ. The acquisition of grain posed a constant challenge to both invaders and defenders. After one of the initial battles at Ch'ŏnggang, residents of Chi county 支縣 (in Sŏnju subprefecture 宣州) fled when they learned Red Turban forces had been sighted nearby. The rebels immediately dispatched a force of their best warriors to secure the grain that had been left behind. Even as approximately 1,000 cavalry troops under the command of General An and Kim Tŭk-pae pursued them, the rebels were unwilling to abandon the precious supplies. Despite the rebels' burden, or perhaps because of it, when the Koryŏ troops finally caught up with the Red Turban contingent, they suffered heavy losses in men, horses, and matériel and were forced to withdraw to Chŏngju.[101]

News of the Red Turbans' repeated victories spread uncertainty and fear down the Korean peninsula. The court tensely debated the defense of such critical sites as the Western Capital. As early as December 26, 1359, such senior officials as Minister of War Yi Am 李嵒 (1297–1364) and Yi Ch'un-bu 李春富 (d. 1371) publicly aired concerns that the Western Capital could not be held. Rather than let the city's granaries fall into rebel hands, some officials proposed burning them. Yi Am rejected such a course of action; denied the city's provisions, the rebels might drive further southward in search of supplies.[102]

Yi Am argued that Koryŏ troops were not yet ready to engage the Red Turbans and proposed that the court trade territory for time. He maintained that if the Western Capital's defenses held too well, the Red Turbans would simply bypass it and move directly against Kaegyŏng. Yi proposed instead that the old and the young of the Western Capital be evacuated eastward and that the granaries be left untouched. Yi felt that such a strategy would feed the Red Turbans' arrogance and slow their march to the south. The city's grain supplies would return to Koryŏ hands once the Western Capital was recaptured.[103] Koryŏ officials were thus cognizant of the rebels' pressing need for supplies and not sanguine about the dynasty's northern defenses.

Residents of the Western Capital shared Yi's worries over the city's fate. When Yi announced his decision to withdraw the defending troops to Hwangju 黄州, ostensibly to wait for all of Koryŏ forces to assemble, residents panicked. Fearing the city's imminent fall, they rushed to convert their grain into lighter, more portable goods. A large bolt of cotton tripled in price from two *tu* 斗 to six.[104] Grain, so dearly coveted by rebels, proved less valuable than liquid assets to residents intent on flight.

Elite Chinese families would have sympathized with the plight of Koreans at this time. In a miscellany written during similarly chaotic conditions in China, *A True Account of the Zhizheng Period*, the scholar Kong Keqi 孔克齊 wrote:[105]

> When I fled [the area affected by rebellion], I tried everywhere to exchange the things in my bags for rice, but without success. When I was able to get something, the price that my goods fetched was less than one tenth their original value. Only gold and silver were urgently wanted. Next were silks and cotton. There was jingle among the people [at the time]: Silver was life, gold was illness, pearls were death. Don't even mention jewelry. By this they meant that all families prized silver. Gold gradually lost value each time it changed hands. No one even brought up pearls, as if they were the dead.
>
> 蓋予避地將所在囊中者徧求易米不可。即得且價不及于前者已十倍之上。惟金銀爲急。絹帛次之。民有謠曰：活銀，病金，死珠子，猶不言翠也。蓋言銀爲諸家所尚。金遇主漸少。珠子則無有問及者，猶死物也。[106]

Although the need to exchange goods for rice in times of crisis was common to both Chinese and Korean refugees, the preference for silver and gold reflects the higher degree of commercialization of the Jiangnan economy.

The Koryŏ court was not idle as the Red Turbans came to control an increasingly large swath of territory in the northwest. On December 31, 1359, the court dispatched nearly half a dozen acting chancellors (*su munha sijung* 守門下侍中) to serve as the ranking military commanders in the northwest and as leading officials in the administration of the Western Capital.[107] The Western Capital itself was the largest and most heavily defended city between Liaoyang and Kaegyŏng. In one essay, the famed scholar Yi Saek 李穡 (1328–96) wrote, "The Western Capital is the root of the dynasty; it controls the northwest."[108] It boasted imposing stone walls that measured more than 24,000 *ch'ŏk* 尺 in circumference and thirteen *ch'ŏk* in height. Perched on the city walls were guard towers from which defenders could hurl down arrows and stones.[109] In case of siege, its residents could rely on nearly fourscore springs and wells for a generous supply of water.[110]

The Red Turban incursions made clear the sorry state of Koryŏ's military forces. First, the court tried to raise more troops. To increase the number of battle-effective soldiers available for the country's defense, the court abolished the customary three-year period of mourning for parents for members of the royal guard.[111] In early January 1360, the court dispatched clerks from government offices to supplement troops in the northwest.[112] Second, the court attempted to raise more horses. All officials with a rank above edict transmitter (*sŭngsŏn* 承宣) were ordered to supply one horse. The court also turned to the affluent Sŏn (Zen) monasteries, registering their monks and horses for possible military service.[113] The repeated efforts to mobilize horses, beginning no later than 1354 and continuing through much of the 1360s, show the importance of cavalry fighting in Northeast Asia at the time. Mounted warriors often determined the outcome of battle.

Despite all these efforts, the Western Capital fell within the month, as Red Turban forces occupied the city on January 17, 1360.[114] The court's immediate response was pragmatic rather than heroic. It dispatched Minister of Revenue Chu Sa-jong 朱思忠 to present fine fabrics, horse saddles and reins, wine, and meat to the Red Turban leaders. Court chronicles note the presentation of gifts was an attempt to gain further intelligence about the rebels' strength.[115] It no doubt was also another effort to buy time in order to better organize defenses against the Red Turbans.

The court's first step to strengthen the military, another set of personnel changes, produced little immediate change. The king dismissed Yi Am, replacing him with Yi Sŭng-gyŏng 李承慶 (d. 1360), a prominent member of the Koryŏ court who during the 1350s had also served in the Yuan administration as a censor and as an Assistant Grand Councilor in the Liaoyang Branch Secretariat.[116] Next Chŏng Se-un 鄭世雲 (d. 1362) was appointed Northwestern Chief Border Inspector (*tosunch'alsa* 都巡察使).[117] Chŏng was one of the most dominant military and political figures of the day. A member of Kongmin's entourage during his years in the Imperial Bodyguard in Daidu, Chŏng had been promoted to third deputy commander (*taehogun* 大護軍) and received honors of the first degree when Kongmin took the throne. He enjoyed the particular favor of the king, favor that Chŏng had occasionally abused for personal ends. In 1356, he had assisted the king in his efforts to purge the Ki family and by 1361 he was serving concurrently in the Bureau of Military Affairs and as Supreme General of the Soaring Eagles Army.[118]

Despite the changes in command, Chŏng seems to have continued Yi Am's policy of sacrificing the north to buy time for Kaegyŏng. Having seen conditions in Hwangju, Chŏng reported to the throne that the rebels had "stockpiled firewood and repaired the walls of the Western Capital. We have no plans to press them. In order to assuage the people's minds, I would that we do not alarm them [the invaders]."[119]

Little information survives regarding the response of ordinary people in the Western Capital, or northwestern Koryŏ in general, to news of the Red Turbans' incursions. As noted above, many had fled on learning of the invaders' progress. Others organized into armed bands to protect themselves and their grain. For instance, late in January 1360, one official reported to the throne that during his clandestine fact-finding trip to the northwestern counties of Ŭiju and Chŏngju, he learned that ordinary people in the region had killed a group of 150 Red Turban foot soldiers who had been left to guard grain supplies.[120] However, the people of Koryŏ were by no means united in their opposition to the Red Turbans, as many either capitulated or sought their fortunes with the invaders.[121]

What of the view from the court? The Red Turbans did nothing to endear themselves to King Kongmin. On January 29, 1360, they apparently sent another communiqué to the Koryŏ king. The original text is lost, but Kongmin found it offensively arrogant.[122] The king directed much of his available military resources to meet the challenge from the northwest. On February 2, several hundred cavalry troops under the command of Minister of Justice Kim Chin 金蓳 and court eunuch Kim Hyŏn 金玄 raced toward the Western Capital where they triumphed in minor clashes with the Red Turbans.[123] First Deputy Commander Yi Pang-sil too is said to have killed several hundred rebels in earlier fighting at Ch'ŏlhwa 鐵化.[124]

At the same time, however, the king seems to have prepared for the worst. He ordered all officials in the capital to ready arms, servants, saddles, mounts, feed, and grain, evidently in anticipation of military action in the capital itself. The Palace Guard (*Suk'wi* 宿衛) practiced polo in the royal gardens for several weeks in order to hone the riding skills they would need for an emergency escape. At night, it is reported that the king and queen practiced their riding in the Rear Gardens (*Huwŏn* 後苑), an activity the king normally avoided whenever possible.[125]

By late in the first lunar month of 1360, Koryŏ royal forces had begun to position themselves to regain the Western Capital. Early in February, a combined force of 20,000 troops encamped at Saengyang Relay Station 生陽驛, an important post just outside Chunghwa 中和 county along the main royal highway to the Western Capital.[126] The soldiers' suffering began even before battle commenced. Frigid conditions led to frostbite, and many collapsed from the cold.[127]

The Red Turbans apparently commanded a rudimentary intelligence network in Koryŏ, for they learned that the royal armies were poised for a counterattack on the Western Capital. Armed with this knowledge, contend Koryŏ court annals, the Red Turbans "murdered tens of thousands of captives taken at Ŭiju, Chŏngju, and the Western Capital." The rebels stacked the corpses into a ghastly mound.[128] This very round figure should probably be taken with a grain of salt. It seems unlikely that the Red Turbans had either the time or manpower to slaughter so many civilians as they braced for imminent battle.

On February 6, 1360, the royal troops regained the city with relatively little fighting. Civilian casualties, however, were heavy. When

Koryŏ infantry troops broke through the rebel defenses, they reportedly trampled to death more than a thousand residents. The rebels also killed many civilians before they withdrew to Yonggang 龍岡 and Hamjong 咸從, relatively small counties ringed by mountains east of the Western Capital and ten miles from the coast.[129]

Although Koryŏ forces had regained the Western Capital, fighting with the Red Turbans continued for nearly two more months before the last of the invaders withdrew from Koryŏ territory. General An figured prominently in a series of clashes north of the Western Capital.[130] In mid-February, 1360, An's forces engaged Red Turban forces in Hamjong county. The Red Turban troops apparently seized the initiative in battle, assaulting An's men before they had formed ranks. When the royal troops broke ranks and fled, Red Turban elite cavalry trampled them. Only General Yi Sun's 李珣 successful efforts to form a rearguard prevented a complete rout. The Koreans also enjoyed the added support of a contingent of 1,000 troops who arrived under a chiliarch of the northeast (*tungpukmyŏn ch'ŏnho* 東北面千户), Chŏng Sin'gye 丁臣桂.[131]

Heavy fighting in Hamjong continued. Hard-pressed (perhaps by the Koryŏ reinforcements led by commander Yu Tang 柳塘), on March 2, 1360, the rebels took up a position within the city stockades, which were promptly surrounded by Koryŏ cavalry troops. As mounted troops rained arrows down on the beleaguered Red Turbans, the royal infantry forced its way into the stockades. Korean chronicles claim a major victory.[132] After suffering losses of "20,000" men, the remaining Red Turban forces under Generalissimo Shen La 元帥沈剌 and Huang Zhishan 黄志善 withdrew with more than 10,000 men to Pyŏngsan county 甑山縣, about eight miles to the north of Hamjong.[133]

Although the recovery of the Western Capital signaled an important Koryŏ victory, it increased pressure on other northwestern localities. A group of more than 400 rebels had been camped in the valleys of Mount Suk 肅山. When they learned of the defeat at the Western Capital, they returned to Ŭiju, where Commander Yu Tang and his subordinate commander had just completed repairs on the city's walls and gates.[134] Perhaps preferring easier targets, the Red Turbans seized the county seats of Poju 保州 and Chŏngju, before Yu drove them off.[135]

Throughout the remainder of March 1360, Koryŏ forces under General An and Yi Pang-sil gradually forced the Red Turbans northward toward the banks of the Yalu River. Part of the Koryŏ success derived from the effective use of elite cavalry units.[136] Another critical factor was the increasing toll that hunger, fatigue, and cold took on the Red Turbans.[137] After repeated defeats, on March 3, the Red Turbans crossed the treacherous Yalu River. They suffered heavy casualties as "several thousand" men fell through the ice into the deadly waters below.[138]

Despite the hunger, fatigue, and cold of nearly constant flight, the fighting in northern Korea's rugged mountains, and the terrors of crossing the Yalu River, the Red Turbans remained dangerous. Those who survived the harrowing crossing immediately formed ranks on the western bank of the Yalu River. Koryŏ commanders believed any further attacks would drive the desperate rebels to fight to the death. Thus, they withdrew from the field. The rebel forces then became the responsibility of Yuan authorities in Liaodong.

Red Turban stragglers from Ŭiju also escaped without any further clashes, as Yi Pang-sil too elected to rest his exhausted troops and mounts rather than give chase.[139] The harsh north Korean winter exhausted both marauders and defenders; during the final weeks of fighting, decisive victory probably seemed less pressing than survival to combatants on both sides. Although Koryŏ forces could now look forward to rest, food, and warmth, the Red Turbans were still in hostile territory in Liaodong.

The punishing physical conditions of winter warfare probably figured less prominently in the concerns of Generalissimo Yi Sŭng-gyŏng, the man responsible for driving the Red Turbans from Koryŏ soil. He oversaw the Koryŏ counterattack from Saengyang Relay Station. Frustrated at what he perceived as his generals' unwillingness to press the attack and under pressure from the throne for results, Yi fell ill and returned to the capital. Disgraced, Yi did not return to his official duties, claiming continued illness.[140]

Yi was probably not the only one to feel as though things were slipping beyond his control. Red Turban forces had left in their wake a trail of destruction and chaos in much of Northeast Asia, which had until now been cushioned from the most disruptive influences of rebellion elsewhere in the Great Yuan *ulus*. Military campaigns had already changed relations between court centers and local regions as magistrates and commanders in the field had no choice but to improvise. The flow of information, matériel, personnel, and taxes became subject to the vagaries of raids, fear, and local calculation. Koryŏ forces had managed to push the Red Turbans west of the Yalu, but few suffered any illusions about lasting safety. Liaodong did not enjoy even this slight reprieve. Northeast Asia had entered a new and turbulent age.

5
Buffeted in the Storm

The Koryŏ victory over the Red Turbans was cause for both celebration and reflection. In mid-March 1360, commanding generals Kyŏng Ch'ŏn-hŭng, An U, and Kim Tŭk-pae formally submitted news of their triumph to the throne.[1] An's long "congratulatory" memorial dwelt at length on the destruction wrought by the Red Turbans' predations and proposed measures to counter the country's fiscal difficulties, social unrest, and military ineptitude.

The Red Turban invasions revealed ongoing issues of regional autonomy and uncertain loyalties in the northwest. Tensions between the central government located in Kaegyŏng and powerful local elites in the northwest ran throughout Koryŏ history. During the twelfth century, two major revolts in northwestern Korea challenged the central government's control over the region. Local efforts to secure greater autonomy from the central government only increased with the appearance of the Mongols. As Chapter 1 noted, in exchange for a pledge of allegiance, in 1232 the Mongols granted Hong Pok-wŏn, an official from the Western Capital, and his descendents a place in the emerging international Mongol elite and a major say in the governance of northwestern Korea and southern Liaodong. In 1258 Cho Hwi 趙暉 revolted against the Koryŏ government, and in 1269, Ch'oe T'an and nearly "fifty cities" in the northwest under his control surrendered to the Great Yuan *ulus*.[2] The Mongols exploited these tensions between local powerholders in northern Korea and the Koryŏ court, establishing the Tongnyŏng Directorate-General in the northwest and the Ssangsŏng Directorate-General to the northeast.[3]

General An attempted to assuage King Kongmin's worries about further Red Turban raids. He declared (quite erroneously it turned out) that the rebels "have no intention of returning east." Yet, he openly acknowledged, "Many among the Red Turbans skilled in riding and archery were men of our own dynasty." These men, he suggested, were "remnants" of Sŏnsŏng 宣城 (present-day Kyoha 交河, Kyŏnggi province), who must be eliminated lest similar incidents reoccur in the future. By "remnants" An almost certainly was referring to the Koreans who remained loyal to the Yuan *darughachi* Lu Lianxiang, whom Yi Pang-sil had killed in 1354.[4] The Red Turban incursions provided another opportunity to secure greater regional autonomy from the throne.

An wished to lighten the considerable burdens of local populations in the northwest. He noted the prevalence of suicide as evidence of desperate conditions there. "Many hanged themselves; their desperation is without question. In other cases, half of the men and their wives slit each other's throats; their livelihoods were already at an end." In such areas as Anju 安州, Kaju 嘉州, Chŏngju 定州, Suju 隨州, and Kwakju 郭州, An proposed, the people should not be forced to provision officials traveling along the royal highways. Providing food, lodging, mounts, and sometimes even sexual services constituted a great burden. Exacerbating the problem was that many officials, hangers-on, merchants, and others often laid claim to these services without proper authorization. Similar abuses surrounding the use of the *jam*, or relay stations on highways, were a perennial problem throughout the Great Yuan *ulus* and other parts of the Mongol empire.[5]

Eliminating sources of local dissatisfaction would dampen support for Red Turban rebels and others who might challenge the Koryŏ throne. An also urged the king against harsh punishments for those "commoners who had no choice but to grovel before the caitiffs and those officers who had no choice but to flee to the mountains." An likely worried that overzealous investigation into the loyalty of local commoners or the behavior of local officials would only further alienate them. Government authorities, An wrote, should supervise the return of refugees and others who had left their homes during the fighting.[6] During the fighting in the area, local militia forces and royal commanders had seized both slaves and free commoners as war booty.

Finally, An reminded his king, the Mongols were closely monitoring developments in northern Koryŏ. Yuan officials traveling with An's forces reported regularly to Daidu about the progress of the war with the Red Turbans.[7] For better or worse, King Kongmin was not fighting alone.

Koryŏ's moment of triumph was fleeting. Early in April 1360, in another example of the importance of transportation routes in Bohai Bay, seventy boats carrying Red Turban forces landed on the coast of P'ungju 豐州, Sŏhae province, and the inlets near the Western Capital. The invaders burned P'ungju's gates and occupied the city. The Red Turbans seized cash and grain from government warehouses and set administrative offices ablaze.[8] Less than a week later, Red Turbans attacked coastal Anju.[9] Although the majority of Red Turban forces operated on land, given the ease of maritime access to Liaodong, Shandong, and Koryŏ, sea raids were always a threat.

Perhaps the new tide of attacks accounts for the alacrity with which the Koryŏ court seized on victories. Having captured and executed the Red Turban leader Huang Zhishan in mid-April the Koryŏ court dispatched the minister of revenue to Daidu to announce its recent victory. Arriving in Liaoyang, however, the minister discovered that unsettled conditions rendered the road to Daidu impassable. He returned home to Koryŏ.[10]

When Yi Pang-sil managed to inflict light casualties on the Red Turbans and to drive them off the coast of P'ungju,[11] the king presented Yi with a set of a jade belt and chin buckles at a state dinner for his officials.[12] Queen Noguk objected to what she perceived as unwarranted munificence. King Kongmin countered, "It was all Yi Pang-sil's meritorious service that prevented my kingdom from being reduced to rubble and the people from coming to harm. Even if I carved out a piece of my flesh and gave it to him, it would not be sufficient recompense. So much less so these [trifling] things!"[13] The king did not forget the military; days later he "lavishly fêted" those generals who had fought on the northern front.[14]

No sooner had the Red Turbans' raids into Koryŏ been quelled than a widespread drought began. It lasted from spring 1360 to at least the fifth lunar month of 1361. During the fourth lunar month of 1360, the king announced a royal pardon for all criminals imprisoned for offenses less than the second degree in an effort to improve the "harmonious spirit" (*hwagi* 和氣) of the kingdom. In addition to the wrongs endured by unjustly accused prisoners, the king also drew attention to the people's suffering brought about by the recent war and drought.[15] Later the same month, the king reduced his meals to one a day to show his commiseration with those who suffered from the long-standing drought.[16] The same month, the court learned that severe famine in the southern provinces of Kyŏngsang and Cholla had reduced many to starvation.[17]

By no later than the sixth lunar month of 1360, famine had spread to the capital Kaegyŏng. As the price of rice rose, the value of other goods dropped. A bolt of cotton, for example, bought only five *sŭng* 升 of rice. The king ordered 2,000 piculs of rice distributed among the population.[18] During the third lunar month of 1361, Yongju 龍州 reported famine and cannibalism.[19] Outbreaks of banditry followed in the wake of a severe famine in northwestern Koryŏ.[20] By late June 1360, the king was praying for rain at the Royal Ancestral Temple (*T'aemyo* 太廟).[21]

Throughout the distractions of drought, famine, cannibalism, and banditry, the Koryŏ court kept vigilant against further Red Turban attacks. Late in August 1360, the court had dispatched Yi Kong-su 李公遂, Lord of Iksan 益山君 (1308–66), Minister of Revenue Chu Sach'ung, and the eunuch Pang Tojŏkyŏ 方都赤如 (n.d.) to the Yuan court in order to appraise the strength of the rebel forces within China. The mission progressed no farther than Tang Relay Station (Tangzhan 湯站), less than forty miles northwest of the Yalu River on the imperial highway to Liaoyang.[22] There they learned that the road to Daidu was again blocked. The mission's failure enraged the king, who threatened death if they did not complete the journey. Again they ventured forward. This time they made it as far as Shenyang, before impassable roads halted their progress. After waiting in vain for several months in Shenyang for conditions to improve, they returned to Koryŏ.[23] King Kongmin and his court knew that the Red Turbans on Koryŏ soil were one tile in a larger mosaic of turmoil throughout the entire Great Yuan *ulus*. Kongmin wanted to exploit Yi Kong-su's excellent contacts at the Yuan court (see Chapter 7) in order to make better sense of his own plight at home.

Impassable roads were not just an inconvenience; they posed a fundamental threat to the Great Yuan *ulus*. Since Chinggis khan's campaigns in West Asia early in the thirteenth century, the Mongols had devoted enormous energy and wealth to developing a network of roads, bridges, relay stations, and riverine and sea channels to facilitate the flow of people, goods, intelligence, and government documents across Eurasia. These famed networks held the empire together, however loosely. They were among the Mongols' greatest triumphs, and in a real sense they defined the empire. Thus whereas Chinese and Koryŏ writers might bemoan the deterioration of transportation infrastructure in a given area, for thoughtful Mongol elites blocked roads were disturbing evidence that the sinews of empire were dangerously strained.

Perhaps responding to these unsettled conditions in southern Liaodong and North China, early in September 1360 King Kongmin visited Paek'ak 白岳, five *li* north of the county seat of Imjin 臨津. His purpose was to evaluate the area as the site of a new capital.[24] Prior to this, the court had considered relocating the capital to Hanyang 漢陽 (present-day Seoul). Soon after the purge of the Ki family in 1356, the Buddhist monk Pou 普愚 (1301–82), an intimate of the king and his royal preceptor (*wangsa* 王師), proposed moving the capital to Hanyang.[25] He promised that its geomantic power would usher in an age of renewed dynastic vigor. For Kongmin, a new beginning distant from the recent purge and perhaps better situated to withstand military reprisal from the Yuan had its appeal. In fact he had ordered the magistrate of Hanyang to repair the city walls and gates, commence construction of several palaces, and plan the relocation of the capital's political elite. The move to Hanyang was abandoned in the face of Red Turban attacks.[26] Neither would Paek'ak become the new seat of power, although contemporaries did refer to the incomplete royal complex at Paek'ak as the "New Capital."[27] By mid-December, Kongmin had gone so far as to relocate his residence to Paek'ak.[28] The Red Turban wars prevented the move from becoming permanent.

Based on past experience, the Koryŏ court knew that the Yalu River offered no protection from turmoil to the west. Early during the thirteenth century, unstable political conditions in Liaodong led first to incursions into northern Koryŏ by rebel Khitan forces, then Jurchen and Mongol efforts to consolidate control in the region, and finally to the Mongols' increasingly stringent military, economic, and political demands on the Koryŏ throne.[29] A century and a half later, in mid-March 1361, war refugees from the Liaodong region continued to flow into Koryŏ.[30]

The brewing crisis may also have been behind overtures by the Circuit Commander of Liaoyang (*Liaoyang zongguan* 遼陽總官), Gaojianu 高家奴.[31] Early in May 1361, his envoy presented gifts of hunting dogs and drinking cups to the Koryŏ throne.[32] The entries of the *Official History of the Koryŏ Dynasty* and *Abridged History of the Koryŏ Dynasty* provide no explanation of Gaojianu's motives, but one suspects that he may have been attempting to consolidate ties with the Koryŏ court at a time of increasing regional (indeed dynastic) instability. Kaegyŏng was considerably closer to Liaoyang than was Daidu.

Communications between the Koryŏ capital and Daidu were precarious but never completely severed. Early in October 1361, Koryŏ's minister of revenue seized on a moment of stability and clear roads to make his way to Daidu to offer congratulations (for what is not clear) to the Yuan throne.[33] Later the same month, Kongmin reinstated officials in the Branch Secretariat for the Eastern Campaigns.[34] Given the king's efforts to assert greater Koryŏ autonomy during the mid-1350s, his motives for re-establishing the branch secretariat at this point require some comment.[35] As noted in Chapter 3, during the 1356 purge of those closely allied with the Ki family, Kongmin ordered several important officials of the Branch Secretariat for the Eastern Campaigns arrested and executed. In the following months, he abolished the Judicial Proceedings Office and the General Command Office within the secretariat. The Offices of the Left and Right, which constituted the secretariat's administrative core, in contrast, were retained.[36]

The biggest change in both the Offices of the Left and Right and of the secretariat as a whole was that from 1356 on they were run as elements of the Koryŏ royal government. The secretariat's most critical function was communication with the Yuan government, usually through correspondence with the Branch Secretariat of Liaoyang.[37] Kongmin's October 1361 decision to appoint officials to the secretariat probably grew out of his desire for an additional avenue of communication with the Great Yuan *ulus* during a time of crisis in Northeast Asia.

Days later, King Kongmin received an edict from the emperor announcing a general amnesty, because "Han Yao'er and others had revolted and battles raged everywhere."[38] The edict reflects Mongol thinking that events in one part of the Great Yuan *ulus* impacted other areas. The Yuan court wished to strengthen ties with King Kongmin as a member of the wider *ulus* elite. It was also a way to reaffirm its military and administrative supervision.[39]

Immediately following receipt of the news about Han Yao'er's revolt, in November 1361, a large Red Turban force (reportedly 100,000 men) under the command of Cracked-Head Pan, Sha Liuer, and General Zhu 朱元帥 crossed the Yalu River. They used the Longfeng 龍鳳 calendar, a sign of allegiance to Han Lin'er's Red Turban Song regime.[40] Their first target was the administrative seat of Sakju 朔州, a border county approximately twelve miles southeast of the Yalu River and located on the royal highway to Kaegyŏng.[41] Sakju boasted stone fortifications and nearly a dozen spring-fed wells within the city.[42] We do not know whether signals from a half-dozen beacon towers 烽燧 surrounding Sakju alerted defenders in time to prepare the city's defenses.[43]

Although court chronicles claim some victories for Koryŏ troops, the Red Turbans progressed steadily southward. Chaos within the ranks of the Koryŏ officer corps undermined effective defenses. Late in October 1361, Kongmin received news that the commander of Tollogang Myriarchy 禿魯江萬户 on the northern border had "rebelled." Details are scarce, but he reportedly murdered several of his officers. Kongmin ordered the minister of punishments to lead a campaign against the errant officer.[44] Two weeks later, in mid-November, in response to the minister's request, the king appointed Yi Sŏng-gye as superior myriarch of the northeast with orders to assist in the campaign. Yi left at the head of his 1,500 military retainers. By this time, the myriarch and his men had already fled north to Kanggye 江界, a strategic region east of the Yalu River. Yi "captured and executed all of them."[45] Having suppressed the mutiny, Yi turned his attention to the invading Red Turbans. He beheaded more than a hundred rebels, including a commander. He presented one captive to the throne.[46]

Despite Yi's efforts, by December 13, 1361, a reported 5,000 to 10,000 Red Turban troops had taken up position outside the recently fortified Chŏllyŏng Pass 岊嶺 (also known as Chabi Pass 慈悲嶺).[47] Located on the main royal highway linking the Western Capital to Kaegyŏng, this strategic pass was just 24 miles north of the main Koryŏ capital. The pass itself was closely associated with past foreign incursions. Less than a century earlier, in 1269, the powerful Korean military commander Ch'oe T'an had shifted his allegiance from the Koryŏ throne to the Mongols. He controlled much of northern Koryŏ, and Chŏllyŏng marked the southern limit of his power.[48]

The throne hoped that erecting fortifications and stationing men at the pass would stop the Red Turbans. In this, the Koryŏ court drew on common wisdom about the natural defensibility of this site. The scholar-official Yi Chang-yong 李藏用 (1201–72) had stressed its strategic value:

The Chabi Pass Highway twists eighteen times,	慈悲嶺路十八折
A single sword there can hold off ten thousand halberds.[49]	一劍橫當萬戈絶

Outmanned by the Red Turban forces, Yi Pang-sil adopted a defensive posture instead of engaging the invading troops in battle. The court approved his recommendation that people and grain from eight prefectures and counties north of the capital be relocated to the fortified position of Chabi Pass.[50] To boost the morale of his officer corps at this critical juncture, General An U secured rewards from the throne in recognition of their efforts. Kongmin promoted An to supreme commander (*towŏnsu* 都元帥) and granted An greater powers of discretion. "The general oversees matters in the field," the king wrote. "You need not request permission when ordering rewards or punishments." The king also "secretly dispatched" several other officials to assist in the defense of Chabi Pass.[51] Kongmin may have been attempting to secure independent sources of military intelligence from the front.

Despite the pass's natural advantages, the additional manpower, and the government's hopes, 5,000 "iron riders" overran the Koryŏ defenses in a dawn attack. Commanding officers such as An U and Kim Tŭk-pae fled the battle on horseback.[52] Given the scale of royal commitment to the pass's defense in terms of military and personnel resources, this was a momentous defeat. The road to Kaegyŏng now lay open.[53]

Flight from the Capital

Outriders for the Red Turbans quickly advanced southward along the main highway to Hŭng'ŭi Relay Station 興義驛 (about ten miles southwest of the county seat of Ubong 牛峰).[54] An U attempted to regroup his troops at Kŭmgyo Relay Station 金郊驛, just thirty *li* northwest of the capital and a frequent rest stop for emissaries traveling to and from the Great Yuan *ulus*.[55] From the station, the military commander sent word to the court, requesting support from the Capital Troops 京兵.[56]

Realizing the capital's vulnerability, Kongmin planned the evacuation of the royal family. This was not the first time that foreign invaders had imperiled Kaegyŏng. Early during the eleventh century, Khitan armies of the Liao dynasty destroyed much of the capital. After the Khitans withdrew, the reigning Koryŏ king mobilized over 300,000 laborers to reconstruct the city walls, a project that required nearly two decades to complete.[57] These walls, towers, and massive gates had not prevented the Koryŏ court's flight from advancing Mongol armies in the mid-thirteenth century. Would they keep the residents of Kaegyŏng safe from the Red Turbans?[58]

During the fourteenth century, Kaegyŏng was far and away the most important city in Koryŏ. As John Duncan has shown, the capital drew elite aristocratic lineages from throughout the country.[59] One recent study suggests that approximately 500,000 people lived in Kaegyŏng and its immediate suburbs. If so, one-fifth to one-sixth of Koryŏ's total population of between 2.5 and 3 million lived in the capital.[60] These figures strain credulity, yet there is no doubt that the capital was by far the most populous city in Koryŏ and its economic center, where a majority of the country's commerce transpired.[61]

When, early in the tenth century, the Koryŏ founder selected Kaegyŏng as the primary dynastic capital, both the city's proximity to his political base and its natural defenses recommended themselves. Ringed by mountains, the tallest of which, the Song'ak range, towers over 750 meters high, the city lay in a basin at the confluence of three major rivers. In the third lunar month of 1358, King Kongmin had ordered the outer walls repaired.[62] At that time, the outer walls stretched more than fourteen miles in length and followed the area's serpentine topography. The walls contained sections of both stone fortifications and earthen walls. Recent archeological surveys suggest that the outer face of the walls averaged four to five meters in height, and the inner face measured between two and three meters. Defensive trenches dug along the perimeters of the walls account for the discrepancy between the outer and inner heights of the walls. The width of the outer walls of Kaegyŏng tapered from five to seven meters at the base to three to four meters at the top.[63]

Now, in mid-November 1361, King Kongmin attempted to mobilize the men of Kaegyŏng in the city's defense. First, he ordered the people of the capital to repair the city's twenty-five fortified gates.[64] Later the same month, the king attempted to raise new troops to man the capital's impressive defenses. He circulated placards that informed his subjects:

With the exception of private slaves, all those who volunteer, gentlemen of established official descent groups (*sain*) and hereditary local elites (*hyangni*), shall be given official posts. Government slaves shall be manumitted. Or, depending on one's preference, cash and cloth shall be granted.

凡應募者, 除私賤外, 士人鄉吏官之. 宮司奴隸良之. 或賞錢帛聽其所自願。[65]

The king then ordered all those below the rank of duke or marquis to contribute war horses to the royal army, in anticipation of the coming clash with the Red Turbans.[66]

When reports of the Red Turbans' devastating victory at Chabi Pass reached the king, he arranged for women and girls, the old and weak, to leave the capital first. News of their departure, a clear sign that the capital would soon be abandoned, sparked unrest in the city.[67]

Before daybreak and as final preparations for the imminent royal evacuation were under way, An U, Yi Pang-sil, and others rushed to Kaegyŏng. They argued for defending the capital against the Red Turbans. One official bellowed, "I would that Your Majesty remain but a little longer in the capital to enlist troops and to defend the ancestral altar."[68] Kongmin's trusted senior officials such as Hong Ŏn-bak, Kim

Yong 金鏞 (d. 1363), An U, and Yi Pang-sil urged the king to stand with his people and fight to the death.[69] Presumably shamefaced for advocating withdrawal over heroic resistance, the remaining ministers "all looked at one another in silence."

At dawn, the king and his entourage traveled to Minch'ŏnsa Temple 旻天寺, located in the middle of the capital,[70] while his close officials spread out through the city's main boulevards in one last attempt to assemble volunteers for the defense of the capital. An U informed the king of his failed efforts. "Your servants shall remain here to resist the rebels," he offered, but "we ask that Your Majesty leave."[71] The Hallim Academy scholar Yu Suk 柳淑 (1324–68) also favored a move southward. When the Red Turbans took Kwangju 廣州, Yu argued, "A dynasty depends on walls, moats, and supplies [to survive]. At present, the city walls [of the capital] are not complete. There are no stockpiles in the grain warehouses. If perchance the rebels arrive in the western suburbs, what would we do?"[72]

With the king's decision to flee the capital, many officials panicked and simply abandoned their posts. One senior official with close ties to both Kongmin and the Mongol court was singled out for his misplaced priorities. The procession of "wives, servants, goods, carts, and horses" that he led out of the city "was very grand." However, he reportedly left his mother behind.[73] In contrast, Yun Hae 尹侅 (n.d.) stood out for his sangfroid, "chatting and laughing with self-assurance with those in the king's entourage." Just a few years prior to this, Yun had served competently as the prefect of Pokju; in the company of the king, he would soon serve as Troop Inspector Commander of Kyŏngsang province (*Kyŏngsang chŏmgun pyŏngmasa* 慶尚點軍兵馬使).[74]

Leaving behind their subjects and the twenty-eight royal mausoleums surrounding the city, the king, queen, and queen dowager departed the city through the Sung'in Gate 崇仁門 to the Southern Hunting Reserve (Namnyŏp 南獵), from which the party then forded the Imjin River 臨津 to pass the night at the Tosulwŏn Temple 兜率院.

Such records as the *Official History of the Koryŏ Dynasty* and the *Abridged History of the Koryŏ Dynasty* note that only two dozen or so high-ranking officials of the court left the capital with the royal family. "Not a single man" of the royal bodyguard accompanied the king, alleges one source.[75] The evacuation may have been dramatic, but it does not appear to have been overly rushed. Along the banks of the river, the king is said to have gazed back at the mountains and river that surrounded his capital and his home. He may have considered the great change in his fortunes. Five years earlier he had audaciously purged powerful rivals at his court and ordered his armies to retake territory west of the Yalu River, openly defying the Great Yuan *ulus* and ambitiously strengthening royal power at home. Now, as foreign armies bore down on his capital, he had been driven from the palace in the night with a distressingly modest entourage. Whatever his thoughts, Kongmin commented to his companions, "This kind of scenery is just right for you gentlemen to compose matching verses."[76] The flight from the capital would be marked in a suitably cultured fashion.

The officials' versification on the banks of the river contrasted sharply with conditions within the capital. With the king's flight, Kaegyŏng descended into chaos: "Young and old fell prostrate, while children and mothers abandoned one another. The suburbs were filled with those who had been crushed in the rush to escape the capital. The sounds of wailing moved Heaven and Earth."[77]

Through an often eerily deserted countryside, the royal entourage began its journey to the court's new home in the south. In flight, Kongmin and his women presented a poignant sight. The queen was forced to abandon her cart and traveled on horseback, and her serving women were reduced to riding weak and emaciated mounts.[78] When the king and his traveling court, now augmented with a 1,400-man guard, made its way to Ŭmjuk 陰竹, only subprefectural officials remained in the administrative seat. "The clerks and commoners (*imin* 吏民) had taken refuge in the mountain strongholds."[79] The king continued to make military appointments as he moved southward, but news from the north was deeply disturbing. On December 19, 1361, at a royal postal relay station fifty *li* south of Kwangju's county seat, one official reported, "The rebels have already entered the capital. North of Imjin 臨津 is no longer our territory."[80]

During the late Koryŏ period, the loss of control of northern territory had particular resonance. This division marked the initial stage of the Mongols' domination during their invasions of the thirteenth century, incursions that eventually resulted in Koryŏ's complete subjugation.

When the earnest official tearfully reported his failure to gain support from the ranking officials of the Secretariat-Chancellery and the Security Council (Chae ch'u 宰樞) for an immediate counterattack against the Red Turbans, the king replied in a daze, "How can things [have changed] so rapidly?"[81]

Elite families reacted in different ways. Some fled Kaegyŏng to escape the impending Red Turban attack. Han Su 韓修 (1333–84), the newly appointed Grand Master of the Palace and Chancellor of the Royal Academy (*chungtaebu kukja cheju* 中大夫國子祭酒), joined the king in Pokju, where he would take up the duties of Supervisor of Rites (*chŏnwi chŏnkyo* 典儀典校) before returning to the capital the following year.[82] Some fled the capital but did not follow the king. In 1361, Pak Yun-mun 朴允文 and his wife, Woman Kim 金氏, took up residence in Milsŏng 密城, where they apparently remained to the end of their days.[83]

Other elites joined the king's entourage as it traveled southward. Observing the ritual mourning period on his father's death, Yi In-bok had withdrawn from his post as a state councilor. Yi and his younger brother met the king at prosperous Ch'ungju 忠州, a critical transportation hub for overland and river traffic.[84] Kongmin was thrilled and ordered them to join him. After the royal armies recaptured the capital, Yi served as assistant prefect of Kaegyŏng.[85]

From an elite family with decades of government service, Yi Kong-su was fighting the Red Turbans at Chukjŏn 竹田 when the capital fell. "As a solitary rider," Yi "pursued the king's entourage to Ch'ungju." Grateful for support during dynastic crisis, "the king was extremely pleased and treated [Yi] with particular favor and regard."[86] Yi would later figure in reconstruction efforts following the recapture of Kaegyŏng. Even before Red Turban fighting ended in Northeast Asia, Kongmin would send Yi to Daidu to stave off Mongol attempts to dethrone him (see Chapter 7).

The repeated stress in the historical records on the king's great joy over officials joining his entourage suggests his desperation. Driven from the capital, Kongmin seemed painfully aware of his precarious position. Rumors of officials fleeing their posts were common. In important cases, Kongmin had to dispatch trusted attendants to confirm local conditions. The irregular flow of information made false accusations easy, which only heightened the sense of uncertainty.[87]

The king did not take for granted that his ministers would rally to his side. In fact, his reception in many localities was tepid. Observation of proper protocol was rare enough to warrant special mention. Thus the biographer of one official stationed in Kyŏngsang took pains to note he "welcomed and attended [the king], fully observing proper etiquette. The provisions [arranged for the king] were lavish."[88] Perhaps sensing the king's need for pomp, the official arranged an honor guard, a colored pavilion, song, and music. It was "exactly as if it were a lavish spectacle of pleasure outing during a time of great peace." The king and his entourage were deeply grateful.[89] Royal processions should have been awe-inspiring spectacles that caused the people to "revere [the king] as if [he were] Heaven and fear him as if [he were] a deity."[90] Kongmin could not have entertained such lofty aspirations during these years.

During his exile from the capital, the king apparently endured great privation. In Ich'ŏn county 利川縣, the king's soaking garments froze, and he burned kindling to warm himself—a far cry from the creature comforts of the royal palace.[91] Securing appropriate food for the royal entourage presented real problems, since much of the local population fled in anticipation of further southern advances by the Red Turbans.[92] During the king's sojourn in Sangju early in 1362, the local magistrate Ch'oe Chae 崔宰 "did his utmost to provide [for the king], but was deeply concerned not to harm the people. Thus those who requested but did not receive [things and services from Ch'oe] found him a bit lacking."[93]

Perhaps more painful to the king than physical discomfort was the chaos that he witnessed during his progress southward. One of the leading Neo-Confucian scholars of the day and a senior minister, Paek Mun-bo, wrote that when the king and his entourage emerged from the mountains into Kyŏngsang province, they confronted mayhem.

From officials to commoners, all panicked in the face of the chaos. They were like a startled roe or a crouching hare. Although [authorities] issued orders to them, they would not assemble. In his heart, the king worried about them. When he ascended the mountains to look down upon them, [he saw that the scattering refugees] were so numerous and desperate they would fill Heaven and Earth.

官吏洎民，臨亂蒼皇，如驚麕伏兔，罔知措手足。雖令之不能齊。上心憂之。及登嶺下視之，蒼蒼焉茫茫焉，若天地之橫截者。[94]

In contrast, Paek writes, stood Pokju: "A great garrison, mountains tall and waters clear, customs olden and people pure." Unlike the chaos of the north and its desperate refugees, Pokju was a vision of order and confidence, "a canopy of pennants [fluttered above the garrison] and rows of officials without end [stood within]. The palace welcomed the king all arrayed at ease."[95] Pleased and no doubt relieved, the king settled in Pokju.

As an island in the raging sea of anarchy, Pokju had immediately recommended itself to the king. Pokju boasted many attractions. Located in a basin ringed with tall mountains on all sides, Pokju was a natural stronghold that was located sufficiently inland to render the chance of pirate raids unlikely. Several large stone-walled forts, dozens of spring-fed wells, sizable military granaries, and good access to the transport arteries of Kyŏngsang province also welcomed the beleaguered king and his court. The local population also enjoyed a reputation for historical loyalty to the Koryŏ throne. Equally important, more than half the king's retinue was closely linked to Pokju through place of origin, marriage, or previous service in the region.[96] Prominent among them was the Hong clan, family of King Kongmin's mother and his prime minister.

As Kongmin regrouped in Pokju, his subjects in Kaegyŏng suffered grievously at the hands of the Red Turbans. If Koryŏ court chronicles are to be believed, the Red Turbans visited great cruelty upon the city.

They butchered cattle and horses and stretched out the skins to form walls. They filled them with water. When the water froze, people were unable to climb out. They also butchered and roasted men and women. Fully indulging their depravity, some roasted pregnant women's breasts to eat.

殺牛馬張皮爲城，灌水成冰，人不得緣上。又屠炙男女。或燔孕婦乳爲食，以恣殘虐。[97]

Although the Red Turbans drove King Kongmin from his capital and brutalized the residents of Kaegyŏng, others in the Capital Region were more fortunate.

Buddhist Monks and the Red Turbans

Nestled in the Ch'onbo Mountains 天寶山 thirty miles southeast of Kaegyŏng, the Sŏn 禪 (Ch. Chan, J. Zen) Hoeam Temple 檜巖寺 neatly captures the many threads that tied Northeast Asia together under the Mongols. The temple's recently appointed abbot was the renowned monk Naong 懶翁 (also known as Hye Kŭn 惠勤 1320–76).[98] During his years in China from 1348 to 1358, Naong had visited several temples in Daidu and the Jiangnan region (including Mingzhou 明州, the maritime warlord Fang Guozhen's base). While in Daidu, Naong studied under the Indian Chan (Dhyana) master Sunyadisya (Pointing to the Void, Zhikong 指空), an aristocrat who early in the fourteenth century had come to the Yuan to pursue religious cultivation and to teach.[99] Sunyadisya is also thought to have founded the Hoeam Temple in 1328.

After years of travel and adventure in some of the wilder parts of south China, Sunyadisya made his way north "to interview the emperor and propagate the True Dharma."[100] Koryŏ women figured prominently in the Indian monk's progress and offer yet another illustration of their importance in elite Mongol society of the Great Yuan *ulus*. In the thriving southern city of Yangzhou 揚州, the Korean wife of the chancellor of the metropolitan government invited Sunyadisya to hold an ordination in the city. Later the Korean wife of the Directorate of the Imperial Treasury became a follower.[101] She bought a house that she converted into a Buddhist temple for his residence.[102] During the summer of 1328, Sunyadisya preached to a rapt audience of elite women at Yŏnbokjŏng 延福亭 in Koryŏ. After receiving ordination from Sunyadisya, a local Koryŏ official tried to proscribe the use of animals in sacrifices to the city god and to prohibit the raising of pigs.[103] After Sunyadisya's death in 1368, his cranial bones were eventually interred in Hoeam Temple by arrangement of the Indian master's most famous Korean disciple, Naong.[104] Two years later, King Kongmin would venerate these cranial bones before having them relocated to the royal palace.[105]

Thus, by the mid-fourteenth century, Sunyadisya stood as one of the pre-eminent monks in East Asia with close ties to Mongol and Koryŏ elites.[106] "It was held," noted Chinese literatus Song Lian, "that he could foretell the future and that he was three hundred years old. People revered him as if he were a god."[107] His eminence as a religious man perhaps explains contemporary tolerance for his *lèse-majesté*. According to one biography, while in Daidu, Sunyadisya "sometimes referred to himself as the Ruler of the Empress and the imperial concubines as his servants . . . [when] the Emperor [Toghan-Temür] got wind of this, he merely said: 'He is a Prince of the Dharma and has the right to aggrandize himself like this. It implies no reflection on me or my family.'"[108]

Sunyadisya cultivated ties with the Koryŏ community throughout the Great Yuan *ulus*. At the invitation of Empress Ki and her son the heir apparent, Sunyadisya gave at least one sermon at the Yanhua Pavilion 延華閣 within the imperial palace complex in Daidu.[109] As noted above, the Korean wife of a Mongolian official had established the temple where Sunyadisya resided in the capital. At least three Sŏn monks from Koryŏ came to study with the Indian master. These included Muhak chach'o 無學自超 (1327–1403), Paek'un kyŏngha 白雲景閑 (1298–1374), and Naong, all of whom would become influential figures in late Koryŏ Buddhism.[110]

Study with Sunyadisya added considerable sheen to Naong's vita, and he quickly came to the notice of the emperor. In 1355, Toghan-Temür appointed him abbot of Guangji Temple 廣濟寺 in the capital. His biographers claim that the emperor presented Naong with cash, silks, and a monk's robe (*kāsāya* 滿繡) embroidered with gold. The heir apparent offered him another monk's robe and an ivory duster. In the spring of 1358, Naong took leave of his Indian master, received his certification of transmission, and began the journey back to Koryŏ. As he passed through Liaodong, P'yŏngyang, Tonghae, and other places in Northeast Asia, Naong gave sermons on Buddhism (presumably in Korean but perhaps Mongolian or Chinese, given his long stay in Daidu).

By the time he returned to Kaegyŏng late in 1361, Naong was one of Koryŏ's most celebrated Sŏn monks, and the king dispatched a royal eunuch to welcome him into the capital. At his audience with the king and queen, Naong was showered with tokens of royal favor, including an embroidered monk's robe, a crystal duster from the king, and an agate duster from the queen. Kongmin appointed him royal preceptor. By late in the tenth lunar month, he had been appointed abbot of Hoeam Temple. Weeks later, Red Turban forces took the capital.

The new abbot was thus immediately confronted with a major crisis. According to a biographer, a small party of several dozen Red Turban riders appeared at the temple, where Naong received them sternly. Their leader then offered the abbot incense made from aloe wood, paid his respects, and withdrew.[111] Many of the temple monks approached their eminent but still largely unfamiliar leader about evacuating to the south.

Naong declined, saying, "The Buddha need only order and we will be protected. What can the rebels do?" The monks approached him again a few days later with even greater urgency. Overwhelmed by their entreaties, Naong promised that they would depart the following day.

"That night," however,

> the master dreamed of a deity with a black mark on his face. The deity straightened his clothing in respect, offered a salutation, and said: "If you scatter in flight, the rebels will without a doubt destroy the temple. I would that you strengthen your resolve." The next day, when [the master] arrived at the statue of the local tutelary deity, he sat and looked at its face. It was the one that he had seen in his dream.
>
> 夢一神人面有黑誌具衣冠作禮曰衆散賊必滅寺願固師志明日至土地神坐視其皃(貌)則夢所見也。[112]

Naong ordered that offerings be made to the tutelary deity. Although rebel riders came and went several more times, the monks remained at the temple.[113] Despite the protection of the local tutelary deity, the temple apparently did suffer damage in the end. In the 1370s, Naong refurbished the Hoeam Temple, because it "had been destroyed in battle."[114]

Whereas Naong remained at his temple, another eminent Sŏn monk, Pou, accompanied Kongmin to the south. Pou, too, had studied and traveled in China. In the spring of 1346, he arrived in Daidu and settled in the Daguan Temple 大觀寺. Before the year had ended, Pou was explicating the *Prajña Sutra* 般若經 to Toghan-Temür in the imperial palace and officiating at Buddhist masses for the empire's elite. Kongmin had first met Pou in Daidu, when he had been serving in the Yuan *keshig*. Pou's biography claims that the young Kongmin had been deeply impressed by Pou and promised a high position to the Buddhist monk if he were to become the Korean king. Returning to Koryŏ, Kongmin kept his word and in 1356 appointed Pou "royal preceptor," whose duties included administrative supervision of religious institutions in Koryŏ.[115] The newly enthroned ruler apparently sought out Pou's views on political as well as religious questions.[116] The royal teacher figured in royal administration, supervising the repair of the capital's walls on Kongmin's orders in 1358. According to a biography compiled by one of his followers, the same year he also submitted a secret memorial to the king warning of an invasion. During the fall of 1359, Pou perceived a portent of imminent danger to the dynasty. He then ascended Mount Miji 彌智山, where he prepared a rude shelter and let all know that it could serve as a place of refuge in time of crisis. The capital's fall to Red Turban forces in the eleventh lunar month of 1361 was to prove his prophecies accurate (at least to the faithful). When the king established his court in exile at Pokju, Pou was there too. Locals reportedly took shelter in the primitive housing that he had constructed.[117]

The Court in Exile

On January 11, 1362, the royal entourage's travels came to end. It arrived at Pokju county, which became the site of a temporary capital.[118] The king and his entourage may have taken some measure of comfort from the city's sturdy stone walls and circle of warning towers surrounding Koryŏ's new seat of power.

Efforts to regroup began immediately. The king appointed Chŏng Se-un to serve as regional commander 總兵官. This post was part of a mid-fourteenth-century trend in the Yuan *ulus* toward granting wide-ranging authority to single commanders who oversaw campaigns spanning several provinces.[119] Chŏng urged the king to display decisive leadership. First, Chŏng argued, the king must immediately "issue a proclamation taking responsibility for [the fall of the capital] in order to assuage the people's hearts."[120] As a first step toward rallying the country's military forces to expel the Red Turbans, urged Chŏng, the king should dispatch officials to coordinate royal troops stationed in the various provinces in the realm.

Kongmin heeded Chŏng's counsel, and the following edict was promulgated in the king's name.

> When the realm enjoys peace, one favors [civil] ministers; when the realm is imperiled, one favors the [military] generals. How one manages the times and circumstances is completely up to human [choice]. Can one be anything but circumspect? Our dynastic progenitor founded this vast enterprise [of the Koryŏ dynasty], and successive sages have followed one after another. They nurtured the people and fostered their livelihood. When it came to me, I have been complacent in ease and pleasure. I have neglected military affairs, resulting in the Red Turbans' invasion. [I] fled to the south. Every time I think of the ancestral temple and altar of state [in the capital], I cannot bear the pain. I have now dispatched the generals to assemble the troops to attack the rebels.

I have bestowed on Chŏng Se-un the tally and ceremonial axe of supreme military command; he will oversee the armies. He does not need my leave in ordering matters of rewards and punishments. Any military officer or soldier who dares willfully defy his command or report to the throne without going through the proper channels will be punished according to martial law. Ah! The army goes forth on the basis of [military] law. Those who have a dynasty to serve should put the dynasty first, and those who have forgotten their family to be a minister should be anxious to do this. You [officials], understand my extreme concern![121]

天下安注意相。天下危注意將。惟時與勢輕重在人。可不愼哉。恭惟太祖肇創鴻業，列聖相承。休養生民。逮于寡人，狃于宴安。軍旅之事廢而不講，以致紅賊侵犯。播越而南。每念宗社，痛楚何堪。今分遣諸將合兵攻賊。乃授鄭世雲節鉞,往董厥師。賞罰用命不用命。其各處軍官軍人敢有故違節制，及隔越馳聞者，聽以軍法從事。於戲。師出以律，有國之所當先國耳。忘家爲臣之所當急。惟爾士衆體予至懷。

In this proclamation, Kongmin humbled himself and acknowledged at least rhetorically the essential role of his generals. The king's lack of attention to the military had resulted in one of the greatest crimes a ruler could commit—the loss of the dynastic altars, which signaled not only political but also filial failure. Noteworthy is the public stress upon the wide-ranging authority and autonomy Chŏng was to wield during the campaign against the Red Turbans.

Having wrung this public contrition from the king, Chŏng displayed appropriate modesty, noting his humble (that is, nonaristocratic) pedigree and expressing grave doubts about placing the dynasty's fate in his hands. He lost little time, however, in taking command. He immediately began preparations to leave Pokju at the head of the army. He ordered Yu Suk, now serving as a member of the Bureau of Military Affairs and as a Hallim academician,[122] to forcibly conscript additional men. When Yu replied that he had already taken such steps, Chŏng threatened him with death if they arrived late.[123]

Chŏng then turned to Kim Yong, another important political player who often enjoyed the king's special favor. Chŏng sharply criticized him for not aggressively confronting the Red Turbans.[124] Before the year was over, Kim's resentment and fear of Chŏng would contribute to a series of violent deaths at court. However, at the time, Chŏng shone brightly. The Acting Director of the Chancellery (*Susijung* 守侍

中), Yi Am, acknowledged Chŏng's critical role—and power—when he wrote:

The rebels have now violated our territory, and the king and his servitors have fled. We are the laughingstock of the whole country and the disgrace of Koryŏ. Master [Chŏng], you are the first to lead [the country] in the righteous cause. With the symbols of command, you direct the armies. Regaining the safety of the dynastic altars and restoring the dynasty depend on this one action. Only you exert yourself [in this cause]. Day and night, our lord and his ministers eagerly await your triumphant return.

今寇賊闌入，君臣播遷，爲天下之笑，三韓之恥，而公首倡大義。仗鉞行師。社稷之再安，王業之中興，在此一舉。惟公勉之。吾君臣日夜望公之凱還也。[125]

Yi Am was in a position to know. A senior minister at Kongmin's court, Yi had served as a commander assigned to monitor the military generals in northern Koryŏ during the early days of the Red Turban incursions. One of his sons had died in the fighting.[126] Days later, the king added to Chŏng's military titles, appointing him a minister in the Secretariat (*Chungsŏ p'yŏngjangsa* 中書平章事).[127]

As columns of royal troops marched northward to confront the Red Turbans, local magistrates and other officials struggled with the small but dangerous raiding parties that ranged through the country. In mid-January 1362, the court granted swift promotions to officials in Yŏmju 鹽州 who had organized a military force and claimed to have killed more than 140 Red Turban outriders.[128] The magistrate of Wŏnju 原州 died in fighting the marauders, but in Anbyŏnbu prefecture 安邊府, locals elected to surrender when 29 Red Turban riders appeared. At least they feigned surrender. After the third round of celebratory drinks, locals took advantage of the raiders' inebriation and false sense of security to kill them all.[129] The prefect of Kanghwa 江華府 adopted a similar strategy. During a banquet hosted by the prefect in the Red Turbans' honor, locals killed senior leaders of the invaders' contingent.[130]

On occasion, however, Koryŏ subjects did join the Red Turbans. In addition to the men of Sŏnsŏng noted above, late in 1361 a military officer who had fought with Generals An U and Yi Pang-sil was taken captive by Red Turban forces near Anju. The details are unclear, but the Red Turbans made him a generalissimo. In a communication to the Koryŏ throne, he announced plans to lead his "million soldiers" eastward, presumably against Kaegyŏng, and called for an immediate surrender.[131] Although the *Official History of the Koryŏ Dynasty* is silent on the subject, it seems likely that at least a portion of the officer's troops followed him to the Red Turban side. One passage of the *Official History* specially notes the "troops of his standard" (*hwihabyŏng* 麾下兵), distinguishing them from regular forces. At the time, many officers, most famously Yi Sŏng-gye, oversaw "personal troops" (*ch'inbyŏng* 親兵) or "troops of their standard." Troops who enjoyed special ties to the surrendering officer had to chose between loyalty to the king and loyalty to their commander.

From the Western Capital, one man returned with news that more than 10,000 people had fled the rebel-controlled city. He begged Chŏng to send an official to take charge of these refugees. Happy to discover the local population had not accepted Red Turban rule, Chŏng dispatched the minister of rites to maintain control.[132] Chŏng not only oversaw military affairs, he also took an active role in restoring political order.

As his armies struggled to regain control in the north, King Kongmin oversaw his court in the south. The sudden appearance of the royal entourage in Pokju caused a great stir. The king continued many of his daily routines, such as archery practice, sightseeing, and boating. Such activities were now, however, subject to public scrutiny. In mid-January 1362, the king and some of his high officials went boating on the lake near Yŏnghoru Pavilion 暎湖樓. After practicing archery along the lake's edge, the king ate a meal offered by several of his ministers. "A wall of people watched [the king's activities]" notes one account. Reactions varied. Some wept and sighed; others recited prophecies. "An ox roaring loudly; a dragon leaving the water; shallow water turning clear," they intoned. "In the past we had heard of such things; now they have proven true."[133]

More serious court matters also unfolded at the temporary capital. Komgmin placed command of the royal guard in the hands of Cho Ton. His presence at the king's side in a time of dynastic crisis was evidence of Kongmin's successful efforts to bolster the throne's power. As noted in Chapter 3, in 1356 Kongmin re-established control of the Ssangsŏng Directorate-General, a strategic military region on the northeast border that since the thirteenth century had been administered by the Yuan government rather than the Koryŏ throne. The king exploited tensions within the Cho family that commanded the garrison and persuaded Cho Ton to ally himself with the Koryŏ dynasty. In his effort to win over fellow Ssangsŏng officers, Cho appealed explicitly to their common ancestry as fellow Koryŏ subjects. To one of his clansmen, he wrote:

> You were originally a man of Koryŏ. Both your grandfather and mine were from Hanyang. Now you betray your own dynasty to follow rebels. What are you thinking? Abandon rebellion and follow the loyal; leave danger and turn to safety. This is the time [for] meritorious service, reputation, wealth, and status.
>
> 汝本高麗人。爾祖與吾祖皆自漢陽來。今背本國從逆豎獨何心哉? 棄逆從順，去危就安，功名富貴，此其時也。[134]

Cho served the court well in negotiating the recovery of Ssangsŏng and received commensurate rewards and honors.

Despite Kongmin's success with Ssangsŏng, the military campaigns were often conducted with brutality, alienating many influential Koryŏ families and, one suspects, Jurchen elites. Cho Tun nearly succeeded in persuading his nephew Cho So-saeng, one of the ranking Ssangsŏng commanders, to surrender to the Koryŏ throne. Cho So-saeng, however, distrusted the court's promises of amnesty; one lieutenant surrendered himself to the court only to be executed.[135] Cho So-saeng fled northward into Jurchen-populated Yuan territory, where he remained a potential threat to King Kongmin.[136] Thus, Cho Ton was an experienced commander familiar with the cut and thrust of battle, both military and political. He must have been a comforting presence by the king's side, even if he represented the unfinished business of the Cho military family in the northeast.

In Pokju, Kongmin attempted to adhere to the ritual calendar as though he were in the dynastic capital. At the lunar New Year, he offered sacrifices at a local Confucian academy to his royal ancestors' surviving spirit tablets (several had been lost in the flight from the capital). Normally the ritual was conducted at the Ancestral Temple in Kaegyŏng. He was careful to maintain his membership in the Great Yuan *ulus*, sending New Year's felicitations to Toghan-Temür in Daidu.[137] Here again we can see Kongmin's dual identity as successor to the Koryŏ founder and as a member of the pan-Eurasian elite of the Mongol empire.

One month after the court had arrived in Pokju, Koryŏ military forces began final preparations to retake Kaegyŏng. On February 12, 1362, a reported 200,000 royal troops under Generals An U, Yi Pang-sil, Kim Tŭk-pae, and others set up camp in the suburbs east of the capital. General Chŏng oversaw these military forces as they surrounded the city. The battle to regain the capital began before dawn.[138] Advancing to the thundering sound of drums, smaller units of crack Koryŏ troops rushed the city walls. At the time only a little-known commander, the future founder of the Chosŏn dynasty, Yi Sŏng-gye, led 2,000 of his personal troops (親兵) in a charge in the rain and snow against the walls.[139] Several dozen riders under the command of an officer under his standard (*hwiha hogun* 麾下護軍) also rushed forward.[140] Korean accounts report that the Red Turbans had fortified the city, but the sudden dawn attack caught even their elite units unaware.

Koryŏ generals exploited the Red Turbans' temporary disarray to mount a full-scale assault on the capital. They, however, were careful not to force the Red Turbans into a corner. Their primary goal was recovery of Kaegyŏng, not extirpation of the Red Turbans. They thus allowed the invaders egress from two city gates.

In their haste to escape, the Red Turbans "trampled one another to death." The majority of Red Turban losses (Korean claims of "100,000 rebels" beheaded seem exaggerated) occurred during the pell-mell flight.[141] Royal troops recovered such valued symbols of Koryŏ rulership as lost gold, silver, official seals granted by the Yuan court, and arms. The 110,000 Red Turbans who survived the slaughter at the capital withdrew west of the Yalu River.[142] Days later, Chŏng's report on the royal army's victory arrived at the temporary court in Pokju. The king immediately dispatched Yi Taetuyi 李大豆里, an official in the Koryŏ heir apparent's household administration, to present Chŏng with raiment and wine as signs of the throne's gratitude.[143]

One generally well-informed Chinese chronicler with close ties to the Yuan court, Quan Heng, suggests that considerable subterfuge made possible the Koryŏ victory. After the king's flight to Pokju (Quan has him instead escaping to T'amma 耽羅, the present-day island of Cheju):

> His officials presented women [as tribute to the Red Turban leaders] and requested permission to surrender. All the Koryŏ military commanders gave

their daughters [to the Red Turbans] in marriage. With this, the [Red Turban] troops and the Koreans were as if related by marriage. They came and went whenever they wished. The Koryŏ men were thus able to hide their horses in the forest. One night, the king issued an order. With the exception of those who spoke Korean, everyone was to be killed. Both Sha Liuer and Master Guan were killed. Only Cracked-Head Pan and his lieutenant "Lefty Li," leading ten thousand light cavalry soldiers, escaped via a byway to the Western Capital. There they surrendered to Bolod[-Temür]. Later, they would again surrender to Kökö[-Temür].

其臣納女請降，將校皆以女子配之，軍士遂與高麗如姻婭，恣情往來。高麗人因而各藏其馬於林中。一夕，傳王令，除高麗聲音者不殺，其餘並殺之。沙劉二，關先生皆死，惟破頭潘神將左李率輕騎萬人，從間道走西京降孛羅〔帖木兒〕，已而又降擴廓〔帖木兒〕。[144]

Whether through military gallantry or subterfuge, Kaegyŏng had been recovered.

A Place in the Sun: General Chŏng's Report

After retaking the capital, Chŏng sent a long report to the king in his temporary lodgings in Pokju. The document, studded with allusions to Chinese history and drawing freely on passages from the Sinic canon, was almost certainly crafted by a man of letters in Chŏng's employ. It seems safe, however, to assume that it reflected the general's thinking. It is worth quoting at length for the light it sheds on Chŏng's perceptions of his own importance and the place of Koryŏ in the greater Mongol empire.

[Your Majesty] keenly desired to save the world and broadly assembled outstanding men of talent. [I] respectfully accepted your order to serve as military commander. [I] fear troubling your sage intelligence, but I have humbly heard that prosperity and decline are fixed by cycles; order and chaos [unfold] without cease. [Among] the keys for keeping the people in order, defending against rebels is [most] difficult. The Great Prince abandoned Bin, unable to defend against the threat of the Di.[145] [Tang] Xuanzong [r. 712–55] traveled to Sichuan, unable to control the invasions of the hounds.[146] Having eradicated the Red Eyebrow [rebels], the Liu [family's] Han dynasty [206 BCE–220 CE] was revived.[147] Having destroyed the Yellow Turbans, the Cao [family's] Wei dynasty [220–66 CE] succeeded to the legitimate line of dynasties.[148] All these were the workings of fate. They were not solely the outcomes of human action. Midwinter of last year saw a fearsome enemy of awesome strength. In terms of their rapacity, even wild beasts could not compare. When we consider their military operations, even [the famed strategists] Sun [Wu] and Wu [Qi] would have had difficulty matching them.[149] Daily they grew more self-assured. There was no one in the world [who was their equal]. [They] seized on their victories to drive far. They had already run rampant throughout the realm. [The rebels] ventured far and went so far as to enter our territory. Whereupon Koryŏ was greatly shaken.[150] None could withstand their strength. Armies collapsed at their approach. One million warriors were suddenly encamped at the capital's walls. In countless numbers, the people were cast adrift, wandering the roads. Alas, the people fell into the most precarious circumstances. Moreover [was] Your Majesty's flight from the capital. This was verily a deep concern for your generals and ministers. Thus, I led the assembled armies. Thereupon, we assaulted the hordes of barbarians. [Our] troops were irresistible. What difficulty was there in meeting the enemy in battle? The arrogant enemy was overwhelmed; their souls were severed [from their bodies] as soon as they met our blades. [We, I] brought to heel that which no one under heaven had been able to bring to heel. [We, I] executed those whom no one in the world had been able to execute. Fish in the bucket should be killed in order to avoid the [later] difficulty of them escaping through the net. How could the one surprise stratagem of Tian Dan 田單 merit emulation?[151] The eight military formations of Zhuge Liang may serve as a model. Climbing the snows to seize the city, Li Su 李愬 [773–821] seized the lands of Caizhou 蔡州.[152] Forming ranks with their backs against the river, Han Xin 韓信 [?–196 BCE] pulled out the pennants of the Zhao 趙 fortifications.[153] Although the specifics differ, their principle was the same.

I previously inspected the troops in 1359. On that occasion, I swept the rebels from Chosŏn. None of the credit for overcoming the force of later incursions belongs to your ministers. For the most part we humbly were graced by Your Highness's bravery and wisdom. Your heavenly endowed surpassing reverence grew daily. Word of your admirable demeanor spread widely. You observe the rites and music of the Three Dynasties. [Your Majesty] "set about diffusing your civil virtue."[154] That depraved and traitorous beasts have been brought to heel and that bestial invaders have been made to submit is due entirely to Your Majesty's transformative power. It was also due exclusively to [Your Majesty]'s supreme benevolence. The spontaneous nature of principle [is that] after the world is in disarray, the myriad things become whole again. This is the time of restoration. Verily it is the beginning of a renewal. [Would your] minister dare not compete in displaying bravery in military affairs?[155]

軫濟世之心，旁求俊彥。敬承分閫之命。恐累聖明。竊聞興衰有數，理亂無窮。安民之要，禦寇爲難。大王去邠未能防狄人之逼。明皇幸蜀不得制猲㺃之侵。掃赤眉而劉漢重興。破黃巾而曹魏繼統。悉惟時運，匪獨人爲當。去歲之仲冬，直滔天之勍敵。論其肆毒，雖豺虎之莫如。觀其行兵，亦孫吳之難抗。日將自恣世無誰何。乘勝長驅，既橫行於天下，遠引直入。遂大振於海東。怒鋒不可當。望風皆自潰. 百萬精甲奄屯住於都城，億兆斯民蕩流離於道路。嗟哉。黎烝甚於塗炭。況乘輿之遠狩，實將相之深憂。肆舉雲合之兵，遂攻蟻聚之虜。士卒得建瓴之勢。赴敵何難。頑嚚爲破竹之魂迎刃輒解。制天下所不能制。誅一世所不能誅。魚可息於鼎中免難脫於網外。田單一奇何足法。葛亮八陣可爲師。凌雪入城，李愬取蔡州之地。背水爲陣，韓信拔趙壁之旗。事雖不同，義則允合。昔蒐兵於己亥，曾掃賊於朝鮮。再克寇侵之強，皆非臣等之績。玆蓋伏遇殿下勇智天錫，聖敬日躋，遠播休風。遵禮樂於三代。誕敷文德。舞干羽于兩階。梟獍之所以馴，犬羊之以伏，無不關於聖化，亦皆囿於至仁。理之自然，否則復泰。斯乃重興之際，實是更始之初。臣等敢不競奮鷹揚之勇。[156]

In this memorial to the throne, Chŏng strove to make clear his own importance within both Koryŏ and the greater Mongol empire. He opens with a nod to fate. Offering examples from Chinese history, Chŏng noted that whether a dynasty crumbles or enjoys a renaissance is often the outcome of destiny.[157] Yet, the way Chŏng framed the question leaves no doubt that the fortunes of these dynasties lay in the hands of eminent generals. The clear implication is that Chŏng, too, had joined the ranks of such exclusive company. When survival of the Koryŏ dynasty hung in the balance, Chŏng swung the scales in the right direction. To drive home the point, he listed a number of famous generals and strategists from Chinese history. Some he considered his inferiors; others he found worthy of emulation. In either case, his peers, it is suggested, are among the great men of history.

As the reports narrows to contemporaneous conditions, Chŏng first established the seemingly irresistible force of the rebel armies. He described them as "a fearsome enemy of awesome strength. In terms of their rapacity, even wild beasts could not compare. When we consider their military operations, even Sun and Wu would have had difficulty matching them. Daily they grew more self-assured."

Chŏng was careful to portray the Red Turban attacks on Koryŏ as part of the larger wars unfolding throughout the Great Yuan *ulus*: "there was no one in the world [who was their equal]." Later in the memorial, Chŏng returned to this theme. "[We, I] brought to heel that which no one under heaven had been able to bring to heel. [We, I] executed those who no one in the world had been able to execute." Such rhetorical expressions as "in the world" and "under heaven" were clear references to the wider Great Yuan *ulus*.

In the next section of the report, Chŏng turned to the danger that the Red Turban invaders posed to the Koryŏ dynasty. Initially, the enemy forces swept aside Koryŏ armies. Confidence evaporated. "Koryŏ was deeply shaken. None could withstand their strength. Armies collapsed at their approach." Soon, the dynastic capital itself fell. Both the people and the king suffered. "One million warriors were suddenly encamped at the capital's walls. In countless numbers, the people were cast adrift, wandering the roads. Alas, the people fell into the most precarious circumstances. Moreover [was] Your Majesty's flight from the capital." After invoking the "deep concern" of the king's generals and ministers, Chŏng turned to his own contributions.

Ch'ŏng was not the only one to note the Red Turbans' seeming invincibility. Kim Ku-yong 金九容 (1338–84) described the 1361 incursion as follows:

Ravenous beasts seized the royal capital,	豺虎陷京國
Officials were all at a loss.	群臣總不知
Panicked, [men] abandoned their wives and children,	蒼黃失妻子
In chaos, they cast aside their infants.	顛倒棄嬰兒
Smoke and flames surged to the clouds,	煙焰衝雲起
Sorrow filled the land.	山河滿目悲
The impregnable fortress was not held for even a morning's time,[158]	金湯巳未守
Fleeing, where do [we] wish to go?[159]	奔走欲何之

Kim stressed the collapse of Koryŏ defenses, the rapid fall of the capital, the chaos of flight from Kaegyŏng, and the despair over where to go or what to do next. In a slightly later essay, Kwŏn Kŭn 權近 (1352–1409), a leading Korean scholar and literatus of the late fourteenth and early fifteenth centuries, also wrote of the Red Turbans' "boundless force." Using the imagery of a raging flood, Kwŏn noted, "They engulfed everything as they came southward. The entire country fell, and [none] could hinder them."[160]

In Chŏng's version of events, however, Koryŏ troops under his command quickly established their dominance. His "troops were irresistible. What difficulty was there in meeting the enemy in battle? The arrogant enemy was overwhelmed; their souls were severed [from their bodies] as soon as they met our blades." As noted above, Chŏng placed his efforts in a wider context of the Great Yuan *ulus*. Chŏng's point is nearly transparent. In stark contrast to Mongol and Chinese generals in the Yuan, Chŏng stopped the Red Turbans in their tracks, quickly driving them from Koryŏ soil. He had defeated the rebels and saved Koryŏ when all others in the empire had failed.

And what of King Kongmin's role in this epic drama? Chŏng lavishly praised the king's contributions. "None of the credit for overcoming the force of later incursions," he opined, "belongs to your ministers. For the most part we humbly were graced with Your Highness's bravery and wisdom." The sovereign's primary contribution to the restoration of control was moral cultivation. Chŏng catalogued Kongmin's attributes: "his heavenly-endowed surpassing reverence," his "admirable demeanor," his adherence to the rites and music of the Three Dynasties, and his expansive "civil virtue." He concluded: "that the ungrateful beasts have been brought to heel and that bestial invaders have been made to submit is due entirely to Your Majesty's transformative power and supreme benevolence." No mention is made of the king's political leadership, military command, or strategic vision. By the end of the document, there could have been little doubt about who deserved credit for saving the dynasty.

Chŏng ended on a bright, and largely self-serving, note. Having weathered the storm, Koryŏ could now look forward to a time of peace. Invoking the imagery of the Chinese classic, the *Book of Changes*, Chŏng wrote, "The spontaneous nature of principle [is that] after the world is in disarray, the myriad things become whole again. This is the time of restoration. Verily it is the beginning of a renewal." Having saved the dynasty, Chŏng also looked forward to further service on behalf of the throne—"[Would your] minister dare not compete in displaying bravery in military affairs?" However humble the language, it was clear that Chŏng expected to continue to play a prominent, perhaps predominant, role in Koryŏ.

Dangerous Victory

Jealousy and deadly competition had followed the court to the south, as political intrigue swirled through the narrow streets of Pokju. Even as preparations to retake the capital were under way, a conspiracy by Kim Yong against Chŏng Se-un and other leading military figures began to take shape.

Kim worried that if the campaign to regain the capital succeeded, Chŏng, An U, Yi Pang-sil, and Kim Tŭk-pae would win greater favor and influence at court. Kim's fears were fully justified. By this point, Chŏng held the post of manager of the Secretariat, a position "between the two ministers and the three stewards" (*yisang samje* 二相三宰)[161] and had directed the war against the Red Turbans with great autonomy. On the pretext of not wanting to "burden the postal riders," Chŏng submitted news only of major battles to the throne.[162] Much of the campaign was directed in the field, and the king did not receive daily updates from the front, let alone give detailed instructions. As the report quoted above makes clear, Chŏng believed that the king would do well to yield military command, and perhaps much political leadership, to his servitors. The military crisis created by the Red Turban invasions greatly enhanced the generals' power and status.

According to the *Official History of the Koryŏ Dynasty*, Kim Yong decided the best course of action would simply be to kill all potential rivals. He thus forged a royal edict and commanded his nephew Kim Im 金琳, a former minister of works, to secretly instruct An U to execute Chŏng on the king's (falsified) order.[163] Some military officers (including An U who wished to follow "the king's orders") supported the assassination. Yi Saek, a prominent minister, would later opine that fellow officers begrudged Chŏng his great success in the Red Turban Wars.[164] Others voiced strong opposition to the "royal order." Kim Tŭk-pae argued, "at present we have not suppressed the rebels. How can we turn on one another?"[165] On February 17, 1362, shortly after Koryŏ troops regained the capital, An invited Chŏng to a banquet. An's men beat the general to death.[166]

The chronology in the *Official History of the Koryŏ Dynasty* appears to absolve King Kongmin of any complicity in Chŏng's death. According to that account, on February 18, Kongmin received news of the victory at Kaegyŏng whereupon he dispatched a senior official from the heir apparent's administration to travel north to present Chŏng with gifts of clothing and wine as tokens of the king's appreciation.[167] The following day, General Mok Ch'ung-ji 睦忠至 arrived in Pokju with news: "The generals have killed Chŏng Se-un." The *Official History* notes somewhat puzzlingly, "The secret [of Chŏng's death] was not divulged."[168] The brief notice does not make clear who exactly killed Chŏng nor does it specify if it was the generals who kept Chŏng's demise quiet or the court at Pokju.

If, for argument's sake, one assumes that Kongmin possessed no prior knowledge of the plot against Chŏng, he must have been astonished at the news. Just days after the greatest Koryŏ military victory in more than a century, senior military officers, most of whom had been the king's strong supporters from the beginning of his reign, murdered the sovereign's handpicked commanding general without explanation or forewarning. How did the king respond to such a momentous development? The *Official History* chronology holds that the very next day, February 20, he dispatched an official to the north to announce a pardon for the generals involved in the assassination. He further commanded the official to "hasten them [the generals?] to the temporary capital in order to allay their concerns."[169] Was he concerned about alienating his generals just when final victory against the Red Turbans had come within their grasp? Did he fear that his mutinous generals might turn against him next?

The decision to pardon his generals had been reached after debate at Kongmin's court. Senior ministers favored forgiving the generals' transgression. The magistrate of Pokju, Pak Chi-yŏng 朴之英, warned of further incidents. He argued that Yi Pang-sil alone had been behind the murder and that other generals had "suffered harm" in the mutiny. He prophesied additional revolts. Pak's dire remarks gave Kongmin pause. He recalled the pardon and made plans to deploy troops against his mutinous generals.[170]

Two days later, February 22, he received a report from his generals concerning Chŏng. Extant sources reveal nothing of its content. Presumably it contained encouraging news, because a pleased Kongmin once again dispatched his envoy with a pardon and various gifts of gold, silver, and textiles for the generals.[171] The king also promoted Yi Pang-sil, whom Pak Chi-yŏng painted as the conspiracy leader, to the post of a manager in the Secretariat, the post that Chŏng had recently held.[172] Yi's tenure was to be short.

Kim Yong was careful to tie up loose threads. Fearing that his nephew would reveal the plot, Kim arranged his execution. He then counseled the throne, "An U killed your principal general. This is to ignore Your Majesty 是不有殿下也. This crime cannot be pardoned."[173] In the official pronouncement of An's guilt, the throne later would similarly stress the lack of respect for the king.

Reportedly afraid of retaliation, possibly against himself, the king ordered Yu T'ak, a senior general who had fought in China in 1354 and who enjoyed Kongmin's confidence, to greet An U outside the city walls. In an apparent effort to gauge An's intentions, Yu dropped to his knees in front of An and offered him a toast. When An attempted to raise Yu to his feet, Yu replied, "Your lordship has just restored Koryŏ." He refused to stand as an equal with An. An's humble behavior did not ease the king's worries. The next day on March 25, An returned in triumph to the capital and met with Kongmin in the king's temporary quarters. Instead of basking in the king's praise, however, An was harangued by Kongmin and beaten to death by the king's attendants.[174]

An's inert body was dragged from the courtyard. The *Official History of the Koryŏ Dynasty* insists that the king believed that An was not dead but simply unconscious. The king issued a pardon for An and the other leading military commanders. Although they had murdered Chŏng without authorization, he would spare them out of consideration for their service to the crown. Kongmin, however, accepted the recommendations of Kim Yong, Yu T'ak, and others that An had been disloyal and that Kim Tŭk-pae and Yi Pang-sil should be arrested immediately.

The two remaining leading military figures in the campaigns against the Red Turbans were quickly eliminated. On Kongmin's orders, Yi Pang-sil's uncle met him on his way to see the king. While Yi knelt in respect to hear the royal edict that his uncle claimed to hold, Yi was knocked unconscious by a sword-blow. Although Yi regained consciousness and even scaled the compound walls, his escape was brief.

He was hunted down and executed on royal orders. Learning the fates of his comrades, the fifty-year old Kim Tŭk-pae fled. The throne exiled his younger brother, imprisoned his wife, and interrogated his son-in-law. Kim was captured and put to death by beheading. His decapitated head was then displayed in Kim's hometown of Sangju as an example to others.[175]

Thus, within the span of a few weeks, four of the most powerful military commanders of the day, the men who regained the capital and saved the dynasty, were declared enemies of the state, executed, and, in Kim's case, ritually violated and publicly humiliated. Lesser military commanders associated with the four generals also faced considerable danger.[176] Although the *Official History of the Koryŏ Dynasty* lays much of the blame at Kim Yong's feet,[177] it seems likely that the beleaguered Kongmin had at least tacitly approved the intrigue as a way to eliminate potential challengers.[178]

To understand why the king was driven to such lengths, we should recall contemporary political and military conditions. Kongmin and a skeletal court were still in exile in the south, while the four commanders stood at the head of large, battle-tested forces whose loyalty to the king was never taken for granted. However much the king might regret the loss of proven military figures in later battles, the four commanders posed too great a threat to tolerate. With the ultimate victory over the Red Turbans seemingly assured, Chŏng, An, Yi, and Kim became expendable.

Chŏng especially had grown into a dangerously powerful military commander, whose arrogance some at court found insufferable. Many greeted news of Chŏng's death with a dry eye. Senior minister Hong Ŏn-bak commented, "When the Supreme Commander took command of the armies, he was extremely arrogant in word and mien. His misfortune was only to be expected."[179]

The official proclamation announcing An U's guilt in the assassination of Chŏng reveals several concerns. First, it dwells on the great powers granted to Chŏng during the Red Turban wars.

Soaring Eagle Senior General Chŏng Se-un was appointed Supreme Commander. [I] bestowed on him the symbols of command. He was to conduct affairs on My behalf. Repeatedly edicts were promulgated announcing why he had been appointed. All senior and junior generals were subject to his command, rendering them unwilling to dare to violate his orders.

鷹揚上將軍鄭世雲爲總兵官。賜之節越。代予行事。繼降敕書，宣示所以委任之意。大將小將並聽約束。俾無敢違。[180]

The military crisis had put wide powers of discretion and command in the hands of leading generals. The proclamation's explicit mention of this trend suggests that it weighed on the minds of Kongmin and his ministers. Later in the passage, concern with challenges to the king's authority is more plainly stated.

[An] U and the others relied on their meritorious service [in the wars] to become arrogant and overweening. They feuded with [Chŏng] Se-un. Not fearing the great law [of the land], they satisfied their passing fury. The Regional Commander conducted affairs on my behalf, but his subordinates dared to kill him without authorization. This is to deny me. . . . The relative weight [of An's merit and offenses] is clear.

祐等恃功驕恣。構釁世雲。不畏大法，以快一朝之憤。總兵官代予行事，而居下者敢擅殺之。是不有我也。...輕重灼然。[181]

Kongmin acknowledged An's great contribution during the war, "acting as the claws and teeth of the dynasty, fighting in blood for years." However, the edict noted, "the merit of destroying the enemy is momentary. If there is the crime of negating the ruler, it is something that cannot be forgiven in ten thousand generations" 破敵之功一時之所。或有無君之罪，萬世之所不能容. Put in slightly different terms, Chŏng was King Kongmin's surrogate. To kill Chŏng was to deny the king's authority. The way that Kongmin and his close advisors framed the problem, the murder of Chŏng constituted a direct attack on the king. An's crime was treasonous, little short of regicide.

Reactions to Kim Tŭk-pae's death reveal resentment over his unjust end. They also suggest why rivals at court might perceive him with trepidation. The Hallim scholar Chŏng Mong-ju 鄭夢周 (1337–91), Kim's student, secured permission from the throne to bury the corpse. He also wrote a eulogy:

In the past, the Red Turbans violated [our territory]. [Your Majesty] mounted [the royal] carriage and fled [to the south]. The fate of the dynasty hung by a thread. Only His Honor took the lead in advocating the great righteousness [of defending the dynasty]. People from far and wide responded. He himself formulated a plan to snatch victory from an impossible situation. He labored at the enterprise of saving Koryŏ. Whose meritorious service made it possible that people have food to eat and a place to sleep here?

Even if there were crimes, his merit should be allowed to offset them. If his crimes outweighed their merit, he should still have been persuaded to acknowledge his crimes before he was executed. Why, when the sweat of his horses was not yet dry and the songs of his triumphant return not yet still, was his enormous merit (as heavy as Mt. Tai) transformed into blood on a sharp sword? This is why I weep tears of blood and beseech Heaven. I know that his loyal soul and staunch spirit will live forever. He will undoubtedly resent [this injustice] in the netherworld. Alas, Fate. What can be done, what can be done?

往者紅寇闌入。乘輿播越。國家之命危如懸線。惟公首倡大義。遠近嚮應。身出萬死之計，克復三韓之業。凡今之人食於斯寢於斯，伊誰之功歟。雖有其罪以功掩之可也。罪重於功，必使歸服其罪，然後誅之可也。柰何汗馬未乾，凱歌未罷，使泰山之功轉爲鋒刃之血歟。此吾所以泣血而問於天者也。吾知其忠魂壯魄千秋萬歲必飲血於九泉之下。嗚呼，命也。如之何如之何。[182]

Ch'ong's formulation of Kim's deeds put the dynasty and the king in the fallen general's debt. It also posits charismatic authority that galvanized "people from near and far" in a moment of deep crisis. Such power constituted an incipient challenge to Kongmin's authority that required a response. Although the eulogy concludes with reference to Fate, Chŏng's accusation of royal ingratitude is unmistakable.

Snippets in the *Official History of the Koryŏ Dynasty* suggest that survivors from the fallen houses enjoyed a measure of popular sympathy. People showered gifts of food on the now-fatherless teenage sons of Yi and An as they begged in the streets. Those who helped the boys were mindful of the debt owed the generals: "That we can now sleep at night and eat three meals a day is because of the meritorious service of the Three Generals."[183]

The fate of the boys weighed on the king's mind as well. Kongmin learned that General An's son was seen standing by the side of the street sprinkling the ground with wine as an offering to his father.[184] "The king pitied the boy and summoned him to the palace [at this time still in Pokju], where Kongmin inquired about where [or how] the boy was going [to stay or for help]. [The king] sent him home.[185] The military officers panicked and fled. The king summoned [them] and granted [them] wine and food to recognize [their service]."

The puzzling incident was presumably intended to show King Kongmin's regret over An Yu's death by demonstrating his concern for An's son. Summoning the boy to the king's residence was a dramatic gesture of generosity, given that An had just been accused of murdering Kongmin's commanding general, Chŏng Se-un. The gesture was public. Kongmin did not discretely dispatch someone to ask after the boy and quietly send him home. Instead, the king granted him an audience, the content of which was known to Kongmin's military officers. The officers' reaction, panic and flight, is striking if mysterious. In any case, it suggests that the purge of the generals had created an atmosphere of heightened fear and uncertainty at Kongmin's court. Having killed a popular general, Kongmin felt compelled to offer help to his now-orphaned son and to somehow calm his skittish military officers.

The case of Yu Suk indirectly reveals the tensions between Kongmin and his generals and again suggests the tenor of uncertainty at the time. A senior official, Yu had coolly recommended abandoning the capital because its defenses were inadequate to withstand the Red Turbans. He had accompanied Kongmin to Pokju, where he counseled the king as a member of the Bureau of Military Affairs and the Hallim Academy. According to his biography in the *Official History of the Koryŏ Dynasty* and Yi Saek's eulogy, the generals had concluded that Yu must die. An Yu and his fellow commanders reasoned (presumably among themselves), "'[We] have already killed the Supreme Commander.' Then, [someone] further said. 'Yu is at the center [i.e., at the king's side]. He always comes up with unexpected stratagems. He is to be feared. [We] should remove him.'" 擅殺總兵官鄭世雲。則又曰。今既殺總兵官矣。柳某居中。每出奇謀。可畏也。去之便.[186] The generals and their advisors identified Yu with the king and expected retaliation for their actions.

Yu, too, apparently took for granted the dangers of royal association. When he learned of the generals' intentions, he immediately approached the king:

> All of them are enraged and difficult to handle. At present, the only reason that the generals hate your minister is merely because I am at Your Highness'

side. If your Highness were to expel me [from the court], your servant would be merely a commoner. Who [then] would bother with me?

衆怒難犯。今諸將忌臣者，徒以在殿下左右耳。殿下如逐臣，則臣一布衣耳，誰復齒牙間耶。[187]

The king obliged, appointing Yu regent of the Eastern Capital. Yu outlived the generals; he would also outlive Kongmin.

The Dynasty's Future

On March 21, 1362, five weeks after the recapture of Kaegyŏng, King Kongmin left Pokju.[188] He would not arrive in the dynastic capital for nearly a year. During the leisurely progress northward, the king and his retinue sojourned in more than a half a dozen localities. A visit from the king conferred great prestige; it also imposed considerable burdens. Magistrates strove to provide properly lavish accommodations while not unduly taxing local society.

Supporting the court had imposed a considerable burden on the local population of Pokju. In recognition of its efforts, the king upgraded Pokju's administrative status from subprefecture to prefecture and bestowed the title Grand Protectorate of Pacifying the East (*Andong taedo hobu* 安東大都護府). Kim Su-on 金守溫 (1410–81) would later write:

When King Kongmin of the previous dynasty fled the attack of the rebels and graced the south with his presence, he sojourned in this place. He ordered his generals out to do battle. When they recovered the capital in Kaegyŏng, he returned in his palanquin, restored to his rightful place. Because he formulated his grand plans here and was thus able to restore peace to the Great Eastern Kingdom, he bestowed the title Pacifying the East.

前朝恭愍王。避寇南幸。駐蹕是邑。命將出師。克復京城。城輿返正。以其訏謨定命於此。而能復安於大東。故賜號安東。

According to Kim, this new administrative status and royal recognition elevated Pokju to the foremost county of the south. It also led to posts in the highest levels of the government for successive generations for Pokju's leading families.[189] Paek Mun-bo was among many who drew attention to the tax exemptions the king granted Pokju in recognition of the subprefecture's importance during the dynasty's time of crisis.[190] The special administrative designation granted such places as

Pokju enhanced local elites' status without significantly decreasing their autonomy from the central government.[191]

The Koryŏ court's desire to publicly acknowledge Pokju's steadfast loyalty owed something to the fact that military personnel, local populations, court ministers, and even one member of the royal family surrendered to the Red Turbans. Additionally, as noted above, at least one field officer apparently joined the ranks of the Red Turban leaders. The administrative status of several localities in Yangkwang province 楊廣道 were downgraded because their residents had "been among the first to welcome and surrender to" the Red Turbans.[192]

In September 1362, the Censorate announced punishments for more than a half-dozen court officials and high-ranking military officers who had surrendered to the Red Turbans. Their progeny were taken into custody.[193] Although the Censorate excoriated the royal clansman (a grandson of King Ch'ungsŏn) for "abandoning the dynasty and forgetting his kin," it could only "beg that if he is pardoned, then his son be taken into custody and his lands and [subject] people be confiscated as a warning to [his] descendents."[194] There is no evidence that the order of confiscation was ever enforced. The court did invest his son with an aristocratic title before he fled to the Yuan court, where he took a post as a censor.

That a royal kinsman "surrendered" to the Red Turbans, however, does not mean that he betrayed the dynasty.[195] Given how suddenly King Kongmin had fled Kaegyŏng, it should be no surprise that even members of the Koryŏ elite fell into Red Turban hands. There is no evidence that the royal kinsman or other officials joined the Red Turbans. Behind the charges of abandoning the dynasty and royal family seems to be the assumption that the kinsman and court ministers should have fled more quickly, died fighting, or committed suicide. The real offense seems to have been that they were taken captive. This probably explains why, despite the Censorate's heated rhetoric, the king meted out relatively light punishments.

Confronted with evidence of how the Red Turban wars had touched even members of his court and the royal family, King Kongmin would fondly recall idyllic scenes of hunting and boating near the Yŏnghoru in Pokju. Perhaps at the prompting of his minister Yi Saek, the king brushed the calligraphy of the three-character name of the building.

According to Yi, who had accompanied the king to Pokju, the king observed that he "had relied on Andong; it was the place of my restoration." The royal calligraphy was then carved into a plaque to be hung from the front of the Yŏnghoru.[196] The local magistrate actually had to expand the hall before it could support the imposing new plaque.[197]

In the coming months and years, King Kongmin would face great dangers. Although he would later wax nostalgic about Pokju, in the spring of 1362, uncertainty was the leitmotif. Koryŏ forces had recaptured the capital at Kaegyŏng, but the dynasty's future was far from assured. Conditions throughout the country remained unsettled for several years. The bloody purge of Kongmin's generals was a very recent memory. The following year, the king would only narrowly escape an assassination attempt by a trusted official. At nearly the same time, the Yuan court would depose Kongmin and try to put its chosen successor on the throne at the point of a sword.

As people of the day struggled to make sense of Koryŏ's plight, some turned to Chinese history. As noted above, in his report to the throne, General Chŏng had alluded to one of the great events in East Asian history, the 755 An Lushan Rebellion. For centuries, the image of Emperor Xuanzong of the Tang dynasty fleeing the capital at Chang'an in the face of a massive military uprising by a powerful military general stationed along the northeastern border, An Lushan, would retain enormous rhetorical power. The revolt was a watershed event for the Tang court, which never regained full control of the empire. Chŏng raised this specter of dynastic crisis in order to underscore the enormity of his service. He had pulled Koryŏ back from the abyss.

One of the most prestigious and senior officials of the day, Yi Chehyŏn, had earlier invoked the An Lushan rebellion to quite different effect. During the flight from the capital, Yi had gained an audience with King Kongmin in Sangju 尚州. Yi "wiped tears from his eyes and sighed, '[The court] has been driven from the capital. How is this any different from Xuanzong and the An Lushan rebellion?'"[198] For Yi, the dynasty's future was far less assured than Chŏng had suggested.

In any case, the first step to recovery was to return to the capital.

6
In the Wake of the Invasions

Recovery from the Red Turban incursions was slow and uncertain. Years of fighting in Liaoyang took their toll on the local population and economy. In the words of one Ming-period source, "During the late Yuan, warfare wrought havoc [on the region]. Residents scattered and fled. The counties and commanderies of Liaoyang were reduced to weeds and brambles. Those who survived were as if [on the brink of death by] fire or drowning."[1] Indulging in a degree of hyperbole, the editors of the *Official History of the Koryŏ Dynasty* observed, "Not even ruins from the palace in the capital remained. The streets were in ruins. Whitened bones [of the dead] stood in piles [on the streets]."[2] The rebels partially destroyed the royal complex located at the foot of Mt. Aksan 岳山, five *li* north of the densely settled city proper.[3] The Yŏn'gyŏng Palace 延慶宮, where Yuan envoys had so recently been fêted by the king and queen, where important Buddhist rituals were conducted, and where the king himself resided at least briefly, suffered considerable damage. The damage was never to be repaired.[4] For the remainder of the dynasty, Koryŏ kings instead were to reside in the Such'ang Palace 壽昌宮, located inside the Lesser Western Gate.[5] However, given that succeeding Koryŏ kings made use of such places as the Polo Field (Kuchŏng 毬庭), it seems likely that much, perhaps most, of the royal complex's physical plant survived the Red Turbans.

Court Recovery

If most royal palaces weathered the storm, critical facets of court life were profoundly disturbed by the recent warfare. Perhaps the greatest ritual loss suffered during the pell-mell flight from the capital was the disappearance of the spirit tablets of four Koryŏ kings, including those of the founder and Kongmin's father and grandfather, from the Royal Ancestral Temple. These tablets formed a critical part of the royal cult of filial piety; during official state ceremonies royal ancestors were honored with sacrifices and rituals. It was an important way to remember that Kongmin's power and legitimacy originated with his ancestors, to whom he owed a debt of respect and veneration. During his flight from Kaegyŏng, Kongmin had visited two temples that housed portraits of the Koryŏ founder, perhaps seeking strength and guidance in a time of chaos and distress.[6] The loss of the spirit tablets, as the physical markers of his ancestors, was thus a major event and could be read as a sign of dynastic, or at least Kongmin's personal, decline. After Kongmin returned to Kaegyŏng, the spirit tablets were temporarily placed in the Amitabha Temple (Mit'asa 彌陀寺), located near Sŭngin Gate 崇仁門. Replacements for the missing spirit tablets were completed shortly thereafter.[7]

In June 1363, Kongmin wrote in a royal proclamation that "among the great matters of state, sacrifice [to the ancestors] is the most important." Acknowledging that because of the recent unrest, many of the ritual vessels and robes had been lost, he ordered their speedy restoration. The king's royal carriage (*sangnak* 象輅) transported the dynastic founder's spirit tablet back to the Royal Ancestral Temple in Kaegyŏng, and a lesser vehicle (*p'yŏngnak* 平輅) conveyed the remaining tablets. Reflecting the court's continuing disarray, among those officials accompanying the king during the transfer, only forty managed to appear in complete court regalia.[8] The king also ordered the reconstruction of an adjoining pavilion to honor meritorious ministers.[9]

The transfer of the tablets represented something of a ritual challenge. The king, still not yet back in Kaegyŏng, grew infuriated when his officials were slow to provide the necessary historical precedents. The man supervising the specially created bureau devoted to the restoration of the spirit tablets to the capital, Paek Mun-bo, explained that they lacked adequate records at hand to formulate a proper response. A court historian was sent to the Haein Historical Repository 海印史庫 to retrieve a copy of *The Three Ritual Classics, Illustrated* (*Sanlitu* 三禮圖) and Du You's 杜祐 (735–812) classic compendium on governmental and ritual institutions, *Tongdian* 通典. Paek based his recommendations on material found in these written sources as well as information gleaned from elderly caretakers from the royal mausoleums. Simple incompetence further slowed progress. Paek complained that one of the officials involved in the project was illiterate and simply guessed at what he was supposed to be reading.[10]

These were hard times for the people of Koryŏ, including residents of Kaegyŏng. Working through a regency government that oversaw the capital's recovery in his absence, the king took measures to restore order and control, settling refugees and directing relief efforts. Early in May 1362, the court issued 10,000 piculs of grain from the Dragon Gate Granary (Yongmunch'ang 龍門倉) as "relief loans" to the starving in the Capital Region.[11] The next month, the court acknowledged popular discontent over the government's slow and unfair judicial findings (presumably regarding reconstruction matters, but no details survive). In response, Paek Mun-bo proposed pardons, lighter sentences, and quicker decisions.[12] Yet at the same time that the court made magnanimous gestures, it demanded higher taxes to cope with the costs of reconstruction. During the fall of 1362, it levied the new "endless rice" (*mudanmi* 無端米) surtax on the people because "[taxes and supplies] were not forthcoming."[13]

The physical destruction wrought by the Red Turbans required a range of government responses. Established late in 1362, a special administrative bureau strictly enforced the ban on butchering horses and cows, which the Red Turbans had "nearly all killed" during their occupation of Kaegyŏng.[14] The decaying corpses that lay scattered in the capital and its environs were another poignant reminder of the recent carnage visited on the region. As late as spring 1363, the court was still paying men to collect and bury these bodies—three meals a day and one bolt of fabric for every five days of work.[15] Later the same spring, the king ordered regional officials to prevent royal armies from damaging agricultural fields during their marches.[16] No evidence of the order's efficacy survives.

The famed poet Chinese Gao Qi 高啓 (1336–74) provides an unexpected window on conditions in Koryŏ in wake of the fighting. Gao poignantly describes the sad fate of two Koryŏ girls in his "Song of Korean Children."

Korean children, 朝鮮兒
Their lustrous black hair just cut,
Even with their eyebrows. 髮綠初剪齊雙眉
At the evening banquet, they emerge,
Singing and dancing together. 芳筵夜出對歌舞
Cotton and soft furs,
Copper earrings hanging. 木綿裘軟銅鐶垂
Lithe bodies spin and turn,
High voices rise and fall. 輕身回旋細喉轉
[Like] shimmering moons or swaying flowers,
[They] appear to me in my intoxication. 蕩月搖花醉中見
Their foreign songs,
What need is there to ask the translator. 夷語何須問譯人
With deep emotions they speak,
Of the sorrow of leaving home. 深情知訴離鄉怨
When the song ends, they walk over,
To offer greetings to the guests. 曲終舉足拜客前
Like a crow caws in a tree beside the well,
The lights go up. 烏啼井樹蠟燈然
Everyone is amazed [that the girls hail from] Xuantu,
Separated by clouds and sea. 共訝玄菟隔雲海
How did the children,
Come to be here? 兒今到此是何緣
Their master told me,
He once went on a distant envoy mission. 主人爲言曾遠使
Ten thousand *li* with good weather,
We arrived in three days. 萬里好風三日至
Deer walked through the ruins of the palace,
In the wake of rebel predations. 鹿走荒宮亂寇過
Chickens squawked in the deserted hostel station,
I stayed the night. 鷄鳴廢館行人次
In the fourth month the king's city,
Scant wheat stalks. 四月王城麥熟稀
The children walked along the road,
The two crying with hunger. 兒行道路兩啼饑

I purchased them with gold and silver,
  Spending everything I had. 黃金擲買傾裝得
I divided gruel among them,
  We returned by boat. 白飲分餐趂舶歸
I remember the eastern vassal,
  When it submitted to us. 我憶東藩內臣日
Its tribute women are now imperial consorts (or empress),
  Wearing the ceremonial gown of the empress. 納女椒房被褘翟
This tune probably,
  Also circulates at the Jiaofang in the palace. 教坊此曲亦應傳
They attended the emperor on his outings,
  Pleasure day and night. 特奉宸遊樂朝夕
In recent years, the Central Kingdom,
  Rebels remained unchecked. 中國年來亂未鋤
All at once foreign envoy missions,
  Were unable to come to court. 頓令貢使入朝無
The Heir Apparent is happy still,
  To reside in Lingwu. 儲皇尚說居靈武
The high minister plots,
  To survey Xudu [Xuchang 許昌] [as a capital]. 丞相方謀卜許都
By the side of the palace moat,
  Several willow trees. 金水河邊幾株柳
Do they still blow in the spring breezes,
  Unharmed? 依舊春風無恙否
Today's encounter,
  Made me recall past times of peace. 小臣撫事憶昇平
I cry in front of my wine cup,
  More tears than drink.[17] 尊前淚瀉多於酒

Gao remarked in a brief explanatory note that the poem was written after visiting the residence of a certain Proofreader Zhou (Zhou Jianjiao 周檢校), which was almost certainly in Nanjing, China. As Chen Gaohua has argued, this Proofreader Zhou had traveled as an envoy for the powerful Chinese warlord Zhang Shicheng to Koryŏ, where he purchased the abandoned children.[18] The chaos and economic depression limned in the poem depict conditions in Koryŏ in the wake of the Red Turban incursions.

The poem is also a reminder that whether they represented Chinese warlords, Mongol generals, or the Yuan imperial family, envoys brought back news, and in this case living examples, of the unsettled conditions on the peninsula. The intricate network of economic, political, cultural, and military ties that bound Northeast Asia held through the increasingly turbulent decades of the mid-fourteenth century (see Chapter 8).

Koryŏ Countryside

Only scarce information regarding the impact of the Red Turban incursions on the countryside survives. Confucian scholar and Minister of Revenue Yi Tal-ch'ung 李達衷 (1309–85) composed a pair of undated poems, entitled "The Country Wife's Lament," which evoke the quiet desperation and depressed conditions caused by the fighting in rural areas.

Endless rain for weeks at a time,
  It has been long since she lit the fires of the hearth. 霖雨連旬久未炊
The wheat in front of her door,
  Just now rich and full. 門前小麥正離離
Waiting for the sky to clear, she wants to cut the grain.
  The sky clears only to return to rain. 待晴欲刈晴還雨
Those who eat their fill are put to work at corvée labor,
  A full stomach easily grows hungry. 課飽爲傭飽易飢

Her husband dead at the hands of the Red Turbans,
  Her son garrisoned on the border. 夫死紅軍子戎邊
Alone, she ekes out a precarious living.
  Her pole inserted in the earth, 一身生理正蕭然
A bamboo hat on her head.
  As she bends to gather the rice, sparrows alight
  on its top. 插竿冠笠雀登頂
As she shoulders her basket,
  A butterfly brushes her shoulder.[19] 拾穗擔筐蛾撲肩

The poems suggests that despite the absence of a standing central army, the Red Turban wars drew a portion of the male population out of Koryŏ's villages, whether they were casualties of war or men recruited to bolster defenses.

A pair of poems by the eremitic scholar Wŏn Ch'ŏn-sŏk 元天錫 (1330–?) strikes a different if still dark tone. In contrast to Yi, Wŏn stressed the steadfastness and social stability of Koryŏ society shown in the face of the Red Turban invasions. Wŏn, however, then contrasted the image of strength and confidence in crisis with the anxiety of more inescapable dangers—the unsettled accounts at the end of the year and the threat of losing one's lands. The poem may allude to the temporary economic dislocations caused by the Red Turban incursions, but it also speaks to the difficulties of everyday life.

Throughout the land, Wind-blown dusts [of battle] exceed years past.	匝地風塵勝去年
What quarter was not in tumult?	四方何處不騷然
If our dynasty stands firm like a rock, Protecting our livelihoods.	我邦若固盤安業
Heaven will allow these people, To sleep in peace.	天使斯民奠安眠
New Year has come upon everyone unaware,	人皆不覺到新年
Haggard from laboring, a touch of frustration.	醉事劬勞幾悵然
They change with times, the affairs of men.	與世推移男子事
Could they worry that there is nowhere they can sleep in peace?[20]	莫憂無地可安眠

Wŏn was not alone in his concerns about Koryŏ society in the wake of the Red Turban incursions. How much he knew of the people's hardships is unclear, but lingering disorder prompted Paek Mun-bo to extol the virtues of the ancient Chinese sage-kings Yao and Shun and the Chinese *Six Classics* as a way to restore harmony within the kingdom and the cosmos.[21] During the summer of 1362, Paek tried to contextualize Koryŏ's recent turbulence in cosmic terms and argued that the dynasty stood poised on the cusp of a new age. He noted that the numerical categories of Heaven (K. *ch'ŏnsu*, Ch. *tianshu* 天數) were cyclical, with 700 years constituting a Minor Origin of a cycle (K. *sosu*, Ch. *xiaoshu* 小元) and 3,600 years forming a Great Complete Origin of a new cycle (K. *taejusu*, Ch. *da zhouyuan* 大周元).[22] It had been 3,600 years since Tangun had founded Korea, observed Paek. To secure Heaven's protection, the proper movement of Yin and Yang, and the dynasty's longevity at this critical juncture, it was essential that the court reject Buddhism and lend its full support to Neo-Confucianism.[23] There is little evidence that Paek's rhetoric curtailed court patronage of Buddhism.

The Red Turban warfare exacerbated existing economic and political problems in the countryside. In the immediate wake of the fighting,

Kongmin had issued a royal proclamation: "Due to the recent military campaigns, the people are not settled in their livelihoods. Court officials great and small have taken refuge from the fighting in the provinces. [There] they seize lands and exploit the people for their own advantage. The people's livelihood has grown more arduous."[24] Kongmin was aware that warfare had further eroded the royal infrastructure. In mid-1363, he issued an edict noting that recent fighting had worsened the decrepitude of the kingdom's postal relay stations. Particularly disturbing was the illegal seizure of the lands and their revenues set aside to support the upkeep of the stations. He ordered investigations, the restoration of lands, and three-year exemptions for certain kinds of taxes for postal station households in the north.[25]

As John Duncan and others have noted, however, the fight to regain control of the kingdom's resources produced few victories for king and court. In 1388, King U would again prohibit "the powerful" from illegally seizing postal relay station lands.[26] The Red Turban war exacerbated but did not cause weak royal authority over lands and people outside the capital.

Another dimension to the king's efforts to restore harmony was gaining support among at least a portion of his military. Chŏng's assassination and the purge of three other major generals made plain how freighted this issue had become. In mid-April 1362, the king hosted a great state banquet at his temporary palace in honor of those officers who had fought against the Red Turbans.[27] A year later, labor obligations to the state were partially waived for surviving members of military households that had lost men during the war.[28]

Restoring administrative order proved difficult. In mid-September 1362, the Capital Regency Censorate reported that, because of the destruction caused by the recent fighting, "The people have fled and scattered, and the alleys are in ruins. Those who have returned scatter and settle according to false rumors [that circulate throughout the city.]" This was largely due, it was thought, to the provinces' failure to submit tribute and taxes. "Thus," the censorate wrote, "people have nothing upon which to fix, and spurious rumors remain unrefuted. Things grow more desperate each day. I beg that all taxes be submitted to the capital in accord with established practice." The censorate did not elaborate on the perceived connection between stability and taxes. The extant version of the document offers no specifics about how to ensure the flow of taxes into royal coffers. The censorate requested that with the exception of the royal bodyguard, all other officials accompanying the king should return to the capital.[29]

The king's continuing absence slowed the capital's recovery. Late in January 1363, his advisors opined, "The capital is the site of the Royal Ancestral Temple and the root of the dynasty. Your Majesty should return quickly to assure the people."[30] As noted above, six months later in May 1363, many officials still refused to return to the capital.[31] In June, the king again expressed his gratitude for his officials' assistance during the Red Turbans crisis but urged them to resume their duties and "not merely go through motions."[32] Drought compounded the king's difficulties.[33]

Victory over the Red Turbans did not fundamentally change long-term political trends within Koryŏ. The king's inability to order his officials back to Kaegyŏng reflected the limitations of the throne's power. Political rivalry also continued after fighting with the Red Turbans ended. Lingering resentment over what some considered the humiliating defeat at the hands of the Red Turbans provided grist for the political mill. In September 1361, one official blasted senior minister Hong Ŏn-bak: "The chaotic flight to the south in 1361; the loss of the ancestral altars to the enemy; the disgrace of His Highness's exile; they have become an object of ridicule throughout the realm. [These were all because] Your Excellency did not make plans in advance." Now that Hong's son and son-in-law occupied key military and administrative posts, "How could this," the official asked, "not cause the dynasty concern?"[34] Hong's defenders maintained that he had formulated the military strategy for the recovery of the capital.[35]

Other matters proved less contentious. The court was quick to offer thanks for the intercession of the gods. The Koryŏ government had sought supernatural aid throughout these years of invasion and turmoil. Early in January 1360, offerings were made to deities of mountains and streams throughout Koryŏ for their assistance against the Red Turbans.[36] That March, sacrifices were made to the Gods of the City Wall and Moats in gratitude for their help in the war effort. During the tenth lunar month of 1361, offerings were made for the military victory at the altars for deities of rivers, mountains, and stars (*kunmang* 群望).[37] King

Kongmin had established a military shrine (*toksa* 纛祠) when his armies were about to march against the Red Turbans.[38] Sacrifices were offered the first and fifteen day of each lunar month before the temple was abolished in 1377 for reasons of unspecified corruption.[39]

The destruction wrought by the Red Turban invasions would exercise a lasting influence on Koryŏ's administrative, legal, and historical records. During the twelfth lunar month of 1371, nearly a decade after the last Red Turbans had left Koryŏ, the king complained that most household registration records had been lost during the flight from the capital. He ordered that new registers be compiled.[40] One wonders what officials had been using as a basis for tax and corvée during the intervening years. In 1392, one official noted, "during the winter of 1361, the rebels sacked the capital city and almost all public and private documents were lost."[41] In the absence of accurate legal records, he charged, the unscrupulous fabricated land deeds 許文. In contrast, when it was advantageous, those who held original documents claimed that they had been lost during the chaos. In order to impose a degree of order, the court ordered that "henceforth, those without clear documentation for litigation from 1361 shall not be permitted to file suits."[42]

The loss of household registration and deeds of ownership related to slaves that occurred during the Red Turban invasions would be felt for decades to come. Well into the fifteenth century, Chosŏn officials would use the Red Turban fighting of 1361 as an important benchmark for a variety of measures designed to limit litigation related to the contested ownership of slaves. The basic reasoning was that the records before 1361 had been lost and that, except for those who could demonstrate clear proof of ownership, officials would not process litigation claims.[43] However, one should not conclude that the problem of slave litigation was new in 1361, no more than one should attribute all land flight or rural poverty to the fighting as some nearly contemporaneous observers sometimes implied. Slaves constituted an integral part of the socioeconomic foundation of the Koryŏ and Chosŏn dynasties, and throughout the fourteenth century, the Koryŏ court established special bureaus to process such litigation related to status, ownership, sale, and donation of slaves.[44] The Red Turban invasion of 1361 became a convenient benchmark for late Koryŏ and early Chosŏn officials to delimit what they often described as endless and, from the state's point of view, profitless litigation.

Historical documents, too, suffered grave damage during the invasions. Rushing to preserve at least a portion of dynastic records before the Red Turbans seized Kaegyŏng, officials in the Bureau of History managed to bury some of their materials. Perhaps in a search for buried valuables, the invaders apparently found them. When Koryŏ forces retook the capital, soldiers disposed carelessly of surviving records they happened upon.[45]

Late in October 1362, the Capital Regency (*Yudo chae-ch'u* 留都宰樞, the first- and second-grade officials of the Secretariat-Chancellery and the junior second-grade officials of the Security Council)[46] reported to the crown that the Royal History Archives had been destroyed in the wake of the Red Turban occupation. The *Veritable Records*, chronologically arranged accounts of the kingdom's major events of each ruler's reign based on official documents, "lay scattered and exposed on the ground." Normally, only the king and select ministers were allowed to consult the *Veritable Records* since they contained detailed information on the court and affairs of state. An official was assigned to collect and store these records.[47] During the ninth lunar month, the Capital Regency Censorate had already notified the court of the parlous condition of the draft histories for the *Veritable Records*, which had been temporarily relocated to the Temple of Confucius. Warning that without prompt action the records might be lost forever, the Censorate had requested that court historians air out the materials (only "three cabinets and a dozen or so boxes" survived) in preparation for more permanent storage. The Censorate also requested that armed guards be posted.[48] Plans to relocate surviving records to the archives at Haein Temple 海印寺 were eventually rejected; conditions in the wake of the loss and recapture of the capital were deemed too unsettled.[49]

One source claims that only one-fifth of the dynastic records (*kukjŏn* 國典) were ever recovered after the chaos of the Red Turban invasions.[50] Before the Red Turban incursions, the well-known scholar-officials Yi Che-hyŏn, Paek Mun-bo, and Yi Tal-ch'ung had begun preparation of a chronicle of the Koryŏ dynasty arranged by reign period. During the evacuation of the capital and the flight to the south, their notes and initial drafts were lost. Only Yi Che-hyŏn's account of the founder's reign survived.[51]

It is not clear what toll the Red Turban campaigns took on the king. Driven from his capital, he believed at times that he would never return. He clearly felt that the flight had entailed hardship for his beloved wife, Queen Noguk. In the funerary inscription for his wife's tomb in the eastern foothills close by Unamsa Temple 雲巖寺 (located near Kongmin's own tomb), the king recalled that while in Daidu, they had "experienced both the bitter and the sweet." He then turned to the difficulties they had encountered, singling out the Red Turbans—"When we returned east [to Koryŏ], we had to again put down revolts. In 1361 the Red Turban rebels attacked the capital, and we fled to the south."[52]

During his slow progress from Pokju to Kaegyŏng, Kongmin continued many of his customary activities. In May 1362 (at the same time that government granaries were supplying grain to the starving in Kaegyŏng), the king watched archery contests and other entertainers near the Western Gate of Sangju, distributing 50 bolts of fabric as a token of his beneficence.[53] A week later, the king practiced his archery at the Southern Tower and ordered his close ministers to play polo for his divertissement.[54] Both archery and polo had been regular parts of Kongmin's life before his flight from Kaegyŏng.

Pecuniary worries followed Kongmin to the south. Prime Minister Hong informed the king that the court's silver and gold were dangerously depleted and that Kongmin's expenditures were "unrestrained." "What," asked Hong accusingly, "is to be done about the royal fisc?" Kongmin stared at Hong without uttering a word. The king's silence infuriated Hong, a senior minister who had secured key posts for his son and son-in-law and who was related to the king through Kongmin's mother. Once he withdrew, Hong exclaimed, "What sort of arrogance is this not to adopt my proposals!" Yi Che-hyŏn, an even more senior minister, was more sympathetic to the king's plight. He, too, had suffered through similar reactions by the king, but Yi's response was pity for his sovereign.[55]

During his years away from the capital, the king interacted more closely (however unintentionally) with his subjects than he would have in the royal palace. In mid-October 1362, unaware of the rider's identity, pedestrians in the streets of Sangju accosted the king at least twice while he practiced his nocturnal equestrian skills incognito.[56] The king's secret outings were not new; late in August, he had begun slipping out the city's Western Gate to improve his mounted archery.[57] In fact, the king established a special bureau of mounted archery in 1362.[58] Recent warfare had demonstrated the importance of cavalry forces, whether deployed on behalf of the dynasty or the king.

After leaving the relative security of Sangju early in September, the king and his party were more vulnerable. Downpours struck the postal relay station at Wŏn'am 元岩; the rains soaked their tents, and several members of the entourage died in the flooding.[59] Days later, flooding was so severe that the king ordered that ten boats be constructed so that he could continue northward along an alternate route.[60]

Given the entourage's atrocious behavior, locals were probably eager to see the king's men on their way as soon as possible. During their sojourn in Sangju, the king's entourage stayed in the homes of local residents. Many guests reportedly took advantage of their status to violate the wives, concubines, sons, and daughters of their hosts. When the party arrived at Ch'ŏngju 清州 in mid-September 1362, the king had to issue orders forbidding residents from fleeing. Few listened.[61] Most were probably relieved to learn that Ch'ŏngju had been considered but rejected as the new site of the capital. Officials in the Censorate argued that it was cramped and too vulnerable to the coastal raiding of Japanese pirates.[62]

In January 1363, the king and his advisors decided that until repairs to Kang'an Hall 康安殿, the king's principal living quarters in the royal compound, were complete, Kongmin would stay at Hŭngwang Temple 興王寺, located south of the capital.[63] A new administrative bureau was specially created to oversee his temporary residence.[64] During January and February, the king slowly made his way northward, stopping every few days.[65]

On March 3, 1363, nearly fifteen months after the Red Turban incursions had driven Kongmin out of Kaegyŏng, the king returned to the capital, or at least its southern suburb.[66] Officials greeted their sovereign at his new apartments in Hŭngwang Temple. Days later, the king remarked to the Capital Regency *chae-ch'u*, "I did not dream that I would be able to return to the capital city. I owe it all to the efforts of my ministers."[67] In his new "temporary palace," the king hosted banquets at the temple for his court ministers,[68] held Buddhist services,[69] and when the weather was good, enjoyed outings to nearby scenic spots.[70] His stay south of the capital, however, was not always so idyllic.

On April 15, 1363, the ambitious Kim Yong, a senior official and longtime supporter of Kongmin, attempted to kill the king.[71] Fifty of Kim's men attacked the king's temporary quarters at the temple. Putting the royal bodyguard to flight (collusion or mere incompetence?), they killed one eunuch attendant and several officials.[72] The king owed his escape to his eunuchs. As the assassins made their way to the king's sleeping quarters, one eunuch carried the king out on his back. Another eunuch who resembled the king pretended to be his lord. Kim's men cut down the stand-in.[73] The king escaped by hiding in the queen dowager's quarters. His Mongol wife sat in the doorway of this room, preventing the soldiers from entering.[74] Although willing to commit regicide, the assassins balked at harming a member of Mongolian aristocracy. From his hiding spot, the king overheard snippets of the assassins' conversation. Several of Kongmin's most senior ministers officials were already dead.[75]

Although the details are unclear, General Ch'oe Yŏng 崔瑩 (1316–88) and royal troops from the capital saved the king from further harm.[76] The grateful king quickly announced rewards for all those even slightly involved in his rescue and exiled the officers responsible for the royal bodyguards' dismal performance.[77] Kim himself was arrested, exiled, and eventually executed for his crimes.[78] Like so many developments in Koryŏ, Kim's abortive coup was closely tied to the political imperatives of the Yuan court (see Chapter 7).

Liaodong in the Wake of the Red Turban Invasions

Even as the Koryŏ court attempted to restore order within its borders, the lingering threat of the Red Turbans involved the Koreans with the Daidu court and local Mongol commanders. Late in April 1362, the Mongol Gaojianu, the associate administrator of the Liaoyang Branch Secretariat (*Liaoyang xingsheng tongzhi* 遼陽行省同知), clashed with remnants of the Red Turbans moving northward from Koryŏ.[79] He claimed to have killed more than 4,000 men in battle and to have captured the rebel leader Cracked-Head Pan. Gaojianu informed the Koryŏ court of his victory.[80] In mid-June, Gaojianu dispatched an additional envoy to the Koryŏ court, this time to request troops for further engagements with the Red Turban forces.[81]

In mid-September 1362, the Yuan court dispatched Hindu 忻都, an Academician Reader-in-waiting (*shidu xueshi* 侍讀學士) from the Academy of Scholarly Worthies in Daidu to bestow raiment and wine on Kongmin on the occasion of his victory over the Red Turbans. Hindu relayed the emperor's message that Koryŏ forces were to cooperate with Gaojianu in a pincer attack against the Red Turbans in the region between Gaizhou 蓋州 and Haizhou 海州 in southern Liaodong.[82] The Koryŏ court had been closely following the progress of the Red Turbans. Kongmin had recently dispatched diplomatic personnel to Liaoyang to secure the latest intelligence regarding the Red Turbans' strength and location.[83]

Perhaps as a result of the Yuan's urging and their own intelligence reports, late in September 1362, Kongmin ordered a joint Yuan-Koryŏ attack on the Red Turbans. The king appointed one of his most senior and trusted ministers, Yu T'ak, to oversee the northwestern forces. During the 1350s, Yu had commanded coastal myriarchies and later had fought under the Mongol Toqto'a against Chinese rebels. At this time, Kongmin appointed a dozen other men to head provincial defenses.[84] Before the armies set forth, however, Yuan forces apparently defeated the Red Turbans, and the king canceled the appointments.[85]

Although Koryŏ's borders had been secured, Liaodong's troubles continued. In mid-January 1363, Daning in western Liaodong fell yet again to Red Turbans forces.[86] The chronology is slightly unclear, but Chinese sources note that during "spring" of the same year, remnants of Master Guan's forces had left Koryŏ, sacked Shangdu once again, and suffered defeat at the hands of a Mongol commander, who eventually induced them to surrender.[87] Master Guan's survivors had to have crossed Liaodong to reach Shangdu; it seems safe to assume that their passage occasioned at least minor chaos.

The Shangdu palaces were never repaired, and the century-long tradition of dual capitals under the Yuan came to an end.[88] In time, the sack of Shangdu assumed greater significance. Noting that "for hundreds of miles around Shangdu, Red Turban forces were everywhere," one observer writing slightly later cast the loss of the imperial palace in the north as a portent of the dynasty's final collapse.[89]

For the fleeing Toghan-Temür, the ruins left by the Red Turbans were a harsh reminder of how dramatically the world had changed. In his memoir of the seventeen months following the Yuan court's flight from Daidu, *A Personal Account of the Emperor's Northern Tour* 北巡私記, the Chinese official Liu Ji 劉佶 noted that in September 1368, after the Yuan emperor and his relatively small entourage had abandoned Daidu and were traveling north to Shangdu, they passed through Juyong Pass. Built at great expense early during Toghan-Temür's reign to revitalize Mongol rule, Juyong Pass was an inspired declaration of imperial rule, carved in stone, proclaimed in six languages, and buttressed with Buddhist notions of rulership. Less than three decades later, it may have seemed more a tribute to hubris than optimism. Evidence of the destruction by the Red Turban forces was everywhere. As Liu remarked, "The roads were desolate. There was not a single soldier at the pass. When His Majesty's carriage arrived, neither were there any provisions for his meal. The emperor sighed deeply, saying, 'If I had not left the capital, how would I have known that things outside [the capital] stood like this.'"[90]

Gaojianu maintained relations with Kongmin's court after the Red Turbans ceased to threaten Koryŏ soil. Late in 1362, he presented the king with four head of lamb and a request for the hand of a Koryŏ maiden. Gaojianu's attentions were not unrequited; King Kongmin gave him the daughter of a Korean bureaucrat.[91] Late in 1366, as head of the Liaoyang Branch Secretariat, Gaojianu sent Kongmin sparrow hawks, a kind of hunting bird.[92] A few months later, Gaojianu sent envoys bearing hunting hounds.[93] Gaojianu would continue to be a critical actor in the northeast for the next several decades, first as a supporter of the Yuan court and later as a broker in relations between the fledgling Ming dynasty and the Koryŏ court.[94]

Chinese sources from the Ming period indicate that the unsettled conditions of the late Yuan, especially the Red Turban war, opened the way for Gaojianu's rise as a warlord. In a pattern common elsewhere in the Great Yuan *ulus* during the mid-fourteenth century, Gaojianu began by organizing local populations and building mountain fortresses. According to these sources, these men formed the core of Gaojianu's military forces that captured Cracked-Head Pan.[95] It is not clear whether Gaojianu received his position as associate administrator in the Liaoyang Branch Secretariat for his service against the Red Turbans, as is sometimes claimed. In any case, he owed his prominence and influence with the Yuan court to the turbulence in the northeast.

After Toghan-Temür's flight to the steppe in 1368, Gaojianu's independence grew. He used the military forces he commanded against the Red Turbans in Liaodong in order to resist the growing Ming threat. During the early 1370s, he took refuge in several mountainous regions near Liaoyang, rebuffing Ming overtures for surrender.[96] In 1372 he and Naghachu raided Koryŏ territory bordering Liaodong.[97] However, like scores of Yuan commanders in the northeast, he eventually succumbed to the Ming court (which offered promises of official position, recognition of his leadership over subordinate populations, the possibility of settlement in the capital, and generous gifts in cash and textiles), traveling to Nanjing in early summer 1372 to acknowledge Zhu Yuanzhang as the holder of the Mandate of Heaven.[98]

In 1376 Gaojianu employed the Red Turban wars in his efforts to mend fences with the Koryŏ court. Recalling their cooperation against the Red Turbans, he said, "I jointly formulated plans with Bayan-Temür [King Kongmin] to kill Sha Liuer and Cracked-Head Pan. At that time, nearly all the officials in the royal capital [of Kaegyŏng] had faith in me."[99] Gaojianu tried to use past military collaboration against the Red Turbans to bolster his new role as a broker between the Ming and Koryŏ courts.[100]

The emergence of the Mongol general Naghachu (d. 1388) as the most powerful military figure in Liaodong may similarly be traced to the Red Turban wars. Koryŏ court annals go so far as to suggest that he essentially wrested his position from a weakened Yuan court. "During the military fighting of the late Yuan, the barbarian caitiff Naghachu, based on his possession of the Shenyang region, was called [or called himself] head of the branch secretariat (*xing sheng cheng xiang* 行省丞相)."[101] By the late 1360s, Naghachu was the most important Mongol commander in Liaodong. He played a prominent role in the region's military and political developments (including relations between the Ming and the Koryŏ dynasties) until his surrender to the Chinese in 1387.[102]

Naghachu proved a more threatening presence for King Kongmin's court (and later the Ming dynasty) than Gaojianu. Late in March 1362, Koryŏ forces in the northeast repeatedly clashed with Naghachu, who defeated them handily. In response, the king dispatched Yi Sŏng-gye (and one assumes his personal military forces).[103] During the seventh lunar month of 1362, the court received reports that Naghachu and "several tens of thousands of troops" had encamped near Hongwŏn 洪原 (present-day Hamgyŏng).

At Naghachu's side was Cho So-saeng, the former commanding officer of the Ssangsŏng Directorate-General, who had been driven out of the city in July 1356 when King Kongmin's troops reasserted the Koryŏ court's control of the region (see Chapter 3). Korean chronicles claim a great victory for the future founder of the Chosŏn dynasty in these battles: "[The invading forces] were almost completely annihilated; they abandoned an enormous amount of armor and weapons."[104]

Midway through the fighting, Naghachu claimed that his incursion into Koryŏ territory had been inadvertent, resulting from his single-minded pursuit of the Red Turban leaders Sha Liuer, Master Guan, and Cracked-Head Pan. "It was not [my intent]," stressed Naghachu, "to invade your honorable border."[105] Such chronicles as the *Official History of the Koryŏ Dynasty* and the *Abridged History of the Koryŏ Dynasty* view Naghachu's explanation with deep skepticism, noting, "the dynastic founder [Yi Sŏng-gye] was aware of his duplicity."[106] As dubious as they may have been about Naghachu's claims, imminent incursions by the Red Turbans were in fact reported by the army commander of the northwest (*sŏ'buk pyŏngmasa* 西北兵馬使) at approximately this time (late in July).[107] Naghachu on occasion presented a more genial face to the Koreans. During the fall of 1367, Naghachu sent envoys with a gift of horses to King Kongmin.[108]

Although Naghachu remained a potential threat to Koryŏ in Liaodong, other challenges to Kongmin's power in Northeast Asia faded in the years following the Red Turban Wars. When in 1356 King Kongmin retook the strategic Ssangsŏng Directorate-General in northeast Korea, Cho So-saeng and his supporters had fled to Jurchen-held lands rather than surrender. In the following years, they remained beyond the control of the Koryŏ throne, which worried that they might create troubles for the king by appealing to the Yuan authorities in Liaodong.[109] As noted above, early in the 1360s, Cho seems to have cooperated with Naghachu's forces. During the summer of 1362, however, Cho, his key supporters, and their families were killed by a Jurchen *darughachi*, Suoyinshan 所音山, and the Circuit Overseer, Buqa 總管不花.[110]

Cho's death did not stabilize the border region. In addition to Gaojianu and Naghachu, unspecified Jurchen forces clashed with Koryŏ troops of the "northern province commander" (*sakpangto tojihwisa* 朔方道都指揮使) in May 1362.[111] Later the same year, the king sent an official to try to "pacify the Jurchen border region," suggesting that frictions continued.[112] As Yuan control in the region receded, military skirmishes, trade, migration, and diplomacy between Jurchen lands and Koryŏ filled the vacuum.

The Red Turban Wars did not fundamentally change the position of Koreans in Liaodong. Large Korean communities continued in Liaoyang and Shenyang. In fact, they would survive the fall of both the Yuan and the Koryŏ dynasties.[113] However, as effective Yuan control of the region diminished, the Koryŏ king's position in Liaodong may have grown stronger. In mid-May 1366, a Koryŏ diplomatic mission returning from Daidu was intercepted at Liaoyang. An unidentified "group of bandits" surrounded the mission. Hoping to intimidate the group, a senior envoy displayed presents of clothing and wine that the Yuan throne had given to the Koryŏ king. He also produced an edict issued by the Yuan heir apparent. The "bandits" responded, "That thing is not good for anything." However, out of their regard for the Koryŏ king, they released the mission.[114] One reading of the incident is that during the 1360s, the Koryŏ throne enjoyed a better reputation or greater influence in Liaodong than the Yuan heir apparent, who was being groomed to succeed as emperor.

Unsettled conditions south of Liaodong periodically rendered travel between Kaegyŏng and Daidu uncertain. In mid-November 1368, Koryŏ envoys en route to the Yuan capital reached Liaoyang only to turn back because "the road was impassable."[115] Since the Yuan court had abandoned Daidu early in September to rapidly approaching Ming armies, one suspects that diplomatic uncertainty rather than local security may explain the envoys' early return.

At least some believed that the Koryŏ throne had a say in Liaodong during the early years of Ming rule. According to an April 1371 entry of the *Official History of the Koryŏ Dynasty*, when the "Northern Yuan Liaoyang [Branch Secretariat] Administrator" Liu Yi 劉益 considered transferring his loyalty to the Ming, he first contacted the Koryŏ king. "Since Liaoyang was originally our territory," an entry from a Koryŏ chronicle reads, "if our dynasty were to request [it of the Ming], it would be possible to avoid relocating [his population]" 若我國請命可免遷徙.[116] The passage suggests that regional elites and the Ming dynasty recognized the Koryŏ throne's interest in the Korean communities of Liaodong and that King Kongmin would have a say in which groups might be safely incorporated into the Ming. Even after Liu joined the Ming and received an appointment as commander of the recently established Dingliao Garrison 定遼衛, he sent envoys to the Koryŏ court with felicitations on Kongmin's birthday.[117] From 1367 to 1370, nearly half a dozen leading figures from the Liaoyang Secretariat dispatched envoys to the Koryŏ throne. This steady flow of gifts and personnel between Mongolian and Chinese military men in Liaodong with the Koryŏ throne had clear parallels elsewhere in the Great Yuan *ulus*.

Koryŏ Relations with the Yuan Court

Even during King Kongmin's exile in the south, the Yuan and Koryŏ courts continued to exchange envoys. Early in June 1362, the emperor dispatched Ki Ch'ŏn-yong 奇田龍, a junior supervisor in the Yuan heir apparent's household administration, to the Koryŏ court, where he presented the king with raiment and wine.[118] Late in June the king dispatched an envoy bearing local tribute to Daidu,[119] and in mid-July the court sent Yi Cha-song 李子松 (d. 1388) to the Yuan capital to announce the Koryŏ triumph over the Red Turbans.[120] At this time, the Koryŏ envoy Yi also turned over to the Mongols more than twenty official seals, including imperial seals.[121] These seals, important symbols of political power and legitimacy, had fallen into the Red Turbans' hands during their occupation of Shangdu and other administrative seats in Northeast Asia. Koryŏ troops had recovered them after the recapture of Kaegyŏng. Early in October 1362, the king led his assembled officials outside the city walls of Ch'ŏngju 清州 to show their respect to a formal communication of New Year's felicitations for the Yuan throne (presumably before the envoy began his journey to Daidu). Kongmin commanded several of his senior ministers to compose poems to mark the occasion. In his preface to their collected poems, Paek Mun-bo made sure to praise Kongmin's "sincerity . . . in serving the [our] Liege Lord and revering His commands."[122]

As noted above, Mongol commanders in Liaodong were in frequent contact with Kongmin, updating him on military developments, requesting troops for joint operations, and occasionally skirmishing along the border. Thus in the face of the recent warfare, economic hardship, halting efforts at administrative reconstruction, and factional sniping within his court, Kongmin (whatever "anti-Yuan" sentiments he may have harbored in his heart)[123] continued to fulfill his political and military obligations toward the Great Yuan *ulus*. In spite of (or precisely because of) such devotion, King Kongmin soon became embroiled in the fierce court struggles that were to wrack the entire empire.

7
A New King of Koryŏ

If Kongmin and his court expected some sign of gratitude for their efforts against the Red Turbans or some expression of common purpose from their liege lord, they were destined for disappointment. In mid-December 1362, the king learned of the Yuan court's dramatic new plans for the Koryŏ throne. The Mongols had announced a new king of Koryŏ, Tash-Temür 塔思帖木兒.[1] Ch'ungsŏn's son (by a palace woman) and Kongmin's uncle, Tash-Temür was a member of the royal Wang family. Amid vague charges of conspiracy, he had left Koryŏ when Kongmin came to the throne in 1356 and settled in Daidu.[2] At some point, he apparently had taken the tonsure but then returned to lay life.[3] Now, he had become a pawn in a vast international intrigue. The proposed heir apparent was to be a kinsman of Empress Ki, Slave of the Three Jewels (K. Sambono, Ch. Sanbaonu 三寶奴); senior posts would go to Kim Yong and Ch'oe Yu.[4]

Why, in a moment of unprecedented dynastic crisis, would the Yuan court expend precious resources and energy on an apparently peripheral escapade?[5] Later court chronicles such as the *Official History of the Yuan Dynasty* and the *Official History of the Koryŏ Dynasty* ascribe the decision to Empress Ki's desire for revenge against King Kongmin.[6] Generally well informed private accounts provide similar explanations. In 1356, Kongmin had killed many of her clansmen. "You are now grown," the empress scolded her son the heir apparent at this time. "Why do you not avenge me?"[7]

As early as 1356, the empress had considered the newly invested Sim Prince (Toqto'a-Buqa) as a possible replacement for King Kongmin. The prince, however, demurred. According to the editors of the *Official History of the Koryŏ Dynasty*, Toqto'a-Buqa's decision "won the approbation of all under heaven," which suggests that political elites of the time considered him a highly viable candidate for the throne.[8] As late as fall 1368, after the Mongol court had been driven from Daidu, Empress Ki was still pressuring her son to order the Mongol general Naghachu to attack Koryŏ for its "transgressions."[9]

Simple revenge or something more? Until recently, the Tash-Temür incident has eluded systematic study, lost in the forgotten years between the suppression of the Red Turbans and the establishment of ties with the fledgling Ming dynasty.[10] Most studies that mention the Yuan's abortive efforts to replace Kongmin accept at face value fourteenth- and fifteenth-century explanations.[11] In the only essay devoted to the incident, Min Hyŏn-gu instead characterizes the abortive coup as a primarily intra-Korean affair and places events in the context of Korean efforts to secure independence from the Mongols. Min maintains that Empress Ki and others wished to replace King Kongmin because of his anti-Yuan policies, which Min holds had wide support throughout Korean society.[12] As I show below, the incident in fact was tied to even broader developments in Northeast Asia. Whereas Min stresses that the abortive coup completed Koryŏ's escape from the empire, I believe the incident reveals much about the place of Koryŏ in the crumbling Great Yuan *ulus*, the continuing impact of the Red Turban incursions, the workings of court politics in both Daidu and Kaegyŏng, and the role of elite women in the Great Yuan *ulus*.

Kongmin immediately moved to gather information and muster support for his position. As his first step, he appointed his minister of personnel as inspector-general of the northwest. This was the slightest of bureaucratic fig leaves intended to cover his real purpose, verification of reports from Daidu.[13] Weeks later, he sent a diplomatic mission to the Yuan court with felicitations on the emperor's birthday.[14] Its members no doubt devoted much of their energies to tracking the latest developments there. In mid-January 1363 Kongmin sent the influential court minister Kim Yong to "console" the mother of Ki Ch'ŏn-yong. As noted in Chapter 6, Ki was an official in the Yuan heir apparent's household administration who in June 1362 had been sent with gifts to King Kongmin. Kongmin now bestowed lands and fields on his mother.[15]

Perhaps feeling greater urgency to return to his capital, in mid-March 1363 Kongmin arrived at his temporary quarters south of Kaegyŏng. Soon thereafter, Kongmin sent two envoys to the Yuan court with several memorials for the emperor. Composed by the famed writer Yi Saek on behalf of the king, the first document was entitled "A Report on Conditions Following the Defeat of the Red Turbans." It stressed the Koryŏ dynasty's loyalty to the Mongol empire, its sedulous efforts to keep the Mongol court informed of developments, and its unswerving commitment to offering tribute to Daidu. The Red Turban wars, however, had thrown such exemplary relations into chaos.

> Who could have anticipated that we would suffer from rebel [attacks]? Soon, [passage] to the court was severed. First fighting spread to P'yŏngyang. Later it engulfed Kaegyŏng. That in every battle we intentionally appeared weak to the enemy was not because we thought over much of our own interests. [Thus] when we counterattacked, we completely destroyed the enemy. That we did not avoid the difficulties of the flight to the south was not because of ourselves, but to lessen the worry over [attack against the Yuan] from the east.[16]
>
> 豈意遭罹寇賊。俄而隔絶朝廷。前平壤之蔓延。後開城之燹及。每鋒以示弱。故非多算之所爲。不旋踵而合攻，竟使隻輪之無返。其不避南遷之困。蓋欲寬東顧之憂。[17]

Here the Red Turban incursions become evidence of Kongmin's devotion to the Yuan. Warfare, not Koryŏ duplicity or disloyalty, disrupted normal diplomatic relations. Kongmin highlights his country's suffering in order to prove his loyalty to the Mongol court. Red Turban victories in Koryŏ were not a product of Koryŏ's military failure. Rather, Kongmin chose to sacrifice his lands, people, and capital in order to alleviate the threat against the Yuan. Kongmin's flight to Pokju, which might otherwise be construed as royal incompetence or military weakness, is held up as an act of devotion to the Great Yuan *ulus*. The phrase "worry over attack from the east" 東顧之憂 (literally "the worry of looking over one's shoulder to the east") exactly paralleled the description of Chagha'an-Temür's contribution to the empire in 1362. Because of Chagha'an-Temür's military victories in Henan, Toghan-Temür no longer had a "worry over attack from the south" 南顧

之憂.[18] Put in slightly different terms, King Kongmin painted himself as among the most stalwart defenders of the realm.

The second document was a congratulatory epistle celebrating Yuan victories over the Red Turban forces in southernmost Liaoyang.[19]

[Through] Your Grace's virtue, dynastic fortunes have grown [even] more prosperous. At the pacification of the demon rebels, all the realm joins in celebration. Your Majesty's benevolence extends to all things. You are virtuous and love the living. [Like King Xun] dancing with shields and feathers between the staircases of the palace, [You] have brought to submission the recalcitrant. Through encouraging [the cultivation of] endless fields and mulberry trees, [You] try to bring about stable livelihoods for the people.

[You] did not exterminate the rebels, and their strength grew without end. They drove deeply right to P'yŏngyang. They gathered again and once more violated Kaegyŏng. When we considered the responsibilities entrusted to us as vassal, we could not leave the rebels for our lord. Thereupon, we issued our entire army, our heart united with the troops.[20] As expected, relying on Your Majesty's Grace, again and again we decimated the villains. Who would have anticipated that remnants of the enemy would cling to their lives in lairs in Haizhou and Gaizhou? Following the commands of your generals, our troops followed [Your forces]. Bolstering [Your] military strength, we displayed our terrible awe. The sprouts of villainy were suppressed. The surviving blackguards surrendered. At that time, [the realm] entered a time of peace and tranquility. Your Sagely Transformative [virtue] has already spread throughout the realm; within our territory, [the Red Turbans'] predations have ceased. Your overflowing favor extends as far as our humble state. Would your minister dare not reverently adhere to the protocol of court visits and increase prayers for Your health?[21]

大人之造，基緒彌隆。妖寇之平，寰區共慶。皇帝陛下仁敦及物。德洽好生。干羽兩階，謂昏迷之可格，耕桑萬里，欲黎庶之載安。誅討不加，猖狂未已。長驅而直低箕壤。再聚而復污松京。自念爲寄，維藩不可遺君。以賊發軍，盡口與士同心，果仗皇靈累殲醜類。何枝黨之餘喘尚海蓋之爲栖。聽帥指而往。從助兵威而耀示。姦萌銷沮殘蘖降投。時升泰平，聖化既敷於率土。境絶陵侮。洪恩偏及於小邦。臣敢不恪修朝聘之儀。益貢康寧之祝。

Both documents stress Koryŏ's loyalty to the Yuan throne in a time of spreading military crisis. The second piece highlights the Korean military's prowess on the battlefield. Unaided by Yuan forces, Kongmin's soldiers destroyed the Red Turbans active in his lands. The rebels' shattered remnants fled Koryŏ and sought refuge in southern Liaoyang. Kongmin is careful to credit his victories to "His Majesty's Grace," a rhetorical construction that reappears in later memorials to the Yuan throne. Kongmin then reminds Toghan-Temür that Koryŏ forces had also figured in the Liaodong victories at Haizhou and Gaizhou. The not-so-subtle message might be boiled down to "discarding proven allies in dangerous times is a recipe for disaster."

The irony of the message may have crossed King Kongmin's mind during these months. Having acquiesced to the murder of his leading generals (whose successes figured so prominently in communications to the Yuan), he was arguably in a much weaker position to regain the throne. Stripped of his title by the Yuan and bereft of military commanders, he was also more susceptible to domestic challenges. At least this was how Kim Yong, a leading official and intimate of the king, viewed matters. As noted in Chapter 6, on April 15, 1363, Kim tried to kill the king in his temporary quarters south of the capital. His plans may have had an international dimension. The late Kim Sang-gi and, more recently, Min Hyŏn-gu have suggested that Kim's abortive coup was part of efforts by Empress Ki and Ch'oe Yu to remove Kongmin from power.[22] Perhaps Kim Yong felt that, given Kongmin's ambiguous status in the Mongol empire, the risk of punishment for regicide was offset by the prospects of rewards from Empress Ki and the heir apparent. Although Kim's coup proved abortive, his actions illustrate how precarious the Yuan throne's announcement of his dethronement had rendered Kongmin's position.

The Red Turban invasions continued to figure in relations between Koryŏ and the Yuan. Late in May 1363, King Kongmin sent a series of communiqués to the Yuan emperor, the Secretariat, and the Household Administration of the Heir Apparent. The Koryŏ throne's decision to pursue its interests on three different fronts reflects a sure command of shifting political developments in Northeast Asia. The emperor and the heir apparent did not see eye to eye on many issues.[23] During the decade preceding the Yuan court's flight from Daidu, Empress Ki and Ayushiridara attempted to effect Toghan-Temür's retirement and the heir apparent's enthronement several times.[24] To register his displeasure publicly, at one point the emperor conspicuously avoided his empress for several months. The tensions led to several purges at court and eventually bled into the military realm. During the mid-1360s, the emperor and the heir apparent would favor two competing generals/warlords in North China, Bolod-Temür (d. 1365) and Köke-Temür (d. 1375), respectively. The generals' open and violent rivalry developed into one of the most pressing issues facing the Yuan dynasty. That Toghan-Temür and his chosen successor diverged on such a signal matter bespeaks the Koryŏ court's wisdom of courting each man separately.

Voicing the opinion of "officialdom and the elders" from the Koryŏ court, the first memorial asked why the Yuan had failed to dispatch envoys to Koryŏ. The Yuan had neither acknowledged Koryŏ tributary missions nor granted the official calendar for the new lunar year. Given King Kongmin's conscientious observation of all tribute responsibilities, the memorial argued, the Yuan's attitude could only be the result of lies spread in Daidu by Koreans opposed to the king.

Addressed to the Secretariat, the second memorial reviewed the Red Turbans' predations in Northeast Asia, noting that the rebels originated in China.

Recently the Red Turbans attacked Shangdu, violating the imperial palace; they sacked Liaosheng, torching the area's towns. The rebels from Shandong crossed the sea and joined them. Their strength was staggering. In the spring of 1359, all the envoys from our humble country were killed while returning from Daidu, where they had offered New Year's felicitations. At the end of the year, the rebels came and sacked P'yŏngyang; we thereupon destroyed them. During the winter of 1361, Sha Liu'er, Master Guan, and others, numbering more than 100,000, again suddenly arrived. We lured them in with an empty city. Finally we captured them. The other remaining bands in Gaizhou and Haizhou dared not attack again. Our humble country contributed to these successes. It has been more than a decade since rebels everywhere have risen up. There are still those who have yet to be vanquished. The rebels in the east have been completely suppressed in four or five years. The Son of Heaven need not worry about his eastern flank, and the court need not suffer from the burden of a distant campaign. Our king's meritorious service is perhaps no less than any of your generals.[25]

邇者紅賊犯上都。污穢宮闕。攻破遼省。焚蕩郡邑。山東之賊航海而來。與之相合。勢甚猖獗。己亥之春，小邦賤价賀正而迴，盡爲所害。至其年冬，來寇平壤，隨即殄滅。至辛丑冬沙劉，關先生等十餘萬眾又復奄至。誘以空城，卒以擒獲。蓋海餘黨不敢復肆。小邦有力焉。四方賊起十有餘年，尚有未盡平者。東方之寇，四五年間便致廓清。天子無東顧之憂，朝廷無遠討之勞。我王之功，未必在諸將之下也。

The memorial then raised an old complaint—that Koreans who opposed the king were spreading lies in Daidu, misleading the Yuan court. Why should Koryŏ, a faithful tributary state, be viewed in the same light as the rebel forces, asked the memorialists. In fact, the rebels might "still receive pardons and even become high officials; what, then, about our king who had rendered meritorious service without fault?"[26] Here the Koryŏ court referred to the Yuan's ongoing negotiations with such Chinese warlords as Fang Guozhen and Zhang Shicheng, which involved pardons for past offenses in exchange for promises of future assistance. The contrast between the Koryŏ king and the often murderous capriciousness of Fang and Zhang is anchored in the phrase "the Son of Heaven need not worry about his eastern flank."

Again, the memorials stressed Kongmin's popular support at home.

Our king is cautious and circumspect; he fears the authority of Heaven; his virtue is without blemish. The people cherish his virtue. It is for this reason that against the predations of the Red Turbans and the attacks of the [Japanese] pirates, he triumphed in every battle. [Thus] we have not failed [to obey] [Your] order to oversee the east. If [You] suffer these blackguards to carry out their treacherous plans, this is for the [Yuan] Court itself to eliminate its protective shield and to wrest away our mother and father.[27]

我王小心謹慎。畏天之威。德罔有缺。民懷其德。是以紅賊之逼，寇之侵，每戰每克。不辱釐東之命。若被不逞之徒。得行奸計，是朝廷自撤其藩籬而奪我父母也。

Descriptions of Koryŏ as the Great Yuan *ulus*'s "protective shield" or "eastern shield" date to the thirteenth century, when the phrases appeared in the context of Qubilai's struggles against Nayan's supporters.[28]

The memorial to the Household Administration of the Heir Apparent echoes these same points—the king's scrupulous observation of his duties toward the Yuan, the support of the aristocrats and the people for the king, and his military successes.

The Koryŏ court was attempting to persuade the Yuan court that it would be foolish to listen to the unprincipled rumormongering of those Koreans in Daidu opposed to King Kongmin. The Mongols would lose a proven military ally in Kongmin and incur broad opposition during a

time of crisis. To forsake the Korean king was "for the [Yuan] Court itself to eliminate its protective shield."

King Kongmin's efforts bore little fruit. A month after the memorials had been dispatched to Daidu, a Yuan envoy, Lijianu 李家奴, made his way to the Koryŏ border along the Yalu River. The Koryŏ court was chary of the Yuan envoy. He was rumored to hold an imperial proclamation from the emperor dethroning Kongmin. If a direct order from the Yuan emperor were made public, Kongmin would be left with little room to negotiate. However weakened the Mongol empire might be, open rebellion was not a road lightly taken. This was especially true in the wake of the Red Turban invasions and the growing problem of coastal piracy. To gain time and to avoid a dangerous stalemate, Kongmin and his advisors prevaricated. The envoy was an imposter, or might be, they announced. An official sounded out the envoy's intentions before allowing Lijianu into Koryŏ territory.[29]

One week later, Kongmin's worries grew. A Koryŏ official returned from the Yuan court with news confirming that the emperor had installed Tash-Temür (sometimes designated by his title Tŏkhŭng-gun 德興君) as the new Koryŏ king.[30] As the king bolstered border defenses in the northwest, in mid-July the Yuan envoy was admitted into Koryŏ territory. Koryŏ authorities immediately detained the members of the envoy's entourage and interrogated them about Tash-Temür's enthronement.[31]

The Koryŏ government attempted to impress the Yuan envoy with its strength, even as subjects who feared forced military service briefly rioted at the capital's edge.[32] In mid-August, court officials received Lijianu outside the Sŏn'ui-mun 宣義門 Gate with a military parade. During Lijianu's brief sojourn in Kaegyŏng, the Koreans pressed the king's case, first with gifts—gold belt-buckles, horse saddles, sets of clothing, and bolts of ramie cloth—and then a banquet. Lijianu and his assistant declined to deliver a memorial protesting the change to the emperor. The envoy did, however, agree to relay a memorial to the heir apparent.[33]

Emperor Shizu 世祖 [Qubilai], pleased that King Ch'unggyŏng 忠敬王 [i.e., King Wŏnjong] was the first in the realm to come to court and offer tribute, married his daughter to Ch'ungnyŏl-wang. Further [Qubilai] permitted [us] to preserve our country's customs unchanged to the present day. Tŏkhŭng-gun Tash-Temür was born to King Ch'ungsŏn and a former palace woman who married Paek Mun-kŏ. The villainous minister Ch'oe Yu vilified the [Koryŏ] court to seize my royal throne. [It has gone so far] even to trouble the Celestial Armies. In generational terms, we are nephew and uncle. How [can this be]?! I humbly hope to explain myself in a memorial. [I hope that] in your Heavenly Sagacity, you will apprehend Tash-Temür, Ch'oe Yu, and the others and return them to this humble state in order to satisfy the fury of the people of our dynasty.[34]

世祖皇帝嘉我忠敬王先天下朝覲之功釐降帝女于忠烈王且許不革國俗以至于今德興君塔思帖木兒是忠宣王出宮人嫁白文擧所產者也而奸臣崔濡誣告朝廷奪我王位至煩天兵其於世爲甥舅之意何哉伏望敷奏天聰執塔思帖木兒崔濡等歸之小邦以快國人之憤。

The missive tries to undermine Tash-Temür's qualifications to take the throne. He was not the offspring of the queen or principal consort, only the lowly son of "a former palace woman." The king contrasts this questionable pedigree with his own line, which goes back to Qubilai. Further, he stresses that Qubilai did not impose the Mongols' form of succession on Koryŏ. Instead of an open and often bloody contest among all male descendents of Chinggis khan to determine who should lead the *ulus*, the Koryŏ throne was to go to the offspring of the king and his primary consort (who was of aristocratic birth) or elder brother to younger brother. With Kongmin's letter in hand and having viewed yet another military demonstration, on August 20, 1363, Lijianu departed Kaegyŏng for Daidu.[35]

The offers of gifts, lavish banquets, and displays of power had little effect. By January 1364, Tash-Temür's entourage was encamped in Liaodong. He was awaiting the arrival of cavalry forces that would escort him through Koryŏ territory to Kaegyŏng, where he would take the throne. The news rocked the Koryŏ court.[36] It was not, however, completely unexpected. King Kongmin had stationed An U-gyŏng 安遇慶, a leading general and a veteran of the recent wars with the Red Turbans, at Ŭiju, the first important Koryŏ city east of the Yalu River. From there, An had ordered his commanders to take up positions along the river itself.[37] During the pre-dawn hours of the first day of the new lunar year (1364/2/4), Ch'oe Yu (AKA Ch'oe Temür, Ch'oe Temür-Buqa) led 10,000 imperial Yuan troops across the Yalu River.[38]

Although the Mongol throne had ordered the soldiers to escort Tash-Temür, Ch'oe felt compelled to offer further incentives. The Koryŏ generals in the Northern Territory were there against their wills, Ch'oe assured the men. Once the Koreans learned that a new king, Tash-Temür, had been named, they were certain to surrender or simply abandon their positions. He promised rich booty to his Mongolian and North China soldiers. The wives, concubines, and property of Koryŏ ministers would be their reward for what he painted as an easy victory.[39]

Instead of welcoming the Yuan forces, however, An's men raised the alert. Ch'oe moved immediately against Ŭiju. From the city walls, An and more than seventy subordinate officials watched the enemy's approach. "Cavalry and infantry divided into seven groups; they advanced together amid beating war drums and battle cries." Despite fierce Koryŏ resistance and the personal heroics of a Mongolian commander in the Koryŏ army, the Yuan forces overwhelmed the defenders, who withdrew to the south. Ch'oe's men drove further southeast and occupied Sŏnju 宣州.[40] The king rushed in reinforcements. They included such proven military commanders as Ch'oe Yŏng (who had most recently saved the king during Kim Yong's abortive coup d'état) and Yi Sŏng-gye, who commanded 1,000 elite cavalry troops. Their arrival boosted the Koryŏ defenders' sagging morale.[41]

Frigid temperatures and severe food shortages wrought havoc among the troops in northwestern Koryŏ. Korean chronicles observed, "the soldiers were so cold and hungry that they could not remain upright."[42] Another report noted, "A *tu* 斗 of rice was exchanged for a horse. One after another, people died of hunger along the road. Deserting soldiers filled the roads as they begged. Their faces were pale and emaciated."[43] General Ch'oe Yŏng attempted to staunch the flow of deserters and restore discipline through summary execution of those who abandoned their units.[44] As was often the case during the Red Turban wars, Kongmin seems largely unaware of his soldiers' piteous state. The editors of the *Official History of the Koryŏ Dynasty* complained, "Those ministers in charge obstructed [the flow of information] and did not report [on conditions]. . . . Inspecting envoys merely looked at one another on the road. The king didn't even know the true state of the military."[45]

At this point, the situation looked grim. One senior minister convinced Kongmin to relocate the capital to the south as a way to gain time and remain beyond the reach of the Yuan forces. Kongmin was dissuaded only when another advisor objected that Tash-Temür posed far less of a challenge than the recently defeated Red Turbans had. Furthermore, he asked, "If the king were to flee, who from areas north of the capital would follow the king?" Instead, he argued Kongmin should personally lead the troops against Tash-Temür.[46] Although Kongmin neither fled the capital nor took to the battlefield, the exchange suggests the importance of the Red Turban wars as a reference point and the king's worries about his subjects' loyalty.

At Chŏngju 定州 to the east, General An's fortunes turned.[47] The rapid pace of the Yuan army's drive eastward overstretched its forces. At the head of a small elite group of 300 cavalry troops, An scored a major victory, capturing an enemy general. In an effort to break the spirit of the Yuan forces, An executed the general in front of the invading army.[48]

Discord among the Koryŏ commanders, however, threatened to undermine An's initial success. Observing that fellow commanders were unwilling to commit themselves to battle, Yi Sŏng-gye remarked imprudently on their cowardice. Stung, the officers responded that Yi might like to face the enemy alone the next day. Despite his concern about betrayal and a perilous moment in battle when his mount became trapped in mire, Yi survived the day. The Yuan forces were put to flight.[49] By February 21, 1364, Ch'oe's troops burned their camp at Suju 隨州, crossed the Yalu, and fled.[50]

Yuan and Koryŏ chronicles characterized Ch'oe's campaign as a complete rout. Out of the 10,000 men from the Yuan armies, "only seventeen riders returned to the capital."[51] Min Hyŏn-gu has suggested that most of the Yuan forces crumbled after the defeat at Suju and safely returned to Yuan territory. The image of seventeen lonely riders, Min proposes, refers to the survivors of a smaller anti–King Kongmin Korean unit within the Yuan forces.[52]

This was a major military victory for Koryŏ, which had not defeated Mongol armies on Korean soil for more than a century, and reflected the growing experience and skill won through recent battles with the Red Turbans. Although extant chronicles leave many of the details unclear, the Koryŏ generals turned initial defeats into ultimate victory by deflecting the Yuan drive against Kaegyŏng, where Tash-Temür was to be installed as the new king. The Yuan commanders probably saw a chance to smash the apparently ineffective main Koryŏ army before moving south. If General An and his officers had been given an opportunity to regroup, they would have posed a serious threat to Tash-Temür's fledgling rule and perhaps even sever the Mongol army's return route back across the Yalu River.

Immediately after putting Ch'oe to flight, General An sent an impassioned letter to the commander of the Posuofu 婆娑府, the Yuan commandery located on the western bank of the Yalu river, across from Ŭiju.[53] The document is worth quoting at length to see how An justified the legitimacy of Kongmin's sovereignty. Equally important, it shows his efforts to convince the Yuan commander to take action against Ch'oe (without sanction from the imperial throne).

For more than 400 years, since the Grand Progenitor, the Wise and Sagely Great King, established the dynasty, the legitimate transmission [of the throne] has been passed down through the offspring of the principal wife. [When] the prior king began to serve the [Mongol] court, [Yuan] Shizu [Qubilai] ordered that no change was to be made in local customs. The king's eldest son of his principal wife, King Ch'ungnyŏl, married a [Mongol] princess. They produced King Ch'ungsŏn. King Ch'ungsŏn also married a [Mongol] princess. They produced King Ch'ungsuk. [In terms of] obligation, [they] were lord and minister. [In terms of family relations] they were father and son-in-law. Our present king, the son of Ch'ungsuk's principal wife, served [in the *kesig*] at the imperial court for more than ten years. His accomplishments were noteworthy. He married a [Mongol] princess and is a son-in-law [of the Yuan throne]. He succeeded to the legitimate line of succession. He has scrupulously observed the protocol of the small serving the great.

Unfortunately, the Red Turbans have stalked the realm, preying on Heaven's people. Whatever direction they have turned, their strength has been fearsome. [Even] Imperial Awe had difficulty controlling [them]. During the winter of *kihae/jihai* 己亥 [1359], Manager of Affairs Mao [Gui] and Administrative Assistant Huang [Zhishan], and others, more than 100,000 rebels violated the Eastern Country. They reached as far as the Western Capital. Our armies launched a great assault [and] swept every single one of them [from the country]. Again in the year *sinch'uk/xinchou* 辛丑 [1361], Sha Liu'er, Manager of Affairs Pan, Master Guan, et al., more than 300,000 rebels entered deep [into our lands]. They captured the royal capital. Our king was enraged. The generals roused themselves to bravery. They completely annihilated the [rebel] hordes. The dynastic altars were made secure. The people were blessed [with peace]. We have already submitted to the Secretariat accounts of our two victories.

Because the people of the east believed that the Liege Dynasty would be certain to reward generously, we had craned our necks and looked North with great expectations.

Little did we think that a member of our own dynasty, Ch'oe Yu, would harbor grievances and spin tales of calumny to mislead His Majesty, causing our ruler even to lose his post and to have Tash-Temür, the illegitimate son of a discarded concubine of King Ch'ungsŏn, to become king. From 3,000 *li* away, he comes from a distance to burden Heaven's people. In serving our prior king, Ch'oe and his ilk were sycophantic and appeased [the king]. They led [the king] into unrighteous [activities]. In the year *kyemi/guiwei* 癸未 [1343], he went south and did not return. This was really brought about by Ch'oe Yu and his ilk. Whenever men of our dynasty speak of this, never is there an occasion when they do not cry bitterly and shed tears. Now Ch'oe and the others use their obstreperous cries to drown out our great merit and to remove our king. Moreover, it has rendered the innocent people of this dynasty unable to repose in peace. This is [why they are] criminals of the dynasty.

Our king sent as envoys Minister Yi Kong-su, Ryu In-u, and Hŏ Kang. [He sent] Hong Sun to offer felicitations on the New Year and to express gratitude for Your Benevolence; on the occasion of the Imperial Birthday, we also [sent an envoy]. Again to express felicitations upon the occasion of the empress's birthday, we sent an envoy to report [to the throne]. Ch'oe Yu and the others conspired to block [these missions]. They seized the tribute gifts. Formal letters of communication were unable to reach [the throne]. They detained the envoys.

Further, Emperor Shizu [Qubilai] commanded [us] not to change local customs. Succession through the principal consort has long been practiced. [Ch'oe] Yu and the others manipulated the court to establish a son of a secondary wife as king. [This is] changing local customs and thus rendering Shizu's rescript an empty writ. [In this sense] he is a criminal to the realm.

The people of this dynasty beat their breasts and gnash their teeth, saying "A treacherous minister, a disobedient son." If the people were to lay their hands on him, they would execute him. From antiquity, there have been laws for this. The crimes of [Ch'oe] Yu and his ilk do not permit [mere] execution. Even if his heart and stomach were to be cut out, there would certainly be no censure from the court. Everyone is furious. All the people have been saying with one voice that a great army must be raised to punish [Ch'oe] Yu and other evildoers. We will not cease until we eat his flesh and sleep on his skin. The talk is tumultuous. It cannot be held back. It is largely settled that one million crack troops will go forth in a punitive campaign against the treasonous group from Koryŏ. Brambles will grow up in the wake of the army's march.

Once a great army is assembled, the horses' heads will point northward. Even if prohibited, the people's hearts are enraged. Their anger is like a fire. Whatever it touches will burst into flame. The innocent throughout the realm will suffer its calamity. The personages of all bureaus should immediately lead their family members to enter mountain fortresses. [They should] avoid from a distance [the coming] military clash. Further, [we will] single out Ch'oe Yu and the traitorous Koryŏ faction. Do not visit misfortune upon all troops.

Whoever is able to apprehend [Ch'oe] Yu and his ilk, submit their [decapitated] heads, and surrender. Not only would the anger of this dynasty be dissipated, the Liege Dynasty would know that Ch'oe and his ilk, having deceived Heaven and flouted the law, had been rightly punished for their crimes. It would offer generous rewards.

This official, having carefully investigated [matters], has acted. Further, [you] should immediately report to the Branch Bureau of Military Affairs and act in unison.[54]

本國自太祖神聖大王創業，垂正統嫡承襲四百餘年，元王始事朝廷，世祖皇帝命不改土風，元王嫡子忠烈王尚公主，生忠宣王。忠宣王亦尚公主，生忠肅王，義爲君臣，親爲甥舅。今我國王忠肅王之嫡子，入侍天庭十有餘年，頗著功績，尚公主爲駙馬，承正統蒞下國，事大之禮恪謹一心。不幸紅賊橫行天下，剝殘天民，所指火烈，天威難制越。己亥冬僞名毛平章黄院判等賊十餘萬闌入東國至于西京。我軍大發一掃無餘。又於辛丑年沙劉潘平章關先生等賊三十餘萬深入王京。吾王赫怒諸將奮勇，盡殲其眾，社稷獲安，人民受賜兩度破賊之事，既以具呈中書省矣。東民以謂上國必厚賞引頸北望。豈慮本國人崔濡等挾其仇怨，具錦誣詞簧惑天聽，使我主上至于失職，以忠宣棄妾孽子搭思帖木兒爲王，三千里外遠勞天民。夫崔濡等事我先王阿諛逢迎，陷於不義。癸未年間南行不返，崔濡惡輩實使之也。本國人言及於此，未嘗不痛哭流涕。今濡等又以笙簧之口掩我大功，廢吾王而使本土無辜之民不遑寧居。此本國之罪人也。吾王使宰相李公遂柳仁雨許綱洪淳等賀正矣，謝恩矣，賀聖節矣，又賀千秋矣，且啓禀矣。濡等互相壅蔽奪其方物表箋，使不得達，拘留使价唯已之從。且世祖皇帝命不改土風，正嫡承襲其來遠矣。濡等冒弄朝廷，立孽庶爲王，改易土風而使世祖皇帝詔旨墜於空虛。此天下之罪人也。本國人搥胷切齒曰，亂臣賊子人，得而誅之古有常憲。如濡之輩罪不容，誅雖刳心腹，必無朝廷之議，大小奮慍雷然一辭必舉大兵往討濡等惡輩，食肉寢皮，然後已。物議洶涌不可止遏。今以精兵百萬往討高麗逆黨約已定矣。師之所過荊棘生焉。大軍一舉馬首指北，雖加禁厲人心憤怒氣炎如火，所觸必焚。天下無辜忍受其禍。本職所管各部人物即宜收帶家口，早入山寨遠避軍鋒又區別崔濡等高麗逆黨毋使諸色軍馬濫及於禍有能捕濡等惡輩傳首納款不唯本國釋怒上國亦知濡等欺天亂法正伏其辜將有厚賞本職。參詳即便施行又當飛報行樞密院同知施行。

An's missive paints Ch'oe as the common enemy of the Yuan and Koryŏ courts. First, he stresses the Koryŏ royal family's pedigree and loyalty to the Yuan. An then recounts Koryŏ's recent military triumphs over the Red Turbans, who challenged Yuan authority east and west of the Yalu River. Invocation of Koryŏ victories against the Red Turbans was a consistent strategy in all communications with the Yuan throne during these years. It reminded the Mongols that they were fighting a common foe, that the Koryŏ throne was a valuable military ally, that Kongmin had remained loyal to the Yuan during a time of crisis, and finally that Koryŏ deserved the gratitude of its Mongolian overlords.

In contrast, Ch'oe Yu, insists the letter, betrayed both his Korean and his Mongol lords, abusing their trust and leading them astray. He also violated the commands of Qubilai khan. Justly infuriated, the people of Koryŏ have set their hearts on revenge. An's message to the local garrison commander is not subtle. It promises direct military action against Ch'oe's forces (west of the Yalu) and warns darkly of the destruction that will follow in the fighting's wake. This was no idle threat. Less than a decade earlier, in 1356, Koryŏ armies under General In Tang had swept aside Yuan garrison forces to seize Posuofu and three imperial relay stations. Although Kongmin had returned the relay stations as part of the peace settlement with the Mongols, the Yuan border was no less vulnerable now.[55]

At the same time, however, the Koryŏ court points out that if the Posuofu commander were to apprehend Ch'oe, the demand for vengeance by Koryŏ subjects would be satisfied. The need for a punitive strike into Liaodong would be obviated. Even more critical, such an action was fully congruent with the true wishes of the Yuan court. In fact, the commander could look forward to generous rewards from a grateful ruler.

Did An's letter matter? No response from the Posuofu commander survives. We can only speculate from what the commander did and did not do. He did not apprehend Ch'oe Yu and the ragged band of survivors from the disastrous campaign and turn them over to the Koryŏ government. They straggled back to Daidu. On the other hand, the Posuofu commander provided no reinforcements or military assistance to

Ch'oe after his withdrawal from Koryŏ territory. In this case, quick neutralization of the military and political threat posed by Ch'oe's forces and by the enthronement of Tash-Temür was Kongmin's ultimate goal. An's diplomatic efforts certainly did no harm.

Returning to the battlefields, commanders from Koryŏ's northern border lost no time in relaying their victories to the throne. "The king was pleased." No doubt he was. The whole state of affairs must have been deeply troubling to Kongmin. The Mongols' decision to dethrone him sharply eroded his political legitimacy and authority. The appearance of a large enemy force in the Northwest Territory dangerously stretched his already thin military resources. Pirates continued their predations along Koryŏ's coastlines, seizing grain shipments, taking captives, and pillaging villages. At the same time that Koryŏ troops fought Yuan soldiers, Jurchen tribesmen escalated attacks in the northeast. By mid-February 1364, "everything north of Hwaju 和州 was lost."[56]

One can appreciate Kongmin's celerity in announcing the triumph over Ch'oe's forces. The immediate crisis defused, such commanders as Ch'oe Yŏng and Yi Sŏng-gye were immediately redeployed to the Northeast Territory to stem the Jurchen incursions. By early in March, they had regained the lost lands.[57] Kongmin ordered his officials to meet the returning generals in the suburbs outside the capital "as if welcoming a royal procession."[58] The king had already begun to dispense promotions and rewards to the military.[59] Later, Kongmin would honor his generals with a banquet at his temporary royal quarters.[60]

How widespread was domestic support for Tash-Temür? A number of measures implemented after Ch'oe's columns were driven from Koryŏ are revealing. Early in March, two weeks after the victory, "the lands, houses, and property of treasonous officials were distributed among the generals."[61] No further details are provided. The timing of the confiscations and identity of the recipients, however, suggest that Kongmin now felt sufficiently confident in his position to move against domestic supporters of Tash-Temür. The same day, the king executed Third Deputy Commander (*hokun* 護軍) Pae Cha-bu 裴自富 for collusion with Tash-Temür. Pae had accepted a post in the new king's government.[62]

Such accusations should be viewed with a measure of caution. For instance, the king also ordered the execution of Chu Sa-ch'ung, a deputy war minister, on charges of collaboration with Tash-Temür. Chu had served the throne loyally in the past. In December 1359, King Kongmin had dispatched Chu as his envoy to the Red Turbans when they seized the Western Capital. Chu now loudly insisted on his innocence. He protested, "I have committed no crime. It is two or three officeholders who lack meritorious service [but desire] sudden promotion. [They] have pressed people to death like this."[63] Chu's case suggests that some men at Kongmin's court exploited the atmosphere of fear and uncertainty to advance their careers through false accusation.

The confusion of the time worked to the advantage of men like Ch'oe Yu. The editors of the *Official History of the Koryŏ Dynasty* maintain that he informed the Yuan throne that the dynastic seal of Koryŏ had been lost during the chaos of the Red Turban invasions.[64] Ch'oe then minted a new seal, which he used for his own purposes. The loss of official seals was a serious matter; they were potent symbols of political legitimacy and essential instruments of daily governance. Orders affixed with official seals held great weight and were ignored at grave peril.

The battle of loyalties was also fought in Daidu. Ch'oe Yu and certain segments of the Yuan court actively sought the support of Koreans resident in Daidu for the new regime. According to the *Official History of the Koryŏ Dynasty*, "all men of our dynasty resident in the capital were appointed to illegitimate posts."[65] "Illegitimate posts" here refers to positions within Tash-Temür's nascent government. Perhaps in an attempt to provide at least a pretense for enthroning a new king of Koryŏ, backers of Tash-Temür in the Yuan capital informed the emperor that Kongmin had been killed by Red Turban forces. Given the strategic importance of the Koryŏ for the Yuan at this point, had such rumors proved true, the need for a new king would have been urgent. One of Kongmin's supporters and the head of a mission dispatched to restore his position, Yi Kong-su, leaped to the king's defense. "Our king," Yi wrote, "defeated the Red Turbans; he remains in good health today."[66]

Yi Kong-su's activities during 1364 illustrate how closely bound were the fortunes of Kaegyŏng and Daidu. King Kongmin had sent Yi to the Yuan capital when he learned of plans to transfer the throne to Tash-Temür. Yi was uniquely well qualified for the task. He was Empress Ki's elder first cousin, a tie Ki freely acknowledged.[67] Long before Yi reached Daidu, the empress and the heir apparent sent envoys to greet him. During the last stages of his journey to the capital, he was honored with a series of banquets hosted on behalf of Ki and her son. Soon after his arrival in Daidu, the empress held a banquet for Yi at her palace, the Xingqinggong 興慶宮. She took the occasion to reaffirm their family ties. "You have devoted yourself in filial piety to my mother. This makes you my elder blood brother. Dare I not treat you as my blood brother?"[68]

In defending Kongmin, Yi assumed the role of Ki's fellow clansman. During this first interview with the empress, Yi began, "The king devotes himself to his lord and hates the enemy.[69] He has rendered meritorious service on behalf of the dynasty. [The Yuan throne] should grant a reward to show the four quarters [of the world] to rouse the generals." Turning to family fortunes, Yi continued:

> How is it that [you] have forsaken common fairness? The calamity of *pyŏngsin/bingshen* 丙申 [1356] was caused exclusively by our family's boundless cupidity during a time of prosperity. It was not the fault of the king. Not to know enough to reflect on our transgressions but rather to dethrone a worthy king [lit., "a king with meritorious service"], in days to come we shall certainly become a laughingstock throughout all the realm.[70]

He then beseeched her to speak to the emperor on behalf of Kongmin. Though moved by Yi's words, Empress Ki remained adamant.

She instead wanted to use Yi Kong-su to her own ends. She and the heir apparent, Ayushiridara, pressed Yi to accept a post in Tash-Temür's government. In contrast with most Koreans in Daidu, Yi declined. Dramatically, Yi protested, "Since I am unable to splatter the shafts of Tŏkhŭng-gun's carriage with blood from my neck [in resistance against his efforts to take the throne], how could I endure to accompany him [to Koryŏ]?"

Various prizes were offered in exchange for Yi's support. First, the Yuan court appointed him commissioner of ritual observance. This prestigious position entailed responsibility for some of the most important rituals in Daidu, including offerings at the Ancestral Temple. Citing his inability to speak Chinese and his unfamiliarity with Chinese ritual, Yi declined. He did, however, accept a post in Empress Ki's household administration. He also participated in the Great Sacrifices at the Ancestral Temple. His "flawless observation of the rites" won both respect from the participants and posthumous titles and honors for his grandfather and female relatives from the throne.[71] Here Yi did not accept an official post, but neither did he completely refuse overtures for his cooperation.

During Yi's sojourn in the capital, the heir apparent courted him. On one occasion, he summoned Yi to the Guanghan Hall 廣寒殿, located on Longevity Hill (Wanshoushan 萬壽山) within the imperial city. During the fourteenth century, Longevity Hill was known for its lush vegetation, especially the graceful willow trees that adorned the small island upon which the hill rose. Guanghan Hall was one of the imperial city's jewels. Perched atop Longevity Hill, it overlooked the calm lakes where the imperial family boated among the thick cover of water lilies that often adorned the waters. From its elevation, the hall also commanded an unparalleled view of the entire capital.[72] To gain access to the hall and its occupants was literally and figuratively to ascend the very heights of the Yuan court.

Ayushiridara first appealed to Yi's role as teacher. The heir apparent inquired about the meaning of the term "benevolence and wisdom" (*ren zhi* 仁智).[73] Yi replied, "Loving the people is called benevolence. Distinguishing matters is called wisdom. If a ruler uses these to govern the world, then he will achieve Great Peace."

Perhaps in an effort to tempt Yi with imperial wealth, the heir apparent asked Yi if he had ever seen such splendid columns (literally "columns of gold and jade"). Guanghan Hall's twelve columns enjoyed great renown. Intricately carved with clouds and dragons by imperial craftsmen, the columns were painted with gold.[74] Despite the grandeur and exclusivity of Guanghan Hall, Yi remained unfazed. He responded in classically Confucian language. "[For] a ruler who governs through benevolence, even if he were to reside in a dwelling of rotting timbers, it would be sturdier than metal or stone. If he did not [rule through benevolence], metal and jade would fall short of rotting timbers."

During the interview, the heir apparent honored Yi by allowing him to sit. This was a mark of status also enjoyed by two other guests that day, Wangjianu 王家奴 (Slave of the Wang family) and Bosali 伯撒里, two eminent Mongols who held some of the most prestigious titles of honor at the Yuan court at the time. Yet another court heavy, Tughlugh-Temür (Ch. Tulu Tiemuer 禿魯帖木兒, d. 1364), a current favorite of the emperor, stood playing the zither for the heir apparent's entertainment. Taking the zither from Tughlugh-Temür, the heir apparent strummed fragments of several melodies. "When one does not practice," he observed, "one forgets them." Yi seized the occasion to appeal to his host. Falling to his knees, he implored, "As long as you do not forget your concern for the people, a few melodies on the zither, what harm is there in forgetting them?" Ayushiridara would later relate Yi's words to his father, the emperor, who was boating on the nearby lakes. Toghan-Temür remarked laconically, "We have long known of this venerable worthy. Among your maternal relatives [or in-laws 外家], he is the only [one of worth]."[75]

One might interpret Yi's comments as pious Confucian pontification. Yet given the circumstances of Yi's mission in the capital, it seems likely that Yi was saying something much more specific. Throughout all his remarks Yi was arguing that the heir apparent, as a ruler, must place the interests of the public weal above personal desire. Put with a bluntness not permitted Yi, the message might summarized: Ayushiridara needed to put aside the family vendetta against King Kongmin, a competent king.

Family matters remained a prominent topic of conversation for Yi Kong-su. In a subsequent interview with the empress, Ki returned to causes of "her brother's disastrous fall." Again, Yi minimized Kongmin's culpability. "[Of those who] are greedy for riches and [become objects of] resentment," he insisted, "few escape [calamity]. It [the fall of her brother] was brought about by circumstances. It was not the king's desire."

This insistent lobbying on behalf of the king did not go unremarked. Pak Buqa, a palace eunuch from Koryŏ close to the empress, complained, "Yi Kong-su speaks only on behalf of his lord. How could he consider [the interests of] his relatives?" Ki apparently agreed. She and Yi did not meet again for some time.[76] Implicit in Pak's criticism was the idea that family interests should trump dynastic loyalty. Yi's effort on behalf of his king was the striking exception that proved the rule. Both Yi and King Kongmin took for granted that an appeal to family ties was an effective strategy for advancing the interests of country.

Despite the empress's rebuff and Yi's apparent failure to influence the heir apparent, some believed that Yi imperiled the plan to install

Tash-Temür as the next king of Koryŏ. When Tash-Temür arrived in Liaoyang on the way to Korea, his handler Ch'oe Yu had argued that Yi must be made to leave Daidu. "Yi Kong-su is in the capital. It is impossible to know his intentions. If he were to change in the interim, it would be too late for regret." The accounts in the *Official History of the Koryŏ Dynasty* and Ch'oe's funerary epitaph maintain that he then paid substantial bribes to Tughlugh-Temür and Pak Buqa to ensure Yi's departure from Daidu and return to Koryŏ.[77]

The ambiguity of Yi's position is striking. Ch'oe's comment suggests that in the eyes of some, Yi appeared to support Tash-Temür. Only "if he were to change," that is, to abandon his support for Tash-Temür, would Yi be a matter of concern. At least a portion of the Koryŏ court also viewed Yi with suspicion. The Koryŏ court stripped Yi of a recent promotion to prime minister of the left, when a Koryŏ translation official returned from Daidu with a "false" report that Yi had accepted a similar but higher post in Tash-Temür's government.[78] The narrative details of Yi's biography in the *Official History of the Koryŏ Dynasty* and his funerary epitaph indicate that the authors felt compelled to dispel doubts about Yi's loyalty to Kongmin. As noted above, the *Official History of the Koryŏ Dynasty* includes the dramatic comment that Yi would rather die than accompany Tash-Temür to Koryŏ. Both the *Official History of the Koryŏ Dynasty* and his funerary epitaph include a statement of Yi's unwavering opposition to Tash-Temür's government. He would rather shave his head, become a monk, and withdraw to the mountains than join the imposter king.

Yi's biography in the *Official History of the Koryŏ Dynasty* relates an episode of high drama intended to prove Yi's loyalty.

> When Tŏkhŭng-gun fell, Yi Kong-su conferred with . . . [half a dozen fellow Korean officials in Daidu at the time]. They wrote a note and placed it inside a bamboo staff. They secretly dispatched their attendants . . . to dress in rags and assume the guise of beggars. They took a short cut and reported to the throne: "Ch'oe is again plotting to raise a great army and go eastward. We would that You do not say that Tŏkhŭng-gun is already fallen. Prepare carefully against him." Only then did our dynasty know that Yi Tŭk-ch'un [the Korean translation official noted above] had reported falsely [about Yi's post in Tash-Temür's government].

德興既敗公遂與・・・等爲書納竹杖中潛遣傔從鄭良宋元衣籃縷爲乞人狀從間道報崔濡復謀起大兵而東願勿謂德興已敗謹備之本國始知得春妄。[79]

Prior to this bit of cloak-and-dagger intrigue, the Koryŏ court had considered Yi firmly in Tash-Temür's camp.

As the biography of Yi Kong-su notes, Ch'oe Yu did not abandon his efforts to enthrone Tash-Temür after his initial setback. Upon his return to Daidu, Ch'oe "again sought the support of the powerful. He planned to raise a great army and move eastward."[80] Ch'oe appealed directly to the emperor. If Tash-Temür was placed on the throne, Ch'oe promised Toghan-Temür, "all eligible men will be sent to serve in the guard troops of the Son of Heaven." He also offered visions of Japanese military assistance to the emperor. Ch'oe would "establish Japanese myriarchies in Kyŏngsang and Chŏlla provinces to recruit Japanese men. They would be granted seals of office and serve as reinforcements for our Liege State."[81] In addition to playing on the Yuan's pressing military needs, Ch'oe reassured the emperor that the yearly flow of grain and women from Koryŏ to Daidu would continue without interruption.

Early in October 1364, the Yuan court formally confirmed Kongmin as Koryŏ's king. Although the Mongols' imprimatur was slow to arrive, Kongmin had entertained at least four envoys from regional Chinese military leaders during the spring and summer of 1364.[82] On at least one occasion, Kongmin had dispatched a return mission.[83] The Yuan court itself had continued to send official envoys to inform him of important political developments in Daidu.[84] Nonetheless, final confirmation of his status came as a great relief to Kongmin. The gifts he showered on the bearer of glad tidings, Chang Cha-on 張子溫, the king's principal spokesman in Daidu, reflect Kongmin's spirits. A horse from the royal stables, a gold belt, a nugget of silver, fifty *sŏk* 石 of rice and legumes, and 250 bolts of cotton were Chang's reward.[85] Not only did the Yuan court confirm Kongmin's status, it also presented to him Ch'oe Yu, the man who had caused the king so many sleepless nights.[86] On November 25, 1364, the Koryŏ court executed the would-be kingmaker.[87] Only at this time did Yi receive permission to return from Daidu to Koryŏ.[88]

Three weeks prior to Ch'oe's execution, an envoy from the Yuan court had arrived in Kaegyŏng bearing the official imperial rescript restoring Kongmin to his throne.

Our Shizu [Qubilai] unified the realm. The Koryŏ king [Wang] Ch'ŏl admired his virtue and submitted. He was granted the title of king. Thereupon we became bound by close family ties. It has been many years now. Tribute offerings have [come] without interruption. You, Bayan-Temür, have been able to succeed to your ancestor's enterprise. Your entire reign you have been devout and conscientious. Recently, sorcerer rebels have been rampant. They raided throughout the Liaoxi region. They attacked its battlefields. You were able to formulate marvelous stratagems to secure victory. You eradicated the hordes of miscreants. Official seals and precious jades, you returned to the Imperial Court. You have rendered merit to our family. In truth you added luster to your forefather's glory.

Unexpectedly, Ch'oe Yu secretly hatched a scheming plot. He foolishly hoped to gain advancement. He relied upon the dictatorial minister Shuosijian as a distant relative. He joined with the eunuch Pak Buqa to realize his scheme [of entrapment]. Hugger-mugger they submitted their petition [to the throne] in a memorial. The imperial edict transferred the throne without fault. Thereupon it reached [the point of] warfare. The [whole] region was in tumult. [This matter] caused Me to sigh deeply.

Now not only has common consensus become clear, the judgment of the Censorate concurs. We are just in matters of punishment and reward in regard to this matter. We have dismissed Tash-Temür. We revoke the seals of office given to him and order him to reside in Yongping. Therefore We order Bayan-Temür hereupon to resume his former titles, to watch over his people, and to be Our Eastern Shield. You must not diminish your meritorious service. Receive and obey [this command].[89]

我世祖皇帝混一文軌高麗王曔向風歸附授以王爵遂結懿親迨茲有年朝貢不絶汝伯顔帖木兒克承先業世篤勤勞比者妖賊陸梁轉掠遼霫之境犯其疆場乃能出奇制勝殲除群醜璽章賓玉復歸天府功在我家允有光于前烈不圖崔濡陰萌險譎妄希進用倚權臣搠思監爲葭孚構閹官朴不花爲媒孽矇聾奏請詔旨無辜易位爰及干戈一方騷然朕所深嘆厥今公論昭著重以臺評是用大明黜陟其塔思帖木兒收還印綬俾居永平肆命伯顔帖木兒仍復舊爵綏輯其民爲朕東藩爾其益篤忠孝毋替厥勳尚欽哉。

Toghan-Temür's decision to reinstate Kongmin as king of Koryŏ requires some explanation. As noted above, Tash-Temür enjoyed a modicum of support in Kaegyŏng and apparently widespread support among Koreans resident in Daidu. Despite Yi's efforts, there is no evidence that Empress Ki or the heir apparent abandoned their desire to replace Kongmin with Tash-Temür. Finally, Ch'oe's guarantee of more direct access to Koryŏ military resources and the prospect of Japanese recruits must have held some allure for Toghan-Temür. Despite all these factors, the Yuan court dropped its support of Tash-Temür and Ch'oe Yu. Why?

First, Ch'oe Yu's disastrous military failure along the Yalu River unquestionably rendered the whole scheme far less appealing to the emperor. A long drawn-out campaign was the last thing Toghan-Temür wanted as he faced serious military threats from both Chinese warlords and increasingly autonomous Mongol generals. In its sustained diplomatic efforts, the Koryŏ court portrayed Kongmin as a loyal military ally with a proven record of success against such major military foes as the Red Turbans.[90]

This success certainly compared well both with Ch'oe Yu's bungling efforts against Korean royalists and with the Yuan's inability to suppress rebellion within China. In a pair of undated poems, the Korean literatus Wŏn Ch'ŏn-sŏk celebrated the recapture of the capital from Red Turban forces. In his explanatory preface, Wŏn wrote: "On the eighteenth day of the first lunar month of the year 1362, 100,000 men of the Two Frontiers and Six Provinces . . . arrived at the capital. They attacked from all sides and swept the rebels from the field, allowing our Koryŏ to renew again the royal enterprise [the Koryŏ dynasty]." Wŏn sets a thoroughly Korean context—the battle site, the triumphant Koryŏ military, and the resurrection of the Koryŏ dynasty.

The northern rebels treacherously plot,
  They are no daunting foe. 北寇奸謀未足雄
The glorious enterprise of the Eastern Han,
  Is now even more limitless. 東韓盛業更無窮
Arms of the reeking invaders,
  The dust of battle settled. 腥膻釖戟風塵靜
All people in the realm at peace,
  One day's meritorious service. 四海民安一日功

They offered their loyalty and righteousness,
  Several heroes. 輸忠奮義几英雄
They drilled the Capital Army,
  Stratagems without limit. 振旅京師計莫窮

They completely swept away the recalcitrant villains,
  On the day they pacified and suppressed [the enemy], 掃盡頑兇平盪日
Each hefted their banners and weapons,
  Competing to win honors.[91] 各□□[92]戟竟論功

Wŏn celebrates the Korean triumph, extolling the generals' bravery, loyalty, skillful command, and the decisiveness of the victory. Especially noteworthy is the silence regarding any military assistance from or political debt to the Great Yuan *ulus*, Koryŏ's putative overlord. Wŏn makes the point emphatically—the Koreans defeated the Red Turbans without Yuan help. In fact, the only indirect references to the Mongols appear in such clearly pejorative terms as "Northern Rebels" and "reeking invaders." Northern rebels had been a term for invading Mongol forces of the thirteenth century. Wŏn had used the expression in exactly this way in at least one other of his extant poems.[93] The term "reeking of animals" was a common slur in both China and Korea against steppe peoples. In other words, Wŏn was not too subtly painting the Red Turbans as a more recent form of Mongol invaders. Could he have been suggesting a similar Koryŏ victory over the Yuan to King Kongmin? In any case, Koryŏ confidence in its military strength was growing.

The lesson was not lost on other observers in East Asia. No later than spring 1363, Chinese warlords began courting Koryŏ. Late in May 1363, the powerful Zhang Shicheng, who controlled the rich and prosperous Jiangsu region, sent an envoy to the Koryŏ court with felicitations on its victory over the Red Turbans. His envoy presented Kongmin with silk textiles and a peacock (see Chapter 8).[94] Prior to this, late in December 1362 or early in January 1363, the Mongolian commander of Liaoyang had presented gifts to the Koryŏ throne and requested a bride.[95]

Political developments at the Yuan court also played a critical role in the decision to reinstate Kongmin as king. On August 24, 1364, Bolod-Temür encamped his army outside Jiande Gate 建德門, on the northwestern face of the capital's looming walls.[96] From a Mongol family with a tradition of government service, Bolod-Temür was a veteran of combat, both military and political. Beginning in 1358, he had assumed a series of high-level military commands in North China, where he campaigned from Shandong in the east to Datong 大同 and Jining 冀寧路 (present-day Taiyuan 太原) in the west. He was also the father of Toghan-Temür's other empress, the Qonggirad Bayan-Qutuq. By 1360 he had become embroiled in a complex struggle for power involving Köke-Temür (the Yuan's other leading general) and several competing factions at the court. This struggle, which fatally undermined the Great Yuan *ulus*, has been ably recounted elsewhere.[97] The narrative below focuses on Bolod-Temür, the heir apparent, and Empress Ki.

According to Korean sources, once ensconced in power in Daidu, Bolod-Temür addressed the unresolved issue of who was to occupy the Koryŏ throne. In conference with his senior advisors, Bolod-Temür opined, "The Koryŏ king has rendered meritorious service; he is without fault. He has been ensnared by small men. Should we not first address this wrong?"[98] The emperor then issued an edict restoring Kongmin to the throne and returning Ch'oe Yu to Koryŏ in irons.[99] Bolod-Temür's proposal was part of a more general effort to rectify standing problems at the Yuan court. These included the execution of several of the emperor's favorites, the end of nonessential palace construction, cuts in court expenditure, and a prohibition against Buddhist ceremonies conducted by Tibetan monks.[100]

What was the importance of the Koryŏ throne to Bolod-Temür? No explicit records survive, but it seems likely that Bolod-Temür's efforts to restore Kongmin were related to his struggles with Empress Ki and the heir apparent, Tash-Temür's most important backers at the Yuan court.[101] Bolod-Temür's daughter was the emperor's primary empress, although Toghan-Temür appears to have been more attached to Empress Ki. Relations between Bolod-Temür and the heir apparent, the son of Empress Ki, were poor. Threatened by the heir apparent, late in 1363 two key supporters of the emperor sought refuge with Bolod-Temür in his military stronghold in Jining. Bolod-Temür rebuffed the heir apparent's repeated efforts to apprehend the men.[102]

Ayushiridara charged Bolod-Temür with harboring a treasonous official and intimated that the general's army posed a threat to the court. Late in April 1364, the heir apparent pressured the emperor to take action. Perhaps against his own wishes, the emperor stripped Bolod-Temür of his command and exiled him to Sichuan. Bolod-Temür announced that he did not believe that the edicts represented the emperor's true intentions. He ignored the orders. By early in May, the court had ordered Köke-Temür to move against Bolod-Temür.[103]

Since a direct attack on the heir apparent was not possible, Bolod-Temür attacked Ayushiridara's surrogates. The general placed the blame for misleading the emperor and for corruption on two men closely allied with the heir apparent. He demanded their heads. By mid-May, an army led by one of Bolod-Temür's commanders was poised just south of the capital. Within days, the court announced the exile of the two men; it then turned them over to Bolod-Temür's commander.[104]

Mission accomplished, the army quickly withdrew to Datong. Less than two weeks later, perhaps at the urging of the infuriated heir apparent, the court issued orders for Köke-Temür to attack Bolod-Temür's base at Jining. In response, Bolod-Temür led an army to Daidu, turning aside ineffectual military efforts by the heir apparent to halt his progress. On August 24, 1364, a day after the heir apparent had fled Daidu, Bolod-Temür occupied the capital. In what is reported as a tearful meeting with his son-in-law the emperor, Bolod-Temür and the two men he had sheltered from the heir apparent protested their innocence. The emperor granted Bolod-Temür and his supporters a string of impressive civil and military posts and titles. Unwilling to sample the tender mercy of Bolod-Temür, the heir apparent ignored imperial edicts demanding his return to the capital.[105]

Instead, Ayushiridara worked to build support against Bolod-Temür in the provinces. From his sanctuary in Taiyuan under the protection of Köke-Temür, the heir apparent sent envoys to armies in Mongolia (Lingbei 嶺北), Gansu, Liaoyang, and Shaanxi to urge a joint attack on Bolod-Temür. From the relative safety of Liaoyang, the Chinese official Li Shizhan circulated official government notices wide and far that lambasted Bolod-Temür's action. "One who violates the previous meritorious service of several generations [of ancestors] is called a rebellious son. One who commits the great crime of disregarding the ruler is called a treasonous minister. [Even now] he obstinately sends envoys to explain [away our] myriad questions and to rally the armies in pursuit of a great undertaking."[106] Bolod-Temür was not amused. He had one of his generals attack supporters of Ayushiridara based at Shangdu. He drove the heir apparent's mother, Empress Ki, out of the imperial palace city and put her under house arrest for 100 days.[107]

Late in April 1365, Bolod-Temür visited the empress in her place of banishment. He ordered her to "return to the palace to retrieve her seal and to compose a letter to be sent to the heir apparent." The note written, he turned her out of the palace once again.[108] She would not return until early in July.[109] Several sources claim that Ki gained her release through manipulating Bolod-Temür's lust.[110] At one point, she presented a woman to her captor as a bride.[111] Impatient to consummate the marriage, the story goes, he temporarily waived a proper dowry. During his time in Daidu, Bolod-Temür acquired a harem of more than forty women. Dressed in their finery, his wives marched in procession when Bolod-Temür went to the court. A nearly contemporaneous Chinese observer noted, "Bolod-Temür wallowed in drink and sex. He lost his edge."[112]

Late in July, Bolod-Temür lost his life. Working with the knowledge of the emperor, on July 27, 1365, assassins planted an axe in Bolod-Temür's skull beneath the plums trees of Yanchun Pavilion.[113] He had been on his way to report the victory of his general over supporters of the heir apparent in Shangdu. Laodisha 老的沙, the emperor's maternal uncle whom Bolod-Temür had shielded against the heir apparent, also suffered a wound to the forehead. He managed, however, to escape on horseback. He gathered Bolod-Temür's mother, wife, and son, and fled northward. The emperor issued an order for people in the capital to kill all Bolod-Temür's subordinates. The next day, the emperor ordered the heir apparent to return to Daidu. Accompanying the edict was evidence that the heir apparent's nemesis was no longer a threat: a box containing Bolod-Temür's decapitated head.[114] By early 1366, both Laodisha and Tughlugh-Temür had been executed by order of the throne.[115]

The fortunes of the heir apparent and Empress Ki were mixed. Escorted by Köke-Temür's army, in October 1365 the heir apparent returned to the capital. Empress Ki wanted Ayushiridara to ride the wave of Köke-Temür's military strength right to the throne. The general, however, stopped in the suburbs of Daidu.[116] The emperor kept his throne for several more years. Early in 1366, the Mongol empress

Bayan-Qutuq died. Empress Ki was invested as Toghan-Temür's new primary empress and granted the surname Solongqa 肅良合, Mongolian for "Korean."[117] The formal elevation in status culminated three decades of nearly ceaseless struggle at the court. From a humble palace attendant serving tea, Ki had become the most powerful woman in Eastern Eurasia. Bolod-Temür and his supporters had been the latest men to underestimate Ki's iron will and keen mind. As Koryŏ's military preparations and the intensive diplomatic efforts described above demonstrate, King Kongmin did not commit the same mistake.

The fate of Tash-Temür is wreathed in mystery. As noted above, the Yuan court had placed him under house arrest in Yongping 永平, a prefecture approximately 125 miles east of Daidu. As long as he lived, however, Tash-Temür posed a potential threat to King Kongmin. This must have been obvious to everyone. At the time, Yongping was administratively subordinate to the Liaoyang Branch Secretariat, home to a large Korean population, and closely linked to Koryŏ. In order to remove this threat, early in 1365, Kongmin dispatched an envoy to the Yuan throne requesting that Tash-Temür be placed in his custody. When the king's envoy arrived in Liaoyang, Heilü, the bureau manager of military affairs (*zhi shumiyuan shi* 知樞密院事), informed him: "The emperor has instructed his minister to beat Tash-Temür and return [him] to his native land. At the moment, it happens that he has lesions on his back. When he has recovered, [we] will beat and then return him."[118] The Yuan court's position allowed little room for further pressure, and the Koryŏ envoy returned.[119] Given the paucity of sources, it is difficult to divine the Yuan court's intentions. At the very least, Tash-Temür was to be held in reserve for possible future use in relations with the Koryŏ throne.

In the meantime, however, the Mongol court showed its appreciation of Kongmin's ongoing contributions to the empire. In April 1365, Yuan officials traveled to Kaegyŏng to invest King Kongmin with the title of Grand Marshal (*taiwei* 太尉), a mark of honor from the Mongol throne. Additionally, in recognition of services during the campaign against the Red Turbans, five of the king's ministers were granted titular positions in the Yuan government. The king greeted the Mongol envoys at the Branch Secretariat offices, where he held a banquet on their behalf.[120] Thus, Toghan-Temür granted prestigious titles and public recognition to the Koryŏ court at the same time that he retained Tash-Temür as a potential threat to Kongmin.

To return to the question posed at the outset of this tale, why did the Yuan throne attempt to replace King Kongmin with his clansman Tash-Temür? Empress Ki's desire for revenge certainly may have figured in the decision. As late as 1371, the Koryŏ court highlighted to the Ming court Empress Ki's desire for vengeance after Kongmin's purge.[121] However, considering her intelligence and political savvy, hatred of Kongmin alone cannot account for the attempted change in the throne. Given the military conditions of the time, especially the recent Red Turban wars in Liaodong and Koryŏ, Empress Ki may have been attempting to remove Toghan-Temür's Eastern Shield. King Kongmin had proven Koryŏ's military competence and asserted his desire to resume closer ties with the Yuan throne. If Kongmin were replaced with a biddable client of Empress Ki, the emperor would have been left further isolated, perhaps sufficiently beleaguered that he would yield the throne to Ayushiridara, Empress Ki's son. It should be recalled that Tash-Temür's successor was to be a kinsman of Empress Ki.[122] Thus, if in the future Tash-Temür proved unsatisfactory as a client king, a member of the Ki family would be in position to ascend the Koryŏ throne.

Empress Ki's aggressive pursuit of her son's political interests was fully consonant with Mongolian political culture. During the mid-thirteenth century, "the most intelligent woman in the world," Sorghaghtani Beki, carefully engineered her sons' rise to supreme power.[123] In the process she effected an epochal change in the Mongolian polity, the Toluid line's replacement of the house of Ögödei as the most dominant in the empire. Other women, such as Qubilai's wife Chabui and, later, Empress Dowager Targi, also wielded considerable power at court. One recent study suggests that the wives and mothers of nearly every Mongolian ruler in East Asia exercised considerable power and harbored significant political ambitions. The competition among these women and their followers figured in some of the most prominent political and military incidents of the fourteenth century.[124] Despite her Koryŏ birth, Empress Ki was a member of the empire's elite. Her expectations and behavior were shaped by Mongolian political culture, which permitted strong women a voice in determining the *ulus*'s fortunes.

If Ki's primary interest was placing her son on the throne rather than revenge against Kongmin, what was Toghan-Temür's reason for acquiescing to her demands? In a general sense, Mongol interference in the selection of Koryŏ kings was nothing new. It dated back to the thirteenth century and had only increased during the mid-fourteenth century. However, if we restrict our consideration to Toghan-Temür, the emperor's treatment of Toqto'a is illuminating. Strong, tall, an accomplished rider and archer of good lineage, Toqto'a had played a critical role in eliminating the powerful prime minister Bayan in 1340. Freed from Bayan's dominance, Toghan-Temür began to rule as well as reign. In 1354, Toqto'a's energy, ambition, charisma, and repeated successes alarmed Toghan-Temür, who tacitly approved his dismissal and death. In this case and others, Toghan-Temür had demonstrated a proclivity for eliminating men who grew dangerously powerful, regardless of their contributions to the empire.[125] The marked success of Koryŏ armies against the Red Turbans coupled with Kongmin's past willingness to challenge the Yuan may have caused Toghan-Temür to view Kongmin with new, and deeply suspicious, eyes.

What, then, would Toghan-Temür have made of Kongmin's stress on Koryŏ military strength? Although such conjecture must remain speculative, Toghan-Temür and his advisors may have realized in the end that they still needed Kongmin's support. As the Great Yuan *ulus*'s position vis-à-vis the Chinese warlords to the south deteriorated during the early 1360s, Toghan-Temür probably saw the need for militarily capable allies in the northeast. As later events would show, the northeast did remain a Yuan stronghold long after Toghan-Temür was driven from the Central Plains.

More than seventy years ago, the famed Japanese historian Wada Sei 和田清 wrote, "When one considers the whole affair, it seems likely that the Yuan disliked Kongmin's resistance, and seizing upon the suppression of the rebels on the northern border, attempted to replace him as king, only to fail."[126] Largely correct, Wada's analysis nevertheless overlooks several facets of Yuan-Koryŏ relations. First, Wada was overly dismissive of Koryŏ military ability. For this reason, he did not consider the possibility that Toghan-Temür might perceive Kongmin as a potential threat. Second, Wada's use of "the Yuan" obscures the competing agendas that rived the Mongol court at the time. Third, and relatedly, he underestimated the political influence and ambition of Empress Ki. More recently, Min Hyŏn-gu has rightly drawn attention to Empress Ki's influence but overstates both Korean unity within Koryŏ and the importance of the "anti-Yuan politics" to either the Kaegyŏng or the Daidu court.

Empress Ki's machinations serve as a reminder that family interests often overshadowed concerns of dynasty or country. Neither the Yuan nor the Koryŏ court was monolithic; they seldom spoke with united voices. The ethnic, cultural, linguistic, and political complexity of courts of the Yuan *ulus* guaranteed that such survivors as Empress Ki, Toghan-Temür, Ayushiridara, and King Kongmin were skilled and subtle operators. Historians should never assume that their motives or methods were any less sophisticated than those more familiar to us today.

8
Wider Perspectives

As King Kongmin's struggle to keep his throne shows, the nature of the Great Yuan *ulus* guaranteed that the pursuit of political interest was not rigidly bound by such categories as nation, dynasty, or ethnicity. A century of Mongol empire had broadened perspectives throughout Eurasia. Even as twilight set upon the Great Yuan *ulus*, these wider vistas guided the expectations and behavior of men and women who saw opportunity in decline.

This chapter begins with a brief survey of the diplomatic networks that developed in East Asia during the mid-fourteenth century, with particular attention to the place of Koryŏ. It then examines how the Red Turban wars figured in memory, including the story of Yi Sŏng-gye's rise. It concludes with a consideration of the wider significance of the Red Turban wars in Northeast Asia.

Diplomacy and Trade in a Crumbling Empire

Although King Kongmin continued to fulfill his responsibilities vis-à-vis the Yuan throne, he kept all his options open throughout the 1360s. He exchanged envoys and gifts with nearly every major leader in East Asia: from Toghan-Temür, the Yuan heir apparent, and Empress Ki to Köke-Temür, Bolod-Temür, Naghachu, and Gaojianu, from Zhang Shicheng, Fang Guozhen, and Zhu Yuanzhang to Jurchen chieftains,

Ashikaga *bakufu* authorities, regional officials in Kyūshū, and Yuan provincial governors.

In some ways, this hyperfluidity reflected the fading power of the Great Yuan *ulus* during the 1350s and 1360s. As Yuan control declined, regional powerholders multiplied. Relations between these new powerholders and the Great Yuan *ulus* ranged along a continuum, from basically loyal servants of the throne to open rebels, but nearly all relations involved considerable negotiation. The Yuan throne simply lacked the power to destroy military challengers. Instead it alternately applied military pressure, offered pardons and official posts, appealed to a sense of loyalty to the dynasty or more narrowly the imperial family, promised generous rewards, shifted blame elsewhere, or turned a blind eye to abuses. All such efforts were complicated by parallel strategies employed among the growing ranks of powerholders throughout East Asia. The Great Yuan *ulus*'s decline created both a strong demand and numerous opportunities for diplomacy.

However, in the same way that ambitious men's readiness to consider Chinese, Jurchen, Mongol, and Koryŏ allies grew out of the Mongolian polity's cosmopolitan outlook, the constant jockeying and alliance building of the mid-fourteenth century were perfectly congruent with Mongolian political culture. Joseph Fletcher once argued that "the recurrent, difficult, and often protracted and violent electoral process politicized tribal society down to the level of the *haran* (common people)."[1] Alliances were often fragile, short-lived affairs. Unions of size and duration were the exception rather than the rule. Thus, Mongols kept their noses to the wind, sensitive to shifts in power, appraising the strengths and weakness of potential allies and enemies, always aware that change was the only constant.[2] This outlook was particularly well suited to the 1350s and 1360s.

Not only did heads of state frequently communicate with one another, but emerging regional polities attempted to forge advantageous relations with dynasties and other up-and-comers. For instance, Zhang Shicheng, one of the most important of these regional leaders, dispatched at least seventeen envoys to the Koryŏ court. Beginning no later than 1358, his men presented gifts of crystals, jade buckles, furs, spices, silk textiles, and aloe wood incense. Building ties to Koryŏ promised political and economic dividends.[3] Zhang's envoys often had military titles like myriarch or chiliarch and brought such instruments of war as bows, arrows, and swords. The Koryŏ court took pains to show these envoys great respect. Kongmin appointed prestigious court scholars to draft personal correspondence with Zhang, which noted their friendship. Zhang Shicheng courted Koryŏ more assiduously than rival suitors, but other rebel leaders also made repeated overtures.[4]

Thus, even as Chinese rebel leaders were negotiating titles and official posts with the Yuan court, they actively pursued ties with foreign dynasties. As one might expect in an age of flourishing trade between China and Southeast Asia, one of the rebel leaders, Chen Youliang 陳友諒 (1321–63), even approached the Tran dynasty in Vietnam. In 1354 he sent an envoy requesting a marriage alliance. After suffering several defeats at the hands of Zhu Yuanzhang in 1361, he then requested military assistance. As a way to ingratiate himself with the Tran court, he apparently maintained the fiction that he was the son of Trận Íchtắc 陳益稷, who after being invested by Qubilai in 1286 as king of Annam, had lived out the rest of his days in Hubei province.[5] Chen and Tran are the Chinese and Vietnamese pronunciations, respectively, of the same Sinic character.

Koryŏ, too, was far from idle. As preceding chapters have shown, during the 1350s and 1360s, royal Koryŏ envoys regularly traveled to Daidu to offer felicitations and gifts to the emperor, the empress, the empress dowager, and the heir apparent. They also met with powerful military figures and other political personages outside the Yuan capital. For instance, the Koryŏ court dispatched the official and man of letters Chŏn Nok-saeng 田祿生 (1318–75) on several missions. Chŏn had passed both the Koryŏ civil service examination and the preliminary level of the Yuan examinations held at the offices of the Branch Secretariat for the Eastern Campaigns in Kaegyŏng.[6] Perhaps because of his skill in classical Chinese, which was the written medium of interregional diplomacy, the court employed Chŏn as a diplomatic specialist. In 1362, he was sent to Zhedong, where he likely established contact with the important warlord Fang Guozhen.[7] One of Fang's lieutenants accompanied Chŏn back to Koryŏ in 1364. Fang's envoy presented to the Koryŏ throne aloe incense, bows, arrows, and several books, including the Chinese political encyclopedias *Yuhai* 玉海 and *Tongzhi* 通志.[8]

Again in May 1365, Kongmin sent Chŏn to the Great Yuan *ulus*, this time to Daidu, where he was to present gifts to the Yuan heir apparent, the Sim Prince, and Köke-Temür.[9] In mid-April 1366, Kongmin dispatched Chŏn as an envoy to Regional Commander and Henan Prince Köke-Temür.[10] Köke-Temür had returned from Daidu to his base in Henan a few weeks earlier.[11] Chŏn's diplomatic activities did not pass unnoticed. In fact, "the Yuan heir apparent detested his [Chŏn's] acting as envoy and ordered him to return east [to Koryŏ]."[12] One of Chŏn's subordinates, Kim Che-an 金齊顏, counseled him: "Your Excellency is a great minister. You cannot remain [here in Daidu]. I will stay. I will carry out our mission."[13] King Kongmin considered the mission vital and ensured that Kim had sufficient funds to make the long journey to Köke-Temür's base in Henan.[14]

Kim traveled alone by horse through wartorn North China. Stressing the importance of the mission, Kim explained to Köke-Temür that although Chŏn had been ordered home, the Koryŏ king insisted that his communication be delivered to the general, one of the most important military figures in East Asia. Kim then presented a jade candle 玉燭 and explained that the candle was like Köke-Temür's virtue. If carefully polished, it would shine brightly.

Kim then came to the reason for his visit—military cooperation against rebel forces.

> Our king is brilliant and benevolently martial. He destroyed the hordes of Red Turbans, a million strong. In order to protect the imperial house, he encouraged all under heaven [to rally behind the Yuan]. Now, Your Lordship is famed throughout the realm for loyalty and righteousness. [We] wish east and west to join forces to eliminate the rebels to assist the imperial house.
>
> 我王聰明仁武。坐殲紅賊百萬之衆，以安帝室，爲天下倡。今大王忠義聞天下。欲東西協力削平僭亂，夾輔帝室。[15]

"The great prince," the Korean court annals relate, "was immensely pleased." Extant materials, however, provide few details of the proposed military alliance or its success. Kim phrased the military alliance in terms of a shared loyalty to the Yuan throne. One wonders, however, if Kongmin had not considered a future without the Yuan. Such speculations aside, Kongmin was obviously keen to keep his hand in the game. In mid-June, he dispatched yet another envoy to Köke-Temür.[16]

The Koryŏ throne's interest did not go unrequited. Late in December 1366, Kim returned to Koryŏ with an envoy from Köke-Temür. The man was a secretary in (Köke-Temür's provincial?) Central Secretariat (*Zhongshu jianjiao* 中書檢校) named Guo Yongxi 郭永錫.[17] Guo had passed the Yuan's civil service examination, and one of his first acts in Koryŏ was to visit the Confucian Academy in Kaegyŏng.[18] A few days later, on behalf of Köke-Temür he presented a gift of 100 pieces of gold to King Kongmin. After a few rounds of wine, Guo invited the king's ministers to join him in the composition of linked poetry. It was an awkward moment for the Koryŏ court. "All those around the throne were military men," relates the *Official History of the Koryŏ Dynasty*, "and they looked at each other nonplussed. The king was deeply embarrassed." Early in January 1367, the king fêted Guo. Köke-Temür's envoy declined the sets of clothing, gold belt buckle, and horse saddle that Kongmin offered his esteemed guest.[19]

Others at the Koryŏ court shared in the little humiliations Guo dispensed so liberally. At one point during his stay in Kaegyŏng, Guo offered words of praise to his hosts:

"I have heard that the extraordinariness of Koryŏ's mountains and rivers preserves the customs of Jizi (Kija). I would view your maps, [and documents related to] rites and music, and government administration." [The Koryŏ official Im] Pak said, "If you wish to know about the miraculous nature of my dynasty's mountains and rivers, right now Your Dynasty has the empress and the heir apparent. Are they not the quintessence of their [the mountains' and rivers'] pure energy?" [Guo] Yongxi slapped his knee and exclaimed, "Then we should tell parents throughout the realm to prefer the birth of baby girls over baby boys." Everyone present blushed with shame.

嘗聞高麗山水之異尚有箕子之風，願觀地圖禮樂官制。[林]樸曰欲知我國山水靈異，方今上有皇后太子。豈非鍾其秀氣耶。永錫拊膝高吟曰遂令天下父母心不重生男重生女。左右慚赧。[20]

Although Guo framed his request in terms of cultural links between China and Koryŏ, he wanted the details of Koryŏ's geography and administration. Unwilling to disclose such sensitive information, Im reminded Guo that the empress was Korean and that her son, the heir apparent, was half-Korean. Not to be outdone, Guo restated the matter in terms of gender. Women were a critical feature of Koryŏ political influence at the Yuan court. Koryŏ men did not, however, appreciate reminders of this fact. Few shed tears when Guo departed Kaegyŏng. He traveled to the Western Capital and then to Köke-Temür's lands.[21] One wonders if Guo was the most appropriate man for the mission.

Whatever King Kongmin and his court thought of Guo, they continued their overtures to Köke-Temür. Late in May 1367, the king sent Chang Cha-on on a diplomatic envoy to Henan.[22] Although Köke-Temür is not mentioned by name, since his military base was in northern Henan at this time, it seems likely that Chang visited Köke-Temür. In 1376, a year after Kongmin's murder and eight years after the establishment of the Ming dynasty, Köke-Temür attempted to strengthen ties with the Koryŏ court by appealing to the "extremely cordial exchanges" he had enjoyed with Kongmin.[23] At this time, Zhu Yuanzhang, too, periodically sent envoys and messages to Köke-Temür and others.[24]

Zhang Shicheng was also thought to be interested in a military alliance with the Koryŏ throne. Sometime before 1368, rumors circulated that "Zhang Shicheng of the Yuan is recruiting generals from our [dynasty]." Zhang had recruited Chinese men of learning to his court, and given Toqto'a's precedent of marshaling Koryŏ military resources, the rumor cannot be dismissed out of hand.

Other facets of this international exchange were less overtly political. Pou, the prominent Sŏn monk and confidant to Kongmin, penned a number of short parting poems on the occasion of fellow Sŏn monks setting out for travel and study in China's Jiangnan region. Although the location of these meetings is unclear, at least two pieces were dedicated to Japanese monks.[25] In 1351, the Sŏn monk Naong visited the port city of Mingzhou 明州 (modern-day Ningbo 寧波) along the southeastern coast of China. For centuries, Mingzhou had been a vital economic hub in Southeast and East Asia, attracting merchants from Japan, Korea, Champa, and beyond.[26] It also regularly drew Buddhist monks like Naong. These religious peregrinations contributed to the flow of information through East Asia. It seems likely that during his stay in Mingzhou, Naong not only visited famous temples but also acquired and transmitted intelligence relating to warlords such as Fang Guozhen.[27] Slightly later, a powerful advisor and confidant to Kongmin, the priest Sin-don, dispatched fellow monk Ch'ŏn Hŭi 千禧 to travel to Buddhist temples in lands controlled by Zhang Shicheng. During his travels, Ch'ŏn met with Zhang's brother.[28]

Desired as a possible economic and military ally in the far-ranging wars that raged through the region, Koryŏ was thoroughly integrated into the rapidly changing landscape of East Asia. This fact did not escape the Koryŏ throne, the Mongol court, loyalist generals in the Yuan, or ambitious Chinese rebels. An elegy composed for a leading minister during the Kongmin reign commented explicitly on the importance of international recognition.

> At home, [the king] executed Ki Ch'ŏl. Abroad, he exterminated the Red Turbans. [Kongmin's] civil virtue and military prowess were famed throughout the world. During the late Yuan, all the men who had occupied the southeast [of China], such as Fang Guozhen and Zhang Shicheng, sent envoys to present gifts to our forefather. The brilliance of the restoration brought glory to our ancestors.
>
> 内誅奇轍。外殲紅賊。文德武烈聞於天下。元季東南割據若方國珍張士誠輩皆遣使款獻我先祖。中興之烈有光於祖宗。[29]

By the 1360s, the Yuan needed Koryŏ as much as Koryŏ needed the Yuan; Yuan envoys traveling to Kaegyŏng outnumbered Koryŏ missions to Daidu. Koryŏ was one of the few remaining bulwarks of the increasingly shaky Yuan dynasty.[30] In the months and years immediately following the loss of Daidu in 1368, Yuan officials from Liaodong, Mongolian nobles, and Köke-Temür (newly appointed as prime minister) sent envoys to the Koryŏ court.[31] Some appealed to a history of shared allegiance and the bonds of kinship, while others held out the bright promise of future glory and new marriage alliances.[32] In nearly all cases, the envoys wanted Koryŏ's military, political, or logistical support.[33]

As Mongol control of the provinces eroded, intelligence and diplomatic overtures became more critical throughout the empire. During the 1350s and 1360s, envoys shuttled back and forth among all the major contenders for power in China, including Zhu Yuanzhang.[34] Zhu's later sensitivity to informal diplomacy was a reaction against the hyperfluidity of mid-fourteenth century East Asia—both overland and overseas—and an acknowledgment of its efficacy. As emperor of the new Ming dynasty, he would move vigorously to eradicate all diplomatic contact that occurred outside officially sanctioned channels (both domestically and internationally). It was not coincidental that Zhu linked, however falsely, even domestic political purges to collusion with foreign powers. A 1371 communication to the Koryŏ throne reflects his frustration with his inability to control intelligence within his borders.

The [Koryŏ] eunuch Yi and men of the Mongols, Turkestani, and various other groups come on the pretext of trade [but actually] to spy. Eunuch Yi has come two or three times. When he meets Mongols, he speaks the Mongol language. When he meets ordinary eunuchs, he speaks the Koryŏ language. When he meets men of Han, he speaks the language of the men of Han. How could this sort of spying deceive me?[35]

姓李的火者並達達回回諸色人部來推做買賣打細。李火者來了兩三番也。見達達説達達話，見一般火者説高麗話，見漢兒説漢兒話。 這般打細呵怎中我。

The Ming founder was himself a master of misdirection and subterfuge. Yet, here in the face of polyglot eunuchs who moved easily among several languages and ethnic groups, Zhu Yuanzhang felt compelled to assert his discernment. The fluid, negotiated aspect of the changing order of political and military relations in North China, Liaodong, and Koryŏ extended to broader patterns in Northeast Asia.

Japan, the Greater Yuan Ulus, *and Northeast Asia*

Although this narrative has focused principally on developments on the continent and peninsula, any consideration of Northeast Asia must include the maritime realm. Ships plied sea-lanes stretching from Guangzhou, Fuzhou, and Qingyuan 慶元 (present-day Ningbo) to Shandong, Liaodong, Koryŏ, and western Japan. Archeology provides us an example of the Chinese ships that sailed these waters. During the summer of 1991, local fishermen chanced upon a sunken ship in Bohai Bay, along the coast of Suizhong county, Liaoning province. Underwater archeology revealed that the 20–22-meter-long ship carried a cargo of iron and nearly six hundred pieces of white and black Cizhou porcelains from the Yuan period. Scholars speculate that they came from the kilns of Pengcheng 彭城 (present-day Cixian 磁縣, Hebei province) and were probably transported overland to the important coastal port of Zhigu 直沽 (near present-day Tianjin). Although some Chinese ships bound for Koryŏ and Japan did depart from Zhigu, the location of the Suizhong wreck suggests that it was probably following a coastal route to Liaodong when it sank, probably in the mid-thirteenth century.[36]

Perhaps the most convincing evidence for the scale of international maritime trade was the stunning 1976 discovery of a wreck off the southern coast of Korea. The ship, which sailed out of Qingyuan, carried more than 20,000 pieces of porcelain from China's principal manufacturing centers and twenty-eight tons of copper coins. Although precise dating of the ship is difficult, wooden tallies and coins suggest that it plied the seas during the first half of the fourteenth century. The Ashikaga *bakufu* authorized the ship's journey, and the great Zen temple of Kyoto, Tōfukuji 東福寺, provided a portion of the capital for the venture.[37]

Such evidence makes clear that cultural, commercial, and diplomatic relations among Japan, Koryŏ, and the Great Yuan *ulus* did not end with abortive Mongol campaigns against the Kamakura *bakufu* late in the thirteenth century. Although marked by peaks and valleys, the flow of monks from Japan's leading monasteries to prominent Buddhist centers in the Yuan demonstrates the continuing religious and cultural ties in East Asia under Mongol rule during the fourteenth century.[38] Many of these Japanese monks developed ties to Chinese cultural luminaries of the thirteenth and fourteenth centuries.[39]

Trade quickly resumed after the Mongols' failed efforts to conquer Japan. Qubilai's successors continued to seek commercial profit through overseas trade. Although violence occasionally marred the visits of Japanese merchants to Chinese shores during the first half of the fourteenth century, it was of limited scale and confined to Qingyuan, the officially designated port for international maritime trade.[40] These riots often erupted out of frustration with corrupt local Yuan officials who acted without court approval. In fact, when such incidents did occur, Daidu rigorously investigated charges of abuse and took firm measures to prevent their recurrence. Since the Mongols' rise early in the thirteenth century, international commerce had been a pillar of empire.

The Yuan simultaneously heightened vigilance along the coast. By the 1350s, pirate raids, usually organized and manned by sailors from Tsushima and Kyūshū, began to plague Koryŏ, and to a lesser extent, Yuan shores. However, the Yuan government did not lose interest in lucrative international trade with Japan. Neither did it categorically deny Japanese merchants access to the most lucrative market in the world.[41]

The roots of Japanese piracy lay firmly in Japan. Turmoil in the Great Yuan *ulus*, however, facilitated piracy's westward spread.

From the late 1350s and to the mid-1380s, Japanese pirates targeted coastal areas along Bohai Bay. They preyed primarily on Yuan and Koryŏ ships transporting tax grain from local government offices to their respective capitals in Daidu and Kaegyŏng. These ships traveled close to the shore, whose villages, administrative seats, and most especially rice warehouses were also subject to pirate raids.[42] Even inland areas were vulnerable. In 1352, raiding parties appeared in the suburbs of Kaegyŏng, deeply alarming residents of the capital. Similar attacks followed in 1357, 1358, and 1360.[43] Even the Red Turbans were vulnerable; in 1360, Japanese pirates attacked Red Turban forces in southern Liaodong and seized two affluent cities that the Chinese rebels had occupied (Jinzhou 金州 and Fuzhou 復州).[44]

The flow of Japanese Buddhist monks to the Jiangnan region reflected the ebb and flow of warfare during the last decades of the Yuan. In 1350, as Fang Guozhen closed in on Changguo 昌國, a small island close to Qingyuan and the island of Putuo (a famed pilgrimage site for the Guanyin cult), panic spread rapidly. Even long-term residents like the Japanese monk Ryūzan Tokken 竜山徳見 scrambled to find passage to Japan. A Japanese chronicle from the time notes, "The Great Yuan has completely fallen into decline. The whole world is in turmoil. I fear that there will not be a single day of safety. All the foreign ships have suffered disaster and misfortune."[45]

As Fang and Zhang Shicheng consolidated control over their respective territories during the mid-1350s, however, trade and the flow of Buddhist monks revived. The chaotic years of 1365–67 witnessed a sharp decline in traffic between Japan and the Yuan. But in 1367–68 plans were afoot in Japan to mount a trade mission to the Jiangnan region in order to finance the construction of a hospice in Kyoto.[46] In fact, growing violence in the Great Yuan *ulus* deepened ties between Japan and the continent. Some fearful Chinese literati sought refuge in Japan. Settling in Hakata, Kyoto, and elsewhere, they used their skills in letters, painting, and medicine to good account, winning a place in elite cultural circles and serving as political advisors to Ashikaga authorities. These refugees often brought detailed and sophisticated knowledge of recent developments in areas controlled by Zhang Shicheng and Chen Youliang.[47]

Behind the destructive Japanese piracy of the mid- to late fourteenth century was the assumption that no borders were absolute, that raiding or trading on the seas would yield wealth and power, and that relations with centers of authority (near or distant) were always subject to negotiation. A similar shifting and opportunist quality characterizes the memories and images born out of the Red Turban wars in Northeast Asia.

Memories of the Red Turban Incursions

The themes of death and destruction, bravery and merit, dominated memories of the Red Turban campaigns. Local gazetteers preserved elegiac poems and essays devoted to the Red Turban wars and their attendant damage. Some accounts extol the bravery of local troops, and others trace the roots of contemporary problems to the wars. Both recent and more distant memories did not exist in a vacuum; they were useful political resources put to service in a number of causes. King Kongmin and General Chŏng Se-un had used their success against the Red Turbans to bolster dynastic and personal fortunes. Later, Chosŏn-period writers would invoke Yi Sŏng-gye's bravery and skill in fighting the Red Turbans to legitimate Yi and his descendants.

Some damage went unrepaired for the remainder of the Koryŏ dynasty. Destroyed during the fighting of 1361, the eastern (Taedong 大同) and southern gates (Hamgu 含毬) of the strategic Western Capital remained tangible reminders of the city's suffering during the Red Turban occupation. According to Kwŏn Kŭn's account, the city gates were repaired only in 1392, after the founding of the Chosŏn dynasty, because "when border defenses are not firm, it is verily a matter of concern."[48]

The destruction and suffering caused by the Red Turban invasions worked themselves into memory, folk beliefs, prose, and poetry. Popular legend held that Red Turbans completely eradicated royal Koryŏ troops defending Kŭksŏngjin 棘城鎮 in Hwangju province. The town was abandoned, and in 1452, stone walls erected around its new location.[49] The site became inextricably tied to the destructive violence of war, prompting many passing literati to recall the death and devastation of the past. Ch'oe Suk-jŏng 崔淑精 (1433–80), for example, wrote:

In years past, fierce rebels broke through our border gates; 昔年怒寇闌塞門
They moved through our territory like a fire raging across a plain. 猛燄烈烈如燎原
Driving straight through [the land], they arrived at the foot of the city walls in less than a day; 長驅不日到城下
Inauspicious clouds dense, covering the world. 妖氛漠漠埋乾坤
The Gate Guardsmen fell under attack, blundering the crisis. 期門受敵誤機會
The Southern Armies were thrown in disarray, barbarian tongues a clamor. 南軍狼狽胡語喧
Hundreds of thousands destroyed in a single day. 數十萬人一朝殲
The remaining soldiers scattered in all directions, fleeing in defeat. 餘卒四散仍敗奔
The soldiers and generals, high and low, all reduced to bones. 同將貴賤作枯骨
Ethers of the wronged coalesce, the *yin* clouds gathering. 怨氣結作陰雲屯
The disconsolate winds howl sorrowfully, blowing to the present. 悲風颯颯吹至今
The ancient fort deserted and desolate, the green mountain denuded. 古城廖落蒼山根
I commit to poetry all my feelings, commemorating the noble souls of the deceased. 投詩直欲弔毅魂
Poems last forever, giving voice to the lingering grievances of the dead.[50] 筆端千古攄遺冤

Writing in 1521, Kim An-guk 金安國 (1478–1543) noted the devastation wrought by the Red Turbans on the formerly prosperous county of Munhwa 文化縣, located in what had been the Capital Region during the Koryŏ period.

From the time when the Red Turbans devastated the county, the whitened bones of those who died remained unburied and exposed in the fields, while the miasma caused by those who had died remained agitated; the stench caused an epidemic that spread throughout the province. . . . The towns and villages grew depressed. They [never] did regain the prosperity of yesteryear. The people of the three counties of Munhwa, Hŭngbongsan, and Chaenyŏng were most severely infected. Local officials fell ill and died one after another. None were able to serve out the full three years of their time in office. Nearly all the clerks and slaves perished. [The territory] was nearly ungovernable. The officials and the people, those above and those below, died of illness without cease. Tax and labor obligations to the state went unmet. The people were daily more desperate. Efforts to rescue them were ineffective.

自經紅賊敗殲之後，白骨暴野，沴氣熕冤，薰爲癘疫，轉染一道 . . . 邑里蕭然，非復昔日之殷阜。文化與鳳山載寧三邑被染尤甚。前後守宰死病相繼。無能數三年安其任者。吏卒僕隸之徒彫耗漸盡。殆不能官，官民上下憂死不暇。政庸不舉。民日困悴。拯救無方。

Eventually the county seat was relocated with the hope that the "poison of the epidemic would gradually dissipate without a trace."[51] Elsewhere Kim attributed Hwanghae province's general population decline, land flight, and economic hardship to the fighting of the "late Koryŏ" and disease.[52]

As John Duncan and others have noted, "by the second half of the fourteenth century, local society was in a state of disorder." Seeking relief from crushing rent burdens, abusive landlords, and poor harvests, farmers and even such local elites as *hyangni* abandoned their lands.[53] Even in relatively rich agricultural areas, deserted villages grew common. Duncan argues persuasively that the dire conditions in the countryside owed more to the penetration of the rural economy by powerful descent groups based in the capital than they did to foreign incursions. However, due to the drama and obvious damage of warfare, the Red Turban wars and coastal piracy masked more fundamental long-term socioeconomic developments.

The Red Turban campaigns and the presence of King Kongmin brought the glow of royalty to Pokju, present-day Andong. According to field surveys conducted by the Andong Folk Museum, today several villages maintain small wooden shrines that house simple wooden carvings said to represent variously Kongmin, his mother, and his daughter.[54] The wall painting of one shrine depicts two seated figures, one a regal male with a crown and the other a young girl. Local tradition holds that the girl saved the king from a Red Turban ambush by throwing herself in front of an arrow meant for Kongmin.[55]

Chinese memories of the Red Turban campaigns bear little impress of developments in Liaodong and Koryŏ. One of the few to explicitly mention their impact on Liaodong was the late Ming scholar Zhu

Guozhen 朱國禎 (1557–1632?). In discussing the unprecedented destruction of the late Yuan rebellions, Zhu observed, "Mao Gui and the others seized the opportunity to advance in all directions. From the Yellow River north, all the way beyond the pass to Liaoyang, there was no place not subject to despoliation."[56] In Zhu's mind, Liaoyang represents the outermost fringe of Red Turban activities or, perhaps more accurately, the outer range of his concerns. In many ways, Zhu's perspective mirrors that of most Chinese scholars up to the present.

Memories of unusually close ties between the Chinggisid house and Koryŏ during the mid-fourteenth century find voice in several later accounts of the rise and fall of the Mongols. As Christopher Atwood has noted, the early seventeenth-century Mongolian chronicle, *Altan Tobchi*, preserves a legend of Chinggis khan, in which his fourth wife, Qulan, a Merkid, appears instead as an empress from Korea. One suspects that this remembered version of history had its genesis in Toghan-Temür's marriage to Empress Ki. Atwood notes further that Mongolian legends related "the temptation of Chinggis Qan to flee to the southeast (Korea) or the southwest (Tangut)."[57] It seems likely that again the stories of Chinggis khan and Toghan-Temür are being conflated and that the image of flight to Korea probably originated in a nearly contemporaneous fourteenth-century account by Quan Heng. This tale maintains that as his empire crumbled, Toghan-Temür planned to flee to T'amma Island (present-day Cheju Island, Korea). Both examples suggest the lasting legacy of both Toghan-Temür and the Chinggisid-Koryŏ ties during the tumultuous Red Turban decades.

Others cast memories of the Red Turban wars more positively. As noted above, General Chŏng Se-un touted his own success in a time of military crisis. Kongmin used the warfare as a diplomatic chip in his efforts to retain his throne. In relations with leading Mongolian generals, the king's ministers trumpeted Koryŏ prowess. Chosŏn-period writers were thus treading a well-worn path when they extolled the exploits of future founder of the Chosŏn dynasty, Yi Sŏng-gye, against the Red Turbans.[58] In his funerary inscription for the dynastic founder's tomb, Kwŏn Kŭn wrote:

> During the time of King Kongmin, the Red Turbans rose up, attacking Shangdu and devastating the Liao-Shen region. None under Heaven dared

confront them. In 1361, they occupied the capital. Kongmin fled and dispatched the armies to retake the capital. Our progenitor was first in battle and presented victories [to the throne]. His awesome reputation began to spread. The following year [1362], he drove off the barbarian Naghachu,[59] while the next year [1363] he pursued the monk Wang Tash-Temür. He broke the foe's spirit and repelled the enemy. He was victorious wherever he turned. Because of this, Kongmin relied even more heavily upon him.[60]

恭愍王時，紅賊起。侵犯上都。蹦轢遼瀋。天下莫敢遏其鋒。至正辛丑來陷王京。恭愍播越。遣使克復。我太祖先登獻捷。威聲始振。明年壬寅走胡人納哈出。又明年癸卯逐僧王塔帖木[兒]。摧鋒却敵。所向必克。由是恭愍時倚益重。

Kwŏn notes that Yi's success in the military campaigns against the Red Turbans broadened his reputation and gained King Kongmin's confidence. Yi's efforts against the Red Turbans led to critical assignments in the dynasty's defense.

During the mid-fifteenth century, one of the founder's most celebrated descendents, King Sejong (r. 1418–50), commissioned the *Yongbi ŏch'ŏn ka* 龍飛御天歌 or *Song of the Dragon Flying to Heaven.* Intended in part to legitimate the Yi family's rule, the *Song* combined many elements, including praise and celebration of the founder and his ancestors, prophesy about the Yi family's ascent to power, and implicit moral precepts to future Chosŏn kings.[61] Canto 33 refers to Yi Sŏng-gye's exploits against the Red Turbans.

Bandits besieged the temporary palace:
The Son of Heaven wept.
When he went to give help and deceived the foe,
The bandits ran away.

Bandits looted the capital:
The King took refuge.
He led the van and won,
and the king returned.[62]

Thus, just as King Kongmin's court had attempted to turn Koryŏ's triumph over the Red Turbans into political capital in relations with the Mongol court, decades later the Chosŏn court wove the founder's heroics against the Red Turbans into a story of personal merit and dynastic legitimacy. Chosŏn writers further elaborated on these images in pictorial and verse form.[63]

Significance of the Red Turban Wars

The Red Turban wars in Northeast Asia form one piece in the larger mosaic of the Mongol empire's collapse. Massive physical destruction—towns and cities sacked, agricultural lands abandoned, populations decimated through disease, starvation, and war—accompanied political dislocation and destabilization throughout East Asia. Most of the critical political and cultural centers of Northeast Asia—Shangdu, Liaoyang, P'yŏngyang, and Kaegyŏng—fell to the Red Turbans. With local governance shattered, the Yuan central government briefly lost control of southern Liaodong. It never regained full command. For more than two decades, no one polity controlled the Liaodong region. Mongolian, Jurchen, Chinese, and Korean contenders vied for supremacy in a region marked by military and political fluidity. The contested state of Liaodong deeply influenced relations between the new Ming dynasty and the Koryŏ throne. Thus, the Red Turban wars did much to determine the issues and terrain of Ming-Koryŏ relations during the succeeding thirty or forty years.

The Koryŏ throne saw much of its northern territory slip behind its control. Driven from his capital in 1361, King Kongmin spent nearly two years in temporary quarters. The king's lack of a permanent seat is an emblem of his faltering ability to rein in his scattered officials. Due to incursions by the Red Turbans and Japanese pirate bands, many fled the north to seek refuge in central and southern Koryŏ. One observer noted at the time, "None of the literati (*sadaebu* 士大夫) could reside at peace in their homes."[64] Another official wrote of being driven to "the mountain forests" after Red Turban forces burned his residence in the capital.[65] One can trace at least a portion of these relocations through late fourteenth-century clan genealogies.[66] The perceptions of a depopulated north persisted for decades. During the early fifteenth century, the Chosŏn court would try to repopulate the north by forcibly relocating households from southern provinces.[67]

Some exploited the chaotic situation to consolidate their own economic and political interests at the local level.[68] Proclamations issued during and after the Red Turban wars noted the illegal seizure of lands and unauthorized use of critical infrastructure. Yet even as King Kongmin demanded an end to extra-legal extractions and the seizure of lands, he could ill afford to alienate elites. Instead, since the mid-1350s, the central government had granted honorary titles that conveyed political, economic, social, and military advantages to local elites willing to supply men and arms.[69] Based on an analysis of household registration records and clan genealogies, Hŏ Hŭng-sik has also noted the proliferation of honorary posts. He has further argued that military men dispatched to suppress the Red Turbans often married their sons into the families of local elites where they fought.[70]

The Red Turban campaigns exacerbated existing tensions at Kongmin's court. One gains some sense of these thinly veiled battles in the comments of the senior official and man of letters Yi Che-hyŏn. After the Red Turbans had been repelled, in a conversation with Hong Ŏnbak, Yi compared Koryŏ's circumstances to those of the Wei Kingdom 魏國, a Chinese state of the third century CE.

> The ancients deserved their reputations as stalwarts. The mountains and streams were the treasures of the Wei. If we had fortified our defenses in the first place, victory would have been ensured. We regret that we did not plan early on. If the rebels had fought on the plains, our troops would certainly have been defeated. It was because of rain and snow, taking the rebels unprepared, that we defeated them. This depended on the assistance of our ancestors' mountains and rivers.[71]

古人稱壯哉。山河此魏國之寶也。初若設險守隘制勝可必。恨不早圖也。賊若野戰則我軍必敗。但因雨雪乘賊不虞，故勝之。此賴宗社山河之祐也。

Here Yi undermines any special merit the generals might claim for their role in saving the dynasty from the Red Turbans. By asserting that the incursions befell Koryŏ only because of inadequate preparations, Yi downplays the Red Turbans' military puissance. Further, the Koryŏ victory grew out of the invaders' poor strategy and the natural advantages of geography and weather, not the efforts of the military—or, one might add, the king. One wonders about Hong's reaction. Some at the Koryŏ court singled out Hong for the dynasty's lack of preparation and subsequent defeat at the hands of the Red Turbans. Hong dismissed one such critic for his temerity.[72] Perhaps Yi's seniority granted a degree of protection.

Militarization

The deterioration of the Great Yuan *ulus* ushered in a process of militarization that directly affected all Northeast Asia. As noted in Chapter 3, Koryŏ generals and troops fought side by side with imperial Mongolian, Chinese, and Tibetan forces against Chinese rebels in southeastern China. These campaigns, a product of faltering Yuan control, spurred Koryŏ to strengthen its military. Kongmin's efforts to increase royal power in 1356 led to a brief series of military clashes with Yuan border forces in Liaodong. The prospect of future battles lent greater urgency to efforts to increase the number of men available for military service, improve the economic foundations of military households, ameliorate conditions for active-service soldiers, and mobilize greater numbers of horses for the cavalry.[73] Soldiers' poor morale and unwillingness to engage the Red Turban armies drove home the link between economic security (in the form of adequate land) and military performance in time of crisis.[74]

High-ranking government officials came to exercise increasingly personal control over the armies of Koryŏ, whose loyalty to the central government grew uncertain at best. In response, Kongmin and other late Koryŏ kings attempted to develop their own personal military forces, usually by bolstering the royal guard. The necessity of such efforts reflects the kings' much reduced stature and influence during the late Koryŏ period.[75] Personal military forces continued to play an important role in the political life of the early Chosŏn period.

If one strategy was to emulate powerful military figures, another was to eliminate them. As Chapter 5 argues, Kongmin considered men like Generals Chŏng, An, and others such a threat that he orchestrated their demise. However, unsettled conditions in Northeast Asia repeatedly demonstrated the need for strong military forces. In 1363 the Yuan court announced plans to strip King Kongmin of his crown and replace him with a more malleable clansman. The king retained his throne in large part because Koryŏ troops denied Yuan forces an easy victory. In fact, after some initial losses, the Koryŏ troops routed Yuan armies. The prospect of an extended campaign rendered plans to remove King Kongmin unpalatable to the Yuan leadership.

Although beyond the scope of this work, the Koryŏ throne considered military force an essential tool for navigating the treacherous international waters of the 1370s and 1380s, when both the Ming dynasty and the Great Yuan *ulus* claimed Koryŏ's allegiance.[76] The eventual fall of the Koryŏ dynasty and the rise of Yi Sŏng-gye's new Chosŏn dynasty grew directly out the collapse of the Great Yuan *ulus* and the pan–East Asian militarization it sparked.

In the Great Yuan *ulus*, generals became pivotal actors in the dramas unfolding in Daidu. Bolod-Temür seized control of Daidu, imprisoned Empress Ki, and drove the heir apparent from the capital. Köke-Temür escorted the heir apparent back to Daidu, but incurred the empress's wrath when he refused to place him on the throne. Whatever dangers an expanded military might pose for King Kongmin and Toghan-Temür, it was a necessary evil.[77]

As the need for local military leaders grew acute, magnates throughout the empire gained new prominence. Liaodong was no exception. Regional warlords in southern Liaodong, many of them Mongols with official credentials granted by the Yuan throne, displayed new independence and strength as a result of the Red Turban rebellion. From no later than the mid-thirteenth century, tensions had developed between, on one hand, the Great Khans and advisors who wished to expand the throne's power and, on the other, members of the Mongolian aristocracy who wished to maintain their autonomy. The empire's success depended on rulers' ability to maintain a balance of power. The Red Turban wars marked the final oscillation between center and region in the empire's northeast corner. From this point on, the Yuan court exercised only intermittent control of the region.

Yet, the view from the new Ming court in Nanjing throws into relief a paradox. If the Red Turban wars made possible Naghachu's rise, he owed his survival as an important actor in Liaodong to his decision not to follow Toghan-Temür's rump court to the steppe. Put differently, his power derived in part from his autonomy from the exile Mongol court. The same could be said about Köke-Temür in the northwest and the Mongol Prince of Liang (Vajravarmi, d. 1382) in the southwest.

To the Ming dynasty, however, Naghachu and his armies in Liaodong represented the Yuan's continued puissance and posed a frightening military threat. Zhu Yuanzhang's decision to expend precious military and economic resources to expand Ming rule into Liaodong (including Jurchen lands) reflected his fear of the Mongols and the prospect of the Great Yuan *ulus*'s resurgence. The possibility of partial fragmentation without complete dismemberment inherent in the Mongol polity allowed Naghachu's survival as both a largely independent operator and a last bulwark of the Great Yuan *ulus*.

That being said, the consequences of Red Turban warfare—the destruction of local governmental infrastructure, economic depression, and a sharp decline in population—fatally weakened Yuan control of Liaodong and opened the way for Ming expansion.[78] As was true in many parts of the Mongol empire, the transition was slow, contested, and often destructive.

Military Leaders

Given the prominence of military leaders in Northeast Asia during these decades, some consideration of their similarities and differences is in order here. They shared several common features. They enjoyed more autonomy vis-à-vis central political authorities and exercised more extensive control over local populations and matériel. The actions of military leaders figured prominently at the court, whether in the formulation of strategy, discussions of dynastic fortunes, or factional infighting and alliance building. Finally, no one in Daidu or Kaegyŏng took their obedience for granted.

At the same time, military men often differed in their relations to central political authorities, to local society, and to one another. Although not a native of the region, the Red Turban leader Mao Gui emerged as the single most dominant military leader in Shandong until his assassination in 1359 by a fellow rebel. Mao neither maintained ties to the Yuan throne nor entered into negotiations with the Mongols. Rather, once ensconced in central Shandong, Mao attempted to legitimate his power through affiliation with the Song Red Turban regime, using its calendar, accepting its titles, and issuing orders in its name. Mao also attempted to garner local support by establishing effective local governance. There is no evidence that he dispatched envoys to rebel leaders not affiliated with the Red Turbans. Unlike many aspiring commanders, he made no overtures to Koryŏ. He may have planned a joint attack on Daidu with a fellow Red Turban commander, but the offensive fizzled. Mao did not renew efforts to forge wider alliances. Given his short rule, it seems unlikely that he won widespread or deep loyalty among the farmers or elites of central Shandong.

In contrast, such figures as Naghachu and Gaojianu had deeper ties to their bases of power. Although his early years are unclear, Naghachu was said to have been a descendent of Muqali, a prominent figure in the initial Mongol conquest of Liaodong early in the thirteenth century. Many Mongols influential in Liaodong traced their ancestry back to Muqali. Naghachu had campaigned in central China, but by the early 1360s he returned to Liaodong, where he held a series of high-level appointments from Yuan authorities for the next two decades. Gaojianu's background is murkier, but he also held Yuan offices and titles.

Naghachu's and Gaojianu's relations with the Yuan throne were complex. On one hand, both enjoyed considerable autonomy vis-à-vis the Yuan throne. They conducted independent diplomatic relations with the Koryŏ dynasty, exchanging gifts, brokering alliances, and sometimes browbeating the king. Part of this autonomy inhered in their positions within the Branch Secretariat of Liaodong. However, part of their independence arose from the warfare of the time, when communication grew uncertain and shifting battle conditions required swift decisions. In the case of Naghachu, this latitude of action sometimes violated the interests of the Mongol court; he repeatedly clashed with Koryŏ royal troops in the midst of what should have been a joint campaign against the Red Turbans along the border between Liaodong and Koryŏ.

Perhaps because they enjoyed such autonomy, neither Naghachu nor Gaojianu ever defied the Mongol court. They helped drive the Red Turbans from Liaodong and would later resist Ming expansion into the region. They would also serve as the Yuan throne's spokesmen to Koryŏ after the Mongols withdrew to the steppe in 1368. Eventually both men joined the Ming dynasty. Naghachu's troops were reassigned to various areas, and he was settled in Nanjing. Taking advantage of Gaojianu's ties to Koryŏ, Zhu Yuanzhang kept him in Liaodong, where he was placed in charge of missions to Kaegyŏng and securing Korean mounts.

Koryŏ military men differed in important ways from figures such as Mao Gui, Naghachu, and Gaojianu. The Koryŏ throne generally exercised far greater control over its military leaders than did its counterpart in Daidu. There is no Korean equivalent during these years of Mao Gui, an independent military leader allied with a rebel regime. Although General Chŏng and others gained sufficient power and stature to worry King Kongmin, there is no evidence that they plotted against the throne or contemplated the sort of freelance military campaigns in which Naghachu indulged. They did not appeal to local support for legitimacy. They operated largely within existing Koryŏ administrative structures, exercising military command by leave of the throne.

This should not be taken as a given. During the twelfth century, the Ch'oe family had seized control of the Koryŏ government, subverting royal authority. Late in the thirteenth century, Sambyŏl-ch'o units had openly defied the Koryŏ throne. During the mid-fourteenth century, General Chŏng's contemporaries elsewhere in Northeast Asia enjoyed enormous latitude, a fact of which he must have been aware. A few decades later, General Yi Sŏng-gye would remove the king and create a new dynasty.

King Kongmin's relatively effective control of the military during the 1360s contradicts the usual image of a beleaguered Koryŏ throne, under siege by the central aristocracy and those allied more closely with the Mongols.[79] Several factors explain King Kongmin's surprising success. First was a matter of expectations. Mongolian political culture tolerated a much higher degree of autonomy for its elite, a tendency accentuated during times of chaos. Although the power of the king and his court over the aristocracy, the military, and local society may have paled in comparison with, say, that of a Song emperor, ascriptive status and political power in Koryŏ were more closely tied to the throne than in the Mongolian tradition.

A second reason was military men's lack of deep ties to local society during these decades. Many military leaders in China and Liaodong developed alternative bases of power and authority rooted in local society. No such widespread movements as the Red Turbans developed in Koryŏ. The primary threats to Kongmin's power originated at court—his own and that of the Mongols. His senior ministers engineered several abortive coups to remove him from power through intimidation or murder. Empress Ki orchestrated his brief dethronement. And in 1374, Koryŏ courtiers assassinated him as part of a palace coup. Significantly, however, they put another member of the royal Wang family on the throne.

This last fact relates to the final reason for Kongmin's surprising degree of control over the military relates: the place of Koryŏ's royal family in the Mongol empire. As noted above, in 1388, little more than a decade after King Kongmin's death, General Yi Sŏng-gye removed the reigning king, and in 1392 he had himself declared founder of a new dynasty. The coup d'état may be explained from many perspectives, but one highly salient consideration is time. It corresponded to a major shift in geopolitics in Northeast Asia. After the dynasty's full integration into the Mongol empire, no Korean military commander had ever openly challenged the Koryŏ king. The Koryŏ throne fell only after the Mongols had lost their ability to project military force onto the peninsula. In 1387, Naghachu surrendered to the Ming, depriving the Mongol court of its most effective military commander in Liaodong. To secure Naghachu's surrender, the Ming court offered the most generous settlement package of the thirty-year Hongwu reign.[80] The next year, General Yi flouted royal orders to attack Liaodong; instead he marched against the Koryŏ capital, removed the king, and positioned himself as Korea's next ruler. King Kongmin owed control over his generals in part to his privileged status as an imperial in-law and the protection that it entitled.

Koryŏ and the Empire

The Red Turban campaigns throw light on relations between the Koryŏ and the Yuan ruling houses. During the crises, the Koryŏ court repeatedly, if futilely, sought Yuan military aid, and King Kongmin dispatched royal troops to assist Yuan forces against the remnants of Red Turban forces in Haizhou and Gaizhou following the rebels' withdrawal from Koryŏ. The same conditions that in 1356 tempted King Kongmin to seize greater autonomy for the throne, including military strikes into Yuan-held territory, also unleashed the Red Turbans into Koryŏ, which further weakened his domestic position.

For a time, the Red Turban revolts represented a common experience for the rulers of Koryŏ and the Yuan. The rebels observed no dynastic or national borders, although Koryŏ authorities noted insistently that rebellion originated west, not east, of the Yalu River. In communications to the Yuan court following the invasions, the Koryŏ court explicitly contrasted its success in driving the rebels from Koryŏ with the Yuan's continuing failure to suppress the Red Turbans. The Koryŏ court intentionally misrepresented the invasion's impact. It stressed the dynasty's military successes, skipped lightly over its enormous losses, and overstated the king's support and control at home. These communications also argued that the Koreans' successful defense of their country directly benefited the Yuan; the Mongols would not face a military threat from the east. King Kongmin and his supporters did this because the Yuan court's perceptions still mattered to Koryŏ, in general, and to the king and his court, in particular.

Many scholars have written that the Koryŏ court perceived the Red Turbans' predations in Koryŏ as confirmation of the Yuan's terminal decline. Korean scholarship on the period often stresses an underlying desire for Korean independence (anti-Yuan sentiment) that was frustrated only by the Red Turban wars, piracy, and the narrow self-interest of some court elites. King Kongmin receives much praise for his "anti-Yuan politics," which are portrayed as representing the wishes of his subjects and ministers.

In the preceding chapters, I have instead highlighted Koryŏ's integration into the Great Yuan *ulus*. Beginning late in the thirteenth century, the ruling houses of the Yuan and Koryŏ intermarried. Generations of potential Koryŏ heirs apparent spent their youth in the imperial *keshig*, the training ground for Eurasia's elite. Members of the Koryŏ ruling house ate and drank with Mongol nobles at state banquets in Daidu and Shangdu, hunted with powerful ministers in the suburbs of the Yuan capitals, and received gifts of clothing, food, and books from Mongol emperors. The Koryŏ king and queen regularly fêted Mongolian officials and aristocrats in Kaegyŏng. The Koryŏ throne repeatedly dispatched military forces to campaign with the Great Khan against Jurchen forces, mutinous Koryŏ troops, Japanese samurai, Mongol nobles, and finally Chinese rebels. Many members of the Koryŏ court dressed in Mongolian robes, plaited their hair in Mongolian fashion, listened to Mongolian music, and spoke Mongolian. Simply put, Koryŏ, like so many other polities across Eurasia, was part of the Mongol empire.

Korean scholarship is emerging from the long shadow of Japanese colonial rule. As James Palais, John Duncan, and others have noted, since the 1950s, in implicit or explicit rejection of earlier Japanese emphasis on stagnation and backwardness, Korean scholars have highlighted "internal development."[81] In the case of the Mongol empire, the Japanese influence is twofold. First is Japanese scholarship of the early twentieth century on Korea under Mongol rule, some of which is of extremely high quality even if produced in the service of the Japanese imperial enterprise.[82] In his 1998 *Political History of Koryŏ Under the Mongol Intervention* (*Wŏn kansŏpha ŭi Koryŏ chŏngch'isa* 元干涉下의 高麗政治史), Kim Tang-t'aek explicitly contrasts his work on domestic political developments circa 1270–1356 to previous Japanese scholarship, which he argues was overconcerned with a unidirectional Mongolian influence on Koryŏ.[83] Kim instead focuses on the interplay of Mongolian and Korean political dynamics and interests. Second is the perhaps unconscious tendency to evaluate Koryŏ's experiences within the Mongolian empire in terms of Korea's travails under the Japanese imperial state. In his 2004 *Political History of the Koryŏ* (*Koryŏ chŏngch'isa non* 高麗政治史論), Min Hyŏn-gu, the world's leading historian of King Kongmin's reign, maintains that although Koryŏ was subject to considerable restrictions under "Mongol interference" and that "its autonomy was greatly impaired," it survived as an "independent kingdom."[84] This stress on autonomy and independence is natural, and Min uses them as the central themes of his book, which is subtitled "The Establishment of a Unified Nation and the Trials of an Independent Kingdom." Such a characterization finds support in fourteenth-century perceptions. In his *Compendium of Chronicles*, Rashīd al-Dīn referred to Koryŏ as a *mulkī 'alīhada*, or "independent kingdom."[85] The unspoken assumption seems to be that because the Wang ruling family continued in power, the Koryŏ state was independent. The implicit contrast is with the Song and Jin dynasties, the dominant states in East Asia before the Yuan, which the Mongols removed from power and whose territories were then subject to direct rule by the Great Yuan *ulus*.

Part of the problem is our understanding of "empire," especially the Mongol empire. In a recent essay on empire in the early modern transatlantic context, Jack Greene points out the pitfalls of anachronistic standards of empire, more specifically "the coercive and centralized model of imperial organization derived from late-nineteenth- and early-twentieth-century empires." "In this conception," he notes, "empires were political entities in which colonies were presided over by powerful nation-states with vast administrative and coercive resources to enforce their claims to sovereignty."[86] Although individual Mongol courts made periodic efforts at centralization and the Chinggisid political style laid greater stress on unity than other strains within the wider Mongolian tradition, the Mongol empire demonstrated considerable flexibility vis-à-vis local regimes, tolerated a relatively high degree of local autonomy, seldom made administrative efficiency its highest priority, and rarely imposed its cultural norms on conquered populations in the sedentary world. Put simply, the conception and functioning of fourteenth-century Mongol empire differed in important ways from those of the Japanese imperial state, which at different times imposed Japanese language, religion, names, law codes, penal practices, and more on the Korean population.

Few would argue that Korea as a political, cultural, and social entity disappeared during the Mongol period. Long-standing patterns and trends continued.[87] By stressing Koryŏ's incorporation into the Mongolian empire, I most emphatically do not deny agency to the people and interests of Koryŏ. I fully agree with Min's observation that "the major question is how to understand the state under these conditions and how to approach the historical changes of this period."[88]

Yuan control in Koryŏ was not absolute, and it was never meant to be so. The central aristocracy, the king and his close associates, and other newcomers to political power pursued their individual interests. They, however, did have to consider the Great Yuan *ulus* in their calculations. Multiple nodes of political authority complicated political competition in Northeast Asia, as alliances spanned multiple regions, bureaucracies, and language groups. Beginning no later than the 1990s, some Korean scholars (perhaps most prominently Chang Tong-ik) began to move beyond such dichotomous analytical categories as "pro-Yuan" versus "anti-Yuan," or newly ascendant, reform-minded Neo-Confucian elites versus established aristocratic elites with major landholdings who were national traitors or Yuan collaborationists.[89]

As many have shown, empire cannot be maintained through unilateral demands; rather, it depends on balancing military power with negotiation, mediation, and the cooperation of local actors.[90] Korean scholars such as Min Hyŏn-gu, Paek In-ho, and others routinely use terms like "Yuan collaborationists" to describe those who cooperated in one way or another with the Great Yuan *ulus*. Such a conceptualization is unfortunate, since nearly every member of the Koryŏ elite, both established families and *arrivistes*, had little choice but to come to terms with the Yuan. This included the Koryŏ royal family, which Min and others consistently portray as anti-Mongol, but which, as Min and others readily acknowledge, was dependent on Mongol support to maintain its power in Koryŏ. Thus, pinning the political and social ills of the day on "Yuan collaborationists" and "powerful families" (*kwŏnmun sejok* 權門勢族) who derived their influence through ties to the Yuan sheds little light on the nature of power, political dynamics, or pan-regional alliances of the period.[91]

Thus, it is important to view thirteenth- and fourteenth-century Koryŏ both in the context of the longer span of Korean history and as a part of the Mongol empire.[92] This twin perspective is necessary for understanding any region, culture, or polity in Eurasia during these centuries (including the Mongols themselves). This dual awareness is equally critical for appreciating the emergence of the post-Mongol world. Only when one bears in mind the levels of political, economic, cultural, and military integration of Northeast Asia under the Mongols is it possible to grasp the significance of the new order that emerged during the late fourteenth and early fifteenth centuries.

The Red Turban Wars and the New Ming Order

Although beyond the scope of this work, a few words should be said about the new order in Northeast Asia gradually taking shape during the final decades of the fourteenth century. If this account has emphasized the opportunities that chaos presented to men of ambition, I do not underestimate the suffering of the mid-fourteenth century. In fact, we often pass too lightly over how bad these decades were. Conditions varied from region to region, but millions suffered deeply from crop failure, famine, warfare, land flight, and the collapse of effective local governance.

Cannibalism, perhaps the ultimate avatar of social collapse, appears frequently in mid-fourteenth-century writings. Changguzhenyi wrote, "North and south of the Yellow River, from 1344 there were consecutive years of famine and drought; brigands plundered cities and towns in broad daylight; people consumed one another's flesh."[93] Li Jiben struck a similar note: "During the rebellion in North China, there were consecutive years of crop failure. The people were often eaten by starving soldiers. Corpses filled the countryside; the stench filled the air." According to Li, the corpses of those who had fallen from starvation on the roads were boiled in caldrons and distributed to the hungry.[94] In his "Song of the Old Man of Yingzhou," the poet Nasen too mentioned cannibalism: "They cut up the corpses of those who have starved to death, none of the dead remained whole." Describing the devastating impact of Red Turban Song rule in North China, the fourteenth-century observer Ye Ziqi wrote of one commander, "Each time he took a city, he would use the people as grain. When all the people were gone, he would conquer another city. Thus, in his wake was 1,000 *li* of barren earth. Shandong, Hebei, Shanxi, and Liang-Huai were all decimated."[95] Another fourteenth-century writer, Tao Zongyi, mentioned Liang-Huai soldiers' reputation for the consumption of human flesh. They ranked the corpses in terms of delectability; children being best, women next, and men last.[96] As Chapter 2 noted, contemporaries accused Yuan imperial troops of "pillaging the people for food" and using local populations to oil their cooking cauldrons.

Recent historians have detailed the scale of fourteenth-century devastation and its social, economic, and human costs. Full recovery took as much as a century, especially in North China.[97] One cannot understand the rise of Zhu Yuanzhang, Fang Guozhen, Zhang Shicheng, Köke-Temür, Bolod-Temür, Naghachu, Gaojianu, and countless less prominent figures without reference to this widespread destruction. The chaos of these decades is equally important to understanding Zhu Yuanzhang's vision of a new order and his methods for realizing it.

Widespread militarization combined with the lack of clear authority meant that the issue of loyalty and allegiance took on new significance. Tao Zongyi opined, "For more than ten years the realm devoted itself to warfare. There were innumerable ministers who brought shame to the dynasty, generals who brought shame to the armies, and those who were defeated and surrendered or absconded." In Tao's eyes, "Less than one in one hundred or one thousand" exhibited loyalty and bravery.[98] The Chinese literatus Li Shizhan wrote, "Since the unrest, all men throughout the land either demeaned themselves to become rebels or advocated righteousness and killed rebels. Those who did neither secretly harbored the intention to watch and wait, to profit from [others'] misfortune." Li observed with asperity, "This is something that the gods do not tolerate and that heroes do not [deign to] mention."[99]

True perhaps, but the uncertainty of the times led many to weigh all options. Individual and family concerns often trumped devotion to dynasty.[100] The Mongols had created an age in which individual and family interests easily transcended dynastic borders. The Great Yuan *ulus*'s decline gave birth to unusually complex issues of loyalty, allegiance, and identity in Northeast Asia. One suspects that similar issues marked the fall of Mongol rule elsewhere in Eurasia.[101]

One must also wonder about the Red Turban wars' impact on Koryŏ's perceptions of the fledgling Ming dynasty.[102] The Ming founder, Zhu Yuanzhang, had begun as a member of the Red Turban organization, a fact that led many Chinese literati to view him with deep suspicion.[103] With the Red Turban invasions of Koryŏ just a few years in the past, Koryŏ observers likely shared these reservations, even if little such documentary evidence of their attitudes survives.

In a 1373 communication with King Kongmin, Zhu freely acknowledged his three years with the Red Turbans during his mid-twenties.[104] He also explicitly evoked the memory of Master Guan and other Red Turban leaders who had attacked Koryŏ. Unhappy with what he perceived as Koryŏ's intransigence, the Ming founder promised that he would inflict far more damage than had Master Guan.

In the past, [Emperor] Tang Taizong [r. 627–49] failed in his campaigns against you. They did not know how to campaign. Later, [Emperor Tang] Gaozong [r. 650–83] came to destroy your dynasty. Later still, Master Guan, his group of men and women, did not pay attention to propriety. [They] were interested only in sex. For this reason he also failed. At that time, your defenses were good. I, however, will not wage war against you in that way.[105]

在先，唐太宗征恁不得他每不會征。後高宗都滅了恁國來。在後，關先生那波男女不理法度，只耍貪淫。以此上他也壞了。因那上頭恁隄防的是也。我可不那般的明白征恁去。

Even for this formidable new master of the Central Plains, however, squaring ideals with reality was difficult. Much of the problem arose from the fact that the Mongols had established practices and expectations in everything from court protocol and diplomatic niceties to notions of borders and clothing that often survived unquestioned within successor regimes throughout Eurasia. The prominent historian Murai Shōsuke has noted that the Chŏson government, in its attempts to resolve the problem of Japanese piracy during the late fourteenth and early fifteenth centuries, broke with a "fundamental principle of diplomacy in East Asia" by receiving envoys not only from the "king of Japan" but also from regional powers in western Japan.[106] Although this might represent a break from past conventions in East Asian diplomacy, it was entirely in keeping with the diplomatic practices of King Kongmin and the Mongol empire. As shown above, Kongmin cultivated ties with a wide variety of powerful men and women.

The new Ming dynasty also followed many Mongol precedents. Koryŏ eunuchs and palace women attended Zhu Yuanzhang in his palaces. Koryŏ eunuchs (as well as Jurchen and Mongols) served in his diplomatic corps. The new Chinese emperor dressed his imperial guard in *jisün* robes. He continued the Mongol custom of exiling important but potentially dangerous political figures to Koryŏ. In formal diplomatic correspondence with the Koryŏ court, Zhu Yuanzhang referred to Kongmin not only by his Korean name of Wang Ki but also by his Mongol name, Bayan-Temür.[107]

People and forces prominent during Zhu Yuanzhang's rise shaped his tenure as emperor. In Northeast Asia, Zhu attempted to co-opt or destroy such players as the Chinese and Mongol warlords of Liaodong (Liu Yi, Gaojianu, and eventually Naghachu). Both he and the Yuan court sought to capitalize on the relations (often painted in rosy colors) that such men as Köke-Temür, Gaojianu, and the Uyghur scholar Xie Xun had struck with the Koryŏ court. The Mongols cast a very long shadow. Understanding their empire of the mid-fourteenth century is critical to understanding developments that would unfold in the following decades and centuries.

Viewing the Red Turbans and their impact in a regional context should not obscure the importance of dynastic borders during the last half of the fourteenth century. Koryŏ irredentism numbered among the reasons for King Kongmin's 1356 military efforts to seize postal stations west of the Yalu River. Plans to take Liaodong were not abandoned until the fifteenth century.[108] However, the Red Turban period throws into clear relief the permeability of borders in Northeast Asia. In recent centuries, Koryŏ had suffered incursions from powers to the north—the Khitans, Jurchens, and the Mongols—and in the more distant past, attacks by Chinese imperial dynasties—the Qin (221–206 BCE), the Han (206 BCE–220 CE), the Sui (581–618), and the Tang (618–907). The Red Turbans marked the first large-scale military incursion by Chinese forces in seven centuries, and the most important by a non-dynastic Chinese army ever. The Red Turbans' disregard for traditional political borders and their success in recruiting at least a small segment of the Koryŏ population demonstrates the porous nature of the Yuan-Koryŏ border.

For those familiar with Northeast Asia, this high level of interpenetration comes as little surprise. During much of the Mongol period, contending centers of Koryŏ political authority were strung across the entire region. The king reigned from Kaegyŏng. Ruling in the name of their Mongol overlords, Korean magnates controlled much of northern Koryŏ. Korean supervisors in special administrative headquarters in Liaoyang oversaw the Korean population of the Liaodong region. Finally, thousands of Koreans, who were closely associated with the Yuan and Koryŏ thrones, resided in Daidu. In addition to the Mongol princes scattered throughout southern Liaodong, one must also add the overlapping administrative organs of political control in Daidu, Liaoyang, northern Koryŏ, and Kaegyŏng itself. Highly ramified lines of political authority and considerable intrigue resulted.

Another result was a blurring of lines (ethnic, political, cultural, and territorial) that ultimately facilitated the removal of southern Liaodong from the Korean polity. Under the Great Yuan *ulus*, the Liaodong region became more closely incorporated into political, economic, military, religious, social, and cultural systems based in China than had been the case for nearly a thousand years. The Mongols knit together a wide variety of peoples, cultures, and regions into an unprecedentedly large, if short-lived, empire. Liaodong was among those swept along.

Yet, the integration of southern Liaodong with China under the Mongols was not predestined. When the Han dynasty collapsed in the third century CE, Liaodong fell beyond the reach of any Chinese central government. Zhu Yuanzhang would become the first Chinese emperor in more than a millennium to exercise lasting control of Liaodong. Despite the much closer ties that developed between China and southern Liaodong under the Great Yuan *ulus*, the area was still not part of a Chinese polity—it was part of the Great Yuan *ulus*.

The unresolved nature of the question grew clear during the mid-fourteenth century. What would happen to the Liaodong region once the Mongols fell?[109] King Kongmin's actions show that some men of Koryŏ believed that when the Mongol empire collapsed, they should retake what they viewed as properly theirs.[110] The establishment of a vigorous new Chinese dynasty, the Ming, complicated matters. Perhaps more than Koryŏ itself, the Ming founder wished for a clear resolution to the Liaodong question.

Zhu Yuanzhang's answer was a new order with clear, some might argue rigid, borders. Zhu attempted to eliminate the frenetic private negotiations and political communications among fluid centers of power that he knew so well from his days as an aspiring warlord. Wherever possible, countries were to have one paramount leader. Interstate relations were to be conducted on a state-to-state basis with limited private trade and even less tolerance for private diplomacy. Borders were to be clear and, when necessary, closely regulated. This, the Ming founder hoped, would lead to stability, order, and control.

Realizing this vision would mean major changes for Northeast Asia.[111] The marked interpenetration between Koryŏ and the Mongol empire would have to be severed. The contending centers of Koryŏ political authority strung across the region would have to be consolidated into the single person of the Koryŏ king. Through co-optation or extirpation, the role of largely autonomous Mongol warlords such as Gaojianu and Naghachu would have to be eliminated. Fluid border populations would have to be settled and registered as either Ming or Koryŏ subjects. Zhu Yuanzhang's plans required decades to implement and were never fully realized. Yet Northeast Asia emerged from the Yuan-Ming transition profoundly different.

To give just one example by way of conclusion, the collapse of Mongol rule in Northeast Asia transformed the place and perception of Liaodong. The Mongols' many integrating structures had facilitated the flow of people, material, and culture across dynastic and linguistic lines.

As these networks receded in the wake of the Mongols' collapse, Liaodong emerged as a border region, a place where the subjects and agendas of independent dynasties came into contact. Uneasy with unregulated contact, the Ming founder imposed control through a massive military presence in this distant northeast corner of his lands. Despite extensive interaction among Chinese, Korean, Jurchen, and Mongol groups that persisted in the region, until the end of the dynasty Liaodong remained a military zone, governed through garrison bureaucracies and perceived by many educated Chinese as the precarious outer pale of civilization.

Epilogue

On September 10, 1368, Toghan-Temür announced his intention to "pay an imperial visit" to Shangdu. Courtiers greeted the news with stunned silence; a few protested that abandoning the capital was tantamount to ending the dynasty. Only hours later, the emperor and a group of roughly a hundred people, including Empress Ki, several consorts, the heir apparent and his consort, senior ministers, and small children from the imperial family, quietly slipped through the massive wooden doors of the hulking Jiande Gate that guarded the northwestern face of the capital's towering city walls. It was the last time any of them ever saw Daidu. The next day they arrived at Juyong Pass, its stone walls decorated with intricate carvings of Buddhist guardian deities. Part of a defensive bulwark that controlled the main imperial highway to Daidu from the north, Juyong Pass was also a religious and political monument that articulated an all-encompassing Buddhist vision of universal rulership, the *cakravartin*, or wheel-turning ruler, that linked Toghan-Temür to the founder of the Great Yuan *ulus*, Qubilai. Erected in the 1340s to celebrate Toghan-Temür's rise to power, Juyong Pass, now abandoned by fleeing soldiers, was a silent witness to his fall.

Traveling through rain, snow, and high winds, Toghan-Temür and his group arrived at Shangdu by the end of the month. Once a testament to the empire's power, the site of the Yuan court's summer capital, Shangdu now stood desolate, most of its buildings burned to the ground during the repeated Red Turban attacks. Here, the Yuan court spent a miserable winter. Toghan-Temür and his advisors pondered the future: to retake Daidu, to flee to Qara Qorum, to seek the assistance of its ostensible ally Koryŏ, or to call upon Köke-Temür for aid. It tried all and failed in all. In the meantime, court morale collapsed as senior ministers sought solace in drink, in the arms of beautiful Korean concubines, or in righteous indignation with others' lack of loyalty, courage, and intelligence. Under mounting pressure from advancing Ming armies, Toghan-Temür, by now often ill and unable to hold court audiences, withdrew further northward. By the end of July 1369, Toghan-Temür settled precariously at Yingchang, where he monitored developments to the south and considered what to do about the new claimant to the Mandate of Heaven, Zhu Yuanzhang. He never found a solution. On May 23, 1370, Toghan-Temür died of dysentery at Yingchang.

His son, Ayushiridara, whose repeated but abortive attempts to seize power from his father had hastened the collapse of the Great Yuan *ulus*, was now emperor, but his victory was hollow. Two weeks after his father's death, Ming armies attacked Yingchang, capturing thousands of head of cattle and sheep and putting Ayushiridara and his court to flight. Ming forces seized Ayushiridara's son and consort, who were then delivered to Zhu Yuanzhang in Nanjing, where they remained as "guests" until 1374. Despite periodic Ming strikes, the capture of his son, the loss of China's vast resources, and the increasing autonomy of his generals, Ayushiridara as the ruler of the Great Yuan *ulus* still posed the single greatest foreign threat to Zhu Yuanzhang until his death in 1378. Ayushiridara may have derived some slight satisfaction that he outlived Köke-Temür (d. 1375), the general who had remained loyal to Toghan-Temür by refusing to cooperate with Empress Ki's efforts to put her son on the throne in 1365.

It is not clear if Empress Ki was by Ayushiridara's side to share in his success. The time and place of her death remain a mystery. Although she does not figure prominently in modern narratives of the Mongol empire, her memory—and the age—did survive in later Mongol narratives of the Yuan's fall. Seventeenth-century Mongolian chronicles indirectly reflect the importance of Empress Ki and Koryŏ; one of Chinggis khan's Merkid brides is recast as a Korean woman, and Chinggis struggles with the temptation to flee to Korea. This later episode probably grew out of rumors that Toghan-Temür planned to flee to T'amma Island (present-day Cheju) off the coast of Koryŏ. Both details preserve a moment in the history of the Mongol empire that has been almost entirely effaced, a time when Koreans were more essential to the Yuan than Turkestanis and when Koryŏ, Liaodong, and eastern North China were more tightly integrated with Daidu than the capital was with Jiangnan and the rest of southern China.

Just as the fortunes of Toghan-Temür, Ayushiridara, and Empress Ki were deeply shaped by the rise of Zhu Yuanzhang, King Kongmin, too, was pulled into the orbit of the new Son of Heaven. King Kongmin maintained political, personal, and familial ties to the Yuan court and its allies in Northeast Asia, but he also moved at a breakneck pace to establish relations with Zhu Yuanzhang. A man of extraordinary talent, energy, and focus, Zhu was a proven military commander, an inspiring political leader, an industrious state builder, a canny negotiator, and a farsighted strategist. Zhu did not suddenly burst on Kongmin's consciousness in January 1368 when the establishment of the Ming dynasty was announced in Zhu's capital of Nanjing or in September 1368 when the Ming armies drove Toghan-Temür from Daidu. Kongmin possessed a less detailed and nuanced understanding of Zhu Yuanzhang than he did of the Yuan court, but the networks of trade, diplomacy, and personnel that bound so much of East Asia ensured that intelligence related to Zhu had been flowing to Kongmin throughout the 1360s, and perhaps even the 1350s.

Thus when the Ming armies finally drove north to Daidu, Kongmin and his advisors moved quickly but not recklessly. Kongmin had decades of experience using the Mongolian matrix of information and resources to protect his interests and had early developed the ability to distinguish the perspectives and goals of the Yuan court from his own. It was not, however, an easy feat. From his childhood, he had been a privileged member of the Mongol empire; the decade in Daidu had to some extent fused his interests to those of Toghan-Temür and the Yuan court. Yet, it was the early lessons that he had first learned in Daidu and later reviewed in Kaegyŏng—the possibility, indeed inevitability, of sudden, dramatic political reversals; the need for allies regardless of language, place of birth, or cultural background; and the inextricable links between domestic and international fortune—that prepared him to negotiate what would eventually prove to be the last great spasm of the Mongol empire's collapse.

Despite his relative success in navigating the shifting geopolitical landscape of eastern Eurasia, King Kongmin ultimately fell to challenges at home. During the night of October 27, 1374, in a spectacular but poorly understood incident, several members of Kongmin's recently formed royal bodyguard murdered their king. The paternity of his son and successor was contested; rumors swirled that he was the product of a liaison between one of King Kongmin's consorts and Sindon, the Buddhist monk cum political advisor. King Kongmin's death weakened the Koryŏ dynasty. Deeply suspicious about the regicide, Zhu Yuanzhang refused to recognize the new king and issued increasingly bellicose warnings against what he perceived as an intransigent and duplicitous regime. The Koryŏ court's relations with the Yuan warmed, but both the prestige and the strength of the Mongols fell far short of what they had been even just a decade earlier. In 1389 the Koryŏ general Yi Sŏng-gye seized power, and in 1392 he formally announced a new dynasty, the Chosŏn.

Thus, the decade from the mid-1360s to the mid-1370s witnessed a generational transformation that in some ways transcended the Mongol loss of China and the establishment of the Ming dynasty. Most of the principal actors in this study—Toghan-Temür, King Kongmin, Ayushiridara, Empress Ki, Bolod-Temür, and Köke-Temür—died, survived by men who created new dynasties, Zhu Yuanzhang and Yi Sŏng-gye. Yi's dynasty would last until the twentieth century, and Zhu is rightly viewed as a pivotal figure in Chinese history. Yet for all his determination to change Chinese society and by extension all of eastern Eurasia, Zhu Yuanzhang carried with him perspectives and expectations formed during the age of Mongol domination. At the same time that he devoted enormous energy to reviving "Chinese tradition," the Ming founder preserved important elements of the Mongols' structures of domestic rule: he assigned households hereditary occupations and obligations to the state; he maintained the Yuan's large province-size administrative units; and he invested his sons with extensive appanages and granted them wide-ranging military and administrative powers. Internationally, he expanded Ming garrisons into southwestern and northeastern regions that the Mongols had brought into the empire; he incorporated

Mongolian, Jurchen, Korean, Vietnamese, Uyghur, and other personnel into his regime; and he attempted to assuage kingdoms from Champa to Turfan that interpolity relations would remain unchanged from the days of the high Yuan. He also adopted less grand but more lasting features from the Mongols. Almost as soon as he came to power, he decided that mounted soldiers from his honor guard should don Mongolian riding tunics in imperial processions. They were still wearing them when the dynasty fell in 1644.

This book has tried to illustrate the advantages of moving beyond nation-state narratives in understanding East Asian history by recapturing some sense of regional integration under the Mongols. My argument is not that regional integration was unique to the Mongols but that the Mongol empire created a matrix of political, economic, military, cultural, technological, and ethnic connections that differed qualitatively from earlier periods. A logical next step is to consider the question "What happens when empires collapse?" Most histories of the post-Mongolian period focus on a single place or polity, for instance, Ming China or Muscovite Rus, but pay surprisingly little attention to Eurasia as a whole. A more profitable perspective would be to view the Ming, for instance, as one instance of a pan-Eurasian phenomenon—polities that were deeply indebted to the Mongols in terms of political structures, ideas of rulership, and patterns of diplomatic, economic, and cultural interaction but had to carve out new identities in the post-Mongol period. One should see the Ming not only as one of a succession of Chinese dynasties but also as part of a cohort of successor regimes that only gradually emerged from the shadow of the Mongol empire.

Reference Matter

Notes

For complete author names, titles, and publication data on the works cited here in short forms, see the Works Cited, pp. 393–425. The following abbreviations are used in the Notes:

CHC	*Cambridge History of China*
KS	Chŏng In-ji, *Koryŏsa*; MJ refers to the 1908 Meiji typeset edition; Yŏnse to the three-volume facsimile edition produced by Yŏnse University and issued by Kyŏng'in munhwasa in 1972.
YS	Song Lian et al., *Yuan shi*

Introduction

1. Maier, *Among Empires*, p. 7.

2. Kim Ho-dong 金浩東 ("Mong'gol che'guk kwa Tae Wŏn") has offered the provocative argument that the Great Mongol Nation was known as Da Yuan 大元 in those parts of the world that used the Chinese script as the primary form of written language and that contemporaries understood Da Yuan to refer to the entire Mongol empire. I use Great Yuan *ulus* in a narrower sense to refer to the region controlled by Qubilai and his successors rather than to the entire Mongol imperium.

3. For a concise review of Chinese-, Japanese-, and Korean-language scholarship, see O Kŭmsŏng, "Yuanmo dongluanqi de wuzhuang qiyi jituan he xiangcun zhibeiceng."

4. Research on northern China during these centuries remains in short supply when compared with the far more voluminous and generally more sophisticated body of scholarship devoted to the southern half of China, especially the southeast quarter. For warnings against generalizing about the late Yuan rebellions only on the basis on Jiangnan, see Chŏn Sun-dong, "Wŏnmal ŭi nongch'on sahoe wa pallan," p. 93. For recent comments on the rise of Jiangnan, see Paul Smith, "Problematizing the Song-Yuan-Ming Transition," pp. 11–19. Studies on Liaodong during the thirteenth and fourteenth centuries are sparser still.

5. For recent representative works, see Allsen, *Commodity and Exchange in the Mongol Empire*; idem, *Culture and Conquest in Mongol Eurasia*; idem, "Technologies of Governance in the Mongolian Empire"; Sugiyama, *Mongoru teikoku no kōbō*; idem, *Yūbokumin kara mita sekaishi*; and idem, *Gyakusetsu no Yūrasiashi*. See also the recent works by Kim Ho-dong (see note 6 below), who has argued strongly for the need to view the Mongol empire as an integrated whole.

6. For recent discussion of the differing outlooks inherent in the terms *Yeke Mongghol Ulus* and Da Yuan 大元, see Kim Ho-dong, "Monggol cheguk ŭi yŏksasang"; idem, "Monggol cheguksa yŏn'gu wa *Chipsa*," pp. 343–46; and idem, "Mong'gol che'guk kwa Tae Wŏn."

For comments on the multiethnic, composite nature of the Mongol *ulus* and the emergence of the Great Yuan *ulus* in the larger context of Eurasia, see Sugiyama, "Chūō Yūrasia no rekishi kōzu," pp. 67–72. For useful discussion of the shifting meanings of *ulus*, see Elverskog, *Our Great Qing*, pp. 17–23. For analysis of the equitable apportioning of responsibilities and rewards as a defining element of the Mongol empire, see Yokkaichi, "*Jarugechi* kō." Yokkaichi's study is especially useful for his stress on the interplay among *ulus*es of different sizes throughout the empire.

Some see Qubilai's Yuan as an increasingly "'normal' dynasty whose concerns were focused wholly on China and its particular problems and issues." See, e.g., Dardess, "Did the Mongols Matter?," pp. 119–20. He argues, "by the early decades of the fourteenth century, this shift was almost complete." For the full articulation of this argument, see Dardess, *Confucians and Conquerors* (New York: Columbia University Press, 1973).

Overreliance on Chinese-language materials has resulted in distortions of even basic elements of the Mongols' governance, such as the widely accepted four-tiered division of peoples in the Great Yuan *ulus* into Mongols, *semuren* (literally "all categories of peoples," usually glossed as Central and Western Asians), *Hanren* 漢人 (former subjects of the Jin dynasty), and Southerners or *Nanren* 南人 (former subjects of the Southern Song). Since the *semuren* category is said to have enjoyed superior social, political, and legal status vis-à-vis the Chinese, it is often offered as evidence of racial or ethnic discrimination against the Chinese. However, Funada Yoshiyuki ("Genchō jika no shokumokujin ni tsuite") has argued that the term *semuren* originated with Chinese officials as a way to differentiate the Chinese people from other populations and thus to preserve Chinese customs. The term appears only in Sinic-script materials and has no counterpart in contemporaneous Mongolian-, Persian-, or European-language documents. For a cogent summary of Funada's argument, see his "Semuren yu Yuandai zhidu, shehui."

7. For recent studies on the Mongols' influence on the flow of people, goods, technologies, and tastes across Eurasia, see Allsen, *Commodity and Exchange in the Mongol Empire*; and idem, *Culture and Conquest in the Mongol Eurasia* and scholarship cited therein. See also idem, "Circulation of Military Technology in the Mongolian Empire"; and idem, "Technologies of Governance in the Mongolian Empire." For concise review of themes and scholarship related to integration under the Mongols, see Biran, "The Mongol Transformation," pp. 348–53.

8. For discussion of the Mongol conquests and their impact on the Turkic world, see Golden, "'I will giveth the people unto thee.'" For the impact on the Qipchak Turks in particular, see Halperin, "The Kipchak Connection." For the Uyghur diaspora, see Brose, "Uyghur Technologists of Writing and Literacy in Mongol China." Funada Yoshiyuki ("Mongoru jidai ni okeru minzoku sesshoku," p. 19) has written that incorporation of powerful local Chinese into the Mongol power structure "not only redrew the ethnic map of Eurasia, it also changed the identity of those who came into contact with them."

9. Paul Smith, "Impressions of the Song-Yuan-Ming Transition," p. 79.

10. Rossabi, "Foreigners in China"; Franke, "Tibetans in Yuan China"; Rachewiltz, "Turks in China Under the Mongols." As Paul Buell ("Role of the Sino-Mongolian Frontier Zone," pp. 69–70) has shown, such groups as the Khitan played an essential role in bridging steppe and sedentary traditions of governance.

11. For the flow of people and goods between Koryŏ and the Mongol empire, see Kim Wi-hyŏn, *Koryŏ sidae taeoe kwan'gyesa yŏn'gu*, pp. 363–433; and Chang Tong-ik, *Koryŏ hugi oegyosa yŏn'gu*, pp. 133–97. For discussion of "Huihui" (which the author leaves undefined) in Koryŏ, see Xi Lei, "Cong Gaoli wenxian kan Yuandai de Huihuiren." Even prior to the Mongol period, foreigners, especially Chinese, had settled in Koryŏ, albeit on a more modest scale; see Peter Yun, "Mongols and Western Asians in the Late Koryŏ Ruling Stratum," p. 51. For recent historiographical discussion of the maritime dimensions of the Mongol empire, see Yokkaichi, "Mongoru teikoku to kaiiki Ajia." For discussion of the Yuan court's interest in maritime trade, see Sen, "The Yuan Khanate and India."

12. Serruys, *The Mongols in China During the Hung-wu Period*, p. 45. Serruys (ibid., pp. 24–46) was arguing against nationalist explanations of the fall of the

Yuan that saw Chinese resentment of foreign Mongol rule as the most important factor in the fighting of the mid-fourteenth century.

13. This is not to deny the Mongols' well-known propensity to organize populations into groups defined in terms of occupation or peoples, which, in the context of Yuan ruling structures, one Japanese scholar has termed "groupism" (*shūdan shugi* 集団主義). To protect their interests and secure their "shares" of the empire's patrimony, central courts, imperial princes, and influential families dispatched *jarghuchi* (judges) throughout the empire. The resulting pattern of interlocking interests and profit-sharing was another element of integration; see Yokkaichi, "*Jarugechi* kō."

14. Exceptions to this generality include, among other things, short-lived attempts to impose Mongolian marriage customs (most especially the levirate) on Chinese populations and measures to force Muslim communities in China to follow Mongolian practices for the slaughter of livestock. See Birge, "Levirate Marriage and the Revival of Widow Chastity in Yüan China," pp. 120–24; and idem, "Women and Confucianism from Song to Ming," pp. 226–29. State support for Islam (at the expense, for instance, of Buddhism) in the Il-khanate or Confucianism in the Great Yuan *ulus* is an important development in the history of the empire but does not fall under the rubric of the imposition of Mongol custom or values.

15. Allsen notes the similarities among a great many polities and examines the Uyghurs as a case study; see Allsen, "The Yuan Dynasty and the Uighurs of Turfan in the 13th Century." See also his discussion of investiture, service in the *kesig*, and playing several rulers off against one another as Mongol techniques of control (Allsen, *Mongol Imperialism*, pp. 72–75). For discussion of the Sa skya sect and the Mongols, see Otosaka Tomoko, "Genchō Chibetto seisaku"; and Petech, *Central Tibet and the Mongols*. On the Qutlugh Khanid dynasty and the Karts of Herat, see Lane, *Early Mongol Rule in Thirteenth Century Iran*, pp. 96–176. For brief comments on how co-opted elites added a Mongolian facet to their identities, see Funada, "Mongoru jidai ni okeru minzoku sesshoku." When viewed in the wider context of Eurasia, the notion that the Mongols preserved the Koryŏ Wang monarchy and its civil bureaucracy because of the Mongols' "sinicization" seems unlikely; see Palais, "A Search for Korean Uniqueness," p. 434.

16. Several scholars have begun this reconceptualization. Morihira Masahiko has examined Koryŏ's place in the empire through a series of detailed essays, cited in the following chapters. Yi Myŏng-mi ("Koryŏ-Wŏn wangsil t'onghon ŭi chŏngch'ijŏk ŭimi") has offered preliminary comparisons between Koryŏ's place in the empire and that of Uyghuristan. Although Otosaka Tomoko's treatment of the Yuan as a part of "Chinese history" is problematic for

some of the reasons limned above, she does compare the Yuan's treatment of Koryŏ and Tibet in "Genchō no taigai seisaku." Finally, Kim Ho-dong's essay on Koryŏ's strategic significance to Qubilai is informed by an empire-wide perspective. For initial comments, see Kim, "Mong'gol che'guk kwa Koryŏ." For his full argument and documentation, see Kim, *Mong'gol che'guk kwa Koryŏ.* Kim pays particular attention to the impact of the succession struggle between Qubilai and his brother Ariq-Böke on relations with Koryŏ.

17. Underdown, "European Knowledge of Korea During the Yuan Dynasty." It is worth noting that just as contemporaneous observers routinely distinguished North China (Khitai, Khitay, Cathay, etc.) and South China (Machin, Mangi, Manzi, etc.), Rashīd al-Dīn also distinguished between northern Korea (Solangqa, Solanqa) and Korea (Kūlī); see Rashīd al-Dīn, *Jāmi' al-tavārīkh*, 2 vols., ed. by B. Karīmī (Tehran: Eqbal, 1959), 2: 685, translated and cited in Allsen, "Apportioned Lands Under the Mongols," p. 174. Rashīd al-Dīn refers to Koryŏ at least half a dozen times in his account of the Mongols in the *Compendium of Chronicles.*

18. Kim Sang-gi, *Sinp'yŏn Koryŏ sidaesa*, pp. 585–615. Kim argues that the loss of his wife warped the king and led to his "perverted" interest in men.

Chapter 1

1. For an accessible account of the Mongols, including their initial rise, see Morgan, *The Mongols.*

2. For description of steppe political organization in general, and the Mongols in particular, see Fletcher, "Turco-Mongolian Monarchic Tradition in the Ottoman Empire"; and idem, "The Mongols: Ecological and Social Perspectives." Warning against ecological determinism and essentializing steppe, or even Mongol, political structures, Christopher Atwood ("Titles, Appanages, Marriages, and Officials," p. 231) contrasts the "almost purely monarchic and despotic Chinggisid polity" with the more consensual and aristocratic aspects of the Oirats.

3. For an influential formulation of the question, see Jackson, "Dissolution of the Mongol Empire." The four great "khanates" did not constitute the entire Mongolian realm. At least through the first half of the thirteenth century, there was a plethora of *ulus*es of various sizes and strengths. Even after the four major *ulus*es consolidated their power within their spheres of interests, however, members of the Mongolian aristocracy maintained considerable autonomy; see Jackson, "From *Ulus* to Khanate." Jackson overstates the power of the khanate courts vis-à-vis Mongolian princely houses, even during the fourteenth century. For the continuing importance of the descendents of

Chinggis khan's brothers in Northeast Asia, see the subsection "Three Princely Houses of the Eastern Regions" in this chapter.

4. For insightful discussion of these administrative structures and strategies as they apply to areas north and south of the steppe, see Allsen, "Technologies of Governance in the Mongolian Empire." Allsen ("Apportioned Lands Under the Mongols," p. 184) argues that the system of sharing local revenues (as well as war booty, human resources, etc.) with non-local Chinggisid princes "may have been intended as glue to keep the ever-expanding empire together." Yokkaichi Yasuhiro ("Mongoru teikoku no kokka kōzō") stresses revenue-sharing as a critical element of steppe leadership and its continuing importance for the Mongol empire.

5. Boyle, "The Dynastic and Political History of the Il-khans"; Morgan, *Medieval Persia*, pp. 83–84; Biran, *Qaidu*; Adshead, *Central Asia in World History*, pp. 85–86.

6. See the relevant chapters in Franke and Twitchett, eds., *CHC*, vol. 6.

7. Allsen, *Mongol Imperialism.*

8. Biran, *Qaidu.*

9. Endicott-West, "Imperial Governance in Yuan Times"; idem, *Mongolian Rule in China.* Herbert Franke ("The Role of the State," pp. 104–7, 112) has noted that "deliberative and consensus-oriented decision-making" was to be found in the political traditions of the Khitans, Jurchens, and Mongols, even after they established dynastic states.

10. For discussion of this hybridity under the later Qing dynasty, see Perdue, *China Marches West.*

11. Elizabeth Endicott-West ("Merchant Associations in Yuan China," p. 152) argues that "the inability of the post-Qubilai Yuan court to distinguish between a governmental budget and an imperial family budget would eventually contribute to the late Yuan economic crisis."

12. See the essays on Chinese culture under the Mongols in Langlois, ed., *China Under Mongol Rule.* Sugiyama Masaaki has been among the most influential Japanese scholars in the ongoing re-evaluation of the impact of the Mongols on Eurasia. Drawing upon a wide variety of sources, Miya Noriko has demonstrated the vibrancy of intellectual life in China under the Mongols in such areas as geographical knowledge, religion, and publishing; see her collected essays, *Mongoru jidai no shuppan bunka*, and her *Mongoru teikoku ga unda sekaizu.* See also Frederick Mote's comments in "Chinese Society Under Mongol Rule, 1215–1368," in *CHC*, vol. 6.

13. See Ostrowski, *Muscovy and the Mongols*; Komaroff and Carboni, *The Legacy of Genghis Khan*; and Lane, *Early Mongol Rule in Thirteenth Century Iran.*

14. Morita Kenji 森田憲司, "Kin-Gen" 金元, in Tonami et al., *Chūgoku rekishi kenkyū nyūmon*, p. 180. For a thorough review of Chinese scholarship on the Yuan period, see Liu Xiao, *Yuanshi yanjiu.*

15. For useful biographical notes, see Herbert Franke, in Goodrich and Fang, *Dictionary of Ming Biography*, pp. 1290–93; and Fujishima, "Gen no Juntei to sono jidai." The only full-length biography of Toghan-Temür in any language is Qiu Shusen's highly readable *Tuohuan Tiemuer zhuan.* Qiu argues that Toghan-Temür's early traumas deeply shaped his personality and outlook on life.

16. The late Charles Hucker once wrote, "It would probably not be an unreasonable exaggeration to say that his whole reign was devoted to the pursuit of personal pleasures" (*The Ming Dynasty*, p. 7). Because of his inconsistency, unwillingness to accept criticism, profligate lifestyle, and oppression of the people, Toghan-Temür was "a historical personage to be rejected," concludes a more recent evaluation in an influential historical journal in the People's Republic of China; see Yu Yuhe and Huang Kun, "Yuan Shundi jianlun." Another scholar notes that despite a promising beginning as an aspiring reformer, Toghan-Temür eventually developed into the "most muddle-headed and decadent emperor in history" (Lei Qing, "Yuan Shundi xinlun," p. 25).

17. Satō Hiyashi ("Minchō ni okeru Ramakyō," p. 312) identifies these rites as *Bla na med pahi rgyud.* The late fourteenth-century observer Changguzhenyi 長古眞逸 obliquely suggested that some trappings of Tibetan Buddhism were popular beyond Daidu and the imperial family. The Chinese warlord Zhang Shicheng's younger brother, Zhang Shixin 張士信, was thought to have maintained a troupe of "demoness dancers" 天魔舞隊, that is, a female dance troupe that offered their performances as entertainment to Buddhist deities. Toghan-Temür famously kept such a troupe in the imperial palace in Daidu; they were closely associated with Tibetan Buddhism, especially the tantric tradition. On Zhang Shixin's troupe, see Changguzhenyi, *Nong tian si hua, juan shang*, 3a.

18. *YS*, 205.4583 哈麻傳. Qamagh was a Qangli 康里氏 Turk who gained the emperor's favor in part through recommending Tibetan monks to him. In another effort to reduce tantric Buddhism to mere sexual technique, a 1353 entry from the *Official History of the Yuan Dynasty* notes that Qamagh and others "secretly presented" an Indian monk to the emperor "to practice the technique of moving one's *qi* in the bedroom. It is called the *Bla na med pahi rgyud.* They also presented Tibetan monks [who] excelled at tantric methods. The emperor practiced them all" (*YS*, 43.913 順帝本紀六至正十三年). Some historians from the People's Republic of China have uncritically accepted contemporary denunciations of Tibetan Buddhism's influence on Toghan-Temür; see, e.g., Qiu Shusen, *Yuanchao jianshi*, p. 457.

19. See Chen Gaohua, "*Yuan shi* zuanxiu kao" 元史纂修考, *Lishi yanjiu* 歷史研究 1990, no. 4, republished in idem, *Yuanshi yanjiu xinlun*, p. 441; Wang Zhenrong, *Yuanshi tanyuan*, p. 26; and Dardess, "Bibliographic Essay" in "Shun-ti and the End of Yuan Rule in China," p. 717.

20. For the compilation of the "Basic Chronicle of Shundi" 順帝本紀 in the *Official History of the Yuan Dynasty*, see Wang Zhenrong, *Yuanshi tanyuan*, pp. 44–50. Wang notes that although Ming scholars lacked a veritable record for Toghan-Temür's reign, an imperially commissioned committee of scholars conducted an intensive search for relevant documentary evidence, collecting government documents (including those in non-Chinese languages), copying stele inscriptions, and interviewing men familiar with Shundi's reign. The resulting basic chronicle may have paled in comparison with that of Qubilai's reign, but it surpassed those of other fourteenth-century emperors. However, as Kim Ho-dong ("Monggol cheguksa yŏn'gu wa *Chipsa*," pp. 343–44) argues, the particular Chinese historiographical tradition of "Official Dynasty Histories" was a flawed vessel to convey the complexity of the Mongol empire. The shortcomings are apparent when the *Yuanshi* is compared with Rashīd al-Dīn's *Compendium of Chronicles*, which made far more extensive use of Mongolian documentary and oral materials.

21. The most thorough study of the Juyong Pass remains the two-volume work by Murata Jirō et al., *Kyoyōkan*, which includes extensive photographs of the pass from the early twentieth century as well as transcriptions of the many inscribed texts.

22. Berger, "Preserving the Nation," p. 105. In the fourth lunar month of 1354, the court ordered the construction of another "stupa overarching a boulevard" 過街塔 at Lugou Bridge (Marco Polo Bridge), the important transportation hub along the imperial highway west of Daidu and leading to the capital (*YS*, 43.915 順帝本紀至正十四年四月是月).

23. For further discussion of Juyongguan's stupas, see Su Bai, "Juyongguan guojieta gaokao" 居庸關過街塔考稿, in idem, *Zangchuan fojiao siyuan kaogu*, pp. 338–64.

24. Farquhar, "Emperor as Bodhisattva," p. 12.

25. Herbert Franke, "From Tribal Chieftain to Universal Emperor and God."

26. *YS*, 43.918 順帝本紀至正十四年十二月是月.

27. My thanks to Shen Weirong 沈衛榮, director of the Central Eurasian Institute of People's University, for explaining the Tibetan meaning of the Chinese transliteration (pers. comm., June 5, 2006). Shen suggests that the ritual may refer to the obstacle-eliminating ritual of the White Umbrella, *Gdugs dpar zlog sgyur*. For a slightly different translation of this passage, see Cleaves,

"The 'Fifteen Palace Poems' by K'o Chiu-ssu," p. 455*n*123. Cleaves renders *duo si ge er* as *dösger.*

28. *YS*, 43.913 順帝本紀六至正十四年正月丁丑. Circumambulation rites, which resembled exuberant parades, were held in the sixth lunar month in Shangdu; see Ye Xinmin, *Yuan Shangdu yanjiu*, pp. 53–54.

29. These appeals to Chinese traditions were fully congruent with Toghan-Temür's accomplishments in the Sinic tradition. For a laudatory account of the emperor's skills in the Chinese high tradition as well as his abilities as a shipbuilder and clock maker, see Lan Wu, "Yuan Shundi Tuohuan Tiemuer."

30. Fujishima, "Gen no Juntei to sono jidai," pp. 60–61; Zhou Liangxia and Gu Juying, *Yuanshi*, pp. 601–2.

31. For a description of Liaodong's geography in the context of Northeast Asia, see Janhunen, *Manchuria*, pp. 3–8.

32. Early during the eleventh century, the Liao state relocated a portion of locally influential Parhae households that had settled in Liaoyang to populate the Central Capital (modern-day Beijing); see Wittfogel and Feng, *A History of Chinese Society*, p. 288.

33. Early in the eleventh century, the Liao prohibited the subjugated Parhae population from playing polo, which was considered a form of military training. However, in 1038, the Liao emperor announced, "The Eastern Capital, a very important military center, has no hunting ground. Except for polo, how can the people get military training? And, since the Son of Heaven considers All Within the Four Seas as one family, why is there a differentiation between this and that?" The ban was relaxed (ibid., pp. 233–34).

34. For instance, during a 1027 famine in Yan (corresponding roughly to the area around Beijing), plans were formulated to ship grain from Liaodong to Yan. Although the proposal was rejected, it suggests that such trade routes were in use at the time (ibid., p. 165). During the early years of the Liao dynasty, the state apparently hesitated to impose overly heavy economic demands on the recently conquered Liaodong region. They feared, rightly, revolt (ibid., pp. 335–36). Similar fears in 1074 prompted the Liao court to forcibly mobilize large numbers of Liaodong men for work on river dikes (ibid., p. 373).

35. Qiu Shusen, "Yuandai de Nüzhenren," p. 164. During the early twelfth century, the Liao government encouraged "men of Liaodong" to join the army. This was an effort to exploit their perceived animosity toward the Jurchen and Parhae (Wittfogel and Feng, *A History of Chinese Society*, p. 197).

36. Chikusa Masaaki, *Seifuku ōchō no jidai*, pp. 103–5.

37. Allsen argues this position compellingly in both *Commodity and Exchange* and *Culture and Conquest.* Di Cosmo comes to similar conclusions in "Mongols and Merchants on the Black Sea."

38. See Allsen, "Rise of the Mongolian Empire," pp. 352–53; and Franke, "The Chin Dynasty," pp. 257–59. More detailed treatment may be found in Han Rulin, comp., *Yuanchao shi*, 1: 122–27; and Cong Peiyuan, *Zhongguo dongbeishi*, pp. 12–20. As early as 1217–18, the armies of Muqali, the leading Mongol general in the Liaodong and North China theater, numbered at least 100,000 men and included Mongol cavalry, Chinese infantry, border units of mixed ethnic composition (*jiujun*) that had served under the Jin, surrendered Jurchen troops, and Khitans. See Huang Shijian, "Muhuali guowang huixia zhujun kao."

39. Lane, *Early Mongol Rule in Thirteenth Century Iran*, p. 60. For Lane, the collapse of the Khwārazmanshāhnate exacerbated already chaotic conditions, which he traces to the early twelfth century.

40. Hao Jing 郝經, "Wanjuanlou ji" 萬卷樓記 (1244), cited in Aubin, "The Rebirth of Chinese Rule," p. 134. For a detailed examination of one man's effort to understand the chaos caused by Mongol victories in larger historical and cultural contexts as well as his own private terms, see West, "Chilly Seas and East-Flowing Rivers."

41. Aubin ("The Rebirth of Chinese Rule") stresses the opportunistic behavior of both rebels and the powerful military families who joined the Mongols.

42. For a discussion of the princes and the approximate locations of their appanages, see Cong Peiyuan, *Zhongguo dongbeishi*, pp. 50–94.

43. This paragraph draws heavily from Ebisawa, "Mongoru teikoku no Tōhō san'ōke"; and Horie, "Temuge-Occhigin to sono shison." For discussion of the Muqali house during the Yuan period, see Harada, "Genchō no Mokkari ichizoku."

44. Sugiyama, "Kubirai seiken to Tōhō san'ōke." Ebisawa also stressed the importance of the Eastern Princes' support.

45. In Chinese-language records, he is known as Tachaer 塔察兒.

46. Rashīd al-Dīn noted that Tāčar held "a great deal of *ulus* and troops" (cited in Jackson, "From *Ulus* to Khanate," p. 16). Jackson (ibid., p. 33) understates Tāčar's importance and the status of his house.

47. For concise discussion of the princes' privileges and administrations, see Cheng Nina, "Yuandai dui Menggu dongdao zhuwang tongxia yanjiu."

48. Horie, "Mongoru = Genchō jidai," pp. 390–95.

49. Ebisawa, "Mongoro teikoku no Tōhō san'ōke," pp. 33–35; Yokkaichi, "*Jarugechi* kō," p. 15.

50. Endicott-West, *Mongolian Rule in Yuan China*, pp. 89–103.

51. For a brief overview, see Rossabi, *Khubilai Khan*, pp. 222–24.

52. Wang Yun, "Da Yuan gu zhengyi dafu Zhexidao xuanweishi xinggongbu shangshu Sun gong shendaobei." The first half of the quotation is cited in Ebisawa, "Mongoru teikoko no Tōhō san'ōke," p. 40.

53. Bozhulu Chong 孛朮魯翀, "Canzhi zhengshi Wang gong shendaobei" 参知政事王公神道碑, in Su Tianjue, comp., *Guochao wenlei*, *juan* 68, 1367.898; cited in Ebisawa, "Mongoru teikoko no Tōhō san'ōke," p. 40.

54. *YS*, 139.3358 朵爾直班傳.

55. Horie, "Mongoru = Genchō jidai," pp. 397–400.

56. *KS*, 28.441 忠烈王四年七月壬辰. See Ebisawa, "Mongoro teikoku no Tōhō san'ōke," p. 40. Tāčar was not the only Mongolian to control assets in Koryŏ. In 1335, the following command appeared from the Yuan court: "The lands and residences in Koryŏ seized by El-Temür, [his son] Tang Qishi 唐其勢, and Dali 答里 [El-Temür's brother] are to be returned to their king, Aratnasiri [King Ch'ungsuk]." The order was issued in the wake of Tang Qishi's fall from power. See *YS*, 38.829 順帝本紀一至元元年十一月甲午.

57. *YS*, 5.81 世祖本紀中統三年正月庚午; cited in Yi Myŏng-mi, "Koryŏ-Wŏn wangsil t'onghon," p. 31. Cong Peiyuan (*Zhongguo dongbeishi*, p. 373) argues that the Yuan court limited economic contacts for fear that the Koryŏ military would grow too strong.

58. Horie, "Temuge-Occhigin to sono shison," pp. 248–51. Ebisawa, Horie, and Sugiyama pass over the developments of the 1350s and 1360s in complete silence.

59. Yang Ŭi-suk, "Wŏn kansŏpgi Yosimjiyŏk Koryŏin ŭi tonghyang," pp. 19–20.

60. *YS*, 154.3628 洪福源傳. See also *KS*, 130.645–47 洪福源傳. Hong's biography in the *Official History of the Koryŏ Dynasty*, which is listed in the section on "Traitors" (*pan'ŏk* 叛逆), does not accurately reflect the myriad ways the Hong family served the empire.

61. *YS*, 154.3628, 3629, 3633, 3634 洪福源傳.

62. *YS*, "Di li er" 地理二, *juan* 59, 5: 1399. The royal clansman was Wang Chun 王綧, previously sent by the Koryŏ court to Daidu as a royal hostage. Wang's biography in *Official History of the Yuan Dynasty* indicates that prior to 1260, the Mongol court had already placed recently relocated Korean households under Wang's supervision and that in 1262 he had led some of them in the campaign against Li Tan 李璮, a powerful Chinese warlord in Shandong province who had revolted against Mongol rule. See *YS*, 166.3891 王綧傳. For a brief discussion of Li's revolt, see Rossabi, *Khubilai Khan*, pp. 62–67. In 1270, Wang served in a joint Mongol-Korean force to suppress Im Yŏn's abortive coup d'état; in that campaign he commanded "1,300 households of apportioned people" 部民一千三百户, presumably the Koreans noted above. On Wang Chun's sons, see *YS*, 166.3891–92 王綧傳.

63. Kim Ku-chin, "Wŏndae Yodong chibang ŭi Koryŏ kunmin," pp. 470–74. For concise discussion of several waves of Korean relocation and immigration

into Liaodong during the thirteenth and fourteenth centuries, see Yang Xiaochun, "Shisan-shixi shiji Liaoyang, Shenyang diqu Gaoli yimin yanjiu." For detailed consideration of Shenyang's administrative structures, including those dedicated to the governance of Korean populations, see Yang Xiaochun, "Yuandai Shenyanglu de jigou shezhi jiqi bianqian."

64. For recent discussion, see Yang Ŭi-suk, "Wŏn kansŏpgi Yosimjiyŏk Koryŏin ŭi tonghyang," pp. 30–35.

65. This paragraph is based on *YS*, 154: 3627–34 洪福源傳.

66. Jie does not appear to have had any special tie to Liaodong. In 1314, he won his first appointment to a post in the Hanlin Academy. On the occasion of the 1357 imperial offerings, his son, Jie Hong 揭汯 (1304–73), probably in his capacity as a Hanlin scholar, would later compose a prayer essay on behalf of the throne for the Beizhen Temple 北鎮廟, dedicated to the spirit of the Yiwulü Mountains 醫巫閭山, located in present-day Beizhen, Liaoning province. This would be the last recorded offering from the throne at Beizhen Temple during the Yuan dynasty. See Luo Xiyi, *Manzhou jinshizhi*, 5.31b–33a, pp. 17350–51. Sonoda Kazuki (*Manshū kinsekishi kō*, 1: 212–13) incorrectly transcribes Jie Hong's name as Jie Fa 法.

The poem is entitled "Presented to the Brothers Adjutants Hong" ("Zeng Hong canjun xiongdi" 贈洪参軍兄弟). I take *ch'amgun/canjun* as an abbreviation of *ch'amgunsa/canjunshi* 参軍事. Hucker notes that the term "adjutant" was a title for aides in princely establishments (Hucker, *Dictionary of Official Titles*, pp. 517–18). In this case, it seems likely that the Hong brothers served as aides in the Sim Prince's establishment. A contemporaneous use of the title *ch'amgunsa/canshi* as an adjutant in the household of the Sim Prince is found in stele inscriptions. In communications with the abbots of Jiangnan temples, Wang Chang dispatched an Adjutant Hong Yak 参軍洪鑰 and an Adjutant Hong Yak 参軍洪瀹. The variation in the personal name seems likely a result of scribal error, with one character written with a water radical and the other with a metal radical. In modern Korean, the pronunciation is identical. The inscriptions appear in Kitamura Takai, "Kōraiō Ō Shō no sūButsu," pp. 130, 132. The same Hong Yak appears in two 1314 entries of the *Official History of the Koryŏ Dynasty*. In the first, it is explained that he was in the Southern Capital (Namgyŏng) as an adjutant of the Koryŏ heir apparent. He loaned Yuan paper cash to several Koryŏ officials dispatched by the reigning Koryŏ king to purchase books in the Jiangnan region. The ship carrying the Koryŏ officials had been wrecked, and the officials had come ashore with little more than the clothing on their backs. The second entry notes that in response to a request by Hong Yak, the Yuan emperor bestowed a large number of Chinese books from the former Song imperial library on the Koryŏ throne. See *KS*, 34.532

忠肅王元年六月庚寅, 七月甲寅. If this line of reasoning is correct, it would neither preclude nor confirm the possibility that the Hong brothers were related to the descendents of Hong Pok-wŏn. The poem, however, unmistakably identifies the brothers with Liaodong.

67. Ching and Nan, respectively in modern Korean. Yang Longzhang has suggested that this line should be understood as a reference to the superior quality of the family (pers. comm., Aug. 13, 2007).

68. Jie Xisi, "Zeng Hong canjun xiongdi" 贈洪參軍兄弟, in *Jie Wenan gong quanji* (*Sibu congkan*), 77:. 50; cited in Chang Tong-ik, *Wŏndae Yŏsa charyo chipnok*, p. 290.

69. It is unclear whether the description of the location of the princedom of Shen (which I take as Shenyang) as in the southeast refers to Liaoyang circuit or reflects Gong's uncertain grasp of Liaodong's geography.

70. One suspects that here "ruler" refers to the Sim Prince rather than the Yuan emperor. Wang Chang, the Sim Prince at the time, however, spent most of his time in Daidu rather than Liaoyang.

71. Gong Su, "Zeng Hong zicong canjun Shenwang chu goushu fengzhi chengyi" 贈洪子淙參軍瀋王處購書奉旨乘驛, *Cun hui zhai gao* 存悔齋稿 (Siku quanshu, *bieji* 4, vol. 1199); cited in Chang Tong-ik, *Wŏndae Yŏsa charyo chipnok*, p. 289.

72. Kim Hye-wŏn, "Koryŏ hugi Sim (yang) wang," p. 39.

73 Some argue that Ch'ungsŏn was the first to acquire the title. See Yi Sŭng-han, "Koryŏ Ch'ungsŏnwang ŭi Simyangwang p'ibong"; and Zhang Daiyu "*Yuan shi* Gaoli fumawang fengwang shiliao kaobian," pp. 47–48.

74. To reward their loyalty, Haishan invested more than a dozen men as princes of the first rank ("single-character princes" 一字王); see Chen Dezhi et al., *Zhongguo tongshi*, 13: 463; and Hsiao, "Mid-Yuan Politics," p. 508. For discussion of Ch'ungsŏn's role in the succession struggle following the emperor Temür's death and his privileged status at the courts of Haishan and Ayurbarwada, see Yi Sŭng-han, "Koryŏ Ch'ungsŏnwang ŭi Simyangwang p'ibong," pp. 26–42.

75. Kim Hye-wŏn, "Koryŏ hugi Sim (yang) wang," p. 43. The communities consisted of approximately 400 households and several dozen headmen. Yang Xiaochun ("Shisan-shisi shiji Liaoyang, Shenyang diqu Gaoli yimin yanjiu," p. 41) also notes the formation of these communities.

76. In 1310, responding to the Sim Prince's request, the Mongol emperor Haishan ordered officials of Shenyang circuit "not to overstep their jurisdiction" (*Koryŏsa chŏryo*, 23.23a, p. 598 忠宣王二年五月). Whether the contested jurisdiction referred to relocated Korean communities in Liaodong or populations within the kingdom of Koryŏ, Ch'ungsŏn's political influence is clear.

77. Korean scholarship generally refers to the second Simyang Prince as Wang Ko, although the character 暠 can be read as either Ko or Ho (Ch. Gao or Hao). In the interests of consistency, I have used the pronunciation Ko throughout.

Kim Hye-wŏn, "Koryŏ hugi Sim (yang) wang," pp. 43–56. The extent of the Sim Prince's political control in Liaodong is unclear. Some Korean scholars assume that the Korean population of Shenyang was the foundation of the prince's power on the larger Koryŏ political stage. Kim Ku-chin ("Wŏndae Yotong chibang ŭi Koryŏ kunmin," p. 485) maintains, "from the time of King Ch'ungsŏn onward, the existence of the Sim Prince was inseparably linked to Koryŏ's domestic political situation. It goes without saying that those Koreans who had joined the Yuan and were living in Shenyang Circuit were the support behind the power of the Sim Prince faction." He offers no evidence for this assertion. In contrast, Kim Kyŏngnae ("Simyangwang e taehan ilgoch'al," p. 95) argues persuasively that "more than the Liaodong region, support for the Sim Prince came from within Koryŏ." Yi Sŭng-han ("Koryŏ Ch'ungsŏnwang ŭi Simyangwang p'ibong," p. 65) argues that the Sim Prince "exercised control over the Koryŏ émigrés in the Liaoyang and Shenyang region," but acknowledges that "it is not possible to know specifically how the Simyang Prince exercised control over the Koryŏ émigrés in the Liaoyang-Shenyang region." Yi (ibid., p. 70*n*87), like Kim, maintains that efforts to enthrone the Sim Prince, Ko, owed far more to intra-Korean political competition than Mongolian "dissolution policies" designed to fragment Koryŏ.

78. On the two Mongol traditions of control of territory and control of populations, see Jackson, "Dissolution of the Mongol Empire," pp. 191–93.

79. Much Korean scholarship stresses the Mongol court's division of authority and power in Liaodong among several competing families as a more effective way to subjugate Korean communities in both Liaodong and Koryŏ itself. For a recent example, see Yang Ŭi-suk, "Wŏn kansŏpgi Yosimjiyŏk Koryŏin ŭi tonghyang," pp. 20–35.

80. For the evolution of administrative structures in Shenyang, see Yang Xiaochun, "Yuandai Shenyanglu de jigou shezhi jiqi bianqian." As Yang notes, Shenyang administrative structures were inseparably linked to Korean communities in the region.

81. No Ki-sik's ("Wŏn-Myŏng kyoch'egi ŭi Yodong kwa Yojin," p. 11) observation that with the establishment of the Liaoyang Branch Secretariat, "the regional administrative apparatus became identical with that of the center (i.e., China proper)" is not persuasive. The large Korean communities, their systems of governance, and the concentration of Mongolian aristocrats in the region

guaranteed that the secretariat bureaucracy would not be as important as its counterparts in areas such as, say, Jiangnan.

82. The description of Liaodong's administrative structures is based largely on Cong Peiyuan, *Zhongguo dongbeishi*, pp. 32–37.

83. *YS*, 154.3630 洪福源傳附洪俊奇傳.

84. Rashiduddin Fazlullah (Rashīd al-Dīn), *Compendium of Chronicles*, p. 445. This and other passages related to Koryŏ require further research in terms of contemporaneous perceptions of Liaodong and Koryŏ.

85. "Polity Prince" is from Allsen, *Culture and Conquest in Mongol Eurasia*, p. 21. Farquhar (*The Government of China*, p. 18) renders it simply as "prince" and notes the equivalent in Mongolian was *gui ong*.

86. *YS*, 139.3353 朶兒只傳.

87. *YS*, 39.843–44 順帝本紀至元四年三月辛酉; 139.3353 朶兒只傳. In 1338, Dorji's uncle (Naimantai 乃蠻台) was invested as Polity Prince (reportedly through the influence of Bayan). As Harada Rie ("Genchō no Mokkari ichizoku," p. 81) notes, there is some discrepancy in the *Official History of the Yuan Dynasty* as to when Dorji lost the title of Polity King. The "Biography of Naimantai" indicates that it was 1337, but the "Biography of Dorji" and the "Basic Chronicles of Shundi" give 1338. For a genealogical chart of the Muqali house, see Harada, pp. 66–67.

88. *YS*, 139.3355 朶兒只傳. The death of Naimantai had made possible Dorji's reacquisition of the title. In 1342, the court had appointed Naimantai as Minister of the Left of Liaoyang Branch Secretariat but allowed him to demure on the basis of his advanced age. Naimantai had been serving as Minister of the Left of the Lingbei Branch Secretariat in Mongolia (*YS*, 139. 3352 乃蠻台傳). During the mid-1340s, a sixth-generation descendent of Muqali, Dorjibal (Ch. Duoer zhiban 朶爾直班, 1314–53), served as the Manager of Governmental Affairs (*pingzhang zhengshi*) of the Liaoyang Branch Secretariat (*YS*, 139.3358 朶爾直班傳).

89. Nasen 迺賢, "Xing lu nan" 行路難, *Jintai ji* 金臺集, 2.7b–8a.

90. *YS*, 42.900 順帝本紀至元十二年五月乙酉. The entry provides no further details.

91. *YS*, 139.3355 朶兒只傳; 44.926 順帝本紀至正十五年六月是月. His son, whose name is transliterated in Chinese as Anmuge shili 俺木哥失里, inherited Dorji's title of Polity Prince.

92. Like other Mongol nobles, the Muqali house held a portfolio of revenue sources drawn from several territories within the *ulus*, including Dongping and Jiangnan; see *YS*, 95.2427–28 食貨志歲賜勳臣, cited in Harada, "Genchō no Mokkari ichizoku," p. 90*n*64.

93. *YS*, 35.778 文宗本紀至順二年二月壬申.

94. *YS*, 35.786 文宗本紀至順二年六月壬戌.

95. *YS*, 35.784 文宗本紀至順二年四月甲子. In the third lunar month, the court had ordered the Liaoyang Branch Secretariat to issue two months' supply of grain from nearby granaries to another 14,500 households in Liaoyang. These households were subordinate populations of the Shou Prince 壽王 (Tuolichu 脱里出), the Yangdi Prince 陽翟王 (Tiemuerchi 帖木兒赤), the Xiping Prince 西平王 (Guanbuba 管不八), and the Chang Prince 昌王 (Balashili 八剌失里) who "lived in Liaoyang" (*YS*, 35.781 至順二年三月癸卯).

96. *YS*, 35.785 文宗本紀至順二年五月戊戌.

97. Chen Gaohua, "Yuandai de liumin wenti," pp. 138–39, 141–42.

98. For discussion of Qaidu, see Biran, *Qaidu*.

99. For a detailed biography of Lian by Hsiao Ch'i-ch'ing (Xiao Qiqing), see Rachewiltz et al., eds., *In the Service of the Khan*, pp. 480–99.

100. The account of Nayan is based primarily on Zhou Liangxia and Gu Juying, *Yuanshi*, pp. 318–22. See also Hiroe Miyaaki, "Nayan no hanran ni tsuite"; Yao Dali, "Naiyan zhi luan zakao"; and Li Zhian, "Make Boluo suoji Naiyan zhi luan kaoshi."

101. Tao Zongyi, "Yinding zihao" 銀錠字號, *Nancun chuogeng lu*, 30.377.

102. *KS*, 30.469 忠烈王十四年三月壬寅.

103. *KS*, 30.469–75.

104. Kim Ku-chin, "Wŏndae Yodong chibang ŭi Koryŏ kunmin," pp. 476–77. Kim does not connect the abolition of Tongnyŏngbu to Mongol aristocrats' challenge to the central government at the time. He speculates that although the territory itself was returned to the Koryŏ court, most of the population was relocated to Liaodong. A similar view is expressed in Yang Ŭi-suk, "Wŏn kansŏpgi Yosimjiyŏk Koryŏin ŭi tonghyang," p. 19.

105. *KS*, 30.469 忠烈王十四年四月乙卯; Chang Tong-ik, *Koryŏ hugi oegyosa yŏn'gu*, p. 37.

106. *KS*, 30.470–72 忠烈王十四年四月庚午, 忠烈王十五年六月癸卯; 忠烈王十五年八月壬戌. Qubilai canceled the proposed campaign against Qaidu in the tenth lunar month of 1289 (*KS*, 30.472 忠烈王十五年十月庚申).

107. *KS*, 30.471 忠烈王十五年二月丙寅. Providing such an amount of grain was difficult, and the king dipped into the royal treasury to meet the quota. The Koreans shipped the grain by sea to Gaizhou. Storms sank nine of the forty-four ships, resulting in significant loss of life and grain (*KS*, 30.471–72 忠烈王十五年三月辛卯, 三月己亥, 十月乙丑).

108. Many of Nayan's supporters were relocated to coastal Dinghai county 定海縣 in southeastern China (Qingyuan circuit 慶元路, in present-day Zhejiang). See Yang Yu (1285–1361), *Shan ju xin yu*, 2.216–17; and Tao Zongyi, "Pan dang gao qian di" 叛黨告遷地, *Nancun chuogeng lu*, 2.30–31. Jackson ("From

Ulus to Khanate," p. 34) notes that Nayan's troops were "redistributed among the imperial family" and that Qubilai "went on to suppress the agents (*darughachis*) appointed by these princes to superintend their assignments in China." He does not, however, mention that control of the house remained in the hands of descendents of Belgütei. For brief comments on Yang Yu and his miscellany, see Franke, "Some Remarks on Yang Yü."

109. Yun Ŭn-suk ("K'ubillai k'an ŭi chung'ang chipkwŏnhwa") has stressed that the Eastern Princes remained influential even after Nayan's revolt and that Qubilai's efforts to extend the power of the central court did not mean an end to princely autonomy.

110. See, e.g., *YS*, 35.793 文宗本紀四至順二年十一月癸未.

111. Cong Peiyuan, *Zhongguo dongbeishi*, pp. 31–32.

112. Hsiao, "Mid-Yuan Politics," p. 541.

113. For discussion of El-Temür, including his ties to Koryŏ, see Ma Juan, "Yuandai Qincharen Yan Tiemuer shiji kaolun."

114. The preceding paragraphs draw from Hsiao, "Mid-Yuan Politics," pp. 541–45; Zhou Liangxia and Gu Juying, *Yuandai shi*, pp. 599–602; Chen Dezhi et al., *Zhongguo tongshi*, 13: 490–95; and Cong Peiyuan, *Zhongguo dongbeishi*, pp. 398–400.

115. Qiu (*Tuohuan Tiemuer zhuan*, p. 7) casts the conflict in terms of El-Temür versus the armies of Liaodong and Shaanxi.

116. *YS*, 176.4115 劉德溫傳; cited in Wu Songdi, *Zhongguo renkoushi*, 3: 390.

117. Farquhar (*Government of China*, p. 272) indicates that the commission began in the 1320s as the Military Commission for the Qipchaq Imperial Army 欽察親軍都督府. More details here are needed on where it was based, the extent of its power, and its impact on the Eastern Princes.

118. *YS*, 32.721 文宗本紀天曆元年十一月丙戌.

119. *YS*, 32.728 文宗本紀天曆二年正月癸酉.

120. Six hundred fifty households were registered in the "Zhaozhou, Menggu, and Jurchen agricultural colonies" of the Liaoyang Branch Secretariat; see *Jingshi dadian xu lu* 經世大典序錄, cited in Su Tianjue, *Guochao wenlei* (*Sibu congkan, chubian jibu* 初編集部), 41.459; and in Su Tianjue, *Yuan wen lei* (same work retitled under Qing), 41.77b, 1367: 544. Japanese and Chinese scholars debate the location of Zhaozhou during the Yuan period; one view is that it was located near Fuyu 扶餘, Jilin province; another holds that it was about 50 miles west of present-day Harbin. It seems to have been garrisoned in the wake of Nayan's revolt. For bibliographic details regarding likely sites of Zhaozhou, see Horie, "Mongoru = Genchō jidai," p. 407*n*43.

121. Yi Kok, "Han kong haengsang Han kong sindo pimyŏng" 有元故亞中大夫河南府路總管兼本路諸軍奧魯總管管內勸農事知河防贈集賢直學士輕車都尉高陽侯謚正惠韓公行狀韓公神道碑銘, *Kajŏng chip*, 12.9a, reprinted in *Han'guk munjip ch'onggon*, 3: 172; Su Tianjue, "Yuan gu Yazhong dafu Henanfulu zongguan Han gong shendao beiming" 元故亞中大夫河南府路總管韓公神道碑銘, *Cixi wen'gao*, 17.279–81.

122. Yi Kok, *Kajŏng chip*, 12.9b–10a, 3: 172.

123. Han's three sons also pursued official careers within the Mongol empire. As was common in elite society, they used both Korean and Mongolian names (Temür-Buqa, "Slave of Avalokitesvara" 觀音奴, and Jangso 承壽).

124. *KS*, 109.309 崔瀣傳; Yi Kok, "Ch'oe kun myoji" 大元故將侍郎遼陽路蓋州判官高麗國正順大夫檢校成均大司成藝文館提學同知春秋館事崔君墓誌, in *Kajŏng chip*, 12.5a, reprinted in *Han'guk munjip ch'onggon*, 3: 164.

125. *KS*, 109.307 安軸傳 (MJ ed.); Yi Kok, "An kong myojimyŏng" 大元故將侍郎遼陽路蓋州判官高麗國三重大匡興寧府院君領藝文館事謚文貞安公墓誌銘, *Kajŏng chip*, 11.10a, reprinted in *Han'guk munjip ch'onggon*, 3: 172, reprinted in *Han'guk munjip ch'onggon*, 3: 172, 3: 166. It is not clear when An returned to Koryŏ. Claiming previous responsibilities (presumably as magistrate of Gaizhou), An initially declined Ch'ungsuk's appointment.

126. Yi Kok, *Kajŏng chip*, 11.11b, reprinted in *Han'guk munjip ch'onggon*, 3: 172, 3: 167.

127. Translation of office based on Farquhar, *Government of China*, p. 414.

128. *KS*, 109. 309 安軸傳.

129. *KS*, 109.311 趙廉傳.

130. Yi Saek, "Yi kong myojimyŏng" 李公墓誌銘, *Mok'ŭn sŏnsaeng mungo*, reprinted in *Han'guk munjip ch'onggon*, 5: 126–27; *KS*, 112.352 李仁復傳.

131. Writing slightly later, Ye Ziqi 葉子奇, a Chinese scholar and memoirist, would complain of the Mongols' discrimination against Chinese in the Yuan bureaucracy. He would similarly invoke the rhetoric of talent without borders. "How can human design outdo Heaven's creation? How can it compare with the equal distribution of Heaven's allotment? There is no division between north and south. Appoint [men] exclusively according to talent. Employ [men] exclusively according to wisdom." 人謀豈能奪天造哉。孰若均平天施。無有南北之分。惟才是任。惟賢是使。(Ye Ziqi, "Za zu pian" 雜俎篇, *Cao mu zi*, *juan* 4 *xia*, p. 81).

132. Yi Kok, "Ki Yodong Ch'oe Hong yang yŏmbang kae hyang'in" 寄遼東崔洪兩廉訪皆鄉人, *Kajŏng chip*, 16.5b, reprinted in *Han'guk munjip ch'onggon*, 3: 198.

133. See the patron list of the 1352 stele inscription for the Shenyang City God temple, in Luo Xiyi, *Manzhou jinshizhi*, 5.26a–27b, pp. 17347–48; and Sonoda, *Manshū kinseki shikō*, 1: 207–8. Several of the administrative titles that appear on the stele do not appear in the *Official History of the Yuan Dynasty*; see

Yang Xiaochun, "Shenyang Yuan Zhizheng shiernian *Chenghuangmiao ji*." The translation "Directorate-General" (*ch'onggwanbu* 總館府) is based on Farquhar, *The Government of China*, p. 414.

134. Cong Peiyuan, *Zhongguo dongbeishi*, p. 16.

135. For a biographical sketch of Muqali, see Rachewiltz et al., eds., *In the Service of the Khan*, pp. 3–8.

136. Cong Peiyuan, *Zhongguo dongbeishi*, pp. 17–18.

137. Chen Gaohua, "Lun Yuandai de junhu," p. 76.

138. For discussion of the Yuan's efforts to expand and consolidate its influence in southern Siberia (i.e., northeastern Liaodong) during the late thirteenth and early fourteenth centuries, see Cheng Nina, "Yuanchao dui Heilongjiang xiayou Nuzhen." For comparative discussion of Yuan and Ming ambitions in Nurgan, see Nakamura Kazuyuki, "Mongoru jidai no Tōsei-sensuibu." Both Cheng and Nakumura note the example of Zhang Cheng to illustrate different points.

139. "Jinzhou Dunwu xiaowei guanjun shang baihu Zhang Cheng mubei" 金州敦武校尉管軍上百户張成墓碑, in Sonoda, *Manshū kinsekishi kō*, 1: 203–6; Luo Xiyi, *Manzhou jinshizhi*, 5.19b–25a. For a photographic reproduction of the stele inscription, see *Beijing tushuguan cang Zhongguo lidai shike taben huibian*, 50: 163. On Mongol names during this time, see Serruys, "Some Types of Names Adopted by the Mongols." My thanks to Thomas Allsen for bringing this article to my attention.

140. The title is noted in the 1349 stele inscription "Kaiyuansi sanmen ji" 開元寺三門記. See *Beijing tushuguan cang Zhongguo lidai shike taben huibian*, 50: 55.

141. Su Tianjue, "Huang Yuan zeng taipu kaifu yitong sansi Kangjing Xing gong shendaobei" 皇元贈太傅開府儀同三司康靖邢公神道碑, in author's *Cixi wen'gao*, 15.244–46. The Gao 高 family of Liaoyang also gained high posts in the central and local governments through military service under the Mongols (*YS*, 41.3614–15 高宣傳).

142. For the evolution of the Koryŏ political system, including relations among the monarch, local elites, and central officials, see Duncan, *Origins of the Chosŏn Dynasty*.

143. Yang Ŭi-suk, "Wŏn kansŏpgi Yosimjiyŏk Koryŏin ŭi tonghyang."

144. The most prominent being Cho Hwi 趙暉 and T'ak Ch'ŏng 卓青.

145. Pang Tong-in, "Tongnyŏngbu ch'ip'e soko"; Kim Wi-hyŏn, *Koryŏ sidae taeoe kwan'gyesa yŏn'gu*, pp. 364–66. This was part of a larger problem for the Koryŏ throne, loss of control over men and resources in the countryside during the thirteenth and fourteenth centuries; see Duncan, *Origins of the Chosŏn Dynasty*, pp. 182–88.

146. For mid-thirteenth-century efforts at centralization under Möngke khan, see Allsen, *Mongol Imperialism.* Tensions of relative degrees of power and autonomy ran through much of Qubilai's reign.

147. Pak Ok-gŏl, "Koryŏmal pukbang yumin kwa ch'uswae"; Kim Wi-hyŏn, *Koryŏ sidae taeoe kwan'gyesa yŏn-gu*, pp. 368–75; Yang Ŭi-suk, "Wŏn kansŏpgi Yosimjiyŏk Koryŏin ŭi tonghyang," pp. 17–19, 23; Kim Sunja, "Wŏn kansŏpgi min ŭi tonghyang," p. 376. Yang and others stress that Koreans were attracted by prospects of lighter tax and corvée obligations in areas beyond Koryŏ control.

148. The Chinese/Korean title of this bureau, 征東行中書省, better reflects its origins. Farquhar's rendering as "Branch Central Secretariat for Koryŏ" suggests a misleading analogy to other branch secretariats established within former Song and Jin territories and is probably best avoided. Abortive efforts to bring Koryŏ under more direct Mongol administrative control involved petitions to establish a "Branch Central Secretariat for Koryŏ."

149. Kitamura Hideo, "Kōrai ni okeru seitōgyōsei ni tsuite"; Chang Tong-ik, *Koryŏ hugi oegyosa yŏn'gu*, pp. 13–109. As Chang notes, the secretariat was among the most important administrative institutions in Koryŏ at the time. When the king was absent, the head of the secretariat ran the kingdom in his stead (pp. 48–49). For a recent synopsis of Kitamura's findings in Chinese, see Cheng Nina, "Yuandai Chaoxian bandao Zhengdong xingsheng yanjiu." For useful analysis of how relations between Qubilai and Koryŏ were shaped by wider developments in East and Central Asia, see Kim Ho-dong, *Mong'gol cheguk kwa Koryŏ.*

150. Secondary scholarship from South Korea often refers to those who derived their power from relations with the Yuan as "pro-Yuan," "Yuan dependents," or "Yuan sympathizers." Scholars like Paek In-ho heap great abuse on "national traitors" who sacrificed national unity to advance personal and family interests; see his "Koryŏ hugi puWŏn seryŏk ŭi hyŏngsŏng kwa seryŏkhwa." Although collaboration with the Mongols certainly aggravated political tensions within Koryŏ, motivations and methods varied widely. Excessive stress on betrayal of an anachronistic nation obscures this complexity.

151. For a concise articulation, see Peter Yun, "Foreigners in Korea During the Period of Mongol Interference." For full description and documentation, see idem, "Foreigners in Koryŏ Ruling Stratum."

152. For introductory remarks on the Eurasian trade sphere, see Sugiyama, *Mongoru teikoku no kōbō*, 2: 189–94; and idem, *Dai Mongoru no jidai*, pp. 168–73.

153. Peter Yun, "Rethinking the Tribute System," p. 146.

154. For gift-giving in the context of the Mongols' patrimonial political style, see Allsen, *Commodity and Exchange in the Mongol Empire*, pp. 52–57.

155. Scholars debate the location of the Sim Prince's residence. Early Japanese and much Korean scholarship puts his establishment in the Liaodong region. See Marugame, "Gen-Kōrai kankei no ichikusari"; Okada, "Gen no Shin-ō to Ryōyō gyōshō"; and Kim Ku-chin, "Yŏ-Wŏn ŭi yŏngt'o punjaeng." See also Yang Ŭi-suk, "Wŏn kansŏpgi Yosimjiyŏk Koryŏin ŭi tonghyang," pp. 33–36. Yang (p. 35) understands the term Sim/Shen Residence (Simbu/Shenfu 瀋府) as an abbreviation of *Simyangro kwanbu/Shenyanglu guanfu* 瀋陽路管府. Kitamura Hideo ("Kōrai jidai no Shin-ō") argues persuasively that the Sim Prince and his establishment were in Beijing. Chang Tong-ik (*Koryŏ hugi oegyosa yŏn'gu*, p. 144) also places the Sim Prince in Beijing.

156. On Koryŏ-Yuan economic relations, see Chang Tong-ik, *Koryŏ hugi oegyosa yŏn'gu*, pp. 133–49. Earlier work by Ch'ŏn Hae-jong ("Yŏ-Wŏn muyŏk ŭi sŏng'gyŏk") stressed the limited and largely exploitive character of Koryŏ-Yuan trade. Zhang Xuehui ("Shilun Yuandai Zhongguo yu Gaoli de maoyi," p. 65) argues that tabulating which side profited more through the tribute trade is difficult given the great variety of goods involved.

157. For discussion of changes in Yuan currency policies during the mid-fourteenth century and the resultant economic instability of the 1350s, see Miyazawa, "Gendai kōhanki no heisei to sono hōkai."

158. Wi Ŭn-suk, "Wŏn kansŏpgi poch'o ŭi yŭt'ong kwa kŭ ŭimi."

159. Pak P'yŏng-sik, "Koryŏ hugi ŭi Kaegyŏng sang'ŏp," pp. 221, 230. The examples provided in Zhang Xuehui, "Shilun Yuandai Zhongguo yu Gaoli de maoyi," p. 65, are reminiscent of the *ortoq*. The Koryŏ economy was smaller, less monetized, and less geared to international trade than was that of China during the Song-Yuan period or even Japan during the Kamakura and Muromachi periods.

160. Cong Peiyuan, *Zhongguo dongbei shi*, pp. 371–77.

161. Chen Gaohua, "Cong *Lao Qida, Piao tongshi* kan Yuan yu Gaoli de jingji wenhua jiaoliu"; Zhang Xuehui, "Shilun Yuandai Zhongguo yu Gaoli de maoyi," pp. 67–69. For an annotated translation of the primer into Japanese, see Kin Bunkyō 金文京, *Rō Kitsudai*. The primer was updated periodically during the Chosŏn period to reflect changes in vernacular Chinese. For brief comments on differences between Chosŏn period editions and the recently discovered Yuan edition (the "old edition") in terms of vocabulary, social custom, and grammar, see Chen Gaohua, "Jiuben *Lao Qida* shu hou."

162. Travel across the border between Koryŏ and Liaodong remained a prominent feature of Northeast Asia throughout the Yuan period and into the Ming; see Pak Sŏng-ju, "Koryŏmal Han-Chunggan ŭi yumin."

163. Yang Ŭi-suk, "Wŏn kansŏpgi Yosimjiyŏk Koryŏin ŭi tonghyang," pp. 22–23.

164. Chang Tong-ik, *Koryŏ hugi oegyosa yŏn'gu*, pp. 149–93.

165. Pak Ok-gŏl, "Koryŏmal pukbang yumin kwa ch'uswae," pp. 121–22, 131–34; Yang Ŭi-suk, "Wŏn kansŏpgi Yosimjiyŏk Koryŏin ŭi tonghyang," pp. 17–23.

166. Wang Chongshi, "Yuandai ruju Zhongguo de Gaoliren," p. 157.

167. For extended discussion, see Cong Peiyuan, *Zhongguo dongbeishi*, pp. 188–295. See also Yao Dali, "Yuan Liaoyang xingsheng gezu de fenbu," pp. 45–56.

168. For relay stations and overland routes in Liaodong, see Cong Peiyuan, *Zhongguo dongbeishi*, pp. 139–80. For Koryŏ, see Morihira, "Kōrai ni okeru Gen no tanseki." As Morihira notes, the transport system made use of existing Koryŏ stations. He further observes that although the overall routes remain fairly constant, individual stations were established and abolished in response to changing circumstances.

169. Sugiyama Masaaki stresses the maritime dimensions of the Mongol empire in all his broader works.

170. The specifics are drawn from Chen Gaohua, "Yuanchao yu Gaoli de haishang jiaotong"; and Cong Peiyuan, *Zhongguo dongbeishi*, pp. 180–87.

171. Chen Gaohua and Shi Weimin, *Zhongguo jingji tongshi*, pp. 373–74.

172. Kwŏn Kŭn 權近, "Sachae sogam Pak Kang chŏn" 司宰少監朴強傳, *Yangch'on chip* 陽村集, 21.17b; reprinted in *Han'guk munjip ch'onggan*, 7: 216.

173. For a preliminary discussion of the impact of the Mongols on the Korean diet, see Yu Ae-ryŏng, "Monggo ka Koryŏ ŭi Yukryu sikyong e mich'in yŏnghyang."

174. Endicott-West, *Mongolian Rule in China*, pp. 81–86; Namujila, "Yuandai Hanren Menggu xingming kao," pp. 12–13.

175. Namujila, "Yuandai Hanren Menggu xingming kao," pp. 10–12. Mongolian influences in fashion, and even language, did not suddenly disappear with the fall of the Yuan; see Serruys, "Remains of Mongol Customs." Late in the fifteenth century the Ming court was still trying to eliminate them among the general population, and early during the sixteenth century Ming emperors themselves wore Mongolian riding tunics and caps; see Robinson, "The Ming Court and the Legacy of the Yuan Mongols."

176. Buell, "Pleasing the Palate of the Qan"; Allsen, *Culture and Conquest in Mongol Eurasia*, pp. 127–40.

177. Allsen, *Commodity and Exchange in the Mongol Empire*, pp. 76–78.

178. For a contemporary note on the popularity of Koryŏ boots, see Tao Zongyi, "Chushi menqian quexue" 處士門前怯薛, *Nancun chuogeng lu*, 28.346.

179. Xi Lei, *Yuandai Gaoli gongnü zhidu yanjiu*, pp. 14–28.

180. Ibid., p. 51.

181. For examples of Korean wives and consorts of high-ranking Mongol and Chinese officials, see Kim Sang-gi, *Sinp'yŏn Koryŏ sidaesa*, p. 575. For more

extensive discussion, see Xi Lei, *Yuandai Gaoli gongnü zhidu yanjiu*, pp. 136–58. For intermarriage between *semuren* men (including those of Turkic, Uyghur, and Indian descent) and Korean women, see Ma Juan, "Yuandai semu Gaoli tonghun juli."

182. Quan Heng and Ren Chongyue, *Gengshen waishi jianzheng*, p. 96; cited in Shi Weimin, *Dushizhong de youmumin*, p. 106. On the Mongols' preference for Korean serving girls, see the early Ming writer Ye Ziqi, "Za zhi pian" 雜制篇, *Cao mu zi, juan* 3 *xia*, p. 63.

183. Shi Weimin, *Dushizhong de youmumin*, pp. 106–17.

184. Quan Heng, *Gengshen waishi*, *xia*.9b (*Yuandai biji xiaoshuo*, 3.530).

185. Zhang Yu, *Nian xia qu*, in Ke Jiusi et al., *Liao Jin Yuan gongci*, p. 13.

186. Perhaps best known for his poetry, Nasen gained a post as a Hanlin compiler and later served as a military advisor to Senggeshiri 桑哥失里. Contemporary literary luminaries marveled at his skill in Chinese poetry; see Chen Yuan, *Yuan Xiyuren huahuakao*, pp. 56–57. Leading lights from the late Yuan provided the calligraphy for the first edition of his collected works, *Jin tai ji*, which gained praise for its exquisite quality even in the succeeding Ming dynasty; see Ye Sheng, "Yuan *Jin tai ji* keben" 元金臺集刻本, in *Shuidong riji*, 8.92.

187. Chen Gaohua, "Yuandai shiren Naixian shengping shiji kao," p. 251.

188. Nasen, "Xinxiang ao" 新鄉媼 (Old Lady of Xinxiang), *Jin tai ji*, 1.33b–34b; also in *Yuanshixuan chuji* 元詩選初集, in *Siku zhenben*, series 11, no. 173; cited in Chang Tong-ik, *Koryŏ hugi oegyosa yŏn'gu*, p. 180n145. Chang excerpts only the portion of the poem that refers directly to Koryŏ, thus obscuring the contrast between impoverished Chinese commoners and bejeweled Koryŏ women in the imperial palace. For an alternative translation of the last portion of the poem, see Ch'en Yuan, *Western and Central Asians in China Under the Mongols*, p. 122.

189. For detailed discussion of exchanges between Koryŏ and Yuan scholars in such varied contexts as diplomatic missions, literati outings, and informal social gatherings, see Chang Tong-ik, *Koryŏ hugi oegyosa yŏn'gu*, pp. 194–234.

190. Bi Aonan, "Yuan Renzong cishu Gaoli zakao."

191. For instance, as a member of King Ch'ungsŏn's entourage in Daidu, the scholar Paek Yi-jŏng 白頤正 spent a decade in the Yuan capital. He returned to Koryŏ with several copies of *The Complete Works of Cheng and Zhu* 程朱全書, which he used when instructing his students; see Paek Mun-bo, "Munhŏngong Yijae sŏnsaeng haengsang" 文憲公彝齋先生行狀, *Tam'am munjip iljip*, 2.18b, reprinted in *Han'guk yŏktae munjip ch'ongsŏ*, 12: 135; also reprinted in *Han'guk munjip ch'onggan*, 3: 317 See also Gui Xipeng, *Yuandai jinshi yanjiu*, pp. 153–62. For a brief discussion of the emergence of an increasingly but never completely Daoxue-dominated civil service examination during the

first half of the fourteenth century, see Elman, *A Cultural History of Civil Examinations in Late Imperial China*, pp. 29–37.

192. Chang Tong-ik, *Koryŏ hugi oegyosa yŏn'gu*, pp. 229–32. Chang especially notes the importance of Yuan scholars serving in their capacity as the supervisor of Confucian schools (*Ruxue tiju* 儒學提舉) within the Branch Secretariat for the Eastern Campaigns.

193. Qiu Shusen, "Yuandai de Nüzhenren," pp. 162–63.

194. Franke, "Tibetans in Yuan China."

195. On evidence of Tibetan Buddhism in Koryŏ, see Chŏn Chongsŏk, "Kōrai bukkyō to Gendai Ramakyō to no kankei." Pointing to a portrait in which the Japanese emperor is dressed as a monk holding Buddhist instruments in each hand, Sugiyama Masaaki (*Dai Mongoru no jidai*, p. 273) has speculated that the Japanese emperor GoDaigo's 後醍醐 marked interest in tantric Buddhism may have been adopted from the Mongols' court in Daidu. Calling GoDaigo "a child of the Mongol age," Sugiyama proposes that the emperor's interest in paper money, stronger monarchal powers, and reforms to palace organization was inspired by the Mongols' example. On the brief Mongol patronage of Tibetan Buddhism in Persia, see Morgan, *The Mongols*, p. 125.

196. Chinggis khan granted special economic and legal privileges to holy men whose powers impressed him. Under his successors, privileges and responsibilities (offering efficacious prayers for the health and longevity of the imperial ruler, family, and enterprise) grew increasingly codified as did the chancellery forms used to designate them. See Atwood, "Validation by Holiness or Sovereignty"; and Jackson, "The Mongols and The Faith of the Conquered."

197. For instance, large groups of Koryŏ monks were periodically summoned to the Daidu court to copy in gold Buddhist sutras. See the 1298 stele account "Koryŏ Hongsin kukjon t'a-myŏng / Gaoli Hongzhen guozun taming" 高麗弘眞國尊塔銘, reprinted in Liu Xihai, *Haidong jinshi yuan*, pp. 17657–58. For the activities of Koryŏ merchants and monks in China, see Chen Gaohua, "Cong *Lao Qida, Piao tongshi* kan Yuan yu Gaoli de jingji wenhua jiaoliu."

198. Morihira, "Dai Gen urusu to Kōrai bukkyō."

199. Ōhara, "Kōrai kokuō *Taizōkyō* kara mita Genchō no shūkyō seisaku." Ōhara examines several expensive sutras commissioned by Koryŏ kings during the latter half of the thirteenth and early fourteenth centuries and concludes that in terms of production and text, they were influenced by those compiled at the Yuan court.

200. Morihira, "Dai Gen urusu to Kōrai bukkyō," pp. 25–28. For tax exemptions for religious organizations in Rus and the Yuan, see Atwood, "Validation by Holiness or Sovereignty."

201. For an example from 1340 involving Ko Yong-bok 高龍卜 (?–1362), a Koryŏ eunuch serving in the Bureau for the Empress's Administration, see the stele inscription "Huayan tang jingben ji" 華嚴堂經本記, reproduced in *Beijing tushuguan cang Zhongguo lidai shike taben huibian*, 50: 6. In response to a request by a Koryŏ monk sojourning in Dongfeng 東峰 Temple, near Fangshan 房山, home to a famous Buddhist enclave south of Daidu, Ko contributed funds for repair of the Garland Flower Sutra inscribed on stone and stored at the temple; see Jia Zhidao 賈志道, "Chongxiu Huayan jingben jilüe" 重修華嚴經本記略, reproduced in Yu Minzhong, (*Qinding*) *Rixia jiuwenkao*, *juan* 131, 4: 2116–17. Yu's account incorrectly gives Ko's name as Yong Pok-go. For a brief biographical note on Ko, see *Han'guk pulgyo inmyŏng sajŏn*, p. 26.

202. Ŭi Ŭn-sok, "Wŏn kansŏpgi poch'o ŭi yŭt'ong kwa kŭ ŭimi," pp. 586–87. For analysis of Koryŏ patronage of Buddhist art and prayers offered for the longevity of Mongol emperors during this time, see Chŏng Ŭn-u, "Koryŏ hugi Pulgyo misul ŭi huwŏnja."

203. For a discussion of the Mongolian term *aimaq* during the late Koryŏ and Chosŏn periods, see Kim Ch'ang-su, "Sŏngjung aemago." On the Mongolian terms used for royal guard units, see Pelliot, "Les Mots Mongols dans le *Korye sa*," pp. 261–62. Immediately upon his accession, King Ch'ungnyŏl organized the Koryŏ men who had accompanied him during his time at the Mongol capitals into his own *keshig*, called the *qorchi* (K. *horjŏk* 忽赤), or "quiver bearers." The usage derived directly from the Mongol empire; see *KS*, 82.651 兵二宿衛. The *qorchi* unit survived until 1390, when it was renamed the more Sinic-sounding Personnel Attendants 近侍, which in fact had its origins in the northern conquest dynasties on the continent; see *KS*, 82.652 兵二宿衛; and Hucker, *Dictionary of Official Titles*, p. 167.

204. The system was introduced into Tibet as the *k'ri skor* (Petech, *Central Tibet and the Mongols*, pp. 50–64). It was also introduced into southern Siberia, among the so-called Water Tatars (Shui dada), where it served as an instrument of both military and civilian administration (Cheng Nina, "Yuanchao dui Heilongjiang xiayou Nüzhen," pp. 72, 75–77).

205. An example of an imperial order of appointment for a Koryŏ myriarchy dated 1334 and written in the 'Phags pa script surfaced in Seoul more than a decade ago. For an initial account based on a photocopy of what appears to be a transcribed version of an original, see Bao Xiang, "Hancheng faxian de Basibazi wenxian."

206. The paragraphs above draw mainly from Kwŏn Yŏng-guk, "Wŏn kansŏpgi Koryŏ kunje ŭi pyŏnhwa." See also Min Hyŏn-gu, "Koryŏ hugi kunje ŭi chŏngch'ijŏk kyŏngjejŏk kiban."

207. The Chinese poet Wang Yun 王惲 (1227–1304) composed a short poem entitled "To the Koryŏ Heir Apparent."

Clouds like embroidered silk redden the waves, the Yalu River.	霞綺紅潮鴨綠清
His bearing is exactly like his father the king's heroic appearance.	風姿渾是父王英
The intricacies of rites of ritual and music resemble those of Zhou institutions.	禮文曲折猶周制
His pleasing visage is like looking on a nephew of the Han.	脂澤涵濡見漢甥
In the room, we chatted, this feeling.	衡宇接談今日款
In Zhongtang, I accompanied you at the banquet, this sentiment.	中堂陪晏嚮來情
[This time] At the Phoenix Pool, is worthy of remembrance.	鳳凰池上應回憶
I am grateful for the additional melody.	慙愧朱絃一再行

In *Qiujian xiansheng da quan wenji* 秋澗先生大全文集, *juan* 22; reprinted in Chang Tong-ik, *Wŏndae Yŏsa charyo chipnok*, p. 126.

208. The preceding paragraphs draw heavily from Kim Hyŏng-su, "Wŏn kansŏp ŭi kuksokron kwa t'ongjeron." These tensions over adoption of Yuan institutions became closely intertwined with political struggles among rivals for the Koryŏ throne. On the Yuan's failed efforts to change the Koryŏ slave system, see Chang Tong-ik, *Koryŏ hugi oegyosa yŏn'gu*, pp. 84–87.

209. See Paek In-ho, "Koryŏ hugi puWŏn seryŏk ŭi hyŏngsŏng kwa seryŏkhwa," p. 321. See also idem, *Koryŏ hugi puWŏn seryŏk yŏn'gu*.

210. Liu Yingli et al., *Da Yuan hunyi fangyu shenglan*, pp. 5 (混一諸道之圖) and 8 (遼陽).

Chapter 2

1. For a brief biography of Toqto'a that hews closely to the perspective of the *Official History of the Yuan Dynasty*, see Takahashi Takuji, "Ushōshō Dattatsu."

2. This paragraph is based on Qiu Shusen, *Tuohuan Tiemuer zhuan*, pp. 67–74; and Dardess, "Shun-ti and the End of Yüan Rule in China," pp. 571–72. The most thorough analysis of Toqto'a in any language remains Dardess's *Conquerors and Confucians*, which informs much of this chapter.

3. Qiu Shusen, *Tuohuan Tiemuer zhuan*, p. 75. For the use of painting and poems in "restoration" efforts during the reign of Tuq-Temür (r. 1329–32), see Weitz, "Art and Politics at the Mongol Court of China."

4. For a concise description of the reforms and their limitations, see Wang Mingjun et al., "Shilun Yuanchao monian de 'Zhizheng genghua.'"

5. For a contemporary description of the damage, see Gong Shitai (1298–1362), "He jue" 河決, *Wanzhaiji* 玩齋集, 1.9a–10b, p. 526.

6. Nasen, "Zeng Zhang zhiyan nangui" 贈張直言南歸, *Jin tai ji*, 2.7b.

7. Sun Chengze, *Yuanchao diangu biannian kao*, 8.30a–33b.

8. As Qiu Shusen (*Tuohuan Tiemuer zhuan*, pp. 117–34) notes, both the debate about the impact of the Yellow River project and the spread of rebellion began nearly as soon as the proposal was made.

9. See Ye Ziqi, "Tan yi pian" 談藝篇, *Cao mu zi*, *juan* 4 *shang*, p. 75.

10. In 1351, the court also hired more than 10,000 men, spending several tens of thousands of *ding* of cash, to dredge the badly silted Zhigu River 直沽河, an important water route to Daidu. The project was completed successfully in less than three months (*YS*, 184.4243 崔敬傳).

11. Quan Heng, *Gengshen waishi*, 1.9a (reprinted in *Yuandai biji xiaoshuo*, Hebei, 3.529); idem and Ren Chongyue, *Gengshen waishi jianzheng*, p. 71.

12. *YS*, 184.4244 崔敬傳. For further details of the recruiting efforts, see Meng Fanqing, "Yuanchao monian haiyun yu chouliang," pp. 229–30.

13. Quan Heng, *Gengshen waishi*, 1.11a, 3.533; idem and Ren Chongyue, *Gengshen waishi jianzheng*, p. 87. For other measures to ensure adequate supplies of grain for Daidu, see Meng Fanqing, "Yuanchao monian haiyun yu chouliang," pp. 229–31.

14. Li Shizhan, "Shang Zhongshu zong bingshu" 上中書總兵書, *Jingji wenji*, 1.5b–6a; also in Li Xiusheng, *Quan Yuan wen*, 50.129.

15. For discussion of Qubilai's desire "to reach out and appeal to the traditional Chinese scholars and Confucians," see Rossabi, *Khubilai Khan*, pp. 131–35. Chinese historians often cast the matter in terms of Qubilai's "progressive" nature; see, e.g., Qiu Shusen, *Yuanchao jianshi*, pp. 133, 136.

16. For insightful discussion of Daidu as the convergence of (a) the steppe and the sown and (b) overland and maritime trade routes, see Sugiyama, "Kubirai to Daito." For a useful review of Japanese and Chinese debates regarding the impact of Chinese and Mongolian traditions on Daidu's spatial configuration and the geopolitical imperatives behind the selection of Beijing as a site for the capital, see Watanabe Ken'ya, "Daito kenkyū no genjō to kadai."

17. Wu Songdi, *Zhongguo renkoushi*, pp. 587–88.

18. For description of these relocated populations, see Allsen, *Commodity and Exchange in the Mongol Empire*; and idem, *Culture and Conquest in Mongol Eurasia*, *passim*.

19. Weidner, "Aspects of Painting and Patronage at the Mongol Court," p. 46.

20. For a discussion of Marco Polo's accounts of these miracles, see Otosaka, "Make Boluo zhuzuozhong suo miaoshu de Zangchuan fojiao."

21. Jing, "Financial and Material Aspects of Tibetan Art," p. 213.

22. Jing, "Portraits of Khubilai Khan and Chabi by Anige"; Watt, *When Silk Was Gold*, pp. 95–99.

23. Yamamoto, "Mongoru jidai ni okeru Chibetto-Kanchikan no kōtsū to tanseki," esp. pp. 97–109. Most of Yamamoto's information dates from records related to the use of the postal relay system early during the fourteenth century.

24. For preliminary discussion of Tibetan Buddhism's significance at the Ming court through the early sixteenth century, see Robinson, "The Ming Court and the Legacy of the Yuan Mongol."

25. *Cakravartin* has been defined as "a ruler the wheels of whose chariot roll everywhere without hindrance" (William Edward Soothill, *A Dictionary of Chinese Buddhist Terms* [London: K. Paul, Trench, Trubner and Company, 1937], p. 469). Qubilai was particularly associated with Mañjuśrī, the Boddhisattva of Wisdom. For biographical information on 'Phags pa, see Rossabi, *Khubilai Khan*, pp. 143–46.

26. Ishihara, *Chibetto bukkyō sekai*, pp. 8–18, 33–34.

27. Ibid., pp. 26–32.

28. Chen Gaohua, "Yuandai Daidu de huangjia fojiao," pp. 2–5.

29. For detailed discussion of the construction of the halls of imperial portraiture, the materials used in the imperial portraits, and imperial patronage of the temples, see Nakamura Jun, "Gendai Daito no chokukenjiin o megutte"; and Jing, "Financial and Material Aspects of Tibetan Art," pp. 232–36.

30. Endicott-West, *Mongolian Rule in China*; Franke, "The Role of the State," pp. 111–12; cf. Dardess, "From Mongol Empire to Yuan Dynasty"; and idem, "Did the Mongols Matter?" pp. 124–25. Mid- and late fourteenth-century observers were generally critical of the corruption, laxity, and often predatory nature of Yuan local administration of their day; see Paul Smith, "Impressions of the Song-Yuan-Ming Transition," pp. 89–94.

31. Farquhar, "Structure and Function in the Yuan Imperial Government."

32. *YS*, 40.862 順帝本紀至正元年十二月癸亥; 40.864 順帝本紀至正二年九月丁丑; 41.874 順帝本紀至正六年三月戊申; 41.877 順帝本紀至正七年四月庚寅; 42.889 順帝本紀至正十年十月是月; 43.909 順帝本紀至正十三年四月戊戌.

33. *YS*, 41.874 順帝本紀至正六年三月辛未; Hu Cuizhong, *Yuanshi xubian*, 13.10b.

34. *YS*, 41.874 順帝本紀至正六年五月丁亥; Hu Cuizhong, *Yuanshi xubian*, 13.10b. It seems likely that it was an "inside job."

35. For discussion of the supply and consumption of Daidu's grain, see Mo Shumin, "Yuandai Daidu de liangshi yu xiaofei."

36. *YS*, 39.838 順帝本紀至元三年正月戊申; 39.842 順帝本紀至元三年九月丙寅; 39.846 順帝本紀至元四年十二月甲午; 40.854 順帝本紀至元六年二月己亥.

37. *YS*, 39.846 順帝本紀至元四年十二月甲午.

38. *YS*, 41.872 順帝本紀至正五年四月丁卯.

39. Yi Kok, "Sop'o ki" 小圃記, *Kajŏng chip*, *kwŏn* 4; cited in Chen Gaohua, "*Kajŏng chip*, *Mo'kŭn ko* yu Yuanshi yanjiu," p. 330.

40. Yi Kok, "Sasa sŏl" 市肆說, *Kajŏng chip*, *kwŏn* 7; cited in Chen Gaohua, "*Kajŏng chip*, *Mo'kŭn ko* yu Yuanshi yanjiu," pp. 330–31.

41. *YS*, 41.881 順帝本紀至正八年三月壬戌.

42. *YS*, 43.918 順帝本紀至正十四年是歲.

43. *YS*, 187.4295 貢師泰傳.

44. *YS*, 205.4585 搠思監傳.

45. *YS*, 187.4296 貢師泰傳.

46. *YS*, 45.937 順帝本紀至正十七年五月丙申; Hu Cuizhong, *Yuanshi xubian*, 15.2b. In 1351, plans to update outdated tax assessments were tabled for fear that "they would drive the people to banditry" (*YS* 185.4258 李稷傳).

47. In 1353, the influential ministers Wugusun Liangzhen 烏古孫良楨 and Uriyangqadai (Ch. Wuliang hetai 悟良哈台) had proposed the plan to introduce agricultural colonies in the Capital Region. They were placed in charge of agricultural colonies in order to remedy "shortfalls in military grain supplies." The initial harvest proved bountiful (*YS*, 187.4289 烏古孫良楨傳; 138.3346 脫脫傳).

48. Hu Cuizhong, *Yuanshi xubian*, 14.21b.

49. *YS*, 45.936 順帝本紀至正十七年四月丙午. Li Shizhan advocated culling the old and weak from the ranks of the military and putting them to work in the fields as a way to support superior troops in the field; see Li Shizhan, "Shang Zhongshu zong bingshu," *Jingji wenji*, 1.9a; also in Li Xiusheng, *Quan Yuan wen*, 50.130–31.

50. *YS*, 45.946 順帝本紀至正十九年二月是月.

51. See *YS*, 188.4311–12 邁里古思傳; Tao Zongyi, *Nancun chuogeng lu*, 10.124–26. Tao objected to the behavior of both men. He faulted Mailigusi for defying orders and criticized Baizhuge for sacrificing the interests of the dynasty to personal animosity and jealousy. Elsewhere Tao noted that Mailigusi's fall was closely tied to local competition among Yuan officials for control of militia forces ("Zao wu you bao fu" 造物有報復, *Nancun chuogeng lu*, 23.283–84). For a discussion of Mailigusi in the context of local defense and local politics, see Wang Ting, "Xixiaren Mailigusi yu Yuanmo Liangzhe difang de shouhu."

52. For an example from the mid-1350s in Shandong, see *YS*, 184.4244 崔敬傳. See also Hu Cuizhong, *Yuanshi xubian*, 13.7b.

53. *YS*, 43.918 順帝本紀至正十四年是歲.

54. *YS*, 204.4552 朴不花傳; 114.2880 后妃一. An entry from the seventh lunar month notes floods, locusts, and a major famine in the capital (*YS*, 45.944 順帝本紀至正十八年七月是月).

55. *YS*, 46.958 順帝本紀至正二十一年是歲.

56. Li Jiben (*js.* 1357), "*Beihuang zalu* xu" 備荒雜錄序, *Yishan wenji*, 4.14b–15a; also in Li Xiusheng, *Quan Yuan wen*, 60.985.

57. Li Jiben, "Liu Yishi zhuan" 劉義士傳, in Li Xiusheng, *Quan Yuan wen*, 60.1028.

58. Ding Kunjian, "Cong shihuan tujing kan Yuandai de youshi zhi feng."

59. Chen Gaohua, "Yuandai shiren Naixian shengping shiji kao," pp. 250–52. Nasen's forefathers were Qarluq Turks from the Ili River valley, who during the early thirteenth century had been incorporated into the Mongol armies and traveled east, where they settled in Henan. Nasen grew up in the prosperous Jiangnan county of Yinxian 鄞縣. In addition to Chen's article, see also Zhang Yingsheng, *Yuandai Huizu wenxuejia*, pp. 193–96.

60. Nasen, "Yingzhou laoweng ge" 潁州老翁歌, *Jin tai ji*, 1.39–41a.

61. See, e.g., the comments of the censor Gao Yuankan 高原侃 regarding extravagant burial customs in the capital, Xia Xie, (*Xinjiao*) *Ming tongjian*, *juan* 1, 1: 208 太祖洪武元年十二月辛未. Shortly later, Zhu Yuanzhang would attribute the fall of the Yuan to "the tendency to extravagance among the people" and the lack of proper social distinctions (ibid.).

62. A poem by Li Fu 李黼, collected in Ye Ziqi, "Tan sou pian" 談藪篇, *Cao mu zi*, *juan* 4 *shang*, p. 79; quoted in Suzuki Chūsei, *Chūgokushi ni okeru kakumei to shūkyō* (Tokyo: Tōkyō daigaku shuppankai, 1974), pp. 73–74; cited and translated in Shek, "Ethics and Polity," p. 98.

63. Zhou Wensun 周聞孫 (1307–60), "Yishi Luo Mingyuan miaobei" 義士羅明遠廟碑, in Li Xiusheng, *Quan Yuan wen*, 51.149.

64. These paragraphs draw from Yang Ne, *Yuandai bailianjiao yanjiu*. See also Chan, "The White Lotus-Maitreya Doctrine"; Shek, "Ethics and Polity"; and ter Haar, *White Lotus Teachings*. See also Wu Han's classic but dated essay "Mingjiao yu Da Ming diguo." Scholars debate the place of Manicheanism in the religious rebellions of the late Yuan period. Early scholarship by Wu Han and Hok-lam Chan (and more recently Richard Shek) argues that the Prince of Light/Radiance *ming wang* 明王 reflected Manichean traditions. Others, most notably ter Haar and Yang Ne, reject such a connection, arguing that the reference to *ming wang* should be understood in a more purely Buddhist context. Reversing his earlier position, Hok-lam Chan has recently argued against Manichean influences, citing primarily the work of Yang Ne. See Chan, "The 'Song' Dynasty Legacy," esp. pp. 117–23.

65. For a biographical note by John Dardess, see *Dictionary of Ming Biography*, pp. 485–88. For more detailed discussion, see Yang Ne, *Yuandai bailianjiao yanjiu*, pp. 157–73.

66. Jiajing period *Guangping fuzhi* 廣平府志, 15.20b–21a, reprinted in *Tianyige cang Mingdai fangzhi xuankan* 天一閣藏明代方志選刊 (Shanghai: Shanghai guji shudian, 1982), vol. 5.

67. Chan, "The 'Song' Dynasty Legacy," pp. 96–102.

68. Chen Gaohua, "Yuandai nongmin qiyijun minghao xiaoding," p. 95.

69. Ibid., p. 96. More recently Hok-lam Chan ("The 'Song' Dynasty Legacy," pp. 124–29) has argued against overly strict distinctions between these groups and views the term Tianwan as "a fabrication after the fact" by early Ming authorities, who were determined to undermine the legitimacy of the Song restoration. On the Tianwan regime based in Qishui (present-day Hunan province), see Yang Ne, *Yuandai bailianjiao yanjiu*, pp. 135–55. For overviews of the Song regime, see Han Rulin, *Yuanchaoshi*, pp. 111–23; and Qiu Shusen, "Yuanmo Hongjinjun de zhengquan jianshe," pp. 95–100.

70. Xia Xie, (*Xinjiao*) *Ming tongjian*, 至正十五年正月, 1: 11.

71. See *YS*, 187.4289 烏古孫良楨傳.

72. For the role of the *keshig* in Mongol relations with Koryŏ, see Chapter 3.

73. Xiao Qiqing, "Yuandai de suwei zhidu," pp. 71–72; idem (Hsiao Ch'i-ch'ing), *The Military Establishment of the Yuan Dynasty*, pp. 34–38.

74. Xiao Qiqing, "Yuandai de suwei zhidu," pp. 83–84.

75. Ibid., pp. 88–90; Hsiao Ch'i-ch'ing, *The Military Establishment*, pp. 44–47.

76. Xiao Qiqing, "Yuandai de suwei zhidu," pp. 89–91.

77. Luoyang in Henan and Linyi 臨沂 (later replaced by Puzhou 濮州) in Shandong were key military centers. This section draws heavily on Xiao Qiqing, "Yuandai de zhenrong zhidu," pp. 118–19; and idem (Hsiao Ch'i-ch'ing), *The Military Establishment*, pp. 51–53.

78. Xiao Qiqing, "Yuandai de zhenrong zhidu," p. 126. As Elizabeth Endicott-West (*Mongolian Rule in China*, pp. 81–82) has noted, occasionally provincial governors (*darughachi*) were Chinese.

79. For a detailed description of military households and the corruption they faced, see Chen Gaohua, "Lun Yuandai de junhu," esp. pp. 85–89.

80. Xiao Qiqing, "Yuandai de zhenrong zhidu," pp. 125–31; idem (Hsiao Ch'i-ch'ing), *The Military Establishment*, pp. 62–63. Some near-contemporary observers attributed the Yuan's ultimate collapse to the decadence and self-indulgence of the hereditary military families; see, e.g., Ye Ziqi, "Ke jin pian," *Cao mu zi*, *juan* 3 *shang*, p. 48; and Changguzhenyi, *Nong tian si hua*, *juan shang*, 3a.

81. Mongolian generals also hired soldiers from among the local population. For an instance from 1352 in central China, when the Mongol commander

Tash-Bātur assembled a reputed 20,000 men as "righteous soldiers," see *YS*, 142.3395 答失八都魯傳. Scattered evidence indicates that Mongolian officers were quite happy to use Chinese militias and requested that such reinforcements be recruited. For examples from 1352, see Liu Mengcong, "Jiao bu fan zei" 剿捕反賊, *Nantai beiyao*, pp. 251, 254–56.

82. Teraji Jun ("Hō Kokuchin seiken no seikaku," p. 31) has argued that the Dai 戴 family, a prosperous elite family with interests in fishing, logging, and agriculture, forged ties with Fang Guozhen as a way to protect its economic concerns at a time when the Yuan's ability to maintain local order was collapsing.

83. Yamane, "'Genmatsu no hanran' to Minchō shihai no kakuritsu," pp. 24–29.

84. At least one writer voiced resentment that the court did not adequately reward men who responded to the Yuan government's calls for help, noting that few gained major posts after the initial wave of rebellion was suppressed; see Li Jiben, "Shu Liu Yuqing zhuan hou" 書劉禹卿傳後, in Li Xiusheng, *Quan Yuan wen*, 60.990.

85. For examples penned by the early Ming writer and official Yang Shiqi 楊士奇 (1365–1444), see "Gu Huaiyuan jiangjun Chengdu youwei zhihui tongzhi zeng Pingjiangbo Chen gong shendao beiming" 故懷遠將軍成都右衛指揮同知贈平江伯陳公神道碑銘, *Dongli wenji*, 12.174; "Gu Yazhong dafu Ningguofu zhifu Chen gong zhi bei" 故亞中大夫寧國府知府陳公之碑, ibid., 14.201; "Gu Lingxue jushi Xiao Anzheng mubeiming" 故凌雪居士蕭安正墓碑銘, ibid., 17.245; "Ouyang Sanfeng muzhiming" 歐陽三峰墓誌銘, ibid., 18.260.

86. Yang Song 楊崧 (mid-fourteenth century), "Luzhou Xu tongzhi zhuan" 廬州許同知傳, in Li Xiusheng, *Quan Yuan wen*, 51.60.

87. A number of Qarluqs, Naimans, and Tanguts registered as Mongolian military households settled in Puyang and developed extensive ties of marriage, study, and military service. Bayan was only one of several such men in Puyang who developed strong interests in Confucianism, education, and local community during the fourteenth century. See the series of commemorative essays and eulogies penned during the 1350s by Pan Di 潘迪 in Li Xiusheng, *Quan Yuan wen*, 51.5–31. For brief comments on the Tangut community in Puyang, see Funada, "Mongoru jidai ni okeru minzoku sesshoku," p. 24.

88. "Boyan Zongdao zhuan" 伯顏宗道傳, in the Zhengde edition of *Daming fuzhi* 大名府志, 10.80b; cited in Chen Gaohua, "Du 'Boyan Zongdao zhuan,'" p. 451.

89. Chen Guohua, "Du 'Boyan Zongdao zhuan,'" p. 451.

90. For a biographical note by John Dardess, see *Dictionary of Ming Biography*, pp. 724–28. See also Frederick Mote, "Rise of the Ming Dynasty," in *CHC*, vol. 7, pt. I, pp. 21–22.

91. Such leading Chinese officials as Li Shizhan tried to persuade Chagha'an-Temür to put aside his personal rivalries in northwest China and to concentrate on the rebellions in Shandong; see, e.g., Li Shizhan, "Yu Chahan Pingzhang shu" 與察罕平章書, in *Jingji wenji*, 1.11a–12b; also in Li Xiusheng, *Quan Yuan wen*, 50.139–41.

92. For a brief discussion of Toqto'a and his dismissal, see Dardess, "Shun-ti and the End of Yüan Rule," pp. 572–80.

93. In 1366, after Toqto'a had been politically rehabilitated, three Mongolian censors wrote to the throne petitioning for posthumous titles for him: "The villainous and treacherous schemed against a great minister, resulting in the change of generals on the eve of battle. The decline in our dynasty's military strategy began with this; deficits in tax revenue began with this; banditry run rampant began with this; the desperation of people's lives began with this. If Toqto'a had not died, how would the realm have come to such dire straits as today?" (*YS*, 138.3349 脱脱傳). The Chinese scholar Li Jiben followed nearly identical arguments in his request that Toqto'a be posthumously invested; see his "Dai qi feng gu taishi zhongshu youchengxiang Tuotuo wen" 代乞封故太師中書右丞相脱脱文, in *Yishan wenji*, in Li Xiusheng, *Quan Yuan wen*, *juan* 1880, 60: 1054–55. Writing just after the collapse of the Yuan in China, Ye Ziqi ("Ke jin pian," *Cao mu zi*, *juan* 3 *shang*, p. 43) similarly attributed the "fall of the Yuan dynasty" to Toqto'a's dismissal.

94. Tan Qian, *Guo que*, 1.266. Sugiyama Masaaki (*Mongoru teikoku no kōbō*, p. 222) observes laconically: "Zhu Yuanzhang's good fortune was the gift of the pride of Toghan-Temür's feeble Great Mongolian Nation." He concludes that but for the emperor's decision, the Ming dynasty might never have been. Here, Sugiyama echoes centuries-old views.

95. Tao Zongyi, "Ji Long ping" 紀隆平, *Nancun chuogeng lu*, 29.357; Ye Ziqi, "Tan sou pian" 談藪篇, *Cao mu zi*, *juan* 4 *shang*, p. 72. Ye held that a jealous rival of Toqto'a persuaded the emperor to issue the edict for his recall and exile.

96. See Li Zefen, "Yuandai moqi cunwang guanjian renwu Tuotuo," pp. 751–52.

97. See *YS*, 40.868 順帝本紀至正三年八月戊戌; 41.874 順帝本紀至正六年三月戊申; 41.876 順帝本紀至正六年十二月壬寅; 41.877 順帝本紀至正七年二月己卯; Hu Cuizhong, *Yuanshi xubian*, 13.5a, 7b, 10b.

98. Su Tianjue, "Shandong jianyan sanshi" 山東建言三事, *Cixi wen'gao*, 27.453. The late fourteenth-century writer Tao Zongyi ("Huashan zei" 花山賊, *Nancun chuogeng lu*, 28.351) would later argue that the inability of the imperial

troops to suppress small groups of bandits led directly to the proliferation of larger groups in places like Henan.

99. Su Tianjue, "Shandong jianyan sanshi," in *Cixi wen'gao*, 27.453–56. In a guide to governance written a few decades prior to this time, Wang Jie 王結 (1275–1336; *Shan su yao yi*, p. 362) advocated more preventative measures to eliminate banditry, including early schooling, inculcating a sense of proper social station, admonitions by local elders for those who strayed, and only then punishment by government officials for the recalcitrant.

100. The following paragraphs draw on Chen Guohua, "Shuo Yuanmo Hongjinjun," pp. 24–25.

101. *YS*, 186.4281 成遵傳. Cheng wrote further that for those who enjoyed comparative safety north of the Yellow River, "even if they had to flay their skins and beat their marrow to supply military provisions [to troops who defended the river], none among them would complain deeply." In 1356, Dong Tuanxiao 董摶霄 maintained that the Yuan's most pressing task was control of the Yellow and Huai rivers, which he thought possible only through the establishment of a series of military bases north and south of the Yellow River (*YS*, 187.4304 董摶霄傳).

102. For a leading Yuan official's comments on Huai'an's strategic importance, see *YS*, 187.4304 董摶霄傳.

103. *YS*, 45.935 順帝本紀至正十七年二月壬申.

104. Qiu Shusen, "Mao Gao shiji kaolüe," pp. 33–34.

105. Bi Gong et al., *Liaodong zhi*, 8.7a 雜志三遼長編; *Quan Liao zhi*, 6.41 外志史考.

106. Zhang Zhu 張翥, "Fang gong shendao beiming" 方公神道碑銘, *Taizhou jinshi lu* 台州金石錄, *juan* 13, in Li Xiusheng, *Quan Yuan wen*, 48.607.

107. The Mongol prince was Mainu 買奴, who garrisoned Yidu (*YS*, 45.936 順帝本紀至正十七年三月甲午).

108. Under the military leadership of Dong Tuanxiao, Ji'nan had repulsed Red Turban attacks through 1357. Shortly after Dong's transfer north, Ji'nan fell (*YS*, 187.4305–6 董摶霄傳).

109. *YS*, 188.4309 王英傳. The account is also found in the 1565 *Qingzhou fuzhi*, 15.9a.

110. *YS*, 45.935 順帝本紀至正十七年正月辛卯; Hu Cuizhong, *Yuanshi xubian*, 15.1a. The *Official History of the Yuan Dynasty* notes *sub anno* 1357 that "in this year, [the emperor] ordered that throughout the realm militias were to be consolidated. All the heads of circuits, prefectures, subprefectures, and counties are to concurrently serve as defense commissioners" (*YS*, 45.940 順帝本紀至正十七年是歲). In March 1358, the court discussed proposals to consolidate nearly a dozen mountain fortresses in Shanxi province under the com-

mand of several high-ranking officials in the central government. Lesser local posts were to be established to oversee actual military operations (*YS*, 45.941, 順帝本紀至正十八年二月己巳).

111. For one example, see Li Jiben, "Fang Shi jia zhuan" 房氏家傳, in *Yishan wenji*, vol. 173, 5.6a; in Li Xiusheng, *Quan Yuan wen*, 60.1031.

112. For instance, the militia myriarch 義兵千户 Yu Bao 余寶 murdered his commanding officer to join Mao's forces (*YS*, 45.940 順帝本紀至正十七年是歲). A militia brigade leader 義兵萬户 joined Mao in the eighth lunar month (*YS*, 45.944 順帝本紀至正十八年八月辛巳). Referring to the defection of the important militia leader Tian Feng 田豐, the early Ming historian Hu Cuizhong (*Yuanshi xubian*, 15.1a) noted tartly that the militia forces "were not enough to defend against the [rebel] enemy but perfectly sufficient to assist the enemy." See also Quan Heng, *Gengshen waishi*, *xia*.1a, reprinted in *Yuandai biji xiaoshuo*, 3.535; idem and Ren Chongyue, *Gengshen waishi jianzheng*, p. 91. Militia forces from nearly all of China proper defected to various rebel groups. For other examples, see Hu Cuizhong, *Yuanshi xubian*, 15.1b, 3a, 4b.

For an instance of several families relocating to neighboring Hejian, see Li Jiben, "Fang Shi jia zhuan," vol. 173, 5.6a; in Li Xiusheng, *Quan Yuan wen*, 60.1031. In 1357 "county elders" in Dongping, Shandong, had organized local men in militias. The following year, however, many fled with their families to Hejian.

113. *YS*, 140.3370 太平傳. Commoners were to receive posthumous titles, and the descendants of officeholders were to inherit the posts of those who died in the line of duty.

114. Li Shizhan, "Shang Zhongshu zongbingshu," *Jingji wenji*, 1.10b.

115. Xia Yizhong 夏以忠, "Zhaoyou Linghui gong miao beiji" 昭佑靈惠公廟碑記, in Yu Minzhong, (*Qinding*) *rixia jiuwen kao*, *juan* 129, 4: 2076.

116. Ibid.

117. Su Tianjue, "Lun Henan xiecong guawu" 論河南脅從詿誤, in *Cixi wen'gao*, 27.460–62.

118. *YS*, 45.941 順帝本紀至正十八年二月癸酉; Qiu Shusen, "Mao Gao shiji kaolüe," pp. 34–35.

119. Based in Linqu 臨朐, in 1357, Mao Gui's lieutenant Li Hua 李華 arrogated an official title, strengthened the city walls, and built two gates (1565 *Qingzhou fuzhi*, 11.31a). The rebel attacks sparked wall-strengthening efforts throughout much of the province. For references to developments in Anqiu 安丘 and Rizhao 日照, see 1565 *Qingzhou fuzhi*, 11.31b, 33b. The editors of the *Qingzhou Prefectural Gazetteer* attribute part of Gaoyuan's successful defense against the Red Turbans to the magistrate's inspired efforts to organize a local militia, dig a defensive moat, and build a fort (ibid., 13.36b). One writer

inveighed against rebels whose housing, carts, guards, symbols of office, and clothing "all arrogated those of imperial bureaus" (Zhou Wensun, "Sheng wei guan yuan li Chen jun ji gong xu" 省委官掾吏陳君紀功序, in Li Xiusheng, *Quan Yuan wen*, 51.142).

120. Qiu Shusen, "Youguan Mao Gui de yixie shishi," p. 22.

121. A 1359 bronze seal for the office of 管軍總管府 cast by the "Ministry of Rites" and using the Longfeng 龍鳳 calendar of the Song regime is preserved in the Ji'nan Municipal Museum (Li Xiaofeng and Yang Dongmei, "Ji'nanshi bowuguan cang gudai tongyin xuanshi," p. 49). The Yidu Branch Secretariat issued a bronze seal for Jinning county 津寧縣 (present-day Ningjin 寧津, Hebei province) (Qiu Shusen, "Yuanmo nongmin zhengquan jifang tongyin," p. 80).

Military seals from other contemporaneous regimes have been found elsewhere in China. A round copper seal inscribed with the title 管軍萬户府 cast by the "Ministry of Rites" during the Taiping reign is thought to have been produced during the mid-1350s by Xu Shouhui's Tianwan 天完 regime; see Shi Shuqing, "Yuanmo Xu Shouhui nongmin zhengquan de tongyin," pp. 9–11. In addition to a copper seal inscribed with the title "generalissimo" 元帥 and cast by the Ministry of Rites in "the eleventh month, sixth year of the Longfeng reign," at least two land deeds dated with the Longfeng calendar have been uncovered in Han Lin'er's capital in Anhui; see Lu Maocun, "Jieshao Han Lin'er Song zhengquan de yizu wenwu." In all cases, the pervasive influence of Yuan institutions is clear. For color photographs of coins and administrative and military seals from rebel regimes, see National Museum of Chinese History, *A Journey into China's Antiquity*, 4: 50–51.

122. Li Shizhan, "Shang Zhongshu zongbing shu" 上中書總兵書, in *Jingji wenji*, 1.6a–b; also in Li Xiusheng, *Quan Yuan wen*, 50.129; cited in Chen Guohua, "Shuo Yuanmo Hongjinjun," p. 24.

123. Such flight was not restricted to the Capital Region. Based on conditions in Linchuan 臨川, Jiangxi, Hu Xingjian 胡行簡 (*js.* 1342) wrote that the collapse of local administration, including the flight of terrified civil and military officials, often meant that local populations had to organize their own defenses; see his "Huiyuan ji" 晦園記, *Chuyinji* 樗隱集, *Siku quanshu zhenben*, vol. 344, 4.2a–b; Li Xiusheng, *Quan Yuan wen*, 56: 45.

124. *YS*, 188.4307 劉哈剌不花傳.

125. Li Shizhan, "Shang Zhongshu zongbing shu," 1.7b–8a; Li Xiusheng, *Quan Yuan wen*, 50: 129–30.

126. Tao Zongyi, "Qi lian" 旗聯, *Nancun chuogeng lu*, 27.342. Tao suggests that Mao Gui's strike against the capital was prefigured in one of the early pro-

nouncements by the Red Turbans that included a "drive direct into the region of You and Yan" (the area surrounding Daidu) and the restoration of the Song.

127. *YS*, 140.3370 太平傳. The He family owed its prolonged success to service in the *keshig*, intimate familiarity with Mongols (including language, customs, intermarriage), and firm grounding in Chinese culture. He Weiyi's son was one of the few Chinese men allowed to marry into the imperial Yuan family and had been granted a Mongol legal status; see Wu Haitao, "Cong Yuandai Heshi jiazu de xingsheng."

128. *YS*, 188.4307 劉哈剌不花傳; 45.942 至正十八年三月乙卯.

129. *YS*, 46.956–57 至正二十一年六月乙未至八月. News of Chagha'an-Temür's success in retaking the important city of Ji'nan and capturing rebel leaders led Li Shizhan (*Jingji wenji*, 1.14b–15a) to conclude that Yidu would soon fall without much effort. He appears to have been acutely aware, however, of how critical Chagha'an-Temür had become to the dynasty, cautioning him (in poetry) to be circumspect and not endanger himself and the dynasty through needless bravado.

130. "Chahan Tiemuer ji Kongmiao bei" 察罕帖木兒祭孔廟碑, in *Shanzuo jinshizhi* 山左金石志, *juan* 24; in Guojia tushuguan shanben jinshi zu, *Liao Song Yuan shike wenxian quanbian*, 1: 746.

131. *YS*, 140.3370 太平傳.

132. Silbergeld, "In Praise of Government," p. 186.

133. Li Shizhan, "Shang Zhongshu chengxiang shu" 上中書丞相書, in *Jingji wenji*, 1.2a–b; also in Li Xiusheng, *Quan Yuan wen*, 50.126–27. See also the slightly later comments of Ye Ziqi, "Ke jin pian," *Cao mu zi*, *juan* 3 *shang*, p. 49.

134. *YS*, 186.4267–68 張楨傳.

135. Zhang Zhu, "Yunsi timing ji" 運司題名記, 1840 *Ji'nan fuzhi* 濟南府志, *juan* 65, in Li Xiusheng, *Quan Yuan wen*, 48.598. Köke-Temür refurbished the offices of the Tax Transport and Salt Monopoly Commission and established a shrine to his late father in one of the buildings.

136. Chen Gaohua, "Lun Zhu Yuanzhang he Yuanchao de guanxi," esp. p. 321.

137. Langlois, "Song Lian and Liu Jin on the Eve of Joining Zhu Yuanzhang."

138. Li Shizhan, "Yu Quannan zuocheng shu" 與泉南左丞書, *Jingji wenji*, 1.13b; also in Li Xiusheng, *Quan Yuan wen*, 50.142. Li commented explicitly on the international trade that generated the port's great wealth. On occasion Li used the opposite rhetorical strategy, stressing the Great Yuan's *ulus*'s dire conditions in order to urge prompt action. For instance, when Bolod-Temür seized power, he wrote, "Today the situation of the dynasty has the air of imminent expiration; it does not have the majesty of a glorious revival. It has the inclination to

willingly accept death; it does not have the determination to rescue [itself] from disaster"; cited in Chen Zuren 陳祖仁 (1314–68), "Hanlin chengzhi Chuguo Li Gong xingzhuang" 翰林承旨楚國李公行狀, in Li Shizhan, *Jingji wenji*, 6.35b. Li's son, Li Jiben, who was active in North China during the last years of Yuan rule there and into the early Ming, was far less given to such optimistic rhetoric. For one of his few invocations (with a strong emphasis on that peace would come *in the future*), see Li Jiben, "Song Chen dushishi huan Zhedong xu" 送陳都事使還淛東序, in Li Xiusheng, *Quan Yuan wen*, 60.968.

139. Meng Fanqing, "Yuanchao monian haiyun yu chouliang," p. 237.

140. Li Shizhan, "Ping Shandong lubu" 平山東露布, *Jingji wenji*, 5.4a–b; also in Li Xiusheng, *Quan Yuan wen*, 50.135.

141. Ibid., *Jingji wenji*, 5.8a–b; also in Li Xiusheng, *Quan Yuan wen*, 50.137.

142. The 1444 edition adds the character *nu* 弩 here.

143. The 1444 edition has *cheng* 誠 instead of *xie* 誠. The translation here uses *xie* over *cheng*.

144. See Li Jiben, "Song Neishi qianyuan Dong gong Jingning fu Hejianlu zongguan xu" 送内使簽院董公景寧赴河間路總管序, in Li Xiusheng, *Quan Yuan wen*, 60.966–67. Writing during the mid-1350s, Liu Shangzhi 劉尚質 (*js.* 1327) commented that even a decade earlier in the 3,000-*li* stretch between central Shandong and Shanxi, "there were only two county magistrates." Presumably, he meant two men worthy of notice; see his "Da Yuan Jiangzhou zhizhou Peng hou qusi zhi bei" 大元絳州知州彭侯去思之碑, in Li Xiusheng, *Quan Yuan wen*, 51.72.

145. The following paragraphs draw from Chen Guohua, "Shuo Yuanmo Hongjinjun," pp. 23–25.

146. *YS*, 45.945 順帝本紀至正十八年十二月癸酉.

147. For comments on royal hunting lodges as military depots and as military targets, see Allsen, *The Royal Hunt in Eurasian History*, pp. 220–21.

148. *YS*, 44.921–922 順帝本紀至正十五年正月丙子, 閏月是月.

149. YS, 45.949 順帝本紀至正十九年是歲.

150. The passage appears in *YS*, 186.4273–74 陳祖仁傳; the quotations appear on p. 4173. The memorial is included in Sun Chengze's *Yuanchao diangu biannian kao*, 8.41a–b. The "Basic Chronicle Account of the Shundi Emperor" notes that Chen petitioned to end palace repair in Shangdu in the fifth lunar month of 1362 (*YS*, 46.959 順帝本紀至正二十二年五月己未).

151. *YS*, 140.3371 太平傳.

152. *YS*, 206.4596–97 阿魯輝帖木兒傳; 45.952–53 順帝本紀至正二十年是歲.

153. *YS*, 45.952 順帝本紀二十年九月癸未.

154. *YS*, 45.945 順帝本紀十八年十二月癸酉.

Chapter 3

1. *YS*, 144.3433 答里麻傳; cited in Chang Tong-ik, *Koryŏ hugi oegyosa yŏn'gu*, p. 51*n*66. Chang notes the passage as evidence of the humiliation that royal envoys endured when using the seals of the Branch Central Secretariat for Korea.

2. Kongmin was the posthumous temple name granted by the Ming court after the king's murder in 1374. In the interest of convenience, the king is called by his posthumous title throughout this study. For a useful overview of King Kongmin and the challenges he faced, see Clark, "Autonomy, Legitimacy, and Tributary Politics," pp. 18–32.

3. For a detailed description of the male Mongol's coiffure during the mid-thirteenth century, see Rubruck's "Report to King Loius IX of France," p. 88.

4. Kim Sang-gi, *Sinp'yŏn Koryŏ sidaesa*, p. 562. For description of the so-called plait-line robes during the Yuan period, see Dang Baohai, "The Plait-line Robe"; and Yang Ling, "Yuandai de bianxian'ao."

5. See, e.g., *KS*, 30.471 忠烈王十五年五月癸未, where King Ch'ungnyŏl and his Mongol princess viewed a polo match as part of festivities to mark the spring Tan-o 端午 Day.

6. Kwŏn Kŭn, "Sachae sogam Pak Kang chŏn" 司宰少監朴強傳, in idem, *Yangch'on chip* 陽村集, 21.18a; reprinted in *Han'guk munjip ch'onggan*, 7: 216.

7. For a brief description of the *huchuang*, see Shi Weimin, *Dushizhong de youmumin*, p. 33. Use of *huchuang* continued even after Mongol hairstyles had been prohibited at the Koryŏ court. For instance, Kongmin and a close advisor (the Buddhist priest Sin-don 辛旽) reclined on a *huchuang* as they reviewed potential royal consorts (*KS*, 132.675 叛逆傳六辛旽傳). In some cases, the Mongolian-style throne invited questions of status and proper hierarchy, for instance when Sin-don was criticized for violating proper social distinctions. He should not have been seated on equal terms with the king on the *huchuang* (*KS*, 113.355 李存吾傳).

8. During these decades, most Koryŏ kings used both Mongol and Korean names (Kim Sang-gi, *Sinp'yŏn K'oryŏ sidaesa*, p. 560).

9. Little is known about the activities of her father, Bolod-Temür. See *YS*, 107.2728 宗室世系表: 魏王阿木哥位; and Hambis, *Le chapitre cvii du Yuan che*, pp. 133–35*n*9. Bolod-Temür was a relatively common name. Her father was not the same Bolod-Temür discussed at length in Chapter 7, the father of Toghan-Temür's first empress.

10. The most comprehensive study of the place of marriage alliances in the Mongol empire, especially eastern Eurasia, is George Zhao's highly informative *Marriage as Political Strategy and Cultural Expression*.

11. The following paragraphs draw heavily from Morihira, "Fuma Kōrai kokuō no seiritsu." On the marriage alliance between the Mongol imperial and the Koryŏ royal families, see also Xiao Qiqing, "Yuan-Li guanxizhong de wangshi huanghun." See also Wang Chongshi, "Yuan yu Gaoli tongzhi jituan de lianyin." For a preliminary discussion of errors contained in the *Official History of the Yuan Dynasty* related to the investiture of Koryŏ son-in-law kings, see Zhang Daiyu, "*Yuan shi* Gaoli fumawang fengwang shiliao kaobian." For a convenient overview in English, see George Zhao, "Control Through Conciliation." For a critical review of Chinese, Japanese, and Korean scholarship related to the marriage ties between the Koryŏ royal house and the Yuan imperial family, see Morhihira, "Kōrai ōke to Mongoru kōzoku no tsūkon kankei ni kan suru oboegaki." Morihira stresses the need for closer examination of the political ramifications of each marriage.

12. For extensive discussion of the Mongol conquest of Koryŏ and Koryŏ resistance efforts, see Henthorn, *Korea: The Mongol Invasions.*

13. Morihira, "Fuma Kōrai kokuō no seiritsu"; Yi Myŏng-mi, "Koryŏ-Wŏn wangsil t'onghon," pp. 19–20.

14. Yi Myŏng-mi, "Koryŏ-Wŏn wangsil t'onghon," pp. 47–50; Kim Hodong, *Mong'gol che'guk kwa Koryŏ*, pp. 88–90. Yi's effort to consider royal marriages between the Yuan and Koryŏ courts in the wider context of the Mongol empire and its workings is a welcome corrective to the comparatively narrow perspective from which much past scholarship has viewed the question. Morihira ("Kōrai ōke to Mongoru kōzoku no tsūkon kankei ni kan suru oboegaki") similarly calls for the Koryŏ-Yuan marriages to be contextualized in the wider developments of the entire Mongol empire.

15. Kim Ho-dong, *Mong'gol che'guk kwa Koryŏ*, pp. 83–120.

16. On military rule, see Shultz, *Generals and Scholars.*

17. Duncan, *Origins of the Chosŏn Dynasty*, p. 190.

18. Miao Wei, "Gaoli Zhongliewang zai Zhongguo," p. 48. Miao consistently (and incorrectly) identifies the Great Yuan *ulus* as China.

19. Henthorn, *Korea: The Mongol Invasions*, pp. 173–93; Hatada, "Nihon to Kōrai."

20. Kim Ho-dong ("Mong'gol che'guk kwa Koryŏ," p. 9) goes so far as to say that Koryŏ was the "strategic cornerstone" of Qubilai's position in East Asia. Kim examines the marriage tie in terms of the shifting political dynamics of the Mongol empire. As Kim (*Mong'gol che'guk kwa Koryŏ*, p. 88) notes, the fact that the powerful Eastern Princes supported Qubilai in the succession struggle with Ariq-Böke may have figured in the Koryŏ throne's decision to ally with Qubilai.

21. *YS*, 107.2728 宗室世系表魏王阿木哥位; Hambis, *Le chapitre cvii du Yuan che*, p. 133.

22. See the genealogical chart of Mongolian princesses in *YS*, 109.2761 表第四諸公主表; *KS*, 35.542 忠肅王十一年八月戊午; and Hambis, "Histoire de Corée," pp. 197–98.

23. Yi Myŏng-mi, "Koryŏ-Wŏn wangsil t'onghon," pp. 58–60. Morihira ("Kōrai ōke to Mongoru kōzoku no tsūkon kankei ni kan suru oboegaki"), however, rightly notes that the Koryŏ royal family did not establish marriage ties in the Mongol aristocracy beyond the house of Qubilai.

24. Duncan (*Origins of the Chosŏn Dynasty*, p. 164) notes the importance of Mongol consorts, who "invested great power in the personal retainers, eunuchs, and other men of non-*yangban* origins, promoting them to key offices in the palace and bureaucracy." On the impact of Mongolian princesses at the Koryŏ court, see George Zhao and Richard Guisso, "Female Anxiety and Female Power."

25. For discussion of a recently excavated example from Inner Mongolia, see Su Dong, "Yijian Yuandai guguguan."

26. *Koryŏsa chŏryo*, 23.27b, p. 600 忠宣王三年二月; 23.29b, p. 601 忠宣王三年十二月.

27. *KS*, 世家忠烈王二十二年十二月; cited in Kim Sang-gi, *Sinp'yŏn Koryŏ sidaesa*, p. 561*n*81.

28. Kim Sang-gi, *Sinp'yŏn Koryŏ sidaesa*, pp. 585, 606–14.

29. Rashīd al-Din, *Compendium of Chronicles*, 2: 445, 448.

30. Rossabi (*Khubilai Khan*, p. 143) notes, "The 'Phags-pa lama's younger brother married a Mongol princess, as did his nephew, and, later, one of his grandnephews." For a brief comparison of Uyghurs and Koreans as imperial in-laws, see Yi Myŏng-mi, "Koryŏ-Wŏn wangsil t'onghon," pp. 77–79. For discussion of the Uyghurs in the Mongol empire, see Allsen, "The Yüan Dynasty and the Uyghurs of Turfan," esp. pp. 247–48.

31. Manz, *Rise and Rule of Tamerlane*, p. 14.

32. Morihira, "Kōrai ōika no kisoteki kōsatsu." Cf. Pak Okgŏl, "Koryŏmal pukbang yumin kwa ch'uswae," pp. 142–43. The communities in southern Manchuria are also noted in Kim Hye-wŏn, "Koryŏ hugi Sim (yang) wang," p. 43. The Koryŏ court took an active part in establishing and supporting these communities. In 1279, the court ordered that wealthy Koryŏ families be selected from the provinces and resettled in the region from Shenyang and Liaoyang to the Yalu River. Supplied with incomes, the communities were to have formal community heads, who served in rotation, and were to include people competent in the Chinese and Mongolian languages. Among their responsibilities was the maintenance of the postal relay stations (*KS*, 82.657–58 兵志二站驛). In a 1370 passage from the *KS*, the Koryŏ throne noted that after Mongolian princesses had been given in marriage to Koryŏ kings, the Yuan throne

had "set aside the land of Liao-Shen to cover part of their expenses" (Peter Lee, ed., *Sources of Korean Civilization,* 1: 363). Under the Mongols, similar communities (伊里干) were provided with lands, exempted from taxes and corvée responsibilities to the Koryŏ throne, and charged with the capture and care of hunting falcons. See Kim Sunja, "Wŏn kansŏpgi min ŭi tonghyang," p. 372, esp. note 17. Kim stresses that the removal of such households from state tax rosters imposed greater burdens on those that remained.

33. Morihira, "Kōrai ōke to Mongoru kōzoku no tsūkon kankei ni kan suru oboegaki," pp. 26–28. These were the so-called *chu zhen wang jia* 出鎮王家.

34. For discussion of the close ties between the *keshig* and Mongol administration during the early and mid-thirteenth century, see Allsen, "Guard and Government." For changes in the leadership structure of the *keshig* during the thirteenth and fourteenth centuries across the empire, see Atwood, "Ulus Emirs, Keshig Elders, Signatures, and Marriage Partners." For comments on the integrative functions of the *keshig*, see Sugiyama, *Dai Mongoru no sekai*, pp. 79–83.

35. On the privileged political and financial status of members of the *keshig*, see Hsiao Ch'i-ch'ing, *The Military Establishment of the Yuan Dynasty*, pp. 34–44. As Hsiao notes, given the large size of the *keshig*, status and privilege varied considerably. For a useful warning against trying to read Yuan political history through the lens of traditional Chinese categories and administrative nomenclature, which often slight the centrality of the *keshig*, see Qu Wenjun, "Yuandai quexue xinlun." Charles Melville ("The Keshig in Iran," p. 135) notes a similar tendency of both modern and contemporary accounts to overlook the royal household of the Il-khans, which he argues was the "nucleus or core of the imperial government."

36. Morris Rossabi (*Khubilai Khan*, pp. 143, 221–22) notes that the Tibetan monk Phyag na rdo rje lama, 'Phagsa pa's younger brother, had been raised at the Mongol court and that 'Phags pa's nephew, Dharmapalaraksita, had resided at the Mongol court since infancy—a fact that did not endear him to many Tibetan clerics.

37. Morihira, "Genchō keshike seido to Kōrai ōke."

38. For evocations of the Mongol capitals during the Yuan, see Ye Xinmin, *Yuan Shangdu yanjiu*; Shi Weimin, *Dushizhong de youmumin*; Chen Gaohua, *Yuan Daidu.*

39. On the banquets, the *jisün*, and their significance, see Shi Weimin, *Dushizhong de youmumin*, pp. 110–23; and Allsen, *Commodity and Exchange in the Mongol Empire*, 19–26. Allsen (ibid., pp. 77–82) suggests a West Asian origin for the *jisün*. For discussion of the term "Colors Banquet," see Han Rulin, "Yuandai zhamayan xintan." For quantification of the considerable meat and alcohol

consumed at the banquets, see John Smith, "Dietary Decadence and Dynastic Decline in the Mongol Empire."

40. Sugiyama, *Mongoru teikoku no kōbō*, 2: 199–200; Allsen, "Robing in the Mongolian Empire."

41. Mote, "Yuan and Ming," p. 209.

42. See the "Preface" of one of Zhou Boqi's 周伯琦 poems on such a banquet in Cleaves, "The 'Fifteen Palace Poems' by K'o Chiu-ssu," pp. 447–48*n*91. Many of these poems are conveniently assembled in Ke Jiusi et al., *Liao Jin Yuan gongci.*

43. *KS*, 31.492 忠烈王二十六年六月壬子; *Koryŏsa chŏryo*, 22.17b, p. 573 忠烈王二十六年六月壬子. For Chinese descriptions of the splendor of Colors Banquets in Shangdu, see Ye Xinmin, *Yuan Shangdu yanjiu*, pp. 47–48.

44. *KS*, 109.302 李兆年傳; *Koryŏsa chŏryo*, 25.15b, p. 641 忠肅後八年五月辛酉.

45. *KS*, 36.552 忠惠王元年正月己酉; 忠惠王元年四月癸卯. For a detailed examination of the seasonal migrations of the Yuan *ulus* court and their relation to earlier nomadic pastoralist traditions, see Kim Ho-dong, "Mong'gol che'guk kunjudŭl." As Ma Juan ("Yuandai Qincharen Yan Tiemuer shiji kaolun," pp. 103–4) notes, Ch'ung-hye and El-Temür's friendship carried over into the political realm. El-Temür proposed Ch'ung-hye as a replacement to Ch'ungsuk, and Ch'unghye appealed to El-Temür to block efforts to establish a Branch Secretariat for Koryŏ. For the extraordinary spread of Qipchaqs across Eurasia during the Mongol period, see Halperin, "The Qipchaq Connection."

46. Xu Huili, "Beijing Zhihuasi faxian Yuandai cangjing."

47. For discussion of Wang Chang's patronage of Buddhism in the Great Yuan *ulus* and Koryŏ, see Kitamura Takai, "Kōraiō Ō Shō no sūButsu."

48. This paragraph is drawn largely from Yi Sŭng-han, "Koryŏ Ch'ungsŏnwang ŭi Simyangwang p'ibong"; and Kim Tang-t'aek, *Wŏn kansŏpha ŭi Koryŏ chŏngch'isa*, pp. 72–83. In contrast, Miao Wei 苗威 ("Gaoli Zhongxuanwang yu Zhongguo") argues unpersuasively that Ch'ungsŏn was uninterested in political power. She holds that his three decades in the Great Yuan *ulus* should be ascribed to his "China complex."

49. Because of the vagueness of surviving accounts, the exact reasons for Ch'ungsŏn's banishment are unclear and often debated. Several passages in the *Official History of the Koryŏ Dynasty* indicate the immediate cause was the jealous calumny of a Korean eunuch at the Yuan court. Kitamura Takei ("Kōraiō Ō Shō no sūButsu," pp. 122–23), among others, follows this argument. Gui Xipeng ("Yuan Yingzong zhe Gaoli Zhongxuanwang") argues compellingly that Shidebala exiled Ch'ungsŏn because of his close connection with the

Empress Dowager Targi, who had emerged as a critical political threat. In other words, Ch'ungsŏn was an important player at the Yuan court. Because of his privileged status as Qubilai's grandson, an imperial in-law, and his role in putting Haishan on the throne, he was considered dangerous enough to merit exile. For a less persuasive argument that attributes Ch'ungsŏn's exile to his desire to preserve Koryŏ's distinctiveness through opposition to transforming Koryŏ into a branch secretariat like those found in the Great Yuan *ulus* proper, see Wang Ting and Ni Shangming, "Gaoli Zhongxuanwang zhe Tufan shijian zaixi."

50. Min Hyŏn-gu, "Chŏngch'ika rosŏ ŭi Kongminwang," pp. 274–75. In 1349, Toqto'a had established the Hall of the Upright Root as part of his efforts to revitalize scholarship (Qiu Shusen, *Tuohuan Tiemuer zhuan*, pp. 78–79).

51. Kwŏn Kŭn, "Sachae sogam Pak Kang chon," *Yangch'on chip*, 21.17a, reprinted in *P'yojŏn yongjin Han'guk munjip ch'onggan*, 7: 216. Kongmin's companion Pak Ch'ŏn-bu 朴天富 stuck by Kongmin's side when many others threw their lot in with Kongmin's nephew, whom the Mongols initially put on the Koryŏ throne instead of Kongmin.

52. *KS*, 112.357 偰遜傳. For brief comments on Xie's family, see Goodrich and Fang, *Dictionary of Ming Biography*, 559.

53. For instance, the eunuch Sin So-bong 申小鳳 was among those who served Kongmin during the prince's eleven years in Daidu. When Kongmin took the throne, Sin was made a merit minister of the first order and would later supervise Kongmin's queen's tomb during the mourning period (*KS*, 122.525–26 申小鳳傳).

54. The following paragraphs on Ch'unghye draw heavily from Kim Tang-t'aek, *Wŏn kansŏpha ŭi Koryŏ chŏngch'isa*, pp. 101–24.

55. *KS*, 36.553 忠惠王元年閏月戊子. Ch'unghye was not alone in adopting Mongolian fashion. The famous Tibetan monk 'Phags pa also wore Mongolian clothing, incurring resentment among fellow Tibetans (Rossabi, *Khubilai Khan*, p. 143).

56. See Hsiao Ch'i-ch'ing, "Mid-Yuan Politics," *CHC*, 6: 500.

57. Mongolian reconstruction follows Hambis, "Histoire de Corée," p. 201.

58. For an accessible account of Toqto'a's machinations, see Qiu Shusen, *Tuohuan Tiemuer zhuan*, pp. 70–74.

59. Kim Tang-t'aek, *Wŏn kansŏpha ŭi Koryŏ chŏngch'isa*, p. 109.

60. Hwang Un-yong, "Koryŏ Kongminwangdae ŭi taeWŏn Myŏng kwan'gye," p. 5. Duncan (*Origins of the Chosŏn Dynasty*, pp. 173–75, 187–89) notes the serious limitations of the scope, duration, and efficacy of the fourteenth-century efforts at reform. In perhaps the most comprehensive analysis of Kongmin's reforms, Kim Ki-tŏk ("14 segi huban kaehyŏk chŏngch'i ŭi") comes to

similar conclusions about the lack of fundamental change during the fourteenth century, observing that policies resulted in an amelioration rather than true reform of socioeconomic problems. See also the brief remarks by Pak Chong-gi, "14 segi ŭi Koryŏ sahoe," p. 24.

61. For comments on Soviet scholars, see Halperin, *Russia and the Golden Horde*, p. 45.

62. Kim Tang-t'aek, *Wŏn kansŏpha ŭi Koryŏ chŏngch'isa*, p. 113. Senior Korean scholar Min Hyŏn-gu ("Chŏngch'ika rosŏ ŭi Kongminwang") makes the identical argument in regard to King Kongmin—perceptive men were naturally anti-Mongolian because they perceived the national disgrace and suffering inflicted by the Mongols.

63. For a useful critique of the concept of "anti-Yuan" reforms prior to 1351, see Pak Chong-gi, "14 segi ŭi Koryŏ sahoe," pp. 20–24. Pak notes that our understanding of various reform policies of the fourteenth century is inseparable from understanding of the composition of Koryŏ's ruling elite, which had changed significantly over the preceding two to three decades.

64. Cf. Kim Tang-t'aek (*Wŏn kansŏpha ŭi Koryŏ chŏngch'isa*, pp. 126–51), who argues that most of the Koryŏ bureaucracy deeply resented the king's arrest and death in exile. He points to the fact that many senior officials petitioned the Yuan court to pardon Ch'unghye. Kim holds that the incident deepened dissatisfaction with the Yuan among the Koryŏ bureaucracy. Several unproven assumptions inform Kim's analysis. First, there is no evidence that the men who petitioned the Yuan court represented the views of the majority of the Koryŏ bureaucracy. Second, resentment of domestic political foes whose power was based in the Yuan is not necessarily the equivalent of resentment of the Yuan itself. Third, Kim does not address the possibility that resentment of "pro-Yuan forces" arose not from their ties to the Yuan as much as from the fact that they were political and social upstarts.

65. On the privileges that son-in-law status brought the Koryŏ throne, see Xiao Qijing, "Yuan-Li guanxizhong de wangshi huanghun," pp. 118–21.

66. *Koryŏsa chŏryo*, 26.9a, p. 668 恭愍王元年正月.

67. For the significance of astronomy to the Mongols, see Allsen, *Culture and Conquest in Mongol Eurasia*, pp. 175, 205–7.

68. For astronomical exchanges among China, Persia, and Inner Asia under the Mongols, see ibid., pp. 161–75.

69. *Koryŏsa chŏryo*, 26.14a, p. 670 恭愍王元年四月癸卯.

70. Ibid., 26.22a, p. 674 恭愍王二年九月乙丑.

71. For a brief overview of the conspiracy, see Kim Sang-gi, *Sinp'yŏn Koryŏ sidaesa*, pp. 553–54. See also *Koryŏsa chŏryo*, 25.17b–18b, pp. 642–43 忠肅後八年八月.

72. When Ch'oe violated the recent widow of a Koryŏ minister, her brother, a eunuch at the Yuan court, reported the matter to Mongol authorities, who dispatched a member of the *keshig* to interrogate Ch'oe in Koryŏ (*Koryŏsa chŏryo*, 25.28a, p. 647 忠惠後四年四月丙申). The incident neatly captures the myriad ties that bound Koryŏ and the Great Yuan *ulus* and how individuals negotiated the Mongolian matrix.

73. *KS*, 131.669 崔濡傳.

74. *Koryŏsa chŏryo*, 26.11a, p. 669 恭愍元年三月.

75. *KS*, 38.582–83 恭愍王三年六月辛卯.

76. *KS*, 111.334 柳濯傳; 111.330 廉悌臣傳. Critics attributed his actions to a desire to curry Mongol favor in his efforts to improve his position at the Koryŏ court.

77. *KS*, 111.334 柳濯傳.

78. *YS*, 43.915 順帝本紀六至正十四年五月是月.

79. *KS*, 38.583 恭愍王三年六月癸卯. The envoys included Bayan-Temür, a native of Koryŏ whose Korean name was Kang Su-yong 康舜龍. His uncle Kang Yun-ch'ung 康允忠 was an influential statesman at the Kongmin court with close ties to the Yuan. For a short biographical note, see Min Hyŏn-gu, "Koryŏ Kongminwang ŭi panWŏnjŏk kaehyŏk chŏngch'i e taehan ŭi chŏn'gae kwasŏng," p. 251.

80. Kang Sŏng-mun, "Koryŏmal Hongt'ujok ch'imgo e kwan han yŏn'gu," pp. 212–13.

81. *KS*, 38.580–81 恭愍王二年七月乙亥.

82. *KS*, 38.576 恭愍王元年二月戊戌.

83. Morihira, "Kōrai ōke to Mongoru kōzoku no tsūkon kankei ni kan suru oboegaki," p. 16. Her father, as noted above, was Bolod-Temür, Wei Prince.

84. *KS*, 38.583 恭愍王三年六月丙午.

85. Chŏng Tu-hŭi, "Koryŏmal sinhŭng muin seryŏk."

86. *KS*, 38.23b–23a 恭愍王三年六月辛亥 (Yŏnse ed., 1: 765; MJ, p. 583).

87. *KS*, 38.24a 恭愍王三年七月癸亥 (Yŏnse ed., 1: 765; MJ, p. 583). The editors of the *Koryŏsa* note that because the Yuan emperor had requested the cream of the Korean army, the king's personal guard was left weak. Feeling vulnerable, the king ordered that "archers" 弓手 be recruited in Sŏhae province.

88. Kim Tang-t'aek, "Koryŏ Kongmin wang ch'o ŭi muchang seryŏk," pp. 28–37.

89. *KS*, 38.24a–b 恭愍王三年七月乙丑 (Yŏnse ed., 1: 765; MJ, p. 583). Ch'oe's position at the Yuan court only poorly reflects the importance of his role. When dispatched to oversee the Korean force's march to Daidu, he held a post in the Directorate for Felt Manufactures 中尚監. The contrast with the official honors bestowed by the Koryŏ court is stark (see below). Early in

November, Yŏm Che-sin returned from the Great Yuan *ulus*, although no reason was provided (*KS*, 38.25b 恭愍王三年十月庚戌 [Yŏnse ed., 1: 766; MJ, p. 584]).

90. *KS*, 110.330 廉悌臣傳; *Koryŏsa chŏryo*, 26.25b–26a, p. 676 恭愍王三年七月.

91. *KS*, 38.583–84 恭愍王三年七月癸酉, 三年七月辛巳.

92. *KS*, 38.583 恭愍王三年七月癸酉.

93. *KS*, 38.584 恭愍王三年十一月丁亥.

94. In regard to this incident, the Chinese writer Ye Ziqi ("Ke jin pian," *Cao mu zi, juan* 3 *shang*, p. 53) wrote that one contingent of troops (the *Mao hulu jun* 毛葫蘆軍) had already mounted the city walls only to meet with rebuke by "someone jealous of their merit" for pressing the attack without authorization from Toqto'a. By the time the Yuan forces regrouped for a coordinated attack on Gaoyou, the opportunity had already passed, and the city did not fall. In both versions, the attack on Gaoyou seems to have been hampered by a lack of clear command and fatally undermined by jealousy within the officer corps.

95. *KS*, 38.26a–b 恭愍王三年十一月丁亥 (Yŏnse ed., 1: 766; MJ, p. 584).

96. *KS*, 38.27a–b 恭愍王四年正月庚午 (Yŏnse ed., 1: 767: MJ, pp. 584–85). King Kongmin received the Yuan emissary outside the Sŏnwimun 宣義門.

97. *YS*, 42.891 順帝本紀五至正十一年五月辛亥.

98. *KS*, 38.585 恭愍王四年五月是月. It is possible that this report reflects the situation prior to Toqto'a's dismissal.

99. Individual commanders were still returning to Koryŏ in the fifth lunar month of 1356 (*KS*, 39.387 恭愍王五年五月丙戌).

100. As noted in Chapter 1, most Korean scholarship uses the pronunciation "ko" for the Sim Prince's personal name.

101. *YS*, 43.916 順帝本紀六至正十四年九月甲子.

102. Kim Hye-wŏn, "Koryŏ hugi Sim (yang) wang," pp. 34–36.

103. *YS*, 44.928 順帝本紀七至正十五年十一月辛亥; *KS*, 39.586 恭愍王五年二月辛亥; *Koryŏsa chŏryo*, 26.30b, p. 678 恭愍王五年二月.

104. The interpretation of Kongmin's actions as "anti-Yuan" seems to have originated with the eminent Japanese scholar Ikeuchi Hiroshi; see his "Kōrai Kyōmin'ō." For a recent example of the anti-Yuan interpretation, see Ch'ae Su-hwan, "Koryŏ Kongmin wangdae." No Kye-hyŏn (*Yŏ Mong oegyosa*, p. 334) calls them "anti-Mongol policies." Although such nomenclature carries a clearer ethnic connotation, No consistently refers to the Great Yuan *ulus* as the Mongols or Mongolia.

105. The foremost scholar of this period, Min Hyŏn-gu ("Koryŏ Kongminwang ŭi panWŏnjŏk kaehyŏk chŏngch'i e taehan il koch'al," pp. 49–50), generally uses the term "anti-Yuan" to characterize Kongmin's actions. For detailed

analysis of the background of the men invested as merit officials for their roles in the purge, see idem, "Koryŏ Kongminwangdae ŭi 'Chu Ki Ch'ŏl kongsin' e taehan kŏmt'o." In the conclusion to this article, Min acknowledges that the purge was less about "anti-Yuan" sentiments than an attempt to remove a clear challenge to the throne. He maintains, however, that the purge harmonized well with the undercurrent of anti-Yuan feeling throughout Koryŏ at the time. Pak Chong-gi ("14 segi ŭi Koryŏ sahoe," pp. 23–24) has rejected the idea of anti-Yuan reforms prior to Kongmin's reign, but notes that "everyone can agree about" the anti-Yuan character of Kongmin's reforms. Kim Ki-tŏk ("14 segi huban kaehyŏk chŏngch'i," pp. 498–99) argues that the anti-Yuan measures were a necessary precondition for the most difficult task of domestic reforms. He acknowledges that elements of the anti-Yuan measures were undone soon after their implementation (p. 500) and that the domestic reforms were nearly a complete failure (p. 504).

Explicitly rejecting the nationalistic interpretation, Peter Yun ("Rethinking the Tribute System," pp. 155–56) stresses Kongmin's sense of danger vis-à-vis the Mongols. He notes the abortive efforts to incorporate Koryŏ into the empire through the establishment of a branch secretariat and the Mongols' repeated dethroning of Koryŏ kings.

106. Ikeuchi ("Kōrai Kyōmin'ō," p. 121–26) was perhaps the first to draw attention to the forced quality of Kongmin's accusations against Ki and others. Ikeuchi's argument that Kongmin's true motivation was greater autonomy from the Yuan has long since become standard in Japanese and Korean scholarship.

107. For a convenient chart listing those killed, their posts, and their relations, see Min Hyŏn-gu, "Koryŏ Kongminwang ŭi panWŏnjŏk kaehyŏk chŏngch'i e taehan il koch'al," pp. 74–75.

108. Duncan (*Origins of the Chosŏn Dynasty*, pp. 165–66) describes the Haengju Ki as a typical Koryŏ "powerful family" (*kwŏnmun sejok* 權門勢族), a small portion of whom actively cultivated ties with the Mongols. For brief review of changing interpretations of the term(s) *kwŏnmun sejok*, see Pak Chong-gi, "14 segi ŭi Koryŏ sahoe," pp. 20–22.

109. Qiu Shusen, *Tuohuan Tiemuer zhuan*, p. 58.

110. This paragraph draws heavily from Yi Yong-bŏm, "Ki Hwanghu," pp. 465–73. See also Herbert Franke's biographical note on Toghan-Temür in Goodrich and Fang, *Dictionary of Ming Biography*, pp. 1291–92. Danashiri had tried to shield one of her brothers who plotted against Bayan and Toghan-Temür in her palace. He was discovered and executed in her presence, his blood splattering her robes. For a useful introduction to Empress Ki, see

George Zhao and Richard Guisso, "Female Anxiety and Female Power," pp. 35–39.

111. Tao Zongyi, "Hou de" 后德, *Nancun chuogeng lu*, 26.327; *YS*, 114.2879 后妃一.

112. Yi Yong-bŏm ("Ki Hwanghu," p. 473) calls it Koryŏ's most nimble diplomatic response since Ch'ungnyŏl's initiatives of the thirteenth century.

113. *YS*, 41.883 順帝本紀四至正八年十二月. Early during the Ming dynasty, imperial clansman Zhu Youdun would express a similar sentiment about Empress Ki in one of his poems about Yuan court life.

Fair skin and rosy cheeks, a yielding willow waist.
Who knows that fortune is, the bud of disaster.
The woman of Koryŏ, first invested [as empress].
Cold and overcast in June, great snows blow.

Zhu, *Yuan gong ci yi bai shou*, in Ke Jiusi et al., *Liao Jin Yuan gongci*, p. 21.

114. See Yi Yong-bŏm, "Ki Hwanghu," pp. 487–91. See also the brief note in Farquhar, *The Government of China*, p. 324.

115. *YS*, 45.948 順帝本紀八至正十九年七月庚子.

116. For discussion of Chaghan-na'ur under the Yuan, see Zhou Qingtao, *Yuan Meng shizha*, pp. 271–89. During the early fourteenth century, Ghazan khan established a similar practice in the Il-khanate. In exchange for covering the expenses for the princesses' needs, particular villages were exempted from taxes and other obligations. See Khwandamir (1475–1535), "Story Eighteen: On Making Arrangements for the Imperial Shilān and those of the Princesses," *Habibu's-siyar* vol. 3, pt. 1, p. 105.

117. Fighting in Jiqing had been so severe in 1347 that the court had sent a Mongolian prince, Bolod-Buqa, to lead a campaign of suppression against "bandits/rebels" there (*YS*, 41.878 順帝本紀四至正七年九月甲子).

118. An entry in the *Official History of the Yuan Dynasty* for 1334 notes a request by officials of the Central Secretariat to send two ships on maritime missions to generate profits for the empress (*YS*, 38.824 順帝本紀元統二年十一月戊子). For comments on the connections between Mongolian princesses and their commercial agents (often members of the *ortoq*) in the wider context of the empire, see Allsen, "Mongolian Princes and Their Merchant Partners," pp. 110–11. Earlier in the fourteenth century, the Household Service for the Empress had included gold and silver from Liaoyang in its portfolio (*YS*, 27.605 英宗本紀至治元年七月辛丑; 27.615 英宗本紀至治元年十一月甲午). In 1327, mining assets were transferred to the Central Secretariat (*YS*, 30.676 晉宗本紀泰定四年正月壬子).

119. As early as 1342, "most of the palace eunuchs were Koryŏ men." Some complained that the palace eunuchs had grown too influential (Quan Heng,

Gengshen waishi, *shang*.5b [*Yuandai biji xiaoshuo*, 3.522]; Quan Heng and Ren Chongyue, *Gengshen waishi jianzheng*, p. 40, does not include these lines). In 1340, the Yuan prohibited "people of Koryŏ and other regions" from making their own sons into eunuchs as a way to avoid taxes and corvée service (*YS*, 40.861 順帝本紀三至正元年六月戊午). Earlier, in 1338, the Yuan had issued a ban against "the acquisition of Koryŏ women and eunuchs" (YS, 39.845 順帝本紀二至元四年八月己巳).

120. *YS*, 204.4551–52 朴不花傳. For discussion of Pak in the context of growing eunuch power during the late Yuan, see Fu Leshu, "Yuandai huanhuo kao," pp. 163–66.

121. Quan Heng, *Gengshen waishi*, *xia*.1b (*Yuandai biji xiaoshuo*, 3.522); Quan Heng and Ren Chongyue, *Gengshen waishi jianzheng*, p. 96.

122. Zhu Youdun, *Yuan gong ci yi bai shou*, in Ke Jiusi et al., *Liao Jin Yuan gongci*, p. 26.

123. Xi Lei, "Yuanchao gongtingzhong de Gaoli nüxing," p. 212.

124. Tao Zongyi, "Hou de" 后德, *Nancun chuogeng lu*, 2.21.

125. Sun Chengze, *Yuanchao diangu biannniankao*, 8.35b–36b.

126. See the biographical note by Edward Dreyer and Hok-lam Chan in Goodrich and Fang, *Dictionary of Ming Biography*, pp. 15–17.

127. According to Quan Heng, Empress Ki had played a key role in To-qto'a's reinstatement in 1347; see Quan Heng, *Gengshen waishi*, *shang*.6b–7a (*Yuandai biji xiaoshuo*, 3.524–25); and Quan Heng and Ren Chongyue, *Gengshen waishi jianzheng*, pp. 50–51. For discussion of tensions between the heir apparent and the emperor, see Han Zhiyuan, "Aiyoushilidala yu Yuanmo zhengzhi." Han's analysis understates Empress Ki's influence. Contemporary Chinese officials praised Ayushiridara for his commitment to Confucianism and the Chinese cultural tradition. For one example among many related to an eight-character piece of calligraphy the heir apparent presented as a gift to a favored official, see Gong Shitai, "Huang taizi ci shuba" 皇太子賜書跋, *Wanzhaiji*, 8.31a–b, p. 659; also in Li Xiusheng, *Quan Yuan wen*, 45.197. As Herbert Franke ("Could the Mongol Emperors Read and Write Chinese") has noted, several fourteenth-century Mongol emperors, including Toghan-Temür, bestowed samples of their calligraphy on officials. For a brief discussion of the accomplishments of Toghan-Temür and Ayushiridara in the Chinese cultural tradition, see Luo Xianyou, "Yuanchao zhudi Hanhua shuyi," pp. 73–74. Luo's treatment of the problem is marred by the complete omission of any facet of Yuan court life beyond "Chinese cultural tradition," even things like Tibetan Buddhism that figure prominently in Chinese-language documents.

128. Ye Ziqi, "Ke jin pian," *Cao mu zi*, *juan* 3 *shang*, p. 49. In Ye's dour appraisal, the excessive favor shown Empress Ki hastened the Yuan's fall.

129. *YS*, 114.2880–81 后妃一. See also Herbert Franke's biographical note on Toghan-Temür in Goodrich and Fang, *Dictionary of Ming Biography*, pp. 1292.

130. For discussion of the involvement of another fourteenth-century empress, Budashiri, in commissioning Buddhist art, see Jing, "Financial and Material Aspects of Tibetan Art," pp. 231–32. For the patronage activities of the Mongol Princess Sengge, see Weidner, "Aspects of Painting and Patronage at the Mongol Court," p. 48.

131. Kim Hyŏng-u, "Hosŭng Chigong yŏn'gu," p. 10.

132. Mount Kŭmgang regularly received incense offerings from the Yuan throne (*KS*, 111.330 廉悌臣傳).

133. Mongolian reconstruction follows Hambis, "Histoire de Corée," p. 203.

134. Yi Kok, "Koryŏ Yŏnboksa chongmyŏng" 高麗演福寺鐘銘, reprinted in Liu Xihai, *Haidong jinshi yuan*, 8.9a, 23: 17661. The text also appears in Yi Kok's *Kajŏngjip*, 7.13a–14a, reprinted in *Han'guk munjip ch'onggan*, 3: 147. However, the list of subscribers and their titles is not included in the text preserved in Yi's collected writings. The Koryŏ king and his wife were listed first among the subscribers. Following them were many members of the Branch Secretariat for the Eastern Campaigns and Koryŏ aristocrats. Several characters differ from the stele inscription found in Liu's *Haidong jinshi yuan*. The text does not specify at which temple on Kŭmgangsan the bell was made.

135. For brief comments on the bell, see Suematsu, "Kōrai Empukuji shōmei." For translation of the Sanskrit and Tibetan passages into Japanese, see Yuyama Akira, "Empukuji Dōshō no Bongo meibun oboegaki." For a rubbing of the phrases "Long live the emperor" 皇帝萬歲 and "May Buddha increase in brilliance daily" 佛日增輝, see *Daitō kinsekisho/Taedong kŭmsŏksŏ*, p. 102.

136. For examples, see 1348 敬天寺石塔 (景福宮), in Yi Nan-yŏng, *Han'guk kŭmsŏkbun ch'ubo*, p. 58; 1344 重興寺青銅縷銀香爐 (奉恩寺), p. 58; 1346 兜率山飯子 (held at Kannon Temple, 對馬下縣縣郡豆酘村觀音堂 Tsushima prefecture, Japan), p. 69; 1305 大德九年銘判子 (held at National University, Kyŏngju Annex), p. 70.

137. Wang Chang, who held the titles of Sim Prince and King of Koryŏ, was also an active patron of Buddhism in both Daidu and Jiangnan (several Chan and Pure Land sect temples) and Koryŏ; see Kitamura Takai, "Kōraiō Ō Shō no sūButsu," pp. 126–35. He offered devotions at the Jiangnan temples as an official imperial agent (御香使).

138. Yi Kok, "Koryŏ Yŏnboksa chongmyŏng," reprinted in Liu Xihai, *Haidong jinshi yuan*, 8.9a, 23: 17661. The text also appears in Yi Kok, *Kajŏngjip*, 7.13a–14a, reprinted in *Han'guk munjip ch'onggan*, 3: 147.

139. The mass burials call to mind the devastation of the Black Death at roughly the same time in West Asia. For discussion of developments in Anatolia, see Schamiloglu, "The Rise of the Ottoman Empire," pp. 262–73.

140. *YS*, 204.4552 朴不花傳. The editors of the *YS* denigrate these efforts, commenting that "Buqa wished to engineer momentary good name" for Empress Ki. The relief effort no doubt was intended to burnish the empress's image. Nonetheless, her patronage met a desperate need. The relief efforts are also mentioned in *YS*, 114.2880 后妃一. The temple was located in the southern part of Daidu. See Yu Minzhong, (*Qinding*) *rixia jiuwen kao*, *juan* 155, 4: 2497–98. Zhang Zhu 張翥 (1287–1368) composed a stele account of the temple with details of the relief efforts entitled "Shan hui zhi bei" 善惠之碑. The account is not included either in Yu Minzhong (*Qinding*) *rixia jiuwen kao* or Li Xiusheng, *Quan Yuan wen*. In a 1358 poem, Zhang Zhu (*Shui an shi ji*, 1.13a) referred to corpses along the roadside, children abandoned by their mothers, disease, famine, overflowing government burial pits, and birds and wild animals converging on the carrion south of the capital's walls. Later in a 1361 piece written again just outside the walls of Daidu, he described the devastation of the time: "White bones [cover] the Central Plains, ten-thousand new ghosts. / The spirits of righteous men, the rainbow pierces the sun" 白骨中原萬鬼新。義士精靈虹貫日 (Tao Zongyi, "Zhang Hanlin shi" 張翰林詩, *Nancun chuogeng lu*, 14.176). A rainbow, especially a white one, can be an emblem of war; the sun can represent the ruler.

141. In 1356, the emperor ordered court scholars to propose appropriate posthumous titles and aristocratic positions for Empress Ki's relatives (*YS*, 44.930 順帝本紀七至正十六年二月丙寅).

142. Zhu Youdun, *Yuan gong ci yi bai shou*, 元宮詞一百首, in Ke Jiusi et al., *Liao Jin Yuan gongci*, p. 22. Also cited in Zhu Youdun, *Yuan gong ci* 元宮詞, cited in Kim Sang-gi, *Sinp'yŏn Koryŏ sidaesa*, p. 575*n*118. Kim lists Zhu Su as the author, a common error.

143. See, e.g., *KS*, 37.566 忠惠(復位)五年十月癸未.

144. *KS*, 38.580 恭愍王二年正月丙子.

145. Translation and reconstruction of the Mongolian term follow Rachewiltz, *The Secret History of the Mongols*, p. 86. For the etymology of the term, see ibid., pp. 607–9. Pelliot ("Les Mots Mongols dans le *Korye sa*," p. 257) calls it a *festin de fiançailles*. Ikeuchi ("Kōrai Kyōminō," p. 118) glosses it as "an established ritual of the Mongols wherein the clan assembles and prays for the prosperity of its progeny."

146. *KS*, 37.581 恭愍王二年八月庚子, 乙巳.

147. *KS*, 131.666 奇轍傳; cited in Ikeuchi, "Kōrai Kyōmin'ō," p. 118. Punctuation follows Ikeuchi.

148. *KS*, 38.580 恭愍王二年七月乙亥. No Kye-hyŏn (*Yŏ-Mong oegyosa*, p. 337) notes the connection between the heir apparent's investiture and the timing of the banquet but does not place Kongmin's action in the context above.

149. It is also worth noting that on the eve of the Ki purge and the military strikes north of the Yalu River, Kongmin had sponsored a series of three Buddhist offerings dedicated to the health and longevity of the Yuan emperor and the Yuan heir apparent. Yu Yŏng-suk ("Wŏnjŭng kuksa Pou wa Kongminwang ŭi kaehyŏk chŏngch'i," pp. 168–69) argues that this apparently compliant attitude was an attempt to lull the Yuan into a false sense of security. Part of Yu's evidence is that even more offerings were dedicated to Kongmin, his queen, his mother, and his officials. It seems more likely that Kongmin, like his predecessors, complied with his religious obligations as a member of the Mongol empire.

150. *KS*, 131.666 奇轍傳.

151. *KS*, 38.581 恭愍王二年九月壬申.

152. *YS*, 44.921 至正十五年正月戊午.

153. *YS*, 44.931, 至正十六年四月丙寅.

154. *KS*, 131.666 奇轍傳.

155. *KS*, 37.566 忠惠(復位)五年八月丙戌. Kim Tang-t'aek (*Wŏn kansŏpha ŭi Koryŏ chŏngch'isa*, pp. 126–39) has plausibly argued that the warning was intended to forestall attacks on Empress Ki, who understood that her clansmen in Koryŏ were a political liability. Kim further argues, less convincingly, that the establishment of the Directorate for Ordering Politics (Chŏngch'i togam) was an effort by the Yuan government to deflect Koryŏ officials' resentment against the Yuan to Koreans resident in Koryŏ with links to the Mongols.

156. The minister was Cho Il-sin 趙日新; see *KS*, 38.579 恭愍王元年九月己亥; and *Koryŏsa chŏryo*, 26.17b, p. 672 恭愍王元年九月己亥. For analysis of this poorly understood incident, see Min Hyŏn-gu, "Koryŏ Kongminwang ŭi panWŏnjŏk kaehyŏk chŏngch'i e taehan il koch'al," pp. 58–63; and Kim Tang-t'aek, *Wŏn kansŏpha ŭi chŏngch'isa*, pp. 155–61. Kim suggests that the plot reflected Cho's efforts to improve his image in the eyes of Koryŏ officials unhappy with the Yuan by attacking a symbol of Yuan influence, Ki Ch'ŏl. The attempt to gain their support failed. Kongmin and these disgruntled officials decided that Cho must die. See also Min Hyŏn-gu, "Chŏngch'ika rosŏ ŭi Kongminwang," pp. 280–81. One scholar has argued that Cho planned to remove King Kongmin from power; see Yi Sang-sŏn, "Kongminwang kwa Pou," pp. 268–69.

157. Editors of the *Official History of the Koryŏ Dynasty* wrote that the practice began in the second year of his reign; see *KS*, 38.580 恭愍王二年五月乙酉.

158. Chang Tong-ik, *Koryŏ hugi oegyosa yŏn'gu*, pp. 107–8. For instance, although Yi Che-hyŏn may have resented his in-laws' newfound stature, he tried to use to his advantage the fact that Empress Ki was born in Koryŏ in his appeal to restore the throne to King Ch'unghye (*KS*, 110.325 李齊賢傳). In contrast, Ki Ch'ol used his connections at the Yuan court to level criticisms against King Ch'unghye and argue for transforming Koryŏ into a province of the Yuan (*KS*, 108.298 曹益清傳).

159. *KS*, 37.566 忠惠(復位)五年十二月戊午.

160. Kongmin also entertained envoys from other members of the Mongolian aristocracy at his court (*KS*, 38.580 恭愍王二年二月丁卯).

161. Min Hyŏn-gu, "Koryŏ Kongminwang ŭi chŭgwi paegyŏng," pp. 803–4. However such ties did not guarantee the Ki's complete immunity. Wang Hu had played a critical role in execution of Ki clansman, Ki Sam-man. Even after the fall of the Ki clan, its members apparently retained some prestige. According to the *Official History of the Koryŏ Dynasty*, in 1376, one Korean official pressured Wang's widow, a Ki woman, to accept his offer of marriage in an effort to gain her property (*KS*, 110.319 王煦傳附重貴). Yi's biography maintains that he detested the Ki family's newfound stature (*KS*, 110.328 李齊賢傳).

162. Min Hyŏn-gu, "Koryŏ Kongminwang ŭi chŭgwi paegyŏng," p. 804.

163. See *KS*, 110.327 李齊賢傳. Yi Che-hyŏn declined the booty, claiming that he had not rendered any meritorious service in the purge. At least a portion of the lands and property of those killed in the purge (and their slaves) was also to go to the support of military personnel (*KS*, 81.643 兵一).

164. *KS*, 39.587 恭愍五年五月丁酉.

165. Min Hyŏn-gu, "Koryŏ Kongminwang ŭi panWŏnjŏk kaehyŏk chŏngch'i e taehan ŭi chŏngae kwasŏng," p. 240. Min notes that Kongmin's decision to challenge the Yuan during the mid-1350s was predicated on his expectation of local support from members of the Yi family.

166. Min Hyŏn-gu, "Koryŏ Kongminwang ŭi panWŏnjŏk kaehyŏk chŏngch'i e taehan il koch'al," pp. 69–72.

167. Duncan, "Social Background to the Founding of the Chosŏn Dynasty," p. 57.

168. *KS*, 39.588 恭愍王五年五月壬寅.

169. Kim Tae-jung, "Koryŏ Kongminwangdae Kyŏnggun ŭi chaegŏn sido," pp. 72–75. For the royal proclamations, see *KS*, 81.643 "Pyŏng il" 兵一, 恭愍五年六月. As Kim Ki-tŏk ("14 segi huban kaehyŏk chŏngch'i," pp. 485–95, 500) notes, the reforms were of limited efficacy because they required fundamental changes in land tenure and control of manpower and material resources that the court was simply unable to implement.

170. *KS*, 39.5b 恭愍王五年六月乙亥 (Yŏnse ed., 1: 771; MT, p. 588).

171. Kim Hye-wŏn, "Koryŏ hugi Sim (yang) wang," p. 36. The newly minted prince demurred, and the empress set her sights on the Koryŏ royal clansman Tash-Temür (also known by his title Tŏkhŭng-gun). See Chapter 7 for discussion of later efforts to replace Kongmin with Tash-Temür as king of Koryŏ.

172. *KS*, 39.589 恭愍王五年七月戊申.

173. *KS*, 39.589–92 恭愍王五年七月丁酉; 五年十月甲寅; 五年十月戊午.

174. Kim Tang-t'aek, "Koryŏ Kongmin wang ch'o ŭi muchang seryŏk," p. 32.

175. *KS*, 112.353 李仁復傳.

176. In 1340, the young son of the deceased and recently discredited emperor Tuq-Temür had been exiled to Koryŏ. The Chinese censor Cui Jing 崔敬 offered a number of reasons why the son should not be banished to a foreign land, including his youth, the importance of caring for members of the imperial clan, and the emperor's munificence. He concluded his argument with the specter of Koryŏ intervention in Yuan court politics. He wrote, "Settling him beyond the borders would be just enough to make us a laughingstock in neighboring regions and bring humiliation at the hands of foreign countries. Furthermore, the heart of barbarians 蠻夷之心 is unknowable. If [his exile] gave rise to another incident, the consequences would be grave. When my remarks touch upon this, it is truly frightening" (*YS*, 184.4242 崔敬傳). Although not explicit, the penultimate sentence of the passage suggests that the Koryŏ government might use infighting within the Mongol ruling house for its own purposes. In the end, the son was assassinated before he reached Koryŏ (*YS*, 36.806 文宗本紀五至順三年).

Early in the 1330s, similar rumors of collusion had reached the Yuan throne regarding Toghan-Temür. In the seventh lunar month of 1331 (the *YS* leaves the precise date unclear), the ten-year-old Toghan-Temür had been exiled to Taech'ŏng Island 大青島 off the coast of Korea, where he was kept in isolation (*KS*, 36.552, 忠惠王元年七月丁巳; *YS*, 38.815 順帝本紀一). Shortly later, two men, Zhu Temür (K. Chu Temür) 朱帖木兒 and Zhao Gaoyi (K. Cho Ko-i) 趙高伊, told the newly restored Tuq-Temür that unspecified members of the Liaoyang Branch Secretariat and people from Koryŏ were plotting to put Toghan-Temür on the throne. According to the entry in the *Official History of the Koryŏ Dynasty*, these charges were false and "after they revolted, they sought refuge [in Koryŏ]." The Liaoyang Branch Secretariat dispatched representatives to apprehend the plotters. The same entry notes that later "bandits killed the two men on the street" (*KS*, 36.555 忠肅後元年正月庚辰; *Koryŏ chŏryo*, 25.3a, p. 635 忠肅後元年正月庚辰). Much of the incident is unclear. The murder of the conspirators before they could be questioned by Yuan officials is suggestive but far from conclusive. One wonders if these rumors had figured in the Yuan throne's decision to relocate Toghan-Temür from Koryŏ to south China in the twelfth lunar month of 1331 (*KS*, 36.555 忠惠王元年十二月甲寅). In the third lunar month of 1332, officials from the Liaoyang Branch Secretariat took into custody two Korean ministers and brought them to Liaoyang on suspicion of involvement with the plot to enthrone Toghan-Temür. The Central Secretariat also sent investigators to search for weapons (*Koryŏ chŏryo*, 25.4b, p. 635 忠肅王後元年三月).

The Yuan throne consistently used Koryŏ as a place to exile Mongolian aristocrats (*KS*, 33.523 忠宣王二年九月己卯; 36.557 忠肅王後元年二月丙戌).

Chapter 4

1. *KS*, 39.593 恭愍王六年八月丁巳. Kim's appointment is noted in *Koryŏsa chŏryo*, 26.45a, p. 686 恭愍王六年八月, but no mention is made of the Red Turbans.

2. When the Red Turbans invaded Koryŏ, Kim enlisted the services of other civil officials with military expertise. In 1361, Im Pak 林樸, who had passed the civil service examination just two years earlier and had been serving as the bailiff (*samgun* 參軍) of Kaegyŏng, joined his staff as a military advisor and assisted with the court's evacuation to the south (*KS*, 111.346 林樸傳). Translation of post comes from appendix, *Bibliographic Guide*, p. 566.

3. *KS*, 113.366 安祐傳. The post was *u pu taeŏn* 右副代言, which Duncan has translated as "right assistant transmitter." The post is not listed in Hucker, Farquhar, or *Bibliographical Guide* appendix. According to the section on the Bureau of Military Affairs in the "Treatise on Administrative Posts" of the *Official History of the Koryŏ Dynasty*, until Ch'ungsŏn's reign, this post had been called the "royal transmitter" (*sŭngji* 承旨); see *KS*, 76.549–50 百官.

4. Translation of title is tentative. Not listed in Farquhar, Hucker, Duncan, or in the 25 dynastic histories. In 1389, it was renamed the *tochŏl chesa* 都節制使.

5. *KS*, 39.593–94 恭愍王六年十一月庚申.

6. *KS*, 39.19b–20a 恭愍王七年三月甲子 (Yŏnse, 1: 778–79; MJ, 594); *Koryŏsa chŏryo*, 27.2a, p. 687 恭愍王七年三月.

7. *Koryŏsa chŏryo*, 27.1a–b, p. 687 恭愍王七年正月. Orders to commence work were given in the third lunar month (*Koryŏsa chŏryo*, 27.2a, p. 687 恭愍王七年三月).

8. See Hazard, "Japanese Marauding in Medieval Korea."

9. Kim Ki-tŏk, "14 segi huban kaehyŏk chŏngch'i," p. 485.

10. Ibid., pp. 485–86.

11. *KS*, 39.20b 恭愍王七年四月甲子 (Yŏnse, 1: 779; MJ, 594); *Koryŏsa chŏryo*, 27.2b, p. 687 恭愍王七年四月.

12. *KS*, 39.21 恭愍王七年四月丙子 (Yŏnse, 1: 779; MJ, 594).

13. *KS*, 39.21a 恭愍王七年四月戊寅 (Yŏnse, 1: 779; MJ, 594). For a brief note on the temple, see Yi Chŏng, *Han'guk pulgyo sajŏn*, p. 255.

14. *KS*, 39.21a 恭愍王七年四月己卯 (Yŏnse, 1: 779; MJ, 594).

15. The court ordered relief to the northeast later during the fourth lunar month (*KS*, 39.21b 恭愍王七年四月丁酉 [Yŏnse, 1: 779; MJ, 594]). In one memorial from the summer of 1358, several high-ranking military and civil officials in northern Koryŏ noted "fighting in all directions, grievous hardship and famine" that afflicted the people. They argued that the king should halt construction projects (*Koryŏsa chŏryo*, 27.3b–4a, p. 688 恭愍王七年七月).

16. *KS*, 39.22b, 1: 779; 39.24b–25a, 1: 780–81; *Koryŏsa chŏryo*, 27.3a–b, p. 688 恭愍王七年六月.

17. Yi Haeng, *Sinjŭng Tongguk yŏji sŭngnam*, *kwŏn* 41, "Ch'angsŏng" 昌城, "Kŏnch'i yŏnhyŏk" 建置沿革, 4: 26–27.

18. Cao Shuji (*Zhongguo renkou shi*, 4: 253) suggests that the area north of Daidu, including Liaodong and southern Mongolia, suffered severe population loss during the late Yuan.

19. Noted in Ejima, "Minsho jochoku chōkō," p. 120.

20. For the expansion of Yuan rule into southern Siberia and the military challenges encountered, especially from peoples on Sakhalin Island, see Cheng Nina, "Yuanchao dui Heilongjiang xiayou Nüzhen"; and Enomori, "Jūsan–jūroku seiki no Higashi Ajia to Ainu minzoku."

21. *YS*, 41.867 順帝本紀至正三年二月丁未.

22. *YS*, 41.874 至正六年四月壬子.

23. *YS*, 41.874 至正六年四月丁卯; 41.875 順帝本紀至正六年五月丁亥, 七月丙戌, 41.877 順帝本紀至正七年四月辛巳. See also Rossabi, *The Jurchens in the Yüan and Ming*, p. 9.

24. *YS*, 42.881 順帝本紀至正八年三月辛酉, 丁酉. Ejima Hisao ("Minsho jochoku chōkō," p. 119) characterizes this unrest as a "movement to reclaim ethnic autonomy" by the Jurchens, who suffered from the Mongols' economic and political exploitation. Cong Peiyuan (*Zhongguo dongbeishi*, 3: 427–28) argues that the entries in the *Official History of the Yuan Dynasty* referring to the Üjiyed revolt represent a continuous and spreading uprising. His argument is plausible, but no evidence demonstrates that the individual groups and incidents were part of a single whole.

25. Cong Peiyuan, *Zhongguo dongbeishi*, 3: 248–53.

26. *YS*, 43.910 順帝本紀至正十三年六月癸卯.

27. *KS*, 113.357 偰遜傳. Xie's father was the prominent late Yuan statesman Xie Zhedu 偰哲篤 (*js.* 1315). Xie Xun was also known as Xie Boliao 伯僚 Xun. Serruys (*The Mongols in China During the Hung-wu Period*, p. 290*n*372) mistakenly dates Xie's flight to Koryŏ to 1369.

28. Brose, "Uyghur Technologists of Writing and Literacy in Mongol China," pp. 419–20.

29. Min Hyŏn-gu, "Koryŏ Kongminwang ŭi chŭgwi paegyŏng," p. 804*n*52. The date of the title is from *KS*, 39.600 恭愍王九年八月己丑.

30. *KS*, 113.357 偰遜傳. The Koryŏ throne made systematic use of non-Koreans, often Central Asians, as a way to bolster its position vis-à-vis Korean aristocratic interests (Peter Yun, "Foreigners in Koryŏ Ruling Stratum"). For more on the Xie family, and the Uyghurs in general, in Yuan China, see Brose, "Uyghur Technologists of Writing and Literacy in Mongol China."

31. *KS*, 恭愍王十八年四月丁卯, cited in Wu Han, *Chaoxian Lichao shilu zhong de Zhongguo ziliao*, 1: 13–14.

32. Chŏn Sun-dong, "Sipsa segi huban Myŏng," p. 4*n*10. See also Li Xinfeng, "Ming qianqi fu Chaoxian shichen." Li does not mention the Uyghur connection.

33. *YS*, 201.4506–07 列女傳二. Esen-Qutuq's biography puts the Red Turban seizure of Daning in 1358. However, there is no corresponding mention of such an attack in the "Basic Annals of Shundi" in the *Official History of the Yuan Dynasty*. According to the Basic Annals chronology, the first attacks in the region dated to the final month of Zhizheng 18 (early 1359) but only Liaoyang is mentioned. That being said, the biography of Xie Sun in the *Official History of the Koryŏ Dynasty* notes that Xie fled Daning in the seventh year of King Kongmin's reign (Zhizheng 18, 1358) because Red Turbans were pressuring Daning (see *KS*, 113.357 偰遜傳).

34. *YS*, 201.4506–7 列女傳二.

35. *YS*, 201.4508 列女傳二; Shao Yuanping, *Yuanshi leibian* 元史類編, 38.12a. Note that Zishan si is not listed in the temples section of *Liaodong zhi* 遼東志, *Quan Liao zhi* 全遼志, *Liaoyang zhouzhi* 遼陽州志, or *Liaoyang xianzhi* 遼陽縣志.

36. *YS*, 201.4508 列女傳二; Shao Yuanping, *Yuanshi leibian*, 38.12b. She used the verb *hai* 醢 (to make fish or meat into paste). Temple monks who witnessed Xu's death buried her with her husband after the rebels withdrew. No local gazetteer that I have seen mentions either Xu or her husband.

37. Farquhar (*The Government of China*, p. 288) notes that there were few encampment officials in China proper after 1320.

38. *YS*, 194.4397 忠義傳二. A nearly identical biography may be found in *Beizhen xianzhi* 北鎮縣志, 3.4a.

39. Sonoda, *Manshū kinseki shikō*, 1: 212–13; Luo Xiyi, *Manzhou jinshizhi*, 5.31b–33a, pp. 17350–51.

40. *YS*, 194.4397 忠義傳二; *Beizhen xianzhi*, 3.4a.

41. *YS*, 45.945 順帝本紀八至正十八年十二月癸酉.

42. *YS*, 194.4397 忠義傳二.

43. Ibid.

44. *YS*, 45.945 順帝本紀八至正十八年十二月庚辰.

45. *YS*, 45.946 順帝本紀八至正十九年正月丙午.

46. Qian Qianyi, *Guochu qunxiong shilüe*, 1.25 龍鳳五年(至正十九年)正月丙午.

47. *YS*, 45.947 順帝本紀八至正十九年四月癸亥.

48. Qiu Shusen, "Yuanmo Hongjinjun de zhengquan jianshe," p. 98. For comments on the Red Turban's establishment of branch secretariats, see idem, "Yuanmo nongmin zhengquan jifang tongyin," p. 80.

49. Chen Gaohua, "Shuo Yuanmo Hongjinjun," pp. 24–25.

50. Qian Qianyi, *Guochu qunxiong shilüe*, 1.27 龍鳳五年(至正十九年)七月丙辰.

51. For instance, during the 1340s, a prominent Qonggirad with prestigious ties to the imperial family, Tai-Buqa 太(泰)不花 served as the manager of governmental affairs for Liaoyang (*Liaoyang pingzhang zhengshi* 遼陽平章政事); see *YS*, 142.3381 太不花傳. In 1364, senior Chinese official Li Shizhan took up duties as minister of the left of the Liaoyang Secretariat (*Liaoyangsheng zuocheng* 遼陽省左丞). Li's son would later serve in the Liaoyang administration. See Chen Zuren 陳祖仁, "Hanlin chengzhi Chuguo Li gong xingzhuang" 翰林承旨楚國李公行狀, in Li Shizhan, *Jingji wenji*, 6.36a, 37a.

52. *YS*, 45.948 順帝本紀八至正十九年七月壬辰.

53. This is a Tibetan name, Chösgem.

54. *YS*, 205.4585–87 搠思監傳. Shuosijian remained an influential voice at Toghan-Temür's court until his death in 1365 at the hand of Bolod-Temür. See Chapter 7.

55. *YS*, 45.948 順帝本紀八至正十九年七月戊申. Fojianu had been involved in military affairs in Liaodong since April, when his post had been a manager in the Bureau of Military Affairs.

56. Funada Yoshiyuki ("Mongoru jidai ni okeru minzoku sesshoku," p. 23) has noted that the Mongol emperor Toghan-Temür had recognized He Weiyi as a Mongol and granted him the name Taiping (great peace), which Funada speculates may have derived from the Mongolian *tayibung*, which in turn may have entered Mongolian from Chinese.

57. *YS*, 140.3369 大平傳.

58. *YS*, 140.3371–72 太平傳; *YS*, 45.950 順帝本紀八至正二十年二月戊午.

59. Quan Heng and Ren Chongyue, *Gengshen waishi jianzheng*, p. 98; Qian Qianyi, *Guochu qunxiong shilüe*, 1.27. Esen-Qutuq would later be executed as a consequence of court intrigue and local political competition (*YS*, 140.3372 太平傳).

60. *YS*, 45.950 順帝本紀八至正二十年正月癸卯.

61. *Ming Taizu shilu* 明太祖實錄, 181.1a–b 洪武二十年三月癸酉; *KS*, 辛禑王十二年十二月, 136.12b (Yŏnse ed., 3: 936; MJ, 3: 739).

62. *KS*, 136.739 辛禑王十三年二月. Editors of Ming-period gazetteers used similar language to describe conditions in Liaodong. "Wherever they [Master Guan, Cracked-Head Pan, etc.], passed, they killed and pillaged. [The region] was nearly emptied by [people's] flight" (See "Za zhi san Liao chang bian" 雜志三遼長編, *Liaodong zhi*, 8.7a; "Wai zhi shi kao" 外志史考, *Quan Liao zhi*, 6.41.)

63. *Ming Taizu shilu*, 181.1a–b 洪武二十年三月癸酉; *KS*, 136.739 辛禑王十三年二月.

64. The text reads *qiao cai* 樵采, the "gathering of kindling/firewood" or "those who gather kindling/firewood" (*Hanyu dacidian*, 4: 1316). Given the syntax of the sentence, it seems likely that *qiao cai* was a scribal error for *qiao mi* 樵米, "firewood and grain."

65. *YS*, 142.3401 也速傳.

66. *YS*, 142.3401–2 也速傳.

67. *YS*, 145.3450 月魯不花傳.

68. *YS*, 142.3402 也速傳.

69. Ibid.

70. "Gaomen wu jiefu" 高門五節婦, *Liaodong zhi*, 6.42a; *Ming Taizu shilu*, 144.5b 洪武十五年四月丙午. The Veritable Records do not mention that he was in the military.

71. Fort detail from *Ming Taizu shilu* 明太祖實錄, 144.5b 明洪武十五年四月丙午.

72. The *Ming Veritable Records* note: "His wife, Woman Guo, was Korean and resided in 渾灘. She hanged herself in the horse barn 馬櫪" (*Ming Taizu shilu* 144.5a–6a).

73. *Liaodong zhi*, 6.42b. For a slightly longer and fuller account, see *Ming Taizu shilu*, 144.5a–6a. The Gao family was officially recognized by the Ming court in June 1382 after a former Yuan official, Mingzu 名祖, informed the emperor of the family's travails during the chaos of the dynastic transition.

74. Matsuda, "Kōkin no ran."

75. *KS*, 39.26a 恭愍王八年二月乙酉 (Yŏnse ed., 1: 781; MJ, p. 596); 安祐傳 (Yŏnse ed., 113.2a–b, 3: 468; MJ, p. 367); *Koryŏsa chŏryo*, 27.4b, p. 688 恭愍王

八年二月. As John Dardess ("The Transformations of Messianic Revolt," p. 543) noted nearly four decades ago, this communiqué seems to be the sole extant specimen of an original White Lotus proclamation.

76. As Wu Han noted more than half a century ago, not until the very end of Zhu Yuanzhang's rise to power as a rebel did he attempt to discredit Mongol rule on the basis of "the Sinic-barbarian divide," a rhetorical strain that would appear more frequently after he became emperor. See Wu Han, *Zhu Yuanzhang zhuan*, pp. 94–99; and idem, *Mingshi jianshu*, pp. 22–24. As late as 1364, Zhu Yuanzhang left the door open to rapprochement with the Yuan; see Chen Gaohua, "Lun Zhu Yuanzhang he Yuanchao de guanxi."

77. Chen Gaohua, "Shuo Yuanmo Hongjinjun," p. 25.

78. Pak Ok-gŭl, "Koryŏmal pukbang yumin kwa ch'uswae"; Kim Wi-hyŏn, *Koryŏ sidae taeoe kwan'gyesa yŏn'gu*, pp. 368–75.

79. *KS*, 39.29b 恭愍王八年十一月甲辰 (Yŏnse ed., 1: 783; MJ, p. 597); *Koryŏsa chŏryo*, 27.5b, p. 689 恭愍王八年十一月.

80. *KS*, 39.29b 恭愍王八年十一月戊午 (Yŏnse ed., 1: 783; MJ, p. 597); *Koryŏsa chŏryo* 25.5b, p. 689 恭愍王八年十一月.

81. Li Chengde, "Hongjinjun jin Gaoli qianxi," p. 79.

82. Ibid., pp. 78–79; Han Rulin, *Yuanchaoshi*, p. 119. Han stresses the Koryŏ ruling elite's "extreme hatred" for the Red Turban movement.

83. Lu Nanqiao, "Yuanmo Hongjinjun qiyi," p. 46.

84. Qu Wenjun, "Hongjinjun huodong dui Gaoli zhengju," p. 36.

85. Kang Sŏng-mun, "Koryŏmal Hongt'ujok ch'imgo e kwan han yŏn'gu," pp. 216, 228. Kang argues that the Red Turbans invaded Koryŏ out of a desire for revenge. He maintains that Red Turbans had attempted but failed to win the support of Korean communities in the Liaodong region. Compounding the insult, the Koryŏ government offered lands and economic assistance to Korean refugees fleeing the region. Kang's interpretation is not persuasive on several counts. First, he offers no evidence that the Red Turbans were motivated by vengeance. Second, it is not clear that Chinese at the time viewed Koreans in Liaodong as part of the Koryŏ state.

86. *KS*, 39.29b 恭愍王八年十一月己未 (Yŏnse ed., 1: 783: MJ, p. 597); *Koryŏsa chŏryo* 27.5b, p. 689 恭愍王八年十一月.

87. *KS*, 113.367 安祐傳.

88. Kim Tang-t'aek, "Koryŏ Kongmin wang ch'o ŭi muchang seryok," p. 32.

89. *KS*, 39.30a 恭愍王八年十二月丁丑 (Yŏnse ed., 1: 783; MJ, p. 597).

90. Yi Haeng, *Sinjŭng Tongguk yŏji sŭngnam*, *kwŏn* 53 昌城, 城郭, 4: 28. Stone walls were erected in 1414.

91. *KS*, 39.30a 恭愍王八年十二月戊辰 (Yŏnse ed., 1: 783; MJ, pp. 597–98); 113.2b 安祐傳 (MJ, p. 367); *Koryŏsa chŏryo*, 27.6a, p. 689 恭愍王八年十二月丁卯.

92. *KS*, 39.30a 恭愍王八年十二月庚午 (Yŏnse ed., 1: 783; MJ, p. 598).

93. Ibid.

94. The *darughachi* was Lu Lianxiang 魯連祥, who had been based in Sŏnsŏng 宣城 (present-day Kyoha 交河, Kyŏnggi province); see *KS*, 113.366 安祐傳. The annals of King Kongmin in the *KS* do not mention either Lu Lianxiang or a revolt in Sŏnsŏng from the years KM 2 to KM 7. The name does not appear in the *YS*. An used troops from Yongju 龍州 (present-day Yongch'ŏn 龍川, Northern P'yŏngyang province).

95. *KS*, 39.30a–b 恭愍王八年十二月乙亥 (Yŏnse ed., 1: 783; MJ, p. 367).

96. The fear was probably exaggerated. Mao Gui had been murdered in the fourth lunar month of 1359 in Shandong.

97. *KS*, 113.367 安祐傳.

98. *KS*, 39.30a–b, 1: 783; 113.2b–3a 安祐傳 (Yŏnse ed., 3: 468–69; MJ, p. 367).

99. The court granted General An a gold belt buckle for his initial victory at Ch'ŏnggang (*Koryŏsa chŏryo*, 27.6a–b, p. 689 恭愍王八年十二月乙亥).

100. Ibid.; *KS*, 111.336 慶復興傳. The king would later bestow on Kyŏng honors of the first order for driving the Red Turbans from Koryŏ and for accompanying the king during his evacuation to the south.

101. *KS*, 113.3a 安祐傳 (Yŏnse ed., 3: 469; MJ, p. 367).

102. *Koryŏsa chŏryo*, 27.6b–7a, pp. 689–90 恭愍王八年十二月乙亥.

103. Yi Saek, "Yi Munjŏng kong myojimyŏng" 李文貞墓誌銘, *Mok'ŭn sŏnsaeng mungo*, 17.7a, reprinted in *Han'guk munjip ch'onggan*, 5: 148; also in Kim Yong-sŏn, *Koryŏ myojimyŏng chipsŏng*, p. 567.

104. *KS*, 39.30b 恭愍王八年十二月己卯 (Yŏnse ed., 1: 783; MJ, p. 598); *Koryŏsa chŏryo*, 27.6b–7a, pp. 689–90 恭愍王八年十二月乙亥.

105. *Zhizheng zhiji* is traditionally attributed to Kong Qi. For a convincing case that the author was Kong Keqi, see Gu Cheng, "*Zhizheng zhiji* de zuozhe wei Kong Keqi."

106. Kong Keqi, "Shou shi yong cui" 首飾用翠, *Zhizheng zhiji*, 3.15b.

107. *KS*, 39.30a 恭愍王八年十二月庚午 (Yŏnse ed., 1: 783; MJ, p. 598). Translation of administrative title based on Hucker, *Dictionary*, pp. 329, 431; and Duncan, *Origins of the Chosŏn Dynasty*, p. 22.

108. Yi Saek, "Sŏgyŏng p'ungwŏllu ki" 西京風月樓記, *Mok'ŭn sŏnsaeng mungo*, 1.12a, reprinted in *Han'uk munjip ch'onggan*, 5: 8.

109. In Tu-su, *P'yŏngyangji*, 1.3a.

110. Ibid., 2.17a.

111. *Koryŏsa chŏryo*, 27.6a, p. 689 恭愍王八年十二月丁卯. The three units were the Holjŏk 忽赤, Ch'ung 忠, and Yong 勇. As Pelliot ("Les Mots Mongols dans le *Korye sa*," p. 261) and others have noted, Holjŏk is the transliteration of the Mongolian *qorchi*, "quiver bearer," which was part of Chinggis khan's guard. *Ch'ung* and *yong* mean "loyal" and "brave," respectively.

112. *KS*, 39.31a 恭愍王八年十二月辛巳 (Yŏnse ed., 1: 784; MJ, p. 598).

113. *Koryŏsa chŏryo*, 27.7a, p. 690 恭愍王八年十二月乙亥.

114. *KS*, 39.30b 恭愍王八年十二月丁亥 (Yŏnse ed., 1: 783; MJ, p. 598); 113.3a, 3: 469; *Koryŏsa chŏryo*, 27.7a, p. 690 恭愍王八年十二月丁亥.

115. *KS*, 39.30b 恭愍王八年十二月戊子 (Yŏnse ed., 1: 783; MJ, p. 598); *Koryŏsa chŏryo*, 27.7a, p. 690 恭愍王八年十二月丁亥.

116. *KS*, 39.30b–31a 恭愍王八年十二月戊子 (Yŏnse ed., 1: 783–84; MJ, p. 598); *Koryŏsa chŏryo*, 27.7a, p. 690 恭愍王八年十二月丁亥.

117. *KS*, 39.31a 恭愍王九年正月己丑 (Yŏnse ed., 1: 784; MJ, p. 598). The full title is not listed in Hucker or Duncan. Hucker (*Dictionary*, p. 254) renders *xunchashi* as "touring surveillance commissioner" and notes that during the Tang the official commonly oversaw a multi-prefectural region.

118. *KS*, 113.371 鄭世雲傳.

119. Ibid.

120. *KS*, 39.30b–31a 恭愍王九年正月己亥 (Yŏnse ed., 1: 783–84; MJ, p. 598).

121. See below. Li Chengde's ("Hongjinjun jin Gaoli qianxi," p. 80) claim that "at least 100,000 Koryŏ peasants joined the Red Turban army" strains credulity.

122. *KS*, 113.39.31a (Yŏnse ed., 1: 784).

123. *KS*, 39.31a–b 恭愍王九年正月癸卯 (Yŏnse ed., 1: 784; MJ, p. 598); *Koryŏsa chŏryo*, 27.7b, p. 690 恭愍王九年正月癸卯.

124. *KS*, 39.31b 恭愍王九年正月甲辰 (Yŏnse ed., 1: 784; MJ, p. 598); 113.3a, 3: 469; *Koryŏsa chŏryo*, 27.8a, p. 690 恭愍王九年正月甲辰.

125. *KS*, 39.31b 恭愍王九年正月癸卯 (Yŏnse ed., 1: 784; MJ, p. 598); *Koryŏsa chŏryo*, 27.7a, p. 690 恭愍王九年正月癸卯. The comments about Kongmin's "fear of mounting horses" are striking given that riding seems to have been a favorite pastime while on the road in the south. The editors of both the *Official History of the Koryŏ Dynasty* and the *Abridged History of the Koryŏ Dynasty* criticize the king for his lack of equestrian skill in particular and martial prowess in general. This is perhaps another sign that even during the mid-fifteenth century, the time of the chronicles' compilation, the military ethos of the late Koryŏ period remained strong.

126. *KS*, 39.598 恭愍王九年正月丙午. Information on the location of Saengyang Station is from Yi Haeng, *Sinjŭng Tongguk yŏji sŭngnam*, *kwŏn* 52, "Chunghwagun" 中和郡, "Yŏkwŏn" 驛院, 4: 2.

127. *KS*, 39.598 恭愍王九年正月丙午; 113.367 安祐傳.

128. *KS*, 39.31b–32a 恭愍王九年正月丙午 (Yŏnse ed., 1: 784; MJ, p. 598); 113.367 安祐傳; *Koryŏsa chŏryo*, 27.8a, p. 690 恭愍王九年正月甲辰.

129. *KS*, 39.32a 恭愍王九年正月丁未 (Yŏnse ed., 1: 784; MJ, p. 598); 113.3a–b, 3: 469; *Koryŏsa chŏryo*, 27.8a, p. 690 恭愍王九年正月甲辰. Accounts differ about who trampled the people to death. The *Koryŏsa chŏryo* account puts the blame on the residents themselves, and the *KS* notes that it was the fault of the troops. For more information on Yonggang, see Yi Haeng, *Sinjŭng Tongguk yŏji sŭngnam*, *kwŏn* 52, "Yonggang," 4: 4–6. Yonggang boasted a stone fortress about two miles north of the administrative seat, in the Osŏksan 烏石山. Local tradition held that the Tang emperor Taizong had been unable to take the fort during his attempted invasions of Korea. It is unclear if residents took refuge there during the Red Turban invasion.

130. On February 14, 1360, the court promoted General An to serve as commander of myriarchy of civilian and military households of Anju (*Anju kunmin manhobu tomanho* 安州軍民萬户府都萬户), and Yi Pang-sil was to serve as commanding myriarch (*sangmanho* 上萬户). See *KS*, 39.32a 恭愍王九年正月乙卯 (Yŏnse ed., 1: 784; MJ, p. 598); 113.3b 安祐傳, 3: 469; *Koryŏsa chŏryo*, 27.8a, p. 690 恭愍王九年正月甲辰.

131. *KS*, 113.36b 安祐傳, 3: 469; *Koryŏsa chŏryo*, 27.8b, p. 690 恭愍王九年二月己未.

132. *KS*, 39.598 恭愍王九年二月壬申; 113.4a 安祐傳, 3: 469.

133. *KS*, 39.598 恭愍王九年二月壬申. See Yi Haeng, *Sinjŭng Tongguk yŏji sŭngnam*, *kwŏn* 52, "Yonggang," 4: 12–13.

134. Translation of posts based on Hucker, *Dictionary*, p. 301.

135. *KS*, 113.4b 安祐傳, 3: 469; *Koryŏsa chŏryo*, 27.8b–9a, pp. 690–91 恭愍王九年二月辛酉.

136. *KS*, 39.32b 恭愍王九年二月癸酉; 113.4b 安祐傳, 3: 469; *Koryŏsa chŏryo*, 27.9a–b, p. 691 恭愍王九年二月癸酉.

137. *KS*, 113.4b 安祐傳, 3: 469.

138. *KS*, 39.32b 恭愍王九年二月癸酉 (Yŏnse ed., 1: 784; MJ, pp. 598–99); 113.4b 安祐傳, 3: 469; *Koryŏsa chŏryo*, 27.9b, p. 691 恭愍王九年二月癸酉.

139. *KS*, 113.4b 安祐傳, 3: 469; *Koryŏsa chŏryo*, 27.9b, p. 691 恭愍王九年二月癸酉.

140. *Koryŏsa chŏryo*, 27.9b, p. 691 恭愍王九年二月癸酉; *KS*, 39.599 恭愍王九年二月壬午.

Chapter 5

1. *KS*, 39.32b 恭愍王九年三月戊子 (Yŏnse ed., 1: 784; MJ, p. 599); *Koryŏsa chŏryo*, 27.9a, p. 691 恭愍王九年三月.

2. Nishino, "Kōraichō ni okeru Hokuhō Ryōkai chiiki ni tsuite." Nishino stresses that these regional tensions preceded the Mongol period.

3. Kim Ku-chin, "Yŏ-Wŏn ŭi yŏngt'o punjaeng."

4. Lu Lianxiang does not appear in the *YS*. The annals of KM 2–7 in *KS* do not mention either Lu or a revolt in Sŏnsŏng.

5. For cases from China, see Rossabi, *Khubilai Khan*, pp. 121, 168. The Il-khanate ruler Ghazan attempted to eliminate "shakedowns" by imperial messengers (Khwandamir, *Habibu's-siyar*, p. 100).

6. Su Tianjue had advocated nearly identical policies in the wake of revolts in Henan province during the 1340s; see Chapter 2.

7. *KS*, 113.5a–6b 安祐傳 (Yŏnse ed., 3: 470; MJ ed. 369).

8. *KS*, 39.32b–33a 恭愍王九年三月己酉 (Yŏnse ed., 1: 784–85; MJ, p. 599); *Koryŏsa chŏryo*, 27.9b–10a, p. 691 恭愍王九年三月己酉.

9. *KS*, 39.33a 恭愍王九年三月甲寅 (Yŏnse ed., 1: 785; MJ, p. 599). The specific locality was Sŏngwŏnp'o 城垣浦.

10. *KS*, 39.33a 恭愍王九年三月乙卯 (Yŏnse ed., 1: 741; MJ, p. 599); *Koryŏsa chŏryo*, 27.10a, p. 691 恭愍王九年三月己酉.

11. *KS*, 39.33b 恭愍王九年四月己未 (Yŏnse ed., 1: 785; MJ, p. 599).

12. *KS*, 39.33b 恭愍王九年四月癸酉 (Yŏnse ed., 1: 785; MJ, p. 599); *Koryŏsa chŏryo*, 27.10b, p. 691 恭愍王九年四月.

13. *KS*, 113.7a, 3: 471; *Koryŏsa chŏryo*, 27.10a–b, p. 691 恭愍王九年四月.

14. *KS*, 39.33b 恭愍王九年四月癸未 (Yŏnse ed., 1: 785; MJ, p. 599); *Koryŏsa chŏryo*, 27.10a–b, p. 691 恭愍王九年四月.

15. *KS*, 39.33b 恭愍王九年四月丙戌 (Yŏnse ed., 1: 785; MJ, p. 599); *Koryŏsa chŏryo*, 27.10b, p. 691 恭愍王九年四月.

16. *KS*, 39.40a 恭愍王九年四月丙戌 (Yŏnse ed., 1: 785; MJ, p. 599); *Koryŏsa chŏryo*, 27.10b, p. 691 恭愍王九年四月.

17. *KS*, 39.40a 恭愍王九年四月丙戌 (Yŏnse ed, 1: 785; MJ, p. 599).

18. *Koryŏsa chŏryo*, 27.11b, p. 692 恭愍王九年四月.

19. Ibid., 27.13b, p. 693 恭愍王十年三月丁巳.

20. Ibid., 四月辛巳.

21. *KS*, 39.37b 十年五月丁卯 (Yŏnse ed., 1: 787; MJ, p. 601).

22. During the Ming, a Tang Relay Station Fort 湯站堡 was located southeast of Liaoyang and lay on the route for Korean delegations in the Ming; halfway between Tangzhan Fort and Liaoyang city proper was the Koryŏ

House. Tangzhan Fort probably takes its name from the Tang River 湯河, which flowed east of Liaoyang; see *Quan Liao zhi*, 1.498.

23. *KS*, 39.5a 恭愍王九年七月辛未 (Yŏnse ed., 1: 786; MJ, 599–600); *Koryŏsa chŏryo* 27.12a, p. 692 恭愍王九年七月.

24. *KS*, 39.4b 恭愍王九年七月乙卯 (Yŏnse ed., 1: 785; MJ, p. 599). Seoul had previously served as the southern capital during Sukjong's 肅宗 reign (1096–1105).

25. For a short biography of Pou in English based on his epitaph, see Vermeersch, *Power of the Buddhas*, pp. 412–13.

26. Yi Sang-sŏn, "Kongminwang kwa Pou," pp. 274–78. Yi argues that Pou's motivations for moving the capital to Hanyang were that it was closer to his home region and would serve to consolidate his political position at the court.

27. *KS*, 39.35a 恭愍王九年七月乙卯 (Yŏnse ed., 1: 786: MJ, 599).

28. *KS*, 39.35b 恭愍王九年十一月辛酉 (Yŏnse ed., 1: 786; MJ, 600).

29. For an overview, see Henthorn, *Korea: The Mongol Invasions*, pp. 14–30.

30. *KS*, 39.35b–36a 恭愍王十年二月辛卯 (Yŏnse ed., 1: 786; MJ, 600). As noted in Chapter 4, the first waves of Korean families in Liaodong returned to Koryŏ in 1359.

31. Literally, "Slave of the Gao family." As Henry Serruys ("Some Types of Names Adopted by the Mongols," pp. 353–55) has noted, this construction was common during the Yuan period.

32. *KS*, 39.37a 恭愍王十年四月辛巳 (Yŏnse ed., 1: 787; MJ, p. 600); *Koryŏsa chŏryo*, 27.13b, p. 693 恭愍王十年四月.

33. *KS*, 39.38a 恭愍王十年九月庚申 (Yŏnse ed., 1: 787; MJ, 601); *Koryŏsa chŏryo*, 27.15b, p. 694 恭愍王十年九月.

34. *KS*, 39.38b 恭愍王十年九月癸酉 (Yŏnse ed., 1: 787; MJ, p. 601); *Koryŏsa chŏryo*, 27.15b, p. 694 恭愍王十年九月.

35. Chang Tong-ik (*Koryŏ hugi oegyosa yŏn'gu*, p. 37) and others have noted that in such times of crisis as Nayan's 1287 revolt in Liaodong, the Yuan court had granted a greater measure of autonomy to Koryŏ in an effort to gain its assistance. This included appointing the Koryŏ king to head the Koryŏ Branch Secretariat.

36. For discussion of these changes, see ibid., pp. 78–79.

37. Ibid., pp. 78.

38. *KS*, 39.38b–39a 恭愍王十年九月癸酉 (Yŏnse ed, 1: 787–88; MJ, p. 601); *Koryŏsa chŏryo*, 27.15b, p. 694 恭愍王十年九月. The *Koryŏsa chŏryo* entry only mentions the amnesty.

39. According to the *YS* (42.893 順帝本紀五至正十一年十二月辛丑), Han Yao'er was taken captive in January 1352 when Esen-Temür recaptured

Shangcai 上蔡. Han was then transported to Daidu, where he was executed. Was there really such a delay in information, or had Han Yao'er and others become metonyms for the Red Turban rebellions as a whole? According to *KS* (38.584 恭愍王四年正月庚午), the Koryŏ court received news of Han's death early in 1355.

40. *KS*, 113.369 安祐傳.

41. *KS*, 39.39a–b 恭愍王十年十月丁酉 (Yŏnse ed., 1: 788; MJ, p. 601); *Koryŏsa chŏryo*, 27.16a, p. 694 恭愍王十年十月丁酉. The Red Turban forces are estimated at 200,000 men strong in An U's biography in *KS*, 113.7a 安祐傳 (Yŏnse ed., 3: 471; MJ, 113.369).

42. Yi Haeng, *Sinjŭng Tongguk yŏji sŭngnam*, *kwŏn* 53, "Sakju," "Kwaksŏng" 郭城, 4: 32.

43. Ibid., "Pongsu" 烽燧, 4: 32.

44. *KS*, 39.601 恭愍王十年九月丙子. A tributary of the Yalu River, Tollogang flows south of Kanggye. The date of the establishment of the myriarchy at Kanggye is unclear, with some entries from the *Official History of the Koryŏ Dynasty* indicating that it was created in 1361 and others before that time. For brief discussion of the historical geography and strategic significance of Tollagang and Kanggye during the late fourteenth century, see Ikeuchi, "Kōrai Shin-u chō ni okeru Tetsuryō mondai," pp. 239–43.

45. *KS*, 39.601 恭愍王十年十月乙未.

46. *KS*, 39.602 恭愍王十年十一月辛酉.

47. Ibid., 癸亥.

48. In Tu-su, *P'yŏngyangji*, 1.2a.

49. Yi Haeng, *Sinjŭng Tongguk yŏji sŭngnam*, *kwŏn* 41, "Sŏhŭng" 瑞興, "San-ch'ŏn" 山川, 3: 22; "Kojŏk" 古蹟, 27.

50. *KS*, 113.369 安祐傳.

51. Ibid.

52. *KS*, 39.602 恭愍王十年十一月癸亥; 113.369 安祐傳.

53. The famous fifteenth-century official and writer Yang Sŏngji 梁誠之 (1415–82) would repeatedly refer to the failure to hold Chabi Pass against the Red Turbans in his discussions of Chosŏn military policy; see his *Nuljae chip* 訥齋集, 4.25a, 4.44b, reprinted in *Han'guk munjip ch'onggan*, 9: 342, 351.

54. *KS*, 39.40b 恭愍王十年十一月乙丑 (Yŏnse ed., 1: 788; MJ, p. 602). For poems on the Hŭng'ŭi Postal Station, see Yi Haeng, *Sinjŭng Tongguk yŏji sŭngnam*, *kwŏn* 42, "Upong," "Yŏkwŏn" 驛院, 3: 24.

55. Kwŏn Kŭn, "Yŏklugi" 驛樓記, in Yi Haeng, *Sinjŭng Tongguk yŏji sŭngnam*, *kwŏn* 43, "Kang'ŭm" 江陰, "Yŏkwŏn" 驛院, 3: 43.

56. *KS*, 113.8a–b, 3: 471; *Koryŏsa chŏryo*, 27.17b, p. 695 恭愍王十年十一月癸亥. On Kongmin's efforts to revitalize the Capital Army, see Kim Tae-jung, "Koryŏ Kongminwangdae Kyŏnggun ŭi chaegŏn sido."

57. Han Chae-yŏm (1775–1818), *Koryŏ kodo chŏng*, 1.26b, p. 57. Han draws his information from the *Koryŏsa*, "Geography Treatise."

58. The outer city wall was 29,700 "paces" (*po* 步) in circumference (Yi Haeng, *Sinjŭng Tongguk yŏji sŭngnam*, *kwŏn* 4, "Kaegyŏngbu sang, sŏngkwak" 開城府上，城郭, 1: 141). According to this account, all the city gates had fallen into disrepair by the time of compilation, that is, the mid-fifteenth century.

59. Duncan, *Origins of the Chosŏn Dynasty*, pp. 52–98.

60. Pak Yong-un, *Koryŏ sidae Kaegyŏng yŏn'gu*, pp. 156, 164, 167; idem, "Kaegyŏng in the Age of Koryŏ," pp. 100–101.

61. Pak P'yŏng-sik, "Koryŏ hugi ŭi Kaegyŏng sang'ŏp." Pak stresses the growth of private markets and their growing importance for both elites and the royal family. However, state involvement in markets was far more pervasive in Koryŏ than in the Song dynasty or the Great Yuan *ulus*.

62. *Koryŏsa chŏryo*, 27.2a, p. 687 恭愍王七年三月.

63. Information on Kaesŏng's topographical setting and outer walls is drawn from Mizutani Masayoshi, "Kōrai no shuto Kaijōjō ni tsuite no kenkyū." This is an annotated translation of two articles by Ch'in Yon-ch'ol, a scholar from the People's Republic of Korea who surveyed Kaesŏng's walls.

64. *KS*, 39.39b 恭愍王十年十月己亥 (Yŏnse ed., 1: 788; MJ, p. 601).

65. *KS*, 81.643 兵志一五軍; *Koryŏsa chŏryo*, 27.16b, p. 694 恭愍王十年十月壬寅. Pirate attacks prompted Koryŏ officials to put the capital on alert and to "select men from among the wards 坊 and *ri* 里 communities to serve as soldiers" (*KS*, 110.317 金倫傳附希祖). During the second half of the fourteenth century, escalating military demands drove the Koryŏ government to include slaves and servants in its armies (Min Hyŏn-gu, "Koryŏ hugi kunje ŭi chŏngch'ijŏk kyŏngjejŏk kiban," p. 337).

66. *KS*, 39.40a 恭愍王十年十一月丁巳 (Yŏnse ed., 1: 788; MJ, pp. 601–2); *Koryŏsa chŏryo*, 27.17b, p. 695.

67. *Koryŏsa chŏryo*, 27.17b, p. 695 恭愍王十年十一月癸亥. When Yuan and Koryŏ forces clashed along the northern border in 1356, the court attempted to prohibit the flight of panicked residents of Kaegyŏng from the capital (*KS*, 39.589 恭愍王五年七月壬午).

68. *KS*, 113.8b–9a 安祐傳 (Yŏnse ed., 3: 471–72; MJ, p. 369); *Koryŏsa chŏryo*, 27.18a, p. 695.

69. *KS*, 111.332–33 洪彥博傳; Kwŏn Kŭn, "Hong sijung hwi Ŏn-bak" 洪侍中諱彥博, *Yangch'on chip*, 35.19a, reprinted in *Han'guk munjip ch'onggan*, 7: 315; *Koryŏsa chŏryo*, 27.17b, p. 695 恭愍王十年十一月癸亥. Kongmin's mother was

Hong's aunt. He had been named a merit official of the first degree for his part in the anti-Ki purge.

70. Located near Sulyuk Bridge 水陸橋 in Hajichŏn, Kaegyŏng (Yi Chŏng, *Han'guk pulgyo sachŏn*, pp. 187–88). For Minch'ŏnsa Temple's ties to Ch'ungsŏn and the Yuan, see Han'guk yŏksa yŏn'guhoe, ed., *Koryŏ ŭi hwangdo Kaegyŏng*, p. 103. In happier days, Kongmin and his queen had made outings to the temple (*KS*, 38.580 恭愍王二年四月戊戌). In 1353, the king donated Yuan paper money to the temple, when it held Benevolent King services 仁王道場 in order to "pacify the troops" 鎮兵 (*KS*, 38.580 恭愍王二年三月甲午).

71. *KS*, 113.8b–9a 安祐傳 (Yŏnse ed., 3: 471–72; MJ, p. 369); *Koryŏsa chŏryo*, 27.18a, p. 695 恭愍王十年十一月癸亥.

72. Yi Saek, "Yu Suk myojimyŏng" 柳淑墓誌銘, *Mo'kŭn sŏnsaeng mungo*, 18.4a, reprinted in *Han'guk munjip ch'onggan*, 5: 154. Also in Kim Yong-sŏn, *Koryŏ myojimyŏng chipsŏng*, p. 601. Note that Yu's biography in the *Koryŏsa* (112.351) has Hwangju 黄州, not Kwangju.

73. *KS*, 111.331 廉悌臣傳.

74. See Yi Saek, "Yun Hae myojimyŏng," *Mo'kŭn sŏnsaeng mungo*, 18.14b–15a, reprinted in *Han'guk munjip ch'onggan*, 5: 159–60; also in Kim Yong-sŏn, *Koryŏ myojimyŏng chipsŏng*, pp. 606–7. After the recapture of Kaegyŏng, Yun received honors of only the second degree, a slight that Yun bore with grace.

75. *KS*, 81.643 兵志一五軍. The Koryŏ censorate made the claim in 1362 as part of its indictment against the parlous state of the kingdom's military, most especially the uselessness of the royal guard.

76. *KS*, 39.40b–41a 恭愍王十年十一月丙寅 (Yŏnse ed., 1: 788–89; MJ, p. 602); *Koryŏsa chŏryo*, 27.18a, p. 695 恭愍王十年十一月癸亥.

77. *KS*, 113.8b–9a 安祐傳 (Yŏnse ed., 3: 471–72; MJ, p. 369); *Koryŏsa chŏryo*, 27.18a, p. 695 恭愍王十年十一月癸亥.

78. *KS*, 39.602 恭愍王十年十一月丁卯.

79. *KS*, 39.41b 恭愍王十年十一月壬申 (Yŏnse ed., 1: 789; MJ, p. 602); *Koryŏsa chŏryo*, 27.19a, p. 696 恭愍王十年十一月壬申.

80. *Koryŏsa chŏryo*, 27.18b, p. 695 恭愍王十年十一月癸亥; Yi Haeng, *Sinjŭng Tongguk yŏji sŭngnam*, *kwŏn* 6, "Kwangju" 廣州, "Yŏkwŏn" 驛院, 1: 12.

81. *Koryŏsa chŏryo*, 27.18b, p. 695 恭愍王十年十一月癸亥. Translation of *chae ch'u* follows Duncan, *Origins of the Chosŏn Dynasty*, p. 27.

82. Yi Saek, "Han Mun Kyŏng kung myojimyŏng" 韓文敬公墓誌銘, *Mo'kŭn sŏnsaeng mungo*, 15.26a, 5: 135. Also in Kim Yong-sŏn, *Koryŏ myojimyŏng chipsŏng*, pp. 612–13. "Grand master" and "chancellor" follow Hucker, *Dictionary*, pp. 194, 299. *Chŏnwi* 典儀 is rendered "supervisor of rites" in ibid., p. 504. *Chŏnkyo* 典校 is not listed in Hucker or Farquhar.

83. Chŏng Mongju 鄭夢周, "Pak Yun-mun ch'ŏ Kimsi myojimyŏng" 朴允文妻金氏墓誌銘, *P'o'ŭn munjip* 圃隱文集, 續錄一, reprinted in Kim Yong-sŏn, *Koryŏ myojimyŏng chipsŏng*, p. 581.

84. Yi Haeng, *Sinjŭng Tongguk yŏji sŭngnam*, *kwŏn* 14, "Hong Kwidal ki" 洪貴達記, "Ch'ungju" 忠州, 1: 7.

85. Yi Saek, "Yi In-bok myojimyŏng" 李仁復墓誌銘, *Mo'kŭn sŏnsaeng mungo*, 15.10b, reprinted in *Han'guk munjip ch'onggan*, 5: 127; also in Kim Yong-sŏn, *Koryŏ myojimyŏng chipsŏng*, pp. 585–86. His biography in the *KS* (112.352–53 李仁復傳) omits his travels to Pokju.

86. Yi Saek, "Yi Kong myojimyŏng" 李公墓誌銘, *Mo'kŭn sŏnsaeng mungo*, 16.10a, reprinted in *Han'guk munjip ch'onggan*, 5: 157. Also in Kim Yong-sŏn, *Koryŏ myojimyŏng chipsŏng*, p. 571.

87. For the case of a minister who had formerly served in the Bureau of Personnel, see Kwŏn Kŭn, "Yu myŏng Chosŏn guksi Mun'gan Kong An myobimyong pyŏng sŏ" 有明朝鮮國謚文簡公安墓碑銘並序, *Yangch'on chip*, 38.2a–b, reprinted in *Han'guk munjip ch'onggan*, 7: 332.

88. *KS*, 111.332 李嵒傳. The official was Yi Am's son, Yi Kang.

89. Sŏ Kŏjŏng 徐居正 (1422–88), "Song Ch'ungch'ŏng kamsa Yi kong sisŏ" 送忠清監司李公詩序, *Saga chip* 四佳集, *munjip* 文集, 6.3b, reprinted in *Han'guk munjip ch'onggan*, 11: 271.

90. *KS*, 107.284 權近傳. Kwŏn was decrying the lack of decorum of King U's night rides when he left the palace accompanied by only a few companions.

91. *KS*, 39.43a 恭愍王十年十一月辛未 (Yŏnse ed., 1: 789; MJ, p. 602); *Koryŏsa chŏryo*, 27.18a, p. 695.

92. See, e.g., conditions at Ŭnjuk 陰竹 county (*KS*, 39.42a–b 恭愍王十年十一月壬申 [Yŏnse ed., 1: 789; MJ, p. 602]).

93. Yi Saek, "Ch'oe Kong myojimyŏng" 崔公墓誌銘, *Mo'kŭn sŏnsaeng mungo*, 15.24a, reprinted in *Han'guk munjip ch'onggan*, 5: 134; also in Kim Yong-sŏn, *Koryŏ myojimyŏng chipsŏng*, p. 596. Although removed from office at this time, he would later serve as a censor and gained an aristocratic title (*KS*, 111.344 崔宰傳).

94. Paek Mun-bo, "Yŏnghoru Kŭmbang ki" 映湖樓金牓記, *Tam'am munjip iljip*, 2.9a–b, reprinted in *Han'guk munjip ch'onggan*, 3: 313: *Han'guk yŏktae munjip ch'ongsŏ*, 12: 116–17; also reprinted in Yi Haeng, *Sinjŭng Tongguk yŏji sŭngnam*, *kwŏn* 24, "Andong" 安東, "Nujŏng" 樓亭, 2: 7–8.

95. Paek Mun-bo, "Yŏnghoru Kŭmbang ki," *Tam'am munjip iljip*, 2.9a–b, reprinted in *Han'guk munjip ch'onggan*, 3: 313: *Han'guk yŏktae munjip ch'ongsŏ*, 12: 116–17; also reprinted in Yi Haeng, *Sinjŭng Tongguk yŏji sŭngnam*, *kwŏn* 24, 2: 8.

96. This description of Pokju and court personnel links to the region is drawn largely from Kim Ho-jong, "Kongminwang ŭi Andongmongjin e kwan-

han il yŏn'gu." See also Yi Kyŏng-hĭ, "Koryŏmal Honggŏnjok ŭi ch'im'ip," pp. 54–64.

97. *KS*, 39.43a 恭愍王十年十一月辛未 (Yŏnse ed., 1: 789; MJ, p. 602); *Koryŏsa chŏryo*, 27.18b–19b, p. 695–96 恭愍王十年十一月辛未. Matthew Paris would include a similar barbarity in a 1245 entry of his chronicle based on information taken from an Englishman in the service of the Mongols as recorded by Yvo of Narbona. "Virgins were deflowered until they died of exhaustion; then their breasts were cut off to be kept as dainties for their chiefs, and their bodies furnished a jovial banquet to the savages" (Ronay, *The Tartar Khan's Englishman*, p. 231). Rumors of the Mongols' cannibalism were common among Europeans of the day (Jackson, *The Mongols and the West*, p. 140). As Lu Nanqiao ("Yuanmo Hongjinjun qiyi," p. 46), who is sympathetic to the Red Turbans, points out, however, claims of cannibalism must be viewed with skepticism, since this was a common way to vilify and dehumanize the enemy. Besides, Lu notes, the Red Turbans were vegetarians!

98. For an English-language biographical note on Naong based on his epitaph, see Vermeersch, *Power of the Buddhas*, pp. 411–12.

99. The monk's personal name was Dhyana badra. For a biographical study, see Kim Hyŏng-u, "Hosŭng Chigong yŏn'gu"; cf. Sørensen, "Lamaism in Korea During the Late Koryŏ Dynasty," pp. 75–76.

100. The translation is adopted from Waley, "New Light," p. 372. I thank my colleague Sen Tansen for bringing this article to my attention.

101. The official's name was Chagha'an-Temür, no relation to the eminent Mongol general of the late Yuan of the same name.

102. Waley, "New Light," p. 372.

103. *KS*, 35.546 忠肅王十五年七月庚寅; cited in Chen Gaohua, "Yuandai laihua," p. 64.

104. Waley, "New Light," pp. 373–74.

105. *KS*, 42.632 恭愍王十九年正月甲寅. Prior to this, they had been housed at the Wangryun Temple 王輪寺, where King Kongmin viewed them. See also Chen Gaohua, "Yuandai laihua," p. 64.

106. Chen Gaohua ("Yuandai laihua," p. 63) notes that several Indian monks traveled to China during the Yuan period.

107. Song Lian, "Ji zhao yuan ming da chanshi bifeng jin gong sheli tabei" 寂照圓明大禪師壁峰金公舍利塔碑, in *Song Lian quanji* 宋濂全集 (Hangzhou: Zhejiang guji chubanshe, 1999), 2: 661; cited in Chen Gaohua, "Yuandai laihua," p. 64.

108. Waley, "New Light," p. 360. Similar attitudes toward senior Buddhist clerics held in Koryŏ at the time. Buddhist monks like Sin-don were not held rigorously to normal social hierarchies. "Previously he was a member of the

sangha. [Observance of such social hierarchies] were rightly put aside. There was no need to upbraid him for his lack of manners." Once he became a minister, however, he was expected to follow court etiquette (*KS*, 112.355 李存吾傳).

109. Kim Hyŏng-u, "Hosŭng Chigong yŏn'gu," p. 10.

110. Ibid., pp. 14–23.

111. Kak Hong 覺宏, "Naong hwasang haengsang" 懶翁和尚行狀, *Naong chip* 懶翁集, in *Han'guk yŏktae munjip ch'ongsŏ*, 25: 258. This detail is not included in Yi Saek's biography of Naong.

112. Yi Saek, "Hoeamsa sŏn'gak wangsabi" 檜巖寺禪覺王師碑, in Chōson sōtokufu, *Chōson kinseki sōran*, 1: 501.

113. Kak Hong, "Naong hwasang haengsang," *Naong chip*, in *Han'guk yŏktae munjip ch'ongsŏ*, 25: 258. This detail is not included in Yi Saek's biography of Naong.

114. Naong claimed that Sunyadisya had previously made plans to refurbish the temple and that he had a responsibility to realize his master's wishes (Yi Saek, "Hoeamsa sŏn'gak wangsabi," in Chōson sōtokufu, *Chōson kinseki sōran*, 1: 499; Kim Hyŏng-u, "Hosŭng Chigong yŏn'gu," p. 18, also refers to this passage).

115. In 1356 Pou was appointed abbot of Kwangmyŏng Temple 廣明寺.

116. Yi Sang-sŏn ("Kongminwang kwa Pou") argues that Pou played an often "decisive role" in such major political events of Kongmin's early reign as the execution of Cho Il-sin, the purge of the Ki family, and the preparations to relocate the capital to Hanyang (present-day Seoul). Evidence for Pou's ties to the Ki purge is sparse. In "Wŏnjŭng kuksa Pou wa Kongminwang ŭi kaehyŏk chŏngch'i," a more detailed essay, Yu Yŏng-suk similarly argues that Pou became a key spiritual and political advisor to the king. Yu notes that before each major "anti-Yuan" political incident of Kongmin's reign, he met with Pou.

117. Yu Ch'ang 維昌, "Pou haengsang" 普愚行狀, appended to Pou, *T'aego hwasang ŏrok*, 48a, 25: 595.

118. *KS*, 39.42b 恭愍王十年十二月壬辰 (Yŏnse ed., 1: 789; MJ, p. 602).

119. On this trend, see Matsuda, "Kōkin no ran," pp. 8–11. Köke-Temür also received this appointment (Matsumoto, "Minsho no Sōheikan," pp. 40–41). Matsumoto discusses the evolution of the title during the first decades of the Ming dynasty.

120. Prior to this, Chŏng had repeatedly urged the king to make such a proclamation (*KS*, 118.372 鄭世雲傳).

121. *KS*, 113.372 鄭世雲傳.

122. Yi Saek, "Yu kong myojimyŏng" 柳公墓誌銘, *Mo'kŭn sŏnsaeng mungo*, 18.4a, reprinted in *Han'guk munjip ch'onggan*, 5: 154; also in Kim Yong-sŏn, *Koryŏ myojimyŏng chipsŏng*, p. 602.

123. *KS*, 113.372 鄭世雲傳.

124. Ibid.

125. Ibid. Translation of *susijung* is based on Hucker, *Dictionary*, p. 423, and takes *su* as "acting." This passage is not included in Yi Saek's biography of Yi Am.

126. Yi Saek, "Yi Mun-jŏng kong myojimyŏng" 李文貞墓誌銘, *Mo'kŭn Sŏnsaeng mungo*, 17.7a, reprinted in *Han'guk munjip ch'onggan*, 5: 148; also in Kim Yong-sŏn, *Koryŏ myojimyŏng chipsŏng*, p. 567.

127. *KS*, 39.43a 恭愍王十年十二月丙申 (Yŏnse ed., 1: 790; MJ, p. 603); *Koryŏsa chŏryo*, 27.18a, p. 631. Title not included in list of titles in *Bibliographical Guide to Traditional Korean Sources*. Rendering in text based on explanation of Yuan usage (Hucker, *Dictionary*, p. 386).

128. *KS*, 39.43a 恭愍王十年十二月丁酉 (Yŏnse ed., 1: 790; MJ, p. 603); *Koryŏsa chŏryo*, 27.20a, p. 696 恭愍王十年十二月壬辰.

129. *Koryŏsa chŏryo*, 27.20a–b, p. 696 恭愍王十年十二月壬辰. See also Kwŏn Kŭn, "Kŭkjŏknu ki" 克敵樓記, *Yangch'on chip*, 13.3b–5a, reprinted in *Han'guk munjip ch'onggan*, 7: 143–44. A hall was constructed to commemorate the victory.

130. *KS*, 39.603 恭愍王十年十二月丁酉; *Koryŏsa chŏryo*, 27.20b, p. 696 恭愍王十年十二月壬辰. One wonders about the credibility of claims that "hereafter, the rebels did not dare enter the prefect's jurisdiction."

131. *KS*, 39.601 恭愍王十年十一月庚戌, 丙辰.

132. *KS*, 113.372 鄭世雲傳. The minister of rites was Yi Sun.

133. *KS*, 39.42b–3a 恭愍王十年十二月乙未 (Yŏnse ed., 1: 789–90; MJ, pp. 602–3). See also *Koryŏsa chŏryo*, 27.20a, p. 696 恭愍王十年十二月壬辰. Days earlier, the king had practiced archery beneath the Western Tower (*KS*, 39.42b 恭愍王十年十二月甲午 [Yŏnse ed., 1: 789; MJ, p. 602]).

134. *KS*, 111.342 趙暾傳.

135. The officer killed was Cho Yŏng-jŏk 趙英赤. Others like Cho To-jok 趙都赤 were granted posts in the commandery and rewarded with symbols of royal favor like "gold passes" 金牌 (*KS*, 39.588 恭愍王五年六月己未).

136. *KS*, 111.342–43 趙暾傳.

137. *KS*, 40.1a 恭愍王十一年正月戊申 (Yŏnse ed., 1: 791; MJ, p. 603); *Koryŏsa chŏryo* 27.20b, p. 696 恭愍王十一年正月.

138. The dating is uncertain. It appears in an entry from February 12, 1362. The passage reads that "before dawn of the 乙未" the fighting began. Earlier in the entry, the Korean troops arrived and took up positions around the capital. Is it possible the attack took place less than twenty-four hours after the troops arrived? The rapid attack would certainly explain the Red Turban's insufficient vigilance. If so, the date should be 乙丑. The next 乙未 appears in

the second lunar month—March 15, 1362. However, many entries in the *Koryŏsa* appear before March 15, 1362.

139. *KS*, 40.1a–b 恭愍王十一年正月甲子 (Yŏnse ed., 1: 791; MJ, p. 603). For further details of Yi Sŏng-gye's heroics, including his wounds (spear cut in right ear), his head count (seven or eight men), and the inspiring example of his valor, see *KS*, 113.9a 鄭世雲傳 (Yŏnse ed., 3: 472; MJ, 374–75).

140. *KS*, 113.9a–b, 3: 472.

141. The figure of 100,000 heads appears in *KS*, 40.1a–b 恭愍王十一年正月甲子 (Yŏnse ed., 1: 791; MJ, p. 603).

142. *KS*, 40.1a–b 恭愍王十一年正月甲子 (Yŏnse ed., 1: 791; MJ, p. 603); 113.9a 鄭世雲傳 (Yŏnse ed., 3: 472; MJ, p. 374).

143. *KS*, 40.1b 恭愍王十年正月庚午 (Yŏnse ed., 1: 791; MJ, p. 603).

144. Quan Heng and Ren Chongyue, *Gengshen waishi jianzheng*, p. 108.

145. This is an allusion to Taiwang (that is, the grandfather of King Wen), who yielded his territory of Bin in northwestern Shaanxi province (approximately 80 miles northwest of present-day Xi'an) to the encroaching Xianyun 獫狁 from the steppe. Mencius would later celebrate his decision as sparing his people from suffering. See Mencius, "Liang Hui Wang zhang ju xia" 梁惠王章句下, in Yang Bojun 楊伯峻, ed., *Mengzi yizheng* 孟子譯證 (Beijing: Zhonghua shujua, 1960, sixth printing 1984), passages 2.3, pp. 30–31, and 2.15, pp. 50–55. For an English translation of these passages, see D. C. Lau, *Mencius* (Hammersmith, Eng.: Penguin, 1976, 1988), pp. 62, 71–72.

146. The "invasions of the hounds" refers to the 755 An Lushan rebellion that nearly destroyed the Tang dynasty. For discussion of the revolt and its impact, see Charles Peterson, "Court and Politics in Mid- and Late T'ang," and Michael Dalby, "Court Politics in Late T'ang Times," in *CHC*, vol. 3, pt. 1, pp. 468–97 and 561–71, respectively.

147. For treatment of the Red Eyebrow rebellion and the revival of the Han dynasty, see Hans Bielenstein, "Wang Mang, the Restoration of the Han Dynasty, and Later Han," in *CHC*, 1: 243–251. Liu Xiu 劉秀 (7 BCE–57 CE; r. 25–57) reigned as the first emperor of the Eastern Han.

148. For brief comments on the role of Yellow Turbans in the fall of the Han, see B. J. Mansvelt Beck, "The Fall of the Han," in *CHC*, 1: 366–69. For brief discussion of the legitimacy of the Wei dynasty, see ibid., pp. 373–76.

149. Both the Spring and Autumn period Sun Wu 孫武 and the Warring States period Wu Qi 吳起 were famed military strategists and writers.

150. Professor Nakasuna Akinori 中砂明德 of Kyoto University has suggested that this phrase should be rendered as "[I, Chŏng,] wielded great power in Koryŏ" (pers. comm., Oct. 2006).

151. A Warring States period military strategist, Tian Dan was famed for his use of deception. For his biography, see Sima Qian 司馬遷, *Shiki kaichū kōshō* 史記會注考證, ed. Takigawa Kametarō 滝川亀太郎 (Tokyo: Tōyōbunka gakuin kenkyūjo, 1932–34; reprinted—Taibei: Hongshi chubanshe, 1982), 82.997–99. For an English translation, see Sima Qian, *Records of the Grand Historian of China*, pp. 30–35.

152. Famed for his skill in mounted archery, clever stratagems, and solicitous treatment of his troops, Military Commissioner Li Su (d. 821) attacked Caizhou one snowy night in 817 to capture Wu Yuanji 吳元濟 and bring the Huaixi 淮西 region under imperial control (Liu Xu, *Jiu Tangshu*, 15.461).

153. For Han Xin's exploits, see Sima Qian, "Marquis of Huai-yin," *Records of the Grand Historian of China*, 1: 214–17.

154. The passage is from "The Counsels of the Great Yu" 大禹謨 section of the *Shujing* 書經. James Legge translates the passage as follows: "The emperor also set about diffusing his accomplishments and virtue more widely. They danced with shields and feathers between the two staircases of the court" (Legge, *The Shoo king*, pt. II, chap. 3, 21, in his *Chinese Classics*, 3: 66–67).

155. The last two lines are not clear to me. 致清明於會朝，戴仲鼇抃之誠，佇瞻望於行在. The North Korean translation runs something along the lines of "through our joy and sincerity, a new and brilliant court has come about. The world, too, will certainly quickly become bright and clear. Respectfully we wish Your Majesty long life" (10: 118). The line 致清明於會朝 seems to derive from the "Da ya da ming" 大雅大明 section of the *Shijing* 詩經, 肆伐大上，會朝清明, which Legge has rendered as "Wu smote the great Shang. That morning's encounter was followed by a clear bright day" (*The She king*, Book One, Ode II, *Chinese Classics*, 4: 436).

156. *KS*, 113.372 鄭世雲傳.

157. Ibid.

158. Translation tentative.

159. Kim Ku-yong, *Ch'ŏk'yakjae hak'ŭm chip* 惕若齋學吟集, *sang* 上 7a. Describing the 1359 incursion, Kim began with the image of "ravenous beasts" and closed with "the stalwarts fled, shouldering their halberds," that is, the royal army was helpless before the Red Turban forces.

160. Kwŏn Kŭn, "Kŭkjŏknu ki" 克敵樓記, *Yangch'on chip*, 13.4a, reprinted in *Han'guk munjip ch'onggan*, 7: 143.

161. Translation tentative and is based on Hucker, *Dictionary*. "Two ministers" may refer to the heads of the Two Departments (*yangbu*), the Secretariat-Chancellery and the Security Council; see Duncan, *Origins of the Chosŏn Dynasty*, p. 27.

162. *KS*, 113.372 鄭世雲傳.

163. *KS*, 40.1b 恭愍十一年正月己巳 (Yŏnse ed., 1: 791; MJ, p. 603).

164. Yi Saek, "Chŭng sajung Chŏng kong hwasang ch'an pyŏng sŏ" 贈侍中鄭公畫像讚並序, in *Mo'kŭn sŏnsaeng mungo*, 12.7a, reprinted in *Han'guk munjip ch'onggan*, 5: 104; also in *Han'guk yŏktae munjip ch'ongsŏ*, vol. 20, part 6, p. 268.

165. *KS*, 113.370 安祐傳.

166. *KS*, 40 恭愍王十二年正月己巳 (Yŏnse ed., 1: 791; MJ, p. 603); *Koryŏsa chŏryo*, 27.22a 恭愍十二年正月甲子, p. 697.

167. *KS*, 40.1b 恭愍王十二年正月庚午 (Yŏnse ed., 1: 791; MJ, p. 603).

168. *KS*, 40.603–4 恭愍王十二年正月辛未.

169. *KS*, 40.604 恭愍王十二年正月壬申.

170. *Koryŏsa chŏryo*, 27.22b–23a, pp. 697–98 恭愍王十二年正月甲子.

171. *KS*, 40.604 恭愍王十二年正月甲戌; *Koryŏsa chŏryo*, 27.22b–23a, pp. 697–98 恭愍王十一年正月甲子.

172. *KS*, 40.604 恭愍王十二年正月乙亥.

173. *KS*, 113.370 安祐傳.

174. *KS*, 40.604 恭愍王十二年二月乙巳. The account in the basic annals of King Kongmin maintains that the attendants acted on Kim Yong's orders and without the king's knowledge.

175. *KS*, 113.370–71 安祐傳; *KS*, 40.604 恭愍王十二年三月丁未. The basic annals account dates Kim's execution to March 27, 1362.

176. Having served with An U, Hŏ Yu 許猷 was among the purge targets. Only at the intercession of Kim Yong did Hŏ avoid execution. He and his son were instead exiled to an island where they served as common soldiers in lookout towers before being recalled to the court (*KS*, 105.247–48 許珙傳附猷).

177. Much secondary scholarship follows the *KS* version. See Kang Chuchin, "Kongminwang ŭi Koryŏ chegŏn undong kwa samwŏnsu."

178. Kongmin's generals were not above murder themselves. During the Red Turban wars, Hŏ Yu, at the time a 兵馬使 who had served in Kongmin's retinue during his decade in Daidu, killed a military commander "on the basis of an old grievance." When the king discovered the matter, he "detested him" but imposed no punishment or demotion (*KS*, 105.247 許珙傳附猷).

179. *KS*, 113.372 鄭世雲傳.

180. Yi Saek, "Choe samwŏnsu kyosŏ" 罪三元帥教書, *Mo'kŭn sŏnsaeng mungo*, 11.19b, reprinted in *Han'guk munjip ch'onggan*, 5: 98; also in *Han'guk yŏktae munjip ch'ongsŏ*, 6: 247.

181. Yi Saek, "Choe samwŏnsu kyosŏ," *Mo'kŭn sŏnsaeng munjip*, 11.19b, reprinted in *Han'guk munjip ch'onggan*, 5: 98; also in *Han'guk yŏktae munjip ch'ongsŏ*, 6: 247.

182. Chŏng, "Che Kim Tŭk-pae mun" 祭金德培文, *Ŭn sŏnsaeng munjip* 隱先生文集, 1a, reprinted in *Han'guk munjip ch'onggan*, 5: 599; *KS*, 113.371 安祐傳.

183. *KS*, 113.371 安祐傳. The text does not specify when or where the boys begged. One imagines that if they were begging in Kaegyŏng, the local population would have been especially grateful, given the atrocities the city had suffered at the hands of the Red Turbans.

184. *KS*, 113.371 安祐傳. Translation is tentative. The passage is open to several translations. The first question revolves around a character, which both the Yŏnse edition and the Meiji-period typeset edition indicate should be 祼, *kwan/guan*, or "libation in offering." North Korean translation renders the passage "standing barefoot by the road" 발가 벗고 길가에 있다는, taking the character as 裸 *ra/luo* (*Puk'ŏk Koryŏsa*, 10: 112). The original text reads: 其幼子祼/裸立道旁哀之召留禁中問其所歸遣之麾下士驚潰王召賜酒食勞之.

185. The sentence could also be translated as "[the king] exiled him" or "[the king] pardoned him."

186. Yi Saek, "Yu kong myojimyŏng" 柳公墓誌銘, *Mo'kŭn sŏnsaeng munjip*, 18.4a, reprinted in *Han'guk munjip ch'onggan*, 5: 154; *KS*, 112.351 柳淑傳. When rewards were being determined for military service in the successful campaign against the Red Turbans, one man complained to Yu Suk that some like Kim Yong's nephew Kim Yim had received high posts far beyond what they deserved. Yu comforted him, saying, "Everyone knows that those who are jealous in the beginning are not jealous in the end." His words suggested that he knew more than others at the court of dark plots and just desserts.

187. Yi Saek, "Yu kong myojimyŏng," *Mo'kŭn sŏnsaeng munjip*, 18.4a, reprinted in *Han'guk munjip ch'onggan*, 5: 154; *KS*, 112.351 柳淑傳.

188. *KS*, 40.2b 恭愍王十一年二月辛丑 (Yŏnse ed., 1: 791; MJ, p. 604); *Koryŏsa chŏryo*, 27.23a–b, p. 698 恭愍王十一年二月. One account suggests that Kongmin left Pokju only after considerable urging by his prime minister, Hong Ŏn-bak (*KS*, 111.333 洪彥博傳).

189. Kim Su-on, "Tong'an nujŏng kwanp'ung nu" 東安樓亭觀風樓, *Tongguk yŏjichi*, *kwŏn* 24, 2: 6.

190. Paek Mun-bo, "Yŏngharu Kŭmbang ki" 映湖樓金牓記, *Tam'am munjip iljip* 淡庵集逸文, 2.9b, reprinted in *Han'guk munjip ch'onggan*, 3: 313; *Han'guk yŏktae munjip ch'ongsŏ*, 12: 117; also reprinted in Yi Haeng, *Sinjŭng Tongguk yŏji sŭngnam*, *kwŏn* 24, "Andong," "Nujŏng," 2: 8.

191. Hatada, "Kōrai-Ichō jidai," p. 54.

192. *KS*, 56.251 地理志一. Residents reportedly paid a hefty bribe to Kim Yong in order to regain their administrative status.

193. *KS*, 40.608 恭愍王十一年九月庚戌.

194. *KS*, 91.45 宗室二.

195. The kinsman, like other members of the Koryŏ elite, was quick to use his connections at home and at the Yuan court to advance his own interests

when stymied by the throne's efforts to rein in elite privilege (*KS*, 91.45 宗室二).

196. Yi Saek, "Yi Saek ch'ansŏ" 李穡讚序, in Yi Haeng, *Sinjŭng Tongguk yŏji sŭngnam, kwŏn* 24, "Andong" 安東, "Nujŏng" 樓亭, 2: 9.

197. Kim Chong-jik 金宗直, in Yi Haeng, *Sinjŭng Tongguk yŏji sŭngnam, kwŏn* 24, "Andong" 安東, "Nujŏng" 樓亭, 2: 10.

198. *KS*, 110.327 李齊賢傳. The time of the encounter is not clear. The passage suggests that they met in Sangju before the Red Turbans were put down. However, the king and his entourage did not pass through Sangju until they began their return from Pokju after the recapture of Kaegyŏng.

Chapter 6

1. "San Liao changbian" 三遼長編, *Liaodong zhi* 遼東志, 8.7a; "Waizhi shikao" 外志史考, *Quan Liao zhi* 全遼志, 6.41a.

2. *KS*, 40.4a 恭愍王十一年三月丁巳 (Yŏnse ed., 1: 792; MJ, p. 604).

3. Yi Haeng, *Sinjŭng Tongguk yŏji sŭngnam, kwŏn* 5, "Kaesŏngbu sang" 開城府上, "Sansŏn" 山川, 1: 132.

4. Ibid., "Kojŏk" 古蹟, 1: 160. See also *KS*, 38.582 恭愍王三年二月丙申; 38.583 三年六月己酉.

5. Yi Haeng, *Sinjŭng Tongguk yŏji sŭngnam, kwŏn* 5, "Kaegyŏngbu ha," "Kojŏk," 1: 162. Yi Sŏng-gye would eventually take the throne in this palace.

6. Vermeersch, *The Power of the Buddhas*, p. 347*n*110. Vermeersch shows that portraits and statues of the Koryŏ founder were distributed in many parts of the kingdom; Chosŏn kings also commissioned portraits and statues of the Koryŏ founder (ibid., pp. 347–48).

7. *KS*, 112.354 白文寶傳; 61.326 禮志三諸陵.

8. *KS*, 61.326 禮志三諸陵.

9. *KS*, 40.28b 恭愍王十二年五月丁亥 (Yŏnse ed., 1: 804; MJ, p. 614).

10. *KS*, 112.354 白文寶傳.

11. *KS*, 40.4b 恭愍王十一年四月庚寅 (Yŏnse ed., 1: 792; MJ, p. 605); *Koryŏsa chŏryo*, 27.25b, p. 699 恭愍王十一年四月甲子.

12. Paek Mun-bo, *Tam'am munjip iljip*, 2.5b, 12: 109.

13. *KS*, 79.615 食貨志二科斂.

14. *KS*, 77.574 百官志二諸司都監各色.

15. *KS*, 40.17a 恭愍王十二年三月乙巳 (Yŏnse ed., 1: 799: MJ, p. 609).

16. *KS*, 84.693 刑法志一職制.

17. Gao Qi, "Chaoxian er ge" 朝鮮兒歌, in *Gao Taishi da quanji* 高太史大全集, *juan* 2; reprinted in *Sibu congkan, chubian jibu* 初編集部, 81: 21–22; cited in Chang Tong-ik, *Wŏndae Yŏsa charyo chipnok*, p. 364. Chang's punctuation of this poem and others should be used with caution. I thank Professor Kang-i Sun

Chang of Yale University for suggesting several improvements to this translation (pers. comm., Sept. 22, 2005).

18. Chen Gaohua, "Yuanchao yu Gaoli de haishang jiaotong," p. 356; reprinted in idem, *Yuanshi yanjiu xinlun*, p. 371.

19. Yi Tal-ch'ung, "Chŏnbu t'an" 田婦歎, *Chejŏng sŏnsaeng munjip*, 1.9b, in *Han'guk yŏktae munjip ch'ongsŏ*, 34: 40; *Han'guk munjip ch'onggan*, 3: 277

20. *Un'gok sisa* 耘谷詩史 (1858 wood-block ed.), 1.9b–10a, reprinted in *Han'guk yŏktae munjip ch'ongsŏ*, 2201: 31–32.

21. *KS*, 112.354 白文寶傳.

22. For comments on the term "origin" (Ch. *yuan*, K. *wŏn*) in the thought of Dong Zhongshu, see Kung-chuan Hsiao, *A History of Chinese Political Thought*, pp. 484–89, esp. p. 488.

23. Paek Mun-bo, "Ch'ŏkbulso" 斥佛疏, *Tam'am munjip iljip*, 2.1a–b, reprinted in *Han'guk munjip ch'onggan*, 3: 309; *KS*, 112.354 白文寶傳.

24. *KS*, 40.612 恭愍王十二年四月丙午. In 1362, the Censorate complained that officials in the provinces were forcing such extra-legal impositions as local specialties, wine, and meat upon populations. They then offered these "tribute items" as bribes to powerful ministers in the capital. See *KS*, 84.623 刑法一職制.

25. *KS*, 82.658–59 兵志二站驛.

26. *KS*, 82.659 兵志二站驛; cited in Kim Ki-tŏk, "14 segi huban kaehyŏk chŏngch'i," p. 468*n*68.

27. *KS*, 40.4a 恭愍王十一年三月辛酉 (Yŏnse ed., 1: 792; MJ, p. 604).

28. *KS*, 81.644 兵志一五軍.

29. *KS*, 40.11a 恭愍王十一年八月丙申 (Yŏnse ed., 1: 796; MJ, p. 607).

30. *KS*, 40.14b 恭愍王十二年正月丁未 (Yŏnse ed., 1: 797; MJ, p. 609).

31. *KS*, 40.24a–b 恭愍王十二年四月丙午 (Yŏnse ed., 1: 802; MJ, p. 612).

32. *KS*, 40.28a–b 恭愍王十二年五月庚午 (Yŏnse ed., 1: 804; MJ, p. 614).

33. *KS*, 40.28b 恭愍王十二年五月丁丑 (Yŏnse ed., 1: 804; MJ, p. 614). The king banned the making of wine because of the drought.

34. *Koryŏsa chŏryo*, 27.31a, p. 702 恭愍王十年八月乙酉; *KS*, 111.333 洪彥博傳.

35. Kwŏn Kŭn, "Hong sijung hwi Ŏn-bak," *Yangch'on chip*, 35.19a–b, reprinted in *Han'guk munjip ch'onggan*, 7: 315.

36. *KS*, 63.354 禮志五雜祀; Hong Ponghan (1713–78), *Chŏngbo munhŏn pigo*, 61.19b, 1: 809.

37. *KS*, 63.354 禮志五雜祀.

38. *Tok* (Ch. *daò*, *dú*) refers to a large pennant or flag for military forces or guards. This may refer to a special ceremony with offerings to ensure victory in battle on the eve of a military campaign.

39. *KS*, 63.354 禮志五雜祀.

40. *KS*, 79.604 食貨志二户口.

41. *KS*, 85.716 刑法志二訴訟.

42. Ibid.

43. Sudō, "Sensho ni okeru nuhi no bensei to suisatsu," pp. 9–11, 20, 43, 50. In 1414, the Chosŏn court ordered that new registers be compiled and that the "old registers" from the Koryŏ dynasty be burned (ibid., pp. 18–20).

44. Ibid., pp. 2, 33.

45. *KS*, 111.346 林樸傳.

46. Reading *chae-ch'u* as a contraction of *chaesin* and *ch'usin*; see Duncan, *Origins of the Chosŏn Dynasty*, p. 26.

47. *KS*, 40.13a 恭愍王十一年十月乙亥 (Yŏnse ed., 1: 797; MJ, p. 608).

48. *KS*, 40.11b 恭愍王十一年八月丙申 (Yŏnse ed., 1: 796; MJ, p. 607).

49. *KS*, 112.353–54 白文寶傳. King Kongmin issued the orders from Ch'ŏngju 清州.

50. *KS*, 111.346 林樸傳.

51. *KS*, 110.331 李齊賢傳.

52. *KS*, 89.27 魯國大長公主傳.

53. *KS*, 40.4b 恭愍王十一年 四月丁亥 (Yŏnse ed., 1: 792; MJ, p. 605).

54. Ibid., 乙未 (Yŏnse ed., 1: 792; MJ, p. 605).

55. *KS*, 111.333 洪彦博傳.

56. *KS*, 40.13a 恭愍王十一年 十月癸酉 (Yŏnse ed., 1: 797; MJ, p. 608).

57. *KS*, 40.10a 恭愍王十一年 八月癸辰 (Yŏnse ed., 1: 795; MJ, p. 607).

58. *KS*, 77.574 百官志二諸司都監各色習射都監.

59. *KS*, 40.10b 恭愍王十一年八月戊子 (Yŏnse ed., 1: 795; MJ, p. 607).

60. Ibid., 庚寅 (Yŏnse ed., 1: 795; MJ, p. 607).

61. Ibid., 壬辰 (Yŏnse ed., 1: 795; MJ, p. 607).

62. *KS*, 40.5a–b 恭愍王十一年六月丙申 (Yŏnse ed., 1: 793; MJ, p. 605).

63. *KS*, 40.14b 恭愍王十二年正月丁未 (Yŏnse ed., 1: 797; MJ, p. 609).

64. *KS*, 77.574 百官志二諸司都監各色興王都監.

65. *KS*, 40.14b–15a (Yŏnse ed., 1: 797–98; MJ, pp. 608–9).

66. *KS*, 40.15a 恭愍王十二年二月癸未 (Yŏnse ed., 1: 798; MJ, p. 609).

67. Ibid., 甲申 (Yŏnse ed., 1: 798; MJ, p. 609).

68. Ibid., 乙酉 (Yŏnse ed., 1: 798; MJ, p. 609).

69. *KS*, 40.17a 恭愍王十二年三月庚申 (Yŏnse ed., 1: 799; MJ, p. 610).

70. Ibid., 辛亥 (Yŏnse ed., 1: 798; MJ, p. 610). The king visited Songryŏng 松嶺, north of Hŭngwang Temple.

71. *KS*, 40.17a–b 恭愍王十二年閏月辛未 (Yŏnse ed., 1: 799; MJ, p. 610).

72. Incidents like this would eventually prompt Kongmin to strengthen the royal guard. For a discussion of his Chaje Guard 子弟衛, see Yi Yong-ju, "Kongminwangdae ŭi Chajeui e kwanhan soyŏn'gu."

73. *KS*, 122.525 安都赤傳.

74. *KS*, 89.26 魯國大長公主傳.

75. These included Yu T'ak and Hong Ŏn-bak (*KS*, 112.351 柳淑傳; 111.333 洪彦博傳). Hong's biography stresses his bravery and refusal to flee, even when he had advance news that the conspirators were on their way to his residence. Equally striking is his apparent lack of concern about the king's safety. He insisted on first eating his breakfast and then painstakingly dressing himself as befitting his status as prime minister. Indeed he (and the editors of the *Official History of the Koryŏ Dynasty*) seemed far more interested in his death than his obligation to his lord in a time of crisis.

76. *KS*, 40.17a–b 恭愍王十二年閏月辛未 (Yŏnse ed., 1: 798; MJ, p. 610).

77. *KS*, 40.17b–23a 恭愍王十二年閏月辛未, 乙酉 (Yŏnse ed., 1: 799–802; MJ, pp. 610–12).

78. *KS*, 40.24a 恭愍王十二年閏月癸巳; 40.28a 恭愍王十二年四月己未 (Yŏnse ed., 1: 802, 804; MJ, p. 612, 614).

79. The combination of *xingsheng* and *tongzhi* is not listed in Hucker. A *xingsheng* in Yuan was usually headed by *chengxiang* (which Hucker renders grand councilor, rank 1B—note that *xingsheng* can also refer to "a senior provincial-level official, especially a Yuan dynasty Overseer [*ta-lu-hua-ch'ih*]," Hucker, *Dictionary*, p. 246).

80. *KS*, 40.4b 恭愍王十一年四月丙子 (Yŏnse ed., 1: 792; MJ, pp. 604–5); *Koryŏsa chŏryo*, 27.25a, p. 699 恭愍王十一年四月.

81. *KS*, 40.5a 恭愍王十一年五月乙丑 (Yŏnse ed., 1: 793; MJ, p. 605).

82. *KS*, 40.10b–11a 恭愍十一年八月乙未 (Yŏnse ed., 1: 795–96; MJ, p. 607); *Koryŏsa chŏryo*, 27.28a, p. 702 恭愍十一年八月乙酉.

83. *KS*, 40.10b 恭愍十一年八月甲午 (Yŏnse ed., 1: 795: MJ, p. 607).

84. Yu had been serving as vice minister 左政丞. On the changes in administrative nomenclature (including the post of vice minister) during Kongmin's reign, see Hwang Un-yong, "Koryŏ Kongminwangdae ŭi taeWŏn Myŏng kwan'gye." He notes the reintroduction of the post of vice minister on p. 5. The others had been serving as *miljiksa* 密直使.

85. *KS*, 40.12a 恭愍十一年八月庚戌 (Yŏnse ed., 1: 796; MJ, p. 608).

86. *YS*, 46.962 順帝本紀至正二十三年正月乙巳; Qian Qianyi, *Guochu qunxiong shilüe*, *juan* 1, p. 36.

87. *YS*, 46.963 順帝本紀至正二十三年三月是春; Qian Qianyi, *Guochu qunxiong shilüe*, *juan* 1, p. 36.

88. *YS*, 45.949 順帝本紀至正十九年是歲. A 1362 request to halt repair of the palaces indicates that efforts were made to restore the emperor's residence in Shangdu, but the dynasty fell before the construction's completion. See *YS*, 46.959 順帝本紀至正二十二年五月己未.

89. Kong Keqi, *Zhizheng zhiji*, 1.1b–2a.

90. Liu Ji, *Beixun siji*, 1b.

91. *KS*, 40.14a 恭愍十一年十二月癸巳 (Yŏnse ed., 1: 797; MJ, p. 608); *Koryŏsa chŏryo*, 27.23b, p. 703.

92. *KS*, 41.12b 恭愍王十五年八月己卯 (Yŏnse ed., 1: 817; MJ, p. 624). As a sign of his merciful disposition, the king released the birds.

93. *KS*, 41.13b 恭愍王十五年十二月癸酉 (Yŏnse ed., 1: 818; MJ, p. 625). Gaojianu's post had changed to associate administrator of the Liaoyang Branch Secretariat.

94. For Gaojianu's later role, see Robinson, "Northeast Asian Borderlands: 1350–1500" (unpublished ms).

95. "San Liao chang bian," *Liaodong zhi*, 8.7a; "Wai zhi shi kao," *Quan Liao zhi*, 6.41a–b.

96. *Ming Taizu shilu*, 56.7a–b 洪武三年九月是月; 66.4b–5a 洪武四年六月壬寅.

97. *KS*, 40.646 恭愍王二十一年正月甲戌.

98. *Ming Taizu shilu*, 76.1a–b 洪武五年九月丁巳.

99. *KS*, 133.686 辛禑王二年六月.

100. In 1379, King U would reverse roles, asserting that Kongmin and Naghachu had "called each other brother." King U pledged that he would "serve [Naghachu] as a father" (*KS*, 134.6b 辛禑王五年 六 月癸未; Yŏnse ed., p. 888; MJ, p. 700).

101. *KS*, 40.604 恭愍王十一年二月己卯.

102. For a biographical note by Hok-lam Chan, see *Dictionary of Ming Biography*, pp. 1083–85. See also Serruys, "Mongols Ennobled During the Early Ming," pp. 211–13.

103. *KS*, 40.2b 恭愍王十一年二月甲辰 (Yŏnse ed., 1: 791; MJ, p. 604).

104. *KS*, 39.7b–8a 恭愍王十一年七月 (Yŏnse ed., 1: 771; MJ, p. 605).

105. *KS*, 40.5b–10a 恭愍王十一年七月 (Yŏnse ed., 1: 793–95; MJ, p. 606).

106. Ibid.

107. *KS*, 40.10a 恭愍王十一年七月庚戌 (Yŏnse ed., 1: 795; MJ, p. 607).

108. *KS*, 41.17a 恭愍王十六年十月己未 (Yŏnse ed., 1: 820; MJ, p. 626).

109. Late in August 1357, the Koryŏ court worried that Cho would seize on "procuring gold nuggets" for tribute to the Yuan as an opportunity to bring charges against the court in administrative offices of Liaoyang. The areas of Ssangsŏng presented tribute of gold to the Yuan court every year (*KS*, 39.18a–b

恭愍王六年八月戊午 [Yŏnse ed., 1: 777; MJ, p. 593]). Driven from Ssangsŏng, in mid-May 1358, Cho had taken control of Haiyang (Kor. Haeyang 海陽), approximately 150 miles to the northeast in Jurchen lands. His control was not total, however, and a Jurchen chieftain from Haiyang named Ölje-Buqa 完者不花 led 1,800 people to Koryŏ in search of succor—"to surrender" (*KS*, 39.21b 恭愍王七年五月甲辰 [Yŏnse ed., 1: 779; MJ, p. 594]). Leaders from Haiyang Myriarchy periodically sent gifts of hunting falcons to the Koryŏ throne (*KS*, 134.32a 辛禑王七年十一月癸未 [Yŏnse ed., 1: 901; MJ, pp. 710–11]; 134.34a 辛禑王八年閏月 [Yŏnse ed., 1: 902; MJ, pp. 711]). After sending his son as a hostage, in 1382 Jintong-Buqa joined the Koryŏ dynasty, and his people were settled in the Toknour 禿魯兀 region (just west of Tanch'ŏn 端川, Hamgyŏng province 咸境); see *KS*, 134.33b 辛禑王八年二月 (Yŏnse ed., p. 902; MJ, p. 711); 134.34a 辛禑王八年閏月 (Yŏnse ed., p. 902; MJ, p. 711).

110. *KS*, 40.10a 恭愍王十一年七月庚戌 (Yŏnse ed., 1: 795; MJ, p. 607).

111. *KS*, 40.4b 恭愍王十一年四月丙戌 (Yŏnse ed., 1: 792; MJ, p. 605).

112. *KS*, 40.608 恭愍王十一年十二月癸未.

113. For discussion of Korean communities in Ming-period Liaodong, see Kawachi Yoshihiro, "Mindai Ryōyō no Tōneiei ni tsuite"; and Piao Yan 朴彥, "Mindai ni okeru Chōsenjin no Ryōtō ijū."

114. *KS*, 41.623 恭愍王十五年四月庚申.

115. *KS*, 41.627 恭愍王十七年十月癸酉. Upon his return to Koryŏ, the envoy was beaten and sent to Daidu again.

116. *KS*, 43.642 恭愍王二十年閏月己未 (1371/4/27). See *Puk'ŏk Koryŏsa*, 4: 181. Hwang Un-yong ("Koryŏ Kongminwangdae ŭi taeWŏn Myŏng kwan'gye," p. 11) translates the passage into Korean as follows: "Because Liaoyang is originally the territory of Koryŏ, if we were to surrender to the Ming, if the Koryŏ court were to offer its support [for our case], we would be able gain exemption from relocation." Hwang argues that most at the time considered Liaodong as the former territory of Koguryŏ, that Koryŏ could well succeed to that position, and that many Koreans continued to live in the region, which was not considered different from the Korean homeland. For brief remarks on this passage, see Wang Wei et al., *Zhong Chao guanxishi*, p. 62.

117. *KS*, 43.642 恭愍王二十年五月癸丑 (1371/6/14). When Liu joined the Ming, he brought the areas of Jinzhou 金州, Fuzhou 復州, Gaizhou 蓋州, and Haizhou 海州, all located along the coast of southern Liaodong (*KS*, 43.642 恭愍王二十年四月戊戌 [1371/5/30]).

118. *KS*, 40.5a 恭愍王十一年五月丁巳 (Yŏnse ed., 1: 793; MJ, p. 605); *Koryŏsa chŏryo*, 27.25b, p. 699 恭愍王十一年五月.

119. *KS*, 40.5a 恭愍王十一年六月戊寅 (Yŏnse ed., 1: 793; MJ, p. 605).

120. *KS*, 40.5b 恭愍王十一年六月丙申 (Yŏnse ed., 1: 793; MJ, p. 605).

121. Ibid.

122. Paek Mun-bo, "Ch'a Kongbuknu ŏngchesiun pyŏngsŏ" 次拱北樓應製詩韻並序, *Tam'am munjip iljip*, 1.2a–3a, reprinted in *Han'guk munjip ch'onggan*, 3: 305–36; *Han'guk yŏktae munhip ch'ongsŏ*, 12: 88–90. The incident is noted in *KS*, 40.608 恭愍王十一年九月辛酉. Paek had been in Kaegyŏng during the poetry assembly but was asked to write the preface.

123. Early in 1362, Kongmin did restore pre-Mongol period administrative titles and nomenclature, an act that many scholars offer as evidence of his nationalism; see *KS*, 40.4a 恭愍王十一年三月甲子 (Yŏnse ed., 1: 792, MJ, p. 604). The restoration, however, proved short-lived.

Chapter 7

1. *KS*, 40.608 恭愍王十一年十二月癸酉.

2. *KS*, 39.592 恭愍王五年十月戊午. Late in 1356, the Koryŏ court had requested that the Yuan court turn Tash-Temür over to its authority. In Daidu, he "cast aspersions and confused the hearts of the people," presumably in regard to the rightful king of Koryŏ (Peter Lee, ed., *Sourcebook of Korean Civilization*, pp. 362–63).

3. *KS*, 38.574 恭愍王庶文; *Koryŏsa chŏryo*, 26.7b, p. 667 忠定王三年十月. Ikeuchi ("Kōrai Kyōmin'ō," p. 124) argues that Tash-Temür was not behind the conspiracy, noting that he was probably seen as a potential candidate for the throne.

4. *KS*, 131.669 崔濡傳; Quan Heng and Ren Chongyue, *Gengshen waishi jianzheng*, p. 116. This rendering of Sambono is from Serruys, "Some Types of Names Adopted by the Mongols," p. 354. The "Three Jewels," as Serruys notes, refer to the Triratna, that is the Buddha, the Law, and the Clergy.

5. After their flight to the steppe, the Mongol Yuan court (and Naghachu) maintained a keen interest in Koryŏ's royal succession. In February 1375 (after Kongmin's murder), the Yuan attempted to put the current Sim Prince, Toqto'a-Buqa (Wang Ko's son), on the Koryŏ throne (*KS*, 133.683 辛禑元年正月; *Koryŏsa chŏryo*, 30.1b, p. 749 辛禑世家元年正月). Reports from border garrisons that the Sim Prince, his mother, and several Koreans of the Yuan court were on their way caused considerable unrest at the court (*KS*, 133.686 辛禑王元年六月). As early as November 1374, rumors about such a plan had reached the Koryŏ court (*KS*, 45.664–65 恭愍王二十三年九月辛巳). For Koryŏ officials sympathetic to the Yuan court, placing the Sim Prince on the Korean throne seemed a logical move in the wake of Kongmin's murder (*KS*, 133.686 辛禑王二年七月; 134.702 辛禑王五年十月己巳). Later in 1376, King U approved a petition that awards be distributed to civil and military officials who had foiled the plot (*KS*, 133.689 辛禑王二年十月壬申).

6. *YS*, 114.2881 后妃一. The quotation along with a notice of the abortive dethronement of Kongmin also appears in the basic chronicle of Toghan-Temür under the year 1362 (*YS*, 46.962 順帝本紀九至正二十二年是歲). See also *KS*, 131.669 崔濡傳; *Koryŏsa chŏryo*, 27.34a, p. 703 恭愍王十二年三月壬寅.

7. The same quotation about revenge also appears in Quan Heng, *Gengshen waishi*, *xia*.14a (reprinted in *Yuandai biji xiaoshuo*, 3.541); Quan Heng and Ren Chongyue, *Gengshen waishi jianzheng*, p. 116.

8. *KS*, 91.47 宗室二. His qualifications included service in the *keshig* of the Yuan heir apparent (*YS*, 42.889 順帝本紀十年十一月丙辰).

9. Liu Ji, *Beixun siji*, 2a.

10. Such major studies of Koryŏ-Yuan relations as Kim Tang-t'aek, *Wŏn kansŏpha ŭi Koryŏ chŏngch'isa*; Chang Tong-ik, *Koryŏ hugi oegyosa yŏn'gu*; and No Kye-hyŏn, *Yŏ Mong oegyosa*, do not mention the incident.

11. See Yi Yong-bŏm, "Ki Hwanghu," p. 509; Wang Chongshi, "Yuan yu Gaoli tongzhi jituan de lianyin," p. 41; Qiu Shushen, *Tuohuan Tiemuer zhuan*, p. 231; and Kim Sang-gi, *Sinp'yŏn Koryŏ sidaesa*, pp. 598–99. Otosaka ("Genchō no taigai seisaku," p. 44) notes Empress Ki's desire for vengeance but sees the incident as another example of the Yuan throne's attempt to interfere in the Koryŏ succession process, especially since its choice was not Kongmin's son. Han Woo-keun (*History of Korea*, pp. 180–81) briefly describes the incident but jumbles the chronology, dating events to after 1368.

12. Min Hyŏn-gu, *Koryŏ chŏngch'isa non*, pp. 346–47. This builds on a dual-level analysis, that is, a strong undercurrent of anti-Yuan sentiment running throughout Korean society and the particulars of individual political incidents, which Min has used in his previous essays on King Kongmin. I discovered Min's essay only after this chapter had been completed and part of it published elsewhere; see Robinson, "Mongoru teikoku no hōkai to Kōrai Kyōmin'ō no taigai seisaku."

13. *KS*, 40.608 恭愍王十一年十二月癸酉.

14. Ibid., 癸巳.

15. *KS*, 40.608 恭愍王十二年正月癸卯.

16. I thank Professor Nakasuna Akinori of Kyoto University for improving the translation of this passage.

17. Yi Saek, "P'yŏng Hongjok hu chinjŏng p'yo" 平紅賊後陳情表, *Mo'kŭn mungo*, 11.1a–b, reprinted in *Han'guk munjip ch'onggan*, 5: 89; *Han'guk yŏktae munjip ch'ongsŏ*, vol. 20, pt. 6, pp. 210–11; *KS*, 40.609 恭愍王十二年三月壬寅 (1363/3/17).

18. Gui Yang 歸暘 (1305–67), "Naiman gong shengci ji" 迺蠻公生祠記, reprinted in *Quan Yuan wen*, 51.110.

19. *KS*, 40.609 恭愍王十二年三月壬寅.

20. My thanks to Professor Nakasuna Akinori for help with the translation of these two sentences.

21. Legge renders the expression *kangning* as "soundness of body and serenity of mind"; see "The Great Plan," *The Shoo King*, Part V, Bk. IV, in *The Chinese Classics*, 2: 343.

22. Kim Sang-gi, *Sinp'yŏn Koryŏ sidaesa*, pp. 596–97; Min Hyŏn-gu, *Koryŏ chŏngch'isa non*, p. 332. See *Koryŏsa chŏryo*, 27.34a, p. 703 恭愍王十二年三月壬寅.

23. For detailed discussion of Ayushiridara's position at the Yuan court, see Han Zhiyuan, "Aiyoushilidala yu Yuanmo zhengzhi." For more general discussion of the place of the heir apparent in the Yuan polity, see Chen Yiming, "Lun Yuandai taizi canzheng wenti."

24. *YS*, 114.2880–82 后妃一.

25. *KS*, 40.25b–26a 恭愍王十二年四月甲寅 (Yŏnse ed., 1: 803; MJ, pp. 612–13).

26. *KS*, 40.26b 恭愍王十二年四月甲寅 (Yŏnse ed., 1: 803; MJ, pp. 612–13).

27. Ibid. (Yŏnse ed., 1: 803; MJ, p. 613).

28. *KS*, 30.469 忠烈王十四年三月壬寅.

29. *KS*, 40.28b 恭愍王十二年五月丁亥 (Yŏnse ed., 1: 804; MJ, p. 614).

30. *KS*, 40.29a 恭愍王十二年五月壬戌 (Yŏnse ed., 1: 805; MJ, p. 614).

31. *KS*, 40.29b 恭愍王十二年六月辛丑 (Yŏnse ed., 1: 805; MJ, p. 615).

32. *KS*, 40.31a 恭愍王十二年六月戊申 (Yŏnse ed., 1: 806; MJ, p. 615).

33. *KS*, 40.30a–b 恭愍王十二年七月甲戌 (Yŏnse ed., 1: 806; MJ, p. 615).

34. *KS*, 40.29b 恭愍王十二年七月甲戌 (Yŏnse ed., 1: 805; MJ, p. 615).

35. *KS*, 40.615 恭愍王十二年七月戊寅.

36. *KS*, 40.616 恭愍王十二年十二月.

37. *KS*, 113.374 安遇慶傳.

38. *KS*, 40.616 恭愍王十三年正月丙寅.

39. *KS*, 131.670 崔濡傳.

40. The officer was Heilü 黑驢 (*KS*, 113.375–6 崔瑩傳).

41. *KS*, 40.616 恭愍王十三年正月丙寅; 113.374 安遇慶傳.

42. *KS*, 40.617 恭愍王十三年正月壬午.

43. *KS*, 113.374 安遇慶傳.

44. *KS*, 113.375–76 崔瑩傳.

45. *KS*, 113.374 安遇慶傳. When King Kongmin learned of his troops' privations, he reduced his meals as a sign of his royal empathy (*Koryŏsa chŏryo*, 27.41a, p. 707 恭愍王十二年七月).

46. *Koryŏsa chŏryo*, 27.41b, p. 707 恭愍王十二年八月.

47. Details of the fighting are sketchy. The Yuan forces entered at Ŭiju and then moved southward to Sŏnju. It is not clear whether the main army then turned eastward to Chŏngju or if the army split. Later, Ch'oe and Yi Sŏng-gye

clashed with Yuan (or perhaps Jurchen) troops at Suju, which is also in the northeast. It may be that the Yuan forces were attempting to divide Koryŏ defenses by approaching Kaegyŏng from the northwest and northeast. This, of course, was not the strategy the Mongols had pursued in their thirteenth-century campaigns against Koryŏ. Perhaps Ch'oe Yu and Tash-Temür hoped to gather supporters from former Ssangsŏng personnel or Jurchen groups in the region.

48. *KS*, 113.374 安遇慶傳.

49. *KS*, 113.375 安遇慶傳.

50. *KS*, 40.617 恭愍王十三年正月癸未.

51. *YS*, 46.962. The same figure also appears in Quan Heng, *Gengshen waishi*, *xia* 14b (reprinted in *Yuandai biji xiaoshuo*, 3.542); and Quan Heng and Ren Chongyue, *Gengshen waishi jianzheng*, p. 116.

52. Min Hyŏn-gu, *Koryŏ chŏngch'isa non*, pp. 334, 343.

53. The communication was given to the inspector of stages (Ch. *tuotuo hesun* 脱脱禾孫, M. *todqosun*). Farquhar (*The Government of China*, p. 418) notes that with the exception of Gansu, by 1332, the post had largely been abolished.

54. *KS*, 113.373–74 安遇慶傳.

55. *KS*, 39.588 恭愍王五年六月癸丑.

56. *KS*, 40.616–17 恭愍王十三年正月庚辰.

57. *KS*, 40.617 恭愍王十三年正月己丑 (1364/2/27), 辛卯 (1364/2/29), 二月乙未 (1364/3/4); *KS*, 113.375–6 崔瑩傳.

58. *KS*, 40.617 恭愍王十三年二月戊戌.

59. Ibid., 丙申,丁酉.

60. Ibid., 甲寅.

61. Ibid., 己亥.

62. Ibid. "Third deputy commander" comes from *A Bibliographical Guide to Traditional Korean Sources*, p. 560.

63. *Koryŏsa chŏryo*, 27.40b, p. 706 恭愍王十二年五月.

64. *KS*, 131.669 崔濡傳.

65. Ibid. One official, who had passed the Koryŏ civil service examination, allied himself with Tash-Temür while in Daidu on court business, returned to Koryŏ when the coup failed, and began to cultivate cotton with seeds he acquired in China. He apparently avoided any serious punishment (*KS*, 111.347–48 文益漸傳).

66. *KS*, 111.346 林樸傳.

67. There is some confusion about their exact relation. The *Koryŏsa chŏryo* account describes him as Ki's 外從兄. The *Koryŏsa* calls him her 内兄. The relation is not made explicit in Yi Saek's funerary account. Kim Tang-t'aek (*Wŏn*

kansŏpha ŭi Koryŏ chŏnghch'isa, p. 163) refers to Yi as Empress Ki's "older cousin on her mother's side" 외사촌 오빠.

68. *KS*, 112.349 李公遂傳; Yi Saek, "Yi Kong-su myojimyŏng," in *Mok'ŭn mungo*, 18.11a, reprinted in *Han'guk munjip ch'onggan*, 5: 158; also in Kim Yong-sŏn, *Koryŏ myojimyŏng chipsŏng*, pp. 571–72; *Koryŏsa chŏryo*, 27.34b, p. 703. See also Kwŏn Kŭn, "Yi Yŏngch'ŏm hwi Kong-su" 李領僉諱公遂, *Yangch'ŏn chip*, 35.16b, in *Han'guk munjip ch'onggan*, 7: 313.

69. The phrase reads 今王勤敵愾, probably a variation of 勤王禦敵, "support the ruler [during a time of crisis] and defend against the enemy." For a nearly contemporaneous usage, see Quan Heng, *Gengshen waishi*, *xia* 8b (reprinted in *Yuandai biji xiaoshuo*, 3.550); and Quan Heng and Ren Chongyue, *Gengshen waishi jianzheng*, p. 147.

70. *KS*, 112.349 李公遂傳; Yi Saek, "Yi Kong-su myojimyŏng," *Mok'ŭn mungo*, 18.11a–b, 5: 158; also in Kim Yong-sŏn, *Koryŏ myojimyŏng chipsŏng*, p. 572; *Koryŏsa chŏryo*, 27.34b–35a, pp. 703–4.

71. Yi Saek, "Yi Kong-su myojimyŏng," *Mok ' ŭn mungo*, 18.11b, 5: 158; also in Kim Yong-sŏn, *Koryŏ myojimyŏng chipsŏng*, p. 572. See also Kwŏn Kŭn, "Yi Yŏngch'ŏm hwi Kong-su," *Yangch'ŏn chip*, 35.16b, in *Han'guk munjip ch'onggan*, 7: 313.

72. Description of the hill and hall from Chen Gaohua, *Yuan Daidu*, pp. 56–57.

73. The reference is perhaps to Book VI of *The Analects*. "The Master said, 'The wise find joy in water; the benevolent find joy in mountains. The wise are active; the benevolent are still. The wise are joyful; the benevolent are long-lived'" (D. C. Lau, trans., *The Analects* [New York: Penguin Books, 1988], p. 84).

74. Chen Gaohua, *Yuan Daidu*, p. 56.

75. *KS*, 112.349 李公遂傳; Yi Saek, "Yi Kong-su myojimyŏng," *Mok'ŭn mungo*, 18.12a–b, 5: 158; also in Kim Yong-sŏn, *Koryŏ myojimyŏng chipsŏng*, p. 572.

76. *KS*, 112.349 李公遂傳; Yi Saek, "Yi Kong-su myojimyŏng," *Mok'ŭn mungo*, 18.12b, 5: 158; also in Kim Yong-sŏn, *Koryŏ myojimyŏng chipsŏng*, p. 573.

77. *KS*, 112.349 李公遂傳; Yi Saek, "Yi Kong-su myojimyŏng," *Mok'ŭn mungo*, 18.12b, 5: 158; also in Kim Yong-sŏn, *Koryŏ myojimyŏng chipsŏng*, p. 573; *Koryŏsa chŏryo*, 27.35a, p. 704.

78. *KS*, 112.349 李公遂傳.

79. *KS*, 112.349–50 李公遂傳. As he passed through the Western Capital on the way to Daidu, Yi stopped at a temple for the founder of the Koryŏ dynasty, where he vowed that he would not return home until Kongmin had been restored to the throne (*KS*, 112.349 李公遂傳).

80. *KS*, 131.670 崔濡傳.

81. Ibid. The currency of such notions is not clear. As early as 1270, the Japanese Zen priest Tōgen Eian wrote that the Mongols wished to incorporate Japanese warriors into their armies: "With the strength [of Japan and the Mongols] combined, no country could resist. That is why the Mongols now desire to subjugate Japan" (Conlan, *In Little Need of Divine Intervention*, p. 201).

82. *KS*, 40.617–18 恭愍王十三年四月甲辰, 四月甲寅, 六月乙卯, 七月丁亥.

83. *KS*, 40.618 恭愍王十三年五月癸酉.

84. Ibid. 戊寅. The Yuan informed the Koryŏ court of the fall of Shuosijian and Pak Buqa and Bolod-Temür's appointment as defender-in-chief 太尉.

85. *KS*, 40.618 恭愍王十三年九月己巳. Other members of the Koryŏ lobby received rewards on their return from Daidu (*KS*, 40.618 恭愍王十三年九月乙酉). Occasions like the presentation of gratitude provided opportunities for Koryŏ officials and members of the Mongol court to observe one another directly. For instance, Bolod-Temür was reportedly much impressed with the simplicity of speech, grave appearance, and unflappable manner of one of the Koryŏ envoys, Yi In-bok, at the imperial audience with the emperor in Daidu (*KS*, 112.353 李仁復傳).

86. *KS*, 40.618 恭愍王十三年九月己巳.

87. *KS*, 40.619 十一月辛酉.

88. Kwŏn Kŭn, "Yi Yŏngch'ŏm hwi Kong-su," *Yangch'ŏn chip*, 35.16b, in *Han'guk munjip ch'onggan*, 7: 313.

89. *KS*, 40.618 恭愍王十三年十月辛丑.

90. The Yuan censor Nürin (Ch. 紐燐) submitted a memorial sharply critical of Ch'oe at this time. His arguments and language strongly resemble those contained in appeals from the Koryŏ court to various branches of the Yuan government. It seems likely that Nürin was allied with the Koryŏ court and had been provided with talking points by supporters of Kongmin (*KS*, 131.670 崔濡傳).

91. Wŏn Ch'ŏn-sŏk, *Un'gok sisa* 耘谷詩史, 1.15a–b, 2201: 42–43.

92. Nonstandard characters: 扠 without the dot; 旌 with 正 instead of 生.

93. Wŏn Ch'ŏn-sŏk, *Un'gok sisa* 耘谷詩史, 1.4a–b, 2201: 20–21.

94. *KS*, 40.612 恭愍王十二年四月壬子; *Koryŏsa chŏryo*, 27.37b, p. 705 恭愍王十二年四月壬子.

95. *Koryŏsa chŏryo*, 27.33b, p. 703 恭愍王十一年十二月.

96. *YS*, 46.967 順帝本紀至正二十四年七月戊子.

97. Dardess, *Conquerors and Confucians*, pp. 118–56; Mote, "Rise of the Ming Dynasty," in *CHC*, vol. 7, pt. I, pp. 19–23; Zhou Liangxia and Gu Juying, *Yuanshi*, pp. 659–67; Chen Dezhi et al., *Zhongguo tongshi*, 13: 543–47, 14: 390–94.

98. *KS*, 112.350 李公遂傳; Yi Saek, "Yi Kong-su myojimyŏng," *Mok'ŭn mungo*, 18.13a, reprinted in *Han'guk munjip ch'onggun*, 5: 159; also in Kim Yong-sŏn, *Koryŏ myojimyŏng chipsŏng*, p. 573.

99. *KS*, 112.349 李公遂傳; Yi Saek, "Yi Kong-su myojimyŏng," *Mok'ŭn mungo*, 18.13a, reprinted in *Han'guk munjip ch'onggun*, 5: 159; also in Kim Yong-sŏn, *Koryŏ myojimyŏng chipsŏng*, p. 573.

100. *YS*, 204.4604 逆臣傳 (Bolod-Temür's biography); *YS*, 46.968 順帝本紀至正二十四年八月是月; Quan Heng, *Gengshen waishi*, *xia* 5b (reprinted in *Yuandai biji xiaoshuo*, 3.544); Quan Heng and Ren Congyue, *Gengshen waishi jianzheng*, p. 125. The question of the Koryŏ throne does not appear in Chinese accounts.

101. The early Ming writer Ye Ziqi ("Ke jin pian" 克謹篇, *Cao mu zi*, *juan* 3, *shang*, pp. 45, 55) maintained that Bolod-Temür wished to eliminate Ayushiridara as heir apparent to the Yuan throne. Bolod-Temür would then position his own grandson, the young son of Bayan Qutuq, as Toghan-Temür's successor.

102. *YS*, 46.965 順帝本紀至正二十三年; 207.4602 逆臣鐵失傳至正二十三年十月. The two men were Laodisha 老的沙 and Tughlugh-Temür. A Qarluq Turk, Laodisha was the emperor's maternal uncle. The emperor had repeatedly tried to persuade the heir apparent not to pursue his grievance against Laodisha. Although the majority of entries in the *YS* portray the two refugees as outlaws, the biographies of Köke-Temür and Bolod-Temür note explicitly that the emperor had secretly ordered Bolod-Temür to protect the men (*YS*, 141.3390 擴廓帖木兒傳; 207.4602 逆臣孛羅帖木兒傳). For a brief discussion of Laodisha, with an emphasis on his identity as a Muslim Turk, see Ma Juan, "Yuandai Halaluren Laodisha shulüe," pp. 128–30. Ma suggests that the Chinese *sha* should be understood as "shah." See also the similar comments of Yang Zhijiu, *Yuandai Huizu shigao*, pp. 231–32. Yang notes the rarity of Muslims in the very highest government posts during the late Yuan. Part of Laodisha's decision to seek refuge with Bolod-Temür grew from the recent purges carried out against censors who dared to air public criticism of powerful figures like Empress Ki and the heir apparent. Offending censors were reassigned, stripped of their posts, and, in at least one case, exiled to Turfan. Laodisha had been serving as a censor. See Zhao Yongchun and Lan Ting, "Yuan Shundi shiqi de dangzheng ji qi weihai," p. 27. On the role of the Censorate in factional struggles during Toghan-Temür's reign, see Liu Yanbo, "Lüelun Shundi shiqi tongzhi jieji neibu douzheng de tedian," pp. 18–19.

103. *YS*, 46.966 順帝本紀至正二十四年三月辛卯, 四月甲午; 207.4602–3 逆臣鐵失傳. The biographies of Köke-Temür and Shuosijian note that Shuosijian and Pak Buqa had falsely charged Bolod-Temür and Laodisha with treason (*YS*, 141.3390 擴廓帖木兒傳; 205.4587 搠思監傳).

104. *YS*, 46.966 順帝本紀至正二十四年四月丁未; 207.4603 逆臣鐵失傳; 205.4587–88 搠思監傳. The two men were Shuosijian and the Korean eunuch Pak Buqa. The emperor approved calls from one censor to exhume and to violate Shuosijian's corpse because of the severity of his crimes. The family property was confiscated and his son sent into exile.

105. *YS*, 46.967–68 順帝本紀至正二十四年七月，八月，十月己未; 207.4603 逆臣鐵失傳.

106. Chen Zuren 陳祖仁, "Hanlin chengzhi Chuguo Li Gong xingzhuang" 翰林承旨楚國李公行狀, in Li Shizhan, *Jingji wenji*, 6.36a. The text reads: 達積世之先勳名曰逆子犯無君之大惡號爲賊臣仍拘執來使以釋群疑獎勵諸軍以圖大舉. Li took up his position as Minister of the Left of the Liaoyang Secretariat.

107. *YS*, 207.4604 逆臣鐵失傳; 141.3390 擴廓帖木兒傳; Quan Heng, *Gengshen waishi*, *xia* 5b (reprinted in *Yuandai biji xiaoshuo*, 3.544); Quan Heng and Ren Chongyue, *Gengshen waishi jianzheng*, p. 125. Quan Heng's wording suggests that her removal was part of Bolod-Temür's efforts to revitalize the court, which also included cuts in court spending, construction, and so forth discussed above. Quan noted that she stayed outside Houzai Gate 後(*sic*)載門, which was located on the northern wall of the imperial city, in front of the present-day Youth Palace in Jingshan Park. The character *hou* 厚 was also used for the gate (Chen Gaohua, *Yuan Daidu*, p. 53).

Empress Ki's biography in the *YS* (14.2881 后妃一) maintains that although Bolod-Temür requested that Ki be removed from the palace, the emperor "did not respond." It notes explicitly that Bolod-Temür "falsified an order" to have her put under house arrest.

108. *YS*, 46.969 順帝本紀至正二十五年四月庚寅; 114.2881 后妃一.

109. *YS*, 46.969 順帝本紀至正二十五年六月乙巳.

110. The biography of Empress Ki notes that she "again presented beautiful women to Bolod-Temür several times. Only after one hundred days did she return to the palace" (*YS*, 114.2881 后妃一).

111. Quan does not note whether the woman was Korean. Empress Ki often presented leading court officials with Korean beauties as part of her patronage network (see Chapter 3). Such a practice was completely in keeping with earlier Mongolian practices whereby the Great Khan distributed women and other prizes among deserving military commanders and members of the imperial family.

112. Quan Heng, *Gengshen waishi*, *xia* 6a (reprinted in *Yuandai biji xiaoshuo*, 3.545); Quan Heng and Ren Chongyue, *Gengshen waishi jianzheng*, p. 128. Reports that explain the prominent presence of women around Bolod-Temür solely in

sexual terms reflect Chinese social and political attitudes rather than the realities of Mongol political culture in which women often played key roles.

113. The date of Bolod-Temür's assassination comes from his biography in *YS*, 207.4604. Dardess gives the date as August 16 in *Dictionary of Ming Biography*, p. 724. Among Bolod-Temür's many sins was the seizure of one of the emperor's favorite consorts (Quan Heng, *Gengshen waishi*, *xia* 6a [reprinted in *Yuandai biji xiaoshuo*, 3.545]; Quan Heng and Ren Chongyue, *Gengshen waishi jianzheng*, p. 129).

114. *YS*, 207.4605; 46.970 順帝本紀至正二十五年七月丙戌.

115. For Laodisha's death, see *YS*, 46.970 順帝本紀至正二十五年十月丁未. For Tughlugh-Temür's demise, see *YS*, 46.971 順帝本紀至正二十五年十二月是月.

116. *YS*, 46.970 順帝本紀至正二十五年九月; 104.2881 后妃一; Quan Heng, *Gengshen waishi*, *xia* 7a (reprinted in *Yuandai biji xiaoshuo*, 3.547); Quan Heng and Ren Chongyue, *Gengshen waishi jianzheng*, p. 132.

117. *YS*, 114.2881 后妃一.

118. *KS*, 41.620 恭愍王十四年正月戊辰; *Koryŏsa chŏryo* 28.9a, p. 713 恭愍王十四年正月.

119. Less than two months later, the Koryŏ throne would follow up with gifts to Heilü. The king sent Yi Cha-song to Liaoyang with presents of "white gold" and a saddle for Heilü (*KS*, 41.620 恭愍王十四年二月丙辰).

120. *KS*, 41.620 恭愍王十四年三月己巳. Less than three weeks later, Kongmin would send Yi Cha-song to Daidu to express his gratitude for the honorary titles. He used the occasion to remind the Yuan throne that despite his devotion to the Mongols, he had just narrowly escaped disaster as a result of the emperor's decision to act on the false charges made against him. Here he refers to the Tash-Temür incident (*KS*, 41.620–21 恭愍王十四年三月戊子).

121. *KS*, 43.646 恭愍王二十一年三月庚戌. The Koryŏ court was explaining why the Ming and Koryŏ courts should take a united stance against the son of Ki Ch'ŏl, Manager Sa'id Temür 平章賽因帖木兒, who, the court claimed, was attempting to mislead Ming officials in Liaodong and instigate border clashes out of hatred for the Koryŏ dynasty.

122. Quan Heng and Ren Chongyue, *Gengshen waishi jianzheng*, p. 116. The heir apparent was to be the Ki kinsman, Sambono.

123. Description from Rashīd al-Dīn, *The Successors of Genghis Khan*, p. 199.

124. George Zhao and Richard Guisso, "Female Anxiety and Female Power."

125. For concise discussion of the major factional battles of Toghan-Temür's reign, including both plots against the emperor and his efforts to

remove potential rivals like Toqto'a and later Köke-Temür (in 1367), see Zhao Yongchun and Lan Ting, "Yuan Shundi shiqi de dangzheng ji qi weihai."

126. Wada Sei, "Minsho no Manshū keiryaku," p. 92. Min Hyŏn-gu (*Koryŏ chŏngch'isa non*, p. 329) makes the same point.

Chapter 8

1. Fletcher, "The Mongols," p. 26.

2. Fletcher, "Turco-Mongolian Monarchic Tradition," pp. 240–41.

3. Chen Gaohua, "Yuanchao yu Gaoli de haishang jiaotong," pp. 355–56; reprinted in idem, *Yuanshi yanjiu xinlun*, pp. 370–72.

4. Kim Hye-wŏn, "Koryŏ Kongminwangdae taeoe chŏngch'aek kwa Han-in kun'ung"; Suematsu, "Raimatsu Sensho ni okeru taiMin kankei," pp. 132–36. Suematsu stresses the economic motivation behind these contacts, and Kim argues persuasively that they also had important military and political components. More recent scholarship undermines Suematsu's contention that trade between Koryŏ and China had "largely been discontinued since the rise of the Yuan" (Suematsu, p. 136). See works by Chen Gaohua cited above.

5. See Wada Hirotoku, "Genmatsu no gun'yū to Betonamu," pp. 44, 68.

6. *KS*, 112.354 田祿生傳.

7. Chŏn Nok-saeng, *Ya'ŭn irjip* 埜隱逸集, 6.9a, 12: 506. This chronology of Chŏn's life merely indicates that he was sent to Zhejiang, but an explanatory note adds that at the time Fang Guozhen controlled Zhejiang. Chŏn's biography in the *Official History of the Koryŏ Dynasty* omits all mention of his activities as a foreign envoy (*KS*, 112.354–55 田祿生傳).

8. Chŏn Nok-seng, *Ya'ŭn irjip*, 3.3a, 12: 434. See *KS* 40.618 恭愍十三年六月乙卯 (1364/7/22). Wang Yinglin 王應麟 (1223–96) compiled the *Yuhai*; Zheng Qiao 鄭樵 (1104–62) produced the *Tongzhi*.

9. *KS*, 41.621 恭愍十四年四月辛丑 (1365/5/4). His post at the time was censor-in-chief 監察大夫. The eunuch Pang Chŏl 方節 accompanied him on the mission. In the fifth lunar month of the next year, the Koryŏ throne sent another envoy to Köke-Temür (*Koryŏsa chŏryo*, 28.21b, p. 719 恭愍王十五年五月). At approximately the same time that Chŏn set out for Daidu, an envoy from Zhang Shicheng arrived at the Koryŏ court (*KS*, 41.621 恭愍十四年四月辛卯 [1365/4/24]). It seems curious that whereas Chŏn arrived in Daidu without incident, one Koryŏ official found conditions at the time sufficiently unsettled that that he was unable to take up his post as pacification commissioner of the Northeast Region 西北面都巡慰使 (*KS*, 41.621 恭愍十四年四月辛丑 [1365/5/4]). The *Official History of the Koryŏ Dynasty* indicates that Chŏn was sent with gifts for the heir apparent, the Sim Prince, and Köke-Temür. Chinese accounts make clear that the Yuan heir apparent left Daidu and arrived in Jining

冀寧 no later than the eighth lunar month of 1364 (至正二十四年八月乙巳). He would not return until Bolod-Temür had been killed. According to the "Basic Chronicle of the Shundi Emperor" in the *Official History of the Yuan Dynasty*, the heir apparent returned to Daidu escorted by Köke-Temür and his military forces in the ninth lunar month of 1365 (*YS*, 45.970 至正二十五年九月; 141.3391 察罕帖木兒傳).

10. *KS*, 41.623 恭愍王十五年三月庚子; Chŏn Nok-seng, *Ya'ŭn irjip*, 3.b, 12: 435; 6.10ab, p. 508. At the same time, Kongmin offered his congratulations to the Yuan heir apparent on his safe return to Daidu (*KS*, 41.623 恭愍王十五年三月庚子). As Chapter 7 noted, Bolod-Temür had driven the heir apparent out of the capital. King Kongmin was keeping all his options open.

11. *YS*, 141.3391 察罕帖木兒傳.

12. *KS*, 104.230 金方慶傳附金齊顏傳. The *Koryŏsa chŏryo* (28.23a, p. 720 恭愍王十五年六月) notes: "The heir apparent did not wish [us] to send an envoy to Henan."

13. *KS*, 104.230 金齊顏傳. See also Chŏn Nok-seng, *Ya'ŭn irjip*, 3.4a, 12: 436; *KS*, 41.624 恭愍王十五年六月壬戌.

14. *Koryŏsa chŏryo*, 28.23a, p. 720 恭愍王十五年六月.

15. *KS*, 104.230 金方慶傳.

16. *KS*, 41.623 恭愍王十五年五月乙酉 (1366/6/12).

17. *KS*, 41.624 恭愍王十五年十一月辛丑 (1366/12/25).

18. Ibid., 十二月戊申 (1367/1/1).

19. Ibid., 辛亥 (1367/1/4).

20. *KS*, 111.346 林樸傳.

21. *KS*, 41.625 恭愍王十五年十二月己未 (1367/1/12).

22. Ibid., 十六年五月戊寅 (1367/5/31). Little more than a year later, Kongmin would send Chang to meet with Zhu Yuanzhang in Nanjing (*KS*, 41.627 恭愍王十七年十一月丁未 [1368/12/20]). Chinese sources like the *Ming Taizu shilu*, *Guo que*, and *Ming shi* omit Chang's mission, although the *Official History of the Koryŏ Dynasty* maintains that Zhu Yuanzhang was deeply gratified by Chang's visit.

23. *KS*, 133.688 辛禑王二年十月.

24. Qian Qianyi, *Guochu qunxiong shilüe*, 11.244–52. See also *Ming Taizu shilu* 明太祖實錄, 吳王元年四月辛亥 3.3a; Tan Qian, *Guo que*, 2.333. Köke-Temür detained at least one of Zhu's envoys. In response, Zhu's regime penned a series of missives decrying such shabby treatment. These communications form a disproportionately large proportion of Qian's chapter on Köke-Temür. Qian's biography of Köke-Temür as well as his biography and the basic chronicle of Toghan-Temür (the Shundi emperor) from the *Official History of the Yuan Dynasty* omit mention of Köke-Temür's diplomatic relations with other

regimes at the time, probably to minimize his legitimacy. Recognition by foreign polities figured prominently in domestic legitimacy.

25. Pou, *T'aego hwasang ŏrok*, 48a, 25: 564–66. The basic chronicle of King Kongmin in the *Official History of the Koryŏ Dynasty* does not mention these ties (恭愍王十四年四月辛丑, 恭愍王十五年四月庚子, 恭愍王十五年六月壬). In 1367, envoys from "Japan" brought gifts to the Koryŏ throne (*KS*, 41.626–27 恭愍王十七年正月戊子, 十七年七月乙亥). For discussion of Japan's ties to the Yuan during the mid-fourteenth century, see below.

26. For discussion of Mingzhou's place in the wider context of the East China Sea, see Enomoto, "Meishū shihakushi to Higashi Shinakai bōekiken."

27. Kak Hong, "Naong hwasang haengsang," in Hye Kŭn, *Naong chip*, 25: 249. This detail is not included in Yi Saek's biography of Naong.

28. Kim Hye-wŏn, "Koryŏ Kongminwangdae taeoe chŏngch'aek kwa Han-in kun'ung," p. 83.

29. *KS*, 111.338 慶復興傳.

30. Kim Hye-wŏn, "Koryŏ Kongminwangdae taeoe chŏngch'aek kwa Han-in kun'ung," pp. 111–12.

31. *KS*, 42.640 恭愍王十九年九月乙巳.

32. *KS*, 41.630 恭愍王十八年九月己亥; 41.630 恭愍王十八年十月乙酉; 42.632 恭愍王十九年三月甲午; 43.644 恭愍王二十年九月癸丑; 44.652 恭愍王二十二年二月乙亥; 133.688–89 辛禑王二年十月.

33. During the last months of 1368, Toghan-Temür repeatedly asked Koryŏ to contribute troops and grain in support of the Great Yuan *ulus* (Liu Ji, *Beixun siji*, 2a–b, 3a).

34. For instance, in spring 1367, "Fang Guozhen secretly dispatched someone to contact Köke-Temür and Chen Youding. [Zhu Yuanzhang] sent a communication rebuking him" (Zhang Tingyu et al., *Ming shi*, 1.15 至正二十七年四月).

35. *KS*, 44.654 恭愍王二十二年七月壬子.

36. Zhang Wei, *Suizhong Sandaogang Yuandai chenchuan*, pp. 82–127, 134–38.

37. Sugiyama, *Dai Mongoru no jidai*, pp. 9–20; Verschuer, *Across the Perilous Sea*, pp. 95–97.

38. Enomoto, "Junteichō zenpanki ni okeru Nichi-Gen kōtsū," pp. 19–27.

39. Chen Gaohua, "Shisi shiji lai Zhongguo de Riben sengren."

40. Maritime trade also took place in ports in Fuzhou to the south.

41. Enomoto, "Nihon ensei yikō ni okeru Genchō no wasen taisaku."

42. Enomoto, "Genmatsu nairanki no Nichi-Gen kōtsū," pp. 2–3.

43. Murai Shōsuke, "Wakō to Chōsen" 倭冦と朝鮮, pp. 186–87; idem, *Bunretsu suru Ōken to shakai*, pp. 174–75.

44. *YS*, 139.3363 紐的該傳.

45. Enomoto, "Genmatsu nairanki no Nichi-Gen kōtsū," p. 8. Quotation from *Shōyōshū* 証羊集, in Tōkyō daigaku shiryō hensanjo, *Dai Nippon shiryō* 大日本史料, ser. 7, 27: 614, cited in Enomoto, p. 7.

46. Enomoto, "Genmatsu nairanki no Nichi-Gen kōtsū," p. 5. Enomoto sees the last decade or so of the Yuan as a critical turning point for Sino-Japanese relations. The unsettled conditions and precarious trade contributed to a long-term decline in interest among Japanese monks in Zen study in China. Those who traveled to Ming China during the fifteenth century were often more interested in literature than religious training (ibid., p. 22).

47. Enomoto, "Jūyon seiki kōhan, Nihon ni torai shita hitobito."

48. Kwŏn Kŭn, "P'yŏngyangsŏng Taemunnu ki" 平壤城大門樓記, *Yang-ch'on chip*, 12.b, reprinted in *Han'guk munjip ch'onggan*, 7: 135; Yi Haeng, *Sinjŭng Tongguk yŏji sŭngnam*, *kwŏn* 51, "P'yŏngyang" 平壤, "Nujŏng," 4: 20.

49. See Yi Haeng, *Sinjŭng Tongguk yŏji sŭngnam*, *kwŏn* 41, "Hwangju," "Ko-jŏk," 3: 9.

50. Ibid.

51. Kim An-guk, "Munhwahyŏn yich'i ki" 文化縣移治記, *Mojae chip* 慕齋集, 11.16b–17a (microfilm p. 6-17).

52. Kim An-guk, "Kyo Hwanghaedo kwanch'alsa mosŏ" 教黃海道觀察使某書, *Mojae chip*, 19.19b (microfilm p. 5-19).

53. Duncan, *Origins of the Chosŏn Dynasty*, pp. 182–87; quotation appears on p. 184. See also Kim Sun-ja, "Wŏn kansŏpgi min ŭi tonghyang," pp. 379–88.

54. For a color photograph of one such shrine and a painting of Kongmin and his queen, see Yi Ki-tam, *Kongminwang kwa ŭi taehwa*, p. 245.

55. Andong minsok pangmulgwan, *Andong ŭi tongje*, pp. 6–7, 14–15, 114–16, 123. I thank Mr. Yi Hŭisŭng 李憙承 of the Andong Folk Museum for kindly providing me with materials relating to the local religious shrines in Andong devoted to King Kongmin and his queen. The Notdaribalgi folk play performed each October at the Andong Folk Festival is also said have its roots in King Kongmin's time in Andong. Tradition holds that when the royal entourage arrived just outside Pokju, a brook barred its way. Local women formed a human chain over which Queen Noguk forded the brook. See Institute of Andong Culture at Andong National University, *A Cultural and Historic Journey into Andong*, pp. 35, 151–52.

56. Quoted in Tan Qian, *Guo que*, 1.300.

57. Christopher Atwood, "How the Mongols Rejected the *Secret History*," unpublished essay. I thank Professor Atwood for kindly sharing this paper with me. George Zhao ("Control Through Conciliation," p. 9*n*22) has also noticed this discrepancy.

58. For an early example of the Red Turbans as the first of the founder's "major victories," see *KS*, 137.41a (Yŏnse ed., 3: 967; MJ, p. 763;). Yi had seized power by this point.

59. Naghachu, too, is woven into the tale of Yi's prowess. The fifteenth-century editors of the *Official History of the Koryŏ Dynasty* were careful to include Naghachu's 1376 observation that he nearly lost his life in fighting against Yi (*KS*, 133.19a–b, p. 874 辛禑王二年十月).

60. Kwŏn Kŭn, "Kŏnwŏnryŏng tobibyŏng pyŏngsŏ" 有明諡康獻朝鮮國太祖至仁啓運聖文神武大王健元陵神道碑銘並序, in *Yangch'on chip*, 36.6b–7a, reprinted in *Han'guk munjip ch'onggan*, 7: 318–19; also included in Yi Haeng, *Sinjŭng Tongguk yŏji sŭngnam*, *kwŏn* 11, "Yangju" 楊州, "Yŏngmo Kŏnwŏnryŏng" 陵墓健元陵, 2: 11. The "Stone Inscription Version" 石刻本 of the eulogy included in Kwŏn's collected works does not mention the Red Turbans' attacks on Shangdu or the Liaodong region. See ibid., 36.14a–b, reprinted in *Han'guk munjip ch'onggan*, 7: 322; and "Kŏnwŏnryŏng chisŏkmun" 健元陵誌石文, *Yangch'on chip*, 39.4b, reprinted in *Han'guk munjip ch'onggan*, 7: 339.

61. See McCann, "Song of the Dragons Flying to Heaven."

62. Translation by Peter Lee, *Songs of Flying Dragons*, p. 186.

63. In 1446, King Sejong commissioned a painting of scenes from the *Song*, which were then further celebrated in verse by leading court ministers; see Pak P'aeng-nyŏn 朴彭年 (1417–56), "P'aljundo song pyŏngsŏ" 八駿圖頌並序, *Pak Sŏnsaeng yigo* 朴先生遺稿, 1.11b–14b, reprinted in *Han'guk munjip ch'onggan*, 9: 59–60; Sŏ Kŏ-jŏng 徐居正 (1420–88), "P'aljundo haeng" 八駿圖行, *Saga chip, sijip*, 3.1a–2b, reprinted in *Han'guk munjip ch'onggan*, 10: 259; Sŏng Sam-mun 成三問 (1418–56), "P'aljundo myong pyŏng'in" 八駿圖銘並引, *Sŏng kŭnbo chip* 成謹甫集, 2.11b–15a, reprinted in *Han'guk munjip ch'onggan*, 10: 196–98; and Sin Suk-ju (1417–75), "P'aljundo pu pyŏngsŏ" 八駿圖賦並敘, *Pohanjae chip* 保閑齋集, 1.5a–11a, reprinted in *Han'guk munjip ch'onggan*, 10: 10–13.

64. Paek Mun-bo, "P'an samsasa iljŏk Son gong sajang sisŏ" 判三司事一直孫公賜杖詩序, *Tam'am munjip iljip*, 2.8a–b, reprinted in *Han'guk munjip ch'onggan*, 3: 312; *Han'guk yŏktae munjip ch'ongsŏ*, 12: 115–16.

65. Yi Tal-ch'ung, "Kyerim bu-in hu chaesa p'yo" 雞林赴任後再辭表, *Chejŏng sŏnsaeng munjip*, 2.3b, 34: 61.

66. Hŏ Hŭng-sik, *Koryŏ sahoesa yŏn'gu*, pp. 452–53.

67. For periodic efforts by the Koryŏ court to repopulate the north early during the dynasty, see Nishino, "Kōraichō ni okeru Hokuhō Ryōkai chiiki ni tsuite," pp. 107–8.

68. One official complained in the 1350s that military officers in the recently established anti-piracy garrisons of Cholla province "abused the [people of the] subprefectures and commanderies to establish their authority; [they] put

to work garrison soldiers to advance their private [interests]" (*KS*, 112.354 田祿生傳).

69. Chŏng Tu-hŭi, "Koryŏmal sinhŭng muin seryŏk ŭi sŏngchang kwa ch'ŏmsŏrjik ŭi sŏrch'i."

70. Hŏ Hŭng-sik, *Koryŏ sahoesa yŏn'gu*, p. 191.

71. *KS*, 113.328 李齊賢.

72. *KS*, 111.333 洪彥博傳.

73. Hong Yŏng-wi, "Kongminwang ŭi panWŏn chŏngch'aek." Hong overstates the importance of the 1356 "anti-Yuan" policies but provides useful details.

74. *KS*, 111.339 金續命傳.

75. Yagi Takeshi 矢木毅, "Kōrai ni okeru gunreiken no kōzō to sono henshitsu."

76. Yi Hyŏng-u, "Koryŏ Kongminwangdae ŭi chŏngch'ijŏk ch'uiwa musang syeryŏk."

77. The late fourteenth-century commentator Tao Zongyi noted at this time, "Armies are murderous instruments. War subverts virtue. The sage uses them only because he has no choice." Tao was less concerned with politics than with how war brutalized society and eroded moral values; see "Yue min kao" 越民考, *Nancun chuogeng lu*, 10.125. Tao later related the story of a man who travels to hell and is taken to the edge of pond. When lictors rub pond mud on his chest, he is suddenly cold and bitterly hungry. He realizes that in an earlier lifetime he had been a Qin general, who had slaughtered 40,000 Zhao troops who had surrendered. Tao offered it as a cautionary tale for military men who enjoyed killing people ("Wei jiang shi sha" 為將嗜殺, *Nancun chuogeng lu*, 13.161–62).

78. Cong Peiyuan (*Zhongguo dongbeishi*, 3: 439) makes a similar point: "Thus, we can say the Middle Army of the Red Turbans contributed to the removal of obstacles and opened the way for the entrance of the Ming armies into the Northeast and the final liquidation of the remnant forces of the Yuan."

79. Min Hyŏn-gu (*Koryŏ chŏngch'sa ron*, pp. 340, 344) stresses that Kongmin personally directed the campaign against the invading Yuan forces in 1364 from Kaegyŏng. The evidence for such a claim is thin.

80. Wang Shizhen, "Zhu xiang lu zhong shang" 諸降虜重賞, *Yanshantang bieji* 弇山堂別集, 14.258.

81. Palais, "A Search for Korean Uniqueness."

82. See Chang Tong-ik, *Koryŏ hugi oegyosa yŏn'gu*, pp. 2–3.

83. Kim Tang-t'aek, *Wŏn kansŏpha ŭi Koryŏ chŏngch'isa*, p. 1.

84. Min Hyŏn-gu, *Koryŏ chŏngch'isa non*, p. 20.

85. Kim Ho-dong, *Mong'gol cheguk kwa Koryŏ*, p. 99.

86. Greene, "Transatlantic Colonization and the Redefinition of Empire," p. 268. I thank my colleague Antonio Barrera for bringing this work to my attention.

87. For a cogent articulation of the need to understand the fourteenth century in terms of long-term developments, most particularly those that grew out of the late twelfth century, see Pak Chong-gi, "14 segi ŭi Koryŏ sahoe."

88. Min Hyŏn-gu, *Koryŏ chŏngch'isa non*, p. 20.

89. Chang goes so far as to point out that some Mongolian influences, such as efforts to reform the Koryŏ slave system, were actually positive. Many of the essays in the 1994 edited volume *14 segi Koryŏ ŭi chŏngch'i wa sahoe* 14 세기고려의정치와사회 (Politics and society in fourteenth-century Koryŏ) similarly challenge simple bifurcations. See the introduction by Pak Chong-gi, who notes that such widely accepted historical notions as the stark contrast between the new "literati" elite and the old "powerful families" simply do not bear scrutiny. This is a central argument of Duncan's *Origins of the Chosŏn Dynasty*.

90. Chang Tong-ik (*Koryŏ hugi oegyosa yŏn'gu*, p. 125) has criticized past scholarship that dwelt exclusively on the oppressive Mongol rule of Korea with little consideration of either the positive consequences of Yuan influence or of Koryŏ motives or reactions.

91. Min Hyŏn-gu (*Koryŏ chŏngch'isa non*, p. 20) lays many of the ills of the day at the feet of these anti-reform, pro-Mongol "powerful families."

92. Kim Ho-dong's *Mong'gol che'guk kwa Koryŏ* is an important step in this direction.

93. Changguzhenyi, *Nong tian si hua, juan shang*, 3a.

94. See Li Jiben, "Liu Yishi zhuan" 劉義士傳, in *Quan Yuan wen*, 60.1028.

95. Ye Ziqi, "Ke jin pian," *Cao mu zi*, p. 51.

96. Tao Zongyi, "Xiang rou" 想肉, *Nancun chuogeng lu, juan* 9, p. 113.

97. For an overview of North China during the early Ming, state-sponsored recovery efforts, and related scholarship, see Robinson, *Bandits, Eunuchs, and the Son of Heaven*, pp. 31–33.

98. Tao Zongyi, "Zhong lie" 忠烈, *Nancun chuogeng lu*, 14.169.

99. Li Shizhan, "Yu Yuanshuai Zhu Mingshu shu" 與元帥朱明叔書, in *Quan Yuan wen*, 50.162.

100. Discussing developments in Shandong during the late Yuan, one Ming observer wrote that "among the people of Juzhou 莒州, nine of ten households abandoned their plows and took up arms. Local magnates grew in ambition; the poor grew more constrained daily" ("Zhizhou Zhao Lin ji" 知州趙麟記, *Qingzhou fuzhi*, 8.17b).

101. In a discussion of developments in the West Asian kingdom of Kart during the fourteenth century, Lawrence Potter ("Herat Under the Karts," p. 198) has written, "Loyalties seem primarily guided by pragmatic considerations. When the chips were down, political necessity overrode allegiance to one's own ethnic group."

102. For discussion of later Korean views of the Ming founder, see Seung B. Kye, "The Posthumous Image and Role of Ming Taizu in Korean Politics."

103. For an evocative account of how one young member of the Jiangnan elite came to terms with Zhu Yuanzhang's regime during the Yuan-Ming transition, see Mote, *The Poet Kao Ch'i*.

104. *KS*, 44.655 恭愍王二十二年七月壬子.

105. Ibid. I thank my colleague Wu Yue for improving this translation.

106. Murai, "Wakō to Chōsen," p. 192.

107. *KS*, 136.741 辛禑王十三年五月.

108. Pak Wŏnho, "The Liaotung Peninsula Invasion Controversy."

109. For discussion of developments in Liaodong during the early decades of the Ming, see Woodruff, "Foreign Policy and Frontier Affairs," pp. 26–119.

110. Irredentist claims were not new. Early in eleventh century, the Koryŏ court had attempted to exploit a revolt in the Liao's Eastern Capital to retake territory east of the Yalu River lost to the Khitan in earlier fighting. The campaign ended in failure (Wittfogel and Feng, *A History of Chinese Society*, p. 420*n*101). During the 1370s and 1380s, the conflicting ambitions of the Ming and Koryŏ governments in Liaodong would severely complicate their relations.

111. I take up this question in a separate work, tentatively titled "Northeast Asian Borderlands: 1350–1500."

Works Cited

Adshead, S. A. M. *Central Asia in World History*. New York: St. Martin's Press, 1993.

Allsen, Thomas. "Apportioned Lands Under the Mongols." In Anatoly Khazanov and André Wink, eds., *Nomads in the Sedentary Worlds*. Richmond, Surrey: Curzon Press, 2001, pp. 172–90.

———. "The Circulation of Military Technology in the Mongolian Empire." In Nicola Di Cosmo, ed., *Warfare in Inner Asian History*. Leiden: Brill, 2002, pp. 265–92.

———. *Commodity and Exchange in the Mongol Empire*. Cambridge: Cambridge University Press, 1997.

———. *Culture and Conquest in Mongol Eurasia*. Cambridge: Cambridge University Press, 2001.

———. "Guard and Government in the Reign of the Grand Qan Möngke, 1251–59." *Harvard Journal of Asiatic Studies* 46, no. 2 (1986): 495–521.

———. "Mongolian Princes and Their Merchant Partners, 1200–1260." *Asia Major* 2, no. 2 (1989): 83–126.

———. *Mongol Imperialism: The Policies of the Grand Qan Möngke in China, Russia, and the Islamic Lands, 1251–1259*. Berkeley: University of California Press, 1987.

———. "Rise of the Mongolian Empire and Mongol Rule in North China." In Herbert Franke and Denis Twitchett, eds., *Cambridge History of China*, vol. 6, *Alien Regimes and Border States*. Cambridge: Cambridge University Press, 1994, pp. 321–413.

———. "Robing in the Mongolian Empire." In Stewart Gordon, ed., *Robes and Honor: The Medieval World of Investiture*. New York: Palgrave, 2001, pp. 305–13.

———. *The Royal Hunt in Eurasian History*. Philadelphia: University of Pennsylvania Press, 2006.

———. "Technologies of Governance in the Mongolian Empire: A Geographic Overview." In David Sneath, ed., *Imperial Statecraft: Political Forms and Techniques of Governance in Inner Asia, Sixth–Twentieth Centuries*. Bellingham: Center for East Asian Studies, Western Washington University, 2006, 117–40.

———. "The Yüan Dynasty and the Uighurs of Turfan in the 13th Century." In Morris Rossabi, ed., *China Among Equals*. Berkeley: University of California Press, 1983, 243–80.

Andong minsok pangmulgwan 安東民俗博物館. *Andong ŭi tongje* 安東의 洞祭. Andong-si: Andong minsok pangmulgwan, 1994.

Atwood, Christopher. *Encyclopedia of Mongolia and the Mongol Empire*. New York: Facts on File, 2004.

———. "Titles, Appanages, Marriages, and Officials: A Comparison of Political Forms in the Zünghar and Thirteenth-Century Mongol Empires." In David Sneath, ed., *Imperial Statecraft: Political Forms and Techniques of Governance in Inner Asia, Sixth–Twentieth Centuries*. Bellingham: Center for East Asian Studies, Western Washington University, 2006, pp. 207–43.

———. "Ulus Emirs, Keshig Elders, Signatures, and Marriage Partners: The Evolution of a Classic Mongol Institution." In David Sneath, ed., *Imperial Statecraft: Political Forms and Techniques of Governance in Inner Asia, Sixth–Twentieth Centuries*. Bellingham: Center for East Asian Studies, Western Washington University, 2006, 141–73.

———. "Validation by Holiness or Sovereignty: Religious Toleration as Political Theology in the Mongol World Empire of the Thirteenth Century." *International History Review* 26, no. 2 (2004): 237–56.

Aubin, Françoise. "The Rebirth of Chinese Rule in Times of Trouble." In S. R. Schram, ed., *Foundations and Limits of State Power in China*. London: School of Oriental and African Studies, University of London; Hong Kong: Chinese University Press, 1987, pp. 113–46.

Bao Xiang 包祥. "Hancheng faxian de Basibazi wenxian" 漢城發現的八思巴字文獻. *Neimenggu daxue xuebao* (*Zhexue shehuixue ban*) 內蒙古大學學報 (哲學社會學版) 1994, no. 2: 36–39.

Beijing tushuguan cang Zhongguo lidai shike taben huibian 北京圖書館藏中國歷代石刻拓本匯編. 1989– . (Vols. 48–50 cover the Yuan.)

Berger, Patricia. "Preserving the Nation: The Political Uses of Tantric Art in China." In Marsha Weidner, ed., *Latter Days of the Law*. Lawrence: Spencer Museum of Art and University of Kansas in association with University of Hawai'i Press, 1994, pp. 89–123.

Bi Aonan 畢奥南. "Yuan Renzong cishu Gaoli zakao" 元仁宗賜書高麗雜考. *Wenxian* 文獻 1998, no. 4: 193–99.

Bi Gong 畢恭 et al. *Liaodong zhi* 遼東志. Comp. 1443. Rev. 1488 and 1529. Reprinted in Jin Yufu 金毓黻, ed., *Liaohai congshu* 遼海叢書. Dalian: Liaohai shushe, 1932.

Biran, Michal. "The Mongol Transformation: From the Steppe to Eurasian Empire." *Medieval Encounters* 10, nos. 1–3 (2004): 339–61.

———. *Qaidu and the Rise of the Independent Mongol State in Central Asia.* Richmond, Surrey: Curzon, 1997.

Birge, Bettine. "Levirate Marriage and the Revival of Widow Chastity in Yüan China." *Asia Major*, 3d ser., 8, no. 2 (1995): 107–46.

———. "Women and Confucianism from Song to Ming: The Institutionalization of Patrilineality." In Paul Smith and Richard von Glahn, eds., *The Song-Yuan-Ming Transition in Chinese History.* Cambridge: Harvard University Asia Center, 2003, pp. 212–40, 429–37.

Boyle, John. "The Dynastic and Political History of the Il-khans." In idem, ed., *Cambridge History of Iran*, vol. 5, *The Saljuq and Mongol Periods.* Cambridge: Cambridge University Press, 1968, 413–17.

Brose, Michael. "Uyghur Technologists of Writing and Literacy in Mongol China." *T'oung Pao* 91 (2005): 396–435.

Buell, Paul. "Pleasing the Palate of the Qan: Changing Foodways of the Imperial Mongols." *Mongolian Studies* 13 (1990): 57–81.

———. "The Role of the Sino-Mongolian Frontier Zone in the Rise of Cinggisqan." In Henry Schwarz, ed., *Studies on Mongolia: Proceedings of the First North American Conference on Mongolian Studies.* Bellingham: Center for East Asian Studies, Western Washington Press, 1979, pp. 63–76.

Cao Shuji 曹樹基. *Zhongguo renkou shi* 中國人口史, vol. 4, *Ming shiqi* 明時期. Shanghai: Fudan daxue chubanshe, 2000.

Ch'ae Su-hwan 蔡守煥. "Koryŏ Kongminwangdae ŭi kaehyŏk kwa chŏngch'ijŏk chibae seryŏk" 高麗 恭愍王代의 改革과 政治的 支配勢力. *Sahak yŏn'gu* 史學研究 55–56 (Sept. 1998): 133–62.

Chan, Hok-lam 陳學霖. "The 'Song' Dynasty Legacy: Symbolism and Legitimation from Han Liner to Zhu Yuanzhang of the Ming Dynasty." *Harvard Journal of Asiatic Studies* 68, no. 1 (2008): 91–133.

——. "The White Lotus-Maitreya Doctrine and Popular Uprisings in Ming and Ch'ing China." *Sinologica* 10, no. 4 (1969): 211–33.

Chang Tong-ik 張東翼. *Koryŏ hugi oegyosa yŏn'gu* 高麗後期外交史研究. Seoul: Iljogak, 1994.

———. *Wŏndae Yŏsa charyo chipnok* 元代麗史資料集錄. Seoul: Sŏul taehakkyo ch'ulp'anbu, 1997.

Changguzhenyi 長古眞逸. *Nong tian si hua* 農田私話. Baoyantang biji 寶顏堂秘笈 ed. [late sixteenth, early seventeenth century], Guangji series 廣集, pt. 4 第四.

Chen Dezhi 陳得芝, Ding Guofan 丁國範, et al., eds. *Zhongguo tongshi* 中國通史, vol. 13, *Yuan shiqi* 元時期. Shanghai: Shanghai renmin chubanshe, 1997.

Chen Gaohua 陳高華. "Cong *Lao Qida, Piao tongshi* kan Yuan yu Gaoli de jingji wenhua jiaoliu" 從《老乞大》《朴通事》看元與高麗的經濟文化交流. *Lishi yanjiu* 歷史研究 1995, no. 5: 45–60.

———. "Du 'Boyan Zongdao zhuan.'" 讀伯顏宗道傳. *Yuanshi ji beifang minzushi yanjiu jikan* 元史及北方民族史研究集刊 10 (1986). Reprinted in idem, *Yuanshi yanjiu lungao* 元史研究論稿. Beijing: Zhonghua shuju, 1991, pp. 450–53.

———. "*Gengshen waishi* zuozhe Quan Heng xiaokao" 《庚申外史》作者權衡小考. *Yuanshi luncong* 元史論叢 4 (1992). Originally published under pseudonym, Wen Ling 溫嶺. Reprinted in idem, *Chen Gaohua wenji* 陳高華文集. Shanghai: Shanghai cishu chubanshe, 2005, pp. 548–49.

———. "Jiuben *Lao Qida* shu hou" 舊本《老乞大》書後. *Zhongguoshi yanjiu* 中國史研究 2002, no. 1. Reprinted in idem, *Chen Gaohua wenji* 陳高華文集. Shanghai: Shanghai cishu chubanshe, 2005, pp. 407–18.

———. "*Kajŏng chip, Mok'ŭn ko* yu Yuanshi yanjiu" 《稼亭集》,《牧隱稿》與元史研究. In Hao Shiyuan 郝時遠 and Luo Xianyou 羅賢佑, eds., *Meng Yuan shi ji minzushi lunji: Jinian Weng Dujian xiansheng danchen yibai zhounian* 蒙元史暨民族史論集—記念翁獨健先生誕辰一百周年. Beijing: Shehui kexue wenxian chubanshe, 2006, pp. 321–35.

———. "Lun Yuandai de junhu" 論元代的軍户. *Yuanshi luncong* 元史論叢 1 (1982): 72–90. Reprinted in idem, *Yuanshi yanjiu lungao* 元史研究論稿. Beijing: Zhonghua shuju, 1991, pp. 127–55.

———. "Lun Zhu Yuanzhang he Yuanchao de guanxi" 論朱元璋和元朝的關係. *Xueshu yuekan* 學術月刊 1980, no. 5. Reprinted in idem, *Yuanshi yanjiu lungao* 元史研究論稿. Beijing: Zhonghua shuju, 1991, pp. 316–27.

———. "Shisi shiji lai Zhongguo de Riben sengren" 十四世紀來中國的日本僧人. *Wenshi* 文史 18 (1983): 131–49.

———. "Shuo Yuanmo Hongjinjun de sanlu beifa" 說元末紅巾軍的三路北伐. *Lishi jiaoxue* 歷史教學 1981, no. 5: 21–25.

———. "Yuanchao yu Gaoli de haishang jiaotong" 元朝與高麗的海上交通. *Chindan hakpo* 震檀學報 71–72 (1991): 348–58.

———. *Yuan Dadu* 元大都. Beijing: Beijing chubanshe, 1982.

———. "Yuandai Dadu de huangjia fojiao" 元代大都的皇家佛教. *Shijie zongjiao yanjiu* 世界宗教研究 1992, no. 2: 2–6.

———. "Yuandai de liumin wenti" 元代的流民問題. *Yuanshi luncong* 元史論叢 4 (1992): 132–47.

———. "Yuandai laihua Yindu sengren Zhikong shiji" 元代來華印度僧人指空事輯. *Nanya yanjiu* 南亞研究 1979, no. 1: 63–68.

———. "Yuandai nongmin qiyijun minghao xiaoding" 元代農民起義軍名號小訂. *Nankai daxue xuebao* 南開大學學報 1979, no. 2: 95–96.

———. "Yuandai shiren Naixian shengping shiji kao" 元代詩人迺賢生平事蹟考. *Wenshi* 文史 32 (1990): 247–62.

———. *Yuanshi yanjiu xinlun* 元史研究新論. Shanghai: Shanghai shehui kexueyuan chubanshe, 2005.

Chen Gaohua 陳高華 and Shi Weimin 史衛民. *Zhongguo jingji tongshi: Yuandai jingji juan* 中國經濟通史: 元代經濟卷. Beijing: Jingji ribao chubanshe, 2000.

Chen Yiming 陳一鳴. "Lun Yuandai taizi canzheng wenti" 論元代太子參政問題. *Neimenggu shehui kexue* 内蒙古社會科學 1992, no. 1: 81–88.

Ch'en Yuan (Chen Yuan 陳垣). *Western and Central Asians in China Under the Mongols.* Trans. from the Chinese by Ch'ien Hsing-hai and L. Carrington Goodrich. Los Angeles: Monumenta Serica, 1966.

———. *Yuan Xiyuren huahuakao* 元西域人華化考. 1923. Reprinted—Shanghai: Shanghai guji chubanshe, 2000.

Cheng Nina 程尼娜. "Yuanchao dui Heilongjiang xiayou Nüzhen Shuidada diqu tongxia yanjiu" 元朝對黑龍江下游女眞水達達地區統轄研究. *Zhongguo bianjiang shidi yanjiu* 中國邊疆史地研究 15, no. 2 (2005): 69–77.

———. "Yuandai Chaoxian bandao Zhengdong xingsheng yanjiu" 元代朝鮮半島征東行省研究. *Shehui kexue zhanxian* 社會科學戰線 2006, no. 6: 157–62.

———. "Yuandai dui Menggu dongdao zhuwang tongxia yanjiu" 元代對蒙古東道諸王統轄研究. *Liaoning shifan daxue xuebao (shehui kexueban)* 遼寧師範大學學報 (社會科學版) 27, no. 5 (2004): 115–18.

Chikusa Masaaki 竺沙雅章. *Seifuku ōchō no jidai* 征服王朝の時代. Tokyo: Kōdansha, 1992 [1977].

Ch'in Yon-ch'ol. "Kōrai no shuto Kaijōjō ni tsuite no kenkyū" 高麗の首都開城城についての研究. Trans. from the Korean by Mizutani Masayoshi 水谷昌義. *Chōsen gakuhō* 朝鮮学報 117 (1985): 1–42.

Chŏn Chong-sŏk 全宗釋. "Kōrai bukkyō to Gendai Ramakyō to no kankei—Ramakyō no eikyō o chūshin ni" 高麗仏教と元代喇嘛教との関係—喇嘛教の影響を中心に. *Indogaku bukkyōgaku kenkyū* 印度学仏教学研究 35, no. 2 (1987): 677–79.

Ch'ŏn Hae-jong 全海宗. "Yŏ-Wŏn muyŏk ŭi sŏng'gyŏk" 麗元貿易의性格, *Tongyang sahak yŏn'gu* 東洋史學研究 12–13 (1978): 43–53.

Chŏn Nok-seng 田祿生. *Ya'ŭn irjip* 埜隱逸集. 1738 ed. Reprinted in *Han'guk munjip ch'onggan*, vol. 3.

Chŏn Sun-dong 全淳東. "Shipsa segi huban Myŏng ŭi tae Koryŏ-Chosŏn chŏngch'aek" 14 世紀 後半 明의 對高麗 朝鮮政策. *Myŏng Ch'ŏngsa yŏn'gu* 明清史研究 5 (1996): 1–20.

———. "Wŏnmal ŭi nongch'on sahoe wa pallan: Hwapuk chibang ŭl chungsim ŭro" 元末의 農村社會와 反亂— 華 北 地 方 을 중심으로—. *Ch'ungbuk taehakpo mun'in hakchi* 忠北大學報文人學志 6 (1991): 91–121.

Chŏng In-ji 鄭麟趾. *Koryŏsa* 高麗史. 1454. Reprinted—Tokyo: Kokusho kankōkai, 1908; and ed. Yŏnse taehakkyo, Tongbanghak Yŏn'guso 延世大學校東方學研究所. Seoul: Kyŏng'in munhwasa, 1972.

Chŏng Tu-hŭi 鄭杜熙. "Koryŏmal sinhŭng muin seryŏk ŭi sŏngchang kwa ch'ŏmsŏljik ŭi sŏlch'i" 高麗末新興武人勢力의 成長과 添設職의 設置. In Han'guk sahak nonch'ong, Yi Chae-yong paksa hwallyŏk ki'nyŏm kanhaeng wiwŏnhoe 韓國史學論叢, 李載 X 博士還曆紀念刊行委員會, ed., *Han'guk sahak nonch'ong: Yi Chae-yong paksa hwallyŏk ki'nyŏm* 韓國史學論叢: 李載 X 博士還曆紀念. Seoul: Hanul, 1990, pp. 280–98.

Chŏng Ŭn-u 鄭恩雨. "Koryŏ hugi pulgyo misul ŭi huwŏnja" 高麗後期佛教美術의 후원자. *Misul yŏn'gu* 16 (2002): 81–103.

Chōsen sōtokufu 朝鮮総督府, comp. *Chōsen kinseki sōran* 朝鮮金石総覧. Seoul, 1919.

———. Chōsen koseki zufu 朝鮮古蹟図譜. Seoul: Chōsen sōtokufu, 1915–35. Reprinted in *Chōsen kōko shiryō shūsei* 朝鮮考古資料集成. Tokyo: Shupan kagaku sōgō kenkyūjo; Osaka: Hatsubaimoto sōgakusha, 1982.

Clark, Donald. "Autonomy, Legitimacy, and Tributary Politics: Sino-Korean Relations in the Fall of the Koryŏ and the Founding of the Yi." Ph.D. diss., Harvard University, 1978.

Cleaves, Francis. "The 'Fifteen Palace Poems' by K'o Chiu-ssu." *Harvard Journal of Asiatic Studies* 20, no. 3/4 (1957): 391–479.

Cong Peiyuan 叢佩遠. *Zhongguo dongbeishi* 中國東北史, vol. 3. Changchun: Jilin wenshi chubanshe, 1998.

Conlan, Thomas. *In Little Need of Divine Intervention: Takezaki Suenaga's Scrolls of the Mongol Invasions of Japan*. Ithaca: Cornell East Asia Series, 2001.

Daitō kinsekisho / Taedong kŭmsŏksŏ 大東金石書. Keijō: Keijō teikoku daigaku, Hōbungakubu 京城帝国大学法文学部, 1932.

Dang Baohai 党寶海. "The Plait-line Robe: A Costume of Ancient Mongolia." *Central Asiatic Journal* 47, no. 2 (2003): 198–216.

Dardess, John. *Conquerors and Confucians: Aspects of Political Change in Late Yüan China*. New York: Columbia University Press, 1973.

———. "Did the Mongols Matter?" In Paul Smith and Richard von Glahn, eds., *The Sung-Yuan-Ming Transition in Chinese History.* Cambridge: Harvard University Asia Center, 2003, pp. 111–34.

———. "From Mongol Empire to Yüan Dynasty: Changing Forms of Imperial Rule in Mongolia and Central Asia." *Monumenta Serica* 30 (1972–73): 117–65.

———. "Shun-ti and the End of Yüan Rule." In Herbert Franke and Denis Twitchett, eds., *The Cambridge History of China*, vol. 6, *Alien Regimes and Border States, 907–1368.* Cambridge: Cambridge University Press, 1994, pp. 561–86.

———. "The Transformations of Messianic Revolt and the Founding of the Ming Dynasty." *Journal of Asian Studies* 29, no. 3 (1970): 539–58.

Di Cosmo, Nicola. "Mongols and Merchants on the Black Sea Frontier in the Thirteenth and Fourteenth Centuries: Convergences and Conflicts." In Reuven Amitai and Michal Biran, eds., *Mongols, Turks, and Others.* Leiden: Brill, 2005, pp. 391–424.

Ding Kunjian 丁崑健. "Cong shihuan tujing kan Yuandai de youshi zhi feng" 從仕宦途徑看元代的游士之風. In Xiao Qiqing (Hsiao Ch'i-ch'ing) 蕭啓慶, ed., *Meng Yuan de lishi yu wenhua* 蒙元歷史與文化. Taibei: Taiwan xuesheng shuju, 2001, pp. 635–50.

Duncan, John. *The Origins of the Chosŏn Dynasty.* Seattle: University of Washington Press, 2000.

———. "The Social Background to the Founding of the Chosŏn Dynasty: Change or Continuity?" *Journal of Korean Studies* 6 (1988–89): 39–79.

Ebisawa Tetsuo 海老沢哲雄. "Mongoru teikoku no Tōhō san'ōke ni kansuru shomondai" モンゴル帝国と東方三王家に関する諸問題. *Saitama daigaku kiyō kyōiku gakubu (jimbun-shakaikagaku)* 埼玉大学紀要教育学部 (人文・社会科学) 21 (1972): 31–46.

Ejima Hisao 江島寿雄. "Mindai jochoku no uma" 明代女直の馬. *Shien* 史淵 63 (1954). Reprinted in idem, *Mindai Shinsho no jochokushi kenkyū* 明代清初の女直史研究. Fukuoka: Chūgoku shoten, 1999.

———. "Minsho jochoku chōkō ni kansuru nisan no mondai" 明初女直朝貢に関する二三の問題. *Shien* 史淵 58 (1953). Reprinted in idem, *Mindai Shinsho no jochokushi kenkyū* 明代清初の女直史研究. Fukuoka: Chūgoku shoten, 1999.

Elman, Benjamin. *A Cultural History of Civil Examinations in Late Imperial China.* Berkeley: University of California Press, 2000.

Elverskog, Johan. *Our Great Qing: The Mongols, Buddhism, and the State in Late Imperial China.* Honolulu: University of Hawai'i Press, 2006.

Endicott-West, Elizabeth. "Imperial Governance in Yüan Times." *Harvard Journal of Asiatic Studies* 46, no. 2 (1986): 523–49.

———. "Merchant Associations in Yüan China: The Ortoy." *Asia Major* 2, no. 2 (1989): 127–54.

———. *Mongolian Rule in China: Local Administration Under the Yuan*. Cambridge: Harvard Council on East Asian Studies, 1989.

Enomori Susumu 榎森進. "Jūsan–jūroku seiki no Higashi Ajia to Ainu minzoku—Gen-Min to Sahalin to Ainu no kankei o chūshin ni" 十三–十六世紀の東アジアとアイヌ民族—元・明とサハリンとアイヌの関係を中心に. In Haga Norihiko 羽下徳彦, ed., *Kita Nihon chūseishi no kenkyū* 北日本中世史の研究. Tokyo: Yoshikawa kōbunkan, 1990, pp. 223–68.

Enomoto Wataru 榎本渉. "Genmatsu nairanki no Nichi-Gen kōtsū" 元末内乱期の日元交通. *Tōyō gakuhō* 東洋学報 84, no. 1 (2002): 1–31.

———. "Junteichō zenpanki ni okeru Nichi-Gen kōtsū" 順帝朝前半期における日元交通. *Nihon rekishi* 日本歴史, no. 640 (2001): 18–34.

———. "Jūyon seiki kōhan, Nihon ni torai shita hitobito" 十四世紀後半、日本に渡来した人々. *Harukanaru chūsei* 遥かなる中世 20 (2003): 25–54.

———. "Meishū shihakushi to Higashi Shinakai bōekiken" 明州市舶司と東シナ海貿易圏. *Rekishigaku kenkyū* 歴史学研究, no. 756 (2001): 12–22.

———. "Nihon ensei yikō ni okeru Genchō no wasen taisaku" 日本遠征以後における元朝の倭船対策. *Nihonshi kenkyū* 日本史研究, no. 470 (2001): 58–82.

Farquhar, David. "Emperor as Bodhisattva in the Governance of the Ch'ing Empire." *Harvard Journal of Asiatic Studies* 38, no. 1 (1978): 5–34.

———. *The Government of China Under Mongolian Rule*. Stuttgart: F. Steiner, 1990.

———. "Structure and Function in the Yüan Imperial Government." In John Langlois, ed., *China Under Mongol Rule*. Princeton: Princeton University, 1981, pp. 25–55.

Fletcher, Joseph. "The Mongols: Ecological and Social Perspectives." *Harvard Journal of Asiatic Studies* 46 (1986): 11–50.

———. "Turco-Mongolian Monarchic Tradition in the Ottoman Empire." *Harvard Ukrainian Studies* 3–4 (1979–80): 236–51.

Franke, Herbert. "The Chin Dynasty." In idem and Denis Twitchett, eds., *The Cambridge History of China*, vol. 6, *Alien Regimes and Border States, 907–1368*. Cambridge: Cambridge University Press, 1994, pp. 215–320.

———. "Could the Mongol Emperors Read and Write Chinese." In idem, *China Under Mongol Rule*. Aldershot, Eng.: Ashgate Publishing; Brookfield, VT: Variorum, 1994, pt. V, pp. 28–41.

———. "From Tribal Chieftain to Universal Emperor and God: Legitimation of the Yuan Dynasty." In idem, *China Under Mongol Rule*. Brookfield: Variorum Press, 1994, 296–328.

———. "The Role of the State as a Structural Element in Polyethnic Societies." In S. R. Schram, ed., *Foundations and Limits of State Power in China.* London: School of Oriental and African Studies, University of London; Hong Kong: Chinese University Press, 1987, pp. 87–112.

———. "Some Remarks on Yang Yü 楊瑀 and His *Shan-chü hsin-hua* 山居新話." In idem, *China Under Mongol Rule.* Aldershot, Eng.: Ashgate Publishing; Brookfield, VT: Variorum, pt. II, pp. 302–8.

———. "Tibetans in Yuan China." In John Langlois, ed., *China Under Mongol Rule.* Princeton: Princeton University Press, 1981, pp. 296–328.

Franke, Herbert, and Denis Twitchett, eds. *The Cambridge History of China*, vol. 6, *Alien Regimes and Border States, 907–1368.* Cambridge: Cambridge University Press, 1994.

Fu Leshu 傅樂淑. "Yuandai huanhuo kao" 元得官禍考. *Yuanshi luncong* 3 (1983): 157–66.

Fujishima Tateki 藤島建樹. "Gen no Juntei to sono jidai" 元の順帝とその時代. *Ōtani gakuhō* 大谷学報 49, no. 4 (1970): 50–65.

Funada Yoshiyuki 船田善之. "Genchō jika no shokumokujin ni tsuite" 元朝治下の色目人について. *Shigaku zasshi* 史学雜誌 108, no. 9 (1999): 43–68.

———. "Mongoru jidai ni okeru minzoku sesshoku to Aidenteitei no shosō" モンゴル時代における民族接触とアイデンテイテイの諸相. In Imanishi Yūichirō 今西裕一郎, ed., *Kyūshū daigaku 21 seiki COE puroguramu Higashi Ajia to Nihon: kōryū to hen'yō* 九州大学 21 世紀 COE プログラム「東アジアと日本: 交流と変容」. Fukuokashi: Kyūshū daigaku, 2007, pp. 19–29.

———. "Semuren yu Yuandai zhidu, shehui" 色目人與元代制度，社會. *Mengguxue xinxi* 蒙古學信息 2 (2003): 7–16.

Golden, Peter. "'I will giveth the people unto thee': The Cinggisid Conquests and Their Aftermath in the Turkic World." *Journal of the Royal Asiatic Society* 10, no. 1 (2000): 21–41.

Gong Shitai 貢師泰 (1298–1362). *Wanzhaiji* 玩齋集. *Wenyuange Siku quanshu*, vol. 1215. Reprinted—Taibei: Shangwu yinshuguan, 1983.

Goodrich, L. Carrington, and Chaoying Fang, eds. *Dictionary of Ming Biography, 1368–1644.* New York: Columbia University Press, 1976.

Greene, Jack. "Transatlantic Colonization and the Redefinition of Empire in the Early Modern Era." In Christine Daniels and Michael Kennedy, eds., *Negotiated Empires: Centers and Peripheries in the Americas, 1500–1820.* New York and London: Routledge, 2002, pp. 267–82.

Gu Cheng 顧誠. "*Zhizheng zhiji* de zuozhe wei Kong Keqi" 《至正直記》的作者爲孔克齊. *Yuanshi luncong* 6 (1997): 227–31.

Gui Xipeng 桂栖鹏. *Yuandai jinshi yanjiu* 元代進士研究. Lanzhou: Lanzhou daxue chubanshe, 2001.

———. "Yuan Yingzong zhe Gaoli Zhongxuanwang yu Tufan yuanyin tanxi" 元英宗謫高麗忠宣王於吐蕃原因探析. *Zhongguo bianjiang shidi yanjiu* 中國邊疆史地研究 10, no. 2 (2001): 43–48.

Guojia tushuguan shanben jinshi zu 國家圖書館善本金石組, ed. *Liao Song Yuan shike wenxian quanbian* 遼金元石刻文獻全編. Beijing: Beijing tushuguan chubanshe, 2003.

Haar, B. J. ter. *White Lotus Teachings*. Leiden: E. J. Brill, 1992.

Halperin, Charles. "The Kipchak Connection: The Ilkhans, the Mamluks, and Ayn Jalut." *Bulletin of the School of Oriental and African Studies, University of London* 63, no. 2 (2000): 229–45.

———. *Russia and the Golden Horde: The Mongol Impact on Medieval Russian History*. Bloomington: University of Indiana, 1985.

———. "Russia in the Mongol Empire in Comparative Perspective." *Harvard Journal of Asiatic Studies* 43, no. 1 (1983): 239–61.

Hambis, Louis. *Le chapitre cvii du* Yuan che*: les généologies imperials mongoles dans l'historie chinoise officielle de la dynastie mongole. Avec les notes supplémentaires par Paul Pelliot. T'oung Pao* suppl. no. 38. Leiden: Brill, 1945.

———. "Notes sur l'histoire de Corée à l'époque mongole." *T'oung Pao* 45 (1957): 151–218.

Han Chae-yŏm 韓在濂 (1775–1818). *Koryŏ kodo chŏng* 高麗古都徵. Reprinted in Yi T'aejin 李泰鎮, ed. *Chosŏn sidae sajŏn yŏkji* 朝鮮時代私撰邑誌. Seoul: Han'guk inmunkwa hakwŏn, 1989, vol. 6.

Han Rulin 韓儒林. "Yuandai zhamayan xintan" 元代詐馬宴新探. In idem, *Qiongluji* 穹廬集. Shanghai: Shanghai renmin chubanshe, 1982, pp. 247–54.

Han Rulin 韓儒林, comp. *Yuanchao shi* 元朝史. Beijing: Renmin chubanshe, 1986.

Han Woo-keun. *History of Korea*. Seoul: Eul-Yoo Publishing, 1970.

Han Zhiyuan 韓志遠. "Aiyoushilidala yu Yuanmo zhengzhi" 愛猷識理達臘與元末政治. *Yuanshi luncong* 元史論叢 4 (1992): 183–95.

Han'guk munjip ch'onggan 韓國文集叢刊, *see* Minjok munhwa ch'ujinhoe.

Han'guk pulgyo inmyŏng sajŏn 韓國佛教人名辭典. Ed. Yi Chŏng 李政. Seoul: Pulgyo sidaesa, 1993.

Han'guk yŏktae munjip ch'ongsŏ 韓國歷代文集叢書, *see* Munjip p'yŏnch'an wiwŏnhoe.

Han'guksa yŏn'guhoe 한국사연구회. *Koryŏ ŭi hwangdo Kaegyŏng* 고려의 황도개경. Seoul: Ch'angjak kwa Pip'yŏngsa, 2002.

Harada Rie 原田理恵. "Genchō no Mokkari ichizoku" 元朝の木華黎一族. In *Tsuitō kinen ronsō* henshū iinkai 追悼記念論叢編集員會, ed. *Mindai*

Chūgoku no rekishiteki isō: Yamane Yukio kyōju tsuitō kinen ronsō 明代中国の歴史的位相: 山根幸夫教授追悼記念論叢. Tokyo: Kyūko shoin, 2007, 2: 65–90.

Hatada Takashi 旗田巍. "Kōrai-Ichō jidai ni okeru gunkensei no ichi keitai" 高麗李朝時代における郡県制の一形態. In idem, *Chōsen chūsei shakaishi no kenkyū* 朝鮮中世社会史の研究. Tokyo: Hōsei daigaku, 1992. Originally published in *Wada hakase koki kinen Tōyōshi ronsō* 和田博士古稀記念東洋史論叢. 1962.

———. "Nihon to Kōrai: Mōko shūrai o chūshin ni shite 日本と高麗—蒙古襲来を中心にして. *Kankoku bunka* 韓国文化 4, no. 10 (1982).

Hazard, Benjamin. "Japanese Marauding in Medieval Korea: The Wako Impact on Late Koryo." Ph.D. diss., University of California, Berkeley, 1967.

Henthorn, William. *Korea: The Mongol Invasions*. Leiden: E. J. Brill, 1963.

Hŏ Hŭng-sik 許興植. *Koryŏ sahoesa yŏn'gu* 高麗社會史研究. Seoul: Asea munhwasa, 1981.

Hong Pong-han 洪鳳漢 (1713–78). *Chŭngbo munhŏn pigo* 增補文獻備考. 1770. Reprinted—Seoul: Kojŏn kanhaenghoe, 1957.

Hong Yŏng-wi 洪榮義. "Kongminwang ŭi panWŏn chŏngch'aek kwa Yŏm Che-sin ŭi kunsa hwaldong" 恭愍王의 反元政策과 廉悌臣의 軍事活動. *Kunsa* 軍事 23 (1991): 91–122.

Horie Masaaki 堀江雅明. "Mongoru = Genchō jidai no Tōhō san *urusu* kenkyū josetsu" モンゴル=元朝時代の東方三ウルス研究序説. In Ono Katsutoshi hakushi shōjū kinenkai 小野勝年博士頌壽記念會 ed., *Ono Katsutoshi hakushi shōjū kinen Tōhōgaku ronshū* 小野勝年博士頌壽記念東方学論集. Kyoto: Hōyū shoten, 1982, pp. 377–411.

———. "Nayan no hanran ni tsuite" ナヤンの反乱について (part 1). *Tōyōshien* 東洋史苑 34–35 (1990): 73–91.

———. "Temuge-Occhigin to sono shison" テムゲ-オッチギンとその子孫. *Tōyōshien* 東洋史苑 24–25 (1985): 225–70.

Hsiao, Ch'i-ch'ing (*see also* Xiao Qiqing). "Mid-Yuan Politics." In *CHC*, 6: 490–560.

———. *The Military Establishment of the Yuan Dynasty*. Cambridge: Council on East Asian Studies, Harvard University, 1978.

Hsiao, Kung-chuan. *A History of Chinese Political Thought*. Translated from the Chinese by Frederick Mote. Princeton: Princeton University Press, 1979.

Hu Cuizhong 胡粹中. *Yuanshi xubian* 元史續編. *Siku quanshu zhenben*, series 6, vols. 62–63. Reproduced from Wenyuange 文淵閣 copy. Taibei: Taiwan shangwu yinshuguan, 1976.

Huang Shijian 黄時鑒. "Muhuali guowang huixia zhujun kao" 木華黎國王麾下諸軍考. *Yuanshi luncong* 元史論叢 1 (1982): 57–71.

Hucker, Charles O. *A Dictionary of Official Titles in Imperial China.* Stanford: Stanford University Press, 1985.

———. *The Ming Dynasty: Its Origins and Evolving Institutions.* Ann Arbor: Center for Chinese Studies, University of Michigan, 1978.

Hwang Un-yong 黄雲龍. "Koryŏ Kongminwangdae ŭi taeWŏn Myŏng kwan'gye" 高麗 恭愍王代의 對元明關係. *Tong'guk sahak* 東國史學 14 (1980): 1–14.

Hye Kŭn 惠勤 (Naong 懶翁). *Naong chip* 懶翁集. Reprinted in *Han'guk yŏktae munjip ch'ongsŏ*, vol. 25.

Ikeuchi Hiroshi 池内宏. "Kōrai Kyōmin'ō no Gen ni taisuru hankō no undō" 高麗恭愍王の元に對する反抗の運動. *Tōyō gakuhō* 東洋学報 7, no. 1 (1917): 117–36.

———. "Kōrai Shin-u chō ni okeru Tetsuryō mondai" 高麗辛禑朝における鐵嶺問題. In idem, *ManSenshi kenkyū* 滿鮮史研究, *chūsei* 中世. Tokyo: Yoshikawa kōbunkan, 3: 235–64.

In Tu-su 尹斗壽, comp. *P'yŏngyangji* 平壤志. Preface dated 1590. Reprinted with annotations—Tokyo, 1897.

Institute of Andong Culture at Andong National University. *A Cultural and Historic Journey into Andong.* Seoul: Korean Studies Advancement Center, 2002.

Ishihara Yumiko 石原裕美子. *Chibetto bukkyō sekai no rekishiteki kenkyū* チベット仏教世界の歴史的研究. Tokyo: Tōhō shoten, 2001.

Jackson, Peter. "Dissolution of the Mongol Empire." *Central Asiatic Journal* 22 (1978): 186–244.

———. "From *Ulus* to Khanate." In Reuven Amitai-Preiss and David Morgan, eds., *The Mongol Empire and Its Legacy.* Leiden: Brill, 1999, pp. 12–37.

———. "The Mongols and the Faith of the Conquered." In Reuven Amitai and Michal Biran, eds., *Mongols, Turks, and Others: Eurasian Nomads and the Sedentary World.* Leiden and Boston: Brill, 2005, pp. 245–90.

———. *The Mongols and the West.* Harlow, Eng.: Pearson Education, 2005.

Janhunen, Juha. *Manchuria: An Ethnic History.* Helsinki: Finno-Ugrian Society, 1996.

Jie Qisi 揭傒斯. *Jie Wenan gong quanji* 揭文安文集. Reprinted in *Sibu congkan* 四部叢刊, vol. 242; and *Siku quanshu bieji* 四庫全書别集 4, vol. 1208.

Jing, Anning. "Financial and Material Aspects of Tibetan Art Under the Yuan Dynasty." *Artibus Asiae* 64, no. 2 (2004): 213–40.

———. "The Portraits of Khubilai Khan and Chabi by Anige (1245–1306), a Nepali Artist at the Yuan Court." *Artibus Asiae* 54, no. 1/2 (1994): 40–86.

Kang Chu-chin 姜周鎭. "Kongminwang ŭi Koryŏ chegŏn undong kwa samwŏnsu" 恭愍王의 高麗再建運動과 三元帥. In *Han'gukhak munhŏn yŏn'gu ŭi hyŏnhwang kwa chŏnmang: Asea munhwasa ch'angnip shipjunyŏn ki'nyŏm nonmunjip* 韓國學文獻硏究의 現況과展望: 亞細亞文化社創立十周年紀念論文集. Seoul: Tongsa, 1983, pp. 521–544.

Kang Sŏng-mun 姜性文. "Koryŏmal Hongt'ujok ch'imgo e kwan han yŏn'gu" 高麗末 紅頭賊 侵寇에 關한 硏究. *Yuksa nonmunjip* 陸士論文集 31 (1986): 207–30.

Kawachi Yoshihiro 河内良弘. "Mindai Ryōyō no Tōneiei ni tsuite" 明代遼陽の東寧衛について. *Tōyōshi kenkyū* 東洋史研究 44, no. 4 (1986): 89–127.

Ke Jiusi 柯九思 et al. *Liao Jin Yuan gongci* 遼金元宮詞. Beijing: Beijing guji chubanshe, 1988.

Khwandamir (1475–1535). *Habibu's-siyar*, vol. 3, *The Reign of the Mongol and the Turk*. 1524. Trans. W. M. Thackston. Cambridge: Harvard University, Department of Near Eastern Languages and Civilizations, 1994.

Kim An-guk 金安國. *Mojae chip* 慕齋集. 1574. Reprinted, 1687. Microfilm held in Yenching Library, Harvard University.

Kim Ch'ang-su 金昌洙. "Sŏngjung aemago" 成衆愛馬考. *Tongguk sahak* 東國史學 9–10 (1966): 17–36.

Kim Ho-dong 金浩東. "Mong'gol che'guk kunjudŭl ŭi yangdo sunhaeng kwa yumokjŏk sŭpsok" 몽골帝國 君主들의 兩都巡幸과 遊牧的 習俗. *Chung'ang Asia yŏn'gu* 中央 아시아 硏究 7 (Dec. 2002): 1–25.

———. "Mong'gol che'guk kwa Koryŏ" 몽골제국과 고려. Presented at Seoul University Korean Studies Symposium 2004 서울대학교 한국학 심포지엄, *Han'gukin ŭi sal kwa chŏnt'ong* 한국인의 삶과 전통. Seoul University, May 2004.

———. *Mong'gol che'guk kwa Koryŏ K'ubillai chŏnggwŏn ŭi t'ansaeng kwa Koryŏ ŭi chŏngch'ijok wisang* 몽골제국과 고려 쿠빌라이 정권의 탄생과 고려의 정치의 정치적 위상. Seoul: Sŏul taehakkyo ch'ulpanbu, 2007.

———. "Mong'gol che'guk kwa Tae Wŏn" 몽골帝國과 大元. *Yŏksa hakpo* 歷史學報, no. 192 (2006): 221–53.

———. "Mong'gol cheguk ŭi yŏksasang: kŭ waegok kwa silsang" 몽골帝國의 歷史像—그 歪曲과 實相. In *Che 46 hoe chŏn'guk yŏksahak taehoe* 제 46 회 전국역 사학대회. Seoul: Chŏn'guk yŏksahak taehoe chojik wiwŏnhoe, 2003, pp. 36–44.

———. "Mong'gol che'guksa yŏn'gu wa *Chipsa*" 몽골帝國史 硏究와『集史』. *Kyŏngbuk sahak* 慶北史學 25 (Aug. 2002): 337–52.

Kim Ho-jong 金昊鍾. "Kongminwang ŭi Andongmongjin e kwanhan il yŏn'gu" 恭愍王의 安東蒙塵에 관한 一硏究. *Andong munhwa* 安東文化 1 (1980): 29–50.

Kim Hye-wŏn 金惠苑. "Koryŏ hugi Sim (yang) wang ŭi chŏngch'i kyŏngjejok kiban" 高麗後期瀋 (陽) 王의 政治・經濟的 基盤. *Kuksagwan nonch'ong* 國史館論叢 49 (1993): 27–56.

———. "Koryŏ Kongminwangdae taeoe chŏngch'aek kwa Han'in kun'ung" 高麗 恭愍王代 對外政策과 漢人群雄. *Paeksan hakpo* 白山學報 51 (1998): 61–101.

Kim Hyŏng-su 金炯秀. "Wŏn kansŏp ŭi kuksokron kwa t'ongjeron" 원간섭의 國俗論과 通制論. In Han'guk chungsesa hakhoe, ed., *Han'guk chungse sahoe ŭi che munje* 韓國中世社會의 諸問題. Taegu-si: Han'guk chungsesa hakhoe, 2001, pp. 289–318.

Kim Hyŏng-u 金炯祐. "Hosŭng Chigong yŏn'gu" 胡僧 指空研究. *Tongguk sahak* 東國史學 18 (1984): 1–23.

Kim Ki-tŏk 김기덕. "14 segi huban kaehyŏk chŏngch'i ŭi naeyong kwa kŭ sŏnggyŏk" 14 세기 후반 개혁정치의 내용과 그 성격. In Han'guk yŏksa yŏn'guhoe: 14-segi Koryŏ sahoe sŏnggyŏk yŏn'guban, ed., *14 segi Koryŏ ŭi chŏngch'i wa sahoe* 14 세기고려의 정치와 사회. Seoul: Minŭmsa, 1994, pp. 446–506.

Kim Ku-chin 金九鎭. "Wŏndae Yodong chibang ŭi Koryŏ kunmin" 元代 遼東地方의 高麗軍民. In Yi Wŏn-sun 李元淳, ed., *Yi Wŏn-sun kyosu hwagap ki'nyŏm sahak nonch'ong* 李元淳教授華甲記念史學論叢. Seoul: Kyohaksa, 1986, pp. 496–86.

———. "Yŏ-Wŏn ŭi yŏngt'o punjaeng kwa kŭ kwisokmunje: Wŏndae e issŏ sŏ Koryŏ pont'o wa Tungnyŏng ch'onggwanbu, Ssangsŏng ch'onggwanbu, T'amla ch'onggwanbu ŭi punni chŏngch'aek ŭl chungsim ŭro" 麗・元의 領土紛爭과 歸屬問題—元代 에 있어서 高麗本土와 東寧府・雙城總館府・耽羅總館府의 分離政策을 중심으로—. *Kuksa nonch'ong* 國史論叢 7 (1989): 61–92.

Kim Ku-yong 金九容. *Ch'ŏk'yakjae hak'ŭm chip* 惕若齋學吟集. Reprinted in *Han'guk munjip ch'onggan*, vol. 6.

Kim Kyŏng-nae 金庚來. "Simyangwang e taehan ilkoch'al" 瀋陽王에 對한 一考察. *Sŏngsin sahak* 信誠史學 6 (1988): 71–96.

Kim Sang-gi 金庠基. *Sinp'yŏn Koryŏ sidaesa* 新編高麗時代史. Seoul: Sŏul taehakkyo ch'ulp'anbu, 1985; 3d printing, 1999.

Kim Sun-ja 김순자. "Wŏn kansŏpgi min ŭi tonghyang" 원간섭기 민의 동향. In Han'guk yŏksa yŏn'guhoe: 14-segi Koryŏ sahoe sŏnggyŏk yŏn'guban, ed., *14 segi Koryŏ ŭi chŏngch'i wa sahoe* 14 세기고려의 정치와 사회. Seoul: Minŭmsa, 1994, pp. 365–408.

Kim Tae-jung 金大中. "Koryŏ Kongminwangdae Kyŏnggun ŭi chaegŏn sido" 高麗 恭愍王代 京軍의 再建 試圖. *Kunsa* 軍史 21 (1990): 64–85.

Kim Tang-t'aek 金塘澤. "Koryŏ Kongminwangch'o ŭi mujang seryŏk" 高麗恭愍王初의 武將勢力. *Han'guksa yŏn'gu* 韓國史研究 93 (1996): 27–53.

———. *Wŏn kansŏpha ŭi Koryŏ chŏngch'isa* 元干涉下의 高麗政治史. Seoul: Ilchogak, 1998.

Kim Wi-hyŏn 金渭顯. *Koryŏ sidae taeoe kwan'gyesa yŏn'gu* 高麗時代對外關係史研究. Seoul: Kyŏngin munhwasa, 2004.

Kim Yong-sŏn 金龍善. *Koryŏ myojimyŏng chipsŏng* 高麗墓誌銘集成. 2d ed. Ch'unch'ŏn: Hallim taehakkyo ch'ulp'anbu, 1997.

Kin Bunkyō 金文京, ed. *Rō Kitsudai* 老乞大. Tokyo: Heibonsha, 2002.

Kitamura Hideo 北村秀人. "Kōrai jidai no Shin'ō ni tsuite no ichi kōsatsu" 高麗時代の瀋王についての一考察. *Jinbunkenkyū* 人文研究 (Ōsaka shiritsu daigaku bungakubu) 24, no. 10 (Dec. 1972): 93–144.

———. "Kōrai ni okeru seitōgyōsei ni tsuite" 高麗における征東行省について. *Chōsen gakuhō* 朝鮮学報 32 (1962): 1–73.

Kitamura Takai 北村高. "Kōraiō Ō Shō no sūButsu" 高麗王王璋の崇佛. *Tōyōshien* 東洋史苑 24–25 (1985): 117–41.

Komaroff, Linda, and Stefano Carboni, eds. *The Legacy of Genghis Khan: Courtly Art and Culture in Western Asia, 1256–1353*. New York: Metropolitan Museum of Art; and New Haven: Yale University Press, 2002.

Kong Keqi 孔克齊. *Zhizheng zhiji* 至正直記. Ca. 1365. Baibu congshu jicheng 百部叢書集成 edition, a photolithic reproduction of 1853 edition by 伍崇曜. Reprinted—Taibei: Yiwen chubanshe, 1965.

Kong Qi, *see* Kong Keqi.

Koryŏsa, *see* Chŏng In-ji.

Koryŏsa chŏryo, *see* Nam Su-mun.

Kwŏn Kŭn 權近. *Yangch'on chip* 陽村集; reprinted in *Han'guk munjip ch'onggan*, 7.

Kwŏn Yŏng-guk 權寧國. "Wŏn kansŏpgi Koryŏ kunje ŭi pyŏnhwa" 원간섭기 고려군제의 변화. In Han'guk yŏksa yŏn'guhoe: 14-segi Koryŏ sahoe sŏnggyŏk yŏn'guban, ed., *14 segi Koryŏ ŭi chŏngch'i wa sahoe* 14 세기 고려의 정치 와 사회. Seoul: Minŭmsa, 1994, pp. 131–58.

Kye, Seung B. "The Posthumous Image and Role of Ming Taizu in Korean Politics." *Ming Studies* 50 (2004): 107–30.

Lan Wu 藍武. "Yuan Shundi Tuohuan Tiemuer de wenhua suyang jiqi xintai yanjiu" 元順帝妥歡貼睦爾的文化素養及其心態研究. *Guangxi shifan daxue xuebao* (zhexue shehui kexue ban) 廣西師範大學學報 (哲學社會科學版) 41, no. 1 (2005): 156–60.

Lane, George. *Early Mongol Rule in Thirteenth Century Iran: A Persian Renaissance*. New York: RoutledgeCurzon, 2003.

Langlois, John. "Song Lian and Liu Jin on the Eve of Joining Zhu Yuanzhang." Paper presented at the conference Ming Taizu and His Times. Chinese University of Hong Kong, Mar. 29, 2006.

Langlois, John, ed. *China Under Mongol Rule*. Princeton: Princeton University Press, 1981.

Lei Qing 雷慶. "Yuan Shundi xinlun" 元順帝新論. *Dongbei shida xuebao* (zhexue shehui kexue ban) 東北師大學報 (哲學社會科學版) 1999, no. 3: 20–25.

Lee, Peter. *Songs of Flying Dragons: A Critical Reading*. Cambridge: Harvard University Press, 1975.

Lee, Peter, ed. *Sourcebook of Korean Civilization*, vol. 1., *From Early Times to the Sixteenth Century*. New York: Columbia University Press, 1993.

Legge, James. *The Chinese Classics*, vol. 3.

Li Chengde 李成德. "Hongjinjun jin Gaoli qianxi" 紅巾軍進高麗淺析. *Henan daxue xuebao* (*shehui kexue ban*) 河南大學學報 (社會科學版) 33, no. 4 (1993): 78–83.

Li Fu 李輔. *Quan Liao zhi* 全遼志. 1566. Reprinted—Dalian: Liao hai shu she, 1934; and in *Liao hai cong shu* 遼海叢書, edited by Jin Yufu 金毓紱. Shenyang: Liaoningsheng Xinhua shudian, 1985, vol. 1.

Li Jiben 李繼本. *Yishan wenji* 一山文集. *Siku quanshu zhenben*, series 11, vol. 173. Reproduced from Wenyuange 文淵閣 copy. Taibei: Taiwan shangwu yinshuguan, 1981.

Li Shizhan 李士瞻. *Jingji wenji* 經濟文集. Ming edition (preface dated 1444). Microfilm held at the East Asian Library and the Gest Collection, Princeton University.

Li Xiaofeng 李曉峰 and Yang Dongmei 楊東梅. "Ji'nanshi bowuguan cang gudai tongyin xuanshi" 濟南市博物館藏古代銅印選釋. *Wenwu chunqiu* 文物春秋 2001, no. 2: 47–52.

Li Xinfeng 李新峰. "Ming qianqi fu Chaoxian shichen congkao" 明前期赴朝鮮使臣叢考. In *Ming Qing luncong* 明清論叢. Beijing: Zijincheng chubanshe, 2003, 4: 91–104.

Li Xiusheng 李修生, comp. *Quan Yuan wen* 全元文. Nanjing: Fenghuang chubanshe (formerly Jiangsu guji chubanshe), 2000–2004.

Li Zefen 李則芬. "Yuandai moqi cunwang guanjian renwu Tuotuo" 元代末期存亡關鍵人物脫脫. In idem, *Song Liao Jin Yuan lishi lunwenji* 宋遼金元歷史論文集. Taibei: Liming wenhua shiye, 1991, pp. 748–53.

Li Zhian 李治安. "Make Boluo suoji Naiyan zhi luan kaoshi" 馬可波羅所記乃顏之亂考釋. *Yuanshi luncong* 元史論叢 8 (2001): 33–45.

Liu Ji 劉佶. *Beixun siji* 北巡私記. Late fourteenth century; 1859 edition held in the Kawabata Collection, Faculty of Letters Library, Kyoto University.

Liu Mengcong 劉孟琮, comp. *Nantai beiyao* 南臺備要. Mid-fourteenth century. Reprinted in *Xiantai tongji (wai sanzhong)* 憲臺通紀 (外三種). Hangzhou: Zhejiang guji chubanshe, 2002.

Liu Xiao 劉曉. *Yuanshi yanjiu* 元史研究. Fuzhou: Fujian renmin chubanshe, 2006.

Liu Xihai 劉喜海. *Haidong jinshi yuan* 海東金石苑. 1831. Reprinted in *Shike shiliao xinbian* 石刻史料新編. Taibei: Xinwenfeng, 1977, vol. 23

Liu Xu 劉昫. *Jiu Tangshu* 舊唐書. Beijing: Xinhua shudian, 1975.

Liu Yanbo 劉艷波. "Lüelun Shundi shiqi tongzhi jieji neibu douzheng de tedian" 略論順帝時期統治階級內部鬥爭的特點. *Songliao xuekan (shehui zhexue ban)* 松遼學刊 (社會哲學版) 4 (1997): 16–21.

Liu Yingli 劉應李 et al., eds. *Da Yuan hunyi fangyu shenglan* 大元混一方輿勝覽. Reprinted—Chengdu: Sichuan daxue chubanshe, 2003.

Lu Maocun 慮茂村. "Jieshao Han Liner Song zhengquan de yizu wenwu" 介紹韓林兒宋政權的一組文物. *Wenwu* 1982, no. 9: 91–92.

Lu Nanqiao 盧南喬. "Yuanmo Hongjinjun qiyi ji jinjun Gaoli de yiyi" 元末紅巾軍起義及進軍高麗的意義. 2 pts. *Wen shi zhe* 文史哲 1954, no. 6: 32–38; no. 7: 45–49.

Luo Xianyou 羅賢佑. "Yuanchao zhudi Hanhua shuyi" 元朝諸帝漢化述議. *Minzu yanjiu* 民族研究 1987, no. 5: 67–74.

Luo Xiyi 羅喜頤, comp. *Manzhou jinshizhi* 滿洲金石志. Reprinted in *Shike shiliao xinbian* 石刻史料新編. Taibei: Xinwenfeng chubanshe, 1977, vol. 23.

Ma Juan 馬娟. "Yuandai Halaluren Laodisha shulüe" 元代哈剌魯人老的沙述略. *Huizu yanjiu* 回族研究 2005, no. 2: 128–30.

———. "Yuandai Qincharen Yan Tiemuer shiji kaolun" 元代欽察人燕鐵木兒事迹考論. *Yuanshi luncong* 元史論叢 9 (2005): 98–106.

———. "Yuandai semu Gaoli tonghun juli" 元代色目高麗通婚舉例. *Ningxia shehui kexue* 寧夏社會科學 2002, no. 5: 94–97.

Maier, Charles. *Among Empires: American Ascendancy and Its Predecessors*. Cambridge: Harvard University Press, 2006.

Manz, Beatrice Forbes. *The Rise and Rule of Tamerlane*. Cambridge: Cambridge University Press, 1989.

Marugame Kinsaku 丸亀金作. "Gen-Kōrai kankei no ichikusari: Shin'ō ni tsuite" 元・高麗関係の一齣—瀋王に就いて. *Seikyū gakusō* 青丘学叢 no. 18 (1936): 1–57.

Matsuda Kōichi 松田孝一. "Kōkin no ran shoki Sensai Genchōgun no zenyō" 紅巾の乱初期陝西元朝軍の全容. *Tōyō gakuhō* 東洋学報 75, no. 1 (1993): 1–30.

Matsumoto Takaharu 松本隆晴. "Minsho no Sōheikan" 明初の総兵官. In Mindaishi kenkyūkai 明代史研究会, ed., *Mindaishi kenkyūkai sōritsu san-*

jūgonen kinen ronshū 明代史研究会創立三十五年記念論集. Tokyo: Kyūko shoin, 2003, pp. 37–58.

McCann, David. "Song of the Dragons Flying to Heaven: Negotiating History." In idem, *Early Korean Literature: Selections and Introductions*. New York: Columbia University Press, 2000, pp. 41–45.

Melville, Charles. "The Keshig in Iran: The Survival of the Royal Mongol Household." In Linda Komaroff, ed., *Beyond the Legacy of Genghis Khan*. Leiden: E. J. Brill, 2006, pp. 135–64.

Meng Fanqing 孟繁清. "Yuanchao monian haiyun yu chouliang" 元朝末年海運與籌糧. In Hao Shiyuan 郝時遠 and Luo Xianyou 羅賢佑, eds., *Meng Yuan shi ji minzushi lunji: Jinian Weng Dujian xiansheng danchen yibai zhounian* 蒙元史暨民族史論集—記念翁獨健先生誕辰一百周年. Beijing: Shehui kexue wenxian chubanshe, 2006, pp. 228–41.

Miao Wei 苗威. "Gaoli Zhongliewang zai Zhongguo" 高麗忠烈王在中國. *Dongjiang xuekan* 東疆學刊 17, no. 2 (2000): 47–51.

———. "Gaoli Zhongxuanwang yu Zhongguo" 高麗忠宣王與中國. *Dongjiang xuekan* 東疆學刊 17, no. 3 (2000): 39–45.

Min Hyŏn-gu 閔賢九. "Chŏngch'ika rosŏ ŭi Kongminwang" 政治家로서의 恭愍王. *Asea yŏn'gu* 亞細亞研究, no. 100 (Dec. 1998): 271–96.

———. *Koryŏ chŏngch'isa non* 高麗政治史論. Seoul: Koryŏ taehakkyo ch'ulp'anbu, 2004.

———. "Koryŏ hugi kunje ŭi chŏngch'ijŏk kyŏngjejŏk kiban" 高麗後期軍制의 政治的 經濟的 基盤. In Yukgun ponbu, Kunsa yŏn'gusil 陸軍本部軍事研究室, ed., *Koryŏ kunjesa* 高麗軍制史. N.p., 1983, pp. 323–46.

———. "Koryŏ Kongminwangdae ŭi 'Chu Ki Ch'ŏl kongsin' e taehan kŏmt'o" 高麗 恭愍王代의「誅奇轍功臣」에 대한 檢討. In Yi Ki-baek sŏnsaeng kohŭi ki'nyŏm Han'guk sahak nonch'ong kan wiwŏnhoe 李基白先生古稀紀念韓國史學論叢刊行委員會, ed., *Yi Kibaek sŏnsaeng kohŭi ki'nyŏm Han'guk sahak nonch'ong* 李基白先生古稀紀念韓國史學論叢. Seoul: Iljogak, 1994, 1: 900–29.

———. "Koryŏ Kongminwang ŭi chŭkwi paegyŏng" 高麗 恭愍王의 即位背景. In *Han U-kŭn paksa chŏngnyŏn ki'nyŏm sahak nonch'ong* 韓㳓劤博士停年紀念史學論叢. Seoul: n.p, 1981, pp. 791–808.

———. "Koryŏ Kongminwang ŭi panWŏnjŏk kaehyŏk chŏngch'i e taehan il koch'al" 高麗 恭愍王의 反元的 改革政治에 대한 一考察. *Chindan hakpo* 震檀學報 68 (1989): 49–77.

———. "Koryŏ Kongminwang ŭi panWŏnjŏk kaehyŏk chŏngch'i e taehan ŭi chŏn'gae kwasŏng" 高麗 恭愍王의 反元的 改革政治에 대한의 展開過程. In T'aegwa Hŏ Sŏn-do sŏnsaeng chŏngnyŏn ki'nyŏm Han'guk sahak nonch'ong kanhaeng wiwŏnhoe, ed., *Han'guk sahak nonch'ong* 韓國史學論叢. Seoul: Iljogak, 1992, pp. 236–57.

Minjok munhwa ch'ujinhoe 民族文化推進會, ed. *Han'guk munjip ch'onggan* 韓國文集叢刊. Seoul: Minjok munhwa ch'ujinhoe, 1990–2005.

Ming shi, *see* Zhang Tingyu et al.

Ming Taizu shilu 明太祖實錄. 1418 to mid-17th c. Fascimile reproduction of Guoli Beiping tushuguan cang Hongge chaoben 國立北平圖書館藏紅格抄本. Taibei: Zhongyang yanjiuyuan, Lishi yuyan yanjiusuo, 1961–66.

Miya Noriko 宮紀子. *Mongoru jidai no shuppan bunka* モンゴル時代の出版文化. Nagoya: Nagoya daigaku shuppankai, 2006.

———. *Mongoru teikoku ga unda sekaizu* モンゴル帝国が生んだ世界図. Tokyo: Nihon keizai shinbun shuppansha, 2007.

Miyazawa Tomoyuki 宮沢知之. "Gendai kōhanki no heisei to sono hōkai" 元代後半期の幣制とその崩壊. *Oryō shigaku* 鷹陵史学 27 (2001): 53–92.

Mizutani Masayoshi 水谷昌義. "Kōrai no shuto Kaijōjō ni tsuite no kenkyū" 高麗の首都開城場についての研究. *Chōsen gakuhō* 朝鮮学報, no. 117 (1985): 1–42.

Mo Shumin 默書民. "Yuandai Daidu de liangshi yu xiaofei" 元代大都的糧食與消費. *Yuanshi luncong* 9 (2004): 65–78.

Momoki Jirō 桃木至郎. *Kaiiki Ajiashi kenkyū nyūmon* 海域アジア史研究入門. Tokyo: Iwanami shoten, 2008.

Morgan, David. *Medieval Persia, 1040–1797*. London and New York: Longman, 1988.

———. *The Mongols*. Cambridge: Blackwell, 1986.

Morihira Masahiko 森平雅彦. "Dai Gen urusu to Kōrai bukkyō: Shōkōji hōshi shutsugen no igi ni yosete" 大元ウルスと高麗仏教—松広寺法旨出現の意義に寄せて. *Nairiku Ajiashi kenkyū* 内陸アジア史研究 17 (Mar. 2003): 23–40.

———. "Fuma Kōrai kokuō no seiritsu: Genchō in okeru Kōraiō no chi'i ni tsuite no yobiteki kōsatsu" 駙馬高麗国王の成立—元朝における高麗王の地位についての予備的考察. *Tōyō gakuhō* 東洋学報 79, no. 4 (Mar. 1998): 1–30.

———. "Genchō keshike seido to Kōrai ōke: Kōrai-Genchō kankei ni okeru turghagh no igi ni kanren shite" 元朝ケシケ制度と高麗王家—高麗元朝関係における禿魯花の意義に関連して. *Shigaku zasshi* 史学雑誌 110, no. 2 (Feb. 2001): 60–89.

———. "Kōrai ni okeru Gen no tanseki—rūto no hitei o chūshin ni" 高麗における元の站赤——ルートの比定を中心に. *Shien* 史淵 141 (Mar. 2004): 79–116.

———. "Kōrai ōika no kisoteki kōsatsu: Dai Gen urusu no ichibun kenseiryoku toshite no Kōrai ōke" 高麗王位下の基礎的考察—大元ウルスの一分権勢力としての高麗王家. *Chōsenshi kenkyūkai ronbunshū* 朝鮮史研究会論文集 36 (1998): 55–87.

———. "Kōrai ōke to Mongoru kōzoku no tsūkon kankei ni kansuru oboegaki" 高麗王家とモンゴル皇族の通婚関係に関する覚書. *Tōyōshi kenkyū* 東洋史研究 67, no. 3 (2008): 1–39.

Mote, Frederick. *The Poet Kao Ch'i*. Princeton: Princeton University Press, 1962.

———. "Rise of the Ming Dynasty," in *CHC*, vol. 7, pt. I, pp. 11–57.

———. "Yuan and Ming." In K. C. Chang, ed., *Food In Chinese Culture: Anthropological and Historical Perspectives*. New Haven: Yale University Press, 1977, pp. 195–257.

Munjip p'yŏnch'an wiwŏnhoe 文集編纂委員會, ed. *Han'guk yŏktae munjip ch'ongsŏ* 韓國歷代文集叢書. Seoul: Kyŏngin munhwasa, 1987– .

Murai Shōsuke 村井章介. *Bunretsu suru ōken to shakai* 分裂する王権と社会. Tokyo: Chūō kōron shinsha, 2003.

———. "Wakō to Chōsen" 倭冦と朝鮮. In Teng Weizao 藤維藻 et al., eds., *Higashi Ajia sekaishi tankyū* 東アジア世界史探求. Tokyo: Kyūko shoin, 1986, 182–96.

Murata Jirō 村田治郎 et al. *Kyoyōkan* 居庸関. Kyoto: Zauhō kankōkai, 1955, 1957.

Nakamura Jun 中村淳. "Gendai Daito no chokukenjiin o megutte" 元代大都の敕建寺院をめぐって. *Tōyōshi kenkyū* 東洋史研究 58, no. 1 (1999): 63–83.

Nakamura Kazuyuki 中村和之. "Mongoru jidai no Tōsei gensuibu to Mindai no Nurugan toshi" モンゴル時代の東征元帥府と明代の奴児干都司. In Kikuchi Toshihiko 菊池俊彦 and Nakamura Kazuyuki, eds., *Chūsei no Hokutō Ajia to Ainu* 中世の北東アジアとアイヌ. Tokyo: Kōchi shoin, 2008, pp. 43–64.

Nam Su-mun 南秀文. *Koryŏsa chŏryo* 高麗史節要. 1452. Reprinted—Seoul: Asea munhwasa, 1974.

Namujila 那木吉拉. "Yuandai Hanren Menggu xingming kao" 元代漢人蒙古姓名考. *Zhongyang minzu xueyuan xuebao* 中央民族學院學報 1992, no. 2: 10–13.

Naong 懶翁, *see* Hye Kŭn.

Nasen. *Jin tai ji* 金臺集. *Wenyuange Siku quanshu zhenben* 文淵閣四庫全書珍本, series 11, vol. 173. Reprinted—Taibei: Shangwu, 1981.

National Museum of Chinese History. *A Journey into China's Antiquity*. Beijing: Morning Glory Publishers, 1997.

Nishino Yukio 西野幸雄. "Kōraichō ni okeru Hokuhō Ryōkai chiiki ni tsuite" 高麗朝における北方両界地域について. *Senshū shigaku* 専修史学 20 (Mar. 1988): 101–19.

No Ki-sik 盧基植. "Wŏn-Myŏng kyoch'eki ŭi Yodong kwa Yojin" 元・明 교체기의 遼東과 女眞. *Asia munhwa* 아시아문화 19 (2003): 9–26.

No Kye-hyŏn 盧啓鉉. *Yŏ Mong oegyosa* 麗蒙外交史. Seoul: Kap'in ch'ulp'ansa, 1993.

O Kŭmsŏng 吳金成. "Yuanmo dongluanqi de wuzhuang qiyi jituan he xiangcun zhibeiceng" 元末動亂期的武裝起義集團和鄉村支配層. Paper presented at the conference "Ming Taizu and His Times" 明太祖及其時代. Chinese University of Hong Kong, March 2006.

Ōhara Yoshitoyo 大原嘉豐. "Kōrai kokuō *Taizōkyō* kara mita Genchō no shūkyō seisaku" 高麗国王大蔵経からみた元朝の宗教政策. In Iwai Shigeki 岩井茂樹, ed., *Chūgoku kinsei shakai no chitsujō keisei* 中国近世社会の秩序形成. Kyoto: Kyōto daigaku jinbun kagaku kenkyūjo, 2004, pp. 23–59.

Okada Hidehiro 岡田英弘. "Gen no Shin'ō to Ryōyō gyōshō" 元の瀋王と遼陽行省. *Chōsen gakuhō* 朝鮮学報 14 (1959): 533–42.

Ostrowski, Donald. *Muscovy and the Mongols: Cross-Cultural Influences on the Steppe Frontier, 1304–1589*. Cambridge: Harvard University Press, 1998.

Otosaka Tomoko 乙坂智子. "Genchō Chibetto seisaku no shidō to hensen" 元朝チベット政策の始動と変遷. *Shikyō* 史鏡 20 (1990): 49–65.

———. "Genchō no taigai seisaku: Kōrai-Chibetto kunchō e no shogū ni miru 'naifu' taisei" 元朝の対外政策—高麗・チベット君長への処遇に見る「内附」体制. *Shikyō* 史鏡 38–39 (1999): 30–53.

———. "Make Boluo zhuzuozhong suo miaoshu de Zangchuan fojiao" 馬可波羅著作中所描述的藏傳佛教. *Yuanshi luncong* 元史論叢 8 (2001): 62–69.

Paek In-ho 백인호/白仁鎬. "Koryŏ hugi puWŏn seryŏk ŭi hyŏngsŏng kwa seryŏkhwa" 고려후기 附元勢力의 형성과 세력화. In Han'guk chungsesa hakhoe 韓國中世史學會, ed., *Han'guk chungse sahoe ŭi che munje* 韓國中世社會의諸問題. Taegu: Han'guk chungse sahakhoe, 2001, pp. 319–43.

———. *Koryŏ hugi puWŏn seryŏk yŏn'gu* 고려후기부원세력연구. Seoul: Sejong ch'ulp'ansa, 2003.

Paek Mun-bo 白文寶. *Tam'am munjip iljip* 淡庵文集逸文. 1900 ed. Reprinted in *Han'guk yŏktae munjip ch'ongsŏ*, vol. 12; *Han'guk munjip ch'onggan*, vol. 3.

Pak Chong-gi 박종기. "14 segi ŭi Koryŏ sahoe: Wŏn kansŏpgi ŭi yihae munje" 14 세기의 고려—원 간섭기의 이해문제. In Han'guk yŏksa yŏn'guhoe: 14-segi Koryŏ sahoe sŏnggyŏk yŏn'guban, ed., *14 segi Koryŏ ŭi chŏngch'i wa sahoe* 14 세기고려의 정치 와 사회. Seoul: Minŭmsa, 1994, pp. 13–35.

Pak Ok-gŏl 朴玉杰. "Koryŏmal pukpang yumin kwa ch'uswae" 高麗末 北方流民 과 推刷. *Paeksan hakpo* 白山學報 60 (2001): 109–49.

Pak P'yŏng-sik 朴平植. "Koryŏ hugi ŭi Kaegyŏng sang'ŏp" 高麗後期의 開京商業. *Kuksagwan nonch'ong* 國史館論叢 98 (2002): 215–37.

Pak Sŏng-ju 朴成柱. "Koryŏmal Han-Chunggan ŭi yumin" 高麗末 韓・中 간의 流民. *Kyŏngju sahak* 慶州史學 20 (2001): 171–96.

Pak Wŏnho. "The Liaotung Peninsula Invasion Controversy During the Early Years of the Yi Dynasty." *Social Science Journal* 6 (1979): 148–81.

Pak Yong-un 朴龍雲. "Kaegyŏng in the Age of Koryŏ." *Seoul Journal of Korean Studies* 11 (1998): 79–106.

———. *Koryŏ sidae Kaegyŏng yŏn'gu* 高麗時代開城研究. Seoul: Iljisa, 1996.

———. *Koryŏ sidaesa* 高麗時代史. 6th ed. Seoul: Iljisa, 2002.

Palais, James. "A Search for Korean Uniqueness." *Harvard Journal of Asiatic Studies* 55, no. 2 (1995): 409–25.

Pang Tong-in 方東仁. "Tongnyŏngbu ch'ip'e soko" 東寧府置廢小考. *Kwandong sahak* 關東史學 2 (1982): 71–83.

Pelliot, Paul. "Les Mots Mongols dans le *Korye sa*." *Journal asiatique*, no. 217 (1930): 253–66.

Perdue, Peter. *China Marches West: The Qing Conquest of Central Eurasia.* Cambridge: Harvard University Press, 2005.

Petech, Luciano. *Central Tibet and the Mongols.* Rome: Instituto italiano per il Medio ed Estremo Oriente, 1990.

Piao Yan 朴彦. "Mindai ni okeru Chōsenjin no Ryōtō ijū" 明代における朝鮮人の遼東移住. *Tōyōshi kenkyū* 東洋史研究 67, no. 1 (June 2008): 1–34.

Potter, Lawrence. "Herat Under the Karts: Social and Political Forces." In Neguin Yavara et al., eds., *Views from the Edge: Essays in Honor of Richard W. Bulliet.* New York: Columbia University Press, 2004, pp. 184–207.

Pou 普愚. *T'aego hwasang ŏrok* 太古和尚語錄. Reprinted in *Han'guk yŏktae munjip ch'ongsŏ* 韓國歷代文集叢書, vol. 25.

Qian Qianyi 錢謙益. *Guochu qunxiong shilüe* 國初群雄事略. Ca. 1630. Reprinted—Beijing: Zhonghua shuju, 1982.

Qiu Shusen 邱樹森. "Mao Gui shiji kaolüe" 毛貴事迹考略. *Wen shi zhe* 文史哲 1980, no. 3: 33–35.

———. *Tuohuan Tiemuer zhuan* 妥懽貼睦爾傳. Changchun: Jilin jiaoyu chubanshe, 1991.

———. "Youguan Mao Gui de yixie shishi" 有關毛貴的一些史實. *Yuanshi ji beifang minzushi yanjiu jikan* 元史及北方民族史研究集刊 3 (1978): 21–22.

———. *Yuanchao jianshi* 元朝簡史. Fuzhou: Fujian renmin chubanshe, 1989; 2d ed. 1999.

———. "Yuandai de Nüzhenren" 元代的女眞人. *Shehui kexue zhanxian* 社會科學戰線 2003, no. 4: 161–64.

———. "Yuanmo Hongjinjun de zhengquan jianshe" 元末紅巾軍的政權建設. *Yuanshi luncong* 元史論叢 1 (1982): 91–108.

———. "Yuanmo nongmin zhengquan jifang tongyin de chubu yanjiu" 元末農民政權幾方銅印的初步研究. *Wenwu* 文物 1975, no. 9: 76–87.

Qu Wenjun 屈文軍. "Hongjinjun huodong dui Gaoli zhengju he Yuan-Li guanxi de yingxiang" 紅巾軍活動對高麗政局和元麗關係的影響. *Zhejiang shidaxue xuebao (shehui kexue ban)* 浙江師大學學報 (社會科學版) 25, no. 5 (2000): 34–37.

———. "Yuandai quexue xinlun" 元代怯薛新論. *Nanjing daxue xuebao (zhexue, renwen kexue, shehui kexue)* 南京大學學報 (哲學, 人文科學, 社會科學) 40, no. 2 (2003): 145–51.

Quan Heng 權衡. *Gengshen waishi* 庚申外史. In Zhou Guangpei 周光培, ed., *Yuandai biji xiaoshuo* 元代筆記小說. Shijiazhuang: Hebei jiaoyu chuban, 1994, vol. 3.

Quan Heng 權衡 and Ren Chongyue 任崇岳. *Gengshen waishi jianzheng* 庚申外史箋證. Zhengzhou: Zhongzhou guji chubanshe, 1991.

Rachewiltz, Igor de. *The Secret History of the Mongols: A Mongolian Epic Chronicle of the Thirteenth Century*. Leiden: Brill, 2006.

——. "Turks in China Under the Mongols: A Preliminary Investigation of Turco-Mongol Relations in the 13th and 14th Centuries." In Morris Rossabi, ed., *China Among Equals: The Middle Kingdom and Its Neighbors, 10th–14th Centuries*. Berkeley: University of California Press, 1983, pp. 281–310.

Rachewiltz, Igor de; Hok-lam Chan; et al, eds. *In the Service of the Khan: Eminent Personalities of the Early Mongol-Yuan Period.* Wiesbaden: Harrassowitz Verlag, 1993.

Rashiduddin Fazlullah (Rashīd al-Dīn). *Jami'u't-Tawarikh, Compendium of Chronicles.* Trans: W. M. Thackston. 3 vols. Cambridge: Department of Near Eastern Languages and Civilizations, Harvard University, 1999.

———. *The Successors of Genghis Khan.* Trans. John Boyle. New York: Columbia University Press, 1971.

Robinson, David. *Bandits, Eunuchs, and the Son of Heaven.* Honolulu: University of Hawai'i Press, 2001.

———. "The Ming Court and the Legacy of the Yuan Mongols." In David Robinson, ed., *Culture, Courtiers, and Competition: The Ming Court (1368–1644).* Cambridge: Harvard University Asia Center, 2008, pp. 365–421.

———. "Mongoru teikoku no hōkai to Kōrai Kyōmin'ō no taigai seisaku" モンゴル帝国の崩壊と高麗恭愍王の対外政策. In Fuma Susumu 夫馬進, ed., *Chūgoku Higashi Ajia gaikō kōryūshi no kenkyū* 中国東アジア外

交交流史の研究. Kyoto: Kyōto daigaku gakujutsu shuppankai, 2007, pp. 145–84.

Ronay, Gabriel. *The Tartar Khan's Englishman.* London: Phoenix Press, 1978.

Rossabi, Morris. "Foreigners in China." In John Langlois, ed., *China Under Mongol Rule.* Princeton: Princeton University Press, 1981, pp. 258–95.

———. *The Jurchens in the Yüan and Ming.* Ithaca: China-Japan Program, Cornell University, 1982.

———. *Khubilai Khan.* Berkeley: University of California Press, 1989.

Rubruck, William. "Report to King Loius IX of France." In Peter Jackson, trans., and David Morgan, ed., *The Mission of Friar William Rubruck.* London: Hakluyt Society, 1990.

Sada Kōjirō 佐田弘治朗, ed. *Manshū kyūsekishi* 滿州舊蹟志. Dairen: Minami Manshū tetsudō kabushiki kaisha, 1924–26.

Satō Hisashi 佐藤長. "Minchō ni okeru Ramakyō sūhai ni tsuite" 明朝におけるラマ教崇拝について. Reprinted in idem, *Chūsei Chibettoshi kenkyū* 中世チベット史研究. Kyoto: Dōhōsha, 1986, pp. 287–320.

Schamiloglu, Uli. "The Rise of the Ottoman Empire: The Black Death in Medieval Anatolia and Its Impact on Turkish Civilization." In Neguin Yavara et al., eds., *Views from the Edge: Essays in Honor of Richard W. Bulliet.* New York: Columbia University Press, 2004, pp. 255–79.

Sen, Tansen. "The Yuan Khanate and India: Cross-Cultural Diplomacy in the Thirteenth and Fourteenth Centuries." *Asia Major* 19, no. 1/2 (2006): 299–326.

Serruys, Henry. "Mongols Ennobled During the Early Ming." *Harvard Journal of Asiatic Studies* 22 (1959): 209–60.

———. *The Mongols in China During the Hung-wu Period.* Mélanges chinois et bouddhiques, vol. 11. Bruxelles: L'Institut belge des hautes études chinoises, 1959.

———. "Remains of Mongol Customs in China During the Early Ming Period." *Monumenta Serica* 16 (1957): 137–90.

———. "Some Types of Names Adopted by the Mongols During the Yuan and the Early Ming Periods." *Monumenta Serica* 17 (1958): 353–60.

Shao Yuanping 邵遠平. *Yuan shi lei bian* 元史類編. 1699. Reprinted in vols. 49–58 of *Shiliao congbian xubian* 史料叢編續編. Taibei: Guangwen shuju, 1968.

Shek, Richard. "Ethics and Polity: The Heterodoxy of Buddhism, Maitreyanism, and the Early White Lotus." In Kwang-Ching Liu and Richard Shek, eds., *Heterodoxy in Late Imperial China.* Honolulu: University of Hawai'i Press, 2004, pp. 73–108.

Shi Shuqing 史樹青. "Yuanmo Xu Shouhui nongmin zhengquan de tongyin" 元末徐壽輝農民政權的銅印. *Wenwu* 文物 1972, no. 6: 9–13.

Shi Weimin 史衛民. *Dushizhong de youmumin* 都市中的遊牧民. Changsha: Hunan chubanshe, 1996.

Shultz, Edward J. *Generals and Scholars: Military Rule in Medieval Korea.* Honolulu: University of Hawai'i Press, 2000.

Silbergeld, Jerome. "In Praise of Government: Chao Yong's Painting, *Noble Steeds*, and Late Yüan Politics." *Artibus Asiae* 46, no. 3 (1985): 159–202.

Sima Qian. *Records of the Grand Historian of China.* Trans. Burton Watson. New York: Columbia University Press.

Smith, John. "Dietary Decadence and Dynastic Decline in the Mongol Empire." *Journal of Asian History* 34, no. 1 (2000): 35–52.

Smith, Paul Jakov. "Impressions of the Song-Yuan-Ming Transition: The Evidence from *Biji* Memoirs." In idem and Richard von Glahn, eds., *The Song-Yuan-Ming Transition in Chinese History.* Cambridge: Harvard University Asia Center, 2003, pp. 71–110.

———. "Problematizing the Song-Yuan-Ming Transition." In idem and Richard von Glahn, eds., *The Song-Yuan-Ming Transition in Chinese History.* Cambridge: Harvard University Asia Center, 2003, pp. 1–34.

Song Lian 宋濂 et al., eds. *Yuan shi* 元史. 1368–70. Reprinted—Beijing: Zhonghua shuju, 1976.

Sonoda Kazuki 園田一亀, comp. *Manshū kinsekishi kō* 満洲金石志稿. Dairen: Minami Manshū tetsudō kabushiki kaisha, 1939.

Sørensen, Henrick. "Lamaism in Korea During the Late Koryo Dynasty," *Korea Journal* 33, no. 3 (Autumn 1993): 67–81.

Su Bai 宿白. *Zangchuan fojiao siyuan kaogu* 藏傳佛教寺院考古. Beijing: Wenwu chubanshe, 1996.

Su Dong 蘇東. "Yijian Yuandai guguguan" 一件元代姑姑冠. *Neimenggu wenwu kaogu* 内蒙古文物考古 25, no. 2 (2001): 99–100.

Su Tianjue 蘇天爵 (1294–1352). *Cixi wen'gao* 慈溪文稿. Reprinted—Beijing: Zhonghua shuju, 1997.

———. *Guochao wenlei* 國朝文類. *Sibu congkan, chubian jibu* 初編集部.

———. *Yuan wen lei* 元文類. 1334. *Siku quanshu.* Reprinted—Shanghai: Shanghai guji chubanshe, 1993.

Sudō Yoshiyuki 周藤吉之. "Sensho ni okeru nuhi no bensei to suisatsu to ni tsuite" 鮮初に於ける奴婢の辨正と推刷とについて. *Seikyū gakusō* 青丘學叢 22 (1935): 1–61.

Suematsu Yasukazu 末松保和. "Kōrai Empukuji shōmei" 高麗演福寺鐘銘. *Tōyō gakuhō* 東洋学報 66 (1985): 319–24.

———. "Raimatsu Sensho ni okeru taiMin kankei" 麗末鮮初における対明関係. Seoul: Keijō teikoku daigaku bungakkai, 1941. Republished in idem,

Kōraichōshi to Chōsenchōshi 高麗朝史と朝鮮朝史. Tokyo: Yoshikawa kōbunkan, 1996, pp. 124–291.

Sugiyama Masaaki 杉山正明. "Chūō Yūrasia no rekishi kōzu: sekaishi o tsunaida mono" 中央ユ—ラシアの歴史構図—世界史をつないだもの. In idem, ed., *Iwanami kōza sekaishi* 岩波講座世界史, 11, *Chūō Yūrashia no tōgō* 中央ユーラシアの統合. Tokyo: Iwanami shoten, 1997, pp. 3–89.

———. *Dai Mongoru no jidai* 大モンゴルの時代. *Sekai no rekishi* 世界の歴史, vol. 9. Tokyo: Chūō kōronsha, 1997.

———. *Dai Mongoru no sekai* 大モンゴルの世界. Tokyo: Kadogawa sensho, 1992.

———. *Gyakusetsu no Yūrasiashi* 逆説のユーラシア史. Tokyo: Nihon keizai shinbunsha, 2002.

———. "Kubirai seiken to Tōhō san'ōke" クビライ政権と東方三王家. *Tōyō gakuhō* 東洋学報 54 (1982): 257–315. Reprinted in idem, *Mongoru teikoko to DaiGen urusu* モンゴル帝国と大元ウルス. Kyoto: Kyōto daigaku gakujutsu shuppankai, 2004, pp. 62–126.

———. "Kubirai to Daito: Mongorugata 'Shūtoken' to sekai teito" クビライと大都—モンゴル型「首都圏」と世界帝都, in idem, *Mongoru teikoku to DaiGen urusu* モンゴル帝国と大元ウルス. Kyoto: Kyōto daigaku gakujutsu shuppankai, 2004, pp. 128–67.

———. *Mongoru teikoku no kōbō* モンゴル帝国の興亡. Tokyo: Kōdansha gendai shinsho, 1996.

———. *Yūbokumin kara mita sekaishi* 遊牧民から見た世界史. Tokyo: Nihon keizai shinbunsha, 1998.

Sun Chengze 孫承澤. *Yuanchao diangu biannniankao* 元朝典故編年考. *Siku quanshu zhenben*, series 2, vol. 140.

Tan Qian 談遷 (1594–1658). *Guo que* 國榷. Ca. 1653. Reprinted—Beijing: Zhonghua shuju, 1988 [1958].

Tao Zongyi 陶宗儀. *Nancun chuogeng lu* 南村輟耕錄. 1366. Reprinted Beijing: Zhonghua shuju, 1997 [1959].

Takahashi Takuji 高橋琢二. "Ushōshō Dattatsu" 右丞相脱脱. *Shigaku* 史学 40, no. 1–3 (1967): 89–98.

Teraji Jun 寺地遵. "Hō Kokuchin seiken no seikaku" 方国珍政権の性格. (Hiroshima daigaku) *Shigaku kenkyū* (広島大学)史学研究, no. 223 (1999): 22–41.

Tonami Mamoru 礪波護, Kishimoto Mio 岸本美緒, and Sugiyama Masaaki 杉山正明, eds. *Chūgoku rekishi kenkyū nyūmon* 中国歴史研究入門. Nagoya: Nagoya daigaku shuppankai, 2006.

Underdown, Michael. "European Knowledge of Korea During the Yuan Dynasty." *Études mongoles et sibériennes* 27 (1996): 385–404.

Vermeersch, Sem. *The Power of the Buddhas: The Politics of Buddhism During the Koryŏ Dynasty (918–1392)*. Cambridge: Harvard University Asia Center, 2008.

Verschuer, Charlotte von. *Across the Perilous Sea: Japanese Trade with China and Korea from the Seventh to the Sixteenth Centuries*. Trans. from the French by Kristen Lee Hunter. Ithaca: East Asia Program, Cornell University, 2006.

Wada Hirotoku 和田博德. "Genmatsu no gun'yū to Betonamu: Chin Yūryō, Shu Genshō ni kansuru *Daietsu shiki zensho* no kiji" 元末の群雄とベトナム—陳友諒・朱元璋に関する大越史記全書の記事. *Shigaku* 史学 49, no. 1 (1978): 44, 68.

Wada Sei 和田清. "Min no Taiso to kōkin no zoku" 明の太祖と紅巾の賊. *Tōyō gakuhō* 東洋学報 13, no. 2 (1924): 122–46.

———. "Minsho no Manshū keiryaku" 明初の滿州經略. 2 pts. *Man Sen chiri rekishi kenkyū hōkoku* 滿鮮地理歷史報告 14 (1934): 177–298; 15 (1937) 71–319.

Waley, Arthur. "New Light on Buddhism in Medieval India." *Mélanges chinois et bouddhiques* 1 (1931–32): 355–76.

Wang Chongshi 王崇時. "Yuandai ruju Zhongguo de Gaoliren" 元代入居中國的高麗人." *Dongbei shida xuebao* 東北師大學報 1991, no. 6: 46–49. Reprinted in Diao Shuren 刁書人 et al., eds., *Zhong-Chao guanxishi yanjiu lunwenji* 中朝關係史研究論文集. Jilin: Jilin wenshi chubanshe, 1995, pp. 150–58.

———. "Yuan yu Gaoli tongzhi jituan de lianyin" 元與高麗統治集團的聯姻. *Jilin shifan xueyuan xuebao* 吉林師範學院學報 1992, no. 4: 36–41.

Wang Jie 王結 (1275–1336). *Shan su yao yi* 善俗要義. Reprinted in *Li xue zhi nan (wai san zhong)* 吏學指南 (外三種). Hangzhou: Zhejiang guji chubanshe, 1988.

Wang Mingjun 王明軍, Yang Jun 楊軍, and Zheng Yuyan 鄭玉艷. "Shilun Yuanchao monian de 'Zhizheng genghua'" 試論元朝末年的"至正更化." *Songliao xuekan (shehui zhexue ban)* 松遼學刊 (社會哲學版) 1998, no. 4: 20–23, 34.

Wang Shizhen 王世貞. *Yanshantang bieji* 弇山堂别集. 1590. Reprinted—Beijing: Zhonghua shuju, 1985.

Wang Ting 王頲. "Xixiaren Mailigusi yu Yuanmo Liangzhe difang de shouhu" 西夏人邁里古思與元末兩浙地方的守護. In Hao Shiyuan 郝時遠 and Luo Xianyou 羅賢佑, eds., *Meng Yuan shi ji minzushi lunji: Jinian Weng Dujian xiansheng danchen yibai zhounian* 蒙元史暨民族史論集——記念翁獨健先生誕辰一百周年. Beijing: Shehui kexue wenxian chubanshe, 2006, 282–95.

Wang Ting 王頲 and Ni Shangming 倪尚明. "Gaoli Zhongxuanwang zhe Tufan shijian zaixi" 高麗忠宣王謫吐蕃事件再析. *Huazhong shifan daxue xuebao* (renwen shehui kexue ban) 華中師範大學學報 (人文社會科學版) 45, no. 2 (2006): 70–74.

Wang Wei 王薇 et al. *Zhong Chao guanxishi* 中朝關係史. Beijing: Shijie zhishi chubanshe, 2002.

Wang Zhenrong 王慎榮. *Yuanshi tanyuan* 元史探源. Changchun: Jilin wenshi chubanshe, 1991.

Watanabe Ken'ya 渡辺健哉. "Daito kenkyū no genjō to kadai" 大都研究の現状と課題. *Chūgoku: shakai to bunka* 中国—社会と文化 20 (2005): 520–28.

Watt, James. *When Silk Was Gold: Central Asian and Chinese Textiles.* New York: Metropolitan Museum of Art, 1997.

Weidner, Marsha. "Aspects of Painting and Patronage at the Mongol Court, 1260–1368." In Li Chu-tsing, ed., *Artists and Patrons: Some Social and Economic Aspects of Chinese Painting.* Lawrence: University of Kansas, Kress Foundation Department of Art History and Nelson-Atkins Museum of Art; Seattle: University of Washington Press, 1989, pp. 39–59.

Weitz, Ankeney. "Art and Politics at the Mongol Court of China: Tugh Temür's Collection of Chinese Paintings." *Artibus Asiae* 64, no. 2 (2004): 243–80.

Wen Ling 溫嶺, *see* Chen Gaohua.

West, Stephen. "Chilly Seas and East-Flowing Rivers: Yuan Hao-wen's Poems of Death and Disorder, 1233–35." In Hoyt Cleveland Tillman and Stephen West, eds., *China Under Jurchen Rule.* Albany: State University of New York Press, 1995, pp. 281–304.

Wi Ŭn-suk 위은숙. "Wŏn kansŏpgi poch'o ŭi yut'ong kwa kŭ ŭimi" 원간섭기 寶鈔의 유통과 그의미. In Han'guk chungsesa hakhoe 韓國中世史學會, ed., *Han'guk chungse sahoe ŭi che munje* 韓國中世社會의 諸問題. Taegu: Han'guk chungsesa hakhoe, 2001, pp. 583–99.

Wittfogel, Karl, and Feng Chia-sheng. *A History of Chinese Society: Liao, 907–1125.* Philadephia: American Philosophical Society, 1949.

Wŏn Ch'ŏn-sŏk 元天錫. *Un'gok sisa* 耘谷詩史. Reprinted in *Han'guk yŏktae munjip ch'ongsŏ*, vol. 2201.

Woodruff, Phillip. "Foreign Policy and Frontier Affairs Along the Northeast Frontier of the Ming Dynasty, 1350–1618: Tripartite Relations of the Ming Chinese, Korean Koryo, and Jurchen-Manchu Tribesmen." Ph.D. diss., University of Chicago, 1995.

Wu Haitao 吳海濤. "Cong Yuandai Heshi jiazu de xingsheng kan liangzhong wenhua zhijian de zhongjie juese" 從元代賀氏家族的興盛看兩種文化之間的中介角色. *Yuanshi luncong* 7 (1999): 105–10.

Wu Han 吳晗. *Chaoxian Lichao shilu zhong de Zhongguo ziliao* 朝鮮李朝實錄中的中國資料. Beijing: Xinhua shudian, 1980, vol. 1.

———. "Mingjiao yu Da Ming diguo" 明教與大明帝國. In idem, *Dushi zhaji* 讀書劄記. Beijing: Sanlian shudian, 1961.

———. *Mingshi jianshu* 明史簡述. 1980. Reprinted—Beijing: Zhonghua shuju, 2005.

———. *Zhu Yuanzhang zhuan* 朱元璋傳. 1948. Reprinted—Hong Kong: Xianggang zhuanji wenxueshe, n.d.

Wu Songdi 吳松弟. *Zhongguo renkoushi: Liao Jin Yuan shiqi* 中國人口史遼金元時期. Shanghai: Fudan daxue chubanshe, 2000.

Xi Lei 喜蕾. "Cong Gaoli wenxian kan Yuandai de Huihuiren" 從高麗文獻看元代的回回人. *Neimenggu daxue xuebao (renwen shehui kexue ban)* 內蒙古大學學報 (人文社會科學 版) 38, no. 4 (2006): 18–22.

———. "Yuanchao gongtingzhong de Gaoli nüxing" 元朝宮廷中的高麗女性. *Yuanshi luncong* 元史論叢 8 (2001): 208–14.

———. *Yuandai Gaoli gongnü zhidu yanjiu* 元代高麗貢女制度研究. Beijing: Minzu chubanshe, 2003.

Xia Xie 夏燮. *(Xinjiao) Ming tongjian* (新校)明通鑑. Ca. 1870. Reprinted—Taibei: Shijie shuju, 1978.

Xiao Qiqing (Hsiao Ch'i-ch'ing) 蕭啓慶. "Yuandai de suwei zhidu" 元代的宿衛制度. *Guoli zhengzhi daxue bianzheng yanjiusuo nianbao* 國立政治大學邊政研究所年報 4 (1973): 43–95. Reprinted in idem, *Yuandaishi xintan* 元代史新探. Taibei: Xinwenfeng chubanshe, 1983.

———. "Yuandai de zhenrong zhidu" 元代的鎮戎制度. In *Yaoshi Congwu xiansheng jinian lunji* 姚師從吾先生紀念論集. Taibei: n.p., 1971, pp. 145–64. Reprinted in idem, *Yuandaishi xintan* 元代史新探. Taibei: Xinwenfeng chubanshe, 1983, pp. 113–39.

———. "Yuan-Li guanxizhong de wangshi huanghun yu qiangquan zhengzhi" 元麗關係中的王室皇婚與強權政治. In Zhonghua minguo Hanguo yanjiu xuehui 中華民國韓國研究學會, comp., *Zhong Han guanxishi guoji yantaohui lunwenji* 中韓關係史國際研討會論文集. Taibei: Zhonghua minguo Hanguo yanjiu xue, 1983, pp. 103–23. Reprinted in idem, *Yuandaishi xintan* 元代史新探. Taibei: Xinwenfeng chubanshe, 1983; and idem, *Nei Beiguo er wai Zhongguo: Meng Yuan shi yanjiu* 內北國而外中國: 蒙元史研究. Beijing: Zhonghua shuju, 2007, 2: 766–89.

Xu Huili 許惠利. "Beijing Zhihuasi faxian Yuandai cangjing" 北京智化寺發現元代藏經. *Wenwu* 文物 1987, no. 8: 1–7, 29.

Xue Lei 薛磊. *Yuandai gongting shi* 元代宮廷史. Tianjin: Baihua wenyi chubanshe, 2008.

Yagi Takeshi 矢木毅. "Kōrai ni okeru gunreiken no kōzō to sono henshitsu" 高麗における軍令権の構造とその変質. *Tōhō gakuhō* 東方学報 70 (1998): 291–327.

Yamamoto Meishi 山本明志. "Mongoru jidai ni okeru Chibetto-Kanchikan no kōtsū to tanseki" モンゴル時代におけるチベット•漢地間の交通と站赤. *Tōyōshi kenkyū* 東洋史研究 67, no. 2 (2008): 95–120.

Yamane Yukio 山根幸夫. "'Genmatsu no hanran' to Minchō shihai no kakuritsu" 「元末の反乱」と明朝支配の確立. In *Iwanami kōza, Sekai rekishi* 12, *Higashi Ajia sekai no tenkai*, II 岩波講座・世界歴史 12 東アジア世界の展開. Tokyo: Iwanami shoten, 1971, pp. 17–29.

Yang Ling 楊玲. "Yuandai de bianxian'ao" 元代的辮線襖. *Yuanshi luncong* 元史論叢 10 (2005): 213–24.

Yang Ne 楊訥. *Yuandai bailianjiao yanjiu* 元代白蓮教研究. Shanghai: Shanghai guiji chubanshe, 2004.

Yang Shiqi 楊士奇. *Dongli wenji* 東里文集. Reprinted—Beijing: Zhonghua shuju, 1998.

Yang Ŭi-suk 梁義淑. "Wŏn kansŏpgi Yosimjiyŏk Koryŏin ŭi tonghyang" 元 간섭기 遼瀋地域 高麗人의 동향. *Tongguk yŏksa kyoyuk* 東國歷史教育 1996: 1–39.

Yang Xiaochun 楊曉春. "Shenyang Yuan Zhizheng shiernian *Chenghuangmiao ji* beiyin guanyuan timing de chubu fenxi" 瀋陽元至正十二年『城隍廟記』碑陰官員題名的初步分析. *Yuanshi ji minzu yu bianjiang yanjiu jikan* 元史及民族與邊疆研究 18 (2006): 43–47.

———. "Shisan-shisi shiji Liaoyang, Shenyang diqu Gaoli yimin yanjiu" 十三十四世紀遼陽, 瀋陽地區高麗移民研究. *Zhongguo bianjiang shidi yanjiu* 中國邊疆史地研究 17, no. 1 (2007): 36–45.

———. "Yuandai Shenyanglu de jigou shezhi jiqi bianqian" 元代瀋陽路的機構設置及其變遷. *Zhongguo lishi dili luncong* 中國歷史地理論叢 23, no. 1 (2008): 74–80.

Yang Yu 楊瑀 (1285–1361). *Shan ju xin yu* 山居新語. 1360. Reprinted in *Yu tang jia hua Shan ju xin yu* 玉堂嘉話山居新語. Beijing: Zhonghua shuju, 2006.

Yang Zhijiu 楊志玖. *Yuandai Huizu shigao* 元代回族史稿. Tianjin: Nankai daxue chubanshe, 2003.

Yao Dali 姚大力. "Naiyan zhi luan zakao" 乃顏之亂雜考. *Yuanshi ji beifang minzushi yanjiu jikan* 元史及北方民族史研究集刊 11 (1987): 74–82.

———. "Yuan Liaoyang xingsheng gezu de fenbu" 元遼陽行省各族的分部. *Yuanshi ji beifeng minzushi yanjiu jikan* 元史及北方民族史研究集刊 8 (1984): 45–56.

Ye Sheng 葉盛. *Shuidong riji* 水東日記. Between 1465 and 1472. Reprinted—Beijing: Zhonghua shuju, 1997 [1980].

Ye Xinmin 葉新民. *Yuan Shangdu yanjiu* 元上都研究. Hohhot: Neimenggu daxue chubanshe, 1998.

Ye Ziqi 葉子奇. *Cao mu zi* 草木子. Late 14th c. Reprinted—Beijing: Zhonghua shuju, 1997, 3d ed.

Yi Chŏng 李政, ed. *Han'guk pulgyo sach'al sachŏn* 韓國佛教寺刹事典. Seoul: Pulgyo shidaesa, 1996.

Yi Haeng 李荇 (1478–1534). *Sinjŭng Tongguk yŏji sŭngnam* 新增東國輿地勝覽. 1530. Reprinted.

Yi Hyŏng-u 李亨雨. "Koryŏ Kongminwangdae ŭi chŏngch'ijŏk ch'ui wa musang syeryŏk" 高麗恭愍王代의 政治的 推移와 武將力. *Kunsa* 軍事 39 (1999): 27–68.

Yi Ki-tam 이기담. *Kongminwang kwa ŭi taehwa* 공미왕과의 대화. Seoul: Kojŭwin, 2005.

Yi Kok 李穀 (1298–1351). *Kajŏng chip* 稼亭集. Reprinted in *Han'guk munjip ch'onggan* 韓國文集叢刊, vol. 3.

Yi Kyŏng-hĭ 李慶喜. "Koryŏmal Honggŏnjok ŭi ch'im'ip kwa Tong'an imshi sudo ŭi taeŭng" 고려말紅巾賊의 침입과 東安臨時首都의 대응. *Pusan sahak* 釜山史學 34 (1993): 45–73.

Yi Myŏng-mi 李命美. "Koryŏ-Wŏn wangsil t'onghon ŭi chŏngch'ijŏk ŭimi" 高麗·元王室通婚의 政治的 의미. *Han'guksa ron* 韓國史論 49 (June 2003): 7–81.

Yi Nan-yŏng 李蘭暎, comp. *Han'guk kŭmsŏkmun ch'ubo* 韓國金石文追補. Seoul: Asia munhwasa, 1976.

Yi Saek 李穡 (1328–96). *Mok'ŭn sŏnsaeng mungo* 牧隱先生文稿. Reprinted in *Han'guk yŏktae munjip ch'ongsŏ*, vol. 20; and in *Han'guk munjip ch'onggan* 韓國文集叢刊, vol. 5. See Minjok munhwa ch'ujinhoe 民族文化推進會.

Yi Sang-sŏn 李相瑄. "Kongminwang kwa Pou: Kongminwangch'o wangkwŏn anjŏng ŭi iljo rŭl chungsim ŭro" 恭愍王과 普愚—恭愍王初 王權安定 의 一助 를 中心으로. In Yi Chae-yong paksa hwanyŏk ki'nyŏm Han'guk sahak nonch'ong kanhaeng wiwŏnhoe 李載龒博士還暦紀念韓國史學論叢刊行委員會, ed., *Yi Chaeyong paksa hwanyŏk ki'nyŏm Han'guk sahak nonch'ong* 李載龒博士還暦紀念韓國史學論叢. Seoul: Hanul, 1990, pp. 260–79.

Yi Sŭng-han 李昇漢. "Koryŏ Ch'ungsŏnwang ŭi Simyangwang p'ibong kwa chaeWŏn chŏngch'i hwaldong" 高麗 忠宣王의 瀋陽王 被封과 在元政治活動. *Chŏnnam sahak* 全南史學 2 (1988): 23–73.

Yi Tal-ch'ung 李達衷. *Chejŏng sŏnsaeng munjip* 霽亭先生文集. Reprinted in *Han'guk yŏktae munjip ch'ongsŏ*, vol. 34 (*Han'guk munjip ch'onggan*, vol. 3).

Yi U 李俁 (1637–93). *Taedong kŭmsŏksŏ* 大東金石書. Reprinted—Keijō: Keijō teikoku daigaku hōbungakubu 京城帝国大学法文学部, 1932.

Yi Yong-bŏm 李龍範. "Ki Hwanghu ŭi ch'aeknip kwa Wŏndae ŭi Chajŏng-wŏn" 奇皇后의 册立과 元代의 資政院. *Yŏksa hakpo* 歷史學報 17–18 (1962): 495–513.

Yi Yong-ju 李用柱. "Kongminwangdae ŭi Chajeui e kwanhan soyŏn'gu" 恭愍王代의 子弟衛에 關한 小硏究. In Sohŏn Nam To-yŏng paksa hwa-gap ki'nyŏm sahak nonch'ong kanhaeng wiwŏnhoe 素軒南都泳博士華甲紀念史學論叢刊行委員會, ed., *Sohŏn Nam To-yŏng paksa hwagap ki'nyŏm sahak nonch'ong* 素軒南都泳博士華甲紀念史學論叢. Seoul: T'ae-haksa, 1984, pp. 177–201.

Yokkaichi Yasuhiro 四日市康博. "*Jarugechi* kō: Mongoru teikoku no jūsōteki kokka kōzō oyobi bunpai shisutemu to no kakawari kara" ジャルゲチ考—モンゴル帝国の重層的国家構造および分配システムとの関わりから. *Shigaku zasshi* 史學雜誌 114, no. 4 (2005): 1–30.

———. "Mongoru teikoku to kaiiki Ajia" モンゴル帝国と海域アジア. In Momoki Jirō 桃木至郎, ed., *Kaiiki Ajiashi kenkyū nyūmon* 海域アジア史研究入門. Tokyo: Iwanami shoten, 2008, pp. 23–30.

———. "Mongoru teikoku no kokka kōzō ni okeru fu no shoyū to bunpai: yūboku shakai to teijū shakai, Chūka sekai to Isuramu sekai" モンゴル帝国の国家構造における富の所有と分配—遊牧社会と定住社会, 中華世界とイスラム世界—. In Imanishi Yūrichirō 今西裕一郎, ed., *Kyūshū daigaku 21 seiki COE puroguramu Higashi Ajia to Nihon: kōryū to hen'yō* 九州大学 21 世紀 COE プログラム「東アジアと日本: 交流と変容」. Fukuokashi: Kyūshū daigaku, 2007, pp. 165–81.

Yu Ae-ryŏng 유애령. "Monggo ka Koryŏ ŭi Yukryu sikyong e mich'in yŏng-hyang" 몽고가 고려의 육류 식용에 미친 영향. In *Kuksakwan nonch'ong* 國史館論叢, pp. 221–37.

Yu Minzhong 于敏中, ed. (*Qinding*) *rixia jiuwen kao* (欽定)日下舊聞考. 1785–87. Reprinted—Beijing: Beijing guji chubanshe, 2000 [1983].

Yu Yŏng-suk 俞塋淑. "Wŏnjŭng kuksa Pou wa Kongminwang ŭi kaehyŏk chŏngch'i" 圓證國師 普愚와 恭愍王의 改革政治. *Han'guksa non* 韓國史論 20 (1990): 139–80.

Yu Yuhe 于語和 and Huang Kun 黄昆. "Yuan Shundi jianlun" 元順帝簡論. *Lishi jiaoxue* 歷史教學 1996, no. 9: 46–48.

Yuan shi, *see* Song Lian et al.

Yun, Peter. "Foreigners in Korea During the Period of Mongol Interference." In *Han'guk munhwa sok ŭi oeguk munhwa* 한국문화속의 외국문화 (conference preceedings). Seoul, 2002, pp. 1221–28.

———. "Foreigners in Koryŏ Ruling Stratum During the Period of Mongol Domination." M.A. thesis. University of California, Los Angeles, 1993.

———. "Mongols and Western Asians in the Late Koryŏ Ruling Stratum." *International Journal of Korean History* 3 (2002): 51–69.

———. "Rethinking the Tribute System: Korean States and Northeast Asian Interstate Relations, 600–1600." Ph.D. diss., University of California, Los Angeles, 1998.

Yun Ŭn-suk 尹銀淑. "K'ubillai k'an ŭi chung'ang chipkwŏnhwa e taehan Tongto chewang ŭi taeŏng: 'Nayan pallan' ŭr chungsim ŭro" 쿠빌라이 칸의 중앙집권화에 대한 東道諸王의 대응—'나얀 반란'을 중심으로—. *Chung'ang Asia yŏn'gu* 中央아시아研究 8 (2003): 29–50.

Yuyama Akira 湯山明. "Empukuji Dōshō no Bongo meibun oboegaki" 演福寺銅鐘の梵語銘文覚書. *Tōyō gakuhō* 東洋学報 66 (1985): 325–62.

Zhang Daiyu 張岱玉. "*Yuan shi* Gaoli fumawang fengwang shiliao kaobian" 《元史》高麗駙馬王封王史料考辨. *Neimenggu shehui kexue* (*Hanwen ban*) 内蒙古社會科學 (漢文版) 26, no. 5 (2005): 46–50.

Zhang Tingyu 張廷玉 et al., eds. *Ming shi* 明史. 1736. Reprinted—Beijing: Zhonghua shuju, 1974.

Zhang Wei 張威. *Suizhong Sandaogang Yuandai chenchuan* 綏中三道崗元代沉船. Beijing: Kexue chubanshe, 2001.

Zhang Xuehui 張雪慧. "Shilun Yuandai Zhongguo yu Gaoli de maoyi" 試論元代中國與高麗的貿易. *Zhongguo shehui jingjishi yanjiu* 中國社會經濟研究 2003, no. 3: 63–70.

Zhang Yingsheng 張迎勝. *Yuandai Huizu wenxuejia* 元代回族文學家. Beijing: Renmin chubanshe, 2004.

Zhang Zhu 張翥 (1287–1368). *Shui an shi ji* 蟬菴詩集. *Sibu congkan xubian*, vol. 44. Shanghai: Shangwu yinshuguan, 1934.

Zhao, George Qingzhi. "Control Through Conciliation: Royal Marriages Between the Mongol Yuan and Koryŏ (Korea) During the 13th and 14th Centuries." *Toronto Studies in Central and Inner Asia* 6 (2004): 3–26.

———. *Marriage as Political Strategy and Cultural Expression*. New York and Bern: Peter Lang, 2008.

Zhao, George, and Richard W. L. Guisso. "Female Anxiety and Female Power: Political Interventions by Mongol Empresses During the 13th and 14th Centuries." *Toronto Studies in Central and Inner Asia* 7 (2005): 17–46.

Zhao Yongchun 趙永春 and Lan Ting 蘭婷. "Yuan Shundi shiqi de dangzheng jiqi weihai" 元順帝時期的黨爭及其威害. *Songliao xuekan* 松遼學刊 2 (1994): 23–29.

Zhou Liangxia 周良霄 and Gu Juying 顧菊英. *Yuanshi* 元史. Shanghai: Shanghai chubanshe, 1993.

Zhou Qingtao 周清濤. *Yuan Meng shizha* 元蒙史札. Hohhot: Neimenggu daxue chubanshe, 2001.

Index

Harvard-Yenching Institute Monograph Series

(titles now in print)

11. *Han Shi Wai Chuan: Han Ying's Illustrations of the Didactic Application of the Classic of Songs*, translated and annotated by James Robert Hightower
21. *The Chinese Short Story: Studies in Dating, Authorship, and Composition*, by Patrick Hanan
22. *Songs of Flying Dragons: A Critical Reading*, by Peter H. Lee
24. *Population, Disease, and Land in Early Japan, 645–900*, by William Wayne Farris
25. *Shikitei Sanba and the Comic Tradition in Edo Fiction*, by Robert W. Leutner
26. *Washing Silk: The Life and Selected Poetry of Wei Chuang (834?–910)*, by Robin D. S. Yates
27. *National Polity and Local Power: The Transformation of Late Imperial China*, by Min Tu-ki
28. *Tang Transformation Texts: A Study of the Buddhist Contribution to the Rise of Vernacular Fiction and Drama in China*, by Victor H. Mair
29. *Mongolian Rule in China: Local Administration in the Yuan Dynasty*, by Elizabeth Endicott-West
30. *Readings in Chinese Literary Thought*, by Stephen Owen
31. *Remembering Paradise: Nativism and Nostalgia in Eighteenth-Century Japan*, by Peter Nosco
32. *Taxing Heaven's Storehouse: Horses, Bureaucrats, and the Destruction of the Sichuan Tea Industry, 1074–1224*, by Paul J. Smith
33. *Escape from the Wasteland: Romanticism and Realism in the Fiction of Mishima Yukio and Oe Kenzaburo*, by Susan Jolliffe Napier
34. *Inside a Service Trade: Studies in Contemporary Chinese Prose*, by Rudolf G. Wagner
35. *The Willow in Autumn: Ryutei Tanehiko, 1783–1842*, by Andrew Lawrence Markus
36. *The Confucian Transformation of Korea: A Study of Society and Ideology*, by Martina Deuchler
37. *The Korean Singer of Tales*, by Marshall R. Pihl
38. *Praying for Power: Buddhism and the Formation of Gentry Society in Late-Ming China*, by Timothy Brook
39. *Word, Image, and Deed in the Life of Su Shi*, by Ronald C. Egan
40. *The Chinese Virago: A Literary Theme*, by Yenna Wu
41. *Studies in the Comic Spirit in Modern Japanese Fiction*, by Joel R. Cohn
42. *Wind Against the Mountain: The Crisis of Politics and Culture in Thirteenth-Century China*, by Richard L. Davis
43. *Powerful Relations: Kinship, Status, and the State in Sung China (960–1279)*, by Beverly Bossler

44. *Limited Views: Essays on Ideas and Letters*, by Qian Zhongshu; selected and translated by Ronald Egan
45. *Sugar and Society in China: Peasants, Technology, and the World Market*, by Sucheta Mazumdar
46. *Chinese History: A Manual*, by Endymion Wilkinson
47. *Studies in Chinese Poetry*, by James R. Hightower and Florence Chia-Ying Yeh
48. *Crazy Ji: Chinese Religion and Popular Literature*, by Meir Shahar
49. *Precious Volumes: An Introduction to Chinese Sectarian Scriptures from the Sixteenth and Seventeenth Centuries*, by Daniel L. Overmyer
50. *Poetry and Painting in Song China: The Subtle Art of Dissent*, by Alfreda Murck
51. *Evil and/or/as the Good: Omnicentrism, Intersubjectivity, and Value Paradox in Tiantai Buddhist Thought*, by Brook Ziporyn
52. *Chinese History: A Manual, Revised and Enlarged Edition*, by Endymion Wilkinson
53. *Articulated Ladies: Gender and the Male Community in Early Chinese Texts*, by Paul Rouzer
54. *Politics and Prayer: Shrines to Local Former Worthies in Sung China*, by Ellen Neskar
55. *Allegories of Desire: Esoteric Literary Commentaries of Medieval Japan*, by Susan Blakeley Klein
56. *Printing for Profit: The Commercial Publishers of Jianyang, Fujian (11th–17th Centuries)*, by Lucille Chia
57. *To Become a God: Cosmology, Sacrifice, and Self-Divinization in Early China*, by Michael J. Puett
58. *Writing and Materiality in China: Essays in Honor of Patrick Hanan*, edited by Judith T. Zeitlin and Lydia H. Liu
59. *Rulin waishi and Cultural Transformation in Late Imperial China*, by Shang Wei
60. *Words Well Put: Visions of Poetic Competence in the Chinese Tradition*, by Graham Sanders
61. *Householders: The Reizei Family in Japanese History*, by Steven D. Carter
62. *The Divine Nature of Power: Chinese Ritual Architecture at the Sacred Site of Jinci*, by Tracy Miller
63. *Beacon Fire and Shooting Star: The Literary Culture of the Liang (502–557)*, by Xiaofei Tian
64. *Lost Soul: "Confucianism" in Contemporary Chinese Academic Discourse*, by John Makeham
65. *The Sage Learning of Liu Zhi: Islamic Thought in Confucian Terms*, by Sachiko Murata, William C. Chittick, and Tu Weiming
66. *Through a Forest of Chancellors: Fugitive Histories in Liu Yuan's* Lingyan ge*, an Illustrated Book from Seventeenth-Century Suzhou*, by Anne Burkus-Chasson
67. *Empire of Texts in Motion: Chinese, Korean, and Taiwanese Transculturations of Japanese Literature*, by Karen Laura Thornber
68. *Empire's Twilight: Northeast Asia Under the Mongols*, by David M. Robinson

LaVergne, TN USA
24 November 2009
165096LV00001B/1/P